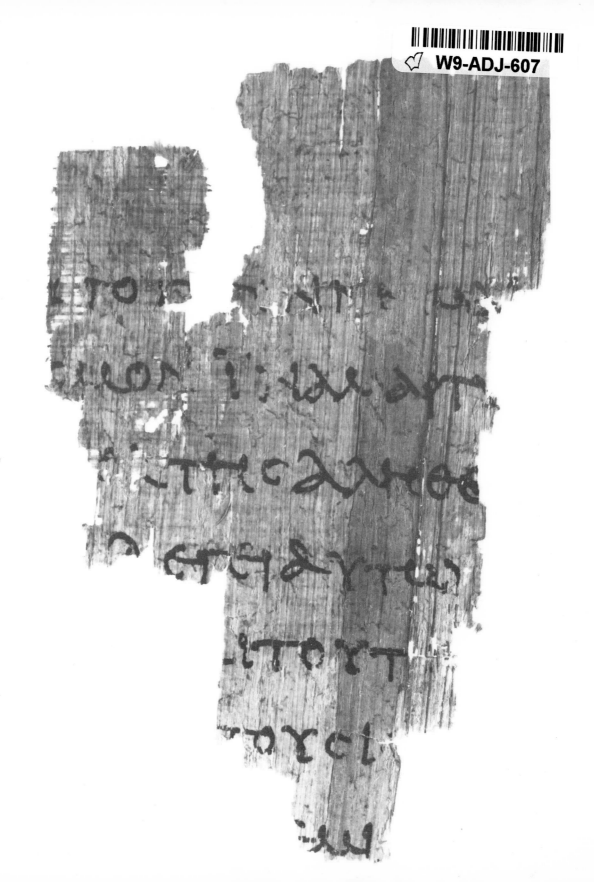

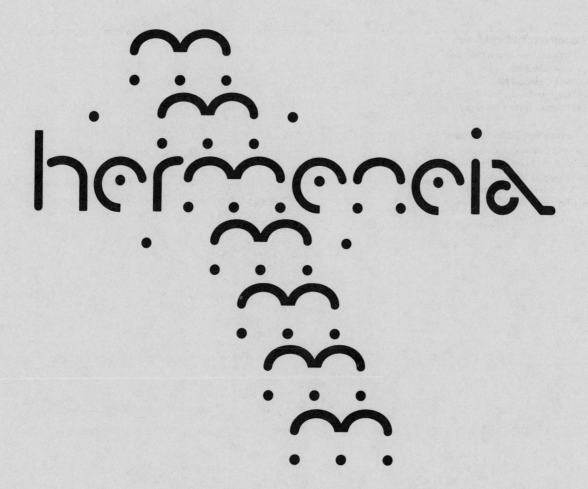

**Hermeneia
—A Critical
and Historical
Commentary
on the Bible**

John 2

A Commentary on the
Gospel of John
Chapters 7–21

by Ernst Haenchen

Translated by
Robert W. Funk

Edited by
Robert W. Funk
with
Ulrich Busse

Fortress
Press

Philadelphia

Translated from the German *Das Johannesevangelium.
Ein Kommentar,* by Ernst Haenchen, pp. 342–614. ©
1980 J. C. B. Mohr (Paul Siebeck), Tübingen.

Library of Congress Catalog Card Number 82-48756
ISBN 0-8006-6015-3

Printed in the United States of America
Design by Kenneth Hiebert
Type set on an Ibycus System at Polebridge Press
K470F84   20–6015

Contents
John 2

Commentary

The name *Hermeneia*, Greek ἑρμηνεία, has been chosen as the title of the commentary series to which this volume belongs. The word *Hermeneia* has a rich background in the history of biblical interpretation as a term used in the ancient Greek-speaking world for the detailed, systematic exposition of a scriptural work. It is hoped that the series, like its name, will carry forward this old and venerable tradition. A second entirely practical reason for selecting the name lies in the desire to avoid a long descriptive title and its inevitable acronym, or worse, an unpronounceable abbreviation.

The series is designed to be a critical and historical commentary to the Bible without arbitrary limits in size or scope. It will utilize the full range of philological and historical tools, including textual criticism (often slighted in modern commentaries), the methods of the history of tradition (including genre and prosodic analysis), and the history of religion.

Hermeneia is designed for the serious student of the Bible. It will make full use of ancient Semitic and classical languages; at the same time, English translations of all comparative materials—Greek, Latin, Canaanite, or Akkadian—will be supplied alongside the citation of the source in its original language. Insofar as possible, the aim is to provide the student or scholar with full critical discussion of each problem of interpretation and with the primary data upon which the discussion is based.

Hermeneia is designed to be international and interconfessional in the selection of authors; its editorial boards were formed with this end in view. Occasionally the series will offer translations of distinguished commentaries which originally appeared in languages other than English. Published volumes of the series will be revised continually, and eventually, new commentaries will replace older works in order to preserve the currency of the series. Commentaries are also being assigned for important literary works in the categories of apocryphal and pseudepigraphical works relating to the Old and New Testaments, including some of Essene or Gnostic authorship.

The editors of *Hermeneia* impose no systematic-theological perspective upon the series (directly, or indirectly by selection of authors). It is expected that authors will struggle to lay bare the ancient meaning of a biblical work or pericope. In this way the text's human relevance should become transparent, as is always the case in competent historical discourse. However, the series eschews for itself homiletical translation of the Bible.

The editors are heavily indebted to Fortress Press for its energy and courage in taking up an expensive, long-term project, the rewards of which will accrue chiefly to the field of biblical scholarship.

The translator and editor of the English edition of this commentary wishes to acknowledge the very considerable contribution of Professor Ulrich Busse and his assistant, Karl-Heinz Pritzen, to the completion of this translation. Without their help the work would not have progressed so rapidly nor with such improved results.

We are also indebted to the Universitat-Gesamthochschule Duisburg for its support of the editorial assistance of our German colleagues.

The translator and editor also wishes to acknowledge the translation counselling of Professor Burton L. Mack of the Claremont Graduate School. In addition to her superb work as typesetter, Charlene Matejovsky performed yeoman's service in verifying and correcting bibliographical entries.

The translator and editor responsible for this volume is Robert W. Funk of the University of Montana.

January, 1984

Frank Moore Cross
For the Old Testament
Editorial Board

Helmut Koester
For the New Testament
Editorial Board

Reference Codes

1. Sources and Abbreviations

a / New Testament

Matt	Matthew
Mark	
Luke	
John	
Acts	
Rom	Romans
1 Cor	1 Corinthians
2 Cor	2 Corinthians
Gal	Galatians
Eph	Ephesians
Phil	Philippians
Col	Colossians
1 Thess	1 Thessalonians
2 Thess	2 Thessalonians
1 Tim	1 Timothy
2 Tim	2 Timothy
Titus	
Phlm	Philemon
Heb	Hebrews
Jas	James
1 Pet	1 Peter
2 Pet	2 Peter
1 John	
2 John	
3 John	
Jude	
Rev	Revelation

b / Old Testament (LXX, Apocrypha)

Gen	Genesis
Exod	Exodus
Lev	Leviticus
Num	Numbers
Deut	Deuteronomy
Josh	Joshua
Judg	Judges
Ruth	
1 Sam	1 Samuel
2 Sam	2 Samuel
1 Kgs	1 Kings
2 Kgs	2 Kings
1 Chr	1 Chronicles
2 Chr	2 Chronicles
Ezra	
Neh	Nehemiah
Esth	Esther
Job	
Ps(s)	Psalms
Prov	Proverbs
Eccl (Qoh)	Ecclesiastes (Qoheleth)

Cant	Song of Solomon
Isa	Isaiah
Jer	Jeremiah
Lam	Lamentations
Ezek	Ezekiel
Dan	Daniel
Hos	Hosea
Joel	
Amos	
Obad	Obadiah
Jonah	
Mic	Micah
Nah	Nahum
Hab	Habakkuk
Zeph	Zephaniah
Hag	Haggai
Zech	Zechariah
Mal	Malachi
1 Kgdms	1 Kingdoms
2 Kgdms	2 Kingdoms
3 Kgdms	3 Kingdoms
4 Kgdms	4 Kingdoms
Add Esth	Additions to Esther
Bar	Baruch
Bel	Bel and the Dragon
1 Esdr	1 Esdras
2 Esdr	2 Esdras
4 Ezra	
Judith	
Ep Jer	Epistle of Jeremiah
1 Macc	1 Maccabees
2 Macc	2 Maccabees
3 Macc	3 Maccabees
4 Macc	4 Maccabees
Pr Azar	Prayer of Azariah
Pr Man	Prayer of Manasseh
Sir	Jesus Sirach (Ecclesiasticus)
Sus	Susanna
Tob	Tobit
Wis	Wisdom of Solomon

c / Pseudepigrapha (and Related Writings)

2 Apoc. Bar.	*Syriac Apocalypse of Baruch*
3 Apoc. Bar.	*Greek Apocalypse of Baruch*
Apoc. Mos.	*Apocalypse of Moses*
As. Mos.	*Assumption of Moses*
1 Enoch	*Ethiopic Enoch*
2 Enoch	*Slavonic Enoch*
Ep. Arist.	*Epistle of Aristeas*
Jub.	*Jubilees*
Mart. Isa.	*Martyrdom of Isaiah*
Odes Sol.	*Odes of Solomon*
Pss. Sol.	*Psalms of Solomon*
Sib. Or.	*Sibylline Oracles*
T. 12 Patr.	*Testaments of the Twelve Patriarchs*

T. Levi	*Testament of Levi*		*Cant.*	*Canticles*
T. Benj.	*Testament of Benjamin*		*Lam.*	*Lamentations*
Acts Pil.	*Acts of Pilate*		*Qoh.*	*Qohelet*
Apoc. Pet.	*Apocalypse of Peter*		*Ps.*	*Psalms*
Gos. Eb.	*Gospel of the Ebionites*		*Sam.*	*Samuel*
Gos. Eg.	*Gospel of the Egyptians*		*Pesaḥ.*	*Pesaḥim*
Gos. Heb.	*Gospel of the Hebrews*		*Šabb.*	*Šabbat*
Gos. Naass.	*Gospel of the Naassenes*		*Sanh.*	*Sanhedrin*
Gos. Naz.	*Gospel of the Nazoreans*		*Seder Olam*	
Gos. Pet.	*Gospel of Peter*		*Rab.*	*Seder Olam Rabbah*
Gos. Thom.	*Gospel of Thomas*		*Šeqal.*	*Šeqalim*
Prot. Jas.	*Protevangelium of James*		*Sukk.*	*Sukka*
			Ta'an.	*Ta'anit*
			Tos.	*Tosefta*

d / Apostolic Fathers

Barn.	*Barnabas*
1 Clem.	*1 Clement*
2 Clem.	*2 Clement*
Did.	*Didache*
Diogn.	*Diognetus*
Herm.	*Hermas*
Man.	*Mandates*
Sim.	*Similitudes*
Vis.	*Visions*
Ign.	*Ignatius*
Eph.	*Ephesians*
Magn.	*Magnesians*
Phld.	*Philadelphians*
Pol.	*Polycarp*
Rom.	*Romans*
Smyr.	*Smyrnaeans*
Trall.	*Trallians*
Mart. Pol.	*Martyrdom of Polycarp*
Pol. Phil.	*Polycarp to the Philippians*

e / Qumran Documents

CD	Cairo (Genizah text of the) Damascus (Document)
Q	Qumran
1QH	*Hôdāyôt (Thanksgiving Hymns)*
1QM	*Milḥāmāh (War Scroll)*
1QpHab	*Pesher on Habakkuk*
1QpNah	*Pesher on Nahum*
1QS	*Serek hayyaḥad (Rule of the Community, Manual of Discipline)*
4QTestim	*Testimonia* text from Qumran Cave 4

f / Rabbinic Texts

B.Meṣ.	*Baba Meṣi'a*
Ber.	*Berakot*
Gen. Rab.	*Genesis Rabbah*
Exod. Rab.	*Exodus Rabbah*
Ketub.	*Ketubot*
Lev. Rab.	*Leviticus Rabbah*
Menaḥ.	*Menaḥot*
Num. Rab.	*Numbers Rabbah*
Midr.	*Midrash*

g / Greek and Latin Authors (including Church Fathers)

Aristophanes		
	Clouds	*Clouds*
	Equites	*Equites*
Ambrosius		
	De fide	*De fide ad Gratianum*
	Enarr. Ps.	*Enarrationes in Psalmos*
Aristotle		
	Pol.	*Politica*
Chrysostom		
	Hom.	*Homiliae*
	In Joh.	*In Johanneum*
Cicero		
	De off.	*De officiis*
	Nat.deor.	*De natura deorum*
Clement of Alexandria		
	Strom.	*Stromateis*
Cyrillus of Jerusalem		
	Hom.	*Homilia in paralyticum*
Euripides		
	Bacchae	*Bacchae*
	Ion	*Ion*
Eusebius		
	H.E.	*Historia ecclesiastica*
Heliodorus		
	Aeth.	*Aethiopica*
Hippolytus		
	Ref.	*Refutatio omnium haeresium*
Irenaeus		
	Adv. haer.	*Adversus haereses*
Isocrates		
	Paneg.	*Panegyricus*
Jerome		
	Vir. ill.	*De viris illustribus*
Jos.	Josephus	
	Ant.	*Antiquitates Judaicae*
	BJ	*Bellum Judaicum*
	C.Apion.	*Contra Apionem*
	Vita	*Vita*
Justin	Justin Martyr	
	First Apol.	*First Apology*
	Dial.	*Dialogus cum Tryphone*

Longus
Pastoralia   *Pastoralia*
Maximus (of) Tyre
Diss.   *Dissertationes*
Orac. Sib.   *Sibylline Oracles*
Origen
Comm. Joh.   *In Johanneum Commentarius*
C. Celsum   *Contra Celsum*
Philo (of Alexandria)
De Abr.   *De Abrahamo*
De cher.   *De cherubim*
De decal.   *De decalogo*
Det. Pot. Ins. *Quod deterius potiori insidiari soleat*
De ebr.   *De ebrietate*
In Flac.   *In Flaccum*
De fuga   *De fuga et inventione*
Leg. all.   *Legum allegoriarum libri*
De mut. nom.   *De mutatione nominum*
De post. Caini *De posteritate Caini*
De somn.   *De somniis*
De spec. leg. *De specialibus legibus*
De virt.   *De virtutibus*
Philostratus
Vita Apoll.   *Vita Apollonii*
Pindar
Pollux   *Pollux*
Plato
De leg.   *De Leges*
Ion   *Ion*
Plutarch
Moralia   *Moralia*
Pomp.   *Pompey*
Sera num.   *De sera numinis vindicta*
ps.-Clem.   pseudo-Clementines
Hom.   *Homilies*
Recog.   *Recognitions*
Suidas
Theodor of Mopsuestia
Comm. Joh.   *In Johanneum Commentarius*

h / Periodicals & Reference Works

AB   Anchor Bible
AER   *American Ecclesiastical Review*
AGJU   Arbeiten zur Geschichte des antiken
        Judentums und des Urchristentums
AGSU   Arbeiten zur Geschichte des
        Spätjudentums and Urchristentums
AJT   *American Journal of Theology*
ALBO   Analecta lovaniensia biblica et
        orientalia
AnBib   Analecta biblica
ANF   *The Ante-Nicene Fathers: The Writings of
        the Fathers down to A. D. 325*, 10 vols.,
        ed. Alexander Roberts and James
        Donaldson (Buffalo: Christian
        Literature Publishing Co., 1885–97;
        reprint Grand Rapids: Wm. B.
        Eerdmans, 1951–56).

Ang   *Angelicum*
ANQ   *Andover Newton Quarterly*
APOT   *The Apocrypha and Pseudepigrapha of the
        Old Testament in English, with
        Introductions and Critical and Explanatory
        Notes to the Several Books*, 2 vols., ed.
        Robert Henry Charles Vol. 1,
        Apocrypha; Vol. 2, *Pseudepigrapha*
        (Oxford: Clarendon Press, 1913).
ARW   *Archiv für Religionswissenschaft*
AsSeign *Assemblées du Seigneur*
ATANT   Abhandlungen zur Theologie des
        Alten und Neuen Testaments
ATR   *Anglical Theological Review*
AUSS   *Andrews University Seminary Studies*
BA   *Biblical Archeologist*
BBB   Bonner biblische Beiträge
BDF   F. Blass, A. Debrunner, and R. W.
        Funk, *A Greek Grammar of the New
        Testament* (Chicago: University of
        Chicago Press, 1961).
BeO   *Bibbia et oriente*
BETL   Bibliotheca ephemeridum
        theologicarum lovaniensium
BEvT   Beiträge zur evangelischen Theologie
BFCT   Beiträge zur Förderung christlicher
        Theologie
BGBE   Beiträge zur Geschichte der biblischen
        Exegese
BHH   *Biblisch-Historisches Handwörterbuch,* ed.
        B. Reicke and L. Rost
BHT   Beiträge zur historischen Theologie
Bib   *Biblica*
BibLeb *Bibel und Leben*
BibS(F) Biblische Studien (Freiburg, 1895–)
BibS(N) Biblische Studien (Neukirchen,
        1951–)
Billerbeck H. L. Strack and P. Billerbeck,
        *Kommentar zum Neuen Testament aus
        Talmud und Midrasch,* 5 vols. (Munich:
        C. H. Beck, 1922–28).
BJRL *Bulletin of the John Rylands University
        Library of Manchester*
BK   *Bibel und Kirche*
BLE   *Bulletin de littérature ecclésiastique*
BLit *Bibel und Liturgie*
BR   *Biblical Research*
BSac *Bibliotheca Sacra*
BT   *The Bible Translator*
BTB   *Biblical Theology Bulletin*
BU   Biblische Untersuchungen
BWANT   Beiträge zur Wissenschaft vom Alten
        und Neuen Testament
BVC   *Bible et vie chrétienne*
BZ   *Biblische Zeitschrift*
BZNW   Beiheft zur *ZNW*
CB   *Cultura bíblica*
CBQ   *Catholic Biblical Quarterly*
CJT   *Canadian Journal of Theology*

ConBNT	Coniectanea biblica, New Testament		MVAG	Mitteilungen der vorderasiastisch-ägyptischen Gesellschaft
ConNT	*Coniectanea neotestamentica*		*Neot*	*Neotestamentica*
CQR	*Church Quarterly Review*		NGG	Nachrichten der Gesellschaft der Wissenschaften in Göttingen
CurTM	*Currents in Theology and Mission*		*NKZ*	*Neue kirchliche Zeitschrift;* from 1934, *Luthertum*
EKKNT	Evangelisch-katholischer Kommentar zum Neuen Testament			
ErJb	*Eranos Jahrbuch*		*NorTT*	*Norsk Teologisk Tidsskrift*
EstBib	*Estudios bíblicos*		*NovT*	*Novum Testamentum*
ETL	*Ephemerides theologicae lovanienses*		NovTSup	Novum Testamentum, Supplements
ETR	*Etudes théologiques et religieuses*		*NRT*	*La nouvelle revue théologique*
EvQ	*Evangelical Quarterly*		*NTApoc*	*New Testament Apocrypha.* Vol. 1: *Gospels and Related Writings*, ed. R. McL. Wilson; tr. A. J. B. Higgins, George Ogg, Richard E. Taylor, and R. McL. Wilson; Vol. 2: *Writings Related to the Apostles; Apocalypses and Related Subjects,* ed. R. McL. Wilson; tr. Ernest Best, David Hill, George Ogg, G. C. Stead, and R. McL. Wilson (Philadelphia: Westminster Press, 1963–1964).
EvT	*Evangelische Theologie*			
ExpTim	*Expository Times*			
FRLANT	Forschungen zur Religion und Literatur des Alten und Neuen Testaments			
Greg	*Gregorianum*			
HeyJ	*Heythrop Journal*			
HibJ	*Hibbert Journal*			
HKNT	Handkommentar zum Neuen Testament			
HNT	Handbuch zum Neuen Testament		NTAbh	Neutestamentliche Abhandlungen
HTKNT	Herders theologischer Kommentar zum Neuen Testament		NTD	Das Neue Testament Deutsch
			NTF	Neutestamentliche Forschung
HTR	*Harvard Theological Review*		NTL	New Testament Library
IB	*The Interpreter's Bible*, 12 vols., ed. G. A. Buttrick et al. (Nashville: Abingdon Press, 1952–1957).		*NTS*	*New Testament Studies*
			OBO	Orbis biblicus et orientalis
			PJ	*Palästina-Jahrbuch*
IDB	*Interpreter's Dictionary of the Bible*, 4 vols., ed. G. A. Buttrick et al. (Nashville: Abingdon Press, 1962–1976).		PTMS	Pittsburgh Theological Monograph Series
			PW	Pauly-Wissowa, *Real-Encyclopädie der classischen Altertumswissenschaft.* Neue Bearbeitung unter Mitwirkung zahlreicher Fachgenossen, ed. Georg Wissowa (Stuttgart: J. B. Metzler, 1893–).
ITQ	*Irish Theological Quarterly*			
Int	*Interpretation*			
JAC	Jahrbuch für Antike und Christentum			
JBL	*Journal of Biblical Literature*			
JJS	*Journal of Jewish Studies*		*RB*	*Revue biblique*
JNES	*Journal of Near Eastern Studies*		*RBén*	*Revue bénédictine*
JPOS	*Journal of the Palestine Oriental Society*		*RevExp*	*Review and Expositor*
JQR	*Jewish Quarterly Review*		*RevistB*	*Revista bíblica*
JR	*Journal of Religion*		*RevQ*	*Revue de Qumran*
JSNT	*Journal for the Study of the New Testament*		*RevScRel*	*Revue des sciences religieuses*
JTS	*Journal of Theological Studies*		*RevThom*	*Revue thomiste*
KD	*Kerygma und Dogma*		RGG	*Religion in Geschichte und Gegenwart*, ed. Kurt Galling (Tübingen: Mohr-Siebeck, ²1927–1932; ³1957–1962).
KEK	Kritisch-exegetischer Kommentar über das Neue Testament			
KNT	Kommentar zum Neuen Testament		*RHE*	*Revue d'histoire ecclésiastique*
LCC	Library of Christian Classics (Philadelphia: Westminster Press).		*RHPR*	*Revue d'histoire et de philosophie religieuses*
			RHR	*Revue de l'histoire des religions*
LCL	Loeb Classical Library (Cambridge: Harvard University Press).		*RivB*	*Rivista biblica*
			RNT	Regensburger Neues Testament
LD	Lectio divina		*RSPT*	*Revue des sciences philosophiques et théologiques*
MPG	Patrologie cursus completus, Series Graeca, ed. Jacques-Paul Migne			
			RSR	*Recherches de science religieuse*
MPL	Patrologia cursus completus, Series Latina, ed. Jacques-Paul Migne		*RTP*	*Revue de théologie et de philosophie*
			RUO	*Revue de l'université d'Ottawa*
MScRel	*Mélanges de science religieuse*		SANT	Studien zum Alten und Neuen Testament
MTZ	*Münchener theologische Zeitschrift*			

SAQ	Sammlung ausgewählter kirchen- und dogmengeschichtlicher Quellenschriften		TTZ	*Trierer theologische Zeitschrift*
			TU	Texte und Untersuchungen zur Geschichte der altchristlichen Literatur
SAWW.PH	Sitzungsberichte der Akademie der Wissenschaften in Wien. Philosophisch-historische Klasse		*TynBul*	*Tyndale Bulletin*
			TZ	*Theologische Zeitschrift*
SBB	Stuttgarter biblische Beiträge		UNT	Untersuchungen zum Neuen Testament
SBFLA	*Studii biblici franciscani liber annuus*		*VC*	*Vigilae christianae*
SBLASP	Society of Biblical Literature Abstracts and Seminar Papers		*VD*	*Verbum domini*
			VSpir	*Vie spirituelle*
SBLDS	Society of Biblical Literature Dissertation Series		*VT*	*Vetus Testamentum*
			WMANT	Wissenschaftliche Monographien zum Alten und Neuen Testament
SBLMS	Society of Biblical Literature Monograph Series		*WTJ*	*Westminster Theological Journal*
SBLSBS	Society of Biblical Literature Sources for Biblical Study		WUNT	Wissenschaftliche Untersuchungen zum Neuen Testament
SBS	Stuttgarter Bibelstudien		*ZAW*	*Zeitschrift für die alttestamentliche Wissenschaft*
SBT	Studies in Biblical Theology			
Scr	*Scripture*		*ZDPV*	*Zeitschrift des deutschen Palästina-Vereins*
SE	*Studia evangelica*		*ZHT*	*Zeitschrift für historische Theologie*
SEÅ	*Svensk exegetisk årsbok*		*ZKG*	*Zeitschrift für Kirchengeschichte*
SHAW.PH	Sitzungberichte der Heidelberger Akademie der Wissenschaften. Philosophisch-historische Klasse		*ZKT*	*Zeitschrift für katholische Theologie*
			ZNW	*Zeitschrift für die neutestamentliche Wissenschaft*
SJLA	Studies in Judaism in Late Antiquity			
SJT	*Scottish Journal of Theology*		*ZRGG*	*Zeitschrift für Religions- und Geistesgeschichte*
SNT	Studien zum Neuen Testament			
SNTSMS	Society for New Testament Studies Monograph Series		*ZST*	*Zeitschrift für systematische Theologie*
			ZTK	*Zeitschrift für Theologie und Kirche*
SPap	*Studia papyrologica*		*ZWT*	*Zeitschrift für wissenschaftliche Theologie*
SPAW.PH	Sitzungsberichte der preussischen Akademie der Wissenschaften. Philosophisch-historische Klasse			

i / General Abbreviations

SR	*Studies in Religion / Sciences religieuses*
ST	*Studia theologica*
SUNT	Studien zur Umwelt des Neuen Testaments
TBl	*Theologische Blätter*
TBü	Theologische Bücherei
TD	*Theological Digest*
TDNT	*Theological Dictionary of the New Testament*, 10 vols., ed. G. Kittel and G. Friedrich; tr. Geoffrey W. Bromiley (Grand Rapids: Wm. B. Eerdmans, 1964–76).
TF	*Theologische Forschung*
TGl	*Theologie und Glaube*
THKNT	Theologischer Handkommentar zum Neuen Testament
TLZ	*Theologische Literaturzeitung*
TQ	*Theologische Quartalschrift*
TRE	*Theologische Realenzyklopädie*
TRev	*Theologische Revue*
TRu	*Theologische Rundschau*
TS	*Theological Studies*
TSK	*Theologische Studien und Kritiken*
TT	*Theologisk Tidsskrift*
TTKi	*Tiddsskrift for Teologi og Kirke*
TToday	*Theology Today*

ca.	*circa*, approximately
cf.	*confer*, compare
chap(s).	chapter(s)
ed(s).	editor(s), edited by
e.g.	*exempli gratia*, for example
esp.	especially
ET	English translation
et al.	*et alii*, and others
f(f).	(and the) following (page[s])
i.e.	*id est*, that is
LXX	Septuaginta
n.	note
n.s.	new series
NT	New Testament, Neues Testament
OT	Old Testament
p(p).	page(s)
Q	Qumran documents
scil.	*scilicet*, namely: to be supplied or understood
ser.	series
s.v.	*sub verbo* or *sub voce* (under the word or lexical entry)
tr.	translated by, translation
v(v)	verse(s)
vg	Vulgate
viz.	*videlicet*, that is to say, to wit
v(v).l(l).	*variae lectiones*, variant readings

2. Short Titles of Commentaries, Studies, and Articles Often Cited

Aland, *Synopsis of the Four Gospels*
   Kurt Aland, ed., *Synopsis of the Four Gospels: Greek English Edition of the Synopsis Quattuor Evangeliorum* (United Bible Societies, ³1979).

Barrett, *John*
   Charles Kingsley Barrett, *The Gospel According to St. John. An Introduction with Commentary and Notes on the Greek Text* (Philadelphia: Westminster Press, ²1978).

Bauer, *Greek-English Lexicon*
   Walter Bauer, *A Greek-English Lexicon of the New Testament and Other Early Christian Literature*, tr. and adapted by William F. Arndt and F. Wilbur Gingrich. Second edition, revised and augmented by F. Wilbur Gingrich and Frederick W. Danker (Chicago and London: University of Chicago Press, 1979) = *Griechisch-Deutsches Wörterbuch zu den Schriften des Neuen Testaments und der übrigen urchristlichen Literatur* (Berlin: A. Töpelmann, ⁴1952, ⁵1958).

Bauer, *Das Johannesevangelium*
   Walter Bauer, *Das Johannesevangelium*, HNT 6 (Tübingen: Mohr-Siebeck, ³1933).

Bauer, *Orthodoxy and Heresy*
   Walter Bauer, *Orthodoxy and Heresy in Earliest Christianity*, ed. Robert A. Kraft and Gerhard Krodel (Philadelphia: Fortress Press, 1971).

Beginnings of Christianity
   F. J. Foakes-Jackson and Kirsopp Lake, eds., *The Beginnings of Christianity*, 5 vols. (Grand Rapids: Baker Book House, 1979).

Belser, *Das Evangelium des heiligen Johannes*
   Johannes Evangelist Belser, *Das Evangelium des heiligen Johannes, übersetzt und erklärt* (Freiburg: Herder, 1905).

Bernard, *John*
   John Henry Bernard, *The Gospel According to St. John: A Critical and Exegetical Commentary on the Gospel according to St. John*, ed. A. H. McNeile. 2 vols. (New York: Charles Scribner's & Sons, 1929).

Bihlmeyer, *Die apostolischen Väter*
   Karl Bihlmeyer, *Die apostolischen Väter*. Vol. 1, *Didache, Barnabas, Klemens I und II, Ignatius, Polykarp, Papias, Quadratus, Diognetbrief*, SAQ, 2, 1 (Tübingen: Mohr-Siebeck, 1924).

Billerbeck
   Hermann L. Strack and Paul Billerbeck, *Kommentar zum Neuen Testament aus Talmud und Midrash*, 5 vols. (Munich: C. H. Beck, 1922–61).

Black, *An Aramaic Approach*
   Matthew Black, *An Aramaic Approach to the Gospels and Acts* (Oxford: Clarendon Press, ²1954).

Bleek, *Beiträge zur Einleitung und Auslegung der heiligen Schrift*
   Friedrich Bleek, *Beiträge zur Einleitung und Auslegung der heiligen Schrift*. Vol. 1, *Beiträge zur Evangelien-Kritik* (Berlin: G. Reimer, 1846).

Braun, *Jean le théologien*
   François-Marie Braun, *Jean le théologien et son évangile dans l'église ancienne* (Paris: J. Gabalda, 1959).

Braun, "Qumran und das Neue Testament"
   Herbert Braun, "Qumran und das Neue Testament. Ein Bericht über 10 Jahre Forschung (1950–1959)." *TRu* 28 (1962) 56–61.

Braun, *La Sainte Bible*
   François-Marie Braun, *L'Evangile selon Saint Jean*, La Sainte Bible 10 (Paris, 1946).

Brown, *John*
   Raymond E. Brown, *The Gospel According to John. Introduction, Translation, and Notes*, 2 vols. Vol. 1, *i–xii*, AB 29 (Garden City: Doubleday, 1966); Vol. 2, *xiii–xxi*, AB 29A (Garden City: Doubleday, 1970).

Büchsel, *Das Evangelium nach Johannes*
   Friedrich Büchsel, *Das Evangelium nach Johannes*, NTD 4 (Göttingen: Vandenhoeck & Ruprecht, ²1935).

Bultmann, *Exegetica*
   Rudolf Bultmann, *Exegetica. Aufsätze zur Erforschung des Neuen Testaments*, ed. Erich Dinkler (Tübingen: Mohr-Siebeck, 1967).

Bultmann, *History of the Synoptic Tradition*
   Rudolf Bultmann, *History of the Synoptic Tradition*, tr. John Marsh (New York: Harper & Row, 1963).

Bultmann, *John*
   Rudolf Bultmann, *The Gospel of John: A Commentary*, tr. G. R. Beasley-Murray (Oxford: Basil Blackwell, 1971) = *Das Evangelium des Johannes*, KEK 2 (Göttingen: Vandenhoeck & Ruprecht, ¹⁰1968).

Bultmann, *Theology of the New Testament*
   Rudolf Bultmann, *Theology of the New Testament*, vol 2. Tr. Kendrick Grobel (London: SCM Press, 1955).

Burney, *Aramaic Origin*
   Charles Fox Burney, *The Aramaic Origin of the Fourth Gospel* (London: Clarendon Press, 1922).

Cullmann, *Peter*
   Oscar Cullmann, *Peter—Disciple, Apostle, Martyr. A Historical and Theological Study* (Philadelphia: Westminster Press, 1953, ²1958).

Dalman, *Sacred Sites and Ways*
   Gustaf Dalman, *Sacred Sites and Ways: Studies in the Topography of the Gospels*, tr. Paul P. Levertoff (London: S. P. C. K; New York: Macmillan, 1935).

Dodd, *Interpretation of the Fourth Gospel*
   Charles Harold Dodd, *The Interpretation of the Fourth Gospel* (Cambridge: Cambridge University Press, 1953).

Dodd, *Tradition*
   Charles Harold Dodd, *Historical Tradition in the Fourth Gospel* (Cambridge: Cambridge University Press, 1965).

Edwards, *John*
Richard Alan Edwards, *The Gospel According to St. John* (London: Eyre & Spottiswoode, 1954).

Ewald, *Die johanneischen Schriften*
Heinrich Ewald, *Die johanneischen Schriften, übersetzt und erklärt*, 2 vols. (Göttingen: Dieterich, 1861).

Fortna, *Gospel of Signs*
Robert T. Fortna, *The Gospel of Signs: A Reconstruction of the Narrative Source Underlying the Fourth Gospel*, SNTSMS 11 (Cambridge: Cambridge University Press, 1970).

Godet, *John*
Frédéric Godet, *Commentary on the Gospel of John*, 3 vols., tr. M. D. Cusin (Edinburgh: T. & T. Clark, 1883).

Guilding, *The Fourth Gospel and Jewish Worship*
A. Guilding, *The Fourth Gospel and Jewish Worship. A Study of the Relation of St. John's Gospel to the Ancient Jewish Lectionary System* (Oxford: Clarendon Press, 1960).

Haenchen, *Acts of the Apostles*
Ernst Haenchen, *The Acts of the Apostles: A Commentary* (Philadelphia: Westminster Press, 1971) = *Die Apostelgeschichte*, KEK (Göttingen: Vandenhoeck & Ruprecht, [14]1965).

Haenchen, *Die Bibel und Wir*
Ernst Haenchen, *Die Bibel und Wir. Gesammelte Aufsätze 2* (Tübingen: Mohr-Siebeck, 1965).

Haenchen, *Gott und Mensch*
Ernst Haenchen, *Gott und Mensch. Gesammelte Aufsätze 1* (Tübingen: Mohr-Siebeck, 1965).

Haenchen, "Johanneische Probleme"
Ernst Haenchen, "Johanneische Probleme." *ZTK* 56 (1959) 19–54. In his *Gott und Mensch. Gesammelte Aufsätze 1* (Tübingen: Mohr-Siebeck, 1965) 78–113.

Haenchen, "Das Johannesevangelium und sein Kommentar"
Ernst Haenchen, "Das Johannesevangelium und sein Kommentar." *TLZ* 89 (1964) 881–98. In his *Die Bibel und Wir. Gesammelte Aufsätze 2* (Tübingen: Mohr-Siebeck, 1968) 206–34.

Haenchen, "Petrus-Probleme"
Ernst Haenchen, "Petrus-Probleme." *NTS* 7 (1961) 187–97. In his *Gott und Mensch. Gesammelte Aufsätze 1* (Tübingen: Mohr-Siebeck, 1965).

Haenchen, "Probleme"
Ernst Haenchen, "Probleme des johanneischen 'Prologs.'" *ZTK* 60 (1963) 305–34. In his *Gott und Mensch. Gesammelte Aufsätze 1* (Tübingen: Mohr-Siebeck, 1965) 114–43.

Haenchen, "Der Vater"
Ernst Haenchen, "'Der Vater, der mich gesandt hat.'" *NTS* 9 (1963) 208–16. In his *Gott und Mensch. Gesammelte Aufsätze 1* (Tübingen: Mohr-Siebeck, 1965) 68–77.

Haenchen, *Der Weg Jesu*
Ernst Haenchen, *Der Weg Jesu. Eine Erklärung des Markus-Evangeliums und der kanonischen Parallelen* (Berlin: Walter de Gruyter, [2]1968).

Hahn, *Hoheitstitel*
Ferdinand Hahn, *Christologische Hoheitstitel. Ihre Geschichte im frühen Christentum*, FRLANT 83 (Göttingen: Vandenhoeck & Ruprecht, 1963).

Heitmüller, "Das Evangelium des Johannes"
Wilhelm Heitmüller, "Das Evangelium des Johannes." In *Die Schriften des Neuen Testaments*, ed. Johannes Weiss (Göttingen: Vandenhoeck & Ruprecht, 1908) 685–861.

Hirsch, *Frühgeschichte 1*
Emanuel Hirsch, *Frühgeschichte des Evangeliums*. Vol. 1, *Das Werden des Markus-Evangeliums* (Tübingen: Mohr-Siebeck, 1941).

Hirsch, *Geschichte der neueren evangelischen Theologie*
Emanuel Hirsch, *Geschichte der neueren evangelischen Theologie* (Gütersloh: Gerd Mohn, 1960–1964).

Hirsch, *Studien*
Emanuel Hirsch, *Studien zum Vierten Evangelium* (Tübingen: Mohr-Siebeck, 1936).

Hirsch, *Das vierte Evangelium*
Emanuel Hirsch, *Das vierte Evangelium in seiner ursprünglichen Gestalt verdeutscht und erklärt* (Tübingen: Mohr-Siebeck, 1936).

Holtzmann, *Das Evangelium des Johannes*
Heinrich Julius Holtzmann, *Das Evangelium des Johannes*, rev. Walter Bauer. HKNT 4 (Tübingen: Mohr-Siebeck, [3]1908).

Jeremias, *Jerusalem*
Joachim Jeremias, *Jerusalem in the Time of Jesus. An Investigation into Economic and Social Conditions during the New Testament Period* (Philadelphia: Fortress Press, 1969) = *Jerusalem zur Zeit Jesu* (Göttingen: Vandenhoeck & Ruprecht, [3]1962).

Jeremias, *Jesus als Weltvollender*
Joachim Jeremias, *Jesus als Weltvollender*, BFCT 33, 4 (Gütersloh: C. Bertelsmann, 1930).

Jeremias, *Rediscovery of Bethesda*
Joachim Jeremias, *The Rediscovery of Bethesda: John 5:2*, New Testament Archaeology 1 (Louisville, KY: Southern Baptist Theological Seminary, 1966).

Käsemann, *New Testament Questions*
Ernst Käsemann, *New Testament Questions of Today*, tr. W. J. Montague and Wilfred F. Bunge (Philadelphia: Fortress Press, 1969).

Käsemann, *The Testament of Jesus*
Ernst Käsemann, *The Testament of Jesus: A Study of the Gospel of John in the Light of Chapter 17*, tr. Gerhard Krodel (Philadelphia: Fortress Press, 1968) = *Jesu letzter Wille nach Johannes 17* (Tübingen: Mohr-Siebeck, 1966).

Kennard, "The Burial of Jesus"
Kennard, J. Spencer, Jr. "The Burial of Jesus." *JBL* 74 (1955) 227–38.

Klein, "Die Verleugnung des Petrus"
Günther Klein, "Die Verleugnung des Petrus.

Eine traditionsgeschichtliche Untersuchung." *ZTK* 58 (1961) 285–328.

Kümmel, *Introduction*
Werner Georg Kümmel, *Introduction to the New Testament*, tr. Howard C. Kee (Nashville: Abingdon Press, 1975).

Kümmel, *NT History and Investigation*
Werner Georg Kümmel, *The New Testament: The History of the Investigation of its Problems*, tr. S. McLean Gilmour and Howard C. Kee (Nashville: Abingdon Press, 1972) = *Das Neue Testament; Geschichte der Erforschung seiner Probleme* (Freiburg: K. Alber, 1958).

Lagrange, *Evangile selon saint Jean*
Marie-Joseph Lagrange, *Evangile selon saint Jean*, Etudes bibliques (Paris: J. Gabalda, ²1925, ⁸1947).

Lawlor and Oulton
Eusebius, *The Ecclesiastical History and The Martyrs of Palestine*, 2 vols. Tr. Hugh Jackson Lawlor and John Ernest Leonard Oulton (London: S. P. C. K, 1927–28).

Leroy, *Rätsel und Mißverständnis*
Herbert Leroy, *Rätsel und Mißvertändnis. Ein Beitrag zur Formgeschichte des Johannesevangeliums*, BBB 30 (Bonn: Peter Hanstein, 1968) esp. 5f., 183–85.

Lightfoot, *St. John's Gospel*
R. H. Lightfoot, *St. John's Gospel. A Commentary*, ed. C. F. Evans (Oxford: Clarendon Press; London: Cumberlege, 1956).

Linnemann, "Die Verleugnung des Petrus"
Eta Linnemann, "Die Verleugnung des Petrus." *ZTK* 63 (1966) 1–32.

Loisy, *Le quatrième évangile*
Alfred Loisy, *Le quatrième évangile* (Paris: A. Picard & Fils, 1903, ²1921).

Luthardt, *Das johanneische Evangelium*
Christian Ernst Luthardt, *Das johanneische Evangelium nach seiner Eigentümlichkeit geschildert und erklärt*, 2 vols. (Nuremburg: Gieger, ²1875).

Maier, *Die Texte vom Toten Meer*
Johann Maier, *Die Texte vom Toten Meer*, 2 vols. Vol. 1, *Übersetzung*; Vol. 2, *Anmerkungen* (Munich: E. Reinhardt, 1960).

Metzger, *The Text of the NT*
Bruce M. Metzger, *The Text of the New Testament: Its Transmission, Corruption, and Restoration* (New York and London: Oxford University Press, 1964).

Michaelis, *Einleitung*
Wilhelm Michaelis, *Einleitung in das Neue Testament* (Bern: B. Haller, ²1954).

Nag Hammadi Library
James M. Robinson, ed., *The Nag Hammadi Library in English* (New York: Harper & Row, 1977).

Nestle
Eberhard Nestle and Erwin Nestle, *Novum Testamentum Graece; apparatum criticum recensuerunt*, rev. and expanded by Kurt Aland and Barbara Aland (Stuttgart: Deutsche Bibelstiftung, ²⁶1979).

Noetzel, *Christus und Dionysus*
Heine Noetzel, *Christus und Dionysus. Bemerkungen zum Religionsgeschichtlichen Hintergrund von Johannes 2, 1–11*, Arbeiten zur Theologie 1 (Stuttgart: Calwer Verlag, 1960).

Regul, *Die antimarcionitischen Evangelienprologe*
J. Regul, *Die antimarcionitischen Evangelienprologe*, Vetus Latina, Die Reste der altlateinischen Bibel, Aus der Geschichte der lateinischen Bibel 6 (Freiburg: Herder, 1969).

Richter, *Studien zum Johannesevangelium*
Georg Richter, *Studien zum Johannesevangelium*, ed. J. Hainz. BU 13 (Regensburg: F. Pustet, 1977).

Ruckstuhl, *Einheit*
Eugen Ruckstuhl, *Die literarische Einheit des Johannesevangeliums* (Freiburg: Paulus, 1951).

Rudolph, *Die Mandäer*
Kurt Rudolph, *Die Mandäer*, 2 vols. Vol. 1, *Prolegomena: Das Mandäerproblem*, FRLANT, n.s., 56; Vol. 2, *Der Kult*, FRLANT, n.s., 57 (Göttingen: Vandenhoeck & Ruprecht, 1960-1961).

Schlatter, *Der Evangelist Johannes*
Adolf Schlatter, *Der Evangelist Johannes. Wie er spricht, denkt, und glaubt. Ein Kommentar zum 4. Evangelium* (Stuttgart: Calwer Veriensbuchhandlung, 1930).

Schnackenburg, *John*
Rudolf Schnackenburg, *The Gospel According to St. John*, 3 vols. Vol. 1, *Introduction and Commentary on Chapters 1–4*, tr. Kevin Smyth (New York: Seabury Press, 1980) = *Das Johannesevangelium*, part 1. HTKNT 4,1 (Freiburg: Herder, 1965); Vol. 2, *Commentary on Chapters 5–12*, tr. Cecily Hastings, Francis McDonagh, David Smith, and Richard Foley (New York: Seabury Press, 1980) = *Das Johannesevangelium*, part 2. HTKNT 4,2 (Freiburg: Herder, 1971); Vol. 3, *Commentary on Chapters 13–21*, tr. David Smith and G. A. Kon (New York: Crossroad, 1982) = *Das Johannesevangelium*, part 3. HTKNT 4,3 (Freiburg: Herder, 1975).

Schwartz, "Aporien"
Eduard Schwartz, "Aporien im vierten Evangelium." NGG (1907) 1: 342–72; (1908) 2: 115–48, 3: 149–88 4: 497–560.

Schweitzer, *The Quest of the Historical Jesus*
Albert Schweitzer, *The Quest of the Historical Jesus: A Critical Study of its Progress from Reimarus to Wrede*, tr. W. Montgomery (New York: Macmillan, 1961) = *Geschichte der Leben-Jesu-Forschung* (Tübingen: Mohr-Siebeck, 1906, ⁶1951).

Schweizer, *Ego Eimi*
Eduard Schweizer, *Ego Eimi. Die religionsgeschichtliche Herkunft und theologische Bedeutung der johanneischen Bildreden, zugleich ein Beitrag zur Quellenfrage des vierten Evangeliums*, FRLANT, n.s., 38 (Göttingen: Vandenhoeck & Ruprecht, ²1965).

Smith, *Composition and Order*
D. Moody Smith, *The Compositon and Order of the Fourth Gospel: Bultmann's Literary Theory* (New Haven and London: Yale University Press, 1965).

Strathmann, *Das Evangelium nach Johannes*
Hermann Strathmann, *Das Evangelium nach Johannes*, NTD 4 (Göttingen: Vandenhoeck & Ruprecht, [11]1968).

Tasker, *John*
R. V. G. Tasker, *The Gospel According to St. John*, Tyndale New Testament Commentaries (Grand Rapids: Wm. B. Eerdmans, 1971).

Thüsing, *Erhöhung*
Wilhelm Thüsing, *Die Erhöhung und Verherrlichung Jesu im Johannesevangelium*, NTAbh 21, 1–2 (Münster: Aschendorff, 1960).

Weiss, *Das Johannes-Evangelium*
Bernhard Weiss, *Das Johannes-Evangelium*, KEK 2 (Göttingen: Vandenhoeck & Ruprecht, 1834, [9]1902).

Wellhausen, *Das Evangelium Johannis*
Julius Wellhausen, *Das Evangelium Johannis* (Berlin: G. Reimer, 1908).

Westcott and Hort
B. F. Westcott and F. J. A. Hort, *The New Testament in the Original Greek*, 2 vols. (Cambridge and London: Macmillan, 1890–1896).

Wette, *Kurze Erklärung*
William Martin Leberecht de Wette, *Kurze Erklärung des Evangeliums und der Briefe Johannes*, Kurzgefasstes exegetisches Handbuch zum Neuen Testament 1,3 (Leipzig: Weidmann, [4]1852).

Wetter, *Der Sohn Gottes*
Gillis Petersson Wetter, *"Der Sohn Gottes," eine Untersuchung über den Charakter und die Tendenz des Johannesevangeliums; zugleich ein Beitrag zur Kenntnis der Heilandsgestalten der Antike* FRLANT, n.s., 9 (Göttingen: Vandenhoeck & Ruprecht, 1916).

Wettstein, *Novum Testamentum Graecum*
J. J. Wettstein, *Novum Testamentum Graecum editionis receptae cum Lectionibus variantibus . . . necnon commentario pleniore . . . opera studio Joannis Jacobi Wetstenii*, 2 vols. (Amsterdam, 1751, 1752).

Wikenhauser, *Das Evangelium nach Johannes*
Alfred Wikenhauser, *Das Evangelium nach Johannes*, RNT 4 (Regensburg: F. Pustet, [2]1957).

Winter, *On the Trial of Jesus*
Paul Winter, *On the Trial of Jesus*, Studia Judaica, Forschungen zur Wissenschaft des Judentums 1 (Berlin: Walter de Gruyter, 1961).

Zahn, *Das Evangelium des Johannes*
Theodor Zahn, *Das Evangelium des Johannes ausgelegt* (Leipzig: A. Deichert, [6]1921).

Page numbers in [ ], following a reference to an
English translation, refer to the original text.

For the convenience of the reader, the reference
codes have been repeated as a part of the front matter
of volume 2. A biographical sketch of Ernst Haenchen
and his work, prepared by Professor D. Ulrich Busse,
appears as an appendix to this volume. An integrated
and augmented bibliography and a comprehensive
index to both volumes round off the work.

The end papers of the Commentary on John are a
reproduction of $\mathfrak{P}^{52}$, which contains a fragment of
John, 18:31–34, 37–38, dating from the early second
century CE. $\mathfrak{P}^{52}$ is the oldest extant fragment of the
New Testament. It is reprinted with the permission of
The John Rylands University Library of Manchester,
England.

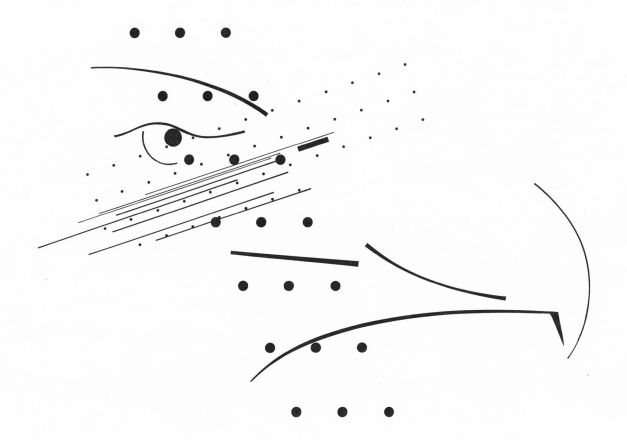

The long discourses in John 7 and 8 present special difficulties. Older scholars, for example, B. Weiss,[1] and their conservative camp followers, like Zahn[2] and Büchsel,[3] owe their psychological mode of interpretation to their fortunate blindness to the dangers that lurk everywhere. But the one who looks closely will note the thin ice that will subsequently give way. In the wake of Wellhausen and Schwartz, it is no longer possible to discover complete and faithful representations of events in the reports of the Gospel of John. The problems are well known and now everything depends on discovering their basis.

In chapters 5 and 6, a miracle is the occasion each time for a discourse of Jesus. That is not the case in chapter 7. The Evangelist must therefore return repeatedly to the preceding miracle at the pool of Bethzatha, set in Jerusalem. But that is not enough. The episode in 7:1–13, consequently, serves as the introduction to the whole.

Even that arrangement was not possible without effort. Chapter 6 ended with the desertion of many disciples following the discourse of Jesus in Capernaum. It is not said that all his Galilean disciples left him at that time; that is wrongly inferred from 6:66–71. In any case, Jesus' further sojourn in Galilee (one can assume that it was months long) would have been difficult for the Evangelist to explain, if he had any serious interest in such questions. In fact, he is concerned with theological problems, not with chronological and topographical issues.

The feast of Tabernacles provides the Evangelist not only with the welcome occasion to move Jesus again out of Galilee and to Jerusalem, this time for the final time, it also permits the Johannine Jesus to make clear, in his conversations with his brothers (as with his mother earlier in 2:4), that he does not follow suggestions given to him, but accepts only divine guidance.

Nevertheless, many things here remain questionable (see the commentary below). It is striking, for example, that up to this point the "world" is mentioned only as the object of the divine plan of salvation. But in chapter 7 the "world" appears for the first time as the anti-divine power, insofar as Johannine theology permits an independent adversary of God to exist at all. The Jews in Jerusalem—the high priests and Pharisees, who are distinguished from the crowd, several times appear in their place—are the indocile representatives of this world. That they are intractable becomes evident, however, only when Jesus attempts, continually, to demonstrate his claim and his mission. He must therefore go to Jerusalem repeatedly as a pilgrim and the festivals provide the apparent occasion for those visits. For it is nowhere said that he participates in the rituals, and the designation of the feast of Tabernacles as the "feast of the Jews" in 7:2 says enough. The attempts of more recent exegetes to discover allusions to the festivals in his discourses have not produced the desired results.[4] Rather, the attempts demonstrate that the wish is the father of the thought, as is so often the case in exegesis.

As a result of the work of Wellhausen and Schwartz—they sometimes also overshoot the mark—it is generally known that the several individual discourse scenes in chapters 7 and 8 do not form a real unity. Both contradictions and repetitions confirm that. The discourse scenes occasionally echo a theological theme, but it would be precipitous to suggest that everything in the Gospel that has one and the same subject originally formed a unity which has been destroyed by a foolish editor or by a catastrophe of unknown nature. Of course, the bulk of what is expected of the reader is not determined at the outset, and one will ask, for example, how the sending of the "officers" to arrest Jesus in verse 32 and their return empty-handed in verse 45 three days later is to be explained: did the Evangelist have in view the reader for whom the two references were separated by about only one page; or is one to accept some kind of disorder, which then of course becomes problematic in its own right; or did the Evangelist make arbitrary use of historical items to serve his own literary and theological purposes? In verse 32, the dispatch of the officers induces Jesus to speak about the short time he will remain with them. In verses 45f., when the minions of the law return with empty hands, their explanation, "No man ever spoke like this man," indirectly portrays the exalted demeanor of Jesus, which is the theme from verse 40 on. The same motif in individual contexts can thus serve

1 *Das Johannes-Evangelium*, 283–354.
2 *Das Evangelium des Johannes*, 374–434.
3 *Das Evangelium nach Johannes*, 93–112.

4 Guilding has gone the farthest in this direction (*The Fourth Gospel and Jewish Worship;* reviewed by Haenchen, *TLZ* 86 [1961] 670–72).

various theological interests, even at the cost of historical probability.

It is highly probable that various traditions have been utilized in so extensive a composition, without our being able, at the same time, to isolate particular sources. The mode of Jesus' argumentation in verses 22f. is typically rabbinic and presupposes forms of knowledge that the Evangelist in other places apparently does not have at his command. Furthermore, the way in which the messiah, who suddenly and mysteriously appears, is mentioned in verse 27 presupposes special knowledge of a rabbinic tradition. It would of course be premature to regard the Evangelist as a man well-read in rabbinics for that reason or to think that the apostle John is thereby "proved" to be the author. The appearance in the same context of completely unhistorical features (the Pharisees as officials) and of such rabbinic tradition shows that one must think of the tradition utilized by the author directly or indirectly as many-layered and variegated. Another example of the difficult position of one who insists on further evidence of the exactness of the author's historical knowledge is to be found in verse 37: is the last day of the feast of Tabernacles, "the great day," the seventh or the eighth day? Exegetes do not agree. For the Evangelist, however, it is probably only a matter of depicting an especially important festival on which Jesus renews his proclamation. As a consequence, one must make an even greater effort than heretofore to discern the aim of the author's message as the most significant factor in his representation of the activity of Jesus.

One further subordinate point in conclusion: the earlier exegetes competely missed the irony with which the Evangelist represents the suppression of the people's decision of faith by the officials. The one-sided historical question posed by earlier exegetes blinded them to other interests. As a result, the picture of the Evangelist was emptied of precision and color.

20. Is Jesus Going to Jerusalem?

Bibliography

Bleek, Friedrich
  "Ueber Joh 7,8, die richtige Lesart (. . .) und den Sinn." In his *Beiträge zur Einleitung und Auslegung der heiligen Schrift.* Vol. 1, *Beiträge zur Evangelienkritik* (Berlin: G. Reimer, 1846) 105–7.

Bornkamm, Günther
  "Joh 7, 10–18: Eine Meditation." *Wissenschaft und Praxis in Kirche und Gesellschaft* 59 (1970) 108–13.

Cottam, Thomas
  "At the Feast of Booths." *ExpTim* 48 (1936/1937) 45.

Dekker, C.
  "Grundschrift und Redaktion im Johannesevangelium." *NTS* 13 (1966/1967) 66–80.

Oke, C. Clarke
  "At the Feast of Booths. A Suggested Rearrangement of John vii–ix." *ExpTim* 47 (1935/1936) 425–27.

Olbricht, Thomas H.
  "Its Works Are Evil (John 7:7)." *Restoration Quarterly* 7 (1963) 242–44.

Schneider, Johannes
  "Zur Komposition von Joh 7, I." *ZNW* 45 (1954) 108–19.

7

1 After this Jesus went about in Galilee; he would not go about in Judea, because the Jews sought to kill him. 2/ Now the Jews' feast of Tabernacles was at hand. 3/ So his brothers said to him, "Leave here and go to Judea, that your disciples may see the works you are doing. 4/ For no man works in secret if he seeks to be known openly. If you do these things, show yourself to the world." 5/ For even his brothers did not believe him. 6/ Jesus said to them, "My time has not yet come, but your time is always here. 7/ The world cannot hate you, but it hates me because I testify of it that its works are evil. 8/ Go to the feast yourselves; I am not going up to the feast, for my time has not yet fully come." 9/ So saying, he remained in Galilee. 10/ But after his brothers had gone up to the feast, then he also went up, not publicly but in private. 11/ The Jews were looking for him at the feast, and saying, "Where is he?" 12/ And there was much muttering about him among the people. While some said, "He is a good man," others said, "No, he is leading the people astray." 13/ Yet for fear of the Jews no one spoke openly of him.

■ **1** "After this": 𝔓⁶⁶ ℵ * D *al* it sy omit the "and," which 𝔓⁷⁵ B read. ℵ and D agree here, as often elsewhere. The imperfects "went about" (περιεπάτει) and "he would" (ἤθελεν) suggest a rather long sojourn in Galilee; it is a half year from the Passover, which was at hand in 6:4, to the feast of Tabernacles. Verse 1b gives as the reason for Jesus' departure that he wanted to avoid the death threat that awaited him in Judea (5:16, 18).

■ **2** For the Evangelist the confrontation of Jesus with the "world" has to take place in Jerusalem, where the high priests and Pharisees who are hostile to Jesus reign. As a consequence, the reasons why Jesus must nevertheless go to Jerusalem have to be introduced. The first is the feast of Tabernacles, which Josephus terms the most important feast of the Jews. The second reason turns out almost to be a counter-reason: Jesus' brothers urge him to go up to Jerusalem to the feast. His brothers were last mentioned in 2:12. If one reads ἔμεινεν ("he stayed") in that passage with 𝔓⁶⁶,[1] then the conversation with his brothers would have taken place in Capernaum, where Jesus gave the great discourse recorded in chapter 6. Since the Evangelist has not reported that Jesus left that place, apart from the "he went about" (περιεπάτει), the present scene could also have taken place in Capernaum. Although it is improbable that Jesus did not leave Capernaum, owing to the statement "he went about" (περιεπάτει), it is still quite possible that he returned once more to Capernaum after wandering about in Galilee and there had his conversation with his brothers. It was perhaps an element in the tradition that Jesus' family remained in Capernaum. The assertion in verse 5 that Jesus' brothers did not believe in him squares with the tradition recorded in Mark 3:21, 31–35, according to which Jesus' family regarded him as possessed and wanted to take him home; the tradition would of course be toned down in the Gospel of John. Interpreters occasionally indicate that James also belonged to these unbelieving brothers; James first came to faith as a result of an appearance of the risen one to him. Yet, however the tradition available to the Evangelist looked to him, it now serves his purposes.

■ **3** Jesus' brothers now urge him to leave (μεταβαίνω could even mean: "move, change one's permanent address") and go to Judea, which, in the context, means Jerusalem. The Jewish-Christian Gospel of the Nazoreans relates that Jesus' mother and his brothers request that he go with them to be baptized.[2] He answers: "Wherein have I sinned that I should go and be baptized by him? Unless what I have said is a sin of ignorance." The scene in Mark 3:31ff. also leads to the Gospel of Thomas, logion 99. Logion 104, however, is reminiscent of the apocryphal tradition preserved by Jerome: "They said to Jesus, 'Come let us pray today and let us fast.' Jesus said, 'What is the sin that I have committed, or wherein have I been defeated?'"[3] The balance of the logion reproduces Mark 2:20. In the apocryphal tradition, the members of Jesus' family are also unbelievers in the sense of the Christian proclamation.

The continuation of the text in John 7:3 is also very difficult: "that your disciples may see the works you are doing." "Your disciples" may be an erroneous substitute for the indefinite subject "one": "that they may also see there (καὶ ἔνθα) the works you are doing." The emendation could be the consequence of an inference from 6:66 that, of those in Galilee, only the twelve remained true and that only in Jerusalem were there still disciples (2:23). The works of which his brothers speak are then the miracles performed in Galilee, works that are reported in 4:46ff. and chapter 6.

■ **4** Verse 4 assumes that people in Jerusalem are not yet aware of Jesus' miracles. Jesus' brothers are not concerned that he heal the sick or perform other miracles in Jerusalem. For them the miracles (which they do not doubt) are the means to become known. Jesus could not remain in hiding, do something in a remote corner like Galilee, and become known only there. It is decisive for his brothers that he be recognized in Jerusalem; for them Jerusalem is the world to which Jesus should reveal himself.

■ **5** Verse 5 correctly emphasizes that Jesus' brothers do not believe in him. For Jesus Jerusalem is the world that is hostile to God, and it hates him, as it here becomes evident for the first time.

■ **6** The response of Jesus is clear in this respect: his

---

1   A reading also attested Hᶜ 053 565 1241 *al* bo Orᵖᵗ, while P⁷⁵ *pm* have ἔμειναν, "they stayed."

2   Fragment 2 found in Jerome, *adv. Pelag.* 3.2. Tr. in Hennecke, *NTApoc* 1: 146f.

3   Tr. H. Koester and T. Lambdin, *The Nag Hammadi Library*, p. 129.

"hour" has not yet come,[4] that hour in which he goes to the cross in accordance with the command of the Father. His brothers are not aware of any special hour, so it is always the right time for them.

■ **7** Since Jesus' brothers serve the world, the world cannot hate them. But the world hates him because he testifies that its works are evil. It follows from this that Jesus can only go to Jerusalem when the Father calls him to do so.

■ **8** The statement of Jesus is important, but its text is unfortunately uncertain: They are to go to the feast. "I am not going" (or: "not yet going") "to the feast, for my time has not yet been fulfilled." Customarily οὐκ ("not") is taken as the original reading (attested by ℵ * D K lat sy^sc) and οὔπω ("not yet") as the reading that smoothes, although the latter is attested by 𝔓^66 𝔓^75 B L T W *al* lat bo sa. But the reading οὐκ contains an internal difficulty: Jesus does not yet know when his time will be fulfilled and the Father will call upon him to die in Jerusalem. Accordingly, he cannot say "not" in accordance with the logic of his situation, but must say "not yet," as in verse 6. From this point of view, the oldest textual witnesses presumably offer the correct reading; this idea was later fastened onto once again, of course, in order to avoid the contradiction that Jesus nevertheless went up to Jerusalem as a pilgrim.

■ **9** Verse 9 brings this scene to a close with the mention of place, as is often the case in the Gospel of John: Jesus remains in Galilee.

■ **10** Verse 10 has caused interpreters a great deal of trouble. Schlatter seems not yet to have noticed the difficulties.[5] In the company of other exegetes, B. Weiss explains it as follows: Jesus did not go up to Jerusalem in a festival caravan (that this caravan would have long since gone to Jerusalem, as indicated by the temporal designation "then," τότε, Weiss overlooks), but went "incognito," as it were, and did so, so that people would not be able to prepare a messianic welcome for him.[6] Weiss does not go into the contradiction to verse 8.[7] Bauer[8] refers to

Wellhausen[9] and Schwartz[10] and explains verse 10 in this fashion: "Since Jesus does not 'go up' (ἀναβαίνω) on this occasion in order to be revealed as the one sent by God, who now returns to the Father," he goes "not openly but in secret" (οὐ φανερῶς, ἀλλ᾽ (ὡς) ἐν κρυπτῷ) to do his work, while at the end of his life he proceeds differently. Strathmann reflects on the matter thus: the brothers want Jesus to perform his works in public—they do not understand the passion of Jesus. "If we understand the rejection of the request of his brothers in this way, it is only an apparent and not a contradiction of fact that Jesus at first categorically refuses to go up to the feast and then goes up after all, but unostentatiously."[11] But his brothers did not speak of a triumphal entry, and Jesus makes his appearance in verses 14 and 37 quite openly.

It remains to consider whether verse 10 is a later insertion. The difficulty is created by the "not" in verse 8: Jesus explains quite definitely that he is not going up to the feast, and then a little later he goes. Verse 10 now makes allowance for this difficulty—quite ingeniously, of course—by representing Jesus as going up in secret and thus not making a proper pilgrimage at all (ἀναβαίνειν). If one omits this verse as a later gloss (in the manuscript tradition the only thing that points to that possibility is an uncertainty regarding word order), the context then becomes clear: Jesus remains in Galilee for the time being.

■ **11** But the Jews wonder whether "he" will appear or not (here we cannot interpret them with certainty as hostile authorities). The "that one" (ἐκεῖνος) is usually interpreted in a derogatory sense: they do not want to pronounce his name. However, there is really only one such "he," which makes Jesus the secret focus of the scene, in a certain sense.

■ **12** Verse 12 even indicates that some are on his side and say that he is a "good" man, while others call him a deceiver of people (which may have been a specifically Jewish reproach). Not one of the groups speaks of him

---

4   The term καιρός here has the same meaning as ὥρα— "the right time" = "hour."

5   *Der Evangelist Johannes,* 189.

6   *Das Johannes-Evangelium,* 288.

7   Weiss reads οὐκ, "not," in verse 8: *Das Johannes-Evangelium,* 288.

8   *Das Johannesevangelium,* 108.

9   *Das Evangelium Johannis,* 34f.

10   "Aporien," 2: 117f.

11   Strathmann, *Das Evangelium nach Johannes,* 128.

aloud "for fear of the Jews"; this shows, as does 9:22, that a confession of Christ inside Judaism has become impossible for the Evangelist. One can only sympathize with him in secret; 9:34 indicates an excommunication from the synagogue, which had taken place at the time of the Evangelist. Hirsch writes of verses 11–13: "This depiction can at least be measured by the famous scenes in Goethe's *Egmont*. There is nothing comparable in ancient literature."[12] That is an intemperate exaggeration. Acts 14:4 and especially Acts 23:9f. exhibit similar examples of the representation of two different groups in Judaism, although the question "Where is he?" does not appear.

■ **13** The pros and cons are not voiced, however, because everyone is anxious not to awaken the wrath of the Jews (the author thinks of the Jews as a dominant class concentrated in Jerusalem). That the speakers in verse 13 are also Jews does not fit the picture depicted there (which is historically impossible) and is not therefore mentioned.

Overview

The Father has sent Jesus: that finally makes understandable a difficulty that has caused some exegetes a great deal of trouble. There is a series of passages in which John represents Jesus as acting in a manner in which no man could or would act. In 2:3 Jesus' mother perhaps asks him, although indirectly, to assist by performing a miracle. Jesus rejects that demand and in doing so addresses his mother with the single word, "woman," as he does later in 19:26. However, a little later he performs the miracle that was requested. The example in 7:3ff. is comparable: his brothers ask him to accompany them to Jerusalem and there to perform miracles. Jesus refuses that request and says that he is not going to Jerusalem. But a few days later he nevertheless goes up to Jerusalem, and in 9:6f. he achieves the sensational miracle of healing the man born blind. Finally, from among a plethora of examples we may focus on the one in 18:6: when Jesus says to the cohort that plans to take him prisoner, "I am he," they fall to the ground. John of course found the miracle at Cana and the collapse of the cohort already related in the tradition; but that does not yet explain why he retained them. However, the explanation becomes clear on the basis of the reason he gives for rejecting his mother in 2:4: "My hour has not yet come." Jesus is not at all dependent upon human motivations, but relies only on the instructions of the Father. The Evangelist makes that clear in chapter 2 with the statement that corresponds to the similar sentence in 7:6: "My time ($\kappa\alpha\iota\rho\acute{o}s$) has not yet come." Even the demand of his closest kin could not move him. In order to make that absolutely clear he does not give Mary the name "mother," but addresses her, as in 19:26, as "woman."

We must, however, consider the words "hour" and "time" more closely. They appear to relate primarily to certain situations in the life of Jesus in which he waits for directions from the Father. But as exegetes have already noted, there is more to it than that. In connection with the term "hour," John thinks of that hour in which Jesus will perform his great act of love on the cross. For the Evangelist, that act of love is already suggested and anticipated in the small act of love in Cana where he rectifies the shortage of wine. The same thing can be said of his appearance in Jerusalem, which his brothers request him to make. Here also John gives the same meaning to the journey to Jerusalem that brings Jesus subsequently to the cross. But this way to the cross, this way to death, owes exclusively to the will of the Father and Jesus' own will. The world with all its might is unable to make him do it.

---

12   *Das vierte Evangelium*, 193f.

21. Jesus at the Feast of the Tabernacles

Feast of the Tabernacles
Bibliography
Allen, Willoughby C.
"St. John vii. 37, 38." *ExpTim* 34 (1922/1923) 329–30.
Bauer, Johannes Baptist
"Drei Cruces." *BZ* 9 (1965) 84–91.
Bertling, D.
"Eine Transposition im Evangelium Johannis." *TSK* 53 (1880) 351–53.
Blenkinsopp, J.
"The Quenching of Thirst: Reflections on the Utterance in the Temple, Jn 7, 37–39." *Scr* 12 (1950) 39–48.
Blenkinsopp, J.
"John 7, 37–39: Another Note on a Notorious Crux." *NTS* 6 (1959/1960) 95–98.
Blindley, T. H.
"Jn 7, 37–38." *Expositor,* 8th ser., 20 (1920) 443–47.
Boismard, Marie-Emile
"De son ventre couleront des fleuves d'eau (Jn 7, 38)." *RB* 65 (1958) 523–46.
Boismard, Marie-Emile
"Les citations targumiques du quatrième évangile." *RB* 66 (1959) 374–78, esp. 374–76.
Braun, François-Marie
"Avoir soif et boire: Jn 4, 10–14; 7, 37–39." In *Mélanges bibliques en hommage au R. P. Béda Rigaux,* ed. A. Descamps and A. De Halleux (Gembloux: Duculot, 1970) 247–58.
Brun, Lyder
"'Floder av levende vand,' (Joh 7, 37–39)." *NorTT* 29 (1928) 71–79.
Burney, Charles Fox
"Our Lord's Old Testament Reference in Joh 7, 37–38." *Expositor,* 8th ser., 20 (1920) 385–88.
Burney, Charles Fox
"The Aramaic Equivalent of ἐκ τῆς κοιλίας in Jn 7, 38." *JTS* 24 (1922/1923) 79–80.
Bussche, Henri van den
"Jésus, l'unique source d'eau vive, Jn 7, 37–39." *BVC* 65 (1965) 17–23.
Bussche, Henri van den
"Leurs écritures et Son enseignement. Jean 7, 14–36." *BVC* 72 (1966) 21–30.
Cortés, Juan B.
"Yet Another Look at Jn 7, 37–38." *CBQ* 29 (1967) 75–86.
Cortés Quirant, J.
"Torrentes de agua viva. ¿Una nueva interpretación de Jn 7, 37–38?" *EstBib* 16 (1957) 279–306.
Daniélou, Jean
"Joh 7, 37 et Ezéch 47, 1–11." *SE* 2 = TU 87 (Berlin: Akademie-Verlag, 1964) 158–63.

Dubarle, André Marie
"Des fleuves d'eau vive (S. Jean VII, 37–39)." *Vivre et penser* 3 = *RB* 52 (1943/1944) 238–41.

Fee, Gordon D.
"Once More—John 7, 37–39." *ExpTim* 89 (1978) 116–18.

Feuillet, André
"Les fleuves d'eau vive." In *Parole de Dieu et sacerdoce* [Festschrift J. J. Weber], ed. E. Fischer and L. Bouyer (Paris and New York: Desclée et Cie, 1962) 107–20.

Flowers, H. J.
"The Displacement of John 7, 37–44." *Expositor*, 8th ser., 22 (1921) 318–20.

Gieseler, J. K. L.
"Vermischte Bemerkungen: zu Joh 7, 38." *TSK* 2 (1829) 137–41.

Goguel, Maurice
"La venue de Jésus à Jérusalem pour la fête des tabernacles (Joh 7)." *RHR* 83 (1921) 123–62.

Grelot, Pierre
"'De son ventre couleront des fleuves d'eau.' La citation scripturaire de Jean 7, 38." *RB* 66 (1959) 369–74.

Grelot, Pierre
"A propos de Jean 7, 38." *RB* 67 (1960) 224–25.

Grelot, Pierre
"Jn VII, 38: Eau du rocher ou source du temple?" *RB* 70 (1963) 43–51.

Hahn, Ferdinand
"Die Worte vom lebendigen Wasser im Johannesevangelium. Eigenart und Vorgeschichte von Joh 4, 10.13f; 6: 35; '7, 37–39." In *God's Christ and His People. Studies in honor of Nils Alstrup Dahl*, ed. Jacob Jervell and Wayne A. Meeks (Oslo: Universitetsforlaget, 1977) 51–70.

Harris, Richard
"Rivers of Living Water (Jn 7, 38)." *Expositor*, 8th ser., 20 (1920) 196–202.

Hooke, S. H.
"'The Spirit Was Not Yet.'" *NTS* 9 (1962/1963) 372–80.

Kilpatrick, George Dunbar
"The Punctuation of John 7, 37–38." *JTS*, n.s., 11 (1960) 340–42.

Kim Pyung-Hak, R.
"Lebendiges Wasser und Sakramentssymbolik." Dissertation, Rome, 1969/1970.

Kohler, Mere
"Des fleuves d'eau vive. Exégèse de Jean 7, 37–39." *RTP* 10 (1960) 188–201.

Kuhn, K. H.
"St. John 7, 37–38." *NTS* 4 (1957/1958) 63–65.

Leanza, Sandro
"Testimonianze della tradizione indiretta su alcuni passi del Nuovo Testamento (Giov VII, 37–38 e altri passi)." *RivB* 15 (1967) 407–18.

Mehlmann, Johannes
"Propheta a Moyse promissus in Jo 7, 52 citatus." *VD* 44 (1966) 79–88.

Menard, Jacques-E.
"L'interprétation patristique de Jean VII, 38." *RUO* (1955) 5–25.

Miguens, M.
"El Agua y el Espíritu en Jn 7, 37–39." *EstBib* 31 (1972) 369–98.

Pancaro, Severino
"The Metamorphosis of a Legal Principle in the Fourth Gospel. A Close Look at Jn 7, 51." *Bib* 53 (1972) 340–61.

Rahner, Hugo
"Flumina de ventre Christi—Die patristische Auslegung von Joh 7, 37–38." *Bib* 22 (1941) 269–302, 367–403.

Sahlin, Harald
"Till förstaelsen av Joh 7, 37–41." *SEÅ* 11 (1946) 77–90.

Schweizer, Eduard
Neues Testament und heutige Verkündigung, BibS(N) 56 (Neukirchen: Neukirchener Verlag, 1969).

Smith, Charles W. F.
"Tabernacles in the Fourth Gospel and Mark." *NTS* 9 (1962/1963) 130–46.

Smothers, Edgar R.
"Two Readings in Papyrus Bodmer II." *HTR* 51 (1958) 109–22.

Stanley, David Michael
"Holy Scripture. The Feast of Tents: Jesus' Self-Revelation." *Worship* 34 (1964) 20–27.

Stiftinger, K.
"Exegesegeschichtliche Studie zu Joh. 7, 37f." Dissertation, Graz, 1970/1971.

Turner, C. H.
"On the Punctation of John 7, 37–38." *JTS* 24 (1923) 66–70.

Waitz, Eberhard
"Zur Erklärung von Joh 7, 22–24." *TSK* 54 (1881) 145–60.

Woodhouse, H.
"Hard Sayings—IX. John 7. 39." *Theology* 67 (1964) 310–12.

7

John 7:14–52

14   About the middle of the feast Jesus went up into the temple and taught. 15/ The Jews marveled at it, saying, "How is it that this man has learning, when he has never studied (with a rabbi)?" 16/ So Jesus answered them, "My teaching is not mine, but his who sent me; 17/ if any man's will is to do his will, he shall know whether the teaching is from God or whether I am speaking on my own authority. 18/ He who speaks on his own authority seeks his own glory; but he who seeks the glory of him who sent him is true, and in him there is no wickedness. 19/ Did not Moses give you the law? Yet none of you keeps the law. Why do you seek to kill me?" 20/ The people answered, "You have a demon! Who is seeking to kill you?" 21/ Jesus answered them, "I did one deed, and you all marvel at it. 22/ Therefore, Moses gave you circumcision (not that it is from Moses, but from the fathers), and you circumcise a man upon the sabbath. 23/ If on the sabbath a man receives circumcision, so that the law of Moses may not be broken, are you angry with me because on the sabbath I made a man's whole body well? 24/ Do not judge by appearances, but judge with right judgment."

25   Some of the people of Jerusalem therefore said, "Is not this the man whom they seek to kill? 26/ And here he is, speaking openly, and they say nothing to him! Can it be that the authorities really know that this is the Christ? 27/ Yet we know where this man comes from; and when the Christ appears, no one will know where he comes from." 28/ So Jesus proclaimed, as he taught in the temple, "You know me, and you know where I come from? But I have not come of my own accord; he who sent me is true, and him you do not know. 29/ I know him, for I come from him, and he sent me." 30/ So they sought to arrest him; but no one laid hands on him, because his hour had not yet come.

31   Yet many of the people believed in him; they said, "When the Christ appears, will he do more signs than this man has done?" 32/ The Pharisees heard the crowd thus muttering about him, and the chief priests and Pharisees sent officers to arrest him. 33/ Jesus then said, "I shall be with you a little longer, and then I go to him who sent me; 34/ you will seek me and you will not find me; where I am you cannot come."

35   The Jews said to one another, "Where does this man intend to go that we shall not find him? Does he intend to go to the Dispersion among the Greeks and teach the Greeks? 36/ What does he mean by saying, 'You will seek me and you will

37   On the last day of the feast, the great day,
      Jesus stood up and proclaimed, "If any
      one thirst, let him come to me and drink.
      38/ He who believes in me, as the scrip-
      ture has said, 'Out of his heart shall flow
      rivers of living water.'" 39/ Now this he
      said about the Spirit, which those who
      believed in him were to receive; for as yet
      the Spirit had not been given, because
      Jesus was not yet glorifed. 40/ When
      they heard these words, some of the
      people said, "This is really the prophet."
      41/ Others said, "This is the Christ." But
      some said, "Is the Christ to come from
      Galilee? 42/ Has not the scripture said
      that the Christ is descended from David,
      and comes from Bethlehem, the village
      where David was?" 43/ So there was a
      division among the people over him. 44/
      Some of them wanted to arrest him, but
      no one laid hands on him.

45   The officers then went back to the chief
      priests and Pharisees, who said to them,
      "Why did you not bring him?" 46/ The
      officers answered, "No man ever spoke
      like this man!" 47/ The Pharisees an-
      swered them, "Are you led astray, you
      also? 48/ Have any of the authorities or
      of the Pharisees believed in him? 49/ But
      this crowd, who do not know the law, are
      accursed." 50/ Nicodemus, who had
      gone to him before, and who was one of
      them, said to them, 51/ "Does our law
      judge a man without first giving him a
      hearing and learning what he does?" 52/
      They replied, "Are you from Galilee too?
      Search and you will see that no prophet
      is to rise from Galilee."

There follow on the segment of narrative set in Galilee three scenes set in Jerusalem: 7:14–36; 7:37–52; 8:12–59. These scenes, in turn, are divided into subscenes. The section 7:14–24 is the first subscene: justification of the sabbath healing. Further subscenes are formed by 7:25–30: the people are divided over Jesus; 7:31–36: Jesus announces his departure; 7:37–44: Jesus promises the spirit; 7:45–52: the hostility of the Pharisees to Jesus.

■ **14** When the feast was already half over, Jesus goes up—the Evangelist has him go immediately into the temple and teach. Nothing is said of Jesus participating in the rituals connected with the feast; the imagination of some exegetes, who have Jesus appear in verse 37 in the midst of water libations, is out of place. He "was teaching": the imperfect again indicates duration. The Evan-

gelist provides no information regarding the place or the content of his teaching. The feast is called Succoth or Booths (in the OT simply חג or חג סוכות; Josephus writes: "At the same time happened to fall the festival of Taber-nacles, which is considered especially sacred and impor-tant by the Hebrews").[1] Originally it was the feast of the vintage; the feast ritual also took the fall rains into consideration, which set in about this time. In the process of historicizing it, the feast was brought into relation to the time when Israel lived in tents, in huts in the wilder-ness. The festival required that Jews live in booths during this week (later an eighth day was added). Μεσαζούσης ("in the midst of") is not only read by D, but also by $\mathfrak{P}^{66}$, and was corrected to μεσούσης, which is more common, by the softening of the guttural sound.[2] Since

1   *Ant.* 8.100: ὁ τῆς σκηνοπηγίας καιρὸς ἑορτῆς σφόδρα
     παρὰ τοῖς Ἑβραίοις ἁγιωτάτης καὶ μεγίστης. Cf.
     Billerbeck, 2: 774–812.

2   Schlatter, *Der Evangelist Johannes*, 190.

according to verse 10 Jesus had already come to Jerusalem, B. Weiss adopts the view that Jesus had already been there in hiding for a spell.[3] Loisy even holds the view that Jesus was there from the outset, but unrecognized, and even thinks that a beginning of docetism is not excluded.[4] Heitmüller believes that a secret stay is possible, but is of the opinion that "the report intentionally leaves the impression of secrecy."[5] Exegetes are united in the view that Jesus did not go up to Jerusalem in a pilgrim's caravan. The thought that Jesus secretly sojourned for a time in Jerusalem is foreign to the Evangelist; rather, he has Jesus go up immediately to the temple and teach. Bultmann would like to reconcile Jesus' rejection of publicity with his subsequent public appearance by pointing out that Jesus remains the hidden revealer for the Evangelist and his works therefore do not lose their character as "hidden" (κρυπτόν).[6] But that imports too much into the text. What Jesus teaches is not stated here; the fact that he teaches forms the presuppositon for what follows.

■ **15** "He does not know letters" (γράμματα οἶδεν): Jewish schooling was oriented to the OT. Thus to "know the scriptures" and to "be educated" are the same thing.[7] "Having never studied" (μὴ μεμαθηκώς): "without being the pupil of a rabbi." According to Zahn,[8] Jesus proves to be an effective haggadist, although he did not enjoy rabbinic training. There is no reason to speak of Jesus as a "genial self-taught man," as does Zahn,[9] nor to conjecture with Bauer that a Jewish polemic was directed against Jesus as an illiterate.[10] The thinking of the Evangelist takes another direction: since Jesus did not enjoy rabbinic schooling, he seems to present teaching that is his own and which has not been taken over from a teacher out of the tradition, as was customary.

■ **16** Yet Jesus denies even this conjecture: "My teaching"—the teaching just presented by him, in which the Evangelist does not want to have him offer the interpretation of the scriptures, but the self-proclamation to be mentioned later—is not "my teaching" (Zahn remarks: "

a brilliant antithesis")[11] although self-conceived. Rather, Jesus offers that teaching that derives from the one who sent him.[12]

■ **17** Verse 17 is formally reminiscent of Num 16:28, where Moses says to the Israelites: "Hereby you shall know that the Lord has sent me to do all these works, and that it has not been of my own accord." But the continuation—the annihilation of the company of Korah—shows that here, unlike the story in John, a miracle is meant to legitimate. On the other hand, Philo is familiar with the picture of the true prophet, who does not speak on his own behalf, but of whom God makes use.[13] On verse 17 Wrede writes: the Evangelist "simply says that in the instance of the opponents of Jesus who do not recognise his teaching as divine the reason lies only in the fact that it is actually towards God that they are disobedient. . . . With this, however, is to be conjoined the idea that unbelief is their guilt; it is wickedness, and they do not *wish* to do the will of him who sent them, 7:17."[14] Bultmann concurs with Wrede.[15] And Bauer also understands the passage in this way: "Misunderstanding relative to the divine sending of Jesus depends on an evil will. Cf. 5:40."[16] The question is just this: What does the author have in mind here as the divine will that is accessible to everyone? The will that one needs only to fulfill in order to know that one is in precise agreement with the teaching of Jesus? Does the Gospel of John presuppose a conscience that speaks to everyone, a conscience that many of course ignore because they do not want to pay attention to it? Lightfoot interprets the passage differently, although it does not appear so at first glance: Jesus "adds that it is open for everyone who wishes to do the will of God (i.e., to believe in him whom God has sent)." But if the "fulfillment of God's will" is the same thing as the acknowledgment that God has sent Jesus, and if Jesus' teaching consists essentially in proclaiming that he is the one sent by God, are we not then stuck in a tautology: Whoever believes that Jesus is a divine emissary will recognize that he has been

3   *Das Johannes-Evangelium*, 290.
4   *Le quatrième évangile*, 497.
5   "Das Evangelium des Johannes," 785.
6   Bultmann, *John*, 294 [221].
7   Bultmann, *John*, 273 n. 3 [205 n. 8].
8   *Das Evangelium des Johannes*, 383.
9   *Das Evangelium des Johannes*, 383.
10 *Das Johannesevangelium*, 109.

11 *Das Evangelium des Johannes*, 383.
12 Cf. Haenchen, "Der Vater," 68–77, especially 71.
13 *De spec. leg.* 1.65.
14 Wrede, *The Messianic Secret*, tr. J. C. G. Greig, The Library of Theological Translations (Greenwood, SC: Attic Press, 1971) 202 and 202 n. 25.
15 *John*, 274 [206].
16 *Das Johannesevangelium*, 109.

sent from God?[17]

This verse has become famous as a consequence of the theology of Ritschl.[18] The verse is customarily interpreted as follows: If one truly follows this prescribed praxis without insight, one will come anon to the knowledge that it derives from God. For that reason, John does not view the matter that way; John does not require such "blind" obedience. In this passage Jesus does not demand that man do what he says (with the prospect of then seeing that it is right); rather, whoever does God's will will know that Jesus is the one sent and that he is completely immersed in God's mission. The doing and the knowing do not form a series, but are different sides of the same event. Accordingly, the Evangelist does indeed know a faith that requires awakening by means of the provocative miracle, but he knows nothing of a "doing the will of God" before one knows that it is God's will. It is more a case of God moving man so that he comes to faith, and less of man doing something out of his own resolve that is passed off as the divine will. That would be a means of getting from below to above, and that is precisely what is foreign to the Evangelist. In this instance, the doctrine of existential decision, which is a modern concept, has misled Bultmann so that he interprets Ritschl as an existentialist. This is the way Ritschl interprets our passage: initially man is to act out of a purely authoritarian faith; later he will come to know that the faith in question has the correct content. Bultmann's doctrine of individual decision overlooks the fact that the decision of faith for the Evangelist is at once human knowledge and divine teaching; no, better: is divine decision, divine creation, in which new knowledge and new readiness for love and obedience are generated simultaneously. There are only a few places where Bultmann presents such an ill-considered doctrine as he does in connection with this passage.

■ **18** Verse 18 appears to provide another means for testing the genuineness of the teaching of Jesus. Whoever speaks on his own authority, seeks his own glory. But for John that is precisely not the case with Jesus: Jesus seeks only the glory of the Father and not his own. For that reason, he does not speak on his own authority, but is true, and in him there is no wickedness.

■ **19** The possibility thus arises of switching from a defensive posture to the offense: Moses gave the law to the Jews— this is irrefragable. And every listener must admit it. But now Jesus reproaches his Jewish auditors: None of you, he says, is fulfilling the law. They therefore constitute the exact opposite of Jesus, in whom there is no wickedness. But to what extent do they not "do" the law? The answer is given at the end of the verse: "Why do you seek to kill me?" (cf. 5:18) The question may be connected to the preceding in this fashion: If you yourselves do not keep the law, why do you want to kill me if I do not keep it?

■ **20** It is only too understandable that the crowd responds that Jesus is possessed: who wants to kill him? The character of the crowd is not altogether clear. On the one hand, Moses has given these people the law; they are therefore Jews. On the other hand, the murmuring of the crowd against Jesus will later be sharply rebuked by the "Jews." In verse 49 the Pharisees speak of "this crowd, who do not know the law; they are accursed" as a group that is despised and rejected by them, that is not identical with them, but rather forms a kind of people who are "Jews" only to a very limited extent. The "Jews" are thus not simply the Jewish people as a whole, but the Jewish people insofar as they deliberately and persistently oppose Jesus.

■ **21–23** The first verse shows that the Evangelist has in mind Jesus' sojourn in Jerusalem described in chapter 5. The Jews then really tried to kill him (5:18). That of course was eighteen months earlier, and our verse appears to attribute that resolve to those now listening to Jesus. In that case, this resolve to kill Jesus would be in disobedience to the command of the law: Thou shalt not kill. But John does not say that. Rather, he expressly recalls the healing of the lame man at the pool of Bethzatha. In verse 21 it is the one work that Jesus did in Jerusalem and that astonishes everyone. Unfortunately, the text at this point is uncertain. Does "therefore" (διὰ τοῦτο) in verse 22 go with what precedes or what follows? In the first case, we should translate: "and for that reason you all marvel." But διὰ τοῦτο is customarily used at the beginning of a sentence, not at the end. Does it therefore go with what follows? "Therefore, Moses has given you

---

17 See the Overview.
18 Cf. Haenchen, "Ritschl als Systematiker," *Gott und Mensch. Gesammelte Aufsätze* 1 (Tübingen: Mohr-

Siebeck, 1965) 409–75, especially 449.

circumcision"—that doesn't make any sense. One endeavors to improve matters by adopting a so-called ellipsis, an omission. Something like this may be supplied: "Therefore, in order to show you that your astonishment has no basis, I say to you . . ."[19]

But that does not put an end to the problems. Up to this point we have assumed that those listening to Jesus do not keep the law of Moses since they seek to kill Jesus. The discussion now turns to Moses, but to a different commandment: circumcision on the eighth day. In a kind of parenthesis, this is said about circumcision: circumcision does not come from Moses, but from the patriarchs. That it is mentioned in this connection is entirely correct. But the entire argument is vitiated by so doing. It is thus probable that this intrusive parenthesis is the disimprovement of an early reader who wanted to guard Jesus' words against the charge of inexactness. When we omit this parenthesis, the sentence reads: Moses gave you the law, and you circumcise a man on the sabbath. That would be the case when the eighth day after birth fell on a sabbath. The Jews thus carry out circumcision on the sabbath in order not to infringe the law of Moses. How can, how may one grumble at Jesus for making a man as a whole well on the sabbath? Those listening to Jesus are here not accused of disobeying the law of Moses, but of the obedience which prompts them to infringe the sabbath. This mode of argumentation corresponds to that of Rabbi Eliezer ben Azariah: "If the sabbath has to take second place already in the case of circumcision, which involves only one member of the body, how much more is it the case with respect to the saving of life?"[20] We learn from Justin that this argument also played a wider role in the dialogue of the community with the Jews: "For, tell me, did God wish . . . those to sin, who are circumcised and do circumcise on the Sabbaths; since He commands that on the eighth day—even though it happen to be a Sabbath—those who are born shall always be circumcised?"[21] Jesus is thus arguing in our passage like the Christian community argued in the time of the Evangelist. Of course a life was not in danger in the case of the healing of the lame man at the pool of Bethzatha. In that respect, the case presented by Rabbi Eliezer is more compelling than the one presented here. The

Evangelist may be reproducing a tradition that was circulating in the community.

■ **24** Since Jesus made an entire man well, it is pointless to charge him with breaking the sabbath. He has greater justification for healing on the sabbath than do those who circumcise. The whole line of argument makes sense of course only when one silently assumes *Num. Rab.* 12f., 203f.: *"the foreskin is a bodily blemish."* In that case, circumcision is to be viewed as the elimination of a "blemish." Of course, further attestation of this point of view is quite late.

Verse 24 concludes with the admonition not to judge by appearances, but to judge with right judgment.

■ **25–30** Verses 25–30 form a new subsection. The contradiction of verse 20 by verse 25 can be explained in part by saying that the Jerusalemites, in contrast to the mass of Galilean pilgrims, knew about the death plot of the authorities. Yet it is surpising that they blab this knowledge about so openly. One ought rather to trust the Evangelist, who is making use of definite motives according to the situation—in this case the death plot— and in so doing lets tensions and contradictions quietly stand.

■ **25** Verse 25 is connected with what follows by the catchword "kill": "Does the circle of leaders perhaps know that he is the Christ?" That is not said simply as a mockery by John, but shows how dependent the people have been made by their spiritual and political leadership.

■ **26** That Jesus, whom they nevertheless want to kill, is permitted to speak unhindered prompts some Jerusalemites to wonder whether the authorities have not finally recognized that Jesus is the Christ. That demonstrates not only the religious immaturity in which the authorities hold the people—what "those in charge" say is decisive—but shifts the entire guilt to them at the same time.

■ **27** Yet it occurs to the people at the same time that their conjecture is impossible: they know where Jesus comes from. In contrast, "we know" that when the Christ comes, no one will know whence he comes. But it will momentarily be shown that this objection is a boomerang: Jesus possesses just that quality whose alleged failure

19   Loisy, *Le quatrième évangile*, 496.
20   *Sanh.* 132a; cf. Billerbeck, 2: 488.
21   *Dial.* 27.5., ANF 1: 208.

they have just adduced against him. Cf. Justin, *Dial.* 8: "But Christ—if He has indeed been born, and exists anywhere—is unknown, and does not even know Himself, and has no power until Elias comes to anoint Him, and make Him manifest to all."[22] Billerbeck points also to *Dial.* 110, where Trypho says: "If they say that the messiah has (already) come (i.e. been born), then it is not yet known who he is; but man will recognize who he is, it is said, when he has become manifest and glorified."[23]

■ **28** "Jesus proclaimed" (ἔκραξεν): this word is used in John 1:15, 7:28, 37, 12:44 to introduce solemn discourse.[24] Zahn again psychologizes: Greatly upset by the cold remarks, Jesus cries out "without regard to the public place in which they were and the sacredness of the temple; he had up to this point been teaching quietly as a rabbi skilled in scripture; but he now calls to the arm-chair politicans of Jerusalem with unmistakable irony. . . ."[25] But the word "teaching" (διδάσκων) shows that John does not have an alteration of the character of the scene in mind. He is not providing a realistic picture of the events on the temple square, but permits everything that is not absolutely necessary to fade away. Jesus is in the peculiar situation of having people know his earthly origins, while not knowing where he is from, that is, from the Father. God is unknown to the Jews, although he is "true,"[26] and they are supposed to know him through the law.

■ **29** Nevertheless, Jesus knows God, since he comes from God and was sent by him. Since the matter of his origin concerns the question whether he is the Christ, Jesus has demonstrated by means of the lack of knowledge on the part of the Jews that precisely that Jewish expectation is fulfilled in himself.

■ **30** His claim now prompts people who are not more closely identified to attempt to arrest him. But no one is able to do that, because his hour has not yet come. Zahn is of the opinion that some of the aroused population of Jerusalem want to perform voluntary police duty, but are afraid of the mass of Galilean pilgrims.[27] But John makes it clear that human decisions and resolution cannot alter the plan of God. No one can touch Jesus until the hour appointed for his crucifixion.

■ **31–36** Verses 31–36 form the second subsection, a kind of interlude or intermezzo. The crowd, which in verse 35 is identified with the Jews, is here manifestly not a unity. Many became believers. The reason they give for becoming believers leads one to suspect at the outset that their faith is not what it ought to be: when the messiah comes, he will not do greater works than Jesus has done.

■ **31** The subsection opens with this bit of information: many of the people become believers. Their faith is of course dubious when they indicate that the coming of the Christ (a figure that differs from Jesus) is a possibility, and when they believe in Jesus on account of his miracles, which are here suddenly assumed to be well known in Jerusalem.

■ **32** This reaction of the crowd now causes the Pharisees (again appearing as officials) to send out their servants to arrest Jesus (did John still know something about the temple police?). The danger in which Jesus finds himself is repeatedly emphasized by John. On the one hand, that prepares the reader for the eventuality of the passion, and, on the other, makes it clear that all moves against Jesus are doomed from the outset to failure.

■ **33** Verse 33 can be interpreted as a reaction of Jesus to this hostility:[28] Although he knows that such moves will not now be effective, he is nevertheless to be with them only a short time longer. He then returns to the one who sent him. The motif "a little longer" (ἔτι μικρόν) is used repeatedly and in various ways (12:35, 13:33, 14:19, 16:18f.). Here it introduces a misunderstanding of the Jews, that is in fact a concealed prophecy.

■ **34** They will seek Jesus and not find him—viz., during the distress of war and the destruction of Jerusalem. With the sentence, "Where I am you cannot come," compare Clement of Alexandria: "Blessed (are) those who are persecuted for my sake, for they will have a place where they cannot be persecuted."[29] And compare

---

22 ANF 1: 199. Cited by Barrett, *John*, 322, in Greek.

23 Billerbeck, 2: 489. But cf. Matt 24:26//Luke 17:23.

24 Cf. Wetter, *Der Sohn Gottes*, 58.

25 *Das Evangelium des Johannes*, 390.

26 ἀληθινός; the word here means the same thing as ἀληθής, 𝔓⁶⁶

27 *Das Evangelium des Johannes*, 392.

28 So Bauer, *Das Johannesevangelium*, 111.

29 *Strom.* 4.41f.

the corrupt form of this saying in the Gospel of Thomas, logion 68.[30]

■ **35** The Jews misunderstand these words and, without knowing it, they pronounce in them a prophecy that had come to pass in the time of the Evangelist: the Christian mission in the diaspora. The Evangelist has in mind not just a mission among hellenistic Jewish Christians; the word "Greeks" (Ἕλληνες) and the fact of the mission to the Gentiles in the time of the Evangelist proves that.

■ **36** Verse 36 repeats once more Jesus' words in verse 34, which the Jews do not understand, and impresses that especially on the reader.

■ **37–44** Verses 37–44 form the next subsection.

■ **37** Verse 37 begins a new subsection, connected to the preceding by a temporal designation. The subsection continues until verse 44.

Interpreters are at odds over whether "the last day of the feast, the great day" means the seventh or the eighth day. The Evangelist probably did not have at his disposal such exact information as Billerbeck provides in his excursus on the feast of Tabernacles.[31] According to Billerbeck,[32] by the last day of the feast the rabbis understand the seventh day, since they reckon the eighth day as a feast in its own right.[33] In support of the seventh day it is alleged there is nothing special about the eighth day, although it has the character of a sabbath (as does the first day), while on the seventh day, the procession circled the altar not one but seven times and the willow branches were beaten on the ground.[34] The words: "If any one thirst" etc. are taken by Billerbeck to be an allusion to the water libations connected with the feast of Tabernacles (they were actually connected with the autumn rains):[35] "Early in the morning on each of the seven days (*Sukk.* 5.1) a priest went to the pool of Siloam accompanied by a large entourage and filled a golden vessel (holding 1.6 liters) with water from the pool; this was accompanied by strains of temple music and the recitation of passages of scripture, such as Isa 12:3. This water was brought back to the temple, amidst loud jubilation and accompanied by music; there, the water together with a jug of wine were poured into silver bowls brought to the altar for that express purpose and thence poured into the ground via tubes. The saying mentioned in the Mishnah is related to the first part of this ritual: Whoever has not seen the joy of drawing water has never experienced joy in his life." This libation was not repeated on the eighth day (contrary to Dodd).[36] However, in verse 37 the reference is to drinking; libation is not mentioned.

■ **38** A further difficulty for the interpretation of verses 37 and 38 has to do with punctuation. One customarily puts a period after "drink" (πινέτω). In that event, the following "He who believes in me" is a nominative absolute that refers to the rest of the sentence following: rivers will flow out of the belly of the one believing in Jesus. But is that really what was intended? The Rabbis took Zach 14:8ff. to refer to the feast of Tabernacles,[37] along with Zach 13:1, Ezek 47:1ff., and Isa 12:3. This tradition goes back to Rabbi Eliezer ben Jacob (90 CE). But John is not alluding to anything like that. In order to approximate the Jewish tradition more closely, although antithetically, some interpreters have taken "He who believes in me" to refer to the preceding. A new sentence would then begin with "As the scripture has said," and that could refer to Jesus: It is out of him that rivers (of the spirit) will flow. In support of this view one can point to a passage quoted by Paul in 1 Cor 10:4 in which water flows out of the rock, a passage developed by the rabbis; this is the rock that accompanied the Israelites on their journey through the wilderness. Paul related this rock as a "spiritual rock" (πνευματικὴ πέτρα) to Christ, who pours out the spirit. In that case, John would be saying something similar here about Jesus.

■ **39** Verse 39 is really an explanation of what precedes in this sense: Jesus' pronouncement was made with a view to those who were to receive the spirit from him, and then he adds: "For the spirit had not yet been given, because Jesus was not yet glorified." Here John is not of

---

30 Cf. Haenchen, Spruch 68 des Thomasevangeliums, *Le Muséon* 75 (1962) 19–29.
31 2: 774–812.
32 2: 490.
33 Billerbeck, 2: 808–12.
34 Billerbeck, 2: 793–99, especially 797.
35 2: 491.
36 *Interpretation of the Fourth Gospel*, 348f.
37 Dodd, *Interpretation of the Fourth Gospel*, 350.

course speaking of the third person of the trinity, but rather of the spirit that is at work in the believers on earth, which Jesus first pours out on his own in John 20:22. Bultmann sees no "reason for omitting v. 39 as a gloss, inserted by the ecclesiastical redactor."[38] Verse 38b does go back to the ecclesiastical redactor. "Only v. 39b could possibly be an editorial gloss, although the view that the community will not receive the Spirit until after Jesus' δοξασθῆναι ['glorification'] is also the view of the Farewell discourses (cf. especially 14:26, 16:7)."[39]

Difficulties are occasioned above all by the word κοιλία, "belly, body." What came to mind was the ancient spring where water bubbled out of the mouth of some figure and thus out of its insides. But such an explanation is overdrawn (see the Overview below).

■ **40f.** "[Some] of the crowd": "some" is to be supplied in accordance with the sense. On this point BDF remarks: "The partitive genitive . . . is being driven out by the use of the prepositions ἐκ (ἀπό, ἐν)."[40] The corresponding expression in Hebrew and Aramaic is מן: cf. Radermacher, who writes that the genitive is being replaced on a broad front and is not a Hebraism.[41]

These verses depict the recognition that follows Jesus' speech: he is regarded as the prophet or even as the Christ. But that provokes another objection: the Christ does not come from Galilee.

■ **42** Verse 42 produces the prooftext: the Christ is of the seed of David and from the village (!) of David, Bethlehem (Micah 5:1, Ps 80:4f., cf. 1:46).

■ **43f.** These verses depict the dissension that arises; some of Jesus' opponents even want to arrest him, but none succeeds, as likewise in verse 30.

In a kind of internal catchword association John renews the motif of verses 30 and 44 ("arrest" means "bring").

■ **45** The last subsection of chapter 7 begins with verse 45.

Only now are the officers mentioned in verse 32 referred to again; they return—after three days—with

tasks unaccomplished and have to face the understandably reproachful question of the high priests and Pharisees: "Why did you not bring him?" The connection with verse 44 is not good, for the servants here are failures for another reason than the men mentioned in verse 30 (and v. 44?): in fact, here the Evangelist begins a new scene that has to do with the justification of Jesus (and in that connection renews the theme of v. 42). It extends as far as verse 52.

■ **46** Verse 46 depicts the authority of Jesus, which does not even permit the officers to undertake an attempt to arrest him: "No man ever spoke like this man."

■ **47** The Pharisees answer in a rage; they are again represented as the superiors of the officers and those standing alongside the reigning authorities: "Are you also led astray?" And then a thematic connection is introduced with verse 26.

■ **48** None of the authorities or the Pharisees has been converted, however. Only in 12:42 is it said that many of the authorities have come to faith, but they did not dare to say it lest they be cast out of the synagogue.

■ **49** Only the people who do not know the law, who are accursed, allow themselves to be misled.[42] Whoever wrote that was really free from the law and yet was somewhat conscious of the contempt with which the Pharisees looked down on uncultured folk.

■ **50** But that is not quite correct: Nicodemus raises an objection—he is represented as one who came to Jesus previously (3:1ff.). The Evangelist now indicates, by means of Nicodemus, that at least one out of this influential circle champions Jesus, although there is only one (cf. 19:39).

■ **51** Nicodemus insists, at least in cautious interrogative form, that the (personified) law judges no one until it has first heard the individual and learned what he or she has done. This statement may have Deut 1:16f. and 19:15 in mind: "judge righteously in the matter," and "you are to have no regard for the appearance of a person." A single witness is not sufficient; there shall be testimony from

38 *John*, 303 n. 5 [229 n. 2].
39 Bultmann, *John*, 303 n. 5 [229 n. 2].
40 BDF §164.
41 *Neutestamentliche Grammatik. Das Griechisch des Neuen Testaments in Zusammenhang mit der Volkssprache dargestellt*, HNT 1 (Tübingen: Mohr-Siebeck, ²1925) 125.
42 Cf. Billerbeck, 2: 494–519.

two or more witnesses. And Nicodemus insists that the one charged must receive a hearing in accordance with the law. He thus plays the law off against the Pharisees. But without success.

■ **52** He is rejected with a prooftext, after which he is suspected of being an earlier secret follower of Jesus: no prophet is to arise from Galilee. However, most manuscripts read "a prophet" without the definite article; yet the article is found in $\mathfrak{P}^{66}$. That could of course be an informed correction. But even this text does not represent an uncontested tradition.[43] "There is no single tribe in Israel from which prophets have not arisen" (*Sukk.* 27b). Seder Olam Rabba 21 is a further generalization: "There is no city in the land of Israel in which there has been no prophet."

Overview

Verse 17 occasions difficulties with this open question: how can we be certain that Jesus has been sent by the Father and that the Father is related to us as Jesus says and expresses in his life? This question is not forbidden to us. John himself has posed it and answered it. If we pay strict attention to his gospel, we will note: although Jesus reveals the Father in word and in deed, he has not, in his earthly works, really found true faith anywhere. John often speaks, to be sure, of Jesus' disciples having faith (2:11), or of people in the crowd having faith (7:31), and even the Jews themselves having faith (8:30f.)—who usually appear as a group to be distinguished from the crowd. Only when one looks more closely does it become evident that this was not yet true faith at all. That becomes abundantly clear in the case of the many Jews in 8:30ff., who—when they had scarcely become believers—take offense and revolt in a shocking way against Jesus. Furthermore, all the best good will in the world does not help the disciples achieve real faith: they simply do not know him. For, when Jesus says to them immediately before the passion: "You now know my Father and have seen him" (14:7), Philip then answers with as much guilelessness as lack of understanding: "Lord, show us the Father, and we shall be satisfied" (14:8). Jesus then has to complain: "Have I been with you so long, and yet you do not know me,

Philip?" (14:9) When the disciples affirm, still later (16:30), that they now really believe that Jesus has been sent from the Father, they receive this disillusioning answer: "Do you now believe? The hour is coming, indeed it has come, when you will be scattered, every man to his home, and will leave me alone." Why have even the disciples not broken through to true faith? John clearly answers in 7:39: "For as yet the spirit had not yet been given, because Jesus was not yet glorified."[44] Only when Jesus has departed from them will he send the holy spirit to them: "On that day you will ask me no questions" (16:23). Only when the resurrected one breathes into them his breath—as God once did in the creation in the case of Adam—only then will they receive the holy spirit and then be capable of true faith (20:22). This coming of the spirit is the birth from above mentioned in Jesus' conversation with Nicodemus, a birth that permits one to see in Jesus the one sent from the Father and, at the same, to see the Father in him. Only then will it be possible to find real peace and genuine joy in the hateful and hostile world (from which, according to 17:15, Christians will not come out). John can also describe this outpouring of the spirit differently; he is not limited to one formula: as the exalted one, Jesus draws all men to himself (12:32), or (since the Father is acting in Jesus) the Father must draw all those chosen to Jesus (6:44). Only when that happens will the hour arrive when the disciples really hear and really know Jesus, the hour when Jesus will really be glorified. Only the risen one or the spirit or the paraclete—John deliberately uses all three expressions deriving from different traditions—will break through the barrier that besets the earthly activity of Jesus, a limit that prompts Jesus to say immediately before the passion: "I have yet many things to say to you, but you cannot bear them now" (16:12).

If, therefore, really to hear and acknowledge Jesus—and thus to be certain that he is the one sent from the Father—is the same thing as the pouring out of the spirit, or the coming of the paraclete, or the return of Jesus, is not then the receiving of the spirit for John a *deus ex machina*, which makes impossible faith possible and therefore permits man by himself to decide to believe or not to believe? No, the spirit is an experience

---

43 Billerbeck, 2: 519.
44 Cf. 16:7 also.

and not a subterfuge. It is no more an illusion than completely sacrificial love is. But just as this love does not effect itself, neither does the spirit produce hearing and knowing. If John says more than once that Jesus saves only those whom the Father has given him, then the same experience comes to expression in this passage, namely that there is no perfect proclamation that can overcome the lack of faith and that man is helpless before the most important question of life in spite of all his good will. John is not advancing "a theory of determinism," anymore than he is positing a theory of the receiving of the spirit: where the word of Jesus does not catch fire (from out of whichever mouth it is spoken), where it does not acknowledge that he "is out of the truth," then we hit upon a mystery that John is confronted with in all its imponderable reality, and can no more illumine than can we. It is—precisely on the view of John—God's mystery.

Something comparable is expressed in verse 39. For one must not overlook the fact that all Jesus' earthly activity remains without echo or the fruit of faith. We are told already in 2:11, to be sure, that Jesus' disciples attached faith to him. But what this sentence taken from the source really means is betrayed by 2:22: only later did the disciples believe the scripture and the words of Jesus. According to 2:23, many in Jerusalem believed in Jesus on the basis of his miracles. But what is wrong with this faith is shown in the continuation: Jesus does not trust them. It does not really require proof that Nicodemus did not really "believe" (chap. 3). The Samaritans do indeed explain in 4:42 that they no longer believe because of the testimony of the woman at the well, but because they themselves have heard him and know that he is true the savior of the world. However, the interweaving of the reasons that is evident in 4:35 warns us against regarding the faith of the Samaritans without further ado as an event within the earthly life of Jesus. The miracle reported in 4:46–54 of course leads to the conversion of the "royal official" and his whole house—

yet only because he has seen "signs and wonders." We cannot say that the lame man in chapter 5 came to faith. The miracle of the feeding is not regarded as a sign at all, according to 6:26, and does not lead to faith. The Jews whose faith is reported in 8:30 prove themselves forthwith to be fierce enemies of Jesus. The blind man who is healed comes to faith in Jesus as the messiah, according to 9:38. And yet the fact that he is cast out of the synagogue shows the connection of this story to a later period. The resurrection of Lazarus produces faith in many according to 11:45; 12:11 points to the same result. Nevertheless, 12:37 records the bitter lament that Jesus has not found faith in spite of the fact that he has performed so many miracles. The disciples' declaration of faith in 16:30 is immediately contradicted by Jesus.

The answer to the riddle is given by 7:39b: prior to the exaltation of Jesus there was no spirit. Only the resurrected Christ can produce the spirit that is promised (20:22). Since, however, the conferral of the spirit can take place only with the parousia, we cannot speak of either Pentecost or of the parousia as an event within the life of Jesus. Both the Synoptics and John have noted the tension between the activity of the earthly Jesus and the risen Christ. The two are counterbalanced in this way: the earthly Jesus does indeed reveal the name of God in word and in miracle, but the risen Christ makes possible saving faith in the Father and him whom the Father has sent, Jesus Christ. John occasionally (16:12) replaces this clean distinction with one that is related: Jesus' preaching remains incomplete, because it is not adequate to enable the hearer to accept; the spirit of truth alone can lead to the whole truth.

22. The Woman Taken in Adultery

Bibliography

Becker, Ulrich

*Jesus und die Ehebrecherin. Untersuchungen zur Text-
und Überlieferungsgeschichte von Joh. 7,53–8,11,*
BZNW 28 (Berlin: A. Töpelmann, 1963).

Blinzler, Josef

"Die Strafe für Ehebruch in Bibel und Halacha.
Zur Auslegung von Joh VIII, 5." *NTS* 4 (1957/
1958) 32–47.

Bornhäuser, Karl

"Jesus und die Ehebrecherin. Zum Verständnisse
des Perikope Joh 8,1–11." *NKZ* 37 (1926) 353–63.

Campenhausen, Hans von

"Zur Perikope von der Ehebrecherin (Joh 7, 53–
8, 11)." *ZNW* 68 (1977) 164–75.

Coleman, B. W.

"The Woman Taken in Adultery. Studies in Texts:
John 7, 53–8, 11." *Theology* 73 (1970) 409–10.

Derrett, John Duncan Martin

"Law in the New Testament: The Story of the
Woman Taken in Adultery." *NTS* 10 (1963/1964)
1–26.

Dieck, C. F.

"Ueber die Geschichte von der Ehebrecherin im
Evangelium Johannis vom juristischen Standpunkte." *TSK* 5 (1832) 791–822.

Eisler, Robert

"Jesus und die ungetreue Braut [Joh 8, 1–11]."
ZNW 22 (1923) 305–7.

Jeremias, Joachim

"Zur Geschichtlichkeit des Verhörs Jesu vor dem
Hohen Rat." *ZNW* 43 (1950/1951) 145–50, esp.
148–50. Also in his *Abba. Studien zur neutestamentlichen Theologie und Zeitgeschichte* (Göttingen:
Vandenhoeck & Ruprecht, 1966) 139–44.

Johnson, A. F.

"A Stylistic Trait of the Fourth Gospel in the
*Pericope Adulterae?" Bulletin of the Evangelical Theo-
logical Society* 9 (1966) 91–96.

Manson, Thomas Walter

"The Pericope de Adultera (Joh 7, 53–8,11)."
ZNW 44 (1952/1953) 255–56.

Merlier, Octave

"Langue et exégèse néotestamentaire: La péricope
de la femme adultère." In Festschrift M. Trianta-
phyllidis (Athens, 1960) 553–61.

Osborne, R. E.

"Pericope adulterae." *CJT* 12 (1966) 281–83.

Riesenfeld, Harald

"Die Perikope von der Ehebrecherin in der frühkirchlichen Tradition." *SEÅ* 17 (1952) 106–11.

Rousseau, François

"La femme adultère. Structure de Jn 7, 53–8,11."
Bib 59 (1978) 463–80.

Salvoni, Fausto

"Textual Authority for Jn 7, 53–8, 11." *Restoration Quarterly* 4 (1960) 11–15.

Schilling, F. A.

"The Story of Jesus and the Adulteress [Jn 8:1–11]." *ATR* 37 (1955) 91–106.

Schnyder, C.

"Ankläger und Angeklagte (Joh 8, 1–11)." *Reformatio* 26 (1977) 641ff.

Steck, R.

"Die Perikope von der Ehebrecherin." In *Zur Feier des 50 jährigen Amtsjubiläums des Herrn Prof. Dr. A. Schweizer. Gratulationsschrift der ev. -theol. Fakultät an der Hochschule Bern zum 29.10.1884* (Bern, 1884).

Trites, Allison A.

"The Woman Taken in Adultery." *BSac* 131 (1974) 137–46.

Wensinck, A. J.

"John VIII, 6–8." In *Amicitiae Corolla. A Volume of Essays Presented to James Rendel Harris, D. Litt., on the Occasion of his Eightieth Birthday*, ed. H. G. Wood (London: University of London Press, 1933) 300–302.

Wikgren, Allen Paul

"The Lectionary Text of the Pericope John 8:1–11." *JBL* 53 (1934) 188–98.

Wittichen, C.

"Zur Markusfrage III: Die ursprüngliche Zugehörigkeit der Erzählung von der Ehebrecherin zum Markusevangelium." *Jahrbücher für protestantische Theologie* 5 (1879) 165–82; 7 (1881) 366–75.

7

53 They went each to his own house, 8. but Jesus went to the Mount of Olives. 2/ Early in the morning he came again to the temple; all the people came to him, and he sat down and taught them. 3/ The scribes and the Pharisees brought a woman who had been caught in adultery, and placing her in the midst 4/ they said to him, "Teacher, this woman has been caught in the act of adultery. 5/ Now in the law Moses commanded us to stone such. What do you say about her?" 6/ This they said to test him, that they might have some charge to bring against him. Jesus bent down and wrote with his finger on the ground. 7/ And as they continued to ask him, he stood up and said to them, "Let him who is without sin among you be the first to throw a stone at her." 8/ And once more he bent down and wrote with his finger on the ground. 9/ But when they heard it, they went away, one by one, beginning with the eldest, and Jesus was left alone with the woman standing before him. 10/ Jesus looked up and said to her, "Woman, where are they? Has no one condemned you?" 11/ She said, "No one, Lord." And Jesus said, "Neither do I condemn you; go, and do not sin again."

The author did not consider the pericope of the woman taken in adultery to be an original part of the Fourth Gospel. It has been inserted after John 7:52 by D and other old Latin manuscripts. But it is missing in the best Greek manuscripts: $\mathfrak{P}^{66}$ $\mathfrak{P}^{75}$ (A) B (C) L N T W X Δ Θ Ψ 33 157 565 892 1241 *al.*

23. The Continuation of the Discourse of Jesus in Jerusalem

Bibliography

Atal, Dosithée
"Die Wahrheit wird euch freimachen." In *Biblische Randbemerkungen. Schülerfestschrift für Rudolf Schnackenburg zum 60. Geburtstag,* ed. H. Merklein and J. Lange (Würzburg: Echter Verlag, 1974) 283–99.

Barth, C. H. W.
"Ueber den Menschenmörder von Anfang—eine exegetische Studie zu Joh 8 v. 44." *Magazin für christliche Prediger* 2, 2 (1824) 35–69.

Bartholomew, Gilbert Leinbach
"An Early Christian Sermon-Drama: John 8,31–59." Dissertation, Union Theological Seminary, 1974.

Blank, Josef
"Predigtmeditationen: Joh 8, 48–59." In his *Schrift-auslegung in Theorie und Praxis,* Biblische Hand-bibliothek 5 (Munich: Kösel, 1969) 207–20.

Charlier, Jean-Pierre
"L'exégèse johannique d'un précepte légal: Jean 8, 17." *RB* 67 (1960) 503–15.

Dahl, Nils Alstrup
"Manndraperen og hans far (Joh 8,44)." *NorTT* 64 (1963) 129–62.

Dahl, Nils Alstrup
"Der Erstgeborene Satans und der Vater des Teufels." In *Apophoreta. Festschrift für Ernst Haenchen zu seinem siebzigsten Geburtstag am 10. Dezember 1964,* BZNW 30 (Berlin: A. Töpelmann, 1964) 70–84.

Dodd, Charles Harold
"A l'arrière-plan d'un dialogue Johannique." *RHPR* 1 (1957) 5–17. In his *More New Testament Studies* (Grand Rapids: Wm. B. Eerdmans, 1968) 41–57.

Egenter, Richard
"Joh 8, 31f. im christlichen Lebensbewusstsein." In *Wahrheit und Verkündigung. Festschrift M. Schmaus II,* ed. Leo Scheffczyk et al. (Munich: Schöningh, 1967) 1583–605.

Grässer, Erich
"Die Juden als Teufelssöhne nach Joh 8, 37–47." In *Antijudaismus im Neuen Testament? Exegetische und systematische Beiträge,* ed. W. P. Eckert et al. Abhandlung zum christlich-jüdischen Dialog 2 (Munich: Chr. Kaiser Verlag, 1967) 157–70.

Hoang Dac-Anh, S.
"La liberté par la vérité." *Ang* 55 (1978) 193–211.

Kern, Walter
"Der symmetrische Gesamtaufbau von Jo 8, 12–58." *ZKT* 78 (1956) 451–54.

Kraft, Heinz
"Untersuchungen zu den Gemeinschafts- und Lebensformen häretischer christlicher Gnosis des

2. Jahrhunderts." Dissertation, Heidelberg, 1950.

Lategan, B. C.
"The truth that sets man free. John 8:31–36." *Neot* 2 (1968) 70–80.

Leenhardt, Franz Johan
"Abraham et la conversion de Saul de Tarse, suivi d'une note sur 'Abraham dans Jean VIII.'" *RHPR* 53 (1973) 331–51.

Lona, Horacio E.
Abraham in Johannes 8. Ein Beitrag zur Methodenfrage, Europäische Hochschulschriften, Series 22; Theologie 65 (Bern: H. Lang; Frankfurt: P. Lang, 1976).

Mollat, Donatien
"L'évangile Jn 8, 45–59: 'Avant qu'Abraham ne fût je suis.'" *AsSeign* 34 (1963) 54–63.

Preiss, Théo.
"Aramäisches in Joh 8, 30–36." *TZ* 3 (1947) 78–80.

Pulver, Max
"Die Lichterfahrung im Johannesevangelium, im Corpus Hermeticum, in der Gnosis und in der Ostkirche." *ErJb* 10 (1943) 253–96.

Riedl, Johannes
"Wenn ihr den Menschensohn erhöht habt, werdet ihr erkennen (Joh 8, 28)." In *Jesus und der Men-schensohn. Für Anton Vögtle*, ed. R. Pesch and R. Schnackenburg (Freiburg: Herder, 1975) 355–70.

Schein, Bruce E.
"Our Father Abraham." Dissertation, Yale University, 1972.

Troadec, Henry
"Le témoignage de la lumière. Jean 8, 12–59." *BVC* 49 (1963) 16–26.

Tuñí Vancells, J. O.
"La verdad os hará libres." Jn 8, 32. Liberación y libertad del creyente en el cuarto evangelio (Barcelona: Herder, 1973).

Würzburger, Karl
"Abrahams Kinder: Überlegungen zu Joh 8, 30–39." *Kirchenblatt für die reformierte Schweiz* 124 (1968) 82–85.

Ziegler, Carl Ludwig
"Erläuterung der schwierigen Stelle Joh 8, 12–59." *Magazin für Religionsphilosophie, Exegese und Kirchengeschichte* 5 (1796) 227–90.

8

12 Again Jesus spoke to them, saying, "I am the light of the world; he who follows me will not walk in darkness, but will have the light of life." 13/ The Pharisees then said to him, "You are bearing witness to yourself; your testimony is not true." 14/ Jesus answered, "Even if I do bear witness to myself, my testimony is true, for I know whence I have come and whither I am going, but you do not know whence I come or whither I am going. 15/ You judge according to the flesh, I judge no one. 16/ Yet even if I do judge, my judgment is true, for it is not I alone that judge, but I and he who sent me. 17/ In your law it is written that the testimony of two men is true; 18/ I bear witness to myself, and the Father who sent me bears witness to me." 19/ They said to him therefore, "Where is your Father?" Jesus answered, "You know neither me nor my Father; if you knew me, you would know my Father also." 20/ These words he spoke in the treasury, as he taught in the temple; but no one arrested him, because his hour had not yet come.

21 Again he said to them, "I go away, and you will seek me and die in your sin; where I am going, you cannot come." 22/ Then said the Jews, "Will he kill himself, since he says, 'Where I am going, you cannot come'?" 23/ He said to them, "You are from below, I am from above; you are of this world, I am not of this world. 24/ I told you that you would die in your sins, for you will die in your sins unless you believe that I am he." 25/ They said to him, "Who are you?" Jesus said to them, "Even what I have told you from the beginning. 26/ I have much to say about you and much to judge; but he who sent me is true, and I declare to the world what I have heard from him." 27/ They did not understand that he spoke to them of the Father. 28/ So Jesus said, "When you have lifted up the Son of man, then you will know that I am he, and that I do nothing on my own authority but speak thus as the Father taught me. 29/ And he who sent me is with me; he has not left me alone, for I always do what is pleasing to him." 30/ As he spoke thus, many believed in him. 31/ Jesus then said to the Jews who had believed in him, "If you continue in my word, you are my disciples, 32/ and you will know the truth, and the truth will make you free." 33/ They answered him, "We are descendants of Abraham, and have never been in bondage to anyone. How is it that you say, 'You will be made free'?" 34/ Jesus answred them, "Truly, truly, I say to you, every one who commits sin is a slave to sin. 35/ The slave does not continue in the house forever; the son continues forever. 36/ So if the Son makes you free, you will be free indeed. 37/ I know that you are descendants of Abraham; yet you seek to kill me, because my word finds no place in you. 38/ I speak of what I have seen with my Father, and you do what you have heard from your father." 39/ They answered him, "Abraham is our father." Jesus said to them, "If you were Abraham's children, you would do what Abraham did, 40/ but now you seek to kill me, a man who has told you the truth which I heard from God; this is not what Abraham did. 41/ You do what your father did." They said to him, "We were not born of fornication; we have one Father, even God." 42/ Jesus said to them, "If God were your Father, you would love me, for I proceeded and came forth from God; I came not of my own accord, but he sent me. 43/ Why do you not understand what I say? It is because you cannot bear to hear my word. 44/ You are of (your) father, the devil, and your will is to do your father's desires. He was a murderer from the beginning, and has nothing to do with the truth, because there is no truth in him. When he lies, he speaks according to his own nature, for he is a liar and the father of lies. 45/ But, because I tell the truth, you do not believe me. 46/ Which of you convicts me of sin? If I tell the truth, why do you not believe me?

47/ He who is of God hears the words of God; the reason why you do not hear them is that you are not of God." 48/ The Jews answered him, "Are we not right in saying that you are a Samaritan and have a demon?" 49/ Jesus answered, "I have not a demon; I honor my Father, and you dishonor me. 50/ Yet I do not seek my glory; there is One who seeks it and he will be the judge. 51/ Truly, truly, I say to you, if any one keeps my word, he will never see death." 52/ The Jews said to him, "Now we know that you have a demon. Abraham died, as did the prophets; and you say, 'If any one keeps my word, he will never taste death.' 53/ Are you greater than our father Abraham, who died? And prophets died! Whom do you make yourself to be?" 54/ Jesus answered, "If I glorify myself, my glory is nothing; it is my Father who glorifies me, of whom you say that he is your God. 55/ But you have not known him; I know him. If I said, I do not know him, I should be a liar like you; but I do know him and I keep his word. 56/ Your father Abraham rejoiced that he was to see my day; he saw it and was glad." 57/ The Jews then said to him, "You are not yet fifty years old, and have you seen Abraham?" 58/ Jesus said to them, "Truly, truly, I say to you, before Abraham was, I am." 59/ So they took up stones to throw at him; but Jesus hid himself, and went out of the temple.

Bultmann has 8:12 follow on 9:41,[1] because in the latter Jesus speaks of seeing. But the Evangelist does not treat a theme in such a way that he assembles all the sayings relevant to that subject in one place, one after the other.

The world is darkness. Jesus is the light that breaks into this darkness and illuminates it. According to Bultmann, Jesus is the light "because he gave us the brightness in which existence itself is illumined and comes to itself, comes to life. . . . The revelation speaks to men who are not merely concerned with the individual problems of the world and their lives, but who are concerned with themselves as a whole, with their authenticity."[2] But the theme of authenticity (in contrast to "they say") is Heidegger speaking, not the Evangelist. Nor does the Evangelist's course set Jesus over against

certain mystery divinities, such as Attis and especially Mithras, as Loisy thinks. "I am" is not a polemic against other "dispensers of light."[3] What John announces is that Jesus neither intends to lead man away from other gods (in which John has no interest), nor to bring them to himself, but to lead them to the one true God, who has sent Jesus as the Father. He is the light of the world that has abandoned God, of the world in which he brings every one who follows him (that is, who believes in him as the one who is sent) to the right way: he indeed refers to himself as "the way" in 14:6, *scil.* to the Father.

■ 13 In these words the faithless Pharisees hear only the unfounded claim of a human being. The warranty that the rabbinic teaching tradition gave to the individual teacher does not support Jesus. Whoever is recom-

1   *John*, 342 [260].
2   *John*, 342 [260].
3   Cf. Bultmann, *John*, 343 [261].

mended only by himself is not credible. That is the great difficulty that goes together with the claim of Jesus of Nazareth, the claim that isolates him from the entire world and that is not covered or guaranteed by human acquiescence.

■ **14** Jesus admits that he gives testimony on his own behalf. But in this case, however, that does not have the consequence of devaluing his testimony. For, Jesus knows whence he comes and whither he goes (John here makes use of a formula derived from Gnosticism), namely, from God to God. His opponents, on the contrary, do not know that, and so they cannot give credence to his claim.

■ **15** They judge according to the flesh, by what stands palpably before them and what can be measured by worldly standards. This thought is extended in a curious way in the brief statement: "I judge no one." This statement is contrasted with the preceding statement, "You judge accordingly to the flesh." In the present text of the Gospel of John, Jesus' judgment is no sooner affirmed than it is denied. In this verse, it is denied. But the affirmative follows in the next verse.

■ **16** "And even if I judge." But that judgment does not refer to others, as is pointed out. Rather, the "judgment" (κρίσις) spoken of in verse 16 is none other than the "judgment" of Jesus. That theme is always the truth of his claim, a claim not only advanced by him but confirmed by the Father.

■ **17f.** In "your" (!) law it is written that the testimony of two men is true (Deut 17:6, 19:15). This rule, which was given for cases of human judgment, is now turned to account on behalf of Jesus: He and the Father are the two witnesses required by the law. This appeal to the Jewish law is questionable, as the next verse makes clear.

■ **19** His opponents ask: Where is your Father? But this question does not disconcert Jesus or the Evangelist, but, on the contrary, proves that those who ask such a question do not know either Jesus or the Father and only betray their ignorance by this query. John uses the Jewish law like a collection of sacred oracles, which one can cite and interpret without reference to the context. This scene also closes with a place designation, as is common.

■ **20** Jesus speaks these words in the treasury, where the story of the poor widow takes place in Mark 12:41ff.; the widow exceeds all other contributors with her small

gift. The Evangelist was presumably no longer aware of anything more specific than this detail circulating in the tradition concerning the temple, so he makes use of it in order to give the teaching of Jesus in the temple some local color. The remark that no one arrested him because his hour had not yet come makes two things clear at once: Jesus' activity in Jerusalem stands under constant threat, and the impossibility that anything would happen to Jesus so long as he stood under the invisible protective umbrella of the divine will.

A new subsection begins with verse 21 and extends through verse 29. The subsection takes up motifs already familiar, but develops them further.

■ **21** Jesus is going away, and soon, and going to the cross and to the Father, and they will seek him in vain, as it has already been explained in 7:33f. But, in that case, it is too late for them; the judgment of God will take place in the destruction of Jerusalem, which is a city standing for the world. When Jesus adds: "Where I am going, you cannot come" (7:34, 36), this leads the Jews to a foolish assumption, which nevertheless contains a kernel of truth that they do not recognize. This prompts the Jews to say:

■ **22** "Will he perhaps kill himself?" Viewed from the human perspective, the manner in which Jesus goes to his death is actually a provocation of death (at least as the Evangelist sees it), which amounts to the same thing as suicide.

■ **23** Verse 23 makes it clear of course that the disposition of Jesus and the Jews is quite different. They cannot go where he is going, to the Father. They are from below, he is from above, from the divine world. They are of this world, Jesus is not of this world. Here the difference is reduced to a kind of maxim, a brief formula, which does not itself appropriate gnostic dualism, but only one of its formulas. For John does not assert, unlike Gnosticism, that the world arose from a fall from God and that man has only to recover his consciousness of his divine essence again. On the contrary, through the Logos, as the agent of creation, the All has come into being. But for this reason, the human world that belongs to the Logos does not want to know anything of the Logos, but remains enclosed within itself. John is able to express this contrast in various ways, a contrast that is broken into enigmatic pieces, as, for example, in this verse with this distinction between "below" and "above." In place of "below," the term "this world" may appear with the same significance, or simply "the world," which corresponds to gnostic usage.

■ **24** Verse 24 provides the explanation for Jesus' enigmatic saying in verse 21b: They will die in their sins, if they do not believe that "I am he." This "I am" ($\grave{\epsilon}\gamma\acute{\omega}$ $\epsilon\grave{\iota}\mu\iota$) sounds mysterious and is intended to sound mysterious. The Christian reader knows that Jesus is the Son of God and the Son of man. But how are the Jews to know that? They can only ask: "Who are you then?"

■ **25f.** These verses constitute a *crux interpretum* (a text presenting special difficulties of interpretation). Some take $\tau\grave{\eta}\nu$ $\grave{\alpha}\rho\chi\acute{\eta}\nu$ as "initially," and translate: "From the beginning I am what I told you," or even: "I am what I told you already from the beginning," which is shattered on the present tense of $\lambda\alpha\lambda\hat{\omega}$ ("I tell"). But one can also understand $\tau\grave{\eta}\nu$ $\grave{\alpha}\rho\chi\acute{\eta}\nu$ as "at all." In that case the best parallel is ps.-Clem. *Hom.* 6.11: "If you do not attend to what I tell you, why do I speak to you at all?"[4]

$"O\tau\iota$ is used to introduce a direct question in Mark 2:16b, 9, 11, 28. In that case, what is being expressed here is the indignation of the one sent by God, who, as in Mark 9:19, meets with constant lack of understanding. However, the continuation of the discourse now becomes difficult. One is led to expect a contrastive particle, "but," as the introduction to verse 26: Jesus does not really want to talk further with the Jews, but because he is under orders from the Father, he will nevertheless continue with his preaching. The question regarding who he is is not immediately answered. Instead of this, Jesus speaks as though an entirely different contrast prevailed: they have asked who he is. He will not speak about himself, but he has much to say and to judge about them. But— and now the answer to the question they asked is to follow—"the one who sent me is true" etc. What Jesus has heard from him he declares to the world ($\kappa\acute{o}\sigma\mu os$).

■ **27** The Jews do not comprehend this time that he is speaking to them of the Father.

■ **28** To this Jesus responds as though they had said it to him: when they have lifted him up, therefore after Easter, they will know that he is the Son of man, namely, when they suffer retribution in the destruction of Jerusalem. It will then be clear that Jesus has not brought his own teaching, but that of the Father.

■ **29** And the one who sent him is beside him unseen. Jesus is only apparently alone. God is with him because he always does what is pleasing to God.

A new subsection begins at this point. It encompasses verses 30–59 and depicts the heightening of the conflict following an initial agreement.

■ **30** It is not really comprehensible that many believe in Jesus as a result of his words, since he has said nothing new and has expressed himself mysteriously in veiled words. However, John uses this alleged faith on the part of many Jews to show that in reality the Jews are anything but believers.

■ **31** The conflict is precipitated here when Jesus promises these new believers that they will truly be his disciples (only), if they hold to his words (or teaching). Their desertion is already hinted at, although faintly.

■ **32f.** In these verses the conflict breaks out: Jesus' words presuppose that his listeners are not yet free, but can only be made free if they "abide," that is, in the truth, abide in Christian faith in Jesus. The word "free" provokes his listeners to respond: as descendants of Abraham we have never been in bondage, we have never been slaves. How can Jesus promise freedom to them?

■ **34f.** In reply, Jesus indicates that every one who sins is a slave of sin; he therefore presumes that they are yet sinners—how they are sinners does not become clear until verse 40. In that event, they are faced with the possibility of condemnation; only Christ and Christians need not fear that.

■ **36** The Jews appear to be free, but they will really be free only as Christians. They indeed invoke their status as sons of Abraham to prove their freedom, but that claim is devastating for them.

■ **37** Jesus knows that they stem from Abraham— biologically; one could also say, according to the flesh. But they seek to kill Jesus because his word has not been received by them, because they do not believe. That serves to sharpen the conflict; Jesus now calls into question their relation to Abraham.

■ **38** He speaks of what he has seen with his Father; but they do what they have heard from the Father. The manuscripts have supplied the article ($\acute{o}$) in the first part of the sentence, and the personal pronoun (μov) in the

4   We find this expression as early as Chrysostom, *Hom.* 53.1 t. 8 p. 311b; Theodore of Mopsuestia, P. 191, Theophylactus and Euthymius.

second. But his words remain enigmatic.

■ **39** Since Jesus and the Jews both assert that their origins are with "the Father," but their behavior differs, the Jews claim that Abraham is their father. Jesus doubts that: as children of Abraham, they would act like he does, and they do not do that at all.

■ **40** For they seek to kill him, which Abraham did not do. And, he is someone who says what he has heard from God and which is therefore the truth.

■ **41** Finally, Jesus becomes even more pointed: they do the work of their father. To this they respond: we are not illegitimate children, and they pass from the claim that Abraham is their father to a second claim, namely, that God is their father. Both assertions mean that they are the people of God.

■ **42f.** On the basis of the assumption that he himself came from God, Jesus is able to reply: they would be obliged to love him if they had indeed come from God. But why then do they not understand his word, that is, why do they not believe?

■ **44** Verse 44 has caused interpreters a great deal of trouble. However, it is to be understood under three stipulations:

(1) One either puts a comma between "father" and "the devil," or strikes out this "father," or adds "Cain";

(2) One reads "father" ($\pi\alpha\tau\rho\acute{o}s$) instead of "the father" ($\tau o\hat{v}\ \pi\alpha\tau\rho\acute{o}s$);

(3) A "your" ($\dot{v}\mu\hat{\omega}\nu$) may have dropped out after $\dot{v}\mu\epsilon\hat{\imath}s$ $\dot{\epsilon}\kappa\ \tau o\hat{v}\ \pi\alpha\tau\rho\acute{o}s$ at an early time.

These stipulations produce the translation: "You are of (your) father, the devil."

The *qui* found in e and Lucifer von Calaris, which leads to a $\ddot{o}s\ \ddot{a}\nu$ ("whoever") instead of $\ddot{o}\tau\alpha\nu$ ("whenever"), offers a possible solution to the conclusion of verse 44: "If anyone speaks lies, he speaks out of his own; for he is a liar and his (i.e., this man's) father," the devil. In that event, it is not necessary to make Cain the father of the Jews, as Hirsch does.[5] The devil is the father of the Jews, and he has no constancy in the truth, that is, he has fallen.

■ **45** Verse 45 is noteworthy in the sense that, after the sharpest conceivable attack, the old train of thought recurs: why do they not believe Jesus, when he tells them the truth? If the Jews are children of the devil, they answer yes, they do not believe him because he tells the truth.

■ **46** No one can convict Jesus of a sin. If he tells the truth, why do they not believe? D *al* omit this verse.

■ **47** Whoever is out of God hears the words of God when they are spoken. Jesus speaks them. The Jews are therefore not out of God, if they do not hear Jesus' words as words of God.

■ **48** The Jews now respond by calling him a Samaritan and saying that he is possessed.

■ **49** Jesus rejoins: he is not possessed, but honors the Father, and they dishonor him (Jesus).

■ **50** He does not seek his own glory; there is another who looks after that for him: God, who is the judge.

■ **51** Jesus closes with the provocative promise: whoever believes in him will never see death.[6]

■ **52** In the view of the Jews, that proves that Jesus is possessed. Abraham has died and the prophets too. How can Jesus promise his followers that they will never see death?

■ **53** Jesus cannot be greater than Abraham, who died, just as the prophets died. What does he make himself out to be? What kind of a position does he claim for himself, arrogate to himself?

■ **54** Jesus responds: if he gives glory to himself, that glory is nothing. The Father glorifies him, the Father that the Jews call their Father.

■ **55** But they do not know him, while Jesus does know him. Were he to assert the opposite, he would be a liar like them. But he does know the Father and he keeps his word.

■ **56** Abraham, the alleged father of the Jews, rejoiced to see my day.[7] Perhaps a rabbinic interpretation of Gen 17:17 lies at the base of "he rejoiced."[8] Abraham would then have seen the day of the Son of man in paradise (Luke 16:22–31).[9]

■ **57** The Jews point to the contradictory character of his claim that he, who is not yet fifty years old—this figure is inferred from John 2:20, and the presbyter

---

5   *Studien,* 78–80.
6   See the Overview.
7   For ἵνα after ἀγαλλιάω, see BDF §392(1a).
8   Cf. Philo, *De mut. nom.* 154ff.
9   Cf. Luke 17:22.

quoted by Irenaeus had already made this inference—[10] believes he has seen Abraham.[11]

■ **58** Jesus replies: Before Abraham was, I am—a reference to his eternal being. The Jews take that as blasphemy.

■ **59** They therefore take up stones to stone him.[12] John does not tell us how Jesus hiding himself is conceived. The thought that a docetic disappearance took place had already occurred to Augustine.[13] But cf. 10:31, 10:39, 12:36, Luke 4:30. The closing sentence, "and went out of the temple," is necessary as an introduction to the following story.

Overview

We may be permitted to set the question of sources aside for chapter 8 and attend the Johannine message itself.

According to that message, God and his acts are completely hidden to man: "No one has ever seen God!" (1:18, 5:37, 6:46). For, this world is alienated from God, and those who represent this "below" for John are the "Jews." He uses them to illustrate that not even the most dazzling signs are able to point them to God. The story of Lazarus is the epitome of this blindness. For John it is also only a sign, which points to the true resurrection, to a life with God, like the healing of the lame man (5:9) mentioned already. The world, this world, is incapable of penetrating to God in and of itself, especially if it thinks it already knows him (8:41).

Rather, according to John, there is a single possibility of obtaining news about the unseen Father: if someone is sent with such information. That brings us to the problem of Johannine christology, which is the most important of all Johannine problems. How John conceives it is indicated by the phrase repeated constantly: "the Father who sent me." Jesus is sent by the Father.

We should first of all be clear about what the phrase, to be sent by the Father, implies. Someone sent represents a sovereign, a supreme authority. The honor that one shows the representative does not apply to his person as such. His significance owes rather to the fact that through him who is really powerful and decisive speaks and acts. The one rightly sent, however, is no *nuntius alienae sententiae* ("bearer of an alien message"), who only mouths foreign words, but is one who places himself entirely in the service of his sovereign. Precisely to the extent that he has the thoughts and wishes of his sovereign in his mind and heart, and rejects everything that is his own, will he be truly identical with his sovereign: he thinks the thoughts of his sovereign, he speaks his words, he adopts his decisions. The more he is taken up into the will of his lord, the more he deserves the honor that is due that one.

The notion of the one sent has been depicted thus far entirely apart from Jesus. However, the description fits Jesus exactly. He is the one sent by the Father for those in the world. Jesus repeats again and again in the Fourth Gospel that he does not speak his own words, but those of his Father (3:34, 7:16, 8:26, 38, 40, 14:10, 24, 17:8); he does not do his own works, but those of his Father (4:34, 5:17, 19ff., 30, 36, 8:28, 14:10, 17:4, 14); he does not carry out his own will, but that of his Father (4:34, 5:30, 6:38, 10:25, 37). If we may formulate pointedly what is said in these texts, we could say: Jesus gains all his significance, according to the Gospel of John, precisely by virtue of the fact that he does not intend to be anything other than the voice and the hands of his Father. On this basis alone does Jesus request honor for himself among men: whoever does not honor him, does not honor the Father who sent him (5:23, 44, 7:18, 8:50, 54). The Jews are therefore completely mistaken when they accuse him of blasphemy: he makes himself equal to God. He actually stands in the place of God as the one sent by him and who is completely at one with the sovereignty of God.

But how does the Evangelist view the world, the κόσμος? One can still speak of the ruler of this world, to be sure (8:44, 12:31, 14:30, 16:11), but that ruler does not put in an appearance himself. Nor do the demons appear as effective powers: the Gospel of John does not contain a single story of an exorcism. The world that is hostile to Christ and inimical to God is represented only by human disbelief, which is embodied in the high priests, the Pharisees, and the Jews generally. Is one permitted to draw from this the conclusion that the Evangelist is a man of the Enlightenment, who "no longer believes in miracles and demons"? By no means!

---

10 *Adv. haer.* 2.22.5.

11 𝔓75 ℵ * 0124 sy^s sa read: ἑώρακεν σε.

12 For a stoning in the temple, cf. Josephus, *Ant.* 17.9.3:

the people stone soldiers of Archaelus in the temple at Passover.

13 Bauer, *Das Johannesevangelium*, 132.

John is obviously persuaded that all the miracles he relates as "signs" really occurred. But the other explanation that one could fall back on also will not do: he has eliminated the demonic powers in order not to detract from Jesus' triumphal power. The Evangelist wants to represent Jesus as the conqueror whose victory is certain even before the battle has begun. But the disappearance of the demons from the earthly scene has a more profound basis: the whole world, the κόσμος, is "darkness" for John.[14] The dividing line between God and the Evil One, between "above" and "below," no longer cuts across earthly events, as it does in the Synoptics; it rather separates this world from the divine world of light, from which Jesus has come and to which he will again return. There is thus no hint that John sees the human world as something bright, optimistic, independent of evil, as does perhaps Mark. The opposite is true: in the Gospel of John the world as a whole is devalued and has sunk into a metaphysical darkness. Salvation consists, as a consequence, in having Jesus, who is the divine emissary from an eternal home, where many mansions await the redeemed, come to earth and awaken in those persons whom God has given him the eternal life that overcomes death. The lordship of Jesus consists of this: God dispenses this life through him. By giving this gift he demonstrates that he is compassionate love.

This true and essential gift of God is, however, invisible. It cannot therefore be either immediately perceived or shown to others. It lies beyond the earthly realm, beyond its possibilities. Events within the earthly realm can therefore only point to this gift at best. One is thus confronted once again with the Johannine doctrine of "signs." All the miracles of Jesus gain their meaning from the fact that they point beyond themselves to the real act of God. We may take, for example, the healing of the man born blind (chapter 9). It is certainly an overpowering deed to give sight to one born blind. But God's majesty is not yet visibile in that act. For whether anyone is blind or has sight is a distinction that lies within the earthly sphere. If, therefore, one does not perceive anything beyond the fact that Jesus has altered something within the earthly sphere by restoring sight to a man born blind, one has not yet caught sight of God's act. One has not yet caught sight of God's majesty. Only when such a healing indicates to us that Jesus is "the light of the world," do we see his "signs" really as signs, as a pointer to God's eternal deed, namely, that Jesus gives men eyes for God.

Furthermore, for the Evangelist, the new existence in the spirit brought by the one sent by God is a gift of God that is invisible as such to earthly eyes. That is demonstrated by Jesus' conversation with Nicodemus. Jesus gives Nicodemus to understand that the one who does not receive an entirely new, heavenly existence from God does not have eyes for God and his works and can perceive nothing of either. Nicodemus' answer indicates that he understands this one thing: Jesus is talking about a form of existence that is new from the ground up. But it seems to Nicodemus that such a thing is impossible. Nicodemus is so firmly imprisoned in the earthly that he can conceive of a new existence only as a second earthly existence. But as such it is entirely out of question—as Nicodemus attempts to show. Jesus' answer endeavors to free him from this captivity by refering him to the spirit. But "spirit" does not mean in the language of the Gospel of John what modern man means by that: it is not intellect, understanding, or élan. We can perhaps best do justice to the Johannine concept of the spirit by translating πνεῦμα, spirit, as "divine reality": "Whoever is not born of the spirit," *scil.* of the divine reality, "cannot see the kingdom of God." "What is born of the flesh," *scil.* of earthly reality, "is flesh" and thus remains within the realm of earthly reality. "What is born of the spirit is spirit" and thus belongs to the realm of divine reality.

What are the consequences for the recognition of the reality of the spirit? Jesus illustrates the situation with the metaphor of the wind (πνεῦμα means both "wind, breath" and "spirit" in Greek): "The wind blows where it wills," without our being able to forecast it. "You hear the sound of it, but you do not know whence it comes or whither it goes. So it is with everyone who is born of the spirit." One senses in such a person something out of the ordinary, something strange. One remarks: here is something special. But one cannot know that this person comes *from God* and goes *to God*, that this person has his or her origin and destiny with God, his or her ultimate

---

14 Cf. 1:5, 10.

home with God. The spirit is invisible to earthly eyes, because the spirit belongs to a different, a higher reality.

The Evangelist tells us what difference this new existence in the spirit makes in the story of the resurrection of Lazarus. What is called "the birth from above" in the conversation with Nicodemus is illustrated in this story in the figure of the resurrection. Jesus says to Martha: "Your brother will rise again." Martha's answer shows that she understands this saying in the sense of the customary belief in the resurrection: "I know that he will rise again in the resurrection at the last day." But that is precisely what Jesus did not mean. His answer discloses something new, something quite different than the Pharisaic belief in the resurrection: "I am the resurrection and the life. He who believes in me, though he die, yet shall he live," although he suffers physical death. "And whoever lives," whoever lives this new, true life, "and believes in me, shall never die." For the one to whom Jesus becomes life, in him Jesus awakens a new, heavenly form of existence. This new life begins in the midst of earthly life and and is not touched by earthly death, but endures forever.

Of what does this new form of existence consist? In fellowship with God, to which Jesus is the way (14:6). When we speak of fellowship with God, we think of a fellowship of shared views and therefore of a particular kind of inwardness. The gift of life that comes through Jesus would then consist in Jesus altering our inner relation to God. That is not entirely incorrect, but it does not say enough on the view of the Evangelist. In the one to whom Jesus gives new life there is born an entirely new human being, a supermundane or heavenly being, or whatever one wishes to call it. This "new existence" is not merely a figure for a change in views, character, or inwardness (for the Gospel of John that would not really be a new existence, but only an alteration within the old). Rather, the Evangelist is saying that Jesus awakens in man an independent spiritual being, that is beyond physical death and does not come to an end with the old

man (8:44), because it belongs to a different, higher reality. That is what it means for Jesus to be here and now "the resurrection and the life"—both in an active sense—and not "the resurrection and the life" in some distant future, at the last day.

A further problem is indicated by 8:51. What is said there is very close to Mark 8:27–9:1. We do not find an exact parallel in John to Mark 8:27–9:1. However, individual aspects of this pericope find echoes in John. The expression in Mark 9:1, "some will not taste death" before the parousia, is characteristically paraphrased in John 8:51: "If any one keeps my word, he will not taste death." In so doing, the expectation of a future parousia is replaced with a conception in which the present takes the place of the future. That corresponds to John's basic disposition to matters. The fourth Evangelist expresses in his own way, in 12:25, what is said in Mark 8:35 and all its synoptic parallels: "He who loves his life loses it, and he who hates his life in this world will keep it for eternal life." The logion regarding the grain of wheat comes just before in John: "Truly, truly, I say to you, unless a grain of wheat falls into the earth and dies, it remains alone"— unless one sows wheat, it cannot multiply; "to be sown in the earth" is understood as a kind of death. That makes contact with the words of Paul in 1 Cor 15:36: "What you sow does not come to life unless it dies." "But"—to return to John—"if it dies, it bears much fruit." It follows from the two texts that the matter was understood then as follows: the grain of wheat that is buried in the earth loses its form and dies. John is not speaking of an eschatological event in the sense of an apocalyptic expectation, but of something that can happen here and now to a person: he can enter into union with God.

24.   The Healing of the Blind Man

Bibliography

A.   John 9:1–41

Bligh, John
"Four Studies in St. John, I: The Man Born Blind." *HeyJ* 7 (1966) 129–44.

Bornhäuser, Karl
"Meister, wer hat gesündigt, dieser oder seine Eltern, dass er ist blind geboren?: Joh. 9, 2." *NKZ* 38 (1927) 433–37.

Bornkamm, Günther
"Die Heilung des Blindgeborenen (Joh 9)." In his *Geschichte und Glaube*, part 2. *Gesammelte Aufsätze*, vol. 4. BEvT 53 (Munich: Chr. Kaiser Verlag, 1971) 65–72.

Brodie, Louis T.
"Creative Rewriting: Key to a New Methodology." In *SBL 1978 Seminar Papers* 2, SBLASP 14 (Missoula: Scholars Press, 1978) 261–67.

Buttmann, Alexander
"Ueber den Gebrauch des Pronomen ἐκεῖνος im vierten Evangelium." *TSK* 33 (1860) 505–36.

Comiskey, J. P.
"Rabbi, Who Has Sinned?" *Bible Today* 26 (1966) 1808–14.

Jong, K. H. E. de
"Joh 9, 2 und die Seelenwanderung." *ARW* 7 (1904) 518–19.

Martyn, James Louis
History and Theology in the Fourth Gospel (Nashville: Abingdon Press, [2]1979), esp. 3–41.

Mollat, Donatien
"La guérsion de l'aveugle-né." *BVC* 23 (1958) 22–31.

Müller, Karlheinz
"Joh 9, 7 und das jüdische Verständnis des Šiloh-Spruches." *BZ* 13 (1969) 251–56.

Porter, Calvin L.
"John 9.38, 39a: A Liturgical Addition to the Text." *NTS* 13 (1966/1967) 387–94.

Reim, Günter
"Joh 9—Tradition und zeitgenössische messianische Diskussion." *BZ* 22 (1978) 245–53.

Steitz, Georg Eduard
"Der classische und der johanneische Gebrauch von ἐκεῖνος," *TSK* 34 (1861) 267–310.

B.   John and OT Judaism

Barrett, Charles Kingsley
The Gospel of John and Judaism, tr. D. M. Smith (London: S. P. C. K.; Philadelphia: Fortress Press, 1975).

Beutler, Johannes
"Die 'Juden' und der Tod Jesu im Johannes-evangelium." In *Exodus und Kreuz im ökumenischen Dialog zwischen Juden und Christen. Diskussionsbeiträge für Religionsunterricht und Erwachsenen-*

bildung, ed. H. H. Henrix and M. Stöhr. Aachener Beiträge zu Pastoral- und Bildungsfragen 8 (Aachen: Einhard-Verlag, 1978) 75–93.

Bleek, Friedrich
"Der Verfasser des vierten Evangeliums beweist durch seine Bekanntschaft mit dem AT sich als einen Juden und Palästinenser. . . ." In his *Beiträge zur Einleitung und Auslegung der heiligen Schrift.* Vol. 1, *Beiträge zur Evangelien-kritik* (Berlin: G. Reimer, 1846) 244–57.

Botha, F. J.
"The Jews in the Fourth Gospel [Afrikaans]." *Theologia evangelica* 2 (1969) 40–45.

Bowman, John
The Fourth Gospel and the the Jews. A Study in R. Akiba, Esther and the Gospel of John, PTMS 8 (Pittsburgh: Pickwick, 1975).

Bowman, John
"The Fourth Gospel and the Samaritans." *BJRL* 40 (1957/1958) 298–329.

Bratcher, Robert G.
"'The Jews' in the Gospel of John." *BT* 26 (1975) 401–9.

Buchanan, George Wesley
"The Samaritan Origin of the Gospel of John." In *Religions in Antiquity. Essays in Honor of E. R. Goodenough,* ed. J. Neusner. Studies in the History of Religions 14 (Leiden: E. J. Brill, 1968) 149–75.

Carroll, Kenneth L.
"The Fourth Gospel and the Exclusion of Christians from the Synagogues." *BJRL* 40 (1957/1958) 19–32.

Cullmann, Oscar
"L'opposition contre le temple de Jérusalem, motif commun de la théologie johannique et du monde ambiant." In his *Des sources de l'évangile à la formation de la théologie chrétienne* (Neuchâtel: Delachaux & Niestlé, 1969) 25–41.

Díez Merino, Luis
"'Galilea' en el IV Evangelio." *EstBib* 31 (1972) 247–73.

Faure, Alexander
"Die alttestamentlichen Zitate im 4. Evangelium und die Quellenscheidungshypothese." *ZNW* 21 (1922) 99–121.

Fischer
"Ueber den Ausdruck *hoi Joudaioi* im Ev. Johannis. Ein Beitrag zur Charakteristik desselben." *Tübinger Zeitschrift für Theologie* 11 (1840) 96–133.

Florival, Ephrem
"'Les siens ne l'ont pas reçu.' Regard évangélique sur la question juive." *NRT* 89 (1967) 43–66.

Franke, August Hermann
Das AT bei Johannes. Ein Beitrag zur Erklärung und Beurtheilung der johanneischen Schriften (Göttingen: Vandenhoeck & Ruprecht, 1885).

Freed, Edwin D.
Old Testament Quotations in the Gospel of John, NovTSup 11 (Leiden: E. J. Brill, 1965).

Freed, Edwin D.
"Did John write his gospel partly to win Samaritans converts?" *NovT* 12 (1970) 241–56.

Freed, Edwin D.
"Samaritan Influence in the Gospel of John." *CBQ* 30 (1968) 580–87.

Fuller, Reginald Horace
"The 'Jews' in the Fourth Gospel." *Dialog* 16 (1977) 31–37.

Grässer, Erich
"Die Antijüdische Polemik im Johannesevangelium." *NTS* 11 (1964/1965) 74–90.

Grässer, Erich
"Die Juden als Teufelssöhne nach Joh 8, 37–47." In *Antijudaismus im Neuen Testament? Exegetische und systematische Beiträge,* ed. W. P. Eckert et al. Abhandlungen zum christlich-jüdischen Dialog 2 (Munich: Chr. Kaiser Verlag, 1967) 157–70.

Gryglewicz, Feliks
"Die Pharisäer und die Johanneskirche." In *Probleme der Forschung,* ed. A. Fuchs. Studien zum Neuen Testament und seiner Umwelt A, 3 (Vienna and Munich: Verlag Herold, 1978) 144–58.

Haupt, Erich
Die alttestamentlichen Citate in den vier Evangelien erörtert (Colberg: C. Jancke, 1871).

Hickling, C. J. A.
"Attitudes to Judaism in the Fourth Gospel." In *L'Evangile de Jean. Sources, rédaction, théologie,* ed. M. de Jonge. BETL 44 (Gembloux: Duculot; Louvain: University Press, 1977) 347–54.

Hilgenfeld, Adolf
"Der Antijudaïsmus des Johannes-Evangeliums." *ZWT* 36 (1893) 507–17.

Hruby, Kurt
"Die Trennung von Kirche und Judentum." In *Theologische Berichte 3. Judentum und Kirche: Volk Gottes,* ed. J. Pfammatter and F. Fürger (Zurich and Cologne: Benziger, 1974) 135–56.

Jocz, Jacob
"Die Juden im Johannesevangelium." *Judaica* 9 (1953) 129–42.

Knight, George A. F.
"Antisemitism in the Fourth Gospel." *Reformed Theological Review* 27 (1968) 81–88.

Leistner, Reinhold
Antijudaismus im Johannesevangelium? Darstellung des Problems in der neueren Auslegungsgeschichte und Untersuchung der Leidensgeschichte, Theologie und Wirklichkeit 3 (Bern: H. Lang; Frankfurt: P. Lang, 1974).

Lowe, Malcolm
"Who were the *IOUDAIOI*?" *NovT* 18 (1976) 101–30.

Lütgert, Wilhelm
"Die Juden im Johannesevangelium." In *Neutestamentliche Studien Georg Heinrici zu seinem 70. Geburtstag (14 März 1914) dargebracht von Fachgenossen,*

Freunden und Schülern, UNT 6 (Leipzig: J. C. Hinrichs, 1914) 147–54.

Martyn, James Louis
History and Theology in the Fourth Gospel (Nashville: Abingdon Press, ²1979).

Matsunaga, Kikuo
"The Galileans in the Fourth Gospel." *Annual of the Japanese Biblical Institute* 2 (1976) 139–58.

Meeks, Wayne A.
"Galilee and Judea in the Fourth Gospel." *JBL* 85 (1966) 159–69.

Meeks, Wayne A.
"'Am I a Jew?' Johannine Christology and Judaism." In *Christianity, Judaism and Other Greco-Roman Cults. Studies for Morton Smith at Sixty.* Part 1, *New Testament,* ed. Jacob Neusner. SJLA 12 (Leiden: E. J. Brill, 1975) 163–86.

Michaels, J. Ramsey
"Alleged Anti-Semitism in the Fourth Gospel." *Gordon Review* 11 (1968) 12–24.

Painter, John
"The Church and Israel in the Gospel of John. A Response." *NTS* 25 (1978/1979) 103–12.

Pancaro, Severino
"The Relationship of the Church to Israel in the Gospel of St John." *NTS* 21 (1974/1975) 396–405.

Purvis, James D.
"The Fourth Gospel and the Samaritans." *NovT* 17 (1975) 161–98.

Reim, Günter
Studien zum alttestamentlichen Hintergrund des Johannesevangeliums, SNTSMS 22 (New York: Cambridge University Press, 1974).

Ruddick, C. T.
"Feeding and Sacrifice—The Old Testament Background of the Fourth Gospel." *ExpTim* 79 (1968) 340–41.

Shepherd, Massey H., Jr.
"The Jews in the Gospel of John. Another Level of Meaning." ATR Supplement 3 (1974) 95–112.

Sikes, Walter W.
"The Anti-Semitism of the Fourth Gospel." *JR* 21 (1941) 23–30.

Schlatter, Adolf
"Der Bruch Jesu mit der Judenschaft." In *Aus Schrift und Geschichte; Theologische Abhandlungen und Skizzen Herrn Prof. D. Conrad von Orelli zur Feier seiner 25-jährigen Lehrtätigkeit in Basel von Freunden und Schülern gewidmet* (Basel: B. Reich, 1898) 1–23.

Schram, Terry Leonard
"The Use of *Joudaioi* in the Fourth Gospel." Dissertation, Utrecht, 1974.

Thoma, Albrecht
"Das Alte Testament im Johannes-Evangelium." *ZWT* 22 (1879) 18–66, 171–223, 273–312.

Wahlde, Urban C. von
"A Literary Analysis of the 'ochlos'-passages in the Fourth Gospel in their Relation to the Pharisees and Jews-material." Dissertation, Marquette University, 1975.

Wiefel, Wolfgang
"Die Scheidung von Gemeinde und Welt im Johannesevangelium auf dem Hintergrund der Trennung von Kirche und Synagoge." *TZ* 35 (1979) 213–27.

Windisch, Hans
"Das johanneische Christentum und sein Verhältnis zum Judentum und zu Paulus." *Christliche Welt* 47 (1933) 98–107, 147–54.

9

1 As he passed by, he saw a man blind from his birth. 2/ And his disciples asked him, "Rabbi, who sinned, this man or his parents, that he was born blind?" 3/ Jesus answered, "It was not that this man sinned, or his parents, but that the works of God might be manifest in him. 4/ We must work the works of him who sent me, while it is day; night comes, when no one can work. 5/ As long as I am in the world, I am the light of the world." 6/ As he said this, he spat on the ground and made clay of the spittle and anointed the man's eyes with clay, 7/ saying to him, "Go, wash in the pool of Siloam" (which means Sent). So he went and washed and came back seeing. 8/ The neighbors and those who had seen him before as a beggar, said, "Is not this the man who used to sit and beg?" 9/ Some said, "It is he"; others said, "No, but he is like him." He said, "I am the man." 10/ They said to him, "Then how were your eyes opened?" 11/ He answered, "The man called Jesus made clay and anointed my eyes and said to me, 'Go to Siloam and wash'; so I went and washed and received my sight." 12/ They said to him, "Where is he?" He said, "I do not know." 13/ They brought to the Pharisees the man who had formerly been blind. 14/ Now it was a sabbath day when Jesus made the clay and opened his eyes. 15/ The Pharisees again asked him how he had received his sight. And he said to them, "He put clay on my eyes, and I washed, and I see." 16/ Some of the Pharisees said, "This man is not from God, for he does not keep the sabbath." But others said, "How can a man who is a sinner do such signs?" There was a division among them. 17/ So they again said to the blind man, "What do you say about him, since he has opened your eyes?" He said, "He is a prophet." 18/ The Jews did not believe that he had been blind and had received his sight, until they called the parents of the man who had received his sight, 19/ and asked them, "Is this your son, who you say was born blind? How then does he now see?" 20/ His parents answered, "We know that this is our son, and that he was born blind; 21/ but how he now sees we do not know, nor do we know who opened his eyes. Ask him; he is of age, he will speak for himself." 22/ His parents said this because they feared the Jews, for the Jews had already agreed that if any one should confess him to be Christ, he was to be put out of the synagogue. 23/ Therefore his parents said, "He is of age, ask him." 24/ So for the second time they called the man who had been blind, and said to him, "Give God the praise; we know that this man is a sinner." 25/ He answered, "Whether he is a sinner, I do not know; one thing I know, that though I was blind, now I see." 26/ They said to him, "What did he do to you? How did he open your eyes?" 27/ He answered them, "I have told you already, and you would not listen. Why do you want to hear it again? Do you too want to become his disciples?" 28/ And they reviled him, saying, "You are his disciple, but we are disciples of Moses. 29/ We know that God has spoken to Moses, but as for this man, we do not know where he comes from." 30/ The man answered, "Why, this is a marvel! You do not know where he comes from, yet he opened my eyes. 31/ We know that God does not listen to sinners, but if any one is a worshiper of God and does his will, God listens to him. 32/ Never since the world began has it been heard that any one opened the eyes of man born blind. 33/ If this man were not from

God, he could do nothing." 34/ They answered him, "You were born in utter sin, and would you teach us?" And they cast him out. 35/ Jesus heard that they had cast him out, and having found him he said, "Do you believe in the Son of man?" 36/ He answered, "And who is he, sir, that I may believe in him?" 37/ Jesus said to him, "You have seen him, and it is he who speaks to you." 38/ He said, "Lord, I believe"; and he worshiped him. 39/ Jesus said, "For judgment I came into this world, that those who do not see may see, and that those who see may become blind." 40/ Some of the Pharisees near him heard this, and they said to him, "Are we also blind?" 41/ Jesus said to them, "If you were blind, you would have no guilt; but now that you say, 'We see,' your guilt remains."

■ **1** "And passing by" (καὶ παράγων): the action continues to take place during the feast of Tabernacles. Earlier interpreters psychologize:[1] these events could not have followed immediately on the heavy scene of chapter 8, for the question of the disciples presupposes a serene frame of mind. In fact, a tradition originally independent might begin with verse 1. One cannot draw conclusions regarding the sequence of individual events from the sequence given in the text. The narrator stipulates that the man in question was blind from birth. The narrator is not concerned with whether the healing took place at the door of the temple or at the gate of the city.

■ **2** On the other hand, in this verse it is presupposed that the disciples (who were last mentioned in 6:66–71) know that the man was blind from birth. It is thus not a question, as it is in 5:6, of miraculous knowledge on the part of Jesus. The Evangelist makes use of the question of the disciples in order to be able to present Jesus' answer. He was not aware of the difficulty. Zahn is of the opinion that Jesus could have initiated a conversation with the blind man in which this circumstance could have been mentioned.[2] But the conversation in 5:6ff. does not provide such a psychologizing explanation for Jesus'

knowledge of the duration of the illness. Is it possible that in an earlier stage of the story it was presupposed that his blindness did not go back to his birth? According to Billerbeck,[3] the rabbis also considered cases in which a child had sinned already in its mother's womb. Bauer's supposition that the hellenistic-Platonic or gnostic doctrine of the pre-existence of the soul comes into play[4] is rightly denied by Bultmann.[5] The explanation of illness as retribution for sin is common in Judaism; the best known representatives are the friends of Job.

■ **3** Jesus rejects this either/or (but only in this instance; the situation is comparable in 11:4):[6] this man's illness provides the occasion to manifest "the works of God." That the readers could have felt this explanation to be inhuman (a man has to suffer the agony of blindness for many years, in order that the power of God may be manifest in his healing) does not enter into the meaning of the story for the narrator, anymore than it does in 11:4. Unlike 6:29, the work of God does not mean faith in Jesus.

Dodd sees the question of theodicy being raised here, as in Luke 13:1–5.[7] But the narrator does not have that in mind as such. Dodd also incorrectly compares this

1 De Wette, *Kurze Erklärung,* 170; Godet, *John,* 2: 359.
2 *Das Evangelium des Johannes,* 434 n. 59.
3 2: 528f.
4 *Das Johannesevangelium,* 133.
5 *John,* 330f. n. 8 [351 n. 2].
6 Bultmann, *John,* 330f. [351].
7 *Tradition,* 186–88.

passage with Luke 11:20//Matt 12:28 (a healing as sign), namely, that the miracle is a sign that the kingdom of God has come. The Evangelist simply does not represent Dodd's realized eschatology. The "signs" do not prove that God's reign has already come, but point indirectly in each case to the fact that Jesus can be the way to God for him.

■ 4 The interchange of "we" and "I" in this verse is striking. Dodd conjectures that a rabbinic aphorism has been used: "The day is short and there is much work to be done; the workers are lazy and the reward is great and the Master of the house is urgent."[8] Rabbi Tarphon (ca. 100 CE) used this proverbial saying in connection with the study of the Torah, although the connection may not have been original. In this context day stands for the normal span of life, and night represents death when one is no longer able to work. The "we" is intended to indicate that the saying applies to the disciples as well.

■ 5 Contrary to expectations, Jesus is here the light of the world so long as he is on earth. That is surprising since for Christians the exalted Lord is the light of the world. But the verse is intended to indicate why Jesus performs the miracle now to be narrated: the miracle will make it obvious that he is the light of the world.

■ 6 The continuation of the story in verse 6 connects up immediately with verse 3: after it is announced in verse 3 that the works of God are to be revealed, Jesus performs the miracle that manifests the works of God. The way in which Jesus makes a poultice out of spittle and dirt and puts it on the eyes of the blind man is surprising by virtue of the gross materials employed in this healing method.[9] Even a mere word is sufficient in 5:8. Moreover, it now appears as though Jesus were not involved in the miracle by himself, but that the water of Siloam is also implicated. This word is therefore etymologically misinterpreted as "Sent," so that, in spite of everything, Jesus turns out to be the healer. Brown recalls that Elisha takes Naiman to the Jordan and has him bathe seven times in the water. The narrator is not

interested in how the blind man finds his way to the pool of Siloam. It is possible that this feature of the source took shape not without allusion to Isa 8:6: "Because this people have refused the waters of Shiloah that flow gently."

The healing of the blind man is therefore depicted as being effected with the means that were employed at that time in Judaism[10] or in paganism,[11] in or by which miraculous cures were sought.[12] Special healing powers were attributed to spittle.

■ 7 On his way to the pool of Siloam the blind man becomes an independent narrative figure, and that is assumed in what follows. Not until 9:35ff. does he meet Jesus again. In translating the name Siloam as "Sent" (probably etymologically inappropriately), the narrator indicates that it is nevertheless Jesus who performs the healing: Jesus is "Sent" by the Father.

We meet the particle $o\mathring{v}v$ ("therefore") in this verse; it appears repeatedly in the narrative segments of the Fourth Gospel. That does not warrant any particular conclusions; Schweizer and Ruckstuhl regard this word as a specific Johannine trait.[13] But when one is investigating the style of a particular writing, it is always a question whether such a "trait" belongs to that particular author, or to the tradition out of which he has created it, or to the literary (or unliterary) layer from which it is derived. The distribution of $o\mathring{v}v$ is remarkably uneven in the Fourth Gospel: it does not appear at all, for example, in the Nicodemus story, so far as I can see; on the other hand, it is astonishingly frequent in the story of the man born blind (from 9:7 on).

■ 8 The mention of the neighbors indicates that the blind man now healed seeks out his old quarters. We now learn that he earlier used to sit at an appropriate spot (in Acts 3:10 it is the door of the temple) and beg. That some do not recognize him as the one who was blind indicates the transformation that he has undergone and thus, indirectly, the reality of the miracle.

■ 9 The dispute over the identity of the man who was

8 *Tradition*, 186; cf. Billerbeck, 2: 529.
9 The reading offered by $\mathfrak{P}^{66}$ $\mathfrak{P}^{75}$ ℵ Θ *pl* Ir[lat] *al*, viz. $\dot{\epsilon}\pi\acute{\epsilon}\chi\rho\iota\sigma\epsilon\nu$ ("anoint") could be derived from verse 11; on the other hand, as Brown (*John*, 1: 372) remarks, it is also possible that $\dot{\epsilon}\pi\iota\tau\iota\theta\acute{\epsilon}\nu\alpha\iota$ ("place on") is taken over by B from verse 15. But the latter suits verse 15 better than it does verse 6, because in v. 15 the recapitualtion is abbreviated.

10 Billerbeck, 2: 15.
11 Petronius 131.
12 The healing in Mark 8:22–26 and the healing of the deaf mute in Mark 7:32–37 are similar.
13 *Einheit*, 198ff.

healed, which is settled by his own assertion, is the preparation for the attempt of the Jews, in verse 18, to deny the identity of the blind man now made to see and so to dispense with the miracle.

■ **10** The reader already knows how he has been healed. When the story of the healing is now retold for the neighbors and repeated later for the Pharisees, that betrays the disbelief of the world, on the one hand, but, on the other, it simultaneously impresses the reality of the miracle on the reader. A similar narrative technique is employed in the threefold repetition of Paul's call in Acts 9, 22, and 26, and in the repetition of the conversion of Cornelius in Acts 10ff.

■ **11** Because unimportant, we are not told where the man who was healed learned the name of Jesus (it is different in the story of the lame man in 5:13). "He anointed" (ἐπέχρισεν) is not an allusion to Christ by accident; it is transmitted as the replacement for "he placed" (ἐπέθηκεν) in verse 6 also.[14] The narrative becomes shorter with each repetition—the reader knows it and should not be bored with the repetition.

■ **12** The man who was cured is now interrogated about Jesus—the name is mentioned in verse 11; the demonstrative "that" (ἐκεῖνος) thus suffices in verse 12. The man who was blind does not know where Jesus is staying; it is therefore necessary to keep asking him about Jesus.

■ **13** He is led to the Pharisees, who once again act as authorities; we do not learn who took him and why he was taken to them. It is important only that the Pharisees now have to assume a defensive posture vis-à-vis a miracle that is very unpleasant to them.

■ **14** Now for the first time it is said that the miracle was performed on a sabbath—as it was in 5:9. Kneading dough (for the poultice) on the sabbath was forbidden as work.[15] That Jesus has committed an infraction of the sabbath law is the occasion, in verse 16, to deny that Jesus "is from God."

■ **15** The man is once again interrogated about the healing, this time by the Pharisees. The healing is now described in the style of a telegram. It becomes evident already at this point that the man formerly blind is not afraid of the authorities like all the others are.

■ **16** When some of the Pharisees now assert that Jesus is

not from God because he breaks the sabbath, that comes as a surprise in the context. But the narrator and his community are persuaded that Jesus comes from God, and that "others" support that claim because no sinner could perform such "wonders" (σημεῖα). In view of the dissension that has broken out, they turn (literally, third person plural) again to the former blind man and ask him his opinion about the man who opened his eyes.

■ **17f.** The answer he gives is that Jesus is a prophet. In order to dismiss this embarrasing testimony, the Jews believe that he had never been blind and healed, and call his parents. This time it is "the Jews" who function as officials.

■ **19** The parents are now asked: is this really your son, who was allegedly born blind? How is it then that he can now see? This scene reveals the perplexity of the opponents. But since healing miracles were allegedly performed at that time, the reaction of the "Jews" is more realistic than it now appears to us.

■ **20f.** The parents reply extremely cautiously: what they are able to testify to are, first, that he is really their son, and, second, that he was really blind. But how he has now come to see or who healed him is unknown to them. One ought to question their son himself; he is old enough to speak for himself.

■ **22** In verse 22 the parents speak out of fear for the "Jews." But it has not been suggested up to this point that the parents were present at the healing or that their son had told them the story. How they came to the knowledge they appear to possess, in spite of their affirmations to the contrary, is not said. Instead, we learn that the "Jews" have already determined to put every one out of the synagogue who confesses Jesus as the messiah. As a consequence, in the time of the narrator and in the circle of his acquaintances, there can no longer have been any Jewish Christians in a Jewish community.

■ **23** Verse 23 emphasizes once more that his parents have abandoned their son for the reason indicated. The difficulty of having a mission among the Jews at that time is thereby made quite evident.

■ **24** They, that is, the Jews, call the man born blind back again; he was apparently not present during the exami-

14 By 𝔓66 𝔓75 D Θ *pl* Ir^lat.
15 Cf. Billerbeck, 2: 530, who refers to *Sabb.* 7.2.

nation of his parents (although that is not specifically mentioned). They treat him almost as though he were already condemned. For, the formula, "Give God the honor," was then employed (although not only then) when a condemned man was required to confess his crime and thus in speaking the truth to give God the honor.[16] The following words show that the opponents have already made up their minds (they therefore see in the man who was healed someone who is potentially condemned): they know that Jesus is a sinner.

■ **25** In sharp contrast to the lame man at the pool in chater 5, the former blind man is not at all intimidated: he does not know whether Jesus is a sinner. But he does know that he was blind and now he sees. Therefore— and this is what is meant—Jesus has performed a miracle on him.

■ **26** As a consequence, he has to tell once more how the healing came about.

■ **27** He now begins to deride them: why do they want to hear it a second time? Have they perhaps not heard enough of it and want to become disciples of Jesus?

■ **28** Understandably, they now lose their patience and revile him: he is a disciple of Jesus, but they are disciples of Moses. Why that is more important is related in the next verse.

■ **29** God has spoken with Moses; that they knew from the Torah. But where Jesus comes from, they do not know. He has no legitimation.

■ **30** Verse 30 brings the blind man's response: That is really a marvel! You are not clear about Jesus' origins, although he has opened the eyes of a man born blind. That constitutes the legitimation that is allegedly missing, as the next verse states.

■ **31** We know (that is, it is generally acknowledged) that God does not listen to sinners, but does listen to the pious, who do his will. Jesus must therefore be a worshiper, who does God's will.

■ **32** Verse 32 underscores the unique character of the miracle, which, as a consequence, is an entirely certain and reliable form of legitimation: there is no precedent for it; no one has ever heard of a man born blind being healed. Verse 33 follows as a consequence:

■ **33** If "this man" were not from God, he could do nothing. That agrees with Jesus' own sayings in the Fourth Gospel, yet is distinguished from them: the man born blind advocates the doctrine formulated by Nicodemus in 3:2, to the effect that Jesus is legitimated by miracles. Only malevolence can overlook this miraculous proof; but the Jews now do.

■ **34** The man who was healed therefore falls into the displeasure of Jesus' opponents: they revile him as one born in utter sin—that is the way they interpret his blindness from birth—and throw him out of the synagogue.

■ **35f.** Jesus reappears in these verses. Up to this point he had been absent bodily, but has remained the real center of the action and counteraction. He asks the man he has healed whether he believes in the Son of man. The blind man immediately understands the designation, "Son of man," in the sense of "Christ" or "messiah," and only wants to learn who he is (as a blind man he had not yet seen Jesus), so that he may believe in him. Although he knows that a man named Jesus has healed him, he has yet to learn through the self-testimony of Jesus that the one who stands before him is actually the one in whom he already has faith.

■ **37** Jesus now solemnly declares himself: You have seen him (he has indeed obtained his ability to see through Jesus), and he who speaks to you is that Son of man.

■ **38** The man who was healed responds with a confession of faith in the Lord and an act of worship: he prostrates himself before Jesus and worships him.

The fact that he is excommunicated from the synagogue indicates the circumstances of a later time.

■ **39** The real action of this scene has come to an end; Jesus' words sum the matter up: for judgment he has come into this world, that the blind may see and those who see may become blind. That is the Johannine form of the synoptic representation of Jesus as accepting sinners and rejecting the religious, the self-justifying. The parable of the Pharisee and tax collector is here acted out, so to speak, in Johannine language and action. The judgment occurs even in the face of the deed of Jesus, which is a blessing and grace to the receiver.

■ **40f.** Verses 40f. provide an illustrative epilogue: some Pharisees cry out in protest because they are called blind

---

16   Billerbeck, 2: 535.

while as disciples of Moses they know who God's messenger is. Jesus now concentrates what he said earlier in one saying: precisely because they assert that they can see are they finally put down as sinners. Forgiveness is no longer possible for them. There is no access to one who has been blinded.

Overview

The healing of the blind man is told in unusual detail. Only the raising of Lazarus in chapter 11 is given comparable coverage in depth. In chapter 9, an artfully constructed source is reproduced virtually without editorial insertion; only verses 4f. stem from the Evangelist, and he has probably added verses 39–41.

Verses 1–7 provide the introduction: a healing story is turned into a conflict over the sabbath by verse 14. The similarity to 5:1–9 has been noted. However, the long discourse of Jesus appended to the event is missing, unlike chapter 5.

Verses 8–12 comprise the first subsection: the neighbors and others who know the former beggar do not want to believe what their eyes tell them: he is the former blind beggar. They are told of the healing by Jesus, whom they can no longer see. The disciples, who put in an abrupt appearance in verses 2f., are not mentioned again. Their only function is to pose the question that is answered in verse 3.

The second subsection extends as far as verse 17: the man who was healed is taken before the Pharisees and has to relate his healing. While the Pharisees debate whether the miracle worker is "from God," since he does not keep the sabbath, the others object: a sinful man could not do such wonders. In response to questioning, the man who was healed replies that he regards the one who healed him as a prophet.

A further subsection consists of verses 18–23: the identity of the man who was healed is called into question—and confirmed. The parents of the former blind man are called in and they confirm that he is their son who was blind from birth, but have nothing to say about his healing—the Pharisees should ask their son himself, since he is old enough. This feature indicates how great is the fear of the Jews, who have already determined to cast anyone out of the synagogue who confesses Jesus as the Christ.

A new hearing follows in verses 24–34. The blind man is questioned once again regarding the circumstances of the healing; he becomes ironic and asks whether the Pharisees want to become disciples of the man who healed him. On the contrary, they proclaim themselves to be disciples of Moses; but they do not know where "he" (that is, Jesus) comes from. To this the man who was healed responds, underscoring very strongly the bent of the healing story: that is quite remarkable, he says, since everyone knows that a man born blind has never yet been healed and that no one can perform such a deed unless he is from God. The Jews then curse him and cast him out of the synagogue.

Verses 35–38 might form the old conclusion: Jesus then makes himself known to the man whom he had healed, who immediately believes in him as the Son of man and worships him.

An epilogue with the theme, blindness and sight, is provided by verses 39–41. Jesus makes the blind see, and those who see blind. The pious steel themselves against Jesus. Pharisees who are present raise an objection to Jesus' pronouncement and receive the answer: because you claim that you see, that is, that you know God, and do not recognize him, for you there is no forgiveness of sin.

The basic thought of this story, what it is designed to teach, is this: the miracle never before heard of, restoring sight to a man born blind, proves that Jesus is "from God." Whoever does not accede to that is blind. It is clear that the theology of this narrative is not that of the Evangelist, but corresponds to the point of view enunciated by Nicodemus in 3:2. For this narrative makes use of the healing story down to the last detail in order to show that the miracle is God's valid legitimation. Accordingly, this story, which is told in an extremely adroit and interesting way and has earned John the reputation of a great dramatist,[17] adopts the point of view of Nicodemus. That is evident in 9:31, where the text says, "If any one is a worshiper of God and does his will, God listens to him." The Evangelist has indicated his own understanding of the story only briefly in verse 5 and in

---

17   Cf. Hirsch, *Das vierte Evangelium*, 235, 245.

9:39: "For judgment I came into this world, that those who do not see may see, and that those who see may become blind." Miracles stories function for the Evangelist only as pointers to something entirely different; he no more doubts the factuality of the miracles than he values them as proof. The Evangelist has therefore taken over a story that is internally alien to him and given it, in verses 4f., what he takes as its authentic meaning: Jesus is the light of the world. The healing points to that—indirectly. That the healing does not constitute proof is shown by the fact that the Pharisees are not persuaded by it and cast the man who was healed out of the synagogue.

Earlier interpreters like Godet, for example,[18] reflect on the sequence of events like this: this event could not have taken place immediately after the heavy scene in chapter 8 because the question of the disciples in verse 2 requires a serene frame of mind; 8:59 could have happened in the morning; 9:1ff. could have followed on the evening of the same day. In place of such thoughts, Zahn wonders how the disciples came to know that the man was blind from birth, and imagines that Jesus could have had a conversation with the blind man in which he learned that fact.[19] Zahn accepts the door of the temple as the place where the healing occurred, while Godet more cautiously conjectures the gate of the city. B. Weiss, who also thinks the place is proximate to the temple (Acts 3:2), calls attention to the healing of the blind man from Bethsaida in Mark 8:22–26.[20] There are two correlative features: both involve the healing of a blind man; and in both spittle plays a role. On the other hand, Mark 8:22–26 corresponds exactly to the healing of the deaf mute in Mark 7:32–37. In this case, too, in addition to the laying on of hands, spittle is used as a medium, and then in a more drastic manner, not in the form of a poultice or dough, but is applied directly to the affected organ. Only the form employed in the Gospel of John permits Jesus to send the man to the pool of "Siloam," which is interpreted in the text to mean "Sent." This circumstance and the proof that in the Gospel of John the man was blind from birth indicates that the Evangelist is using a tradition in which the miraculous is heightened. Insofar as we have synoptic parallels as controls, the miraculous element in all the Johannine stories is heightened, and those stories without synoptic parallels, like the healing of the man born blind (chap. 9) and the raising of Lazarus (chap. 11), eclipse all the miracles related in the Synoptics. What these miracles are supposed to effect in the reader is indicated clearly by John 20:30f., assuming that this is the old conclusion to the "Gospel": "Now Jesus did many other signs in the presence of the disciples, which are not written in this book; but these are written that you may believe that Jesus is the Christ, the Son of God, and that believing you may have life in his name." It is especially easy to observe in the healing story of the man born blind that the author has related the miracle stories with this aim in view. In verses 16, 25, and 31, different expressions are used to call the reader's attention to the fact that God does not hear a sinner; consequently, Jesus must be from God, otherwise he would not have been able to perform this miracle.

---

18   *John*, 2: 359.
19   *Das Evangelium des Johannes*, 435.
20   *Das Johannesevangelium*, 356.

25. Jesus, The Good Shepherd

Bibliography

Ackermann, J. S.
"The Rabbinic Interpretation of Psalm 82 and the Gospel of John: John 10:34." *HTR* 59 (1966) 186–91.

Bammel, Ernst
"'John did no miracle': John 10, 41." In *Miracles. Cambridge Studies in their Philosophy and History*, ed. C. F. D. Moule. (London: A. R. Mowbray, 1965) 197–202.

Becquet, G.
"Jésus, Bon Pasteur, donne vie à une nouvelle communauté (Jn 10,11–18)." *Esprit et vie* 80 (1970) 242–43.

Boismard, Marie-Emile
"Jésus, le prophète par excellence, d'après Jean 10,24–39." In *Neues Testament und Kirche. Für Rudolf Schnackenburg*, ed. J. Gnilka (Freiburg: Herder, 1974) 160–71.

Bruns, J. Edgar
"The Discourse on the Good Shepherd and the Rite of Ordination." *AER* 149 (1963) 386–91.

Derrett, John Duncan Martin
"The Good Shepherd: St. John's Use of Jewish Halakah and Haggadah." *ST* 27 (1973) 25–50.

Emerton, John Adney
"Melchizedek and the Gods: Fresh Evidence for the Jewish Background of John X, 34–36." *JTS*, n.s., 17 (1966) 399–401.

Emerton, John Adney
"Some New Testament Notes." *JTS*, n.s., 11 (1960) 329–36.

Fascher, Erich
"'Ich bin die Tür!' Eine Studie zu Joh X, 1–18." *Deutsche Theologie* 79 (1942) 33–57, 118–33.

Fascher, Erich
"Zur Auslegung von Joh X, 17–18." *Deutsche Theologie* 78 (1941) 37–66.

Fischer, Karl Martin
"Der johanneische Christus und der gnostische Erlöser. Überlegungen auf Grund von Joh 10." In *Gnosis und Neues Testament. Studien aus Religionswissenschaft und Theologie*, ed. K.-W. Tröger (Gütersloh: Gerd Mohn; Berlin: Evangelische Verlagsanstalt, 1973) 245–67.

Friedrichsen, Anton
"Herdekapitlet Joh 10." *SEÅ* 8 (1943) 30–48.

Frisque, Jean and Thierry Maertens
"Deuxième dimanche du temps pascal." *Paroisse et liturgie* 47 (1965) 338–50.

George, Augustin
"Je suis la porte des brebis. Jean 10, 1–10." *BVC* 51 (1963) 18–25.

Giblet, Jean
"Et il y eut la dédicace. Jn 10, 22–39." *BVC* 66 (1965) 17–25.

Hahn, Ferdinand
  "Die Hirtenrede in Joh 10." In *Theologie Crucis—Signum Crucis. Festschrift für Erich Dinkler zum 70. Geburtstag*, ed. C. Andresen and G. Klein (Tübingen: Mohr-Siebeck, 1979) 185–200.

Hanson, Anthony
  "John's Citation of Psalm 82. John 10:33–6." *NTS* 11 (1964/1965) 158–62.

Hanson, Anthony
  "John's Citation of Psalm 82 Reconsidered." *NTS* 13 (1966/1967) 363–67.

Hofius, Otfried
  "Die Sammlung der Heiden zur Herde Israels (Joh 10:16, 11:51f.)." *ZNW* 58 (1967) 289–91.

Iglesias, Manuel
  "Sobre la transcripción 'Hijo de Dios' (Jn 10,36 en P45)." *SPap* 8 (1969) 89–96.

Jonge, Marinus de and Adam Simon van den Woude
  "11Q Melchizedek and the New Testament." *NTS* 12 (1965/1966) 301–26.

Jost, Wilhelm
  "Poimen" Das Bild vom Hirten in der biblischen Überlieferung und seine christologische Bedeutung (Giessen: Kindt, 1939).

Kiefer, Otto
  Die Hirtenrede: Analyse und Deutung von Joh 10, 1–18 (Stuttgart: Katholisches Bibelwerk, 1967).

Kiefer, Otto
  "Le seul troupeau et le seul Pasteur: Jésus et les siens, Jn 10, 1–18." *AsSeign* 25 (1969) 46–61.

Kruijf, Theo C. de
  "Messias Jezus en Jezus Christus." *Theologie en Pastoraat* 63 (1967) 372–78.

Lohfink, Gerhard
  "Kein Wunder in Nazareth." *Katechetische Blätter* 102 (1977) 699–700.

Martin, James P.
  "John 19, 1–10." *Int* 32 (1978) 171–75.

Mary Therese, Sr.
  "The Good Shepherd." *Bible Today* 38 (1968) 2657–64.

Meyer, Paul W.
  "A Note on John 10:1–18." *JBL* 75 (1956) 232–35.

Mollat, Donatien
  "Le bon pasteur." In *Populus Dei. Studi in onore del Card. Alfredo Ottaviani per il cinquantesimo di sazerdozio: 18.3.1966* (Roma: Christen tipografia offset, 1969) 927–68.

Quasten, John
  "The Parable of the Good Shepherd: Jn 10, 1–21." *CBQ* 10 (1948) 1–12, 151–69.

Reynolds, S. M.
  "The Supreme Importance of the Doctrine of Election and the Eternal Security of the Elect as Taught in the Gospel of John." *WTJ* 28 (1965) 38–41.

Robinson, John Arthur Thomas
  "The Parable of John 10, 1–5." *ZNW* 46 (1955) 233–40.

Schneider, Johannes
  "Zur Komposition von Joh 10." *ConNT* 11 (1947) 220–25.

Simonis, A. J.
  Die Hirtenrede im Johannes-Evangelium. Versuch einer Analyse von Johannes 10, 1–18 nach Entstehung, Hintergrund und Inhalt, AnBib 29 (Rome: Päpstliches Bibelinstitut, 1967).

Spitta, Friedrich
  "Die Hirtengleichnisse des vierten Evangeliums." *ZNW* 10 (1909) 59–80, 103–27.

Steinmeyer, Franz Karl Ludwig
  Beiträge zum Verständnis des johanneischen Evangeliums. Vol. 6, *Die Aussagen Jesu im Zehnten Capitel des Johannes* (Berlin: Wiegandt und Grieben, 1891).

Stemberger, Günter
  "Les brebis du Bon Pasteur." *AsSeign* 25 (1969) 62–70.

Villiers, J. L. de
  "The Shepherd and the Flock." *Neot* 2 (1968) 89–103.

Weigandt, Peter
  "Zum Text von Joh 10, 7. Ein Beitrag zum Problem der koptischen Bibelübersetzung." *NovT* 9 (1967) 43–51.

Whittacker, John
  "A Hellenistic Context for Jo 10, 29." *VC* 24 (1970) 241–60.

10

1 "Truly, truly, I say to you, he who does not enter the sheepfold by the door but climbs in by another way, that man is a thief and a robber; **2**/ but he who enters by the door is the shepherd of the sheep. **3**/ To him the gatekeeper opens; the sheep hear his voice, and he calls his own sheep by name and leads them out. **4**/ When he has brought out all his own, he goes before them, and the sheep follow him, for they know his voice. **5**/ A stranger they will not follow, but they will flee from him, for they do not know the voice of strangers." 6/ This figure Jesus used with them, but they did not understand what he was saying to them. 7/ So Jesus again said to them, "Truly, truly, I say to you, I am the door of the sheep. 8/ All who came before me are thieves and robbers; but the sheep did not heed them. 9/ I am the door; if any one enters by me, he will be saved, and will go in and out and find pasture. 10/ The thief comes only to steal and kill and destroy; I came that they may have life, and have it abundantly. 11/ I am the good shepherd. The good shepherd lays down his life for the sheep. 12/ He who is a hireling and not a shepherd, whose own the sheep are not, sees the wolf coming and leaves the sheep and flees; and the wolf snatches them and scatters them. 13/ He flees because he is a hireling and cares nothing for the sheep. 14/ I am the good shepherd; I know my own and my own know me, 15/ as the Father knows me and I know the Father; and I lay down my life for the sheep. 16/ And I have other sheep, that are not of this fold; I must bring them also, and they will heed my voice. So there shall be one flock, one shepherd. 17/ For this reason the Father loves me, because I lay down my life, that I may take it again. 18/ No one takes it from me, but I lay it down of my own accord. I have power to lay it down, and I have power to take it again; this charge I have received from my Father." 19/ There was again a division among the Jews because of these words. 20/ Many of them said, "He has a demon, and he is mad; why listen to him?" 21/ Others said, "These are not the sayings of one who has a demon. Can a demon open the eyes of the blind?"

22 It was the feast of the Dedication at Jerusalem; it was winter, 23/ and Jesus was walking in the temple, in the portico of Solomon. 24/ So the Jews gathered round him and said to him, "How long will will you keep us in suspense? If you are the Christ, tell us plainly." 25/ Jesus answered them, "I told you, and you do not believe. The works that I do in my Father's name, they bear witness to me; 26/ but you do not believe, because you do not belong to my sheep. 27/ My sheep hear my voice, and I know them, and they follow me; 28/ and I give them eternal life, and they shall never perish, and no one shall snatch them out of my hand. 29/ My Father, who has given them to me, is greater than all, and no one is able to snatch them out of the Father's hand. 30/ I and the Father are one." 31/ The Jews took up stones again to stone him. 32/ Jesus answered them, "I have shown you many good works from the

Father; for which of these do you stone me?" 33/ The Jews answered him, "We stone you for no good work but for blasphemy; because you, being a man, make yourself God." 34/ Jesus answered them, "Is it not written in your law, 'I said, you are gods'? 35/ If he called them gods to whom the word of God came (and scripture cannot be broken), 36/ do you say of him whom the Father consecrated and sent into the world, 'You are blaspheming,' because I said, 'I am the Son of God'? 37/ If I am not doing the works of my Father, then do not believe me, believe the works, that you may know and understand that the Father is in me and I am in the Father." 39/ Again they tried to arrest him, but he escaped from their hands. 40/ He went away again across the Jordon to the place where John at first baptized, and there he remained. 41/ And many came to him; and they said, "John did no sign, but everything that John said about this man was true." 42/ And many believed in him there.

■ 1 Verse 1 introduces a brief figurative discourse (see v. 6). To this John connects Jesus' discourse on the good shepherd, since the story of the healing of the blind man, which precedes, did not provide figurative material for this discourse. The theme, "Jesus is the light of the world," is mentioned briefly in (8:12) and 9:5.

"Truly, truly" (ἀμὴν ἀμήν)[1] begins a description of the shepherd that corresponds to oriental relationships; the demeanor of the shepherd gains further definition by comparison with a flatter picture of his counterpart or adversary. From a literary point of view, it is not satisfactory to speak of this counterpart at the outset, and to do so brings negative consequences.

The thief and the robber[2] does not enter in through the door in the sheepfold,[3] in which the sheep are collected at night and guarded by an assistant shepherd; indeed, he would not be admitted, since the door of the sheepfold is guarded by a gatekeeper. Instead, he scrambles over the wall of the enclosure at another point (ἀλλοχόθεν is colloquial Koine for ἄλλοθεν).

■ 2 The shepherd of the sheep, on the other hand, characteristically enters by the door. He is the owner of the sheep. The description is begun with this feature

because the further activities of the shepherd follow from it.

Neither the flock, nor the door, nor the gatekeeper is to be allegorized. This is, in fact, a realistic picture of an oriental shepherd.

■ 3 The gatekeeper opens the door to him (cf. Mark 13:34: ὁ θυρωρός, "doorkeeper," John 18:16f.), and "the sheep hear his voice" (the fact that he calls them is expressed only in this indirect way on account of the following: "he calls his sheep by name"). When Longus says of Damis,[4] "He calls some of them by name" (ἐκάλεσε τινας αὐτῶν ὀνόμαστι), that might be more realistic. Each sheep would not have a special name in a large flock. This limitation is forbidden here, however, because of the underlying theological meaning: Jesus knows each one of his own; each one of them stands in a direct relationship to him.[5] Τὰ ἴδια means "his own (sheep)" (cf. v. 12); a distinction between sheep belonging to different shepherds in the same flock is not intended. Pollux interprets "to shepherd" (ποιμαίνειν) as "to lead out to pasture" (ἐπὶ νόμας ἐξάγειν).[6]

■ 4 "Brought out," ἐξέβαλε: βάλλω, together with compounds derived from it, has a faded sense in Koine (not:

---

1   Cf. 1:51.
2   See Obad 5.
3   An αὐλή is a stone enclosure.

4   Pastoralia 4.26.38.
5   See on verse 6.
6   Pollux 1.250.

"cast out"; 5:7, 18:11; cf. Jas 2:25): "let out, lead, bring out." The repetition of "his own" (ἴδια) suggests a certain emphasis: it indicates the close relationship of the shepherd with "his" sheep. That the shepherd leads his sheep is presupposed already in Ps 80:1f. That the sheep follow him because they recognize his voice shows that they trust him.

■ 5 The antitype follows: the sheep will not follow a stranger, and thus someone they do not trust, because the voice of this person is strange to them. Verse 6 indicates that Jesus has created a story out of the life of the shepherd that, on the view of the narrator, is by no means irrelevant to the situation of Jesus and to the situation of the Christian community.

■ 6 Jesus has spoken a παροιμία, which according to 16:25, 29, is a dark saying or a figure of speech with a hidden meaning. The explanation given by Suidas of παροιμία corresponds to the understanding in the Gospel of John: Suidas defines it as λόγος ἀπόκρυφός (literally, "a hidden word"), which requires an "interpretation" (ἑρμενεία), according to Sir 47:17 (39:3).[7] John does not provide the hidden meaning, however; he only reports that Jesus' hearers did not understand the figure of speech. It is certain that he had Jesus in mind in the figure of the shepherd, as the following makes clear. But that does not mean that it is permitted or even required that the other figures be interpreted allegorically, one and all. For example, these suggestions have been made: "the gatekeeper" (ὁ θυρωρός) means Moses (Chrysostom), or it means the Baptist (Zahn still interprets it this way),[8] or even God (this is Schlatter's view).[9] Nevertheless, the contrast between the good shepherd and the thief and the robber, who are revealed in their relationships to the sheep, would have been the key to the text for the reader. Since Jesus was without doubt the good shepherd for them, it remains to ask what the flock represents. The Fourth Gospel knows nothing of a constituted community with ecclesiastical officials, although that strikes Käsemann as incredible.[10] The community for

which the Evangelist composed his gospel was a group of pneumatics, and that is the way the Jewish-Christian community of the earliest period appeared to him, although he knew of the existence of the twelve.

■ 7 Verse 7 is clearly set off from what precedes. "Truly, truly" is again used to introduced a significant saying of Jesus. Nearly all the manuscripts offer a text in which Jesus is called "the door" of the sheep (meaning, to the sheep). Only sa reads "shepherd" (ποιμήν) instead of "door" (θύρα). That has been regarded as an isolated correction. The same reading is now attested by 𝔓75. Nevertheless, it is judged to be the easier and therefore the later reading, especially since it is supported by verse 11. But both points are questionable. Verse 8 requires that Jesus be spoken of in the immediate context as the shepherd and not as the door. In spite of this, almost all manuscripts read "door" (θύρα). This reading might have arisen as a result of the interpretation of verse 1 in this sense: Jesus is described as the door, since one comes into the community only through him. Jesus is the shepherd of the sheep, from whom they receive everything that is necessary to life, and who shelters, leads, and cares for them.

■ 8 In contrast, verse 8 refers to all who came before him as "thieves and robbers." Bultmann finds an allusion to gnostic redeemer figures here.[11] But what have such figures to do with a controversy with the Jewish community? Furthermore, the text cannot have the OT prophets in mind; their words do indeed belong to "scripture," to which occasional reference is made. Thus, as opposing figures only the Jewish rulers or the high priests and Pharisees come into question, and their tenure of course belongs to the past for the Evangelist, insofar as they appear as officials in Jerusalem. The exegesis of the following must indicate whether this interpretation is sound. The assertion that the sheep did not follow these men admittedly already presents a difficulty. Bauer calls attention to the gnostic book of Baruch, where Baruch,

7 Also compare logion (1) in the Gospel of Thomas: "Whoever finds the interpretation of these sayings will not experience death." *Nag Hammadi Library*, 118.
8 *Das Evangelium des Johannes*, 450.
9 *Der Evangelist Johannes*, 234.
10 *The Testament of Jesus*, 27f.
11 *John*, 376f. [286].

who is sent by God, says to the twelve-year old Jesus: "All the prophets were deceived by you into making false statements."[12] According to Bultmann,[13] "In this saying the Revealer sets himself apart from all other pretended revealers of past ages as the sole Revealer." However, the "I am" sayings do not run "I am and no one else is" (*scil.* the revealer), although the confused passage, 10:7–9, could be so interpreted. Furthermore, when Jesus is here called the good shepherd, that is so because the Father knows and therefore loves him, because he lays down his life. It is the "door" ($\theta\acute{\nu}\rho\alpha$) of the Father that stands behind the activity of Jesus as the shepherd (10:18). In modern interpretations, one reckons with false messiahs, by whom the community is not to be led astray. Yet we cannot prove the existence of such pseudo-messiahs prior to Jesus; rather, they were otherwise thought of only as figures connected with the coming end of the age.

■ **9** Verse 9 shows clearly that the Christ is here understood as the door, through which his own will find salvation (in judgment) and (eternal) pasture. If one strikes the verse as a misunderstanding and misleading gloss, the result is a better connection with (corrected) verses 7f.

There is, however, the possibility of conceiving the entire segment, verses 7–10, as not a part of the original Gospel, as Bauer does:[14] it can be a matter of an early gloss that was occasioned by verse 1 ("Whoever does not go through the door . . ."). That is indeed especially evident in this verse: "Whoever goes through the door, will be saved"—Jesus is here conceived as the door to the sheepfold.

■ **10** Verse 10 speaks in particular of the thieves and robbers, who only want to take advantage of the flock, and thus to live off of the flock, not for the flock. That does not fit the gnostic redeemer, nor does it suit the pseudo-christs. In any case, the Jewish rulers are not elsewhere depicted with these hues, and their relation to Christians was not of the sort that Christians would be called their flock.

■ **11–13** Verses 11–13 clearly constitute a unity of their own. It begins with the words, "I am the good shepherd." That is immediately elaborated upon: the good shepherd sacrifices himself for the sheep. His counterpart in this context is not the thief and the robber—it would be absurd to speak of him here—but the "hireling." The sheep do not belong to the hireling, and he thus does not risk his life for them. That is illustrated by the case of the wolf threatening the flock: the hireling sees the wolf coming and flees. Whether that was the rule is a question in itself. Did the shepherd not have dogs along, so that the hireling would not be seriously threatened? But, supposing that the hireling flees, the wolf then creates a blood bath and destroys the flock to the extent that the animals do not save themselves. It is a question whether we have here a figurative illustration of how the good shepherd behaves. It could also be that the author is thinking in this passage of a situation in the community in which it is being threatened by persecution. In that case, the good shepherd would be the leader who does not save himself in the hour of danger and turns the community, now leaderless, over to the persecutors, while the "hireling" shows his true colors by bolting. This experience connected with times of crisis, if it does lie behind this figure, could have served to allow Jesus to be depicted as the good shepherd. The theme of the death of the shepherd is taken up again briefly at the end of verse 15, and then finally treated in verses 17f. Meanwhile, other thoughts intrude.

■ **14f.** Apart from the conclusion of verse 15, the assertion that Jesus is the good shepherd is amplified with the observation that he knows his own and they know him, and that the relationship between them thereby mirrors the relationship that obtains between the Father and son. "Know" in this context is of course more than an intellectual knowing: it consists of a (two-sided) fellowship. To know one another does not mean to be acquainted; rather, it means to have a living bond.

■ **16** Verse 16 adds the thought that the flock that has

---

12   Bauer, *Das Johannesevangelium,* 140. The reference is to Hippolytus 5.26.29, p. 131. Cf. Haenchen, "Das Buch Baruch," *Gott und Mensch. Gesammelte Aufsätze* 1 (Tübingen: Mohr-Siebeck, 1965) 299–334, especially 304f.

13   *John,* 376 [286].

14   *Das Johannesevangelium,* 139.

been the subject of discussion thus far will be enlarged with other sheep, for whom Jesus will likewise be the shepherd. The final result will be one flock and one shepherd. There is apparently an allusion here to different groups of Christians. The earliest distinction is offered by the Jewish Christian community, whose shepherd Jesus was from the beginning, and the gentile Christians; from the perspective of his earthly life, he will turn them into a single flock only in the future, so that the distinction between them will disappear. Or one could imagine that gentile Christians are thought of only as potential Christians, who will eventually belong to the community. We may thus have something like a counterpart to the scene involving the Greeks in 12:20–36.[15] In that passage, the prospect of winning the "Greeks" is connected with thoughts about the death of Jesus: only by dying does his life bear fruit; then Easter brings the great church.

■ **17f.** Whether the reference to laying down his life in these verses does not constitute a break with what precedes, but is integrally connected with it, is questionable. We must first inquire how "to take" (λαβεῖν) is to be translated: does it mean "take," or does it imply "obtain, receive"? Why does the Father love him? Because he lays down his life—but not as a terminal death: does the resurrection not follow on his death? Is the resurrection Jesus' own deed, so that he restores life to himself? It is probably a case of showing that Jesus' death was his own free act. But matters cannot be left there. For, in that case, it would be the end; Jesus is dead, and death would be victorious. Unless he is to be death's prize, he has to overcome death by rising from the dead—again through his own free act. The freedom of Jesus thereby appears to make the freedom of the Father superfluous. For this reason, verse 18 is added at the conclusion: the death and resurrection of Jesus fulfills the command of the Father. How his freedom and the freedom of the Father are actually related is discussed in verse 29.

The aorist ἦρεν, "took," is puzzling in verse 18; it is attested by 𝔓⁴⁵ B ℵ * syᴾ. 𝔓⁶⁶ reads αἴρει (present tense); there is a gap in 𝔓⁷⁵. One can refer the aorist to an attempt to kill Jesus in the past; but the context does not support that view. Rather, Jesus speaks of the moment in which he dies, as he does in the τίθημι ("lay down, place") that follows.

■ **19–21** Dissension again breaks out among the Jews in view of Jesus' testimony to himself. The author thus indicates the two possibilities that are the consequence of Jesus' self-testimony (and the testimony of his community): the one understands him as possessed; the other argues, to the contrary, that one who is possessed (or his "spirit") cannot open the eyes of the blind. The reference to the miracle thus makes it appear that what is humanly beyond comprehension may nevertheless not be entirely impossible.

■ **22** Verse 22 opens a new segment that extends as far as verse 39. The temporal notices, "feast of Dedication" and "winter," clearly separate this segment from the preceding.

■ **23** Verse 23 provides some local color with the mention of the "portico of Solomon" (cf. Acts 3:11, 5:12). The Evangelist possibly thinks of this portico as an enclosed hall, in which Jesus walks about like a peripatetic on account of the winter.

■ **24** In verse 24 the Jews posed the question that dominates the following dialogue: Is Jesus the Christ or not? Here the Jews want Jesus to say openly (παρρησίᾳ; cf. 11:14) whether he is the Christ. The Evangelist knows well that Christ means "the anointed," as does the term messiah. But he does not use the messianic concept; for him the question is only whether Jesus is the Christ. It is the Christian designation alone that comes into consideration for him. That this question is still an agonizing open question for the Jews is shown by their lack of faith. Bultmann's thought that this question demands an answer that relieves them of the decision, and that Jesus can now reveal himself through an "indirect communication," does not appear to correspond to the thought of the Evangelist.[16] Jesus tells the Samaritan woman that he is the messiah (4:26; and she is not described up to that point as a believer), and in 9:37 he reveals himself to the blind man who was healed as the Son of man. But there are also other passages in which Jesus raises his messianic claim and is so understood by some of the Jews, for example, in 7:41a.

■ **25–30** In the preceding verse the Evangelist intended to

---

15 See the commentary on that passage.
16 *John*, 362 [275].

picture the Jews once more as blind and as still not prepared to believe; at the same time, he intended to create the possibility of a new discourse by Jesus, in which his relation to the Father would be developed. To the imperative, "tell us" (εἰπέ) there corresponds the aorist, "I told (you)" (εἶπον), which is similar sounding: this is a wordplay that cannot be reproduced exactly in German (but in English: "*Tell* us plainly"—"I *told* you"). It is dubious whether we can strike the reference to the works of Jesus in verse 25 with Hirsch,[17] so that this meaning would result: "You do not believe, because you do not belong to my sheep" (v. 26). One certainly ought not to dismiss the statement, "and I give them eternal life" (v. 28), and certainly not verse 29. Rather, the sequence of verses 28 and 29 is especially important. After Jesus has said: "and no one shall snatch them (the sheep given to him) out of my hand," he continues by making the same assertion for the person of God: "My Father, who has given (them) to me, is greater than all (everyone or everything), and no one can snatch them out of the Father's hand." It is precisely on the basis of this presupposition that verse 30 can be understood: "I and the Father are one." Jesus and the Father are not a single person—that would require εἷς—but one, so that Jesus does just what God does. John is a representative of an expressly subordinationist christology. But precisely because Jesus refuses to speak and act on his own, in order to subordinate himself completely to the will of the Father, can the one having faith see the Father in him. Although the Father is greater than the son (John 14:28), Jesus can therefore say (10:30): "I and the Father are one" (naturally not: one person).

■ **31** The Jews "of course" again misunderstand Jesus' words as blasphemy: Jesus, a man, makes himself God. For the Jews that is blasphemy against God, to which they attempt to respond by seeking to stone Jesus.

■ **32** Jesus defends himself: do you propose to stone him on account of the good works that the Father gave him to do?

■ **33** The Jews say, no, not for good works, but because he makes himself God.

■ **34–38** Jesus' response to this charge deviates from everything that has been said up to this point. Ps 82:6 is cited as testimony that God has already called men "gods." If that now stands in "your" law, and the law cannot be annulled, how can the Jews then call him a blasphemer whom God has sent into the world, because he says, "I am God's Son?" It is presupposed that Jesus made this assertion; that must also have been the meaning of verse 30 in the eyes of the author. Accordingly, one ought at least to believe his works and thereby acknowledge that the Father is in him and he in the Father. That is obviously a new form again of earlier assertions: "I am God's Son," and "I and the Father are one."

■ **39** The consequence of this new assertion is of course a fresh misunderstanding on the part of the Jews, who once again want to arrest Jesus. How he eludes them is not explained. Instead, we learn that Jesus departs.

■ **40f.** Jesus departs for a place on the other side of the Jordan, where John first baptized, and stays there. We are told, further, that many people there believed in him because the things John said about him proved to be true. That cannot be true faith of course in the eyes of the Evangelist.

■ **42** It may be more important for the Evangelist, however, that he place Jesus now at a sufficient distance from the location of the following story, so that Jesus cannot immediately arrive at the side of the ailing Lazarus. Of course, the present form of the story does not require such a great distance any more, since Jesus simply waits until Lazarus dies. The stage for the great miracle has thus been set.

Overview

Chapter 10 exceeds the other discourses in difficulty. This chapter, for example, is not set off from chapter 9 in 𝔓⁶⁶ and 𝔓⁷⁵. There are two reasons for introducing a division between the two chapters:

(1) A new theme begins with 10:1 (although the healing of the blind man is mentioned once more in 10:21), viz., the shepherd motif: 10:2, (7,) 11, (12,) 14. In verses 22–39, the question whether Jesus is the Christ is addressed; his opponents are the Jews.

(2) The second reason is that a new section begins with the double amen ("truly, truly").

---

17   *Studien,* 84f.

On the other hand, it is unclear who the opponents are assumed to be in 10:1–21. They are the doctors of the law for Hirsch. "That Jesus leads his own out of bondage to the law into the freedom of the gospel is the deeper meaning of his pronouncement."[18] But this interpretation makes use of Pauline thought and is unwarranted. Bultmann incorrectly assumes that a discourse on light followed upon chapter 9 and reconstructs it out of 8:12, 12:44–50, 8:21–29.[19] Barrett, who also will have nothing to do with rearrangements in this passage either, admits that it is difficult to find a unified train of thought in this passage, which is more a commentary on chapter 9 than a continuation of it.[20] Hirelings refer to the Pharisees, who cast out the blind man rather than caring for him. Strathmann also asserts that 9:40f. forms the introduction to chapter 10: the discourse on the shepherd is directed at the Pharisees.[21] But he must confess: "The discourse on the shepherd, with its sharp attacks, which, however, avoid being unclear about those for whom they are intended, and with the exclusive gruffness of its claims, which, however, lack conceptual precision, and with its continual shift in figures and lapses in thought, and with the puzzling brevity of its hints, in fact, has something corrupt about it."[22] Bauer concedes that 10:21b connects chapters 9 and 10, but that this verse could also be an addition.[23] The interpretation of chapter 10 as referring to the Pharisees is to be abandoned. Bauer is "almost" prepared to accept the view that "the Evangelist has taken over all sorts of alien figures and concepts without the ability to forge them into a unity."[24] In view of these difficulties presented by the text, it is small wonder that Bultmann sought to improve things by making massive rearrangements.[25] He assumes that the Evangelist has again made use of the discourse source, in which the sequence was: 10:11–13, 1–5, 8, 10, 14–15a, 27–30,[26] but he leaves it open whether these fragments of the source had already been expanded by glosses of the Evangelist. The Evangelist may have created the following complex out of his

source: 10:22–26, 11–13, 1–10, 14–18, 27–39. This whole complex was connected to 12:36b, 10:19–21, since these verses presuppose a lengthy discussion. In this procedure, Bultmann proposes to identify the revelatory discourse source on the basis of style, and leaves unexplained how the text came to its present shape as a result of the reworking of the Evangelist. The double reconstruction—the identification of the discourse source and its reworking by the Evangelist—does not seem to us to be tenable. The displacement of such small segments cannot be understood either on the basis of a codex or a scroll. In chapter 10—with its general theme, "the (good) shepherd"—Jesus' relation to his own is treated. It is loosely divided into two parts: Verses 1–21 and verses 22–42. Verses 40–42 form the transition to chapter 11. Only the second part is provided with information about the situation (time, place, etc.). The first part is connected to chapter 9 by means of verse 21b: 10:1–21 develops the role Jesus has played in chapter 9.[27]

The interpretation of this segment has shown that the text still has some traps ready for the investigator. One cannot say that the description is realistic, although the portico of Solomon is once mentioned (10:23). The obscurity of the text owes in part to the fact that the Evangelist has Jesus speak in a way that is comprehensible to his readers, but not, however, to the listeners presupposed in the story. There are some indications which suggest that early interpreters did not get on well with the text and thus did not shrink from altering the text here and there. Verse 8, for example, is continued in verse 10. Verses 11–13 constitute a self-enclosed unit. But these verses seem to describe Jesus as the model of the good church leader. Verse 14 resumes verse 4, and verse 15 follows well. On the other hand, verse 16 introduces a new thought, namely, that of the church arising from the Jewish-Christian and Gentile-Christian communities; that is not at all a Johannine thought. Here the sheep, who were the elect up to this point, have

18 *Das vierte Evangelium,* 254.
19 *John,* 313f. [236f.].
20 *John,* 367f.
21 *Das Evangelium nach Johannes,* 157ff.
22 *Das Evangelium nach Johannes,* 161f.
23 *Das Johannesevangelium,* 142.
24 *Das Johannesevangelium,* 143.
25 *John,* 358–60 [272–74].

26 *John,* 360 [274].
27 See Barrett, *John,* 367f.

become Jewish Christians, to whom the Evangelist is completely indifferent. Since verse 17 follows on verse 15, Hirsch is probably right in ascribing verse 16 to the redactor.[28] In other words, the text in chapter 10 in any case reflects relations between the Christian and Jewish communities that probably obtained toward the close of the first century CE.

Polemic and christology are closely interwoven in this passage. If, on the basis of verses 17f., one asks what John himself thought about the resurrection, and why he did not decline to use the Easter story in this awkward form, one might say two things in response:

(1) John himself assigns the same meaning to the coming of the spirit, the paraclete, and Jesus' return.

(2) His own christology has its roots in the combination of Jesus' earthly life with the experience of the spirit, which incorporates in itself faith in the Father and the one he has sent, Jesus Christ. John was not of the opinion that Jesus stayed dead and rose only in the kerygma of his disciples—in a mere "That," if at all. John is persuaded—one thinks of passages like 10:18 or 17:5—that the descent of Jesus from the Father, described as "the Logos became flesh," has as its counterpart a corresponding ascent to the Father.

---

28   Hirsch, *Studien,* 83.

26. The Raising of Lazarus

Bibliography

Bailey, John Amadee
The Traditions Common to the Gospels of Luke and John, NovTSup 7 (Leiden: E. J. Brill, 1963).

Bleek, Friedrich
"Auslassung der Auferweckung des Lazarus bei den Synoptikern." In his *Beiträge zur Einleitung und Auslegung der heiligen Schrift.* Vol. 1, *Beiträge zur Evangelien-kritik* (Berlin: G. Reimer, 1846) 100–101.

Bonner, Campbell
"Traces of Thaumaturgic Technique in the Miracles." *HTR* 20 (1927) 171–81.

Brodie, Louis T.
"Creative Rewriting: Key to a New Methodology." In *SBL 1978 Seminar Papers* 2, SBLASP 14 (Missoula: Scholars Press, 1978) 261–67.

Cadman, William Healey
"The Raising of Lazarus." *SE* 1 = TU 73 (Berlin: Akademie-Verlag, 1959) 423–34.

Dunkerley, Roderic
"Lazarus." *NTS* 5 (1958/1959) 321–27.

Eckhardt, Karl August
Der Tod des Johannes als Schlüssel zum Verständnis der johanneischen Schriften (Berlin: Walter de Gruyter, 1961), esp. 17–20.

Feuillet, André
Etudes Johanniques, Museum Lessianum Section biblique 4 (Brugges: Desclée de Brouwer, 1962)

Grossouw, William K.
"Ich bin die Auferstehung und das Leben. Glaubst du das?" *Schrift* 9 (1970) 98–102.

Gumlich, Fr.
"Die Räthsel der Erweckung Lazari." *TSK* 35 (1862) 65–110.

Heise, Jürgen
Bleiben. Menein in den Johanneischen Schriften, Hermeneutische Untersuchungen zur Theologie 8 (Tübingen: Mohr-Siebeck, 1967).

Holtzmann, Heinrich Julius
"Das schriftstellerische Verhältnis des Johannes zu den Synoptikern." *ZWT* 12 (1869) 62–85, 155–78, 446–56.

Junker, H.
"Die Auferstehung und das ewige Leben." *Evangelische Erziehung* 16 (1964) 330–33.

Kopp, Klemens
Die heiligen Stätten der Evangelien (Regensburg: F. Pustet, 1959).

Leroy, Herbert
Rätsel und Mißverständnis. Ein Beitrag zur Formgeschichte des Johannesevangeliums, BBB 30 (Bonn: Peter Hanstein, 1968), esp. 5–6, 183–85.

Lewis, Frank Warburton
"A Certain Village—Not Bethany." *ExpTim* 32

(1920/1921) 330.

Martin, James P.
"History and Eschatology in the Lazarus Narrative, John 11.1–44." *SJT* 17 (1964) 332–43.

McNeil, Brian
"The Raising of Lazarus." *Downside Review* 92 (1974) 269–75.

Merli, Dino
"Lo scopo della risurrezione di Lazzaro in Giov. 11,1–44." *BeO* 12 (1970) 59–82.

Michiels, R.
"De opwekking van Lazarus." *Collationes Brugenses et Gandavenses* 21 (1975) 433–47.

Osborne, Basil
"A Folded Napkin in a Empty Tomb: John 11:44 and 20:7 Again." *HeyJ* 14 (1973) 437–40.

Preisker, Herbert
"Wundermächte und Wundermänner der hellenistisch-römischen Kultur und die Auferweckung des Lazarus in Joh 11." *Wissenschaftliche Zeitschrift der Martin-Luther-Universität Halle-Wittenberg* 6 (1952/1953) 519–23.

Reiser, William E.
"The Case of the Tidy Tomb: The Place of the Napkins of John 11:44 and 20:7." *HeyJ* 14 (1973) 47–57.

Reuter, Hans Richard
"Wider die Krankheit zum Tode." In *Schöpferische Nachfolge,* ed. Ch. Frey and W. Huber (Heidelberg: Forschungsstätte der Evangelischen Studien gemeinschaft, 1978) 563ff.

Romaniuk, Kazimierz
"'I am the Resurrection and the Life.'" *Concilium* 60 (1970) 68–77.

Sabourin, Leopold
"Resurrectio Lazari (Jo 11,1–44)." *VD* 46 (1968) 350–60.

Sahlin, Harald
"Lasarus-gestalten (Die Gestalt des Lazarus)." *SEÅ* 37/38 (1972/1973) 167–74.

Sanders, Joseph N.
"Those Whom Jesus Loved: St. John 11,5." *NTS* 1 (1954/1955) 29–76.

Sass, Gerhard
Die Auferweckung des Lazarus. Eine Auslegung von Johannes 11, BibS(N) 51 (Neukirchen-Vluyn: Neukirchener Verlag, 1967).

Scognamiglio, A. R.
"La resurrezione di Lazzaro: un 'segno' tra passato e presente." *Nicolaus* 5 (1977) 3–58.

Schniewind, Julius
Die Parallelperikopen bei Lukas und Johannes (Hildesheim: G. Olms, ²1958).

Stenger, Werner
"Die Auferweckung des Lazarus (Joh 11,1–45). Vorlage und johanneische Redaktion." *TTZ* 83 (1974) 17–37.

Thompson, L. M.
"The Multiple Uses of the Lazarus-Motif in Modern Literature." *Christian Scholar's Review* 7 (1978) 306–9.

Trudinger, Paul
"The Raising of Lazarus—A Brief Response." *Downside Review* 94 (1976) 287–90.

Trudinger, Paul
"A 'Lazarus Motif' in Primitive Christian Preaching." *ANQ* 7 (1966) 29–32.

Wilcox, Max
"The 'Prayer' of Jesus in John XI, 41b–42." *NTS* 24 (1977/1978) 128–32.

Wilkens, Wilhelm
"Die Erweckung des Lazarus." *TZ* 15 (1959) 22–39.

11

1 **Now a certain man was ill, Lazarus of Bethany, the village of Mary and her sister Martha. 2/ It was Mary who anointed the Lord with ointment and wiped his feet with her hair, whose brother Lazarus was ill. 3/ Now the sisters sent to him, saying, "Lord, he whom you love is ill." 4/ But when Jesus heard it he said, "This illness is not unto death; it is for the glory of God, so that the Son of God may be glorified by means of it." 5/ Now Jesus loved Martha and her sister and Lazarus. 6/ So when he heard that he was ill, he stayed two days longer in the place where he was. 7/ Then after this he said to the disciples, "Let us go into Judea again." 8/ The disciples said to him, "Rabbi, the Jews**

were but now seeking to stone you, and are you going there again?" 9/ Jesus answered, "Are there not twelve hours in the day? If any one walks in the day, he does not stumble, because he sees the light of this world. 10/ But if any one walks in the night, he stumbles, because the light is not in him." 11/ Thus he spoke, and then he said to them, "Our friend Lazarus has fallen asleep, but I go to awake him out of sleep." 12/ The disciples said to him, "Lord, if he has fallen asleep, he will recover." 13/ Now Jesus had spoken of his death, but they thought that he meant taking rest in sleep. 14/ Then Jesus told them plainly, "Lazarus is dead; 15/ and for your sake I am glad that I was not there, so that you may believe. But let us go to him." 16/ Thomas, called the Twin, said to his fellow disciples, "Let us also go, that we may die with him." 17/ Now when Jesus came, he found that Lazarus had already been in the tomb four days. 18/ Bethany was near Jerusalem, about two miles off, 19/ and many of the Jews had come to Martha and Mary to console them concerning their brother. 20/ When Martha heard that Jesus was coming, she went and met him, while Mary sat in the house. 21/ Martha said to Jesus, "Lord, if you had been here, my brother would not have died. 22/ And even now I know that whatever you ask from God, God will give you." 23/ Jesus said to her, "Your brother will rise again." 24/ Martha said to him, "I know that he will rise again in the resurrection at the last day." 25/ Jesus said to her, "I am the resurrection and the life; he who believes in me, though he die, yet shall he live, 26/ and whoever lives and believes in me shall never die. Do you believe this?" 27/ She said to him, "Yes, Lord; I believe that you are that Christ, the Son of God, he who is coming into the world." 28/ When she had said this, she went and called her sister Mary, saying quietly, "The Teacher is here and is calling for you." 29/ And when she heard it, she rose quickly and went to him. 30/ Now Jesus had not come to the village, but was still in the place where Martha had met him. 31/ When the Jews who were with her in the house, consoling her, saw Mary rise quickly and go out, they followed her, supposing that she was going to the tomb to weep there. 32/ Then Mary, when she came where Jesus was and saw him, fell at his feet, saying to him, "Lord, if you had been here, my brother would not have died." 33/ When Jesus saw her weeping, and the Jews who came with her also weeping, he was deeply moved in spirit and troubled; and

34/ he said, "Where have you laid him?" They said to him, "Lord, come and see." 35/ Jesus wept. 36/ So the Jews said, "See how he loved him!" 37/ But some of them said, "Could not he who opened the eyes of the blind man have kept this man from dying?" 38/ Then Jesus, deeply moved again, came to the tomb; it was a cave, and a stone lay upon it. 39/ Jesus said, "Take away the stone." Martha, the sister of the dead man, said to him, "Lord, by this time there will be an odor, for he has been dead four days." 40/ Jesus said to her, "Did I not tell you that if you would believe you would see the glory of God?" 41/ So they took away the stone. And Jesus lifted up his eyes and said, "Father, I thank thee that thou hast heard me. 42/ I knew that thou hearest me always, but I have said this on account of the people standing by, that they may believe that thou didst send me." 43/ When he had said this, he cried with a loud voice, "Lazarus, come out." 44/ The dead man came out, his hands and feet bound with bandages, and his face wrapped with a cloth. Jesus said to them, "Unbind him, and let him go."

The last and the greatest miracle story in the Gospel of John begins at this point without any connection to what precedes: the raising of Lazarus. The Synoptics also relate resurrection miracles: the daughter of Jairus (Mark 5:22–43) and the young man from Nain (Luke 7:11–17). The miraculous element in John 11:1–44 is heightened, however, in relation to the synoptic stories. In contrast to the synoptic accounts, there is a clear exaggeration of the miraculous: Lazarus has already been in his grave three days—decomposing—when Jesus raises him (11:39). The Synoptics did not know this story; they would not have failed to include it as the greatest of all the resurrection stories. The persons appearing in the Lazarus legend appear also in the synoptic Gospels, but in completely different contexts (see the Overview).

■ 1 Exegetes such as Wellhausen,[1] Schwartz,[2] Bauer,[3] Hirsch,[4] Bultmann,[5] Fortna,[6] Schnackenburg,[7] and Brown,[8] hit upon special difficulties already in the analysis of verse 1. But these aporias diminish if one does not interrogate the text primarily for historical information. This story was still new to the reader. The narrator—who is not simply identical with the Evangelist, although the latter follows the narrator word for word over long stretches—is first of all obliged to depict the participants and situation for the reader. The central participant is of course Jesus himself. And yet he responds—as miracle worker—to the request conveyed to him. The real driving force that sets the whole action in motion and brings it to an end is the illness of Lazarus; Lazarus is identified by his place of domicile: according to John 1:28, it was "Bethany beyond the Jordan," east of Jericho, located at the middle of the three fords across the Jordan south of the Allenby bridge.[9] As someone who was seriously ill,[10] Lazarus is dependent on the help of others who live in the same village. Those others are Mary and Martha.

■ 2 Mary is already known to the readers and the lis-

1   Das Evangelium Johannis, 52f.
2   "Aporien," 3: 166.
3   Das Johannesevangelium, 148.
4   Studien, 87–90.
5   John, 394 [300].
6   Gospel of Signs, 74–87.
7   John, 2: 316–51,
8   1: 420–37.

9   Cf. Dalman, Sacred Sites and Ways, 87ff.; C. Kopp, Die heiligen Stätten der Evangelien (Regensburg: Pustet, 1969), likewise thinks this location is possible.
10 The word ἀσθενής here, like ἀσθένεια in verse 4, and ἀσθενέω in verses 2f., 6, means someone who is seriously ill.

teners, and the narrator makes use of this fact: she has annointed the Lord with ointment and wiped his feet with her hair. Since that is first related in detail in 12:1–8, some exegetes have taken verse 2 as a later redactional remark.[11] It is a peculiarity of the narrator, however, to introduce participants who are known by some special deed in the community, by referring to that deed when they first appear in the story. Mary is thus introduced in this way here, so that the reader will be informed about her (cf. on Nicodemus: 7:50, 19:39; on Caiaphas: 11:49f. and 18:14; on Judas the betrayer: 6:71, 12:4, 13:2, 18:2, 3, 5; on "the disciple whom Jesus loved": 13:23, 18:15f., 19:26, 20:2, 3, 8, 21:20). Verse 2 coincides precisely with the introductory words of verse 1. With the close of verse 2, the first small subsection is thus rounded off; the situation is depicted out of which the subsequent action will develop.

■ 3 "Now"[12] the sisters send to him (Jesus) with the message (literally, "saying"). They send him a message without mentioning themselves: "Lord, he whom you love is ill." The request is thereby only indirectly expressed.[13] The message is modest and brief: "he whom you love" emphasizes the close relationship of Jesus to Lazarus. Spelled out, the message runs: "Lazarus is sick. Yet you love him. Come quickly! He is very ill." Jesus cannot refuse such a request. Yet matters take an entirely different course.

■ 4 When Jesus hears this message (the messenger immediately disappears, but such trivia are never mentioned; the narrator rarely gives stage directions), he says (to the reader really) something that is remarkable: "This illness is not unto death; it is for the glory of God, so that the Son of God may be glorified by means of it." This remark functions as background: the illness is not of the absolutely fatal kind—yet Lazarus will sink very deeply into the shades of death before Jesus raises him. God's glory does not consist in sparing the faithful life's difficulties, but precisely in refusing to do so, he shows that he is able to make the impossible possible through his Son.

■ 5 Viewed externally, Jesus acts without compassion. The sisters have begged Jesus to come immediately, although indirectly. And so the possibility of misunder-

standing is present: unless Jesus comes, he is without compassion. So that the reader will not misunderstand the peculiar behavior of Jesus, the narrator emphasizes that Jesus loves Martha and her sister, as well as Lazarus. What Jesus does to them by staying away must have been incomprehensible and dreadful for all three. The narrator knows that the reader will also be shocked: what do these cruelties beyond comprehension mean? He therefore assures the readers: Jesus loves all three. Lazarus is mentioned last in order to show that his love for Lazarus is not diminished. It is precisely these last words that carry the emphasis, since Jesus' behavior vis-à-vis Lazarus is the most incomprehensible. The narrator cannot demonstrate Jesus' love at this point; he can only assert it.

If one may generalize about what is being said here of the anguish of the three siblings, one may say that a mystery is revealed that the narrator knows about: God does not spare those he loves from life's difficulties. He anticipates, rather, that believers will understand when Lazarus has to go to this death on behalf of the glory of the God who saves from death. Real love for God includes the willingness to sacrifice everything to God, without knowing whether or how one will get it back.

■ 6 Verse 6 now describes the strange behavior of Jesus that has long been hinted at: when he receives the message, he remains two additional days quietly at the place where he was. B. Weiss proposes to explain this behavior by saying that Jesus was waiting on a sign from God.[14] He knew only that God would not deny him his miraculous help. "That he remained in order to let Lazarus die so he could raise him from the dead (Bretschneider, Strauss, . . . Baur . . .) is excluded by the fact that, according to verse 17, Lazarus must have died shortly after the message reached Jesus." That must mean: even if Jesus had started out at once on the journey of more than thirty kilometers, he would not have arrived in time. But that does not explain the two-day wait of Jesus one whit. Nor does the text give any indication that Jesus was waiting that long on a sign from God. At most, it shifts the inexplicable to God. To be sure, one can point to John 5:19b where Jesus says: The Son can do nothing except what he sees the Father

---

11 Thus Schnackenburg, *John*, 2: 322.
12 The "now" (οὖν) that is typical of the narrative segments in the Gospel of John appears fourteen times in the Lazarus story.
13 Cf. Bultmann, *John*, 397 [302].
14 *Das Johannesevangelium*, 402.

doing. But if one takes that in the sense of B. Weiss' apologetic, one delimits the human in Jesus and threatens to turn him into a puppet. Our passage provides no suggestion of such an understanding. On the contrary, verses 4, 11, and 15 show that Jesus knew very well, by virtue of his supernatural knowledge, that his delay would turn a simple illness into an unheard of miracle, a resurrection from the dead, a miracle that would make faith easier in the view of the narrator.

■ 7 Verse 7 is set off from the preceding by the words, "then after this."[15] With respect to content, this verse begins a new segment that extends as far as verse 11a. The surprising thing is that a journey to Judea is even mentioned, but of Lazarus there is not a word. Then the "after this" ($\mu\epsilon\tau\grave{\alpha}$ $\tau\hat{o}\hat{\upsilon}\tau o$) reappears in verse 11a. That could indicate that verses 7–10 are an insertion,[16] which interrupts verses 6 and 11. The content also supports this suggestion. Jesus addresses his disciples, who are suddenly once again present: "Let us go to Judea again." Presumably the narrator thinks that Jesus is in Perea, at John's old baptismal location; that is the last geographical designation mentioned in 10:40. However, the narrator gives no reason why Jesus proposes to return to Jerusalem.

■ 8 The disciples consequently respond that it makes no sense to go back now to Judea, and they base their negative response to Jesus' suggestion on the experience Jesus had just had there. Perhaps two passages coalesce when they say: "Rabbi,[17] the Jews were but now seeking to stone you" (cf. 8:59), and he had hid himself from them and went out of the temple. But in 10:39 also the hatred of the Jews was vented: "Again they tried to arrest him." But Jesus escaped from their hands. The narrator appears to have both of these events in mind. The objection the disciples have to Jesus' proposal is that danger lurks for him in Judea. What can Jesus respond to that?

■ 9 As orientals are wont to do, Jesus responds to the question with a question: "Are there not twelve hours in the day?" We attribute twenty-four hours to the day, but the Jews distinguished two separate entities: day and night. The day has twelve hours; the remainder belonged to the night. They did not take into consideration that the daylight hours varied with the season. To his question Jesus can expect assent: there are twelve daylight hours, twelve hours of sunlight. John can add to this: If anyone walks during the day, he does not stumble—one thinks of the kinds of roads in Palestine at that time;[18] they were narrow, stone-strewn paths. By day one does not stumble on the stones that lay in the path; for one sees by "the light of the world." We would put it differently today: we see the world in the light of the sun. The continuation of this thought is more difficult to understand.

■ 10 "But if he walks in the night, he stumbles, because the light is not in him." This text has occasioned difficulty for interpreters from the beginning; the manuscript D offers a shrewd conjecture with the reading "in it" (scil. "night"; $\dot{\epsilon}\nu$ $\alpha\dot{\upsilon}\tau\hat{\eta}$) instead of "in him" ($\dot{\epsilon}\nu$ $\alpha\dot{\upsilon}\tau\hat{\wp}$). Fortna concedes that the reconstruction of the text of this saying of Jesus is difficult.[19] There are, however, clues: each time the Evangelist takes up his source again following an interpolation, he goes back to the original point, repeats or paraphrases some words that came before the interruption, and usually provides a temporal connective. It is a question here, however, of whether the Evangelist has undertaken an insertion, or whether an unskilled hand—put to use in the earlier passage in 9:4—is responsible for the insertion. Bultmann is of the opinion that use is made here of a saying from the revelatory discourse source, that ran simply: "Whoever walks by day does not stumble; but if anyone walks by night, he stumbles."[20] The idea that Jesus must use the time that he sojourns on earth in order to perform a miracle appears to us to correspond poorly to the thought of the Evangelist. Further, the hypothesis of a "revelatory discourse source" has not prevailed, and Bultmann must furthermore alter the text to make his interpretation viable. B.

---

15 Cf. the comparable situation in Mark 2:5 and 2:10.
16 Fortna, *Gospel of Signs*, 78, notes this possibility.
17 This is the last time that the disciples address Jesus as "rabbi" ($\dot{\rho}\alpha\beta\beta\acute{\iota}$) in the Gospel of John.
18 Apart from the main Roman roads.
19 *Gospel of Signs*, 78.
20 *John*, 399 [304].

Weiss interprets as follows: "The definite limits of the number of hours in the natural day . . . designates a time of working that is measured out by God," during which nothing could happen to Jesus.[21] In support of this view one can appeal to the phrase, "it was night" (ἦν δὲ νύξ) in 13:30; this phrase of course designates the point at which Judas goes out to betray Jesus.

The core of the difficulty seems to consist only of the discussion of a dubious journey to Judea without any mention of the Lazarus theme in verses 7–10. The Lazarus theme does not come up until verse 11 and introduced only by the phrase "after this" (μετὰ τοῦτο), which was already used in verse 7, and which, on the face of it, is interpolated in the context. In short, the suspicion remains that verses 7–10 are interpolated in order to emphasize the risk of a return to Judea, a risk that of course comes up again in the remark of Thomas.

■ **11** Verse 11 is again clearly separated from what precedes: now, finally, Jesus speaks of Lazarus, for whose sake he is about to go to Judea, to Bethany: "Our friend Lazarus has fallen asleep, but I go to wake him out of sleep." The "after this" (μετὰ τοῦτο), which was used earlier in verse 7, seems to us, as it does to Fortna, to support the view that an insertion ends here with the same phrase with which it began. We may then conjecture that the text prior to the insertion ran something like this: "Thereupon he said to the disciples [v 7a]: Our friend has fallen asleep, but I go to awake him out of sleep" (v. 11). Jesus thereby points in a veiled way to the true situation. According to Leroy, "In respect of the Johannine misunderstanding, it is a case of a variation on the riddle. The function of the riddle, namely, to demonstrate the knowledge of the one being interrogated in front of the interrogator, is exercised by means of the misunderstanding."[22] The veiled riddle in a statement serves to make "the dialogue partner all the more certain of his lack of knowledge. . . . To demonstrate that the dialogue partner is unknowing . . . in the face of the wisdom of Jesus is the tendency of the misunderstanding." This literary form goes together with christology in the Fourth Gospel. "Only because Jesus is the one who knows, and knows the revealed criterion for discipleship, can this form be employed."[23] Further, the

community is dependent on the revelation of Jesus, which, however, is granted to it.

As a consequence, the emphasis is not to be put here on the lack of understanding on the part of the disciples—the Evangelist does not want to represent them at all as ignoramuses—but on the wisdom of Jesus, which is all the more illuminating by contrast. That is entirely consistent with the christology of the source, which to a great extent avails itself of the "divine man" (θεῖος ἀνήρ) concept.

The segment that begins here with the words, "and then he said to the disciples," extends as far as verse 15 and is based on the death of Lazarus, which is the reason Jesus wants to go to Judea. Verse 16 belongs thematically to the segment, 11:7–10: the theme is the danger connected with a return to Judea. New to that theme is Thomas' proposal to participate in the mortal danger for Jesus, while in verses 7–10 only the danger to Jesus is mentioned.

■ **12** Verse 12 shows the lack of understanding on the part of the disciples. Schwartz has adjudged their non-understanding incorrectly as "childish": "They could not believe that it was a medical bulletin that told them of Lazarus' condition."[24] In fact, they do take Jesus' words as a "medical bulletin." For, when Jesus told them that Lazarus had fallen asleep, they knew it could not be a case of falling asleep as one does at night. They therefore believe that Lazarus has taken ill and that he has fallen into a healing sleep after the crisis has passed.[25] Why Jesus is to awake him out of that sleep they of course do not know and they do not broach that question. That Jesus' "going" is a march of several days through Jericho to Bethany is unknown to the narrator, or he would not allow it as a disturbing element of the real world intruding into the mysterious legendary world. For the narrator, of course, the hidden meaning of Jesus' words, which betray his omniscience, is established at the outset. Consequently, there is no aporia for him at this point, and it did not bother him at all that no messenger was really necessary where the omniscience of Jesus was concerned. Put differently, we should not expect that Jesus' statement—that he will awaken Lazarus—will occasion a misunderstanding like that of the disciples.

21   *Das Johannesevangelium*, 403.
22   *Rätsel und Mißverständnis*, 5f., 183–85.
23   Leroy, *Rätsel und Mißverständnis*, 184.

24   "Aporien," 3: 167 n. 2.
25   Cf. Wettstein, *Novum Testamentum Graecum*, 1: 915.

Verse 11b already indicates that the disciples misunderstand.

■ **13** Verse 13 makes it clear what Jesus really means—"sleep" is a favorite euphemism for the harsh reality "has died"—and what the disciples incorrectly inferred from his words.

■ **14** Verse 14 relieves the tension: Jesus now speaks openly (i.e., παρρησίᾳ), without a figure that is open to misunderstanding (cf. John 16:29): "Lazarus is dead"—which belatedly explains the word "fallen asleep" (κεκοίμηται) in verse 11 and Jesus' promise that he will awaken him.

■ **15** Jesus' words are to be understood thus: "I am glad for your sakes that I was not there" (for in that case Lazarus would not have died, but would have been healed by Jesus; see 11:21–32), "so that you may come to faith." The narrator is convinced that the eyewitness to a resurrection will come more readily to faith than the witness of a mere healing.[26] For the christology of the narrator the miraculous deeds of Jesus are demonstrations of power that prove his divine sonship. The situation is different for the Evangelist: the greatest miracles are also events within the mundane world. As such, they have no power of proof: to draw a conclusion from an inner-worldly event to the kingdom of the Father is not valid. The realm of the Father is "entirely other." For that reason, miracles can only be pointers to what is "entirely other"; here, in the case of the resurrection of Lazarus, the true meaning concerns the resurrection of the spiritually dead to fellowship with God, to authentic life. In the source, Jesus' summons to go to Lazarus has now been justified.

■ **16** "Thomas" (Θωμᾶς) is an authentic Greek name,[27] used readily by Jews as a translation of the Aramaic name תְּאוֹמָה ("twin"). Thomas appears in the Synoptics (Mark 3:18, Matt 10:3, Luke 6:15, Acts 1:13) and in the Gospel of John at 11:16, 14:5, 20:24, 26–28, 21:2. The segment 20:24–28 is a later insertion into the source; in it Thomas overcomes his budding doubt in the resurrection[28] when he is convinced, as one of the disciples, of the mundane character of the resurrection by confirmation of the wound in Jesus' side. The Evangelist regards faith that originates in that way as of little value: 20:29.

In the Christian and gnostic Syrian tradition, Thomas (the twin) is identified with Jesus' brother Judas: according to the Abgar legend,[29] "Thomas, one of the twelve apostles," sent Thaddaeus to Edessa. But according to the Syrian report, "Judas, who is also called Thomas, sent" Thaddaeus to Abgar. The designation "Judas Thomas, who is also called Didymos" appears occasionally in the Acts of Thomas.[30]

In Gnosticism, Thomas was the (spiritual) brother of Jesus; so also in the Gospel of Thomas in the introduction and in logia 13 and 114.[31]

The words of Thomas in verse 16 give expression to his fidelity; at the same time, there is an undertone of resignation that betrays the blindness of this disciple to the power of Jesus. In the third place, however, there lies hidden in this saying of Thomas the truth that the way to Bethany will lead ultimately to the death of Jesus. The possibility that this inspired the insertion of verses 7–10 is not excluded.

■ **17** Following the words "when Jesus came," D 33 69 *pm* sy add "to Bethany" (εἰς Βηθανίαν) as a clarifying remark. These words are still lacking in the older manuscripts, 𝔓⁶⁶ and 𝔓⁷⁵, as well as in B C * *pc*. That Jesus was going to Bethany is clear from the following verse. The detailed description does not warrant the judgment that this text is older.

Jesus arrives on the evening of the fourth day (together with the disciples, who are no longer mentioned in the narrative), following the death and burial of Lazarus of Bethany. The soul, according to Jewish belief, lingered in the vicinity of the body three days after death.[32] According to Jewish conviction, consequently, a resuscitation of one who had died was impossible on the fourth day, since the soul would not enter again into the

---

26 On the further development of a story that was originally a healing story into a resurrection narrative, cf. Haenchen, *Der Weg Jesu*, 204–13.

27 BDF §53(2).

28 Cf. the analogous segment in Luke 24:36–43.

29 Eusebius, *H.E.* 1.13.4.

30 On this point, cf. *NTApoc* 1: 278–307 and 2: 442f.

31 On this point, cf. Haenchen, *Die Botschaft des Thomas-Evangeliums*, Theologische Bibliothek Töpelmann 6 (Berlin: A. Töpelmann, 1961).

32 Cf. Billerbeck, 2: 544f.

body that had altered its position. It was all the more impressive for the witnesses of the miracle that Jesus raised Lazarus on the fourth day. The fourth day thus has a special meaning here and is taken over deliberately by the narrator for use in connection with the greatest of all possible resurrection miracles.

■ 18 Verse 18 gives the distance between Bethany and Jerusalem as "about two miles" (fifteen stadia or 3 kilometers). Dalman says that that is inaccurate.[33] But it was not important to the narrator to provide exact geographical data: as usual in the Gospel of John, the number is introduced with "approximately" (ώς) to indicate that the measurements are not exact to the meter. The distance between Bethany and Jerusalem is given in order to explain how it was that many mourners appeared so quickly from Jerusalem.

Wikenhauser writes of the customs connected with the visit of mourners: "The custom of the visit of mourners is ancient (cf. 2 Sam 10:2). It was diligently practiced during Jesus' time and was enjoined by the rabbis. For the consolation of the survivors there was a rather complicated protocol. It began on the way home after the interment and continued for seven days, during which mourners constantly arrived at the house."[34]

Mary remained at home—that was also a part of mourning—in order to receive the mourners and to accept their condolences.

■ 19 Jerusalem is the real domicile of the "Jews" for the narrator. He does not see that the three brothers and sisters in Bethany are Jews also; they belong to the circle of disciples. To console the mourner was an obligation of compassion and a pious and meritorious act.[35] The appearances of Jews to console the bereaved thus corresponds to ancient Jewish custom. From the compositional point of view, it was handy for the narrator to have the Jews present who would later spread reports of the miracle in Jerusalem (11:45).

■ 20 How Martha (and only Martha?) received the news that Jesus had arrived in the vicinity of the village is an insignificant detail left unmentioned by the narrator. One of the sisters had to remain at home in order to accept, with thanks, the condolences of the mourners who were constantly arriving;[36] thus, while Mary performed the receptionist's role at home,[37] Martha hurried out to meet Jesus. As a result, Martha has to play the role of the one who does not yet have perfect faith and who must first be instructed by Jesus.

■ 21 The words of Martha express both her grief and her trust in Jesus at the same time: had Jesus been present, her brother would not have died; where Jesus is present, death must yield. But has Jesus really and definitely come too late? That is not at all her view, as her words in the following verse prove.

■ 22 She rather directs her request indirectly to Jesus, of course in a very gentle and meek manner, to the effect that he might now nevertheless call Lazarus back to life. Her words could not be interpreted to imply anything other than: "I know that God will fulfill your every petition." Confession and petition are thereby inextricably woven together.

■ 23 Verse 23 brings us to what the Evangelist himself introduces into the story, which was perhaps originally continued in verse 28. Jesus' answer is open to misunderstanding and is misunderstood. Jesus' answer, "Your brother will rise again," could be Jesus' promise that he will fulfill her wish and raise Lazarus at once. But it could also refer to the resurrection in the endtime, which will include Lazarus. In that case, Martha's petition would have been refused. Martha's response that she knows that all will be resurrected on the last day sounds a bit peevish as though she had said: "I know that, but I have asked that you raise him here and now." It is not easy for the Evangelist to introduce his own concerns into the text here. It follows from verse 22 that Martha believes it possible that Jesus is able to resurrect her brother here and now. That presents the Evangelist with a certain difficulty. The Evangelist is himself also convinced that the true resurrection takes places at any moment at

---

33   *Sacred Sites and Ways,* 249.
34   *Das Evangelium nach Johannes,* 214.
35   See above and cf. Billerbeck 4, 1: 559–610, especially 592–607.
36   See above.
37   Receiving guests was part of the custom: cf. Luke 10:39.

which eyes are opened and faith becomes a reality—and therefore in the here and now. But here and now does not mean the same thing for him as it does for Martha. For Martha, the fulfillment of her request is her trust that Jesus has the power to make an exception. She has no inkling that the apparent exception is the rule, or why it is, or that it is derived from a different conception of "resurrection." The Evangelist gets out of the difficulty by having Martha simply fall back on the expectation of a general resurrection at the end of time. On the other hand, the Evangelist can point vigorously to the present and to the different quality of this resurrection, which, in fact, still lies beyond the horizon of Martha's faith. Jesus' words produce a rupture in the old, limited horizon: "I am the resurrection and the life; he who believes in me, though he die, yet shall he live."

For the circumspective reader, it becomes evident in this passage how difficult it was for the Evangelist to intrude his interpretation upon the view that, in its own way, was powerful and absolutely convincing for that time; and his own interpretation calls for intimations derived from the miraculous, and intimations are never entirely in concord.

The Evangelist is concerned with the spiritual resurrection in the moment of faith (and one cannot expect that of Lazarus who is dead). For that reason, the really important thing for the Evangelist is that the bodily resurrection be taken as an intimation of the spiritual resurrection, and that becomes visible only in the incidental circumstance that Jesus brings Lazarus back to life here and now. The story in the source does not indicate that this life is actually to be different: Lazarus' relation to God is not altered by his resurrection.

■ **24** The Evangelist has intruded vigorously into the story in order to elucidate his own interpretation of the resurrection question. Martha suddenly forgets that she has asked for an immediate resurrection. Again introduced by the words "I know" ($o\tilde{i}\delta a$), she expresses the Jewish and early Christian expectation of the resurrection: that it would follow on the last day, as one took Ezek 37:1–14 to mean, without implying that it was actually so intended. Ezek 37:1–20 describes the famous vision of the prophet of the valley of dry bones, a valley full of individual bones. At the command of God given through the prophet, the bones assembled themselves into skeletons, which were then covered with sinews, flesh, and skin, and which finally were resurrected. According to the prophet, this vision signifies that God will bring a remnant of the exiles back home and will make them into a great people. It is thus really a question of a "national resurrection," not of a bodily resurrection of a people or of all mankind. It is precisely this "bodily" resurrection of all men on the last day that is imported into the discourse of Jesus (and of the Evangelist) in the redactional insertion in John 5:27–29. The confession of Martha thus exhibits only the common conception (that also became regnant in Christianity), namely, the expectation of a future resurrection,[38] which will be simply a making-alive-again, as in Ezek 37, and that means a bodily and not a spiritual resurrection. The introductory "I know" ($o\tilde{i}\delta a$) makes Martha's response sound like a self-evident and generally acknowledged certainty.

■ **25** Why the Evangelist has to let himself recede from the reader's view first comes to light in verse 25: he can now permit the majestic words of the Johannine Jesus to have their full weight over against this "normal" expectation of the resurrection: "I am the resurrection and the life." "And the life" is omitted by $\mathfrak{P}^{45}$ 1 sy^s Cypr Or. Hardly correctly: the Church Fathers often cite texts that are especially well known only in abbreviated form. A further reason for the omission could have been the fact that only the mention of the resurrection appears to be appropriate to this scene. But this is deceptive, since it is precisely the concept of life that plays a decisive role in what follows. Of course, the concept of the resurrection has an especially good and necessary meaning in connection with the resurrection of Lazarus.

In place of the general resurrection on the last day, which Jesus does not occasion (although he subsequently plays a role as judge), Jesus' saying presupposes another resurrection that follows here and now, in the moment in which a man hears and believes the message of Jesus—presented by Jesus himself or one of his disciples. The real resurrection takes place for the Evangelist at a time when the general expectation does not suppose it to take place, that is, in the here and now, and it consists of

---

38   See on John 5:28f.

something that does not come into its own in the general expectation: in belief in the Son of God, who possesses the power to raise spiritually from the dead. Through it one comes again or for the first time into a right relationship to God and to life, and thereby to a new existence that extends beyond the earthly—uninterrupted by death.[39] Some interpreters of course are of the opinion that one could combine the present and the future resurrections—first comes the "spiritual" and then the bodily—and that one can find the final communion with God expressed in the second. This apologetic harmonization is shattered, however, by the fact that for the Evangelist there is no higher form of communion with God than the one that is attainable in the here and now.

■ **26** In wording that is not exactly simple, verse 26 expresses what death implies, the death of the earthly man, following the spiritual resurrection in the here and now, namely, nothing. If one takes that literally, it then means: the "spiritual" existence in unity with God, which arises in faith, is not a "new self-understanding,"[40] which comes to an end with the earthly passing of man, but is a real entity that differs from the earthly man. It therefore does not end with the death of the earthly man, although we are able to say no more than that it remains united with God. Since no one has ever seen the Father, the new entity, viz., being in faith, "born from above," is also taken up as such into the invisibleness of the Father. The Evangelist expresses that in 5:24 by means of the saying of Jesus: "He who hears my word and believes him who sent me, has eternal life; he does not come into judgment, but has passed from death to life."

The view just sketched is taken, in part, to be "gnostic." It is the case, to be sure, that some gnostics from Valentinian circles have harboured the conviction that every gnostic naturally possesses identity with the divine and is therefore necessarily saved ($\phi\acute{\upsilon}\sigma\epsilon\iota\ \sigma\omega\zeta\acute{o}\mu\epsilon\nu o\iota$: "saved by nature").[41] The gnostic Gospel of Thomas clearly represents another gnostic doctrine: it presupposes that one does not possess salvation once and

for all. Gnostic missionaries have confidence in specific persons, who seem to them to be open to gnostic knowledge: whoever is deeply aware of his distinction from the hostile world has thereby become a "self" that is different from the world; such a person is aware that his being differs from the world and that he has come from the realm of divine light. But now everything depends on whether such a person in fact is not infatuated with the world and all its charms, on whether he is on guard every moment of life vis-à-vis the world, like a highwayman waiting in ambush. If the gnostic disciple does not stick to this the most stringent of all ascetic practices, he dies like all non-gnostics and is completely dissipated in death. That is put graphically in the parabolic narrative in logion 97: "Jesus said, 'The Kingdom of the Father is like a certain woman who was carrying a jar full of meal. While she was walking on a road, still some distance from home, the handle of the jar broke and the meal emptied out behind her on the road. She did not realize it; she had noticed no accident. When she reached her house, she set the jar down and found it empty.'"[42] This logion is a parable of warning that describes the unnoticed loss of the "Kingdom," a loss that is first remarked when it is too late (at the end of life's course). The "Kingdom," the "self," is not something one possesses once and for all. It can be lost while "underway" without the loss being noticed (the Christian equivalent would be: one can lose one's faith without perceiving the loss). Whoever does not have this divine self, from him will his earthly existence also be taken away (in death). On the other hand, in the moment of death, the constant gnostic returns again to the realm of light from which he came, as the "Letter to Rheginus" shows.[43] The situation looks entirely different to the Evangelist. For him there is no one who merely needs to be reminded of his identification with the divine. Rather, "a birth from above" (John 3:3, 5) has to awaken him from spiritual death, and this "birth from above" happens only to those whom the Father himself has given to Jesus. Only thereby does man

---

39   Cf. Schnackenburg, *John*, 2: 352ff.
40   Bultmann, *John*, 258f., 402ff. [194, 307f.].
41   Bultmann, *John*, 487 n. 5 [373 n. 3], incorrectly generalizes the point and extends it to all gnostics.
42   Tr. Thomas Lambdin, *Nag Hammadi Library*, 128.
43   The definitive edition of the "Letter to Rheginus," correctly titled, *The Treatise on Resurrection*, is now: Bentley Layton, *The Gnostic Treatise on Resurrection*

From Nag Hammadi. Harvard Dissertations in Religion 12. Missoula: Scholars Press, 1979.

gain a new existence, an existence that Nicodemus regards as impossible. This existence is a transition from "spiritual" or "religious" death to life (5:24); Jesus is able to grant this transition because, like the Father, he is life.

The words "dead" and "living" are very difficult to represent briefly in German or English terms in the non-literal sense in which the Evangelist uses them. The word "religious" for most people today has a pleasant archaic ring to it; "spiritual death," however, can be misunderstood as eccentricity or as someone who is slightly "touched in the head." "Eternal life" for the Evangelist begins in the midst of this earthly life, and is not thought of in the sense of understanding, reasons, the intellectual, or as the "inner life." For all of that man possesses and confirms already, before he is "born from above," and all of that he possesses and confirms afterwards, up to the time of his earthly death. All of that, which exists "alongside" him, is "qualitatively" different from "eternal life." "Spiritual death" is likewise not the dissolution of the earthly life on the death bed, but concerns the relationship to God that is missing or has been lost.[44]

The mundane aspect of this process is the moment in which one hears and believes Jesus' message. The story of Lazarus, for the Evangelist, is one in which Lazarus hears Jesus' call to life in death, and this is an allusion to the bestowal of new existence in fellowship with the Father and with the son. But an allusion or pointer is not the same thing as that to which it points. When one turns on the turn signal in an automobile to indicate that one is about to alter the direction of travel, that is not the same thing as altering the direction of travel. If one refers death and life symbolically to sinful and sinless existence, that is shattered by verse 25. For, the statement, "he shall live" (i.e., be sinless), "although he die" (i.e., sin) does not make acceptable sense. The Evangelist speaks not only of symbols, he believes that in reality whoever is "born from above" has obtained a supramundane existence and in this new existence will no longer be affected by death, although this man of faith will not be spared death, any more than was Lazarus —or Jesus himself. Nevertheless, this man must "abide, be steadfast" (8:31, 35, 14:17, 15:4–7). The "birth from above" is not automatically effective. On the other hand, it is the will of the Father at the same time that the faithful be kept (17:12). The tension between human obedience and the divine will cannot be avoided in any Christian theological statement.

■ **27** Martha's response is her solemn confession provided by verse 27. Its liturgical tone of course is in striking contrast to her earlier confession in verse 21. Nevertheless, the liturgically stylized confession fulfills its function admirably: Martha can quit the scene on this harmonious note—a scene that is still to be played outside Bethany—and make way for her sister Mary.

■ **28** Of course, a fresh difficulty then appears to emerge. Some commentators have trouble with the fact that the text does not mention Jesus' wish to speak now with Mary. But this difficulty arises from a misunderstanding. The narrator does not see it as his task to provide anything like a police report for the scene. From the words of Martha, which the reader has to take seriously, it emerges that Jesus does, in fact, wish to speak with Mary. His wish does not, therefore, require special mention in the text. The narrator exercises the freedom not to relate things that the reader can derive from the text for himself or herself. The aporias that thwart Schwartz and Wellhausen at every step in their progress through the text are based, for the most part, on their desire to impose a strange style on the narrator with the discipline of a school teacher. Whoever does not adequately observe the freedom of authorial composition should not wonder if he or she does not make exegetical progress in the face of nothing but snares in the text. The narrator thus does not have Jesus explicitly mention that he also wants Mary to come to him. Rather, the close sequence of the two sisters he has taken from the tradition and represented it as well as he could in the way depicted in verse 28. That had the advantage of not interrupting the rapid course of the action by a retarding remark.

■ **29f.** The text of course also presents difficulties that, in the last analysis, owe to the origin of the story. Actually there is no new aspect that Mary's words could reveal. Hirsch of course advocates a different interpretation: the author "has Mary utter the exact first words of the same complaint to Jesus, when she meets him, that Martha earlier uttered—but in a posture of adoration. And so

---

44 [Haenchen was of the opinion that the English phrases, "spiritual life" and "spiritual death" perhaps better represent what the Evangelist had in mind. I have used them throughout to translate *geistlicher Tod* and *geistliches Leben* or their surrogates.—Translator.]

matters progress quite differently. In Martha's case, there is a conversation in which her lack of understanding is revealed in spite of her faith. No word passes between Jesus and Mary after the first, short lament, which is nevertheless worshipful. Mary is silent and Jesus is silent. . . . Because of her silence, Mary is unique among the persons connected with this work . . . the silence of the weeping Mary in front of him brings Jesus to grief and tears. Mary can be understood in no way other than as the picture of the Christian disposition to suffering and death: the grief comes to the one who worships in faith, in expectant but mute petition."[45] What speaks for Hirsch's interpretation in the text are the words: "When she saw him, she fell weeping at his feet." Martha did indeed speak the words of faith in that version of the story employed by the Evangelist: "I know that whatever you ask from God, God will give you" (v. 22). The picture of Martha so constructed is only distorted by the intervention of the Evangelist: it suddenly appears as though she were spiritually deaf and hears in Jesus' words of promise only what is self-evident to all the world, namely, the resurrection at the end of time. In general, Hirsch has not distinguished between the source, which the Evangelist adapts to his own purposes to a certain extent, and the elements the Evangelist has introduced into the source. The most important thing for him was to distinguish the Evangelist from the later redactor. That made it possible for him to depreciate the words of Martha and to insert a picture of faith for Mary—in his overinterpretation especially laudatory—while Mary as yet speaks only the first part of what Martha had already said to Jesus. The narrator could not overlook the fact that the tradition spoke of two sisters.[46] He therefore was compelled to include both in the action without having enough material for doing so. Thus Martha chose the better part in the source of the narrator, a part that the Evangelist and Hirsch have then taken away.

■ **31** Mary departs quickly from the house filled with mourners: this feature is used skillfully as motivation for all the Jews who are present to come with her to Jesus and thus to become witnesses to his act of restoring life to the decaying Lazarus. Of course, matters have not come

that far as yet. Jesus is still standing someplace close to the village (as though mysteriously transfixed, for which, however, the narrator is responsible), where Martha had met him. The layout of the entire scene is skillfully wrought. Lazarus has been entombed somewhere outside the village—Jesus does not know where. Jesus does not go to the house where the mourners are, which would be the customary thing to do, and then Martha comes out to meet him. Mary has learned nothing from the words that Jesus and Martha have exchanged. She does not know what subject was discussed in the conversation between Jesus and her sister. She only knows— and this bit of knowledge is nowhere accounted for— that Jesus awaits her at some particular location along the road. Not until verse 34 is the action shifted to the grave of Lazarus.

■ **32** When Mary sees Jesus, she throws herself at his feet, weeping—this feature is new in the encounter of the two sisters with Jesus—and speaks the same words that Martha had said earlier: "Lord, if you had been here, my brother would not have died." One can interpret that in different ways. Hirsch is of the opinion that the author intended to create contrasting pictures in Martha and Mary: Mary complains as does Martha—but "in a posture of adoration."[47] The author cannot have meant Mary's silence in a negative way: "the silently weeping Mary in front of him drives him to grief and tears."[48] He means to paint her as "the Christian disposition to suffering and death."[49] This goes together with Hirsch's view that the Evangelist was a great poet. On the contrary, one should admit as a matter of fact that the two sisters are not to be understood as contrasting figures. The way in which Mary is called by Martha, the way in which Mary almost repeats the speech of her sister, has the effect of making her appear virtually as the shadow of her sister. In verse 39, she again makes way for Martha, and that contributes to the impression that she is a shadow. After all, it was not the task of the narrator to give a precise and distinguishable characterization of each of the sisters. Incidentally, the substantive repetition of verse 21 in verse 32 has the advantage of once

---

45   *Das vierte Evangelium*, 290f.
46   Cf. Luke 10:38–42.
47   *Das vierte Evangelium*, 290.
48   *Das vierte Evangelium*, 290f.
49   *Das vierte Evangelium*, 291.

again emphasizing for the reader faith in the power of Jesus.

■ **33** Verse 33 has been variously interpreted. Early on there were two textual traditions: a more difficult reading attested by $\mathfrak{P}^{66}$* $\mathfrak{P}^{75}$ B and other witnesses, and a less difficult attested by $\mathfrak{P}^{45}$ $\mathfrak{P}^{66}$ D (Φ) *pc* p sa. One should probably not allow the impression to arise, on the basis of $\mathfrak{P}^{45}$ $\mathfrak{P}^{66}$ D *pc* p sa, that Jesus was given over to emotion. One correctly distinguishes the text and sense of the source and the version of the Evangelist. The source may very well have made use of the preparation of the miracle worker as a literary device.[50] Recent commentators often overlook the fact that "grow angry" (ἐνεβρι-μήσατο) is used absolutely, without object, and so supply the missing object, to the extent that they do not render the offensive expression harmless by means of apologetic interpretations. Bauer[51] and Schnackenburg[52] interpret his "anger" as directed against the Jews and Mary who are weeping (Schnackenburg omits mention of Mary); their weeping shows that they do not have faith in the power of the prince of life who stands before them. They employ this same interpretation in verse 38.

Black takes a different approach.[53] In John 11:33, a Syriac expression has been incorrectly understood and translated. The Syriac expression, *'eth'azaz bᵉruha*, has a broader usage than the corresponding Greek expression, ἐνεβριμήσατο τῷ πνεύματι, "he was deeply moved in his spirit." An attack of rage or anger is not intended. And so the English interpreter can be reconciled to the customary text: "he groaned in his spirit and was troubled." But the source—so it appears to us—has depicted Jesus on the model of the miracle worker as Bonner has characterized him. That is also no doubt the case in John 9:6ff., where Jesus is depicted as a pagan miracle worker, who heals the blind by making a paste out of earth and spittle and putting it on their eyes. From the standpoint of the method of healing, there is thus no objection to the supposition that the source makes use of typical features of miracle workers and is not offended by

them. In any case, there are such cases in the Synoptics (Mark 7:31–36, 8:22–26). The supposition that the Evangelist understood the source to mean that Jesus himself was deeply moved in the face of death and wept like Mary and the Jews is not precluded. The same thing could apply to verse 38. The emphasis for the Evangelist lay at an entirely different point: the resurrection of Lazarus was a pointer to the real resurrection, by means of which a person spiritually dead is taken back into full communion with God.[54]

■ **34** This explanation is supported by the continuation of the story in the words of the source. Jesus asks where Lazarus is interred. This question actually contradicted his omniscience, otherwise often emphasized. This delay of the action is compositionally necessary for the narrator, who can sustain the tension over long stretches of narrative.

■ **35f.** Jesus now breaks out in tears. That is intended to express neither his distress over human faithlessness nor to describe a quiet, dispassionate weeping bridled by reason, contrary to Braun.[55] Rather, in accordance with the explanation given in connection with verse 33, it may now be said candidly how human were Jesus' feelings. That becomes all the more evident when the Jews now say (here they are not at all represented as hostile): "See how he loved him!" What was said in verse 5 is thereby repeated. Of course, those who speak so are not yet aware that this love is able to do more than merely shed tears and share grief as a fellow sufferer.

■ **37** Some of the Jews go still further and refer to the healing of the blind man narrated in chapter 9. What is mentioned here, however, by way of question is immediately revealed to be a prophecy of which they had no premonition.

■ **38** Jesus again intensifies his inner preparation for the miracle[56] and strides to the grave. The story then comes very close to such a high pitch of tension that it is scarcely bearable. It is delayed momentarily by the prosaic bit of information about the gravestone that blocked the

50 Thus Bultmann, *John*, 406 n. 4 [310 n. 4], who finds *voces mysticae* here, following the example of C. Bonner, "Traces of Thaumaturgic Technique in the Miracles," HTR 20 (1927) 171–81.

51 *Das Johannesevangelium*, 152.

52 *John*, 2: 335f.

53 *An Aramaic Approach*, 174–77.

54 See above on verse 25f.

55 *Le Sainte Bible*, 400.

56 See above, on verse 33.

entrance to the grave[57] and the statement of Martha, which in its dreadful realism no longer betrays a scintilla of faith.

■ **39** Jesus gives the command to take away the stone. But now Martha, the sister of the dead man, can no longer contain herself. Her words are to be understood as a passionate outcry: "Lord, by this time there will be an odor, for he has been dead four days." This all too brutally candid characterization of the situation serves as preparation for the coming miraculous deed: a corpse that has already begun to deteriorate will be restored to good health.

It is nowhere said that Lazarus has been enbalmed; further, the pleasant smelling herbs that were placed between the bandages and the corpse served only for the period of the interment. Enbalming of the type practiced by the Egyptians was not common among the Jews.

■ **40** The human, all too human, reaction of Martha is really an expression of doubt in the power of God (Jesus' words now reveal that), whose glory is now revealed. Martha is not thereby reproached as an individual for her lack of faith. It is rather her task—thankless, of course—to demonstrate how difficult it is for all men to conceive so great a miracle.

■ **41f.** These verses make clear that Jesus knew in advance that the Father would fulfill his every request, as Martha had indeed earlier asserted (v. 21). He therefore does not utter the request as a request, but as thanks for something already given. Furthermore, these thanks do not need to be spoken aloud. He speaks them aloud only so that those standing about would know that he, Jesus, is really the one sent by the Father. This designation of his dignity can already have been used by the Evangelist's source. One can concur completely with Käsemann that here again the medium of a "divine man" (θεῖος ἀνήρ) theology is being employed. But in saying that, one has not yet understood the concerns of the Evangelist.

■ **43f.** In these verses the miracle itself is briefly depicted. With a loud voice—the majestic command of a "divine man" (θεῖος ἀνήρ)—Jesus calls out: "Lazarus, come forth." And it happens: the dead man emerges. His feet and hands are still bound with linen bindings; also, Lazarus cannot see the way out of the grave; for a handkerchief still covers his face. The miracle does not therefore consist merely in making the dead to live, but also in the fact that he glides out of the grave—as though he were borne by an invisible hand. That Jesus does not further concern himself with Lazarus' friends, but only says, "Unbind him, and let him go," could belong to an early stage of the tradition, in which Lazarus was not the brother of the two sisters, Mary and Martha. Beyond that, we must also decide whether this feature is to be understood as an aspect of the composition. And that point is also to be treated in the Overview.

Overview

The tensions within the Fourth Gospel are especially noticeable in chapter 11. Critical exegetes in this century have sought to resolve these tensions by means of a relatively simply means: a source has been reworked. Bultmann has correctly judged the solutions offered to be less than satisfactory.[58]

Schwartz believes that originally the story ran: Jesus came to the grave immediately following the burial of Lazarus (a heightening of the miracle at Nain), met the sisters and the Jews there, raised Lazarus, and thereby produced "his own downfall on earth." The text of the original gospel was "later whitewashed."[59]

According to Wellhausen, the Lazarus episode in the basic source is the dénouement. Only verses 1a, 3, 7–10, 16 (17?) and 33–37 have been retained from the underlying source. Everything else stems from a reworking.[60]

Spitta distinguishes an underlying document created by the apostle John[61] from additions of an editor. These derive in part from his own reflections, and in part from other gospel traditions known to him.[62]

Wendt is of the opinion that the words of Jesus belong to an older layer of the tradition.[63] They contain good

57   Billerbeck, 1: 1051.
58   Bultmann, *John*, 395f. n.4 [301 n. 4].
59   "Aporien," 3: 166–71.
60   *Das Evangelium Johannis*, 50–53.
61   *Das Johannes-Evangelium als Quelle der Geschichte Jesu* (Göttingen: Vandenhoeck & Ruprecht, 1910) 401–7.
62   *Das Johannes-Evangelium als Quelle der Geschichte Jesu* (Göttingen: Vandenhoeck & Ruprecht, 1910) 230–

55.
63   *Die Schichten im vierten Evangelium* (Göttingen: Vandenhoeck & Ruprecht, 1911) 97.

historical tradition derived from an eyewitness. The redactor of the discourse layer has formally recoined these words; he probably fixed his memory of the actual words of Jesus only after a long interval. Still later the fourth Evangelist edited these late notes. Nevertheless, one can still recognize the form of the historical Jesus through this double veil. We meet here certain aspects of Jesus that are not equally strongly emphasized by the Synoptics. "The Evangelist" has "mixed synoptic traditions with oral materials of various origins and worked them up in accordance with his own special viewpoints and ideas."[64]

Wendland found this segment to represent a combination of synoptic tradition and free invention, which permits the Evangelist's (n.b.) massive faith in miracles to come to expression.[65]

On the view of Hirsch,[66] what lay before the Evangelist was the story of the resurrection of Lazarus in an abbreviated form. In this version, Lazarus was not the brother but the neighbor of Mary and Martha. "The clear assignment, without remainder, of the expanded and reworked parts to him (i.e., to the Evangelist) and the balance to the source is hardly possible."[67] The story becomes truly living only through the efforts of the Evangelist. The Lazarus story was also a legend in its original form. It did not belong to the circle of the primitive Jerusalem community. "The miracles of Jesus, which might be validly attested as historical, are always . . . recognizable as compassionate demonstrations of love. On the other hand, Lazarus is a purely objective demonstration of divine sovereignty. . . . By incorporating the Lazarus legend the author has endangered his own picture of Jesus."[68]

According to Bultmann, the story of Lazarus stems from the signs source,[69] into which the Evangelist has inserted verses 4, 7–10, 16, 20–32, and 40–42, and "in these, as elsewhere, he employs sayings from the revelation-discourses."[70] In his opinion, the text of the original source looked like this:

[1]Now a certain man was ill, Lazarus of Bethany, the village of Mary and her sister Martha. [3] So the sisters sent to him, saying, "Lord, he whom you love is ill." [5]But Jesus loved Lazarus. [6]So when he heard that he was ill, he stayed two days longer in the place where he was. [11]Afterwards he said to (his disciples): "Our friend Lazarus has fallen asleep, but I go to awake him out of sleep." [12]Then the disciples said to him, "Lord, if he has fallen asleep, he will recover." [14]Then Jesus told them plainly, "Lazarus is dead; and for your sake (so that you may believe), I am glad that I was not there; but let us go to him. [17]Now when Jesus came, he found that Lazarus had already been in the tomb four days. [18]Bethany was near Jerusalem, about two miles off, [19]and many of the Jews had come to Martha and Mary to console them concerning their brother, etc.

The Jews appear here, however, only on account of the Johannine passion narrative. And the Johannine misunderstanding does not belong to the original story. The original narrative could have run something like this:

[1]Now a certain man was ill, Lazarus of Bethany, the village of Mary and her sister Martha. [3]So the sisters sent to him, saying, "Lord, he whom you love is ill." [4]But when Jesus heard it, [6]he stayed two days longer in the place where he was. [7]Then after this he said to his disciples, [11]"Our friend Lazarus has fallen asleep, but let us go to him." [18]Bethany was near Jerusalem, about two miles off. [20]When Martha heard that Jesus was coming, she went out to meet him; but Mary sat in the house. [21] Then Martha said to Jesus, "Lord, if you had been here, my brother would not have died. [22]And even now I know that whatever you ask from God, God will give you." [33]Jesus [34]said, "Where have you laid him?" [35]They said to him, "Come and see." [38]It was a cave and a stone lay upon it. [39]Jesus said, "Take away the stone." Then Martha said to him, "Lord, he already stinks. For he has been dead four days. [43]Jesus called out with a loud voice, "Lazarus, come forth." [44]The dead man came out, bound hand and foot with bindings, and his face was covered with a handkerchief. Jesus said, "Unbind him and let him go."

---

64 *Schichten*, 22.
65 *Die urchristlichen Literaturformen*, HNT 1, 3 (Tübingen: Mohr-Siebeck, 1912) 305–7.
66 *Das vierte Evangelium*, 272ff.
67 *Das vierte Evangelium*, 273.
68 *Das vierte Evangelium*, 275f.
69 *John*, 395 n. 2 [301 n. 2].
70 *John*, 295f. n 4 [301 n. 4].

Brown is right in not being satisfied with the solution of Bultmann.[71] Instead of that solution, he recommends the following: the story transmitted in isolation stems from earlier tradition. With this story, the "pedagogical genius" of John brings Jesus' public ministry to a close.

Undoubtedly the richest reflections are those of Schnackenburg in his excursus on eschatological thought in the Gospel of John.[72] He penetrates more deeply into the problems of present and futuristic eschatology than anyone else. But it is still a question whether futuristic eschatology—with which Martha reckons—can really be combined with present eschatology in the way Schnackenburg seems to think.

It has long been observed that the Lazarus pericope has contacts with other passages in the synoptic gospels, especially the Gospel of Luke. That concerns the name Lazarus, which is the Greek from of the abbreviated form of Eleazar ("God has helped"), and which in the Palestinian Talmud is shortened to Lazar. We know this name preeminently from the Lukan parable of the rich man and Lazarus (Luke 16:19–31). The rich man remains anonymous in this parable, but the poor man is called "God helps," in prophetic anticipation of his final destiny. But the Lukan parable has even closer points of contact with the story of Lazarus' resurrection. In Luke 16:30f., it is stated that even if Lazarus were to rise from the dead and come back to life, the Jews would not be moved to repentance, like the rich man hopes in his torment. That corresponds precisely to John 11:45–53, where the Jews, who are unprepard to repent, resolve to kill Lazarus, who was raised from the dead, and Jesus, who raised him from the dead. That means precisely that what in Luke 16:30f. appears as a mere possibility in a story of Jesus becomes reality in John 11: Lazarus is raised from the dead, and the Jews do not repent but plot murder.

It is not only Lazarus, however, who is mentioned in the Gospel of Luke, but also his two sisters, Martha and Mary: Luke 10:38–40 informs us that they both live in an unnamed village (cf. John 11:1). In the Lukan story, Martha is incessantly occupied with serving (διακονεῖν); in John 12:2 the correlative thing is said of her: "Martha served" (ἡ Μάρθα διηκόνει). The correspondences do not go so far in the case of Mary. Nevertheless, it is said of her in Luke 10:39 that she sat quietly at Jesus' feet at home, and in John 11:20 that "Mary sat in the house." She then hurries of course to Jesus.

But there are also other relationships beyond these. In Luke 7:36–50 it is reported that a woman who was a sinner anointed Jesus and having wet his feet with her tears, wiped them with her hair. A similar scene is played out in John 11:2: Mary anoints Jesus' feet and wipes them with her hair. This story is then told in detail in John 12:1–8, where it takes place following a guest supper in the village of Bethany. The location of the action in Luke is an anonymous "city" (πόλις), but in Mark 14:3 and John 12:1 it is in Bethany. Luke has nothing corresponding to Mark 14:3–9. He perhaps took the view that his anointing story in chapter 7 was a better variant of the Markan anointing.

In this situation, the remedy that is apparently ready to hand is the view that John knew and used the synoptic gospels—or at least one or the other of them. Hirsch especially has worked with this hypothesis. In his opinion, the great author and poet, John, has taken appropriate elements or details out of the Synoptics from time to time, and incorporated a free version of them into his work.

Gardner-Smith published his short but convincing study, *St. John and the Synoptic Gospels,* in 1938.[73] He proved that the fourth Evangelist did not know or use any one of the synoptic gospels, let alone all three.[74] Besides, the confluence of such details would be difficult to explain in any case. In that event, one must take other possibilities into account, especially this one: here we get a sense of the mutations of the oral tradition. Two things in particular can be said in support of this view.

In the first place, some scholars have long since noted that there are connections especially between the third and fourth gospels, which are of very different kinds and reach.[75] To mention only one that was not introduced above: Luke already knows of farewell discourses of Jesus to his disciples. In this case, one would scarcely jump to the conclusion that John had read the third Gospel and had been inspired by it.

In the second place, however, there are observations

71 *John,* 1: 429.
72 *John,* 2: 426–37.
73 (Cambridge: The University Press); see especially 42–50.
74 Cf. the agreement of Dodd, Noack, and J. Jeremias.
75 For example, H. J. Holtzmann, "Das schriftstelle-

that indicate to us that Luke and John are the latest of the gospels.[76] If Luke in chapter 7 and John in chapter 12 report that a woman annointed Jesus, that agrees with Mark 14. But in Mark 14:3 the woman remains anonymous and she anoints his head, while in Luke 7 a woman who is a sinner wets Jesus' feet with her tears at a meal and wipes them with her hair; then she anoints his feet. In John 12:3, Mary anoints the feet of Jesus and wipes them with her hair. Here it can be seen how a tradition fades and is expanded at the same time (the name of the one who anoints is given: Mary). That is not an early form of the tradition. Further, the treatment of Lazarus in John 11:44 as someone who is not a beloved friend and brother of the two sisters, but is treated like the daughter of Jairus in Mark 5:43, shows us that the Johannine story of Lazarus has a long prehistory behind it.

Now one must free oneself from prejudgments, of which we are often not conscious as such. The fact that Matthew and Luke have both made use of Mark prompts the supposition that the oral Jesus tradition came to an end with the so-called great Gospels. Papyrus Egerton 2 shows us how a new gospel can be conceived by a collector of Jesus stories out of very different—and extra-canonical—traditions. The oral tradition existed for a long time alongside the written. In the Introduction §1.6 (volume 1), we have cited the Papias fragment preserved by Eusebius.[77] This same Papias has transmitted a Jewish legend preserved in the Syrian Apocalypse of Baruch in a coarser form than a saying of Jesus transmitted by the disciple of John. The sayings material as well as the narrative material have not been uniformly preserved; often it is only the most impressive words and formulations that resist such mutation. As a consequence, new formations, sayings and stories—or at least comparable sayings and stories—take their rise.

Some scholars are nevertheless convinced that Jesus, like the rabbis later, had his disciples learn by heart the traditions that they were to pass on. But what would the gospels have looked like, had Jesus taken the care with his precise diction that was characteristic of the rabbis? One need only compare the sermon on the mount in Matthew with the discourse on the plain in Luke, or observe the transmutations of the story of the centurion from Capernaum from Matt 8:5–13, through Luke 7:1–10, to John 4:46–54. One then sees that the history of the tradition was more than a literary process. What we possess of written particulars regarding the sayings material and narratives in the gospels might be assessed to a great extent as a mere capturing of the flux of tradition in a given moment, as this or that community, this or that Evangelist, achieved it, and as they conceived that arrested tradition and passed it on. The pipe-dream of Vinzez von Lerinum of the *quod semper et ubique et ab omnibus creditum est* ("what has been believed always, everywhere, and by everybody") at least ought not to cause critical scholarship to dream on. It is of course not always easy to determine whether an evangelist treats his tradition freely or whether he has used a different tradition than is found elsewhere.

At this point, however, another factor enters in and obscures our view of the problems of the tradition, the oral tradition and its mutations. It appears to be self-evident that one tradition employed by an evangelist (a *Q[uelle]*, or a "source") must be older than this gospel and therefore be closer to the reported event. This is the reason for the zealousness of the quest for sources, which at times has dominated scholarship as the problem alleged to be the most important. But that is not to say that a tradition employed by a gospel is the oldest. Yet in very few cases do we know the precise course of the synoptic tradition and the intermediate stages that it touched. Something else goes together with that point: one is indeed often too ready to speak of an "original report" or an original gospel—Schwartz and Wellhausen come to mind—where it was only probable that an evangelist made use of an earlier "gospel." The data for the "life of Jesus" that are available to us are only like the tip of an iceberg, whose real mass is hidden from view,

rische Verhältnis des Johannes zu den Synoptikern," *ZWT* 12 (1869) 62–85, 155–78, 446–56; Schniewind, *Die Parallelperikopen bei Lukas und Johannes* (Hildesheim: G. Olms, ²1958); Bailey, *The Tradition Common to the Gospels of Luke and John* (Leiden: Brill, 1963).

76 If Noack alludes only to the oral tradition and concludes from that that John is as early as Mark and collected the oral tradition for himself, that is shattered on the example to be given momentarily.

77 *H.E.* 3.39.3.

since it is under water. The mention of Chorazin in Matt 11:21 and Luke 10:13 is evidence of the gappiness of the tradition available to us.

Not every "evangelist" was aware of everything that every other evangelist has transmitted. That becomes clear precisely in the story of Lazarus. Had Mark known this the most marvelous of all miracle stories that the NT contains, he would not have withheld it from his readers (assuming that he could have tolerated it in his picture of Jesus). The Lazarus story arose rather late and does not remain unaltered even in the Gospel of John. We are thus faced with the question: how did the fourth Evangelist understand the Lazarus narrative that lay before him (presumably in written form, as part of a gospel)? In connection with 11:25f., Wellhausen has remarked: "If that holds good, then the resurrection of Lazarus is completely superfluous. The saying that is the point of verses 21–27 robs the whole event of all meaning."[78] Wellhausen was certainly a scholar of the greatest range. But he did not raise the issue that he here touched upon. In fact, the story of Lazarus that the Evangelist recapitulates in this passage is in a certain sense highly unsuited to his purpose. Lazarus does indeed return to his old earthly life. In a certain sense, his resurrection from the dead was an event that took place in the world. He presumably soon died again, as John 12:10 hints. There is nowhere the slightest hint that his relationship to God was altered by his resurrection. Eckhardt has endeavored, with pardonable zeal, to fill in the gap: Jesus raised the beloved disciple, John, of whom it was then believed that he would not die again.[79] The Lazarus story is here being spun out again and not much differently than if it were being told anew after many centuries.

The Evangelist may well have intervened in the Lazarus story as it was transmitted to him only in verses 23–27. It was enough for him that he could express the knowledge that was alone important to him, the knowledge at which, in his eyes, the Lazarus story hinted between the lines vividly and graphically: for the Christian complete union with God is not something that sets in some time beyond the grave and decay. Rather, we discover "eternal life" here and now, namely, in union with the Father of Jesus in its fullness and blessedness.

The Evangelist saw a hidden hint in the Lazarus story—but which is revealed in verses 25f. He therefore took the story over. He inserted a tiny clue, like he does in the story of the royal official ($\beta\alpha\sigma\iota\lambda\iota\kappa\acute{o}s$) in 4:48f. or in the Thomas story in 20:29. The story of the healing of the man born blind (chap. 9) is also a hint that Jesus is the light of the world and is to be acknowledged as such.

Some scholars are of the opinion that the Evangelist saw mere symbols in these stories. But a symbol does not effect what the pointing character of this story is able to achieve. The pointing function ($\sigma\eta\mu\epsilon\hat{\iota}\alpha$) can be compared to the turn signals in an auto; that means: the car is about to alter its direction. The actual process of turning the signals on is completely different from the car's change in direction. Similarly, the Evangelist makes use of actual processes, or what he takes to be such, that could point to something "completely other."

The Evangelist was not concerned to create a series of scenes, but to relate events that really took place. The earthly life of Jesus for him was the appearance of the unseen Father in his visible son. The true message of Jesus for him and for all to whom the spirit had been imparted was hidden/revealed in the earthly life of Jesus: hidden for those who did not comprehend this hint (although he firmly believed that Jesus had brought a decaying Lazarus back to life), revealed for those whose eyes the spirit had opened to the pointer to a heavenly meaning of an earthly event.

That the Evangelist found a "gospel" that he alone knew how to read was at once his fortune and his misfortune. This written gospel created by a great poet, a gospel that led from miracle to miracle, was created by someone for whom the divinity of Jesus was narrated palpably, demonstrably. It was unfortunate for the Evangelist that this "gospel of miracles" used by him as a pointer was nevertheless for him also a collection of actual miracle stories. In that case, the miracles of Jesus were only events in the everyday world, events which did not lead to God, only alleged proofs, like the story of Thomas without the last verse, a verse which then corrects the faith of Thomas. It only became a book of the church when a redactor restored the worst, that

78 *Das Evangelium Johannis*, 51.
79 Karl August Eckhardt, *Der Tod des Johannes als Schlüssel zum Verständnis der johanneischen Schriften* (Berlin: Walter de Gruyter, 1961), especially 17–20.

means, the highest, features of the message of the Evangelist to something like sound, normal Christianity; he of course did so by means of additions, like those we so clearly discovered in chapter 5.

The trouble the Fourth Gospel has caused exegetes owes to the fact that the Evangelist has made a "gospel of miracles" the bearer of his own message. For that message a miracle as such—even if it were the resurrection of someone already decaying—remains an event within mundane reality and becomes significant only for those who see a pointer in this event, which remains mundane, to something that is no longer mundane. Jesus' disciples of course regularly misunderstand what he says and does. For, so long as the spirit had not yet been given (cf. 7:39), men, like the Jews, are compelled to misunderstand what Jesus says and does as events within the world. To be sure, Jesus has become flesh, so that believers may see the Father in him. But during his earthly life his disciples must ask him, as Philip does: "Show us the Father." To this Jesus responds: "Have I been so long with you, and yet you do not know me, Philip? He who has seen me has seen the Father."[80] Yet this seeing is first possible when the risen Jesus comes to his disciples and says to them: "Peace be with you. As the Father has sent me, even so I send you." And with these words he breathed on them and said to them: "Receive the Holy Spirit."[81] The event takes place here on a higher level than is said of the creation of man in Gen 2:7: God breathed his spirit into man. The earthly life of Jesus therefore has the sense for John of a revelation of the unseen Father, which becomes visible as such only after its conclusion on the cross and in the receiving of the spirit.

For that reason, John was anything but a docetist. Whoever makes him out to be a naive docetist, as Käsemann does,[82] becomes the victim of a fatal confusion. There are, of course, individual features in the Fourth Gospel, as also in the other three Gospels, in which Jesus is represented as a "divine man" ($\theta\epsilon\hat{\iota}os\ \dot{a}v\acute{\eta}\rho$), or, as Käsemann puts it, as a God walking about on earth. In my judgment, one may get this impression with greater frequency in the avowed "gospel of miracles" used by John as the basis of his own gospel. But neither John nor the Synoptics have had an attack of docetism on account of such features. They were all convinced that a divine being became a bona fide man in Jesus of Nazareth, and that that man led a real human life right up to his death on the cross. Whoever turns the story of the crucifixion into a mere symbol, who reduces it to its significance, to an event that never happened, that person constructs an early Christianity that never was. There is of course a shift in Jesus' words on the cross from Mark's "My God, my God, why have you forsaken me?", to Luke's "Father, into Thy hands I commend my spirit," to John's "It is finished." But that is not enough to turn John into a docetist. He believes in the true man, Jesus, who is at the same time the Son of God. It is for that reason that he became so important for the subsequent development of Christian dogma.

---

80 John 14:8f.
81 John 20:21f.
82 In his book, *The Testament of Jesus.*

27. The Sanhedrin Resolves to Put Jesus to Death

Bibliography

Albright, William Foxwell
  "The Ephraim of the Old and New Testament."
  JPOS 3 (1923) 36–40.

Bammel, Ernst
  "Joh 11,45–47." In *The Trial of Jesus. Cambridge
  Studies in honour of C. F. D. Moule*, ed. E. Bammel.
  SBT 13 (Naperville, IL: Allenson, 1970) 11–40.

Barker, Margaret
  "Caiaphas' Words in Jn 11,50 refer to Messiah be
  Joseph." In *The Trial of Jesus. Cambridge Studies in
  honour of C. F. D. Moule*, ed. E. Bammel. SBT 13
  (Naperville, IL: Allenson, 1970) 41–46.

Dodd, Charles Harold
  "The Prophecy of Caiaphas: John 11,47–53." In
  his *More New Testament Studies* (Grand Rapids: Wm.
  B. Eerdmans, 1968) 58–68.

Ensfelder, J. T.
  "Die Weissagung des Hohenpriesters Kaiphas—ein
  exegetischer Versuch über Joh XI, 50–51." *Theologische Jahrbücher* 1 (Tübingen, 1842) 792–800.

Glusman, Edward F.
  "The Cleansing of the Temple and the Anointing
  at Bethany: The Order of Events in Mark 11 and
  John 11–12." In *SBL 1979 Seminar Papers* 1,
  SBLASP 16 (Missoula: Scholars Press, 1979) 113–
  17.

Grimm, Werner
  "Das Opfer eines Menschen. Eine Auslegung von
  Joh 11,47–53." In *Israel hat dennoch Gott zum Trost.
  Festschrift für Schalom Ben-Chorin*, ed. G. Müller
  (Trier: Paulinus-Verlag, 1978) 61–82.

Grimm, Werner
  "Die Preisgabe eines Menschen zur Rettung des
  Volkes (Joh 11,50)." In *Josephus Studien. Unter-
  suchungen zu Josephus, dem antiken Judentum und dem
  Neuen Testament. Otto Michel zum 70. Geburtstag
  gewidmet*, ed. O. Betz, K. Haacker, and M. Hengel
  (Göttingen: Vandenhoeck & Ruprecht, 1974)
  133–46.

Hofius, Otfried
  "Die Sammlung der Heiden zur Herde Israels (Joh
  10:16; 11:51f)." *ZNW* 58 (1967) 289–91.

Pancaro, Severino
  "'People of God' in St. John's Gospel?" *NTS* 16
  (1969/1970) 114–29.

Schwank, Benedikt
  "Efraim in Joh 11,54." *Erbe und Auftrag* 51 (1975)
  346–51. Also in *L'Evangile de Jean. Sources, rédaction, théologie*, ed. M. de Jonge. BETL 44
  (Gembloux: Duculot; Louvain: University Press,
  1977) 377–83.

Schepens, Prosper
  "Pontifex anni illius (Ev. de saint Jean 11,49.51;
  18,14)." *RSR* 11 (1921) 372–74.

Widengren, Geo
    "The Gathering of the Dispersed." *SEÅ* 41/42
    (1976/1977) 224–34.
Windisch, Hans
    Der zweite Korintherbrief, ed. G. Strecker. KEK 6
    (Göttingen: Vandenhoeck & Ruprecht, ⁹1924,
    1970).

11

45 Many of the Jews therefore, who had come
with Mary and had seen what he did,
believed in him; 46/ but some of them
went to the Pharisees and told them
what Jesus had done. 47/ So the chief
priests and the Pharisees gathered the
council, and said, "What are we to do?
For this man performs many signs. 48/ If
we let him go on thus, every one will
believe in him, and Romans will come
and destroy both our holy place and our
nation." 49/ But one of them, Caiaphas,
who was high priest that year, said to
them, "You know nothing at all; 50/ you
do not understand that it is expedient for
you that one man should die for the
people, and not that the whole nation
should perish." 51/ He did not say this of
his own accord, but being high priest that
year he prophesied that Jesus should
die for the nation, 52/ and not for the
nation only, but to gather into one the
children of God who are scattered
abroad. 53/ So from that day on they
took counsel how to put him to death.
54/ Jesus therefore no longer went about
openly among the Jews, but went from
there to the country near the wilderness,
to a town called Ephraim; and there he
stayed with the disciples. 55/ Now the
Passover of the Jews was at hand, and
many went up from the country to
Jerusalem before the Passover, to purify
themselves. 56/ They were looking for
Jesus and saying to one another as they
stood in the temple, "What do you think?
That he will not come to the feast?" 57/
Now the chief priests and the Pharisees
had given orders that if any one knew
where he was, he should let them know,
so that they might arrest him.

■**45** The miracle produces both faith and disbelief: many
Jewish eyewitnesses from among the crowd of mourners
with Mary (Martha is not mentioned) become believers.
The text of the original source presumably went further
(see the Overview). One can now see how important
these witnesses are for our story: they reassure the
reader that this miracle really took place.

■**46** But some Jews go to the Pharisees, who function
here as the real enemies of Jesus. That contradicts the
Lukan representation of things, but probably corresponds to the relationships that gradually emerged after
Easter. That these witnesses remain disbelievers in the
face of the miracle shows how obdurate they are. The
relationship of these informers to the Pharisees is not
precisely depicted; the details are unimportant to the
narrator.

■**47** The chief priests and the Pharisees (who appear here
as the dominant officials) now call the Sanhedrin
together; however, the latter is at first without advice.
For it is not possible to deny the miracle. The expedient

of explaining the miracle as the work of Beelzebub does not enter the picture (cf. Mark 3:22). But the miracle is not taken as proof for Jesus' messiahship. The situation is simply made clear as a consequence of plain logic: in the opinion of the narrator, who puts himself in the place of the disbelieving Jews, superficial considerations are involved, namely, "This man"—a contemptuous designation, which avoids the name of Jesus—"performs many miracles" (σημεῖα). For the reader that confirms once again that the raising of Lazarus really happened, and yet explains, at the same time, the peculiar logic in accordance with which the success of Jesus makes it necessary finally to put him to death.

■ **48** Verse 48 develops the point just made: if Jesus is permitted to continue to work as he does, eventually everybody will believe in him (i.e., as the messiah), and a political movement will arise that will venerate Jesus as the king of Israel. The consequence will be that the Romans will intervene, occupy the sacred "place" (i.e., the temple), and deport the ruling class. The idea that is often cited in the interpretation of this verse, that one who bestows life must die precisely because he bestows life, does not occur in the text: the resurrection of Lazarus is assessed only as a great miracle, which does not fail to leave its imprint on the masses, especially since other miracles will follow. The leaders of the Jewish people, as depicted by the narrator, think entirely in mundane and political terms. The religious significance of the miracle does not occur to them. That in Judaism the miracles could not be played off against the law—at least not in rabbinic Judaism—plays no role here.

■ **49** In this difficult situation, Caiaphas (whose tenure ran from 18–36 CE) makes the decision as "the high priest of that year." Whether that is meant to say that he was the high priest in office at that time (without any inference regarding the duration of his tenure), or whether the narrator meant to say that the high priests changed each year, is not made clear.[1] Bultmann elects the second: the genitive, "of that year," is "hardly a temporal genitive with the meaning 'in, during,'"[2] but presupposes "that the person of the High Priest changed annually, as was the case with pagan high-priestly officials in Syria and Asia Minor."[3] Since the way in which the narrator

depicts the Jews as official persons is inappropriate, there is much to be said for the view that the expression occurring in verse 49 and in 18:13 is to be understood in Bultmann's sense. Why the narrator represents Caiaphas to the reader as holding office at that time is not made clear until verse 51.

■ **50** Caiaphas reproaches his colleagues on the Sanhedrin for a lack of insight: they do not consider that it is better for one man to die for the people than for the whole nation to perish. That is a cold calculation, which simply assumes that the individual is of less value than the people. If the word λαός ("people") had occurred in place of ἔθνος ("nation"), a religious basis could have been discovered in this statement: it is extremely important that the chosen people as such be preserved, including their (relative) independence under a theocratic regime. But the narrator does not have Caiaphas say that. What concerns the high priest, and the council as a whole, is his and their own power.

■ **51** The narrator now discloses something like a religious motive for Caiaphas' statement, but a very different one, to be sure, than suggested in verse 50. As the high priest for that year, Caiaphas, without being aware of it, has expressed the divine plan that stands behind the death of Jesus. It would really be better for Jesus to die for the people, than for all to die. Here the narrator hints at the salvific significance of the death of Jesus; but he only hints at it. Thus, it does not become entirely clear whether he is thinking of an atoning death on the part of Jesus or some other form of substitution.

■ **52** But the death of Jesus does not simply concern the Jewish people, but all of the children of God who are scattered over the whole earth; they are to be gathered together into a new, great unity. The word "church" is not used. The death of Jesus therefore has universal meaning in the sense that it benefits all Christians.

■ **53** From this day on it is a foregone conclusion that they

---

1   High priests were, in fact, chosen for life, but they were often deposed by the Romans after a short tenure.

2   BDF §186(2).

3   Bultmann, *John*, 410f. n.10 [314 n.2]. Cf. Bauer, *Das Johannesevangelium*, 156.

will put Jesus to death.[4] Perhaps two thoughts intersect here: (1) from this day forward, they scheme about how they can do away with Jesus, and (2) they take the decision on this day to kill him.

■ **54–57** Jesus no longer stays openly among the Jews, that means, within Judea (thanks to his miraculous knowledge, the plot is known to him), but departs for the country near the wilderness, to a "city" called Ephraim, where he tarries with his disciples. The tension in the story mounts: the threat to his life has come into the open. How will Jesus now conduct himself? Will he remain in his hiding place where he is secure? Or will he return to Jerusalem again and to the Jews?

Interpreters have often puzzled over "the city of Ephraim." I have reviewed Guilding's attempt to explain the mention of such a city; the reader is referred to that review.[5] Josephus mentions a "town" called Ephraim, close to Bethel,[6] which Billerbeck wants to identify with grain-rich Chapharaim, which is called Ephraim in the Mishnah.[7] On the other hand, Soggin has in mind a village lying not far from Baal Hazor (2 Sam 13:23), which is perhaps the same place as Aphairema mentioned in 1 Macc 11:34.[8] Dalman advises that it is "the village that today is called *eṭ-Ṭaiybeh,* about 7 kilometers northeast of Bethel."[9] The name undergoes further change in the tradition: D speaks of a χώρα Σαμφουριν, which is Sepphoris; Chrysostom offers Ἐφρατά.[10] Hirsch believes that a place name following "country" became corrupted and can no longer be reconstructed.[11]

Overview

The history of the interpretation of this passage indicates how diverse are the points of view from which this text has been treated. We must limit ourselves here, of course, to a small sample.

Wellhausen as usual is in quest of his beloved territory, that is, of the underlying source.[12] Alien to this source were the many miracles, as well as the high priest Caiaphas and the idea of the sacrifice in verses 50–52—

of this Wellhausen is certain. In fact, the flights of Jesus to Perea (10:40) and to Ephraim (11:54) may be variants of the same flight. From that it follows that the determination of the Sanhedrin is an insertion "to make possible the change in destinations to which Jesus flees. First Jesus goes to Perea. After the officials proceed against him, he no longer feels that he is safe there and goes to a more remote place on the edge of the wilderness." Last of all, the Lazarus story may be inserted between the two variants.

Wellhausen proceeds on the basis of his hypothesis of an underlying source, which stood very close to the historical course of events, and from that point works out a history of the tradition that hangs on the fine thread of that hypothesis.

Schwartz, the master at uncovering "aporias in the Fourth Gospel," interprets differently.[13] To verse 54 he objects: "The words of Thomas in 11:16 were sheer braggadocio and the Sanhedrin was very foolish, for the latter permitted the dangerous man to escape. . . ." Basically, Schwartz employs the same method as his friend Wellhausen: he likewise presupposes an original version, except that he is skeptical about the possibility of recovering it. In his eagerness to find a serious discrepancy between 11:16 and 11:54, he overlooks the fact that the narrator views the situation differently: it is only with the raising of Lazarus that the threat of death becomes so great for Jesus that he flees to the edge of the desert. The role that that composition of the narrator plays in the ways matters are depicted never comes into view for him as such.

On the other hand, Bultmann takes verses 45–54 "as a Johannine composition that has no source behind it."[14] How this creation of the Evangelist is related to verse 11, which he is supposed to have edited,[15] is not discussed.

Strathmann sees himself as "driven to the conclusion that this chapter also does not literally represent a historical event, but is a freely composed symbolic narrative making use of synoptic, particularly Lukan,

4 On βουλεύμαι ("take counsel"), see BDF §392(1a).
5 Guilding, *The Fourth Gospel and Jewish Worship,* 143–53. My review is in *TLZ* 86 (1961) 670–72.
6 *BJ* 4.9.9 (§551).
7 Billerbeck, 2: 546.
8 *Biblisch-theologisches Handwörterbuch zur Lutherbibel und zu neueren Übersetzungen* (Göttingen, 1954, ⁵1964) 1: 421.
9 *Sacred Sites and Ways,* 217f., 268.
10 t. VIII 390c.
11 *Studien,* 25.
12 *Das Evangelium Johannis,* 54.
13 "Aporien," 3: 173.
14 *John,* 409f. n. 8 [313 n. 2]; Bultmann agrees with J. Finegan, *Die Überlieferung der Leidens- und Auferstehungsgeschichte Jesu,* BZNW 15 (Giessen: A.

elements; with the help of a unique 'sign,' this narrative is intended to emphasize once more the truth of the promise made to Martha (vv. 25, 26: the exclusive salvific significance of Jesus expressed in the briefest possible way) and to show, at the same time, that he died as a victim precisely of his mission and his significance." This chapter "discloses its force only when we abandon the attempt to arrive at an apologetic historical understanding. We ought to quit this antique apologetic all the more readily since it does not yield anything really convincing, but at most produces a pacifier."[16] But this notion of Strathmann's that the disciple John is supposed to have created a deeply significant symbolic narrative in order to express the meaning of his master is without convincing cogency, but is itself a final apologetic historical effort, which is only capable of mollification, if that.

Brown also offers such an apologetic when he infers from 18:13 that the deposed high priest Annas still exercised influence and this is a sign of intimate knowledge. In view of such intimate knowledge, the information about Caiaphas as the high priest of that year could not, in turn, betray misinformation about Jewish institutions.[17] Brown takes *Samphourin* (Σαμφουριν) read by D in verse 54 as a corruption of *šēm 'efrayîm* ("whose name is Ephraim").[18] He finds the report of the flight to Ephraim a historical reminiscence,[19] although he sees the story as turning entirely on the saying in verse 50, "It is more to your advantage to have one man die [for the people] than to have the whole nation destroyed";[20] in this he is following Dodd.[21]

This is the judgment of Hirsch: "Insofar as the author is not here freely composing but is reworking tradition, we have to do with a late tradition of legendary character. It is by no means beyond his capabilities freely to invent the procedure of the Sanhedrin in this passage. As always, he simply lets the persons who act express the motives that seem to him to be given and does not hit entirely on the right ones in so doing."[22] However, "it corresponds well" to the situation in Palestine at that

time "if the Sanhedrin shows itself governed by concern that a messianic movement under Jesus could lead to the destruction of the temple and the end of its own governance of the Jewish people."[23] In this there may be a double irony: (1) those who do not believe misunderstand Jesus as a political messiah. (2) Yet what the Sanhedrin fears nevertheless occurs in the year 70 CE. The hierarchy intends to act politically. But because they are only interested in preserving the ecclesiastical bureaucracy and sphere of power and because they are driven by anxiety aimed at avoiding its loss, in the end they bring about what they want to avoid. The words of Caiaphas express a cold lack of faith, which allows the means to justify the aim: the preservation of the Jewish religious community justifies judicial execution. Yet, at the same time, the narrator expresses in these words the profound mystery of Christian redemption: Jesus dies for mankind. "Caiaphas is turned into a prophet, without being aware of it."[24] Whoever closes himself up to God, will nevertheless be used by God as an instrument.[25] "Although we cannot comprehend it, God alone" is "nevertheless effective truth and love. . . ."[26]

The attempt to arrange the exegetes indicated in relation to their aims results in three groups. Some investigators—for example, Wellhausen and Schwartz—attempt above all to reconstruct the development of the present text. Others endeavor to reconcile the events that actually lie behind the text with the text itself—one can, in this instance, for example, point to the names of Guilding and Brown. Others, finally, concern themselves with the elaboration of the theological content of the text. The work of Bultmann, Strathmann, and Hirsch shows that whoever makes this third purpose his goal appears, almost of necessity, to be led to the view that the text is to a great extent a pure composition of the author.

At this point, objections against this third trend arise: the passage contains elements that suggest the use of tradition, and elements that concern both form and content. Of the first sort is the appearance of the word

Töpelmann, 1934) 40f.
15 Bultmann, *John*, 398 n. 3 [303 n. 6].
16 *Das Evangelium nach Johannes*, 174.
17 Brown, *John*, 1: 440.
18 *John*, 1: 441.
19 *John*, 1: 444.
20 *John*, 1: 442.
21 "The Prophecy of Caiaphas (John xi 47–53),"

Neotestamentica et Patristica. Eine Freundesgabe, Herrn Professor Dr. Oscar Cullmann zu seinem 60. Geburtstag überreicht, NovTSup 6 (Leiden: Brill, 1962) 134–43.
22 *Das vierte Evangelium*, 294.
23 *Das vierte Evangelium*, 296.
24 *Das vierte Evangelium*, 297.
25 *Das vierte Evangelium*, 298.
26 *Das vierte Evangelium*, 299.

οὖν ("therefore") that is characteristic of the narrative style in 11:1, 3, 14, 16, 17, 20, 21, 31, 33, 36, 38, 45, 47, 54, which is continued in 11:56 and 12:1, 2, 3, 7, 9. In the segment, verses 23–27, that is especially assigned to the Evangelist, this οὖν does not appear. That it is not to be expected in the drama of verses 41–44 might be taken as obvious, without thereby having to ascribe these verses to the Evangelist. With respect to content, it is foreign to the Evangelist to lay claim to many miracles as in verses 45 and 47f., miracles that are intended to awaken faith (although not in every case just yet); also foreign to him are the further thought that the high priest is turned as such into a prophet without his knowing it, and the mention of a flight of Jesus to the town of Ephraim, which cannot be a pure invention of the Evangelist.

But the real problem of chapter 11 has not come into view with all that. It lies in its significance for the composition of the Gospel of John. The Gospel of John is fundamentally distinguished from the Synoptics by virtue of the beginning of the passion narrative. In the case of the Synoptics, the conflict stories and the eschatological discourse of Jesus makes it evident that an unheard of tension dominates the days in Jerusalem prior to the Passover, to say nothing of the three predictions of the passion by Jesus. But why the high priests and elders actually take Jesus prisoner is a question that remains unanswered—on the human plane, to be distinguished from the mystery of God's will. It is only Jesus' confession before the Sanhedrin, which the latter feels to be blasphemy worthy of death, that is taken to be sufficient basis for the death verdict; this verdict must of course be confirmed and carried out by the Romans. But this basis is provided only after the fact of the imprisonment, so to speak, and not before. In a certain sense, there is thus a gap in the synoptic account, although the pious reader did not feel it. Matters are different in the Gospel of John.

In order to follow through the train of thought in this passage, which is not entirely simple, one must of course very carefully distinguish between the Gospel of John and its "source." Up to this point we have been able to establish that a sharp difference exists between the material used by the Evangelist—which we may represent as "gospel of miracles" lying in front of him—and his reworking of these materials. The material being used constantly emphasizes the number and magnitude of Jesus' miracles as evidence of his rank and power. The fourth Evangelist, on the other hand, sees the miracles merely as pointers to the "wholly other," namely, to the power that Jesus has to disclose the true relationship of his own to God.

We may first examine the "material" of the alleged source, to which the Lazarus story belongs, in all probability. It describes the greatest of Jesus' miracles. Does it provide a rational bridge from there to the passion narrative proper, which begins with the arrest and ends with the cross? At first the miracle of Lazarus does not appear to provide the occasion for the arrest and execution of the miracle worker. But John 11:45–54 causes us to see how the narrator (therefore the author of the source) explains the connection between the miracle and the trial of Jesus. It is not the miracle of Lazarus as such that causes the Sanhedrin to resolve to put him to death. Rather, 11:47f. shows, first of all, that the resurrection of Lazarus is viewed as an example of the many wonders done by Jesus, and in the second place, that the Sanhedrin expected that Jesus would continue to perform such miracles. That corresponds well to the basic disposition of the source as we have repeatedly perceived it. But from all these miracles— those that have taken place and those that are to be expected—there now follows a further consequence for the Sanhedrin, according to the narrator, that determines everything to come: if one permits Jesus to continue to perform such miracles, then all Jews will believe in him. That of course does not conform to the fact that the Sanhedrin has not been influenced by the resurrection of Lazarus, nor to the fact that not all eyewitnesses became believers. Some of these eyewitnesses indeed go straight to the Pharisees and denounce Jesus (11:45). But we will not pursue these side issues further, issues that evidently did not present difficulties to the narrator. Rather, on the basis of the Sanhedrin's fear that all Jews will believe in Jesus, he draws the further conclusion that the Romans will intervene and take the temple away from the reigning hierarchy and deprive them of their authority over the people. But why will the Romans see themselves as prompted to take such measures if all Jews were to come to faith in Jesus? An unexpressed thought is presupposed here: this faith of the people in Jesus will be faith in Jesus as the messiah, as the "king of Israel" (a formula that not only plays a significant role in the passion narrative in the Gospel of John, but also shows up in the Synoptics: Mark 15:9ff., Matt 27:11, Luke 23:2f.), as a national messiah. That has an especially clear parallel in Luke 23:2f.

At this point we are faced with a further question. We have repeatedly observed up to this point that the narrator is looking at the situation in this world and therefore represents it as such. How did he come to this representation? There is a clue to the answer in John 6:14f. At that point Jesus recognizes that the crowd wants to come and make him king on the basis of the miraculous feeding, and he withdraws by fleeing to the mountain. That is to say, there takes place in connection with the feeding precisely what the Sanhedrin fears: the crowd will make the one who can miraculously multiply the loaves into a king (i.e., messiah). A note is thus struck; introduced at this early time is a theme that is not so quickly dropped in chapter 11 as it is in chapter 6, but comes to its full resonance. The verses in John 6:14f. are therefore considerably more important than they appear to the reader of chapter 6.

In accounting for the plot against Jesus, the narrator had nevertheless to overcome a hindrance that we have not yet fully considered. The anxiety of the Sanhedrin that Jesus' successful (miraculous) activity would lead to a conflict with Rome, with the consequence that Jesus had therefore to be done away with in advance, seems not to have been satisfactory for the narrator as an effective "moralistic" basis for the elimination of Jesus. As a result, in the speech of Caiaphas, he has strengthened the moral motive by introducing a widespread saying, which he naturally does not cite as such. In the OT there are only forerunners of it: in 2 Sam 20:20–22 and Jonah 1:12–15 the demand is made that someone be handed over against whom the wrath of God or the superior enemy can be directed. Bultmann cites Josephus[27] in this context, but the intended significance is unclear.[28] Schlatter is also not helpful.[29] On the other hand, Billerbeck provides real parallels from *Rab. Gen.* 94 (60a): "It is better that this man should die, than that everyone be punished on his account." The passage from *Midr. Sam.* 32 §3 (71a): "Is it not better for you to

sacrifice a thousand men, than that your city be destroyed?" does not suit as well. Similarly, *Midr. Qoh.* 9.18 (46a), with comparable meaning. Windisch has adduced examples from Greek and Latin literature.[30] That something is here being drawn from another context is indicated by a linguistic feature: the word ἔθνος is used in the Gospel of John for "the people" only in this passage; in John 18:14, which plays on the saying of Caiaphas, the word for "people" is λαός.

There is, further, a certain bit of tension that remains. Caiaphas speaks of the Jewish people. But the prophecy presumably contained in his words does not refer to Jews but to Christians. This difference is obscured in that the following reference is to "God's children," an expression that otherwise only appears in verse 1:12 in the Gospel of John, and therefore in a passage that does not derive from the Evangelist, in my opinion. But apart from that, the alleged prophecy is questionable, as verse 52 shows. It concerns not only the Christianity that presently exists, but also the Christianity that is to come.

The narrator, consequently, has not only illustrated Jesus' power by means of a very special case in the Lazarus story, but has also employed this event as the point of departure for demonstrating the Sanhedrin's apparent basis for making Jesus silent once and for all. The story of Lazarus thereby becomes, for the narrator, the key in a certain sense to the puzzle of the passion narrative. The feature often emphasized in edifying treatments of this passage, namely, that the prince of life has to die because he gives life, has no basis in the text.

So much for the composition of the underlying source and its understanding of the story of Jesus, especially the passion narrative. We must now answer the second question: how did matters appear to the Evangelist? That is not so difficult. For, it is widely conceded that the Evangelist unmistakably corrects his source in verses 23–27. The miracle of Lazarus serves the purpose for him of demonstrating that Jesus is the "resurrection and the life." However, "resurrection and life" are not his inherent, permanent qualities, but he is able to share them with others, and not just at the end of time, but in the here and now. What is meant by that is that Jesus can make possible the right relationship between God and

---

27 *BJ* 2.103f.
28 *John*, 411 n. 1 [314 n. 3].
29 *Der Evangelist Johannes*, 259.

30 *Der zweite Korintherbrief*, ed. G. Strecker, KEK 6 (Göttingen: Vandenhoeck & Ruprecht, 1970) 185f.

man, to the extent that "the Father" has given him "these persons." Wellhausen's sarcasm, reported above, that the resurrection of Lazarus is superfluous, if verse 25 is valid, shows only that he had not understood the "sign-character" that the story of Lazarus has for the Evangelist. The Evangelist could fully countenance the Lazarus story in this passage: it contains the greatest and the final sign that Jesus gives the world. At the same time, however, verses 45–54 show that the high priests and Pharisees did not recognize the sign: as "friend" (φίλος) of Jesus, Lazarus is the prototype of the chosen disciple that Jesus calls to life. That the Jews misunderstand the kingship of Jesus corresponds entirely to the conviction of the Evangelist. How he conceives Jesus' remark on his kingship is indicated to the reader in detail in the scene with Pilate in 18:33–40; in 18:37 he gives his own interpretation of the kingship of Jesus. The Jews and Caiaphas do not really act out of concern for the chosen people, but out of concern for their own power: that also was a given for the Evangelist. Finally, Jesus' evasion of the danger that threatened by fleeing to an outlying place like Ephraim was completely acceptable to the Evangelist from the point of view of composition. This was because it makes clear to the reader that Jesus could save himself at any time he wished, and that he therefore went to his death of his own free will.

In our search for the theological meaning of the underlying source and of the work of the Evangelist, we must not lose sight of the historical problem that is indeed suggested by the NT itself but not really treated: does the Jesus movement manifest messianic features and was Jesus crucified for that reason? In his book, Eisler attempts to prove that Jesus in fact appeared as a messianic revolutionary, took possession of the temple, and was defeated and executed by Pilate.[31] Drawing above all on Eisler (and Winter),[32] Carmichael repeated this interpretation.[33] There are only scanty clues in the Gospels that Jesus kindled a messianic movement: among the disciples of Jesus, according to Luke 6:15 and Acts

1:13, there was a Simon the Zealot (ὁ Ζηλωτής), who was probably a former member of the nationalistic, religious party of extremists. Presumably, the same person is referred to in Matt 10:4 and Mark 3:18 with the designation Simon the Cananaean (ὁ Καναναῖος); in support of this view, one must assume that the Armaic word is not to be translated as "Cananaean," but is derived from קנא ("Zealot"). Further, one could point to the saying of Jesus: "I have not come to bring peace, but a sword" (Matt 10:34; Luke 12:51) and the puzzling saying about the two swords (Luke 22:36ff.); the account of the blow with a sword at the arrest of Jesus (Mark 14:47; Matt 26:51; Luke 22:50; John 18:10); Jesus' lament over Jerusalem (Luke 23:27–31); his prediction of the destruction of the temple (Mark 13:2; Matt 24:2; Luke 21:6); the alleged saying of Jesus about the temple during his trial (Mark 14:58; Matt 26:61; Acts 6:14; John 2:19, 21); and, finally, the often repeated designation of Jesus as the "king of the Jews" during his trial in all the Gospels. It has often been said that all this betrays the fact that Jesus was executed on account of a messianic-political movement. The community, however, has blunted these incriminating assertions beyond recognition. But the facts may not be so simply explained. Fact one: Jesus takes a direct, violent action that contradicts the most important and universal of his precepts ("love your enemy," and the like). Fact two: that Jesus brings a sword means, in the context, that the unity of the family is destroyed when its members become his adherents— that makes sense only in the period after Easter. The same thing can be said of the saying to buy a sword: the time of the persecution is now. With this Luke has connected the saying about the two swords, which explains how the resistance to the arrest came to pass. The prediction about the destruction of the temple is probably a post-Easter prophecy, which grows into the lament over Jerusalem and the Christian conviction that the destruction of Jerusalem was punishment for the death of Jesus. Prior to 70 CE, it was expected that the

31 Eisler, Ἰησοῦς βασιλεὺς οὐ βασιλεύσας. Die messianische Unabhängigkeitsbewegung vom Auftreten Johannes des Täufers bis zum Untergang Jakobs des Gerechten, nach der neuerschlossenen Eroberung von Jerusalem des Flavius Josephus und den christlichen Quellen, 2 vols. (Heidelberg: Carl Winter, 1929–1930).

32 Winter, On the Trial of Jesus.

33 Carmichael, The Death of Jesus (New York: Macmillan, 1963).

temple would become even greater in the time of the messiah. After 70 CE, the Jews hoped that the temple would be restored to its majesty in the days of the messiah. In that connection, it was usually God who was thought of as the builder. But in the Sibylline Oracles it is the messiah who will rebuild the temple.[34] *Rab. Lev.* 9 (111a), *Rab. Num.* 13 (168b), and *Midr.Cant.* 4.16 (117b)

teach the same thing.[35] The accustion articulated in Luke 23:27–31 that the death of Jesus would bring the destruction of Jerusalem, was answered with a counter-charge on the part of the Jews, that Jesus asserted that he would destroy the temple and in three days raise it up, and this did not occur. Christians sought in various ways to take the sting out of this saying.[36]

---

34   *Orac. Sib.* 5.420ff.
35   Billerbeck, 1: 1003–5.
36   Also cf. the Jewish traditon in Billerbeck, 1: 1027.

28.   The Anointing at Bethany

Bibliography

Bevan, T. W.
  "The Four Anointings." *ExpTim* 39 (1927/1928)
  137–39.

Bruns, J. Edgar
  "A Note on Jn 12,3." *CBQ* 28 (1966) 219–22.

Derrett, John Duncan Martin
  "The Anointings at Bethany." *SE* 2 = TU 87
  (Berlin: Akademie-Verlag, 1964) 174–82.

Fortna, Robert T.
  *The Gospel of Signs. A Reconstruction of the Narrative
  Source Underlying the Fourth Gospel,* NovTSup 11
  (New York and London: Cambridge University
  Press, 1970) 149–52.

Foston, Hubert M.
  "Two Johannine Parentheses." *ExpTim* 32 (1920/
  1921) 520–23.

Glusman, Edward F.
  "The Cleansing of the Temple and the Anointing
  at Bethany: The Order of Events in Mark 11 and
  John 11–12." In *SBL 1979 Seminar Papers* 1,
  SBLASP 16 (Missoula: Scholars Press, 1979) 113–
  18.

Haenchen, Ernst
  *Der Weg Jesu. Eine Erklärung des Markus-Evange-
  liums und der kanonischen Parallelen,* Sammlung
  Töpelmann, 2, 6 (Berlin: Walter de Gruyter,
  1966, ²1968), esp. 462–72.

Holst, Robert Arthur
  "The Relation of John 12 to the So-called
  Johannine Book of Glory." Dissertation, Princeton
  Theological Seminary, 1974.

Jeremias, Joachim
  "Mc 14,9." *ZNW* 44 (1952/1953) 103–7.

Kittlaus, Lloyd R.
  "Evidence from Jn 12 that the Author of John
  knew the Gospel of Mark." In *SBL 1979 Seminar
  Papers* 1, SBLASP 16 (Missoula: Scholars Press,
  1979) 119–22.

Kleist, James A.
  "A Note on the Greek Text of St. John 12,7."
  Classic Journal 21 (1925) 46–48.

Kolenkow, Anitra Bingham
  "The Changing Patterns: Conflicts and the Necessity of Death: John 2 and 12 and Markan Parallels." In *SBL 1979 Seminar Papers* 1, SBLASP 16
  (Missoula: Scholars Press, 1979) 123–25.

Kühne, W.
  "Eine kritische Studie zu Joh 12,7." *TSK* 98/99
  (1926) 476–77.

Legault, André
  "An Application of the Form-Critique Method to
  the Anointings in Galilee (Lk. 7,36–50) and
  Bethany (Mt. 26,6–13; Mk. 14,3–9; Jn 12,1–8)."
  CBQ 16 (1954) 131–45.

Lemonnyer, Antoine
"L'onction de Béthanie (Jean 12,1–8)." *RSR* 18 (1928) 105–17.

Munro, Winsome
"The Anointing in Mark 14,3–9 and John 12,1–8." In *SBL 1979 Seminar Papers* 1, SBLASP 16 (Missoula: Scholars Press, 1979) 127–30.

Prete, Benedetto
"'I poveri' nel racconto giovanneo dell'unzione di Betania (Gv 12,1–8)." *Atti della settimana biblica* 24 (1978) 429–44.

Sanders, Joseph N.
"Those Whom Jesus Loved: St. John 11,5." *NTS* 1 (1954/1955) 29–76.

Schnackenburg, Rudolf
"Der johanneische Bericht von der Salbung in Bethanien (Joh 12,1–8)." *MTZ* (1950) 48–52.

Sybel, Ludwig von
"Die Salbungen." *ZNW* 23 (1924) 184–93.

Weise, Manfred
"Passionswoche und Epiphaniewoche im Johannes-Evangelium. Ihre Bedeutung für Komposition und Konzeption des vierten Evangeliums." *KD* 12 (1966) 48–62, esp. 51–52.

12

1 Six days before the Passover, Jesus came to Bethany, where Lazarus was, whom Jesus had raised from the dead. 2/ There they made him a supper; Martha served, but Lazarus was one of those at table with him. 3/ Mary took a pound of costly ointment of pure nard and anointed the feet of Jesus and wiped his feet with her hair; and the house was filled with the fragrance of the ointment. 4/ But Judas Iscariot, one of his disciples (he who was to betray him), said, 5/ "Why was this ointment not sold for three hundred denarii and given to the poor?" 6/ This he said, not that he cared for the poor but because he was a thief, and as he had the money box he used to take what was put into it. 7/ Jesus said, "Let her alone, let her keep it for the day of my burial. 8/ The poor you always have with you, but you do not always have me."

Introduction

This scene belongs to that material in the Gospel of John that has parallels in the Synoptics: Mark 14:3–9//Matt 26:6–13//Luke 7:36–50. While the event at Bethany takes place in Mark shortly before the entrance into Jerusalem, Luke reports it as taking place during Jesus' ministry in Galilee. Brown goes into detail regarding the relationships of the various reports.[1] Dodd conjectures that one and the same event lies behind the three accounts.[2] Brown decides in favor of the solution of Benoit reported by Legault.[3] According to Benoit, one must distinguish two different events: one in Galilee, and one in Bethany. In Galilee, the action concerns a woman of questionable reputation; one can imagine such a woman undoing her hair in public. On the other hand, in Bethany Mary is expressing her love for Jesus by offering him an expensive gift. But the second incident has been influenced by the first. In fact, a very complicated set of relationships is involved among various facets of the tradition. Contacts with the Synoptics and differences

---

1   *John*, 1: 449–54.
2   *Tradition*, 162–73.
3   A. Legault, "An Application of the Form-Critique Method to the Anointings in Galilee (Lk. 7, 36–50) and Bethany (Mt. 26, 6–13; Mk. 14, 3–9; Jn 12, 1–8)," *CBQ* 16 (1954) 131–45.

from them vary.[4]

■ **1** According to 12:1, Jesus comes to Bethany six days before the Passover, after his stay in the "town called Ephraim" (11:54). This bit of information plays no role, however, in the story that follows; one might conjecture, consequently, that it stood in the underlying source of the Gospel of John. Nothing here points to a "sacred passion week." "The next day" (12:12) is followed by "Now before the feast of the Passover" (13:1), and the arrest (18:1ff.) follows the farewell discoures. Lazarus is mentioned as being present in Bethany and at the meal, but not as master of the house and host. The addition, "whom Jesus had raised from the dead," sounds strange inasmuch as the resurrection had just been related in chapter 11. However, the repetition of the same phrase in 12:9 leads to the supposition that this feature was already firmly connected with the mention of Lazarus' name.

■ **2** Martha looks after the serving, as in Luke 10:40. That is understandable in the Lukan passage since it belongs to the essence of a story about an invitation. But here where a meal is being arranged for Jesus, the presence of this woman is surprising to the Jewish-Christian reader (as it is for the presence of Mary); it becomes understandable only in the light of the tendency of the Gentile-Christian tradition to assemble as many "biblical persons" as possible. In this way, the tradition apparently becomes more graphic.

■ **3** This feature dominates the further depiction. Mary is introduced following Martha; in the course of the tradition, Mary leads up to the Johannine source (the tradition leads from "a woman" in Mark 14:3, to a woman "who was a sinner" in Luke 7:37ff., and thence to Mary Magdalene, "from whom seven demons had gone out" in Luke 8:2). She takes a "Roman" liter (327 grams) of costly, pure nard and anoints Jesus (there is no mention of her breaking an alabaster jar [Mark 14:3]). In this scene only a few items are indicated; where Mary suddenly came up with this expensive ointment is not explored by the narrator: the central point is that she is now able to carry out such an anointing. The text of the source was apparently no longer entirely coherent. When Mary anoints the feet and not the head of Jesus and then wipes the ointment with her hair into the bargain, that does not square with custom—at most a prostitute ran around with her hair loose, and Mary is not that, although she loved Jesus with abandon. That the scent of the nard fills the entire house shows how costly it is.

Hirsch understands the anointing as thanks for the resurrection of Lazarus: "Thanksgiving hovers like an unexpressed, silent prayer in the space around Jesus. . . . The gesture of Mary nevertheless expresses some reserve in the limitless phantasy of her heart, because she is depicted from the beginning as filled with silent adoration."[5] But is that not a romantic overinterpretation that is foreign to the fourth Evangelist, as will immediately be demonstrated?

■ **4** The unexpected tribute (and seemingly effusive, as it appears to us, in contrast to the Luke's version in chap. 7) by the faithful Mary stands in sharp contrast to the reproach leveled at her by Judas. He represents the world, which thinks only of the monetary value of things, although it masquerades as piety: one ought to think of the poor. This is what the disciple who is shortly to betray Jesus says. The character attributed to him in the older tradition is thereby disclosed, just as it becomes evident in verses 5f.

■ **5** "One could have sold this costly ointment"—to whom does it belong, really? It doesn't matter—"for three hundred denarii and given the money to the poor!" That sounds very pious and full of Christian concern for the poor.

■ **6** The reader is expressly informed that Judas does not really care about the poor, but that he is thinking of the 300 denarii that one could have received for this expensive ointment.[6] The deceitful keeper of the cash box would now not come into this sum.

Why did Judas betray the Lord? This is a question that continually plagued the first Christians. The answer is supposed to have been provided by Zech 11:12. The sum mentioned there is admittedly exaggerated in John— increased tenfold. In this passage the tradition is not perturbed that Jesus appointed the least suitable man, a thief, to guard the cash box. The alleged data derived from Zechariah was so suggestive of an apologetic-

---

4   See the Overview.

5   *Das vierte Evangelium*, 303.

6   Three hundred denarii represents what a laborer would earn for three hundred days of work.

psychological interpretation of the passage that further reflection was unnecessary.

■ **7** Jesus' answer begins with the old traditional command: "Let her alone!" This instruction is based on a new interpretation of Mary's act of love: she has anticipated the anointing of his body at death. The wording of the text, in any case, is difficult: "The purpose was that she might keep it"? According to Schlatter, the words are intended to say: "so that she might use what remains in the jar for my corpse."[7] Bultmann interprets similarly: "She must keep it for the day of my burial."[8] Attempts to improve the text are found in $\mathfrak{R}$ *pm*, which omit the ἵνα ("in order that") and replace τηρήσῃ ("she might keep") with τετήρηκεν ("she has kept"). Schmiedel has proposed a conjecture: τηρήσῃ is to be replaced with ποιήσῃ following Matt 26:12: "In pouring this ointment on my body, she has taken care of my burial."[9] However the oldest text may have looked, Mary's act presumably was understood as the anticipation of Jesus' burial and justified as such.

Hirsch interprets: "The thanks to the one who returned Lazarus to life could only be the anointing of the body for death. . . . Among all the persons Jesus meets in the Fourth Gospel," Mary may have come "closest to the mystery of the hour."[10]

■ **8** The other part of Jesus' response now follows: "The poor you have with you always, but you do not always have me." This saying is fulfilled by the certainty of Jesus' death. It was therefore very dear to the community; yet it shows that Jesus consciously went to meet his death and thereby affirmed it. In this connection, one forgets or ignores the other thing that goes together with this: one could have social intercourse with Jesus as another human "thou" only as long as he tarries on earth. Mary's deed now makes use of the last possibilty of human proximity and fellowship.

Joachim Jeremias thinks the story of the anointing is comprehensible only on the basis of the Palestinian distinction between almsgiving and acts of charity.[11] A gift of money to the poor would be almsgiving; the burial of the dead would be a special act of charity, considered higher and more valuable. The explanation that refers to the report in Mark has this against it: the woman is not aware that she is anointing a body for burial. Yet the contrast between almsgiving and acts of charity (which can also be extended to the dead) is not central to the story; rather, the contrast beteen Jesus and the poor is central. In the Johannine version, the story turns on the fact that the poor are always present, but Jesus will soon be present no longer. One ought not to get out of the difficulty by claiming that Jesus should have justified the woman's act on the basis of the rabbinic distinction between almsgiving and acts of charity, the latter of which has a higher value. By doing so—by making Jesus into a rabbi—one buys "Palestinian authenticity" at too high a price.

Overview

The word "tradition" readily awakens the impression that what is involved, especially in the case of biblical tradition, is something fixed, unalterable, a "sacred text," passed from mouth to mouth and from original to copy intact. Papias has such a conception of tradition.[12] Our segment can disabuse us of this erroneous conception. A tradition is rather something living and changing, the development of which can be traced in auspicious cases. That is especially evident in our story. In Mark 14:3–9, Matt 26:6–13, and John 12:1–8, we do indeed have a narrative of the anointing of Jesus in Bethany before his passion. But Luke possesses a story of an anointing of Jesus that occurs at some earlier date, in an unnamed place, and under other circumstances; it has only to be taken into consideration because, in spite of all the differences from Mark and Matthew, it has a series of points of contact with the Johannine version.

The earliest stage of this story that is preserved appears to lie before us in Mark 14. Here the place of the action is designated as Bethany, in the environs of

7   *Der Evangelist Johannes,* 64.
8   *John,* 416 n. 2 [318 n. 4].
9   Paul W. Schmiedel, *The Johannine Writings,* tr. Maurice A. Canney (London: A. & C. Black, 1908) 127 and Nestle-Aland[26] *ad loc.*
10 *Das vierte Evangelium,* 304.
11 "Mc 14,9," *ZNW* 44 (1952/1953) 103–7.
12 See Introduction, §1.6.

Jerusalem, and more exactly, in the "house of Simon the leper." This datum of course admits of various interpretations. This house could once have belonged to Simon, who was a leper, and who was therefore forced to leave his house (lepers could not live in villages in Israel). But, furthermore, it was called the house of Simon, with only the further qualification, "the leper." In that case, the narrator would have had a good knowledge of the place. It has also been conjectured that the house was the property of a leper whom Jesus had cured of his disease. The name was nevertheless retained in an unaltered form (cf. Mark 15:15a). During the transmission of NT stories the imagination is very active and could lead to the further supposition that Simon gave this feast for Jesus out of gratitude for his cure. This must be the case since the participants in the meal lay about on "dinner pillows," supported by the left arm (Mark 14:3). Since one ate the customary meal sitting up, it must have been a festive occasion.

All of that sounds entirely plausible. But that house could also have belonged to a Simon who left it at the onset of his illness. It was now no longer called "the house of Simon," but "the house of Simon the leper." Perhaps he had already been dead a long time; houses sometimes retain their names for long periods. Our text says nothing of a healing of this Simon, and that makes the interpretation of the meal as an expression of thanks for healing questionable also. Whoever lived in this house in the time of Jesus and invited him to dinner cannot be deduced with certainty from a tradition that is apparently so rich in information and apparently so reliable. That is to say, we do not know who invited Jesus to dinner and how large the circle of guests was. It is not at all certain that all the guests belonged to Jesus' disciples. That the woman who did the anointing got into the house during the meal suggests that we must not imagine too strict a list of guests who were admitted.

We learn from Mark only that Jesus was anointed by a woman who managed to get in. Who this woman was, and what prompted her to do the anointing, we do not learn. That "some" reproach her deed is not directed at her as a person. The text does not state that she is a "sinner," a notorious prostitute. On the basis of verse 8, one could suppose that Jesus knew her. But even that remains an uncertain inference. It is precisely because the account of Mark is so sparse in details that the

"tradition" is led to enlarge and thereby alter it.

The woman brought an ἀλάβαστρον with her, a vessel made of glass, clay, or alabaster, in which one kept liquid ointment. Before using, one broke the long, slender neck of the vessel and poured the liquid on the head of the one to be honored—usually only a few drops of the sinfully expensive perfume. It has occasionally been conjectured that the woman broke the alabaster vessel (v 3) so that it could not again be used. One thereby fails to recognize the impossibility of using it more than once. Since the woman poured the oil on the head of Jesus while he was lying at the table, so to speak, she had to stand on the head side of the dinner cushion, which was usually intended for three persons (Luke narrates the anointing of his feet, which presupposes that she stood behind the reclining form). The woman herself says nothing as she performs her act, or the narrator assumes that there is nothing to be said about it. The explanation of the anointing that Jesus himself gives in verse 8 is not to be taken as a description of what the woman herself had in mind with her act. How Jesus understood it was of decisive importance.

The reaction of "some" to this anointing surprises us (vv 4f.). The guests are shocked at the extravagance. The narrator does not divulge whether they are disciples of Jesus or not. They think the costly oil should have been sold and the proceeds given to the poor. There is not a suggestion that this reproach is hypocritical; it is apparently the honest conviction of these men that is being expressed. The "over three hundred denarii" is an evaluation of the narrator, who illustrates the high cost of the oil by means of a huge sum. When the critics get excited at this unheard of extravagance, Jesus is prompted to take the woman under his protection. His "Let her alone!" puts an end at once to the insurgent feeling against the woman. The expression, "do not trouble," suggests an agitated scene like one can well imagine taking place among temperamental orientals. That the protest against the anointing really also touches Jesus himself is overlooked by the narrator. Jesus actually defends himself when he says that they have the poor with them always and could care for them if they wanted to (it is difficult not to hear the ironic question in these words whether their concern for the poor really comes from the heart). In any event, Jesus will not always be with them. And this note gives the story a deadly serious cast—which constitutes what is special about it. The critics are silent from now on. The woman has performed for Jesus the final act of charity—whether she knew it or not is not important. But Jesus knows it and says it. Moreover, the woman has given everything—the narrator appears so to understand the situation—in order to be able to purchase the expensive ointment. But the emphasis of the story does not lie on this point, but on the disclosure of the mystery of death: the woman has anticipated the anointing that really should come at the time of Jesus' burial. According to Mark 16:1ff., Jesus' body was not actually anointed again. When the women came to anoint him, the grave was already empty and the time for anointing was past.

To our surprise, Mark does not permit the story to end with verse 8, but appends another saying of Jesus that at first seems strange. The solemn words are: "And truly, I say to you, wherever the gospel is preached in the whole world, what she has done will be told in memory of her." We do not learn the woman's name. Jesus honors her so highly and yet her name is known to God alone. It is not her name that is here being celebrated; rather, it is her deed that is to be remembered. Just as people in many lands and major cities keep an eternal flame burning in memory of the unknown soldier, so here, too, it appears that a deed is singled out for undying commemoration. But the deed that lives on in the Gospel of Mark is something different. It extols not an unknown soldier who died in the anonymity of battle, but an unknown woman, about whose entire life we know nothing and whose name is included in this forgetfulness. What lives on is her deed, which devotedly honors the master in the hour with what nobody but him knows to be the last act of love and charity that would be shown him in this life.

The story is told in a very similar fashion in the Gospel of Matthew (26:6–13), only more briefly, as is typical of Matthew, since he intends to include a great deal more material in his gospel: one thinks only of the mass of discourse material that is presented over and beyond Mark. That compels the first Evangelist to forego all epic breadth and plastic vividness and limit himself strictly to what he took to be indispensable. And so we have the abbreviated version of Matthew:

> Now when Jesus was at Bethany in the house of Simon the leper, a woman came up to him with an alabaster jar of very expensive ointment, and she poured it on his head, as he lay at table. But when the disciples saw it, they were indignant, saying, "Why this waste? For this ointment might have been sold for a large sum (of money), and given to the poor." But Jesus, aware of this, said to them, "Why do you trouble the woman? For she has done a beautiful thing to me. For you always have the poor with you, but you will not always have me. In pouring this ointment on my body she has done it to prepare me for burial. Truly, I say to you, wherever this gospel is preached in the whole world, what this woman has done will be told in memory of her."

Matthew appends the final saying to the story as does Mark.

Although Matthew tells the story in a similar fashion, some things are nevertheless altered: the unknown "some," whose indignation Mark depicts, have become the disciples. This alteration virtually suggests itself: who other than the disciples could have taken part in the meal in the house of Simon the leper? To this it has to be said: in the gospels the effort is constantly made to fill in what are apparent gaps, to the extent that the context permits the content to be supplied. That process occurs here in a quite obvious way in that the unknown critics of Mark's account are identified as the unknown disciples. Something further is also modified. The question of how much one might have received for the oil is not answered with the amount, "more than three hundred denarii." Nothing depends on the exact amount; to have said something about it would have been to divert attention to something incidental. It is enough to say "for a large sum (of money)" (in the Greek text it is expressed simply as: πολλοῦ, i.e., "for much"). Matthew omits the addition, "if you wish"; that could have sidetracked the train of thought. The next alteration of Matthew is insignificant: the narrator inserts "he became aware of this" (γνούς), by which he lets some of the steam out of the protest, which in Mark is vented as fury. The disciples protest (speak) in their hearts; λέγειν ("to say") is often used to mean "say in one's heart, silently." But because they are the disciples, who rant and rave in Mark with loud protests, the gruffness of the scene is reduced. That does not hinder the progress of the action, for Jesus is aware of what they are saying or intend to say.

According to verse 7, the woman poured the ointment on Jesus' head. But in verse 12 Jesus says: The woman has anointed my body. The corresponding statements in

Mark are in 14:3 and 8. Both Evangelists have borne in mind that the anointing of the dead involves not merely the head, but the entire body. Accordingly, they understand the anointing of the head here as a representative anointing of the (whole) body. This new understanding of the anointing compelled them, in speaking of the anointing of Jesus' head (κεφαλή), to recast the text in accordance with the sense (σῶμα, "body") when Jesus gives his interpretation.

The third Gospel also contains a story of the anointing (Luke 7:36–50). But it is not set in Bethany at the beginning of the passion story; rather, Jesus has been invited to be the guest of a Pharisee somewhere else (Nain is mentioned in 7:11). Jesus accepts the invitation, and reclines with the other guests on dinner cushions. A courtesan of the city hears of this, procures an alabaster vessel filled with oil of myrrh, goes to the house of the Pharisee, and approaches the feet of the reclining guests from behind. As she bends over Jesus' feet, her tears wet his feet. She wipes them with her hair, kisses, and anoints his feet. The conflict does not arise from the reproach of (unnamed) disciples at the extravagance, but from thoughts of the Pharisee about Jesus. If he were a "prophet," reflects the host, "he would have known who and what the woman was who was touching him." The unspoken reproach concerns Jesus directly and the woman only indirectly. This corresponds to the fact that Jesus defends himself and, in the context, thereby defends the woman also.

Things continue to proceed with the usual courtesy with the other guests. "Simon, I have something to say to you" and "What is it, Teacher" are the question and answer of the guest and the host. Jesus tells a story of two men who could not repay loans of 50 and 500 denarii, and the good creditor (δανειστής) forgave the debt of both: "Who would have loved him more?" As expected, the host, Simon, answers: "The one, I suppose, to whom he forgave more." He thereby pronounces the judgment himself that Luke spells out in verses 40–45.

Luke thus might have borrowed the name Simon for the anonymous Pharisee from the Markan tradition, as well as the anointing (which permitted him to expand the accusation in verse 46). The non-synoptic tradition, which was the one predominantly employed, appears to have understood the story as follows: the act of love directed to Jesus by the woman was her response to the forgiveness granted her by God (through the proclamation of Jesus?). The Lukan version is not unambiguous in verse 45.[13] If one assigns the mention of the name Simon and the motif of anointing to Luke the author, as well as the contrast between the woman who was a sinner and the Pharisee, which is worthy of a rhetorician (running from βλέπεις, "you see," in v 44 to εἶπεν, "he said," in v 48), then one gets a fairly good picture of the tradition that Luke used, in addition to individual features drawn from the Markan tradition. Verses 49f. belong entirely to him; verse 49 shows that Jesus was even more than a prophet;[14] verse 50 sounds like it was borrowed from Mark 5:34. That a Pharisee as a representative of the pious customs treated a guest so poorly (no occasion for footwashing, no kiss),[15] has no support in the tradition, but is inferred by Luke from the silence of the tradition with respect to these obvious features. Luke 7:36ff. was therefore not originally a story of an anointing.

The anointing story in John 12:1–8 provides an example of how two stories interpenetrate each other in the process of handing them around and on. One motif leads from the anonymous woman (Mark and Matthew) and "the sinner" (Luke 7) to Mary (Luke 10:38–42 and 8:2) as the one who does the anointing. The "some" (τινες) of Mark is transformed into the "disciples" in Matthew and thence into Judas the betrayer. The accent thereby shifts, although Jesus remains the central character. The idea of the passion is connected with the Bethany tradition, the forgiveness going with grateful love is connected with the invitation to dinner at the house of the Pharisee. Both traditions have two con-

13 See J. Weiss, *Die Schriften des Neuen Testaments*. Vol. 1, *Die drei älteren Evangelien. Die Apostelgeschichte* (Göttingen: Vandenhoeck & Ruprecht, ²1907) 450f.

14 The phrase ὃς καί, "who also," is a means of strengthening the relative by means of καί, "and," that is not uncommon in Luke; e.g., in Acts 1:11 οἳ καὶ εἶπαν, "and who said."

15 See Billerbeck, 1: 426f.

trasting persons: the Johannine tradition sets Mary, who thinks only of Jesus, over against Judas, who thinks only of himself; the Lukan version has the "sinful woman" triumph over the Pharisee. In both cases, Jesus sets the truth off against the men who encounter him. But the Johannine pericope has an entirely different cast. The Johannine version presents a turning point. For a period that is rapidly coming to an end, Jesus is still free, surrounded by friends and disciples. He must also struggle here with non-understanding, and with the evil that lurks there already, awaiting the right opportunity.

Jesus alone really understands the situation. His mention of his burial (ἐνταφιασμός) points to the dark shadow of the passion for the reader. To be sure, the jubilation that his entrance into Jerusalem will arouse, the feeling of powerlessness on the part of his enemies, as though the whole world were flocking to Jesus, can obscure the reality momentarily. But, in fact, the activity of Jesus in the world has already come to its end, and the conclusion to chapter 12 will produce the complaint that there is no faith in spite of all the miracles. Who has ears to hear will readily perceive the sounding of the knell.

29. Anticipation and Menace

Bibliography
Faure, Alexander
"Die alttestamentlichen Zitate im 4. Evangelium
und die Quellenscheidungshypothese." *ZNW* 21
(1922) 99–121, esp. 111, 114.
Soltau, Wilhelm
*Das vierte Evangelium in seiner Entstehungsgeschichte
dargelegt*, SHAW.PH 7 (Heidelberg: Carl Winter,
⁶1916), esp. 9, 12, 24, 26.

12

9   **When the great crowd of the Jews learned
that he was there, they came, not only on
account of Jesus but also to see Lazarus,
whom he had raised from the dead. 10/
So the chief priests planned to put
Lazarus also to death, 11/ because on
account of him many of the Jews were
going away and believing in Jesus.**

■ **9** A transitional section (vv 9–11) follows on the meal
scene in Bethany without any internal connection. The
crowds are not festival pilgrims, but the Jews mentioned
in 11:19, 31, 45, who had also witnessed the resurrection
of Lazarus. They are residents of Jerusalem. Some of
them informed the Pharisees of the resurrection of
Lazarus (11:46). But the large number remaining must
also have returned to Jerusalem in the meantime, since
Jesus had hidden himself in the town of Ephraim (11:54).
This crowd could be identical with the "crowd" ($\H{o}\chi\lambda o\varsigma$)
mentioned in 12:17; yet 12:18 is evidence against this
view: they had only heard of the miracle.

■ **10** The narrator takes note of the fact that the high
priests planned to put Lazarus to death also. The
preceding resurrection story provides the religious
motive for the death resolution of the Sanhedrin: Jewish
obtuseness intends the death of Lazarus as well as that of
Jesus because his raising of Lazarus demonstrates that
Jesus is the dispenser of life. The tradition utilized by the
Evangelist exhibits a very clear trait at this point: for that
tradition the miracles of Jesus establish Jesus' divine
station straightaway and make it visible for everyone,
and it is a sign of groundless obduracy that Jesus'
opponents reject belief even in view of the resurrection
of a body already in the process of decaying and can only
think of how to put the newly resurrected Lazarus back

into his grave.

■ **11** According to 11:45, the raising of Lazarus leads
many to faith; this verse points to the same result. Since
the presence of Lazarus is propaganda for Jesus, Lazarus
must also be eliminated.

Overview

These three verses can scarcely be compared with a
synoptic counterpart. The anointing takes place, in Mark
and Matthew, following the narrative of the triumphal
entry. The anointing in Bethany therefore takes place
during Jesus' activity in Jerusalem. What the synoptic
tradition reports as events in Jericho (Mark/Matt:
Bartimaeus; Luke: Bartimaeus and Zacchaeus) has no
counterpart in the Gospel of John; but the sayings
material (parables; controversy dialogues), reported by
the Synoptics after the entry, also have no counterpart in
John, except for the story of the anointing, which has
strong contacts with the Lukan account, where, however,
it is located in Nain. There follows on chapter 12 in the
Gospel of John, the last verses of which sound like the
end of a gospel, the account of the last meal and the
announcement of the betrayal. The so-called farewell
discourses (chaps. 14–17) follow after that.

We could therefore conjecture that the great gap
created by the omission of the synoptic sayings material

assigned to Jerusalem was filled in the Gospel of John by the farewell discourses, which are quite differently constituted. But the question nevertheless remains whether the Gospel of John consciously rejected the teaching activity of Jesus in Jerusalem and substituted for it the enormous amount of material in the farewell discourses.

But John did not basically make use of the Synoptics up to chapter 12; rather, he took up stories essentially understood as signs out of the non-synoptic tradition. Since John induces the crisis by means of the resurrection of Lazarus, he has to move the cleansing of the temple forward in his account and does not need to report any further controversy with the Jews—apart from the last meal.

Verses 9–11 already prepare for the entry of Jesus into Jerusalem. They show the tension of the people, who not only want to see Jesus, the great miracle worker, but also Lazarus, who was brought back to life from the grave. Many come on his account and become believers as a result of the miraculous proof that he constitutes. The chief priests now resolve, as a consequence, to put Lazarus to death also, since he is living testimony to the miraculous power of Jesus. How that transpires, if at all, the Gospel of John does not tell. In all probability, this naive story, which is so filled with joy at the miracle, was already being circulated prior to the Evangelist. For this resurrection into earthly life is not, for him, the true awakening to eternal life with God that Jesus will dispense with the gift of the spirit.

30. The Entry into Jerusalem

Bibliography

Farmer, William R.
"The Palm Branches in John 12,13." *JTS*, n.s., 3 (1952) 62–66.

Freed, Edwin D.
"The Entry into Jerusalem in the Gospel of John." *JBL* 80 (1961) 329–38.

Gyllenberg, Rafael
"Intåget i Jerusalem och Johannesevangeliets." *SEÅ* 41/42 (1976/1977) 81–86.

Haenchen, Ernst
Der Weg Jesu. Eine Erklärung des Markus-Evangeliums und der kanonischen Parallelen, Sammlung Töpelmann, 2, 6 (Berlin: Walter de Gruyter, 1966, ²1968), esp. 379.

Holst, Robert Arthur
"The Relation of John 12 to the So-called Johannine Book of Glory." Dissertation, Princeton Theological Seminary, 1974.

Patsch, Hermann
"Der Einzug Jesu in Jerusalem. Ein historischer Versuch." *ZTK* 68 (1971) 1–26.

Smith, D. Moody, Jr.
"John 12,12ff. and the Question of John's Use of the Synoptics." *JBL* 82 (1963) 58–64.

12

12 The next day a great crowd who had come to the feast heard that Jesus was coming to Jerusalem. 13/ So they took branches of palm trees and went out to meet him, crying, "Hosanna! Blessed be he who comes in the name of the Lord, even the King of Israel!" 14/ And Jesus found a young ass and sat upon it; as it is written: 15/ "Fear not, daughter of Zion; behold they king is coming, sitting on an ass's colt!" 16/ His disciples did not understand this at first; but when Jesus was glorified, then they remembered that this had been written of him and had been done to him. 17/ The crowd that had been with him when he called Lazarus out of the tomb and raised him from the dead bore witness. 18/ The reason why the crowd went to meet him was that they heard he had done this sign. 19/ The Pharisees then said to one another, "You see that you can do nothing; look, the world has gone after him."

The entry into Jerusalem is represented relatively briefly and recalls the Synoptics. The "finding" of the ass does not appear as a miracle, but as the fulfillment of Isa 40:9/Zech 9:9. It is expressly emphasized that it was only the post-Easter community that discovered this prediction regarding Jesus; Jesus did not therefore deliberately precipitate its fulfillment. The title for Jesus, "the king of Israel," which plays a large role in the Johannine passion narrative, appears here for the first time. Only the crowd coming out to meet him, not his disciples, cry out this title. He does not march in at the head of a troop of Galilean pilgrims, but only with his disciples. The Lazarus event is especially emphasized once again; it was that event that brought him many followers, so that the Pharisees resign themselves with a sigh: There is nothing to be done! The whole world has gone after him. This does not reflect the Johannine concept of "world." And one has the impression otherwise that traditional material is here being transmitted—including the quotation. There is nothing to suggest that a new source begins at this point, as Bultmann thinks.[1] The conclusion of this short pericope provides the connection for what follows. The concept of "the whole world" is thereby expanded from the crowd coming out to meet him to the gentile Christian world. That does not imply that a break comes between verses 19 and 20.[2]

The entry takes place on the fifth day before the Passover, according to 12:1. However, additional correlative temporal notices that would produce a holy week are lacking; 13:1 gives only the additional notice: before the Passover. It will repay us to elucidate the synoptic parallels: Mark 11:1–10//Matt 21:1–11// Luke 19:29–38.

In Mark 11:1–7 there is expressly narrated the miraculous acquisition of the ass. That this scene is lacking in John is determinative for the distinction between John and the Synoptics in general: the Gospel of John omits all of this synoptic material; it provides only the story of the last meal, followed by the long discourses of Jesus. The differences continue after the arrest. The stress in John lies on the representation of the exchange between Jesus and Pilate. It does not depend on tradition, but substitutes for tradition. The spreading out of garments on the road in Mark 11:8 is not mentioned, nor is the circumstance that those following Jesus cry out hosannas. Furthermore, the entry into Jerusalem is eclipsed in John by the Lazarus miracle and its consequences. Lazarus is mentioned as a dinner guest in 12:1, and in 12:17 the significance of his raising is once again brought out. Under these circumstances, it is almost self-evident that the Evangelist could not have taken notice of a minor miracle like the healing of blind Bartimaeus—in the event his tradition contained a counterpart of that story. But that is precisely the question: is the tradition available to him analogous to that available to the synoptic writers?

■ **12** Jesus does not come with a band of pilgrims into the city, but is led only by his disciples. A great crowd of pilgrims of course goes out to meet him when they hear of his coming (v 9), and receive him with palm branches and the cry of Ps 118:26f.

■ **13** While Mark 11:10 has them speak of the coming kingdom of "our father David," Matthew 21:9 reports only that they speak of "David's Son"; verse 13 is the closest to Luke 19:38, where Jesus is also greeted as king. Luke and John presumably follow a later version of the story, which nevertheless had been anticipated by Mark's version of the passion narrative proper, in which the title of king had been used at high risk.

■ **14** The report has the effect of being extremely tight by virtue of the fact that the anointing is narrated prior to the entry and in verse 14 the story of the miraculous finding of the ass is reproduced in the briefest possible form ("he found").

■ **15f.** Only the two OT quotations—Ps 118:26f., in the case of the cry connected with the entry, and Isa 40:9 combined with Zech 9:9—remind the readers that here OT prophecy and the long announced will of God is being fulfilled—unrecognized at first, of course.

■ **17f.** On the other hand, verses 17f. connect up emphatically with the raising of Lazarus: it is this event that caused the large crowd to go out to meet Jesus.

■ **19** At the same time, this feature has further significance: it now becomes understandable why the Pharisees say to each other in resignation: "You see that you can do nothing; look, the world has gone after him!" But this

---

1   *John,* 417 [319].
2   On this point cf. the comment on v 20.

confession on the part of his opponents (which will not, however, prevent them from carrying out their resolution to put Jesus to death) anticipates the following section, which once again permits us to recognize the wider horizon of the the Fourth Gospel.

31. The "Greeks" and Jesus' Discourse on the Hour of His Glorification

Bibliography

Barksdale, J. O.

"Victory of Light. II: Joh 12,20–36." *Japanese Christian Quarterly* 28 (1962) 48–54.

Beauvery, Robert

"Jésus élevé attire les hommes à lui." *Esprit et vie* 80 (1970) 117–19.

Bussche, Henri van den

"Si le grain de blé ne tombe pas en terre (Jn 12,20–39)." *BVC* 5 (1954) 53–67.

Caird, George B.

"Judgment and Salvation. An Exposition of John 12,31–32." *CJT* 2 (1956) 231–37.

Hermann, Rudolf

"Die Prüfungsstunde des Sendungsgehorsams Jesu (Joh 12,20–43[50])." *ZST* 7 (1929/1930) 742–71.

Kossen, H. B.

"Who were the Greeks of John 12,20?" In *Studies in John Presented to J. N. Sevenster on the Occasion of his Seventieth Birthday* (Leiden: E. J. Brill, 1970) 97–110.

Léon-Dufour, Xavier

"Père, fais-moi passer sain et sauf à travers cette heure!" In *Neues Testament und Geschichte. Historisches Geschehen und Deutung im Neuen Testament. Oscar Cullman zum 70. Geburtstag,* ed. H. Baltensweiler and B. Reicke (Tübingen: Mohr-Siebeck; Zurich: Theologischer Verlag, 1972) 157–66.

Moore, W. E.

"Sir, We wish to See Jesus—Was this an Occasion of Temptation?" *SJT* 20 (1967) 75–93.

Potterie, Ignace de la

"L'exaltation du Fils de l'homme (Jn. 12,31–36)." *Greg* 49 (1968) 460–78.

Rasco, Aemilius

"Christus granum frumenti (Jo 12,24)." *VD* 37 (1959) 12–25, 65–77.

Thüsing, Wilhelm

"'Wenn ich von der Erde erhöht bin . . .' (Joh 12,32). Die Erhöhung Jesu nach dem Johannesevangelium." *Bibel und Kirche* 20 (1965) 40–42.

Torrey, Charles C.

"When I am Lifted up from the Earth, John 12:32." *JBL* 51 (1932) 320–22.

Unnik, Willem Cornelis van

"The Quotation from the Old Testament in Jn 12,34." *NovT* 3 (1959) 174–79.

Wrege, Hans-Theo

"Jesusgeschichte und Jüngergeschichte nach Joh 12,20–38 und Hebr 5,7–10." In *Der Ruf Jesu und die Antwort der Gemeinde. Exegetische Untersuchungen Joachim Jeremias zum 70. Geburtstag gewidmet von seinen Schülern,* ed. E. Lohse et al. (Göttingen: Vandenhoeck & Ruprecht, 1970) 259–88.

20 Now among those who went up to worship at the feast were some Greeks. 21/ So these came to Philip, who was from Bethsaida in Galilee, and said to him, "Sir, we wish to see Jesus." 22/ Philip went and told Andrew; Andrew went with Philip and they told Jesus. 23/ And Jesus answered them, "The hour has come for the Son of man to be glorified. 24/ Truly, truly, I say to you, unless a grain of wheat falls into the earth and dies, it remains alone; but if it dies, it bears much fruit. 25/ He who loves his life loses it, and he who hates his life in this world will keep it for eternal life. 26/ If any one serves me, he must follow me; and where I am, there shall my servant be also; if any one serves me, the Father will honor him. 27/ Now is my soul troubled. And what shall I say? 'Father, save me from this hour'? No, for this purpose I have come to this hour. 28/ Father, glorify they name." Then a voice came from heaven, "I have glorified it, and I will glorify it again." 29/ The crowd standing by heard it and said that it had thundered. Others said, "An angel has spoken to him." 30/ Jesus answered, "This voice has come for your sake, not for mine. 31/ Now is the judgment of this world, now shall the ruler of this world be cast out; 32/ and I, when I am lifted up from the earth, will draw all men to myself." 33/ He said this to show by what death he was to die. 34/ The crowd answered him, "We have heard from the law that the Christ remains forever. How can you say that the Son of man must be lifted up? Who is this Son of man?" 35/ Jesus said to them, "The light is with you for a little longer. Walk while you have the light, lest the darkness overtake you; he who walks in the darkness does not know where he goes. 36/ While you have the light, believe in the light, that you may become sons of light." When Jesus had said this, he departed and hid himself from them.

■ 20 Among the pilgrims were also some "Greeks," as verse 20 briefly reports. One might take this to refer to hellenistic Jews from the diaspora. But for the Evangelist they represent the Greek world in general, and thus also the pagan world.

■ 21 For this reason it is reported solemnly and specifically that they make their wish to see Jesus known to Philip from Bethsaida.

■ 22 Their desire to see Jesus is passed on through Philip and his brother Andrew to Jesus himself for the same reason.

■ 23f. And again for the same reason—because these few "Greeks" represent the pagan world that presses to see Jesus—Jesus replies with this observation: the hour has now come when the Son of man is to be glorified. Whether the "Greeks" got to speak with Jesus and what was said if they did, is unimportant by comparison and is therefore not narrated.

■ 24 The peculiarity of the Evangelist is thereby again confirmed: he likes to limit himself to a hint and then let the reflective reader draw the consequences for himself or herself. Yet that is not always so simple—as it is not in our case. The hour of glorification is the hour, first of all, when Jesus is raised up on the cross and dies, as can be discerned from verse 24. There is no way to lordship apart from this death. Underscored by the double "truly," that is made graphic by the saying about the grain of wheat: only if this grain falls into the ground and dies, will it bear much fruit—otherwise it remains alone, isolated, and unproductive, an abortive form of life.

■ 25 The Evangelist thus comes to the theme of Christian martyrdom, which was indeed not alien to Mark at an earlier time (8:27–9:1). Whoever loves his life, and thus keeps and guards it and does not allow it to be threatened, will lose it and it will not become true life; on the other hand, whoever hates his life in this world will keep it for eternal life. Dark undertones are certainly not missing from this promise. Nevertheless, demand to become a disciple in suffering gives way, for the present, to the promise of the blessedness of fellowship with God (and this blessedness is not just a sticky sentimentalism). This "to serve" is not distinguished from the "to deny oneself, to renounce oneself" of Mark. Yet it remains to consider whether this denial of self is perfect love for John. The earthly life is not devalued for John because of the expectation of an imminent end as it is in Paul. But the Johannine relocation of the last hour in the now does not make the slightest bit of difference in the devaluation of this "world" for John. The "eschatological reservation" of Paul appears to be foreign to the Gospel of John. But it nevertheless appears to be retained in a mysterious way: the "lifting up" cannot be extracted from this double aspect of death and glory. The Evangelist does not indicate what the two things are to look like concretely in the life of Jesus' disciples. On this point he leaves his reader with the difficult task of filling out a statement that sounds edifying but remains abstract with the concrete reality of his or her here and now.

■ 26 Jesus gives good assurance that he who serves him and follows him on the difficult path will also reach the heavenly goal of Jesus; him will the Father also "honor." Nevertheless this "honor" does not come after or alongside this earthly life, nor does it lie beyond it, and thus remains a hidden and demanding lordship, a service, that must be carried out in selflessness and self-denial.

■ 27 As verse 27 plainly states, this is not something for Jesus himself that is self-evident and easy: his soul is also perplexed and he is prompted to say, "Father, save me from this hour." This anguish of Jesus, depicted by Mark, is for John only like a small cloud that appears momentarily to darken the sun. It is clear that John here provides that which for him is the essential content of the Gethsemane tradition for him, and he therefore does not refer to it again later. Gethsemane is concentrated, so to speak, in a fraction of a second: "No, for this purpose I have come to this hour" follows immediately. The close and constant union of Jesus with the Father, whom he represents on earth, does not permit the Evangelist to go beyond this hint.

■ 28 Rather, Jesus breaks out immediately in a request to glorify the divine name, and a voice from heaven promises: he will be "raised up, exalted," just as God has already "exalted him" when he became flesh. The word "glorify" is therefore to be understood here in its antithetical double sense. God is glorified when Jesus, whom John depicts as the absolutely obedient embodiment of the divine will, gives himself up entirely to the passion: the divine will triumphs in that hour when God, entering fully into the passion, exhibits his love definitively for his own.

■ 29 Verse 29 emphasizes that the crowd is not permitted to hear the voice of the Father as such, but only perceives that it thundered; others admit that at most they heard an angel speak. This verse is completely comprehensible as an expression of the fact that God's voice cannot be apprehended as a natural phenomenon, as something that can be received and monitored.

■ 30 Verse 30, on the other hand, is difficult. Here Jesus assures them that this voice became audible not on his account, but for the sake of the hearers. Does that mean that Jesus does not need an answer to his petition, because, thanks to his unmarred union with the Father, he does not require such a confirmation? In that case would not only the affirmative answer of God be unnecessary, but also Jesus' own prayer for his own and the Father's sake? Would his prayer be necessary only for the sake of the disciples? Yet, is a prayer, a petition which the petitioner does not need to utter, really in earnest? Is not Käsemann's objection justified here? Is not the Evangelist guilty of a naive docetism? We here catch sight of the greatest difficulty connected with Johannine christology: the existence of Jesus devoted wholly to God, which permits him to become God's revealer, threatens to entrap him in a world in which mortals do not live, a world that is inaccessible to us. For Mark, Jesus has gone into the abyss of what is remote and alien to God, into that terrible divine silence to an hour when one most passionately longs to hear the answer of God and yet does not hear it. The Johannine identification of "I and the Father are one" here reveals its danger: if no one has seen God at any time and the Father and Jesus are one, then Jesus also threatens to disappear into a world that is invisible to us and to become invisible himself.

■ **31f.** The Evangelist has perceived this and in verses 31f. gives his answer. Now, in the moment when Jesus is glorified, crucified, the judgment of the world takes place: the ruler of this world will now be cast out. When Jesus goes to the cross and to death, there is the victory of divine love. The one sent by God, in whom God becomes visible, goes of his own free will, not compelled by a divine will imposed on him from without, to his death on the gibbet. The power that rules in this world and over this world is thereby overcome, or rather, in this moment—which is still outstanding if one consults the historical clock—will it be overcome. To what extent is this the case? Will sin come to an end, war no longer be pursued, violence, rape, and torture cease, deceit fail? Will mourning and despair disappear? Verse 32 gives as an answer: "And I, when I am lifted up from the earth, will draw all men to myself." The word "all" is here an error. Jesus will draw "only" those to him whom the Father has given him and to whom he imparts the spirit as the one exalted to God. For the Evangelist, when he received the spirit and came to understand and believe in Jesus, it is evident that the cross became the glory. But that would be a manner of speaking had it not also applied to his own life. That means: he is now able to affirm the shadow of the cross falling across his own life as the divine radiance, and he has now lost his fear of the lord of this world and his power; he has therefore lost his fear in the face of his own anxiety and despair, and in the face of injustice and suffering perpetrated on him, and is able willingly to say yes to martyrdom, which was a real possibility for Christians in those days. Martyrdom no longer threatens Christians in many lands in this manner. Instead, the "world" encompasses each person with a density and intenseness that makes a retreat into pietistic inwardness no longer appear possible. The influence of the "powers" of state, business, and political parties, of the mass media with their insensible yet all the more effective power is so great, while the silence of God, out of which the "spirit" of consolation only seldom appears to erupt for one or the other, is so inexorable and all-embracing, that the danger of resignation and even despair is overpowering, precisely in the case of those most on guard. To have no anxiety with respect to our own anxiety and even with respect to our own guilt, with which we often unwittingly burden ourselves, sounds like utopia. We thus have no reason to wonder why Christians today do not appear to suffer martyrdom, but rather to wonder that we do not catch sight of its reality simply because the Gestapo has been disbanded and the riot stick does not wave constantly over our heads.

In verses 30–36 we are faced with other questions.

■ **33** If verse 33 is only intended to say that Jesus' exaltation means the crucifixion, that would be a supplementary explanation of something that the Evangelist has long since been telling the reader. But the verse looks like a transition to the following section, where the subject under discussion is again the departure of the redeemer and revealer.

■ **34** The crowd of people curiously appears to understand this as a messianic claim, coupled with an announcement of the passion. On the other hand, they object that the (Jewish) law contains nothing about a withdrawal of the messiah, nor is anything similar actually said in the book of Daniel about the Son of man: he seems to be a figure that lives beyond condescension, who himself only executes judgment, but is not himself subject to judgment. There can be no doubt that questions are here being addressed that did not move a Jerusalem or Galilean crowd, but are of concern to the Christian community in the time of the Evangelist himself. It remains a sore point for them that the revealer has to disappear; yet only they are capable of explaining exaltation as death and recognizing Son of man (who is not mentioned in the preceding passage) as another name for the messiah. If the messiah/Son of man has to die, what kind of a Son of man is that?

■ **35** Jesus' answer in verse 35 takes nothing away from the announcement of the cross: "The light is with you only for a little longer," for a brief time. That requires of those who have faith that they believe in the light and accordingly go their earthly ways so long as they have the light before them. We thereby take note of something peculiar that concerns the Evangelist above all: he was indeed convinced that the community had really only a short time to wait before the departing Jesus was replaced by the spirit, who would lead into all truth. However, Jesus admonishes as though the "a little longer" applies to the post-Easter period as well, as though Christians would be orphans not only for a few normal days or weeks, but for a span of time unknown to us. However, the Fourth Gospel thereby again draws closer to us, who are in danger of being dismayed and frustrated, whether by its doctrine of the spirit and our lack of the spirit. The immediate expectation of the Fourth Gospel does not imply that nothing more need be expected, but that we always have everything to expect and thus cannot simply lounge about. Rather, we are further driven about and remain scared (if we do not permit ourselves to be lulled to sleep by the "world") and learn that we cannot place too cheap a price on the "spirit." The exaltation does not lie behind us, but in front of us, and it is not pure glitter and glory, but blood and sweat and tears on the part of the Christian who wants to remain a Christian or become a Christian. The American negroes once comforted themselves in a world devoid of grace with a song in which it is said: we must all cross over Jordan. That certainly also means that we all, every last one, have to cross over into the promised land. Yet, at the same time, the accompanying certainty is that we all, every last one, have to cross over the boundary of death. That can assist us in understanding the dialectic of "after a little while" and help us recognize the reality of the two poles: on the one hand, the next moment can free me from my anxiety, my loneliness, my guilt, and thus "after a little while" break open the prison in which we are incarcerated and to which we are constantly contributing. But "after a little while" warns us, at the same time, not to wait for "glorification" like the fulfillment of a utopia, but to hold fast to the notion that the way to glory does not bypass the cross that waits for us "after a little while."

32. The Discourse of Jesus (Part two)

Bibliography

Boismard, Marie-Emile
"Le caractère adventice de Jn 12,45–50." *Sacra pagina* 2 (1959) 189–92.

Borgen, Peder
"The Use of Tradition in John 12.44–50." *NTS* 26 (1979/1980) 18–35.

Schnackenburg, Rudolf
"Joh 12,39–41: Zur christologischen Schriftauslegung des vierten Evangelisten." In *Neues Testament und Geschichte. Historisches Geschehen und Deutung im Neuen Testament. Oscar Cullman zum 70. Geburtstag*, ed. H. Baltensweiler and B. Reicke (Tübingen: Mohr-Siebeck; Zurich: Theologischer Verlag, 1972) 167–77.

12

37 Though he had done so many signs before them, yet they did not believe in him; 38/ it was that the word spoken by the prophet Isaiah might be fulfilled: "Lord, who has believed our report, and to whom has the arm of the Lord been revealed?" 39/ Therefore they could not believe. For Isaiah again said, 40/ "He has blinded their eyes and hardened their heart, lest they should see with their eyes and perceive with their heart, and turn for me to heal them." 41/ Isaiah said this because he saw his glory and spoke of him. 42/ Nevertheless many even of the authorities believed in him, but for fear of the Pharisees they did not confess it, lest they should be put out of the synagogue; 43/ for they loved the praise of men more than the praise of God. 44/ And Jesus cried out and said, "He who believes in me, believes not in me but in him who sent me. 45/ And he who sees me sees him who sent me. 46/ I have come as light into the world, that whoever believes in me may not remain in darkness. 47/ If any one hears my sayings and does not keep them, I do not judge him; for I did not come to judge the world but to save the world. 48/ He who rejects me and does not receive my sayings has a judge; the word that I have spoken will be his judge on the last day. 49/ For I have not spoken on my own authority; the Father who sent me has himself given me commandment what to say and what to speak. 50/ And I know that his commandment is eternal life. What I say, therefore, I say as the Father has bidden me."

Introduction

Jesus' discourse ends enigmatically in verse 36b. Jesus has just spoken to his own on the occasion of the coming of the Greeks, and he now hides himself as though "after a little while" had already become reality. Instead of that, the Evangelist—or probably a redactor—takes this report as a complaint and an indictment.

■ **37** Although Jesus has performed many signs before them, as verse 37 reminds us (the healing of the man born blind and the raising of Lazarus are such signs or pointers, which stand many others in good stead), they do not believe in him. The marvel of disbelief seems to be so enormous to the speaker that he can only have recourse to the divine will itself, which was proclaimed already in the prophet Isaiah: our preaching will be futile, and the arm, reign, and power of the Lord remain unacknowledged. We are therefore not the first and only ones who have had a dismal experience with our preaching, but come in a long line of bitterly disappointed proclaimers who are forced to cry out to God because nobody listens. But perhaps things are really different, and worse, if that is possible.

■ **40** In this verse is quoted the Isaiah passage that appears again and again in the NT when the riddle of the ineffectiveness of the Christian proclamation becomes pressing: God himself wills that eyes no longer see and ears no longer hear, and that, as a consequence, there is no salvation.

■ **41** Isaiah is alleged to have said this, according to verse 41, because he saw his, that is, Jesus' glory and spoke of him and not of himself. In this connection, we must bear in mind of course that it is precisely this glory that is the other side of the cross. But we must ask ourselves above all whether we are exempt from this blindness and deafness and whether the prophet was always referring to someone else when he announced the lack of salvation. It is not so certain where the boundaries between us and others lie; perhaps the world shows us only the signs that point to a storm, while Jesus' signs remain hidden to us because we always experience the Father as the hidden God. In other words, because we are unable to escape the "after a little while" and also ought not to escape, because it belongs to the destiny of discipleship.

■ **42** Verse 42 appears of course to offer a consoling message: in spite of everything, many have nevertheless begun to believe in Jesus, even some of the authorities, some of those belonging to the governing circles and groups hostile to Jesus; they do not dare to confess it on account of the Pharisees, who are unbending. But the faith that remains secret is basically sorry consolation and a poor counselor.

■ **43** The reason believers dare not confess their faith lies in the fact that they love the praise of men more than the praise of God, that the "robust realism" that will not yield its claims wants nothing to do, then or now, with the cross and therefore with sacrifice, with commitment and with disappointment ("after a little while") that does not fail to set in.

■ **44f.** Over against this secret faith, Jesus raises his voice once more and repeats his message, which can scarcely be validated in this world: Whoever believes in him, does not really believe in him (the Christian faith does not permit even the Father's emissary to be confused with the Father, the messenger with the one sending the messenger), but precisely in the one sending the messenger, who sends both the messenger (Jesus) and the messengers (the disciples). Only where this confusion is avoided, where Jesus and the pastor or the missionary are not confused with the Father, are the ratios preserved, and the one who does the sending then becomes visible in the messenger.

■ **46** Jesus has really come into the world as light, so that no one who believes in him need be engulfed by darkness (i.e., by anxiety, guilt, despair).

■ **47f.** Jesus does not judge the one who hears his words and does not believe. For he has not come into the world to judge it, but to save it. His word—the word that is scorned, ignored, rejected—will judge such a person, and then not on some mythical last day, but right now, as we know only too well in our solitude before God.

■ **49f.** Jesus is actually only the voice of the Father (the words he speaks in vv 49f. are the last words spoken in public). Now, as before, he does not speak out of himself. And this is precisely what makes it so difficult for us, because the word confronts us in dreadful loneliness, untested and unconfirmed by world history and our own everyday experience, but veiled by that "after a little while."

33.   The Last Supper

Bibliography

Bacon, Benjamin Wisner
  "The Sacrament of the Footwashing." *ExpTim* 43
  (1931/1932) 218–21.
Barton, George A.
  "The Origin of the Discrepancy between the
  Synoptists and the Fourth Gospel as to the Date
  and Character of Christ's Last Supper with his
  Disciples." *JBL* 43 (1924) 28–31.
Bishop, Eric F. F.
  "'He that Eateth Bread with me hath Lifted up his
  Heel against me': —Jn xiii. 18 (Ps xli. 9)." *ExpTim*
  70 (1958/1959) 331–32.
Bleek, Friedrich
  "Ueber den Monathstag des Todes Christi und des
  letzten Abendmahles mit seinen Jüngern und die
  in der Beziehung zwischen Johannes und den
  Synoptikern stattfindende Differenz." In his
  *Beiträge zur Einleitung und Auslegung der heiligen
  Schrift.* Vol. 1, *Beiträge zur Evangelien-Kritik* (Berlin:
  G. Reimer, 1846) 107–56.
Böhmer, Wilhelm
  "Das Fusswaschen Christi, nach seiner sacrament-
  lichen Würde dargestellt." *TSK* 23 (1850) 829–42.
Boismard, Marie-Emile
  "Le lavement des pieds (*Jn*, XIII, 1–17)." *RB* 71
  (1964) 5–24.
Braun, François-Marie
  "Le lavement des pieds et la réponse de Jésus à
  Saint Pierre (Jean XIII,4–10)." *RB* 44 (1935) 22–
  33.
Campenhausen, Hans von
  "Zur Auslegung von Joh 13,6–10." *ZNW* 33 (1934)
  259–71.
Christie, W. M.
  "Did Christ Eat the Passover with his Disciples? or,
  The Synoptics *versus* John's Gospel." *ExpTim* 43
  (1931/1932) 515–19.
Cothenet, Edouard
  "Gestes et actes symboliques du Christ dans le IVe
  Evangile." In *Gestes et paroles dans les diverses familles
  liturqiques*, Bibliotheca "Ephemerides Liturgicae"
  "Subsidia" 14 [Rome] 24 (Rome: Centro Liturgico
  Vincenzio, 1978) 95–116.
Derrett, John Duncan Martin
  "'Domine, tu mihi lavas pedes?' (Studio su
  Giovanni 13,1–30)." *BeO* 21 (1979) 13–42.
Dunn, James D. G.
  "The Washing of Disciples' Feet in John 13:1–20."
  ZNW 61 (1970) 247–52.
Eisler, Robert
  "Zur Fusswaschung am Tage vor dem Passah."
  ZNW 14 (1913) 268–71.
Evdokimow, Paul
  "Etude sur Jean 13,18–30." *Esprit et Vie* (1950)
  201–16.

Fiebig, Paul
  "Die Fusswaschung [Joh 13:8–10]." *Angelos* 3 (1930) 121–28.
Fridrichsen, Anton
  "Bemerkungen zur Fusswaschung Joh 13." *ZNW* 38 (1939) 94–96.
Gerritzen, F.
  "El lavatorio de los pies (Joh 13,1–17)." *Sinite* 4 (1963) 145–64.
Graf, Eduard
  "Bemerkung über Joh 13, 1–4." *TSK* 40 (1867) 714–48.
Grossouw, William K.
  "A Note on John xiii 1–3." *NovT* 8 (1966) 124–31.
Haring, N. M.
  "Historical Notes on the Interpretation of John 13:10." *CBQ* 13 (1951) 355–80.
Jaubert, Annie
  "Une lecture du lavement des pieds au mardi-mercredi saint." *Muséon* 79 (1966) 257–86.
Kassing, Altfrid
  "Das Evangelium der Fusswaschung." *Erbe und Auftrag* 36 (1960) 83–93.
Kelly, John
  "What Did Christ Mean by the Sign of Love?" *African Ecclesiastical Review* 13 (1971) 113–21.
Knox, Wilfred L.
  "John 13. 1–10." *HTR* 43 (1950) 161–63.
Lazure, N.
  "Le lavement des pieds (Jn 13,1–15)." *AsSeign* 38 (1967) 40–50.
Lohmeyer, Ernst
  "Die Fusswaschung." *ZNW* 38 (1939) 74–94.
Lohse, Wolfram
  "Die Fusswaschung (Joh 13,1–20). Eine Geschichte ihrer Deutung." Dissertation, Erlangen, 1966/1967.
Martin, Josef
  Symposion. Die Geschichte einer literarischen Form, Studien zur Geschichte und Kultur des Altertums 17 (Paderborn: F. Schöningh, 1931).
Michl, Johann
  "Der Sinn der Fusswaschung." *Bib* 40 (1959) 697–708.
Moffatt, James
  "The Lord's Supper in the Fourth Gospel." *Expositor*, 8th ser., 7 (1913) 1–22.
Mussner, Franz
  "Fusswaschung (Joh 13, 1–17). Versuch einer Deutung." *Geist und Leben* 31 (1958) 25–30.
Niccacci, Alviero
  "L'unitá litteraria di Gv 13,1–38." *Euntes docet* 29 (1976) 291–323.
Richter, Georg
  "Die Fusswaschung: Joh 13,1–20." *MTZ* 16 (1965) 13–26. Now in his *Studien zum Johannesevangelium*, ed. J. Hainz. BU 13 (Regensburg: F. Pustet, 1977) 42–57.
Richter, Georg
  "Die Deutung des Kreuzestodes Jesu in der Leidensgeschichte des Johannesevangeliums (Joh 13–19)." In his *Studien zum Johannesevangelium*, ed. J. Hainz. BU 13 (Regensburg: F. Pustet, 1977) 58–73.
Richter, Georg
  Die Fusswaschung im Johannesevangelium. Geschichte ihrer Deutung, BU 1 (Regensburg: F. Pustet, 1967).
Robinson, John Arthur Thomas
  "The Significance of the Foot-Washing." In *Neotestamentica et patristica. Eine Freundesgabe, Herrn Professor Dr. Oscar Cullmann zu seinem 60. Geburtstag überreicht*, NovTSup 6 (Leiden: E. J. Brill, 1962) 144–47.
Ru, Gerrit de
  "Einge notities bij de herinterpretaties van de voetwassing." *Kerk en theologie* 30 (1979) 89–104.
Snyder, Graydon F.
  "John 13:16 and the Anti-Petrinism of the Johannine Tradition." *BR* 16 (1971) 5–15.
Sparks, H. F. D.
  "St. John's Knowledge of Matthew. The Evidence of John 13,16 and 15,20." *JTS*, n.s., 3 (1952) 58–61.
Thyen, Hartwig
  "Johannes 13 und die 'kirchliche Redaktion' des vierten Evangeliums." In *Tradition und Glaube. Das frühe Christentum in seiner Umwelt. Festgabe für Karl Georg Kuhn zum 65. Geburtstag*, ed. G. Jeremias, H.-W. Kuhn, and H. Stegemann (Göttingen: Vandenhoeck & Ruprecht, 1971) 343–56.
Weiser, Alfons
  "Joh 13,12–20—Zufügung eines späteren Herausgebers?" *BZ* 12 (1968) 252–57.
Weiss, Herold
  "Foot Washing in the Johannine Community." *NovT* 21 (1979) 298–325.
Wilcox, Max
  "The Composition of Joh 13,21–30." In *Neotestamentica and Semitica. Studies in Honour of Matthew Black*, ed. E. E. Ellis and M. Wilcox (Edinburgh: T. & T. Clark, 1969) 143–56.
Zweifel, Bertrand
  "Jésus lave les pieds de ses disciples. Essai d'exégèse sur Jn 13,1–20." Dissertation, Lausanne, 1965.

13

1 Now before the feast of the Passover, when Jesus knew that his hour had come to depart out of this world to the Father, having loved his own who were in the world, he loved them to the end. 2/ And during supper, when the devil had already put it into the heart of Judas Iscariot, Simon's son, to betray him, 3/ Jesus, knowing that the Father had given all things into his hands, and that he had come from God and was going to God, 4/ rose from supper, laid aside his garments, and girded himself with a towel. 5/ Then he poured water into a basin, and began to wash the disciples' feet, and to wipe them with the towel with which he was girded. 6/ He came to Simon Peter; and Peter said to him, "Lord, do you wash my feet?" 7/ Jesus answered him, "What I am doing you do not know now, but afterward you will understand." 8/ Peter said to him, "You shall never wash my feet." Jesus answered him, "If I do not wash you, you have no part in me." 9/ Simon Peter said to him, "Lord, not my feet only but also my hands and my head!" 10/ Jesus said to him, "He who has bathed does not need to wash, except for his feet, but he is clean all over; and you are clean, but not all of you." 11/ For he knew who was to betray him; that was why he said, "You are not all clean." 12/ When he had washed their feet, and taken his garments, and resumed his place, he said to them, "Do you know what I have done for you? 13/ You call me Teacher and Lord; and you are right, for so I am. 14/ If I then, your Lord and Teacher, have washed your feet, you also ought to wash one another's feet. 15/ For I have given you an example, that you also should do as I have done to you. 16/ Truly, truly, I say to you, a servant is not greater than his master; nor is he who is sent greater than he who sent him. 17/ If you know these things, blessed are you if you do them. 18/ I am not speaking of you all; I know whom I have chosen; it is that the scripture may be fulfilled, 'He who ate my bread has lifted his heel against me.' 19/ I tell you this now, before it takes place, that when it does take place you may believe that I am he. 20/ Truly, truly, I say to you, he who receives any one whom I send receives me; and he who receives me receives him who sent me." 21/ When Jesus had thus spoken, he was troubled in spirit, and testified, "Truly, truly, I say to you, one of you will betray me." 22/ The disciples looked at one another, uncertain of whom he spoke. 23/ One of his disciples, whom Jesus loved, was lying close to the breast of Jesus; 24/ so

Simon Peter beckoned him and said, "Tell us who it is of whom he speaks." 25/ So lying thus, close to the breast of Jesus, he said to him, "Lord, who is it?" 26/ Jesus answered, "It is he to whom I shall give this morsel when I have dipped it." So when he had dipped the morsel, he gave it to Judas, the son of Simon Iscariot. 27/ Then after the morsel, Satan entered into him. Jesus said to him, "What you are going to do, do quickly." 28/ Now no one at the table knew why he said this to him. 29/ Some thought that, because Judas had the money box, Jesus was telling him, "Buy what we need for the feast"; or, that he should give something to the poor. 30/ So, after receiving the morsel, he immediately went out; and it was night.

Introduction

The unusual introduction to this chapter (vv 1–3) reflects an event whose unusual character the Evangelist has taken from a tradition foreign to the Synoptics (but cf. Luke 22:27). An old source lies behind this account, which already related the footwashing rather than the Passover meal. It was probably not meant to represent Jesus as a pious Jew observing the Passover meal (and is thus dejudaizing). The alternative interpretation, that the story viewed him as the Passover lamb, is not hinted at in the Fourth Gospel. The footwashing is the great token of love. Instead of the Jewish concept of "covenant with God," its "meaning" is Jesus' love for his "own."

■ 1 The temporal notice, "before the feast of the Passover" (the thirteenth of Nisan and not the fourteenth, as in the synoptic tradition),[1] does not make it necessary for the Evangelist to accept the view that Jesus celebrated the Passover in Jerusalem: none of Jesus' journeys to Jerusalem in the Gospel of John has the aim of having the Lord participate in the temple cultus. Rather, he goes up only to proclaim his own sending and significance in the temple. The Evangelist himself undoubtedly formulated the striking participial construction that begins with

"knowing" ($\epsilon i\delta\acute{\omega}\varsigma$),[2] in order to prompt his readers to reflect on what Jesus himself knew and what the reader must also know: the decisive hour, which has already been much discussed, lies immediately ahead: the hour of his death. But it quite correctly is not given this designation. It is replaced and solemnly paraphrased with the true and real sense it has as the hour when Jesus "departs out of this world to the Father." This hour thus becomes evident as the limits of this world—although at first only for Jesus, then later also for his own—limits that our world cannot overstep and beyond which the kingdom of the Father stretches with its many mansions ("beyond" does not refer here to either a spatial or to a real temporal concept, as will be shown). That does not imply a mere change in locales,[3] but that "this world" and "the Father" are qualitatively different realms of power. This qualitative distinction plays an extremely important role in Gnosticism, for example, in the transcendence of the "Good One" in the Gnosticism represented by the Book of Baruch,[4] and in the "non-existent God" in the system of Basilides.[5] At this point John comes remarkably close to gnostic terminology.

Understood in the Johannine sense, the hour of death

---

1   Cf. 18:28 with Mark 14:17–23, Matt 26:20–29, Luke 22:14–20.
2   Contrary to Bultmann, *John*, 461 [351].
3   Contrary to Käsemann, *The Testament of Jesus*, 20.
4   Hippolytus, *Ref.* 5.26.25.
5   Hippolytus, *Ref.* 7.20f. Cf. Jonas, *Gnosis und spätantiker Geist.* Vol. 1, *Die Mythologische Gnosis*, FRLANT, n.s., 33 (Göttingen: Vandenhoeck &

Ruprecht, 1934) 94–140, and *The Gnostic Religion. The Message of the Alien God and the Beginnings of Christianity* (Boston: Beacon, ²1963) 48–99.

is nothing to alarm and frighten. Rather, it permits and produces the completion of a great work. When Jesus has loved his own who are in this world—all of his words and works belonging to this demonstration of love that is not at all sentimental—he now gives his own the last and conclusive proof of his love. The footwashing which he is about to perform—for the time being only in private of course—is the anticipation of the cross and expresses the meaning of the cross graphically as a deed of Jesus. This anticipation was necessary since the Evangelist could not represent the death scene itself as an act of love. It is much too much a passion for that purpose—as the tradition has dictated.

But what stood in the source? "During supper" (δείπνου γινομένου; v 2) does not fit after the genitive ἑορτῆς τοῦ πάσχα ("before the Passover"). But it is meant in accordance with the sense. This meal with the footwashing had already replaced the Passover meal in the source.

■ **2** Verse 2 begins with an indication of the situation: a meal[6] is in progress, during which the following events occur. The note to hand Jesus over that the devil had already put it into the heart of Judas Iscariot, Simon's son, derives from older tradition available to the Evangelist.[7] That exhibits a trait similar to the one found in Luke 22:3 but by no means plagarized from Luke. John does indeed speak occasionally of "the lord of this world," but not of the devil or Satan, who has no more place in his view of the life of Jesus than do the many demons so readily reported by the synoptic tradition.[8]

■ **3** The Evangelist could make this feature his own by describing the real status of things by way of effective contrast: Jesus himself knew and the reader, in turn, ought to know that Jesus knows that the Father has given all things into his hands, and that he can therefore act with royal freedom when he now takes on himself the lowliest of all servant's tasks. He knows that he comes from and goes to God, and is thus enveloped in the Father's love and salvific purpose.

"To come from God and go to God" is the formula in Gnosticism that describes the self-consciousness of the perfect gnostic; but here it expresses the special status of Jesus. The act of servitude that Jesus is now to perform stands in contrast to that status. The unprecedented aspect of this act is thereby put in the correct light.

■ **4** The activity introduced by verse 2 now begins in verse 4: Jesus gets up during the meal (the reading γενομένου, "had taken place," in verse 2, seeks to tone down the unprecedented character of this act that breaks through every transmitted form). If one allows "during supper" (δείπνου γινομένου) to stand in verse 2, "from supper" (ἐκ τοῦ δείπνου) is superfluous. On the other hand, it is necessary following on verses 2f. Because this meal is partaken of prior to the Passover, it is not the Passover meal nor the synoptic "last supper," in spite of

6 Cf. Billerbeck, 4: 611–39.
7 The peculiar form of the clause owes to the desire to avoid placing the genitive phrase, "Judas, son of Simon" (Ἰούδας Σίμωνος), which is open to misunderstanding, after "heart" (καρδίαν).
8 The older versions of Haenchen's work view the matter of sources differently. The author writes: "Verse 2 contains only the specific datum as its kernel: 'and as an evening meal was taking place.' Since Jesus is again reclining at the table in verse 12, the footwashing takes place during the meal, while the disciples are reclining on dining pillows, each of which provids places for three persons, and their feet are readily available for washing. Whoever does not have this process in mind—confirmed by verse 23—like the painters in the Middle Ages and Renaissance (for example, Leonardo di Vinci, in his Last Supper) is faced with an unsolvable problem that is already discernible in the reading γενομενον, 'had taken place' = past tense in ℵ D Θ 33 *pl* lat (𝔓⁶⁶ has the scribal variant γεναμενον): Jesus has to wash the feet of the seated disciples after the meal. This verse has therefore been filled out with the clause referring to the devil (τοῦ διαβόλου). But what does that mean? 'When the devil had already made up his mind?' From what is this usage derived? Is it Hebraic? The αὐτόν, 'him,' does not fit; it of course refers to Jesus. Yet is it perhaps better to translate: 'When the devil had already put it in the heart of Judas to turn him over'? But that conflicts with verse 27. However, the beloved disciple was probably inserted only later. That has caused verse 2 to be misunderstood. A further question remains: why does a rather long participial construction with εἰδώς, 'knowing,' come in verse 3, when the content has already been basically expressed in verse 1. Is that intended to neutralize 'the devil' (τοῦ διαβόλου)? Consequently, it could have been the final redactor who filled it out, and that brought it close to the Lukan tradition in 22:3."

all its solemnity. Jesus takes his outer garment off and girds himself about with a towel. The scene appears to be unusually graphic, and our imagination is only too ready to fill it out down to the smallest detail: how the disciples, surprised and touched by the enigmatic act of the master, sit there motionless, not knowing what is happening to them and what they are to do in response. But it is no longer a real footwashing in the mind of the Evangelist: one does not wash twenty-four feet with the water of one washbasin and dry them with a single apron. Rather, the Evangelist depicts the act, the sense of which alone now concerns him, in a form already simplified and simultaneously stylized; it had perhaps already assumed that form as a sacred ritual in the community of the Evangelist.

■ **5** Verse 5 carries the action further, which takes place in front of the silent company (Peter alone is mentioned in this connection): Jesus pours water into a vessel and begins to wash the feet of the disciples and to dry them with the towel about his waist. Joachim Jeremias thinks the article before "washbasin" is a Semitism: it reflects the emphatic state without definite significance.[9] But the washbasin is obviously present for the narrator ($\mathfrak{P}^{66}$ clarifies the word which is rarely attested by expanding it to ποδονιπτήρ: "footbasin"). The tension rises precisely because this verse reports no reaction on the part of the disciples to Jesus' surprising behavior, except when he commences it.

■ **6** Verse 6 finally breaks the tension when Jesus comes to Peter. It is not said (although it is often asserted) that Jesus began his footwashing with Peter. Rather, the phrase, "When he came to Simon Peter," supports the view that others had silently submitted to the act of the master prior to Peter. But Peter says to Jesus—the laconic text only permits us to surmise who is speaking to whom; later manuscripts will clarify this—as he draws back horrified: "Lord, do you wash my feet?"[10] The words "Lord" and "feet" come at the emphatic points of the sentence, at the beginning and the end, in tension with each other and thus depict the fundamental impossibility of the act: how can a teacher wash the feet of a student? The Evangelist could have taken the reaction of Peter directly out of his source. For he understands the

act of Jesus as an act of condescending love that reaches its apex in the cross. The footwashing is essentially identical with the event of the cross as an interpretation, as an explantion of the cross as a deed of condescending love. In this respect, Peter confronts the "scandal of the cross" (σκάνδαλον τοῦ σταυροῦ). Peter perceives the footwashing as something that is not appropriate to Jesus as Lord. Peter now prompts Jesus to explain his act. That occurs in verse 7.

■ **7** Jesus' explanation for his action is given in solemn form: "He answered and said." That is not to be understood in an OT or Jewish sense, but as the expression of the full authority with which the Lord acts. Jesus' response is serene and definite: "What I am doing you do not know now; but afterward you will understand." Jesus' answer allows for the lack of comprehension on the part of the disciple without chastising him and promises an explanation for later. Bultmann has plausibly and justifiably contested the view that Jesus' explanation in verse 12 could be related to this "afterward."[11] This difficulty becomes more acute if verse 12 follows immediately on verse 7. But that is actually the case in the work of the Evangelist, in my opinion; verses 8–11 were inserted at a later time.

■ **8** In this insertion, Peter does not concern himself at all with Jesus' answer, but repeats his objection in stronger form: he will never let Jesus wash his feet. This behavior makes sense only if one understands it as the beginning of a new dialogue now to ensue that does not look forward to the explanation promised by Jesus. Jesus responds to Peter's resistance: If he does not wash him, Peter will have no relationship to him. This OT expression has an exemplar, for example, in 2 Sam 20:1 in the Masoretic text and in the LXX.

■ **9** In verse 9, Peter's passionate rejection of the footwashing in an absurd lack of understanding is transformed into the request to have Jesus wash his hands and head also, as though salvation lay in the quantity of the water. Peter does not cut a good figure in the Gospel of John. He is not the protagonist among the disciples in the good sense, but indicates their lack of understanding. For it is not said that the other disciples comprehend what Jesus is doing. It is of course necessary that one

---

9   *The Eucharistic Words of Jesus,* tr. A. Ehrhardt (New York: Macmillan, 1955) 70 n. 3.

10   *BDF* §319: a conative present.

11   *John,* 467f. [355].

speaker be permitted to speak on behalf of everybody—mass scenes are the exception. There is no mention here of a beloved disciple who is comprehending—he could not have been inserted here without destroying the composition of the scene. It is clear that the behavior of this disciple involves a misunderstanding. Of what that misunderstanding consists, however, is not so easily determined.

■ **10** This verse, which is intended to provide an explanation, is obscure and its wording uncertain. Up to this point, the Evangelist has used the verb νίπτειν for the washing of feet; now, in contrast, the verb λούειν suddenly appears. The short reading (without "except for his feet," εἰ μὴ τοὺς πόδας), offered by ℵ c vg^codd, would imply: whoever has bathed does not need to wash, but is entirely clean. But what then is the point of the footwashing? Thus, the long text read also by 𝔓^66 B C alone appears to make sense: whoever has bathed needs only to wash his feet (or: to have his feet washed). The subordinate clause does not then fit: but he is entirely clean. Apparently the footwashing is understood as a sacramental act that alone makes fellowship with Jesus possible. For the moment let us ignore the fact that one gets into difficulties with the explanation of "to bathe" (λούειν), which seems to refer to baptism, the value of which then surpasses footwashing. Why then must footwashing occur in order to make fellowship with Jesus possible? Nevertheless, the real misunderstanding indicated by verses 8–11 lies elsewhere. Footwashing does of course create fellowship between Jesus and his disciples; it is a striking expression of his sacrifice. But it is that only as such, not as the purely sacramental effect of a washing. Furthermore, two other difficulties arise out of verses 8ff. In the first place, the disciples are said to be clean. That is affirmed and denied in verse 10 in a single breath: they are clean, but not all of them.

■ **11** Jesus says that, as verse 11 adds, because he knew who his betrayer was. But if the disciples are entirely clean as "those having bathed" (λελουμένοι), why do they still need to take part in the footwashing? In the second place, Peter's haughty contradiction in verse 8 of Jesus' instruction in verse 7 is unprecedented in the Fourth Gospel. The Evangelist does not go to work in so clumsy a fashion. It does not improve matters to say that this contradiction on the part of Peter only prompts the reaffirmation of the Lord that there is no fellowship with him apart from footwashing, and the silliness of Peter in then wanting Jesus to wash both his hands and his head is something other than the customary Johannine misunderstanding. It overlooks the real offense that lies in the slave's task to wash feet. The Evangelist certainly frequently depicts the misunderstanding of the disciples. But here the misunderstanding itself is not correctly conceived. The opposition of Peter in verse 8 is directed against the teacher washing the feet of the disciple and thus against self-abasement that exceeds all limits. Bultmann so interprets that what is involved here is the Son of God who became incarnate and not a personal act of love, and he asks why the natural man does not find such an act acceptable.[12] It is to be said in response that it is not a question here of the incarnate Son of God, but of the service of a slave; this act was not expected of a Jewish slave in Israel, but only of a heathen slave. Peter takes offense at the Lord for wanting to demonstrate such service to the follower against all relevant codes, while it really ought only to be the reverse. In any case, that is the way the Evangelist understands the situation, and that is the way it is presupposed by verse 12, to which we now turn.

■ **12** It is clear that the explanation is given in this verse that is promised in verse 7. One can object with Bultmann, of course, that, for the Evangelist, Peter will really be able to understand Jesus' act only when the cross provides the explanation.[13] And yet the Evangelist, who elsewhere is given to conflating the times of Jesus' earthly activity and that of the community, cannot wait here, as an author, until he has related Jesus' death and resurrection. He has to say now what Jesus' enigmatic act means, and cannot have the resurrected Jesus return to the footwashing in chapter 20. In fact, in the theology of the Evangelist—and on this point Bultmann is entirely correct—the significance of who Jesus is and what he provides dawned on the disciples only after the outpouring of the spirit. But that does not alter the fact that Jesus has to speak the salvific words in advance, and not only in this passage, words that will be properly

---

12   *John*, 468–73 [355–61].
13   *John*, 467f. [355].

understood only after the disciples partake of the spirit. Verse 12 can therefore be taken as an immediate development of verse 7: Jesus performs the footwashing on all the disciples, puts his outer garment back on, and reclines again on the dinner cushions. Then he addresses the question of verse 7: do the disciples understand what he has done to them? Evidently not, and so he has to clarify matters, which he does in the following two verses.

■ **13** The explanation begins with the point that they call him "teacher" (rabbi) and "Lord" (*Mari*). They are right in doing so, for so he is. And yet he, as Lord and teacher, has washed their feet. It follows from that that they should wash each other's feet. The fact that here the author speaks only of footwashing, uses only this graphic expression, and does not indicate that the meaning contained in that term is felt to be a problem. But the key term, "love," has already been dropped in verse 1 and it will be further developed in verse 34. And so the Evangelist leaves it at that offensive figure of speech, footwashing, which he explains as a model and example that Jesus gave to the disciples. The behavior of Jesus toward them, his utter devotion (which will of course find its complete and final expression in his death on the cross, although it began already with the incarnation), ought also to determine the behavior of his own toward each other.

■ **14** When as rabbi and Lord Jesus washed the feet of his disciples, that is an act of self-abnegation (out of love), of self-divestment, and the real emphasis lies on this motif of love. The Evangelist also believes that the humiliation—and thus also the cross—can only be properly understood from this perspective. Yet the word love does not appear in this context. Instead, it is said that Jesus has given the disciples an example which they should follow: they should "wash each other's feet," that is, they should not exalt themselves above one another.

■ **15** Verse 15 expresses this meaning rather clearly: Jesus has provided the disciples with an example of how they should behave toward one another. Jesus' act of footwashing is not conceived in this passage as the meaning of the cross (and his entire earthly life), as the salvific self-humiliation of divine love; rather, the relation of one Christian to another really takes the place of the relation of God to man, Jesus to man. The Evangelist was perhaps able to take that notion over because he was concerned

that the love that bound God and Jesus to the disciples should also reign between and among the disciples. In that case, the Evangelist may have confined his intrusion to a minimum. He may have been satisfied to indicate how he really intended the footwashing as a whole to be understood, the footwashing that he reported following a tradition, and which after him, moreover, became completely contradictory and obscure as a result of its sacramental interpretation.

■ **16** Floating sayings material has also become attached to this story, as it were. The saying of Jesus is introduced with "truly, truly, I say to you." The saying, "a servant is not greater than his master; nor is he who is sent greater than he who sent him," appears to be an admonition to humility. The disciples are indeed not greater and not better than their lord. For precisely that reason, Jesus' act in washing their feet is exemplary and paradigmatic. In this respect, verse 16 fits the story of the love that suffers self-humiliation.

■ **17** If they know these things, verse 17 adds in conclusion, they are blessed if they practice what they know. But that is not really the admonition to love—as it will confront us later (v 34) in the discourse of Jesus—but a warning against pride and perhaps also an aversion to suffering. It is quickly forgotten that discipleship is a discipleship in suffering and not in glory, and the Gospel of John, which, more than any other, reduces the passion of Jesus to his humanity and then paints the picture of the heavenly lord with colors that are all the more brilliant, itself stands in dire need of such an admonition.

■ **18–20** With these verses we come once again to a later addition, to a redactional insertion. A similar remark of Jesus appeared earlier in 6:70; there it is firmly anchored in the context. An allusion to it appears also in 15:16, where it likewise corresponds to the context. But in this passage, on the other hand, the verse awkwardly presupposes what is said in verses 21ff., and thereby destroys the tension with which the text is obviously concerned. The purpose of the quotation—indicated in verse 19—is not merely to prepare the reader for the betrayal and to inform the reader that Jesus had exact foreknowledge of it; the quotation of Ps 41:9 also provides the scriptural proof that this betrayal was prophesied in scripture and was therefore contained in God's plan of salvation. Earlier scholars were persuaded that the Synoptics had made use of this passage. Mark 14:18 has Jesus say that one of those eating with him would betray him, and in Mark 14:20, in response to the question about who that one is, Jesus answers only: "one of the twelve, who is dipping bread into the dish with me." It is clear that in this passage Jesus does not dip a morsel in the dish and hand it to Judas, but lets matters rest with the veiled saying. In Matt 26:25, Judas asks, "Is it I?" and receives the not unambiguous affirmative answer: "You have said so." Luke 22:14 introduces an account that is closer to the Johannine version. Yet in verses 21ff. the betrayal is announced with the words, "But behold the hand of him who betrays me is with me on the table." There is no mention of the dish or of dipping into it. Presumably, Luke could not presuppose knowledge of the details of the Jewish Passover meal on the part of his readers. The specific reference to Judas that is prepared for in Matthew is suppressed in John at first because the OT quotation occupies the foreground. It is possible that it was especially important, in view of Jewish (and later heathen) reproaches leveled against Jesus, that he not have remarked that one of his own disciples delivered him into the hands of the Jews. If one takes Mark as the point of departure, Jesus is apparently simply surprised. Verse 19 has Jesus announce the betrayal ahead of time to the disciples, so that it might not destroy their faith once it occurs. This perspective has the reader of the Gospel primarily in view.

Verse 20 does not belong to this context at all; it is loosely connected with verse 16 by means of the catch-word "send" ($\pi\acute{\epsilon}\mu\pi\omega$); formally and with respect to content it is closely connected to Matt 10:40 and could have been taken over by the redactor from that context.

■ **21** The story proper—probably in the form of the source—is continued in this verse and provides the actual prediction of the betrayal, as in Mark 14:19, Matt 26:21, and Luke 22:21. It is introduced in a form that calls the reader's attention to the particulars of the moment: Jesus shows that he is deeply troubled and solemnly expresses the certainty that one of those sitting with him at table will betray him, yet he does so without being specific. In view of verse 18, that is nothing new, and even less so in view of verse 11. Yet in this story the reaction of the disciples is new. No one doubts that this

prediction of Jesus will be fulfilled.

■ **22** Verse 22 is reminiscent of the synoptic parallels, yet it goes its own way: the disciples look at one another, uncertain of whom he could thus speak. But they do not ask, as they do in Mark and Matthew, 'Is it I?'

■ **23** With this verse begins the first of those passages in which the "beloved disciple" is introduced, or, more exactly, the disciple "whom Jesus loved." The Synoptics know of no such favored disciple, and this passage does not give us warrant for reckoning with the historicity of the scene either. Verse 23 reports that this disciple lay at the breast of Jesus. The dinner couch, for three persons, corresponds to the custom of taking festive meals in a reclining position. One lay on one's side, supported by the left arm, so that the right hand was free for eating. In order to make eating easier, the place of the second, middle, participant was located slightly behind the participant to the left, so that his head was about chest high with respect to the person on the left ($\grave{\epsilon}\nu\ \kappa\acute{o}\lambda\pi\omega$). This same arrangement was repeated for the third or righthand participant. This arrangement did not indicate a special relationship. The actual place of honor was the lefthand position.[14] If a disciple thus lay to the right of Jesus, he needed only to bend his head back in order to address a quiet question to him. This is the situation in which that disciple "whom Jesus loved" found himself, according to verse 23.

■ **24f.** This verse is not easily connected with the preceding. Peter can, of course, beckon to the beloved disciple were he lying on any of the dinner couches in the large circle. But then how can he say to him that he would like to know of whom Jesus speaks. An exchange in whispers, of which some interpreters speak, would then be conceivable only if there were complete silence, in which the others at the table would also have heard. The disciple addressed by Peter fulfills the request: he leans back and asks Jesus: Who is it?

■ **26** According to this verse, Jesus answers by telling the disciple that he will dip a morsel in the dish and give it to the (future) betrayer. He then dips the morsel in the dish and gives it to Judas, son of Simon Iscariot.

■ **27** Verse 27, upon close examination, provides two further developments. First, after the morsel, Satan

14   Cf. Billerbeck, 4,1: 41–76; 4,2: 611–39.

enters into Judas. Jesus' word follows: "What you are going to do, do quickly." In this form, both the devil and Jesus' word are simultaneously effective in Judas.

■ **28** This verse indicates that none of the dinner guests understood why he said what he did to Judas. They thus heard what Jesus said to Judas, but they did not hear the exchange among Peter, the beloved disciple, and Jesus.

■ **29** This verse indicates what the disciples imagine Jesus to have meant: some think that Judas, as the treasurer of the group, is to buy something for the feast, while others think that he is to give something to the poor.

■ **30** Verse 30 is made to connect up only with difficulty: only now does Judas take the morsel and immediately go out. But according to verses 26f., Judas had already received the morsel. That indicates that everything is not in order in this scene. The final remark is striking: "It was night" is especially cryptic and effective for the reader precisely because of its possible deep meaning (night of the passion). Thus, in contrast to the other NT representations of the event, here Jesus himself precipitates the deed of Judas. It thus turns out that the betrayal does not surprise Jesus in a much more impressive way than in the mere prediction of the betrayal. If one attributes verses 23–26ab and 28f. to a revision, the result is a report that is much more possible for the Evangelist. But that is not really a compelling reconstruction (see the Overview).

Overview

Hirsch has eliminated the beloved disciple when he asserts: "The author knows of no favored disciple and of no special love for one particular disciple."[15] That may be, but the elimination of the words "whom Jesus loved" does not solve the puzzle in spite of the consideration Hirsch adduces: "Had he [the author] named a particular disciple as the trusted one, the one who occupied the place of honor and was able to direct the question to Jesus, he would have contradicted his whole presentation . . . and besides, he would have directed attention to an entirely new point that would have distracted from the story of Judas. It is evidence of a genuine artistic sense that he was aware of that and thus makes the figure in a position next to Jesus, as required by the action, an

unknown and undetermined subsidiary figure. Whoever understands that, poses no further questions and imagines no further mystery."[16] Yet when Peter requests the disciple allegedly occupying the place of honor to pose a question of Jesus, attention is nevertheless directed to that disciple. Moreover, at least the disciple on the right must now have known who was to betray Jesus. However, that contradicts what is said in verse 28: no one at the table understood what Jesus said to Judas. The beloved disciple must have understood it. One does not solve the problem by eliminating the words "whom Jesus loved", nor has one really dealt with the difficulty if one follows Hirsch further in striking verse 27a ("Then after the morsel, Satan entered into him") and in removing verses 28f.[17] One must rather observe that in all passages where the beloved disciple is treated, he stands in a position of superiority with respect to Peter; this superiority is manifested in various ways, but that is not what is important. The entire scene with Peter is therefore to be considered an insertion. It is now evident that two motifs are competing with each other: one is the morsel given by Jesus that causes Judas to fall into the hands of Satan, the other is the saying of Jesus that sends the betrayer out to perform his deed. It hardly need be asked which of the two is more crass: the magical morsel, with which Satan enters Judas obviously is. We therefore have to accept the view that this feature belongs to a revision that has a coarsening effect. Although the scene with Peter and the beloved disciple is to be omitted, in the text that is left, verse 27b follows immediately on verse 22; in that case, of course, "Judas, son of Simon Iscariot" must be substituted for the simple "him." It is then also the case that Judas did not commit the betrayal in and of himself: Jesus gives him the order to carry it out. But that transpires without the magical morsel and Satan. If the conversation among Peter, the beloved disciple, and Jesus is omitted, then there is no need to eliminate verses 28f. These verses now make good sense. The action takes place now between Jesus and Judas, between the sacrifice and him who is to make the sacrifice and yet who does not have the possibility of making the sacrifice in himself. We are thus left with this situation: the fourth Evangelist does not permit Jesus to be

---

15 *Das vierte Evangelium,* 341.

16 Hirsch, *Das vierte Evangelium,* 341.

17 Hirsch, *Das vierte Evangelium,* 341.

betrayed, to become a deceived sacrifice. Rather, Jesus holds the threads of fate in his hands: he has the power to lay his life down. But Jesus' transcendence was not sufficiently heightened for the redactor, and so, without stylistic skill—the entire scene, from beginning to end, is artificially conceived—he attempts to make Jesus' power more evident and has Satan enter into the hated Judas. And so one of the most remarkable scenes of the Fourth Gospel has been spoiled by a foolish redactor. We will meet him again and again, and each time it will be shown that these intrusions obscure the text. One can not only "lift out" the scenes with the beloved disciple, one can also thereby illumine the text. The remarkable thing is that the beloved disciple basically remains an insignificant figure, whose attraction lies in his name alone and in the quality of the man suggested by the name, but which never becomes visible. That will be demonstrated by 18:15f., 19:26, 20:2, and 21:7, 20.

The manner in which Jesus identifies the betrayer varies from one gospel to another. In this connection two trends are competing with one another. On the one hand, it is happily reported that Jesus precisely identified the betrayer ahead of time; on the other, one ought not to overstep certain bounds in the forecast, otherwise it would become incomprehensible that the disciples continued to tolerate Judas among themselves. Mark appears to offer the oldest tradition. According to Mark, Jesus simply predicted that one of the twelve, who are thought of as sharing a meal with him, will betray him, that is, deliver him over into the hand of his enemies. Obviously, the reproach that Jesus had no premonition of the betrayal (which is probably what happened) troubled Christians, in spite of the fact that his precautionary measures are still recognizable. It is unrealistic for the disciples to look at one another, uncertain about who is meant, when Judas is present. It is clear that in Mark this is not satisfactory: Jesus must at least have indicated that Judas was the guilty party. But this indication, too, is unrealistic: it could have made the other disciples distrustful of Judas. The technique of "dipping in the dish" appears already in the Markan account. It makes good sense in connection with the Passover meal. A biblical prooftext was not given for this betrayal, but

only for the death of the "Son of man."

Luke has omitted the dish and the dipping—it was not comprehensible to his readers. In its place he has indicated the communal character of the meal by the note that the hand of the betrayer was on the table, like the hand of Jesus; he does not seem to assume that each person had a serving tray in front of him. He speaks of the "determination" rather than providing a prooftext. That is more readily understood by Greeks.[18] Since according to Luke the announcement of the betrayal follows immediately upon the distribution of the bread, it could be imagined that in verse 21 Judas receives the morsel just as Jesus gives it to him. That would be the presupposition for the Johannine tradition, which has developed orally from a version that corresponds to the Lukan form. As narrator, John has an unfavorable situation as his point of departure. Judas has been both baptized and washed by Jesus. That is tolerable if the baptism and washing—or only the washing, if verses 8–11 are a later insertion—are understood not as a magical force, but just as an "example." Nevertheless, the Johannine parallel to the announcement of the betrayal is then very remarkable and not very unified. First of all, Ps 41:9 is here introduced as the OT prediction of the betrayal. Then comes the announcement that is poorly appended: One of you will betray me. The beloved disciple, who lies on the dinner couch to Jesus' right, with his head at the height of Jesus' chest, is prompted to inquire further about this matter by Peter. To the question, "Lord, who is it?", Jesus answers: "It is he to whom I give the morsel when I have dipped it." And he dipped the morsel in the dish and gave it to Judas Iscariot. Verse 27a, which now follows, appears to be a later addition: and after the morsel, Satan entered into him. The text proper continues in verse 27b: Jesus said to him: What you are going to do, do quickly. But none of those around the table understood this—except Judas. He takes the morsel and immediately goes out. "And it was night." The opposing tendencies mentioned earlier are especially striking at this point. The reader immediately understands who is meant, and without the help of verse 27a. For it is not the devil that drives Judas out; on the contrary, it is Jesus himself who sends him to do his job.

18   Cf. Acts 2:23, 10:42, 11:29, 17:26, 31.

In this account, verses 18 and 21 are not compatible. Jesus has said earlier that he will be betrayed. Why then is he troubled only in verse 21? In verse 18 an OT passage now appears as a prooftext. It is scarcely especially old—Matthew would certainly have made use of it elsewhere. It shows that some Psalms were read as descriptions of the passion. In this manner Ps 41:9 has been introduced into the passion narrative: "Even my friend, whom I trusted, who ate my bread. . . ." In Hebrew: "Even the man of my peace [i.e., my close friend], whom I trusted, who ate my bread, has raised his heel high against me [i.e., has given me a kick]." LXX Ps 40:10: "For even the man of my peace, on whom I hoped, who ate my bread, has made a powerful blow against me with his heel." Since verse 11 contains a request to be raised up, it is quite understandable why this passage was interpreted with reference to the passion. John here has a later prooftext, one still unknown to the Synoptics. It is therefore all the more unresolved whether it appeared already in the source, stems from the Evangelist, or first made its way into the text at the hand of the redactor.

The word "morsel" (ψωμίον) appears only here in the NT and never in the LXX. The verb ψωμίζειν, "to feed" (active), is known to the LXX, as is the substantive ψωμός in the sense of "bread," as in Ruth 2:14: "And since it was mealtime, Boas said to her: Come and eat and dip your morsel in the wine." The word "morsel" here is פַּת in Hebrew, which means "morsel, crumb." But a connection between this passage and Ps 41:9 cannot be demonstrated. What is new is, first, that Jesus here identifies Judas by means of a gesture. Normally everyone dips into the dish for himself. But one does not need to accept with Hirsch[19] that Judas is thereby characterized as a stranger. To be handed a morsel can also be a special honor. Further, this handing over a morsel is a clear identifying token to the beloved disciple; otherwise it remains incomprehensible to the disciples. There follow two mutually exclusive consequences: in accordance with the first, Satan enters into Judas after the morsel—the supper has been spoken of as infernal. Jesus would then have made Judas fair game for Satan by means of the morsel. That the Evangelist did not intend any such

thing is clear, but is confirmed by the saying of Jesus that follows: "What you are going to do, do at once." This shows how Jesus holds his destiny in his own hands, entirely without magic: he sends Judas out on the previously planned betrayal with a word that everyone hears but nobody except Judas understands. Since he is already close to Judas as a result of handing him the morsel (how is that to be pictured?), he can speak to him softly, without having to use his name and without another feeling that he has been addressed. But this entire segment runs into difficulty with verse 18f. That implies that the tradition of the morsel can be older than its connection with the beloved disciple, although the former here appears in connection with the latter. The special thing now is that the beloved disciple first learns who the betrayer is but does not of course draw a conclusion from that. Naturally, he must not detain Judas and subject him to public censure—that would have produced confusion in the entire story and action. Yet that does not prove that the scene is true to life. What obtains with 20:8 also obtains here. In 20:8 the beloved disciple comes to faith with the resurrection of Jesus, but he does not say a single word to the other disciples about it. Only his preference over Peter is reported, but this preference has no effect on the story. The beloved disciple turns out to be a purely literary figure; he is not real. The story in John 13 with the word of Jesus addressed to Judas is very nice. But it is difficult to say what it would have sounded like without the preceding question of a disciple. Verse 22 is the best prospect for a connecting verse. But the conclusion of verse 26 does not run on smoothly. The words, "he received [it] and" (λαμβάνει καὶ), do not fit; they could be a reminiscence of the account of the last supper, where Jesus took bread and gave it to them. Perhaps we are to read with 𝔓66 and A: "and dipping the morsel" (καὶ ἐμβάψας τὸ ψωμίον). In that case, Jesus would be answering the unspoken question of the disciples, and it would be an answer that betrays nothing, except for Judas, through the word that is spoken, not through the morsel as such. When Jesus gives the morsel to Judas, that only serves to bring the two into close contact. The morsel has no magical significance, nor does the word: Judas knows that he has

---

19 *Das vierte Evangelium*, 388.

been seen through, and knows at the same time that Jesus does not oppose what has been planned. Naturally, it would be better were verse 30 to follow immediately on verse 27. But that proposal is not quite compelling. One cannot eliminate verses 28f. on the strength of suggestion.

A further problem is posed by the traditonal interpretation of verses 14–15. The present text is misunderstood when this interpretation of the text is called "paraenetical" or "ethical." Jesus' action can no more be called "paraenetical" than can the action of his disciples. Jesus' act in washing feet—denoting his self-abnegation to the extent of death—is his salvific act of revelation. One cannot enter into fellowship with him and through him with the "Father" whom he has revealed if one is not prepared for this same act of self-abnegation. Everything turns on this kind of existence, which alone makes unity with the Father and the son possible. To say that this is only something ethical, yet lying below the level of the religious, throws Johannine theology as a whole into confusion. Behavior toward fellow Christians (or fellow human beings) is not to be separated from behavior toward God and Jesus. In this sense, there is no such thing as "pure religion" that permits us to pass the neighbor by and come directly to God. John views the whole of Jesus' earthly life as the revelation and realization of this divine love. He makes this especially clear in his depiction of the last supper of Jesus—and thus at the most conspicuous time possible—during which Jesus gets up and washes the feet of the disciples. Footwashing was a sign of lowly service in those days. In this case, however, it manifests the willing self-abnegation of the Lord and Master; in other words, his utter devotion in love. In accordance with the will of the Father, Jesus was not there for his own sake, but for the sake of those whom the Father had given him. To be there for the sake of others is the love that Jesus proclaims to his disciples as the new commandment (15:12); that love is also the bearing of fruit, as indicated in 15:8. The love that is utter devotion gives life its true content for the first time and in a curious way. All other forms of human behavior: the quest for pleasure, the desire for fortune, striving for power—all these finally leave life empty. Only the water of the love that is utterly devoted can quench the thirst of man. This love gives life its purpose—even if one must die for it. Whoever so loves, with him will the Father and Jesus commune (14:23).

34. The Love Commandment

Bibliography

A. John 13:31–17:26

Ballenstedt, Heinrich Christian
"Die letzten Reden Jesu an seine Jünger, im Geiste Johannes vorgetragen." In his *Philo und Johannes; oder, Neue philosophisch-kritische Untersuchung des Logos beym Johannes nach dem Philo, nebst einer Erklärung und Uebersetzung des ersten Briefes Johannes aus der geweihten Sprache der Hierophanten*, 3 vols. (Braunschweig: F. B. Culemann, 1802); *oder, Fortgesetzte Anwendung des Philo zur Interpretation der Johanneischen Schriften; mit besonderer Hinsicht auf die Frage: ob Johannes der Verfasser der ihm zugeschriebenen Bücher seyn könne?* (Göttingen: H. Dieterich, 1812), esp. 1: 97–118; 2: 69–94.

Baumeister, Theofried
"Der Tod Jesu und die Leidensnachfolge des Jüngers nach dem Johannesevangelium und dem ersten Johannesbrief." *Wissenschaft und Weisheit* 40 (1977) 81–99.

Becker, Jürgen
"Die Abschiedsreden Jesu im Johannesevangelium." *ZNW* 61 (1970) 215–46.

Behler, Gerhard Maria
Die Abschiedsworte des Herrn: Joh 13–17 (Salzburg: O. Müller, 1962).

Bornkamm, Günther
"Die Zeit des Geistes. Ein johanneisches Wort und seine Geschichte." In his *Geschichte und Glauben*, part 1. *Gesammelte Aufsätze*, vol. 3. BEvT 48 (Munich: Chr. Kaiser Verlag, 1971) 90–103.

Boyd, W. J. Peter
"The Ascension according to St. John. Chapters 14–17 not pre-passion but post-resurrection." *Theology* 70 (1967) 207–11.

Boyle, John L.
"The Last Discourse (Jn 13,31–16,33) and Prayer (Jn 17): Some Observations on Their Unity and Development." *Bib* 56 (1975) 210–22.

Bussche, Henri van den
Le discours d'adieu de Jésus; commentaire des chapitres 13 à 17 de l'évangile selon saint Jean, tr. C. Charlier and P. Goidts (Tournai: Casterman, 1959) = *Jesus' woorden bij het Afscheidsmaal; verklaring van de hoofdstukken 13–17 van het Sint-Jansevangelie* (Den Haag: Lannoo, Tielt, 1957).

Carmody, J.
"The 'Death of God' and John 14–17." *Bible Today* 30 (1967) 2082–90.

Gaechter, Paul
"Der formale Aufbau der Abschiedsrede Jesu." *ZKT* 58 (1934) 155–207.

Hauret, Charles
Les Adieux du Seigneur (Jean XIII–XVII). Charte de vie apostolique (Paris: J. Gabalda, 1952).

Huby, Joseph
  Le discours de Jésus après la Cène; suivi d'une étude sur la connaissance de foi dans Saint Jean (Paris: Beauchesne, 1933).
Kundsin, Karl
  "Die Wiederkunft Jesu in den Abschiedsreden des Johannesevangeliums." *ZNW* 33 (1934) 210–15.
Lacomara, Aelved
  "Deuteronomy and the Farewell Discourse (Jn 13:31–16:33)." *CBQ* 36 (1974) 65–84.
Langbrandtner, Wolfgang
  Weltferner Gott oder Gott der Liebe? Der Ketzerstreit in der johanneischen Kirche. Eine exegetisch-religionsgeschichtliche Untersuchung mit Berücksichtigung der koptisch-gnostischen Texte aus Nag-Hammadi, Beiträge zur biblischen Exegese und Theologie 6 (Frankfurt: P. Lang, 1977), esp. 50–69.
Nägelsbach, Friedrich
  "Die Voraussagungen Jesu nach Joh. 14–16 und ihre Folgerungen." *NKZ* 22 (1911) 663–96.
Oehler, Wilhelm
  Das Wort des Johannes an die Gemeinde: Evangelium Johannis 15–17, Johannes-Briefe und Offenbarung des Johannes (Gütersloh: C. Bertelsmann, 1938).
Onuki, Takashi
  "Die johanneischen Abschiedsreden und die synoptische Tradition—eine traditionskritische und traditionsgeschichtliche Untersuchung." *Annual of the Japanese Biblical Institute* 3 (1977) 157–268.
Pass, H. Leonard
  The Glory of the Father. A Study in S. John XIII–XVII (London and Oxford: A. R. Mowbray, 1935).
Riggs, Don Richard
  "John's Persecution Ethic: A Study in the Farewell Discourse." Dissertation, Vanderbilt University, 1969.
Segalla, Giuseppe
  "Il libro dell'Addio di Gesú ai suoi." *Parole di Vita* 15 (1970) 356–76.
Seynaeve, J.
  "Le testament spirituel du Christ. Les discours de la denière Cène (Jn 13–17)." *Orientations Pastorales* 14 (1962) 66–75.
Schneider, Johannes
  "Die Abschiedsreden Jesu. Ein Beitrag zur Frage der Komposition von Joh 13,31–17,26." In *Gott und die Götter.* [FS. E. Fascher] (Berlin: Evangelische Verlagsanstalt, 1958) 103–12.
Stagg, F.
  "The Farewell Discourses—John 13–17." *RevExp* 62 (1965) 459–72.
Steinmetz, Franz-Josef
  "'. . . Und ich gehe nimmer, wann ich gehe—.' Zum Verständnis der johanneischen Abschiedsreden." *Geist und Leben* 51 (1978) 85–99.

Steinmeyer, Franz Karl Ludwig
  Beiträge zum Verständnis des johanneischen Evangeliums. Vol. 8, *Die Scheiderede Jesu an den Kreis der Seinen* (Berlin: Wiegandt & Grieben, 1893).
Swete, Henry Barclay
  The Last Discourse and Prayer of Our Lord. A Study of St. John XIV–XVII (London: Macmillan, 1914).
Walter, Eugen
  Die Mysterien des Wortes und der Liebe. Auslegung der Abschiedsreden des Herrn (Joh. 14–17) (Freiburg: Herder, 1964; Dusseldorf: Patmos Verlag, ²1967).
Zimmermann, Heinrich
  "Struktur und Aussageabsicht der johanneischen Abschiedsreden (Jo 13–17)." *BLit* 8 (1967) 279–90.

B. John 13:31–38

Bornkamm, Günther
  "Zur Interpretation des Johannesevangeliums." *EvT* 28 (1968) 8–25.
Bussche, Henri van den
  "Nu is de Mensensoon verheerlijkt (Joh 13,31–38)." *Collationes Gandavenses* 3 (1953) 97–105.
Cerfaux, Lucien
  "La charité fraternelle et le retour du Christ (Jn 13,33–38)." *ETL* 24 (1948) 321–32.
Charlier, Célestin
  "La présence dans l'absence (Jn 12,31–14,31)." *BVC* 2 (1953) 61–75.
Kelly, John
  "What did Christ Mean by the Sign of Love?" *African Ecclesiastical Review* 13 (1971) 113–21.
Kölbing, F. W.
  "Biblische Erörterungen: Ueber Joh 13,34.35." *TSK* 18 (1845) 685–96.
Lazure, N.
  "Louange au Fils de l'homme et commandement nouveau. Jn 13,31–33a. 34–35." *AsSeign* 26 (1973) 73–80.
Reese, James M.
  "Literary Structure of Jn 13:31–14:31; 16:5–6, 16–33." *CBQ* 34 (1972) 321–31.
Thils, G.
  "De interpretatione Evangelii Sancti Johannis 13,31–14,31." *Collectanea Mechliniensia* 29 (1940) 33–36.
Vellanickal, Matthew
  The Divine Sonship of Christians in the Johannine Writings, AnBib 72 (Rome: Pontifical Biblical Institute, 1977).

31   When he had gone out, Jesus said, "Now is the Son of man glorified, and in him God is glorified; 32/ if God is glorified in him, God will also glorify him in himself, and glorify him at once. 33/ Little children, yet a little while I am with you. You will seek me; and as I said to the Jews so now I say to you, 'Where I am going you cannot come.' 34/ A new commandment I give to you, that you love one another; even as I have loved you, that you also love one another. 35/ By this all men will know that you are my disciples, if you have love for one another." 36/ Simon Peter said to him, "Lord, where are you going?" Jesus answered, "Where I am going you cannot follow me now; but you shall follow afterward." 37/ Peter said to him, "Lord, why cannot I follow you now? I will lay down my life for you." 38/ Jesus answered, "Will you lay down your life for me? Truly, truly, I say to you, the cock will not crow, till you have denied me three times."

■ **31** When Judas has gone out, Jesus is alone—apparently—with his faithful followers. From now on, as far as the end of chapter 16, he speaks only to and with them.

By what means is the Son of man to be glorified, and God in him? Several possibilities present themselves: the means may be that Jesus has identified the betrayer and has simultaneously sent him out to perform his deed, and in so doing, has caused the betrayal and thus the passion to become inevitable. The glorification of God and that of Jesus—the latter comes into view with the former—is therefore not that of an earthly triumph, but that of the passion. Jesus' surrender to death, which he has made graphic in the act of footwashing, is the glory of which Jesus speaks. But why does it only come to pass when Judas has gone out? Because this surrender to death, this extreme love, does not apply to everyone, but only to those whom God and Jesus have chosen. God may indeed love the world—that does not imply that the whole world will be saved, even if God sacrifices himself for it in Jesus. John knows about the mystery that not everyone comes to faith. At the very moment Jesus is speaking these words, he is convinced that no one really believes in him, not even those who were chosen. If Jesus treats them as though they did believe, that is in anticipation of the future when the spirit will be given to those who are truly chosen.

■ **32** The oldest manuscripts have already omitted the words "if God is glorified in him," on the basis of an original scribal error: the scribe skipped from the first "God is glorified in him" to the second "God is glorified in him." That is to say, the scribe intended to write the second phrase when he wrote the first one. The text is therefore to be explained as follows: If God has been glorified in him, then God will be glorified in him, and glorify him at once. After Jesus has burned all his bridges by sending Judas out on his fateful errand, it is but a short time to the cross on Golgatha. There thus speaks here the one about to die—contrary to Käsemann—the one who affirms his death as glorification, and not only because the resurrection will follow after his death. The love of God, which involves the sacrifice of self, is most visible and at its apex on the cross and not on Easter morning. For that reason, John narrates the resurrection abruptly, almost as though it were something ancillary. Jesus thus announces his imminent death. And he strikes a new, intimate tone in this situation by the way he addresses the disciples.

■ **33** The intimate tone is expressed in the address: "Little children." He must now tell them that he is only going to be with them a little while longer. Only a very few hours now separate him from his death, and an only slighter shorter interval from his reunion with his own. They will seek him, and he must now say to them, as he once said to the Jews (7:34), that they cannot go where he is going: to his death. This thought is continued in verse 36.

■ **34f.** Verses 34f. give the commandment of mutual love—in this situation as a new commandment—the love with which Jesus has loved them and has just exemplified in the footwashing. Everyone will know by this love that they are his disciples. In this passage, John does not have in view the worldwide church, but the small band of disciples for whom this Gospel was written.

■ **36** Peter may now ask: Where are you going? A foolish question, as it seems. Jesus is not understood to the last, even by Peter, who is here represented as the spokesman for the disciples. Jesus responds not only with a repetition of what he said earlier, but also with a prophecy: Peter will not follow him now, but no doubt later he will follow him—in death.

■ **37** Verse 37 shows that Peter has understood more than it first appears: he asks, to be sure, why he cannot now follow Jesus, but he affirms that he is prepared to give his life for Jesus. He thereby manifests, of course, a deeper level of non-understanding: he underestimates what he has to do. He therefore receives the answer he does in verse 38.

■ **38** Jesus replies: he will truly not lay down his life now for Jesus, but will deny him three times before the cock crows. Once again, respect is paid to a synoptic motif, but its meaning is that Jesus has foreknowledge of what is to come. He does not go into an unknown future, but knows everything he is to encounter. It is no doubt evident that the denial by his disciples is thereby robbed of its sting. Here Peter does not of course play a prominant role: he exhibits a self-confidence that is unjustified. But nothing is said about the beloved disciple performing any better. He does indeed appear in 18:15f., again as

the counterpart to Peter—as someone known to the high priest. But there he is referred to only as "another disciple"; so that is not strong evidence.

Overview

Bornkamm is of the opinion that: "For what is involved here is not an episodic story in time, but the problem of time and history in general, with which faith is confronted everywhere."[1] That is not correct. At the moment in which the spirit comes to the disciples, this situation is overcome; the new fellowship with Jesus and the Father of course begins at this point. One may therefore only say: this is the situation of all men to whom the spirit has not yet been imparted. The uncertainty attached to the spirit, which modern man is all too inclined to assert, might have been foreign to the Evangelist. On the other hand, the Evangelist also well knew something of the living situation of the disciples in the world, in which they are in need of consolation and strengthening, in short, in which they are in need of the spirit. The paraclete is nothing other than a new form of Jesus; John identifies the return of Jesus, the paraclete, and the coming of the Father. Only so can he combine history and tradition with his experience of the present.

---

1   "Zur Interpretation des Johannesevangeliums," *EvT* 28 (1968) 17.

35. Jesus Discourse on the Situation of the Disciples

Bibliography

A. John 14:1–31

Bacon, Benjamin Wisner
"'In my Father's house are many mansions' John 14,2." *ExpTim* 43 (1931/1932) 477–78.

Bacon, Benjamin Wisner
"Displacement of John 14." *JBL* 13 (1894) 64–76.

Barrett, Charles Kingsley
"'The Father is Greater than I' (Joh 14,28): Subordinationist Christology in the New Testament." In *Neues Testament und Kirche. Für Rudolf Schnackenburg,* ed. J. Gnilka (Freiburg: Herder, 1974) 144–59.

Beauvery, Robert
"Evangiles et homélies. Présentation exégétique des Evangiles de Dimanche [Jn 14,1–12; 14,15–21; Mc 13,33–37]." *Esprit et vie* 79 (1969) 287–91, 317–19, 633–36.

Beck, Dr.
"Ueber Joh 14,1.2." *TSK* 4 (1831) 130–34.

Bertram, G.
"Ev Joh 14,9 und das gnostische Christusbild." *Akten des Internationalen Kongresses, Christ. Arch.* 7 (Berlin: Civitas Vaticanum, 1969) 379–89.

Blank, Josef
"Das Wort, der Geist und die Gemeinde (Joh 14,23–31)." *Am Tische des Wortes* 3 (1965) 28–44.

Blank, Josef
"Predigtmeditationen: Joh 14,23–31." In his *Schriftauslegung in Theorie und Praxis,* Biblische Handbibliothek 5 (Munich: Kösel, 1969) 188–206.

Bleek, Friedrich
"Ueber Joh 14,31 als Beweis der Authentie der johanneischen Reden." In his *Beiträge zur Einleitung und Auslegung der heiligen Schrift.* Vol. 1, *Beiträge zur Evangelien-Kritik* (Berlin: G. Reimer, 1846) 236–39.

Borgen, Peder
"God's Agent in the Fourth Gospel." In *Religions in Antiquity. Essays in Memory of E. R. Goodenough,* ed. J. Neusner (Leiden: E. J. Brill, 1968) 137–47.

Boring, M. Eugene
"The Influence of Christian Prophecy on the Johannine Portrayal of the Paraclete and Jesus." *NTS* 25 (1978/1979) 113–23.

Cignelli, Lino
"Giovanni 14,28 nell'esegesi di S. Ireneo." *Studii Biblici Franciscani Liber Annuus* 27 (1977) 173–96.

Eckle, Wolfgang
Geist und Logos bei Cicero und im Johannesevangelium (Hildesheim: G. Olms, 1978).

Ensley, Eugene C.
"Eternity is Now. A Sermon on Joh 14:1–11." *Int* 19 (1965) 295–98.

Fensham, F. Charles
"I am the Way, the Truth and the Life." *Neot* 2 (1968) 81–88.

Fischer, Günter
Die himmlischen Wohnungen. Untersuchungen zu Joh 14,2f, Europäische Hochschulschriften, Series 23; Theologie 38 (Bern: H. Lang; Frankfurt: P. Lang, 1975).

George, Augustin
"L'évangile Jn 14,23–30: Les venues de Dieu aux croyants." *AsSeign* 51 (1963) 63–71.

Girgensohn, Herbert
"Worte Jesu an die ecclesia viatorum. Betrachtungen zu Joh 14,1–6." In his *Heilende Kräfte der Seelsorge Aufsätze* (Göttingen: Vandenhoeck & Ruprecht, 1966) 177–84.

Gollwitzer, Helmut
"Ausser Christus kein Heil? Joh 14,6." In *Antijudaismus im Neuen Testament? Exegetische und systematische Beiträge,* ed. W. P. Eckert, N. P. Levinson, M. Stöhr. Abhandlungen zum christlich-jüdischen Dialog 2 (Munich: Chr. Kaiser Verlag, 1967) 171–94.

Gundry, Robert H.
"In my Father's House are Many *Monai* (John 14:2)." *ZNW* 58 (1967) 68–72.

Hammer, J.
"Eine klare Stellung zu Joh 14,31b." *Bibel und Kirche* 14 (1959) 33–40.

Klijn, A. J. F.
"John 14,22 and the Name Judas Thomas." In *Studies in John. Presented to Professor J. N. Sevenster on the Occasion of his Seventieth Birthday* (Leiden: E. J. Brill, 1970) 88–96.

Korteweg, T.
"The Reality of the Invisible. Some Remarks on St. John 14,8 and Greek Philosophic Tradition." In *Studies in Hellenistic Religions,* ed. M. J. Vermaseren. Etudes préliminaires aux religions orientales dans l'empire romain 78 (Leiden: E. J. Brill, 1979) 50–102.

Kugelman, Richard
"The Gospel for Pentecost [John 14:23–31]." *CBQ* 6 (1944) 259–75.

La Roche, S.
"Versuch einer Erklärung der Stelle Joh 14,1.2." *TSK* 3 (1830) 114–18.

Potterie, Ignace de la
"'Je suis la Voie, la Vérité et la Vie' (Joh 14, 6)." *NRT* 88 (1966) 907–42.

Rossetto, G.
"La route vers le Père: Jn 14,1–12." *AsSeign* 26 (1973) 18–30.

Simonetti, Manlio
"Giovanni 14,28 nella controversia ariana." In *Kyriakon. Festschrift Johannes Quasten,* ed. P. Granfield and J. A. Jungmann. 2 vols. (Münster: Aschendorff, 1970) 151–61.

Schaefer, O.

"Der Sinn der Rede Jesu von den vielen Wohnungen in seines Vaters Hause und von dem Weg zu ihm (Joh 14,1–7)." *ZNW* 32 (1933) 210–17.

Schnackenburg, Rudolf
"Johannes 14,7." In *Studies in New Testament Language and Text. Essays in Honour of George D. Kilpatrick on the Occasion of his sixty-fifth Birthday,* ed. J. K. Elliott. NovTSup 44 (Leiden: E. J. Brill, 1976) 345–56.

Widengren, Geo
"En la maison de mon Père sont demeures nombreuses." *SEÅ* 37/38 (1972/1973) 9–15.

B. The Paraclete

Bacon, Benjamin Wisner
"The 'Other' Comforter." *Expositor,* 8th ser., 14 (1917) 273–82.

Bammel, Ernst
"Jesus und der Paraklet in Joh 16." In *Christ and Spirit in the New Testament* [Festschrift C. F. D. Moule], ed. B. Lindars and S. S. Smalley (New York: Cambridge University Press, 1973) 199–217.

Barrett, Charles Kingsley
"The Holy Spirit in the Fourth Gospel." *JTS,* n.s., 1 (1950) 1–15.

Bartlett, W.
"The Coming of the Holy Ghost according to the Fourth Gospel." *ExpTim* 37 (1925/1926) 72–75.

Berrouard, M.-F.
"Le Paraclète, défenseur du Christ devant la conscience du croyant (Jn 16,8–11)." *RSPT* 33 (1949) 361–89.

Betz, Otto
Der Paraklet. Fürsprecher im häretischen Spätjudentum, im Johannes-Evangelium und in den neu gefundenen gnostischen Schriften, AGSU 2 (Leiden: E. J. Brill, 1963).

Bornkamm, Günther
"Der Paraklet im Johannesevangelium." In his *Geschichte und Glauben,* part 1. *Gesammelte Aufsätze,* vol 3. BEvT 48 (Munich: Chr. Kaiser Verlag, 1968) 68–89.

Bornkamm, Günther
"Die Zeit des Geistes. Ein johanneisches Wort und seine Geschichte." In his *Geschichte und Glauben,* part 1. *Gesammelte Aufsätze,* vol. 3. BEvT 48 (Munich: Chr. Kaiser Verlag, 1968) 90–103.

Brown, Raymond Edward
"The Paraclete in the Fourth Gospel." *NTS* 13 (1966/1967) 113–32.

Brown, Raymond Edward
"The 'Paraclete' in the Light of Modern Research." *SE* 4 = TU 102 (Berlin: Akademie-Verlag, 1968) 158–65.

Büchsel, Friedrich
Der Geist Gottes im Neuen Testament (Gütersloh: C. Bertelsmann, 1926) 485–511.

Cassien, Bishop
  Le Pentecôte johannique (Paris: Editeurs Réunis, 1939).
Davies, John Gordon
  "The Primary Meaning of παράκλητος." *JTS*, n.s., 4 (1953) 35–38.
Durand, M. G. de
  "Pentecôte johannique et Pentecôte lucanienne chez certains Pères." *BLE* 79 (1978) 97–126.
Floor, L.
  "The Lord and the Holy Spirit in the fourth Gospel." *Neot* 2 (1968) 122–30.
Ghiberti, Giuseppe
  "La rivelazione giovannea del Paraclito." In *Lo Spirito Santo nella liturgia della parola* (Treviso: Editrice Trevigiana, 1968) 7–58.
Holwerda, David Earl
  The Holy Spirit and Eschatology in the Gospel of John; A Critique of Rudolf Bultmann's Present Eschatology (Kampen: Kok, 1959).
Hunt, W. B.
  "John's Doctrine of the Spirit." *Southwestern Journal of Theology* 8 (1965) 45–65.
Hurley, J. M.
  "The Paraclete in the Fourth Gospel." *Bible Today* 36 (1968) 2485–88.
Isaacs, Marie E.
  The Concept of Spirit. A Study of Pneuma *in Hellenistic Judaism and its Bearing on the New Testament,* Heythrop Monographs 1 (London: Heythrop College [University of London], 1976).
Johansson, Nils
  "Parakletoi. Vorstellungen von Fürsprechern für die Menschen vor Gott in der alttestamentlichen Religion, im Spätjudentum und Urchristentum." Dissertation (Lund: C. W. K. Gleerup, 1940).
Johnston, George
  "The Spirit-Paraclete in the Gospel of John." *Pittsburgh Perspective* 9 (1968) 29–37.
Johnston, George
  The Spirit-Paraclete in the Gospel of John, NovTSup 12 (New York and London: Cambridge University Press, 1970).
Kipp, John Lewis
  "The Relationship between the Conception of the 'Holy Spirit' and the 'Risen Christ' in the Fourth Gospel." Dissertation, Princeton Theological Seminary, 1964.
Kothgasser, Alois M.
  "Die Lehr-, Erinnerungs-, Bezeugungs- und Einführungsfunktion der johanneischen Geist-Parakleten gegenüber der Christus-Offenbarung." *Salesianum* 33 (1971) 557–98; 34 (1972) 3–51.
Kothgasser, Alois M.
  "Das Problem der Dogmenentwicklung und die Lehrfunktion des johanneischen Parakleten." Dissertation, Rome, 1968.
Leaney, Alfred Robert Clare
  "The Historical Background and Theological Meaning of the Paraclete." *Duke Divinity School Review* 37 (1972) 146–59.
Leaney, Alfred Robert Clare
  "The Johannine Paraclete and the Qumran Scrolls." In *John and Qumran*, ed. J. H. Charlesworth (London: Chapman, 1972) 38–61.
Locher, Gottfried W.
  "Der Geist als Paraklet. Eine exegetisch-dogmatische Besinnung." *EvT* 26 (1966) 565–79.
Lofthouse, William Frederick
  "The Holy Spirit in the Acts and the Fourth Gospel." *ExpTim* 52 (1940/1941) 334–36.
Martin, Alain G.
  "Le Saint-Esprit et l'Evangile de Jean dans une perspective trinitaire." *Revue reformée* 29 (1978) 141–51.
McPolin, J.
  "Holy Spirit in Luke and John." *ITQ* 45 (1978) 117–131.
Meeks, Wayne A.
  "The Divine Agent and his Counterfeit in Philo and the Fourth Gospel." In *Aspects of Religious Propaganda in Judaism and Early Christianity.* ed. E. Schüssler-Fiorenza. University of Notre Dame Center for the Study of Judaism and Christianity in Antiquity 2 (Notre Dame and London: University of Notre Dame, 1976) 43–67.
Michaelis, Wilhelm
  "Zur Herkunft des johanneischen Paraklet-Titels." *ConNT* 11 (1948) 147–62.
Mowinckel, Sigmund
  "Die Vorstellungen des Spätjudentums vom heiligen Geist als Fürsprecher und der johanneische Paraklet." *ZNW* 32 (1933) 97–130.
Müller, Ulrich B.
  "Die Parakletenvorstellung im Johannesevangelium." *ZTK* 71 (1974) 31–77.
Mussner, Franz
  "Die johanneischen Parakletsprüche und die apostolische Tradition." In his *Praesentia Salutis. Gesammelte Studien zu Fragen und Themen des Neuen Testamentes,* Kommentare und Beiträge zum Alten und Neuen Testament (Düsseldorf: Patmos-Verlag, 1967) 147–58.
Niccacci, Alviero
  "Esame letterario di Gv 14." *Euntes docet* 31 (1978) 209–60.
Patrick, Johnstone G.
  "The Promise of the Paraclete." *BSac* 127 (1970) 333–45.
Pillai, C. J.
  "'Advocate' —Christ's Name for the Holy Spirit." *Bible Today* 30 (1967) 2078–81.
Porsch, Felix
  Pneuma und Wort. Ein exegetischer Beitrag zur Pneumatologie des Johannesevangeliums, Frankfurter Theologische Studien 16 (Frankfurt: Verlag Josef Knecht, 1974).

Porsch, Felix

Anwalt der Glaubenden. Das Wirken des Geistes nach dem Zeugnis des Johannesevangeliums, Geist und Leben (Stuttgart: Katholisches Bibelwerk, 1978).

Potterie, Ignace de la

"L'Esprit Saint dans l'Evangile de Jean." *NTS* 18 (1971/1972) 448–51.

Potterie, Ignace de la

"Parole et Esprit dans S. Jean." In *L'Evangile de Jean. Sources, rédaction, théologie,* ed. M. de Jonge. BETL 44 (Gembloux: Duculot; Louvain: University Press, 1977) 177–201.

Riesenfeld, Harald

"A Probable Background to the Johannine Paraclete." In *Ex Orbe Religionum. Studia Geo Widengren XXIV mense Apr. MCMLXXII quo die lustra tredecim feliciter explevit oblata ab collegis, discipulis, amicis, collegae magistro amico congratulantibus. Pars prior,* Studies in the History of Religion [Supplements to *Numen*] 21 (Leiden: E. J. Brill, 1972) 266–77.

Snaith, Norman H.

"The Meaning of 'the Paraclete.'" *ExpTim* 57 (1945/1946) 47–50.

Synge, F. C.

"The Holy Spirit in the Gospels and Acts." *CQR* (1935) 205–17.

Schlier, Heinrich

"Der Heilige Geist als Interpret nach dem Johannesevangelium." *Internationale Katholische Zeitschrift Communio* 2 (1973) 97–108.

Schlier, Heinrich

"Zum Begriff des Geistes nach dem JE." In *Neutestamentliche Aufsätze. Festschrift für Prof. Josef Schmid zum 70. Geburtstag,* ed. J. Blinzler et al. (Regensburg: F. Pustet, 1963) 233–39.

Schnackenburg, Rudolf

"Die johanneische Gemeinde und ihre Geistererfahrung." In *Die Kirche des Anfangs. Festschrift für Heinz Schürmann zum 65. Geburtstag,* ed. R. Schnackenburg, J. Ernst, and J. Wanke. Erfurter Theologische Studien 38 (Leipzig: St. Benno;

Freiburg: Herder, 1977) 277–306.

Schwegler, Friedrich Carl Albert

Der Montanismus und die christliche Kirche des zweiten Jahrhunderts (Tübingen: L. F. Fues, 1841) 15–151.

Schwegler, Friedrich Carl Albert

Das nachapostolische Zeitalter in den Hauptmomenten seiner Entwicklung, 2 vols. (Tübingen: L. F. Fues, 1846) 338–74.

Villalón, J. R.

Sacrements dans l'Esprit. Existence humaine et théologie sacramentelle, Théologie historique 43 (Paris: Beauchesne, 1977) 277–82.

Windisch, Hans

"Die fünf johanneischen Parakletsprüche." In *Festgabe für Adolf Jülicher zum 70. Geburtstag 26. Januar 1927* (Tübingen: Mohr-Siebeck, 1927) 110–37.

Windisch, Hans

"Jesus und der Geist im Johannes-Evangelium." In *Amicitiae Corolla, A Volume of Essays presented to James Rendel Harris, D. Litt., on the Occasion of his Eightieth Birthday,* ed. H. G. Wood (London: University of London Press, 1933) 34–69.

Windisch, Hans

The Spirit-Paraclete in the Fourth Gospel, tr. J. W. Cox. Facet Books, Biblical Series 20 (Philadelphia: Fortress Press, 1968).

Woodhouse, H. F.

"The Paraclete as Interpreter." *Biblical Theology* 18 (1968) 51–53.

Wotherspoon, Arthur W.

"Concerning the Name 'Paraclete.'" *ExpTim* 34 (1922/1923) 43–44.

14

1 "Let not your hearts be troubled; believe in God, believe also in me. 2/ In my Father's house are many rooms; if it were not so, would I have told you that I go to prepare a place for you? 3/ And when I go and prepare a place for you, I will come again and will take you to myself, that where I am you may be also. 4/ And you know the way where I am going." 5/ Thomas said to him, "Lord, we do not know where you are going; how can we know the way?" 6/ Jesus said to him, "I am the way, and the truth, and the life; no one comes to the Father, but by me. 7/ If you had known me, you would have known my Father also; henceforth you know him and have seen him." 8/ Philip said to him, "Lord, show us the Father, and we shall

be satisfied." 9/ Jesus said to him, "Have I been with you so long, and yet you do not know me, Philip? He who has seen me has seen the Father; how can you say, 'Show us the Father'? 10/ Do you not believe that I am in the Father and the Father in me? The words that I say to you I do not speak on my own authority; but the Father who dwells in me does his works. 11/ Believe me that I am in the Father and the Father in me; or else believe me for the sake of the works themselves. 12/ Truly, truly, I say to you, he who believes in me will also do the works that I do; and greater works than these will he do, because I go to the Father. 13/ Whatever you ask in my name, I will do it, that the Father may be glorified in the Son; 14/ if you ask anything in my name, I will do it. 15/ If you love me, you will keep my commandments. 16/ And I will pray the Father, and he will give you another Counselor, to be with you forever, 17/ even the Spirit of truth, whom the world cannot receive, because it neither sees him nor knows him; you know him, for he dwells with you, and will be in you. 18/ I will not leave you desolate; I will come to you. 19/ Yet a little while, and the world will see me no more, but you will see me; because I live, you will live also. 20/ In that day you will know that I am in my Father, and you in me, and I in you. 21/ He who has my commandments and keeps them, he it is who loves me; and he who loves me will be loved by my Father, and I will love him and manifest myself to him." 22/ Judas (not Iscariot) said to him, "Lord, how is it that you will manifest yourself to us, and not to the world?" 23/ Jesus answered him, "If a man loves me, he will keep my word, and my Father will love him, and we will come to him and make our home with him. 24/ He who does not love me does not keep my words; and the word which you hear is not mine but the Father's who sent me. 25/ These things I have spoken to you, while I am still with you. 26/ But the Counselor, the Holy Spirit, whom the Father will send in my name, he will teach you all things, and bring to your remembrance all that I have said to you. 27/ Peace I leave with you; my peace I give to you; not as the world gives do I give to you. Let not your hearts be troubled, neither let them be afraid. 28/ You heard me say to you, 'I go away, and I will come to you.' If you loved me, you would have rejoiced, because I go to the Father; for the Father is greater than I. 29/ And now I have told you before it takes place, so that when it does take place, you may believe. 30/ I will no

longer talk much with you, for the ruler of
this world is coming. He has no power
over me; 31/ but I do as the Father has
commanded me, so that the world
may know that I love the Father. Rise, let
us go hence."

Introduction

The problem with which the Evangelist struggles in this
chapter consists in this: how is the experience of the spirit
that dominates him and that has given him his new
understanding of Jesus related to the tradition of the
return of Jesus that has been transmitted to him? The
return of Jesus is spoken of in a double sense: on the one
hand, one could designate as the return of Jesus the
appearances of the resurrected one, appearances in
which not a small number of Christians of the first generation participated, according to 1 Corinthians 15. On
the other hand, one could understand by this phrase the
anticipated return of Jesus in glory at the end of time, at
the in-breaking of the reign of God. The Evangelist
believed that there was nothing higher than fellowship
with the Father, and he believed that one could share in
that fellowship here and now through the experience of
the spirit. He therefore interpreted the primitive Christian tradition of the return of Jesus at the end of time as
just another form of what he himself had experienced.
He does not put it simply prosaically: what was earlier
called such and such is really nothing other than the
experience of the spirit. On the contrary, he set the two
expressions alongside each other (linguistically we would
have to say: he set them down one after the other) and
left it to the reader to discover the identity of the traditional and his own, "modern" mode of expression and
perspectives. And he makes this identification clear in
view of the dire need in which Christians found themselves since the departure of Jesus, since the absence of
God, who threatens to become dubious as a consequence.
It is no longer so striking when other concepts are
identified, like commands, words, expressions, in view of
the decisive equation of eschatology and experience of
the spirit. But at the same time we have to reflect: it is
precisely at this point that Jesus' position vis-à-vis the
Father throws good light on his special task. Thus, the
author returns again and again to this theme.

■ **1** The hour of Jesus' death draws quickly closer. His
death will be a terrible shock for the disciples. Those
who thought they would never forsake him will learn
that they will deny him, one and all. Because God is
proximate to them—as to us all—only in Jesus, they will
misunderstand their loneliness as being God forsaken.
For that reason, they now must be consoled, strengthened, encouraged, and admonished with respect to the
decisive matter: Believe in God and believe in me.

■ **2** They will perceive the end of Jesus' earthly life as
something that plunges them into distress, and Jesus'
departure thereby turns out to be for their salvation: he
will prepare a place for them in the presence of God.
Although the Evangelist uses this figure and speaks of
many mansions there, he does not want to be taken
literally: Jesus restores the right relationship with God.
He makes man at home with the Father. Yet the possibilities open to the Evangelist to express the union of the
believer with God through Jesus permit him also to seize
on other figures for that purpose, the expectation of the
endtime above all.

■ **3** When Jesus has prepared a home for his own in the
presence of God, he will come again and take them to
himself, so that they may again be united with him—in
the presence of God. The expectation of the parousia is
thus placed in the service of the Johannine proclamation.
For, verse 3 does not at all mean that the disciples' sense
of being forsaken by God will cease only when Jesus
returns at the end of time.

■ **4–10** These verses lead to the Johannine reinterpretation of the eschatological hope; the reinterpretation
takes the form of a dialogue of Jesus with them made
necessary by non-understanding on their part. Jesus'
words in verse 3 form the evocative occasion: they know
the way to the place he is going. In response, Thomas
explains that they do not know where he is going and
thus accordingly do not know the way. That is not as
incomprehensible as it sounds, since it is the conviction of
the Evangelist that no one has ever seen the Father: he is
simply inaccessible in his transcendence. But it is precisely
in this context that the mission and significance of Jesus
becomes visible: he is the "way," *scil.* to the Father, and as
such the "truth" and the "life," disclosing the divine
truth. For the Gospel of John Jesus is the appearance of
the unseen Father in this world (v 9). In Jesus the Father
who sent him becomes visible to those believing. It is

never said that Jesus is only the "that" of revelation, without making its "what" concrete;[1] there is no mention of this "that" being the negation of all human self-assertion.[2] When Jesus says, as the word of the Father (12:49), "I am the bread of life," "I am the light of the world," "I am the resurrection and the life," the Father is thereby made known as the merciful one, as the loving God—the joyous message is not always to be expressed in Pauline conceptualities. This love as sacrifice finds its final consummation precisely in death. In Jesus' death the love of God is consummated ($\tau\epsilon\tau\epsilon\lambda\epsilon\sigma\tau\alpha\iota$), and fellowship with God for those believing is restored. Thus Jesus' death is swallowed up completed in his revelatory life as regards the Father, and is not something alongside the revelation. Jesus alone reveals the Father. No one comes to the Father except through him. These statements always have in view the logos become flesh, Jesus of Nazareth. For the Evangelist understands perfectly the question about the distinction between the Jesus who proclaims and the Christ proclaimed by the community and endeavors to answer it in his own way. The disciples did not exactly understand Jesus so long as he was with them, as the response of Philip makes clear. They could not yet break through to authentic faith because the spirit had not yet been given prior to the exaltation of Jesus (7:39). Only when the resurrected one has breathed into them, as God once breathed into Adam, does he make true belief in him possible. For that reason, the Evangelist has to have the Jesus of the Gospel say what the "historical Jesus" cannot yet say, because they are not yet able to understand (16:12f.). The Jesus of the Gospel of John thus already speaks as the risen Christ, and thus already with the clarity that only the spirit of truth can give to the disciples. John thereby simultaneously expresses the overarching unity of "Jesus" and the "Christ," a unity he exemplifies in the intertwining of the times in sayings like 5:24f. and 4:35ff. Consequently, the "hour" can already come to pass in the earthly life of Jesus—prior to the passion—which is the cross, and the resurrection, and the return, all rolled into one. Everything is therefore accessible to the believers, who see Jesus no longer. Yes, and more: when Jesus says (20:21), "As the Father has sent me, even so I send you," then the Father becomes visible in the words of the disciples, just as he does in the words of Jesus, and the heaven is open for the believers (1:51). For he is now the one, in his humanity, in whom the believer can see the Father. Not in the way, of course, that the one who has seen Jesus has seen the Father—otherwise the high priests and their adherents must also have seen the Father. Moreover, Jesus makes the Father visible in his entire way of life, including the death that now confronts him: only so can the sacrifice of love be comprehended. But even that is not derived from a retrospective inference from earthly appearances. Only later will it become evident, thanks to the spirit, that Jesus' earthly life can be discerned as the presence of the Father. It is understandable, as a consequence, that Philip can now ask Jesus to show him the Father. In response, Jesus points, in the first instance, to the fact that he and the Father stand in unbroken unity (v 10). But how can that be demonstrated—if there is such a thing as a demonstration appropriate to it? Jesus points to his words, words that he does not speak out of himself, but on behalf of someone else: they are the works that the Father does who is in him. The possibility for the situation following Jesus' departure is thereby already established. Not in the way, of course, that the words of the earthly Jesus are simply transmitted. The Gospel of John as a whole is not a reproduction of the words of the "historical Jesus" designed to preserve them, but an interpretation—a new interpretation—that is based on a completely new understanding of the form and message of Jesus.

■ 11 This completely new understanding is also expressed in verses 11f. These two verses repeat the call to faith in the unity of the Father and Jesus, and point once more to his works, which are nothing other than his words, in view of what he has said up to this point. That is important for the exposition of verse 12.

■ 12 This verse does not prophesy that the disciples will some day be able to raise the dead, and dead that were in the tomb longer than Lazarus at that. The resurrection for which the raising of Lazarus was indeed only a sign is the resurrection of the spiritually dead, as suggested in 5:25f. It cannot be a matter, precisely for that reason, of reproducing the words of the earthly Jesus. Rather, the

1   Bultmann, *Theology of the New Testament*, 2: 66.
2   Bultmann, *Theology of the New Testament*, 2: 67f.

new proclamation, as practiced by the Evangelist himself, will depart drastically from the literal words of the "historical Jesus" and go its own way, without losing its internal contact, however, with what Jesus himself once had said. That will immediately be made clear in his sayings about the paraclete. It is Jesus' departure to the Father that makes the way free for such a new and powerful interpretation and proclamation (end of v 12).

■ **13f.** With verses 13f. we come to a thought familiar to us from the Synoptics (Matt 7:7). It is inserted here in order to emphasize the connection between the earthly Jesus, who now goes to the Father, and his disciples. Their works are placed under his protection, and are therefore conceived as a prayer in his name, which he himself will fulfill. If these verses are not to be taken as a meaningless insertion from the synoptic tradition, one is driven to such an interpretation. That is made all the more necessary by virtue of the fact that they do not really have a parallel in the Synoptics. In the Synoptics, on the one hand, the name of Jesus is presented as an instrument of power, employed to exorcize demons and perform cures, so that the name of Jesus is understood as a competitor superior to the magical names that would otherwise be employed in such cases. On the other hand, the Synoptics also speak of men being persecuted on behalf of the name, that is, because they are Christians, because they belong to the Jesus community. It almost goes without saying that the earthly Jesus did not speak sayings like those recorded in verses 13f. The later Jesus tradition is coming to expression here, yet in the form of a new interpretation that conforms to the Johannine proclamation. Only if we understand verses 13f. in this way is there no break between these verses and the sayings on the paraclete which follow.

■ **15–31** Verses 15–31 are key sayings for understanding the Johannine message precisely because various traditional materials are being employed here, in order to illuminate the same thing from various perspectives.

■ **15** The commandments of Jesus are mentioned first of all, commandments which those who love him observe. Love for Jesus is not taken here as a feeling; the misunderstanding that love is a sentiment is excluded by virtue of the fact that it is represented as obedience to an instruction. That is a statement that is, of course, open to misunderstanding: the fourth Evangelist is not promulgating a new law. But one might well recall what was said

earlier about the example or model. It is a matter of concrete, lived obedience. But how is that made possible? That is answered in verses 16f.

■ **16** Jesus will pray to the Father to send to them another comforter or counselor, who will not be limited in activity, unlike Jesus, to a specific period in the community. The next verse indicates what is meant by the term paraclete, which remains ambiguous and perpetually disputed.

■ **17** The paraclete is more closely defined in this verse: it is the spirit of truth. This designation is of course also open to various interpretations. Yet one should probably understand something concrete by this term: both the Christian community in which the Evangelist lived and the Evangelist himself have experienced the spirit, and that experience has given rise to a new picture of Jesus and a new christology, which the Evangelist has now embodied in the Fourth Gospel as the spokesman for this "movement." This spirit is incomprehensible for the world, for the non-Christian and anti-Christian world. Presumably a kind of fanaticism was involved because those on the outside, from the point of view of this movement which operated from a new center, (how effective was it?), were unable to catch sight of anything that authenticated this movement.

■ **18** It is a different matter for those who belong to this new community, to this "resurrection movement," as verse 18 explains. For them, the spirit of truth is not something unknown and strange, but something from which they have new life—let us not forget that the Johannine Jesus calls himself "the life." The believer is persuaded that he or she is no longer separated from the Father, because one is convinced that he or she has correctly understood Jesus. Verse 18 expresses what has heretofore been described as the sending of the spirit by the Father with the help of another tradition: Jesus will not leave his own destitute; he will come again. This expression, which has heretofore been used in connection with the eschatological expectation of the imminent end, is now substantially transformed: what one earlier referred to as the "return of Jesus" now truly takes place in the sending of the spirit. The history of Jesus thus does not cease with his departure from his disciples; it continues in another form and creates a new chapter that gives real meaning to everything that has gone before.

■ **19** Verse 19 is thus a reference to Jesus' death: his death will remove him from the realm of the visible for the world, but he will again become visible for his own in that he is giving them a new life, not merely a continuation of the previous Christian tradition.

■ **20** According to verse 20, the time of the adolescence of the those who have received the spirit has now come to an end: they now know that they form the same unity with Jesus that binds Jesus to the Father.

■ **21** Verse 21 repeats what was just said, using the concept of the "commandments" of Jesus, which those loving him will fulfill. The ethic of the spirit is not ethical anarchy, but a true ethic with the highest requirements one can imagine: the unlimited sacrifice, like the love with which Jesus loved them in his entire human existence. That implies, at the same time, that separation from the Father has been eliminated for Christians. The Father is no longer the unknown, the big *X,* that can also be nothingness in the end. Rather, the one with great love wears a mask of nothingness. The Christian is promised that the Father will again love him or her and Jesus will make himself known again to that one. Bultmann regularly refers to Jesus in his commentary as the "revealer," *scil.,* of the Father. Oddly enough, John does not make use of this gnostic concept and speaks here, in connection with "making visible," not of making the Father known, but of making himself known. It is precisely because Jesus has so completely rejected his own importance that he can stand in fully for the Father. But verse 21 also prepares for what is to come.

■ **22** Judas—not the Son of Simon, Iscariot—[3] poses a question that was deeply concealed in the preceding dialogue: why will Jesus make himself known only to his own and not to the world? It follows from this remark that the Johannine community knew itself to be a "closed community" more or less. It is not informed by the conscious that it ought to evangelize the world; rather, its mission has internal limitations.

■ **23** Verse 23 discloses those limitations, except that the bounds of the mission are not made entirely clear to us: whoever loves Jesus is obedient; the world does not have this love, it does not catch sight of the true significance of Jesus, and, going together with this, it does not understand the required obedience in life for which Jesus has

provided the model. But the Evangelist completes his statement with an expression he has not used up to this point: he not only says that the Father for his part will love the true disciples, but the Father and Jesus will come to the believers and dwell with them. Reference has occasionally been made to a God-mysticism in the Fourth Gospel. Since, however, Jesus and the Father are one, because the one doing the sending is present in the one being sent, the new statement coming at the close of verse 23 is not so unprecedented as first appears. But what does this statement mean? Does it mean that Jesus and the Father are present and at home in and among the believers? In accordance with what the Evangelist has said up to this point in various ways about the return of Jesus, this expression also can mean nothing other than the authentic Christian's existence in the spirit. It follows from this that the Christian, for example, becomes the bearer of grace and judgment for his or her hearers just as the earthly Jesus was for his (cf. 20:21ff.). Insofar as the Christian gives expression to the message of Jesus, either it is heard by the one addressed or it remains closed to that hearer. That could be understood to indicate a theology of decision. But John follows another course: in the situation in which there is an encounter with the message of Jesus, what becomes visible is "only" whether the one addressed belongs to those whom the Father has given to Jesus. The decision lies with the Father, not with man. Man can no more produce a new birth out of the spirit by taking a decision than he can choose to be born—he cannot select or determine his parents or his place in history by taking a decision. Man remains within "this world" in his own decisions, and there is nothing earthly than can produce the rule of God.[4] The mystery of divine election cannot be transposed to the realm of anthropology. For this reason, there is no such thing as a miracle that constitutes proof of God.

■ **24** Whoever does not love Jesus, does not keep his commandments, for him a life of absolute self-abnegation is not something commanded, not something meaningful as a requirement. But verse 24 admonishes Jesus' own once more not to perceive the word of Jesus

---

3   In sy[s] he is called Thomas, in sy[c] Judas Thomas.
4   See above, 3:3–18.

as his human word, but as the word of the Father who sent him.

■ 25f. The Evangelist is helped over this difficulty, which is apparently only a recurrence of the claim of Jesus to have been sent by the Father, whose claim looks like a check written without adequate funds on deposit, by the reference to the paraclete, the spirit of truth, whom the Father will send in the name of Jesus: the spirit will teach the disciples all things and thus lead them out of the distress of life's riddle and remind them of Jesus' own words. The tension between the two statements, first, that the paraclete alone provides the whole truth, and, second, that the paraclete prompts only the recollection of what Jesus had already said, points up the difficulty occasioned by the meeting of the new experience of the spirit and the old tradition. This experience of the spirit, in which the transcendent side of all earthly history is revealed, takes place in the midst of history, and the Evangelist affirms that. The earthly life of Jesus is therefore important to him because it eliminates the danger that the experience of the spirit will turn out to be a subjective dream. And yet the Evangelist does not simply reproduce the historical past—in that case the experience of the spirit would be reduced to the logia of the historical Jesus, which an ecclesiastical tradition provides. He rather has the historical Jesus interpret the practical knowledge of the spirit and thus takes the historical Jesus up into the new reality of the spirit.

■ 27–31 Verses 27–31 provide the peaceful conclusion to the discourse, which is actually a farewell speech.

■ 27 Jesus leaves the believers his peace, which is not merely a partial and always unsatisfying peace, like the peace the world gives. The hortatory consolation once again resounds: Do not let yourselves be disconcerted and anxious.

■ 28 For, Jesus will indeed return. In fact, his own should actually rejoice over his departure to the Father; for the Father is greater than he. He himself is only the one sent, but the Father who sends him is sovereign. He is the promise, but the Father is the fulfillment. What Jesus says here about his own death applies also to the death of individual Christians. One should not therefore be troubled that Jesus now departs.

■ 29 He had told them this beforehand so that their faith would not be shattered when he departs.

■ 30 He no longer has much to say, for the ruler of this world is coming, and that is death with all its dread. The ruler of this world has no claim on Jesus, and he cannot hold onto him.

■ 31 But Jesus must nevertheless die so that the world may see that he loves the Father, who calls him in the depths of the world and death. Only in Jesus' obedience does it become clear that Jesus does not live for himself, but acts only as the Father charges him.

Verse 31 ends with the summons to rise and go hence. These words are of course reminiscent of Mark 14:42. But there the words that John has condensed into the saying in 12:27 are spoken in Gethsemane. In the Gospel of John, the situation is different: up to this point, Jesus and his disciples were at the last supper and were lying on dinner cushions. Now he calls on them to arise and go hence. Chapters 15–17, accordingly, must be discourses of Jesus spoken along the way, as they cross to Kidron.

36. Jesus the Vine

Bibliography

Beauvery, Robert
"La mission des disciples: demeurer dans l'amour par l'obéissance (Jn 15, 9–17)." *Esprit et vie* 80 (1970) 273–75.

Beauvery, Robert
"Les disciples, communauté à laquelle Jésus donne vie (Jn 15,1–8)." *Esprit et vie* 80 (1970) 242–45.

Borig, Rainer
Der wahre Weinstock. Untersuchungen zu Jo 15,1–10, SANT 16 (Munich: Kösel, 1967).

Braun, Herbert
"Joh 15,1–8." *Göttinger Predigtmeditationen* 23 (1968/1969) 290–93.

Bussche, Henri van den
"La vigne et ses fruits (Jn 15, 1–8)." *BVC* 26 (1959) 12–18.

Dibelius, Martin
"Joh. 15:13: Eine Studie zum Traditionsproblem des Johannesevangeliums." In *Festgabe für Adolf Deissmann zum 60. Geburtstag, 7. November 1926* (Tübingen: Mohr-Siebeck, 1927) 168–86.

George, Augustin
"Les témoins de Jésus devant le monde." *AsSeign* 50 (1966) 30–40.

George, Augustin
"Jésus, la vigne véritable (Jn 15,1–17)." *Logos* 2 (Tokyo, 1960) 148–67.

Grundmann, Walter
"Das Wort von Jesu Freunden (Joh 15,13–16) und das Herrenmahl." *NovT* 3 (1959) 62–69.

Hawkin, David J.
"Orthodoxy and Heresy in John 10,1–21 and 15,1–17." *EvQ* 47 (1975) 208–13.

Jaubert, Annie
"L'image de la vigne (Jean 15)." In *Oikonomia. Heilsgeschichte als Thema der Theologie. Oscar Cullmann zum 65. Geburtstag gewidmet,* ed. Felix Christ (Hamburg: B. Reich, 1967) 93–99.

Lee, G. M.
"New Testament Gleanings." *Bib* 51 (1970) 235–40.

Lee, G. M.
"John 15,14: 'Ye are my friends.'" *NovT* 15 (1973) 260.

O'Grady, John F.
"The Good Shepherd and the Vine of the Branches." *BTB* 8 (1978) 86–89.

Radermakers, Jean
"Je suis la vraie vigne Jn 15,1–8." *AsSeign* 26 (1973) 46–58.

Rosscup, James E.
Abiding in Christ. Studies in John 15. (Grand Rapids: Zondervan, 1973).

Sandvik, Björn
  "Joh 15 als Abendmahlstext." *TZ* 23 (1967) 323–28.
Segalla, Giuseppe
  "La struttura chiastica di Giov 15,1–8." *BeO* 12 (1970) 129–131.
Smith, C. R.
  "The Unfruitful Branches in John 15." *Grace Journal* 9 (1968) 3–22.
Sparks, H. F. D.
  "St. John's Knowledge of Matthew. The Evidence of John 13,16 and 15,20." *JTS*, n.s., 3 (1952) 58–61.
Thyen, Hartwig
  "'Niemand hat grössere Liebe als die, dass er sein Leben für seine Freunde hingibt' (Joh 15,13)." In *Theologia Crucis—Signum Crucis. Festschrift für Erich Dinkler zum 70. Geburtstag*, ed. C. Andersen and G. Klein (Tübingen: Mohr-Siebeck, 1979) 467–81.
Vouga, François
  "'Aimez-vous les uns les autres.' Une étude sur l'église de Jean." *Bulletin de Centre Protestant d'Etudes* 26 (Geneva, 1974) 5–31.

15

1 "I am the true vine, and my Father is the vinedresser. 2/ Every branch of mine that bears no fruit, he takes away, and every branch that does bear fruit he prunes, that it may bear more fruit. 3/ You are already made clean by the word which I have spoken to you. 4/ Abide in me, and I in you. As the branch cannot bear fruit by itself, unless it abides in the vine, neither can you, unless you abide in me. 5/ I am the vine, you are the branches. He who abides in me, and I in him, he it is that bears much fruit, for apart from me you can do nothing. 6/ If a man does not abide in me, he is cast forth as a branch and withers; and the branches are gathered, thrown into the fire and burned. 7/ If you abide in me, and my words abide in you, ask whatever you will, and it shall be done for you. 8/ By this my Father is glorified, that you bear much fruit, and so prove to be my disciples. 9/ As the Father has loved me, so have I loved you; abide in my love. 10/ If you keep my commandments, you will abide in my love, just as I have kept my Father's commandments and abide in his love. 11/ These things I have spoken to you, that my joy may be in you, and that your joy may be full. 12/ This is my commandment, that you love one another as I have loved you. 13/ Greater love has no man than this, that a man lay down his life for his friends. 14/ You are my friends if you do what I command you. 15/ No longer do I call you servants, for the servant does not know what his master is doing; but I have called you friends, for all that I have heard from my Father I have made known to you. 16/ You did not choose me, but I chose you and appointed you that you should go and bear fruit and that your fruit should abide; so that whatever you ask the Father in my name, he may give it to you. 17/ This I command you, to love one another."

■ **1** If one thinks of the discourse that begins with this verse as being spoken while in transit, the result is not a realistic picture. Apparently the Evangelist is not concerned to depict it as such. With the concluding remark in 14:31, the Evangelist has indicated a scanty and vague situation; this discourse is not really located in time and space. One can of course term it a farewell discourse and testament. But it is also something like a cathecism for disciples or a bill of polity. For chapters 15 and 16 indicate how Jesus wants his community to have what he will give them and what they are to expect from the world. The Father, who is greater than Jesus, is depicted here as someone over Jesus. Jesus is the true vine, and his Father is the vinedresser. What does the word "true" (ἀληθινός) imply? It is made clear in what follows that the relationship that exists between Jesus and his own is the one that obtains between vine and branch. Why is it not said: I am like a vine, etc., so that the figurative nature of what is being said is clear? In the first instance, it is not merely a matter of a figure of speech for the Evangelist, but rather of a description that corresponds exactly to the reality of discipleship. Yet Jesus does not dispense the power of earthly life, as a vine does for its branches. He is the true vine, because he imparts true life. He does not provide an animal or vegetable existence, but imparts a spiritual reality. This word is of course too weak. It invites misunderstanding as something intellectual, as something that somehow floats colorless over authentic reality. But that is precisely what the Evangelist does not mean. Spiritual existence is living reality in a concrete time and space, in the midst of history and nature. Yet man, who leads such an existence, is not the victim of his time, at any rate not internally. He lives in contact with his time, but his time does not govern him, because he is given to a different service. One can of course ask whether misunderstandings could not insinuate themselves at this point and whether such a person believes himself to be in the service of the most high within some sort of scheme, while he in fact is subject to the will of a kind of period idol. That is perpetually the case, and spiritual existence, consequently, is not something given once and for all, but something that includes, rather than excludes, the probing reflection on and critical discernment of the spirits.

■ **2** This verse makes clear that spiritual existence is not given once and for all in a second sense: even religion is not perfect, but must be subject to the discipline of its God; whoever bears fruit must ask why he or she does not bear more fruit. John distinguishes between such imperfection, which is perpetually in progress, and the other kind of imperfection, which is sterile and dry and closed to efforts to make it productive. The Father's judgment is proclaimed against this loveless disobedience vis-à-vis Jesus' command. The way in which the Evangelist uses this name for God can be misleading. By "Father" he does not mean the "God of love," but the inscrutable Lord, whose love can be very harsh and can even make use of the gibbet, the cross, in its service. In this sense the Fourth Gospel is not interested in the principal aim of Gnosticism, "rest" (ἀνάπαυσις), the final rest and impassivity.

■ **3** Since that is not the way it is with God and his action toward Christians, it can be said of the disciples in verses 3 and 4a that they are now pure on account of the word that Jesus has spoken to them. But they must "abide" in that word, it must put roots down in them and determine their entire life. Only then do they abide "in him."

■ **4** But verse 4 has still more to say: the branches cannot bear fruit of themselves, but receive their strength and sap from the vine. The believer is not a self-determined person, but one who is always receiving anew, who lays claim to nothing as his or her own accomplishment. And so neither does Jesus claim anything as his own achievement, as he is represented in the Fourth Gospel (and not only here), but places himself entirely in the service of the Father and renounces his own word. He gave himself over entirely to what the Father has effected in him. For that reason, his words were the works of the Father. To empty the person so that the whole fullness of God can flow in is not something, of course, that can be acquired or forced by some technique of self-alienation. It is the mystery of love being enacted. The love of which John speaks and which Jesus wants to see in the disciples is not a passion that is designed to possess, that is intended to take possession of a thing or person, but is that self-abnegation that Jesus illustrates in the footwashing.

■ **5** When verse 5 says that we Christians can do nothing without him, that is not a declaration of bankruptcy, but an expression of the readiness for and confident hope in the fullness that the vine can furnish.

■ **6** Verse 6 paints the opposite picture: in the vineyard, the dry shoots are cut off and piled up, to be burned finally as useless material. That is the fruitlessness of a life dried up by lovelessness and self-assertion; and such a life ends in despair, although, viewed from the outside, it appears to have achieved a great deal, and has even become a dreaded power.

■ **7** Verse 7 once again sets the picture of the good life over against this threat of failure: the good life remains bound to Jesus, and prayers emanating from it will be heard because the ego does not dominate.

■ **8** The faith that "bears fruit" is, as verse 8 instructs us, the glorification of God, in connection with which we must not forget for our part that a certain cross on Golgatha has become the most fruitful of all trees. God does not care for fruitlessness and frustration, and where life may appear futile among God's own, from our point of view, we should reflect that God sees all things.

■ **10** Verse 10 sets Jesus out as the greatest example of love. That can appear surprising and strange since the "Johannine Jesus" is not sentimental and frivolity is remote to him who is on his way to the cross. Further, Jesus could not choose his way of life in accordance with his own preferences; there were also "commandments" for him to fulfill. That he knew how to carry his heavy burden lightly should not mislead us into thinking that his burden was light. It was therefore a fateful delusion when theological liberalism thought it saw in the Johannine Jesus only a god walking about on earth and thus forgot the incarnation, the becoming flesh, which is not merely a manner of speaking or a piece of stodgy tradition. The passion narrative, consequently, was not an embarrassment for the Evangelist, as has been recently asserted again. Over against such an assertion, exegetes like Wilkens, for example, are right when they also perceive a passion gospel in the work of John.

■ **13** To keep us from making a mistake, verse 13 makes it clear that it is the highest form of love that is involved, the kind that lays down its life for its friends. Dibelius once interpreted this verse as a kind of commonplace that had penetrated the Gospel of John and was not integrally connected with its special message. The term love in John 15:13, according to Dibelius, has "the common meaning exclusively, and not the typical Johannine sense ('essential co-existence')."[1] It is quite

possible that the Evangelist has put a current saying about the highest level of love among friends into the mouth of Jesus; but that does not mean that he has not reinterpreted it in his own sense, which would then be translated in a very misleading way with "essential co-existence." "Essential co-existence" suggests that what is involved is the agreement of present entities; the relationship between Jesus and his "friends" is of course not that kind of relationship. The branches are not independent entities in relation to the vine, and the life giving sap does not flow from the branches to the vine, but the other way around.

■ **14** With respect to his friends, Jesus is the one who gives commands, who assigns tasks, as verse 14 indicates.

■ **15f.** If he now rejects the designation "servants" or "slaves" (δοῦλοι) for his friends, he does so because the slave obeys blindly, without insight into the command of his lord and without the joyful understanding heart of a friend. But that does not give them equal status: Jesus has chosen his friends, and not the reverse. He has "appointed" them, determined them, and made them to go and bear abiding fruit. Pride in the success of the mission, which may be what the author has in mind here, is thereby snipped off. But how does the following go together with this: the Father will give them everything they ask in the name of Jesus? Has a piece of synoptic tradition been thoughtlessly inserted here? Another connection is more likely: success derives not from their own activity, but is the fulfillment of a request addressed to God, and therefore a gift. If one assumed a synoptic insertion, a difficulty would continue to exist: why would this saying be inserted precisely at this point?

■ **17** Verse 17 appears to serve the function of forming the transition from the key term "love," which more or less runs throughout this segment, to the hatred of the world, which is the subject of the next section.

---

1   RGG² 3: 354.

37. The Hatred of the World
for the Disciples

Bibliography

A. John 15:18–27

Baumeister, Theofried
"Der Tod Jesu und die Leidensnachfolge des Jüngers nach dem Johannesevangelium und dem ersten Johannesbrief." *Wissenschaft und Weisheit* 40 (1977) 81–99.

Becker, Jürgen
"Die Abschiedsreden Jesu im Johannesevangelium." *ZNW* 61 (1970) 215–46, esp. 230, 236–41.

Becker, Jürgen
"Beobachtungen zum Dualismus im Johannesevangelium." *ZNW* 65 (1974) 71–87, esp. 84–85.

George, Augustin
"L'évangile: Les témoins de Jesus devant le monde." *AsSeign* 50 (1966) 30–40.

McNaugher, John
"The Witnessing Spirit and the Witnessed Christ." *BSac* 88 (1931) 207–19.

B. Johannine Ecclesiology

Allen, E. L.
"The Jewish Christian Church in the Fourth Gospel." *JBL* 74 (1955) 88–92.

Baumbach, Günter
"Die Funktion der Gemeinde in der Welt in johanneischer Sicht." *Zeichen der Zeit* 21 (1971) 161–67.

Baumbach, Günter
"Gemeinde und Welt im Johannes-Evangelium." *Kairos* 14 (1972) 121–36.

Becker, Jürgen
"Joh 3,1–21 als Reflex johanneischer Schuldiskussion." In *Das Wort und die Wörter. Festschrift Gerhard Friedrich zum 65. Geburtstag,* ed. H. Balz and S. Schulz (Stuttgart: W. Kohlhammer, 1973) 85–95.

Bogart, John
Orthodox and Heretical Perfectionism in the Johannine Community as Evident in the First Epistle of John, SBLDS 33 (Missoula: Scholars Press, 1977).

Bousset, Wilhelm
Jüdisch-christlicher Schulbetrieb in Alexandria und Rom. Literarische Untersuchungen zu Philo und Clemens von Alexandria, Justin und Irenäus (Göttingen: Vandenhoeck & Ruprecht, 1915; New York: G. Olms, 1975).

Boxel, Piet van
"Glaube und Liebe. Die Aktualität des johanneischen Jüngermodells." *Geist und Leben* 48 (1975) 18–28.

Braun, François-Marie
"Apostolique et pneumatique selon saint Jean." *RevThom* 71 (1971) 451–62.

Brown, Raymond Edward
"'Other Sheep not of this Fold': The Johannine

Perspective on Christian Diversity in the Late First Century." *JBL* 97 (1978) 5–22.

Brown, Raymond Edward
The Community of the Beloved Disciple (New York: Paulist, 1979).

Brown, Raymond Edward
"Johannine Ecclesiology—The Community's Origins." *Int* 31 (1977) 379–93.

Bussche, Henri van den
"Die Kirche im vierten Evangelium." In *Von Christus zur Kirche. Charisma und Amt im Urchristentum* (Freiburg: Herder, 1966) 79–107.

Conzelmann, Hans
"Paulus und die Weisheit." *NTS* 12 (1965/1966) 231–244. In his *Theologie als Schriftauslegung. Aufsätze zum Neuen Testament,* BEvT 65 (Munich: Chr. Kaiser Verlag, 1974) 167–76.

Cullmann, Oscar
"Von Jesus zum Stephanuskreis und zum Johannesevangelium." In *Jesus und Paulus. Festschrift für Werner Georg Kümmel zum 70. Geburtstag,* ed. E. E. Ellis and E. Grässer (Göttingen: Vandenhoeck & Ruprecht, 1975) 44–56.

Cullmann, Oscar
Der johanneische Kreis. Sein Platz im Spätjudentum, in der Jüngerschaft Jesu und im Urchristentum. Zum Ursprung des Johannesevangelium (Tübingen: Mohr-Siebeck, 1975).

Culpepper, R. Alan
The Johannine School. An Evaluation of the Johannine-School Hypothesis Based on an Investigation of the Nature of Ancient Schools, SBLDS 26 (Missoula: Scholars Press, 1975).

Dahl, Nils Alstrup
"The Johannine Church and History." In *Current Issues in New Testament Interpretation: Essays in honor of Otto A. Piper,* ed. William Klassen (New York: Harper & Brothers, 1962) 124–42.

Dahl, Nils Alstrup
Das Volk Gottes. Eine Untersuchung zum Kirchenbewusstsein des Urchristentums, Skrifter utgitt av det norske videnskaps-akademi i Oslo—Historisk-filosofisk klasse 2, 9 (Darmstadt: Wissenschaftliche Buchgesellschaft, ²1963), esp. 167–74.

Fiorenza, Elizabeth Schüssler
"The Quest for the Johannine School. The Apocalypse and the Fourth Gospel." *NTS* 23 (1976/1977) 402–27.

Gaugler, Ernst
"Die Bedeutung der Kirche in den johanneischen Schriften." *Internationale Kirchliche Zeitschrift* 14 (1924) 97–117.

Grant, Robert M.
"The Fourth Gospel and the Church." *HTR* 35 (1942) 95–116.

Grayston, Kenneth
"Jesus and the Church in St. John's Gospel." *London Quarterly and Holborn Review* 35 (1967) 106–15.

Gryglewicz, Feliks
"Die Pharisäer und die Johanneskirche." In *Probleme der Forschung,* ed. A. Fuchs. Studien zum Neuen Testament und seiner Umwelt A, 3 (Vienna and Munich: Verlag Herold, 1978) 144–58.

Haacker, Klaus
"Jesus und die Kirche nach Johannes." *TZ* 29 (1973) 179–201.

Hartke, Wilhelm
Vier urchristliche Parteien und ihre Vereinigung zur Apostolischen Kirche, I and II, Deutsche Akademie der Wissenschaften zu Berlin, Schriften der Sektion für Altertumswissenschaft 24 (Berlin: Akademie-Verlag, 1961).

Heitmüller, Wilhelm
"Zur Johannes-Tradition." *ZNW* 15 (1914) 189–209.

Howard, Wilbert Francis
Christianity According to St. John (London: Duckworth, 1943).

Hruby, Kurt
"Die Trennung von Kirche und Judentum." In *Theologische Berichte 3. Judentum und Kirche: Volk Gottes,* ed. J. Pfammatter and F. Fürger (Zurich and Cologne: Benziger, 1974) 138–56.

Jonge, Marinus de
"Son of God and Children of God in the Fourth Gospel." In *Saved by Hope. Essays in Honor of Richard C. Oudersluys,* ed. J. I. Cook (Grand Rapids: Wm. B. Eerdmans, 1978).

Kraft, Heinz
"Untersuchungen zu den Gemeinschafts- und Lebensformen häretischer christlicher Gnosis des 2. Jahrhunderts." Dissertation, Heidelberg, 1950.

Kuhl, Josef
Die Sendung Jesu Christi und der Kirche nach dem Johannesevangelium (Siegburg: Steyler, 1967).

Kysar, Robert
"Community and Gospel: Vectors in Fourth Gospel Criticism." *Int* 31 (1977) 355–66.

Langbrandtner, Wolfgang
Weltferner Gott oder Gott der Liebe? Der Ketzerstreit in der johanneischen Kirche. Eine exegetisch-religionsgeschichtliche Untersuchung mit Berücksichtigung der koptisch-gnostischen Texte aus Nag-Hammadi, Beiträge zur biblischen Exegese und Theologie 6 (Frankfurt: P. Lang, 1977).

Lebram, Jürgen Christian
"Die Theologie der späten Chokma und des häretischen Judentums." *ZAW* 77 (1965) 202–11.

LeFort, Pierre
Les structures de l'église militante selon saint Jean. Etude d'ecclésiologie concrète appliquée au IVe évangile et aux épîtres johanniques, Nouvelle Série Théologique 25 (Geneva: Labor & Fides, 1970).

Luck, Ulrich
"Die kirchliche Einheit als Problem des Johannesevangeliums." *Wort und Dienst* 10 (1969) 51–67.

Martyn, James Louis
  History and Theology in the Fourth Gospel (Nashville: Abingdon Press, ²1979).

Martyn, James Louis
  "Clementine Recognitions 1, 33–71, Jewish Christianity and the Fourth Gospel." In *God's Christ and His People; Studies in Honor of Nils Alstrup Dahl*, ed. Jacob Jervell and Wayne A. Meeks (Oslo: Universitetsforlaget, 1977) 265–295.

Martyn, James Louis
  "Glimpses into the History of the Johannine Community. From its Origin through the Period of its Life in which the Fourth Gospel was Composed." In *L'Evangile de Jean. Sources, rédaction, théologie*, ed. M. de Jonge. BETL 44 (Gembloux: Duculot; Louvain: University Press, 1977) 149–76.

Marzotto, Damiano
  L'unità degli uomini nel vangelo di Giovanni, Supplementi alla Rivista Biblica 9 (Brescia: Paideia, 1977).

Meeks, Wayne A.
  "Die Funktion des vom Himmel herabgestiegenen Offenbarers für das Selbstverständnis der johanneischen Gemeinde." In *Zur Soziologie des Urchristentums. Ausgewählte Beiträge zum frühchristlichen Gemeinschaftsleben in seiner gesellschaftlichen Umwelt*, ed. Wayne A. Meeks. TBü 62 (Munich: Chr. Kaiser Verlag, 1979) 245–83 = "The Man from Heaven in Johannine Sectarianism." *JBL* 91 (1972) 44–72.

Meeks, Wayne A.
  "'Am I a Jew?' Johannine Christianity and Judaism." In *Christianity, Judaism and Other Greco-Roman Cults. Studies for Morton Smith at Sixty*. Part 1, *New Testament*, ed. Jacob Neusner. SJLA 12 (Leiden: E. J. Brill, 1975) 163–86.

Miller, John Whelan
  "The Concept of the Church in the Gospel according to John." Dissertation, Princeton Theological Seminary, 1976.

Miranda, Juan Peter
  Der Vater, der mich gesandt hat. Religionsgeschichtliche Untersuchungen zu den johanneischen Sendungsformeln. Zugleich ein Beitrag zur johanneischen Christologie und Ekklesiologie, Europäische Hochschulschriften, Series 23; Theologie 7 (Bern: H. Lang; Frankfurt: P. Lang, 1972).

O'Grady, John F.
  Individual and Community in John (Rome: Pontifical Biblical Institute, 1978).

O'Grady, John F.
  "Johannine Ecclesiology: A Critical Evaluation." *BTB* 7 (1977) 36–44.

O'Grady, John F.
  "Individualism and Johannine Ecclesiology." *BTB* 5 (1975) 227–61.

Painter, John
  "The Church and Israel in the Gospel of John: A Response." *NTS* 25 (1978/1979) 103–12.

Painter, John
  "Christ and the Church in John 1,45–51." In *L'Evangile de Jean. Sources, rédaction, théologie*, ed. M. de Jonge. BETL 44 (Gembloux: Duculot; Louvain: University Press, 1977) 359–62.

Pancaro, Severino
  "'People of God' in St. John's Gospel?" *NTS* 16 (1969/1970) 114–29.

Pancaro, Severino
  "The Relationship of the Church to Israel in the Gospel of St John." *NTS* 21 (1974/1975) 396–405.

Pastor Piñeiro, Félix-Alejandro
  "Comunidad y ministerio en el evangelio joaneo." *Estudios ecclesiásticos* 50 (1975) 323–56.

Pastor Piñeiro, Félix-Alejandro
  La ecclesiologia juanea según E. Schweizer, Analecta Gregoriana 168, Series Facultatis Theologicae (Rome: Gregorian University, 1968).

Peterson, Erik
  "Der Gottesfreund—Beiträge zur Geschichte eines religiösen Terminus." *ZKG* 42 (1923) 161–202.

Radermakers, Jean
  "Mission et apostolat dans l'évangile johannique." *SE* 2 = TU 87 (Berlin: Akademie-Verlag, 1964) 100–121.

Ricca, P.
  "Note di ecclesiologia giovannica." *Protestantesimo* 22 (1967) 148–66.

Richter, Georg
  Studien zum Johannesevangelium, ed. J. Hainz. BU 13 (Regensburg: F. Pustet, 1977).

Segalla, Giuseppe
  "L'esperienza cristiana in Giovanni." *Studia Patavina* 18 (1971) 299–342.

Smith, D. Moody, Jr.
  "Johannine Christianity: Some Reflections on its Character and Delineation." *NTS* 21 (1974/1975) 222–48.

Schelkle, Karl Hermann
  "Kirche im Johannesevangelium." *TQ* 156 (1976) 277–283.

Schmitt, J.
  "Le groupe johannique et la chrétienté apostolique." In *Les groupes informels dans l'église*, ed. René Metz and Jean Schlick (Strasbourg: C. E. R. D. I. C., 1971) 169–79.

Schnackenburg, Rudolf
  Die Kirche im Neuen Testament. Ihre Wirklichkeit und theologische Deutung, ihr Wesen und Geheimnis, Quaestiones Disputatae 14 (New York and Freiburg: Herder, 1961) 93–106.

Schnackenburg, Rudolf
  "Die johanneische Gemeinde und ihre Geisterfahrung." In *Die Kirche des Anfangs. Festschrift für Heinz Schürmann zum 65. Geburtstag*, ed. R. Schnackenburg, J. Ernst, and J. Wanke. Erfurter Theologische Studien 38 (Leipzig: St. Benno;

Freiburg: Herder, 1977) 277–306.

Schweizer, Eduard
"Der Kirchenbegriff im Evangelium und den Briefen des Johannes." *SE* I = TU 73 (Berlin: Akademie-Verlag, 1959) 363–81.

Schweizer, Eduard
Gemeinde und Gemeindeordnung im Neuen Testament, ATANT 35 (Zurich: Zwingli Verlag, 1959) 105–24.

Thyen, Hartwig
"Entwicklungen innerhalb der johanneischen Theologie und Kirche im Spiegel von Joh 21 und der Lieblingsjüngertexte des Evangeliums." In *L'Evangile de Jean. Sources, rédaction, théologie,* ed. M. de Jonge. BETL 44 (Gembloux: Duculot; Louvain: University Press, 1977) 259–99.

Vanderlip, D. George
Christianity according to John (Philadelphia: Westminster Press, 1975).

Wiefel, Wolfgang
"Die Scheidung von Gemeinde und Welt im Johannesevangelium auf dem Hintergrund der Trennung von Kirche und Synagoge." *TZ* 35 (1979) 213–27.

Wilken, Robert Louis
"Collegia, Philosophical Schools and Theology." In *The Catacombs and the Colosseum. The Roman Empire as the Setting of Primitive Christianity,* ed. S. Benko and J. J. O'Rourke (Valley Forge, PA: Judson, 1971) 268–91.

Windisch, Hans
"Das johanneische Christentum und sein Verhältnis zum Judentum und zu Paulus." *Christliche Welt* 47 (1933) 98–107.

15

18 "If the world hates you, know that it has hated me before it hated you. 19/ If you were of the world, the world would love its own; but because you are not of the world, but I chose you out of the world, therefore the world hates you. 20/ Remember the word that I said to you, 'A servant is not greater than his master.' If they persecuted me, they will persecute you; if they keep my word, they will keep yours also. 21/ But all this they will do to you on my account, because they do not know him who sent me. 22/ If I had not come and spoken to them, they would not have sin; but now they have no excuse for their sin. 23/ He who hates me hates my Father also. 24/ If I had not done among them the works which no one else did, they would not have sin; but now they have seen and hated both me and my Father. 25/ It is to fulfill the word that is written in their law, 'They hated me without cause.' 26/ But when the Counselor comes, whom I shall send to you from the Father, even the Spirit of truth, who proceeds from the Father, he will bear witness to me; 27/ and you also are witnesses, because you have been with me from the beginning."

■ **18** The Evangelist lived in a period and environment that were hostile to the Christian community. This hostility led him to inquire after the basis of the world's rejection. The first reason he gives is that Jesus himself had already run up against the hatred of the world and that brought him to the cross. On the basis of chapters 18 and 19, we can say that for him the world is represented by the Jews: as 16:2 shows, they are the originators of the persecution encountered by the community. Since they are putting Christians out of the synagogue (16:2), Jewish Christians are involved, but they are of an unusual variety. It is noteworthy that the Fourth Gospel depicts the Jews as the violent opponents of the community, but without betraying any precise knowledge of Judaism, apart from specific passages of another type. That prompts the conclusion that we are perhaps faced with two different layers of material. The older source employed by the Evangelist still exhibits some exact knowledge of Judaism, since the community (or at least its forefathers) had been put out of the synagogue (cf. 9:22). It is on this basis that the strikingly strong use of the formula, "king of the Jews," in the passion narrative is to be explained; it does not go back to the Evangelist's own composition. This context is to be considered also in connection with 6:15.

The Jews, however, are not really involved as representatives of the world, and the real emphasis lies on the notion of "world." Here we perceive a dualism between the world and the realm of the Father, for which the Evangelist does not have a special concept, a technical term. This suggests that his source did not provide him with a concept corresponding to "world." The real question, however, is this: was the Jewish community, from which Christians were separating themselves—those who were expressing themselves in the source—already permeated with some kind of dualism? That they did not yet have a name for the realm of the Father leads to the view that the new message was being used in a dualistic ("pre-gnostic"?) form by them. In that case, one may also conjecture that a considerable difference already existed between this form of the message and the synoptic tradition. If one considers that the Fourth Gospel must be dated to about 90–100 CE, the source comes at a correspondingly earlier time and is perhaps contemporary with Matthew and Luke. But this community would have come into being at a still earlier time. The surprising thing is that in one sphere of missionary Christianity the synoptic tradition was receding in those days and was being replaced or driven out by a wild tradition. Apparently the mission, to which the "earlier community" of the Evangelist owed its origin, derived from a secondary branch of the Christian mission, whose efforts were directed to the winning of the Jewish community. That would be the kernel of truth in the view that the Fourth Gospel was intended as a missionary tract for Israel. But let us turn from these general considerations back to the text.

■ **19** World and Christianity from the beginning are opposed, are hostile to one another. If Christians were of the world, they would not have to fear persecution (cf. 7:7). That would lead to the view that Christians as such are outside and above the world. The quality which Christians possess from the outset would then distinguish them from the world. But the situation is viewed differently in verse 19: Christians also belong to the world in and of themselves. But Jesus has chosen them out of the world and thereby taken them out of the world. A theology of decision is thus not involved here: it is not possible for each member to enter the kingdom of God by his or her own choice. It is only the miracle of a second birth through the spirit, a basic transformation, that conducts them to this realm and excludes any sense of superiority.

■ **20** This verse points back to 13:16, a saying that follows the footwashing and implies that a slave or servant can expect no better treatment than can his or her master. Then, in verse 20b, there is a positive counterpart that does not fit into this context: if they have kept my word, they will also keep yours. The comparable destinies of lord and servant are certainly being described; but the overarching theme is still the persecution that the two have to endure. As a consequence, Pallis has conjectured that a negative should also be inserted here: "If they have not kept my word, they will not keep yours."[1] This is a poor conjecture because "my" word cannot fail. Moreover, it is to be observed: according to the Gospel of John, even the disciples did not keep Jesus' words, to say nothing of other groups. The way out of this difficulty is therefore to assume that here the times are being intermingled (the time of Jesus and the time of the church), as is often the case in the Gospel of John. But since in this passage Jesus and the disciples are being set over against one another and of both it is being said that some keep their word, this explanation is not possible.

■ **21** Verse 21, furthermore, goes with 20a, but not with 20b: the Christian community will be persecuted "on account of my name," simply because they belong to Christ, because their relation to the Father is not recognized.

■ **22** Another point of view is presented in verse 22: had Jesus not come with his message, the current opponents would be without sin; but now they have no pretext for their sins, no excuse.

■ **23** Verse 23 points once again to the fact that whoever hates Jesus also hates the Father.

■ **24** Following this, verse 24 offers a kind of parallel to

1   Alexander Pallis, *Notes on St. Mark and St. Matthew* (London: Oxford University Press, 1932).

verse 22: if Jesus had not done the works among them that no other has done,[2] their opponents would be guiltless. But they have now seen these works "and hated both me and my Father."

■ **25** Verse 25 brings the entire section to a close; it is foreign to the thought of the Evangelist: this has taken place in order that the will of God might be fulfilled, "They hated me without a cause." The author here is thinking of Ps 35:19:

> Let not those rejoice over me
> who are wrongfully my foes,
> and let not those wink the eye
> who hate me without cause.

and of Ps 25:19:

> Consider how many are my foes,
> and with what violent hatred they hate me.

and of Ps 69:4:

> More in number than the hairs of my head
> are those who hate me without cause;
> mighty are those who would destroy me,
> those who attack me with lies.

Primitive Christianity read the "psalms of the innocent and suffering just" as passion gospels. And the argument being advanced depends on them.

■ **26** In verse 26 a saying about the paraclete again follows, but without connection to what precedes: when the paraclete sent by Jesus comes from the Father, who is the spirit of truth proceeding from the Father, then will he bear witness to Jesus. Here a leveling of the relationship of the Father to the son (i.e., Jesus) vis-à-vis the sending of the spirit appears to be intended: the spirit of truth proceeds from the Father, but he is sent by Jesus. In 14:16 it is said that the Father would give the spirit—in response to a request of Jesus. It is clear what is at stake: what does the Evangelist really mean when he speaks of the paraclete? (Perhaps we could best translate the term as "advocate.") As a closer definition we are told that he is the spirit of truth. The thing that comes first to the mind of the theologian is the third person of the trinity. But it is dubious whether the Evangelist was acquainted with something like the trinitarian dogma and whether he has that in mind here. But he was cer-

tainly aware of something else: a heavenly being, the logos, the son, who became man, and not merely man—the term man is only a concept and not someone who wanders through Galilee in the first century CE—but as a very particular man, namely, Jesus of Nazareth. His earthly existence came to an end on the cross. Then he returned to the Father, already an untouchable entity; he was no longer a man of flesh and blood like us—for we cannot pass through closed doors; and he poured the holy spirit on his own, by breathing on them, just as God did to the lump of clay that was Adam when he made him into a living soul. Thus does the Evangelist depict the work of Jesus and his departing gift, the outpouring of the spirit. But the sayings about the paraclete permit us to recognize that something decisively new became effective with this gift, something that had not yet been given during his earthly life (7:39), namely, the spirit. We know from the letters of Paul that primitive Christianity, as we are prompted to see or divine it here, was an ecstatic Christianity of the spirit. Luke has dated the coming of the spirit on the fiftieth day after the Passover, on Pentecost (Acts 2). He was still aware that speaking in tongues belonged to that event, an ecstatic speech that is unlike human speech—perhaps some took it to be the language of angels. But the spirit expressed itself not in such speaking or stammering, but in a new life; this existence in the spirit was the most important thing for Paul: whoever does not have the spirit of Christ is not a Christian. Indeed, it appears as though Paul has so conceived this being in Christ that as members Christians all together form a huge body of Christ (not a headless torso, for which then Jesus supplies the head). As certainly as Jesus Christ was an individual person for Paul, one to whom he prayed and from whom he received the answer, so were all Christians "in Christ," precisely as members of the great, comprehensive, all-embracing body of Christ. But they also had to live accordingly, and Paul unfortunately had frequently to enjoin them to do so, because the old ways had no more become a thing of the past as completely as one might have wished. The fourth Evangelist had not read the letters of Paul and did not speak Paul's language. But he also was certain that the spirit had been given to Christians, and that had

---

2   Cf. the mode of argumentation in the story of the
     man born blind: 9:15, 25, 30–32.

tremendous consequences for him and his readers. On the one hand, it was said that the spirit had not yet been given during the earthly life of Jesus—apart from Jesus himself. For that reason, the message of Jesus fell on deaf ears and hardened hearts at that time. Only now, when the spirit had opened hearts, could the message of Jesus really be received; the Evangelist then also endeavored to interpret it in a new and comprehensible way for his readers. We cannot say precisely what synoptic sayings material may have reached the Evangelist. In any case, it only rarely finds echoes in the Gospel of John, and it makes no headway against John's new language and its content. Concretely that means, among other things: the imminent expectation of the end that animated primitive Christianity is simultaneously raised to its highest degreee in the Fourth Gospel and abolished—"to abolish, take up into" (*aufgehoben*) Hegel would say.

With the coming of the spirit we are again united with God, with the Father. God, the invisible, has sent us his visible image in Jesus and thereby opened the way to himself. No future can bring us more. Yet we nevertheless do not live in heaven, but always in the world (17:15). "To abide" is therefore a task for Christians. It is not said that the paraclete will assist Christians in this task. In general the position of the spirit remains dubious: is the paraclete someone other than Jesus ("to send another as helper") or does Jesus return in the paraclete? Does the paraclete only remind us of Jesus or does the paraclete first lead us into all truth? Who sends him? Is he a person? Certainly not in the sense that Jesus was a person. The question has to be asked whether sayings regarding the paraclete are being corrected, or whether the Evangelist himself has not quite dealt with the problem of the old and new, continuity and discontinuity. This much however may be clear: the Fourth Gospel does not contain the later doctrine of the trinity, according to which three divine persons, but of one substance, exist together in an ineffable mystery. In this doctrine, on the one hand, the spirit appears as a sort of "person" alongside Jesus, in a way that is not characteristic of either Paul or John. On the other hand, the unity of the spirit with the resurrected Jesus, as it is expressed in the Pauline doctrine of "being in Christ" and as it may

be discerned in John, has retreated.

That the Christian faith is dated from Easter forward and that it is yet indivisibly connected with the preacher from Galilee who was crucified in Jerusalem has not yet today found adequate expression. It also remains an open question whether the Johannine sayings regarding the paraclete are only a remnant of what was once a long series of expressions, or whether they were first inserted into the Gospel in its original form. To say that the resurrected Christ himself will bring the spirit on his return does not square very well with the statement that he will send the spirit as the exalted one. What is being used here as tradition? What does the Evangelist intend to say with this tradition? Since he apparently thinks of various expressions merely as variations of the same message, this message itself is in danger of becoming ambiguous. This one fact alone is clear: the synoptic message of the kingdom has disappeared except for minimal traces; the entire Johannine theology has been developed on the basis of the notion of the Father, whom no one has ever seen, and who therefore sends his son; in his son, however, he cannot be seen so long as the son remains on earth. Jesus' earthly life will become meaningful after the fact when the spirit interprets the life of Jesus as a hidden allusion to a unity with the Father that exists for the time being only in Jesus. But not as a sacrifice, not as the redemption of human sin—sin consists rather in the fact that men do not acknowledge Jesus as the Son of God sent by the Father. Earlier the concept of sin could not really be applied to this idea. These are thoughts that are unprecedented in a doctrine of faith that has been conceived on the basis of Paul, and it is not surprising that the Pauline and Johannine forms of religiosity are customarily combined.

■ **27** While verse 26 speaks of the testimony of the spirit on behalf of Jesus, verse 27 introduces a new thought: the disciples will also give testimony on behalf of Jesus because they were with him from the beginning. That is difficult to understand in the context of Johannine theology since the disciples did not recognize Jesus during his earthly life and the later disciples had not been with him from the beginning.

38. Conclusion of the Address to the Disciples

Bibliography

Bammel, Ernst
"Jesus und der Paraklet in Joh 16." In *Christ and Spirit in the New Testament* [Festschrift C. F. D. Moule], ed. B. Lindars and S. S. Smalley (New York: Cambridge University Press, 1973) 199–217.

Bleibtreu, Walther
"Evang. Joh. 16, 23, 24." *NKZ* 22 (1911) 958–62.

Bream, Howard N.
"No Need to be Asked Questions. A Study of John 16,30." In *Search the Scriptures. New Testament Studies in Honor of Raymond T. Stamm,* ed. J. M. Myers, O. Reimherr and H. N. Bream. Gettysburg Theological Studies 3 (Leiden: E. J. Brill, 1969) 49–74.

Bruns, J. Edgar
"A Note on John 16:33 and 1 John 2:13–14." *JBL* 86 (1967) 451–53.

Carson, D. A.
"The Function of the Paraclete in John 16:7–11." *JBL* 98 (1979) 547–66.

Fascher, Erich
"Johannes 16, 32. Eine Studie zur Geschichte der Schriftauslegung und zur Traditionsgeschichte des Urchristentums." *ZNW* 39 (1940) 171–230.

George, Augustin
"L'Esprit, guide vers la vérité plénière. Jn 16,12–15." *AsSeign* 31 (1973) 40–47.

George, Augustin
"La tâche du Paraclet: Jn 16,5–14." *AsSeign* 47 (1963) 28–36.

George, Augustin
"La nouveauté de pâques: Jn 16,23–30." *AsSeign* 48 (1965) 39–46.

Hatch, William H. P.
"The Meaning of John 16,8–11." *HTR* 14 (1921) 103–5.

Kremer, Jacob
"Jesu Verheissung des Geistes—Zur Verankerung der Aussage von Joh 16,13 im Leben Jesu." In *Die Kirche des Anfangs. Festschrift für Heinz Schürmann zum 65. Geburtstag,* ed. R. Schnackenburg, J. Ernst and J. Wanke. Erfurter Theologische Studien 38 (Leipzig: St. Benno; Freiburg: Herder, 1977) 246–76.

Lindars, Barnabas
"Δικαιοσύνη in Jn 16,8 and 10." In *Mélanges bibliques en hommage au R. P. Béda Rigaux,* ed. A. Descamps and A. De Halleux (Gembloux: Duculot, 1970) 275–86.

Patrick, Johnstone G.
"The Promise of the Paraclete." *BSac* 127 (1970) 333–45.

Rubio Morán, L.
  "Revelación en enigmas y revelación en claridad. Análisis exegético de Jn 16,25." *Salmanticensis* 19 (1972) 107–44.
Smith, D. Moody, Jr.
  "John 16,1–15." *Int* 33 (1979) 58–62.
Stanton, Vincent Henry
  "Convince or convict (John 16,8)." *ExpTim* 33 (1921/1922) 278–79.
Stenger, Werner
  "Δικαιοσύνη in Joh 16,8.10." *NovT* 21 (1979) 2–12.

Zerwick, Maximillian
  "Vom Wirken des Heiligen Geistes in uns. Meditationsgedanken zu Jo 16,5–15." *Geist und Leben* 38 (1965) 224–30.

16

1 "I have said all this to you to keep you from falling away. 2/ They will put you out of the synagogues; indeed, the hour is coming when whoever kills you will think he is offering service to God. 3/ And they will do this because they have not known the Father, nor me. 4/ But I have said these things to you, that when their hour comes you may remember that I told you of them. I did not say these things to you from the beginning, because I was with you. 5/ But now I am going to him who sent me; yet none of you asks me, 'Where are you going?' 6/ But because I have said these things to you, sorrow has filled your hearts. 7/ Nevertheless I tell you the truth: it is to your advantage that I go away, for if I do not go away, the Counselor will not come to you; but if I go, I will send him to you. 8/ And when he comes, he will convince the world of sin and righteousness and of judgment: 9/ of sin, because they do not believe me; 10/ of righeousness, because I go to the Father, and you will see me no more; 11/ of judgment, because the ruler of this world is judged. 12/ I have yet many things to say to you, but you cannot bear them now. 13/ When the Spirit of truth comes, he will guide you into all the truth; for he will not speak on his own authority, but whatever he hears he will speak, and he will declare to you the things that are to come. 14/ He will glorify me, for he will take what is mine and declare it to you. 15/ All that the Father has is mine; therefore I said that he will take what is mine and declare it to you.

16 A little while, and you will see me no more; again a little while, and you will see me." 17/ Some of his disciples said to one another, "What is this that he says to us, 'A little while, and you will not see me, and again a little while, and you will see me'; and, 'because I go to the Father?'" 18/ They said, "What does he mean by 'a little while'? We do not know what he means." 19/ Jesus knew that they wanted to ask him; so he said to them,

"Is this what you are asking yourselves, what I meant by saying, 'A little while, and you will not see me, and again a little while, and you will see me'? 20/ Truly, truly, I say to you, you will weep and lament, but the world will rejoice; you will be sorrowful, but your sorrow will turn to joy. 21/ When a woman is in travail she has sorrow, because her hour has come; but when she is delivered of the child, she no longer remembers the anguish, for joy that a child is born into the world. 22/ So you have sorrow now, but I will see you again and your hearts will rejoice, and no one will take your joy from you. 23/ On that day you will ask me no questions. Truly, truly, I say to you, if you ask anything of the Father, he will give it to you in my name. 24/ Hitherto you have asked nothing in my name; ask, and you will receive, that your joy may be full. 25/ I have said this to you in figures; the hour is coming when I shall no longer speak to you in figures but tell you plainly of the Father. 26/ In that day you will ask in my name; and I do not say to you that I shall pray the Father for you; 27/ for the Father himself loves you, because you have loved me and have believed that I came from the Father. 28/ I came from the Father and have come into the world; again, I am leaving the world and going to the Father." 29/ His disciples said, "Ah, now you are speaking plainly, not in any figure! 30/ Now we know that you know all things, and need none to question you; by this we believe that you came from God." 31/ Jesus answered them, "Do you now believe? 32/ The hour is coming, indeed it has come, when you will be scattered, every man to his home, and will leave me alone; yet I am not alone, for the Father is with me. 33/ I have said this to you, that in me you may have peace. In the world you have tribulation; but be of good cheer, I have overcome the world."

■ **1f.** What did Jesus say to the disciples to keep them from being scandalized and led astray? He told them of the coming persecution, which would make the hatred of the world evident. The world sees the disciples as—at best—a small minority being led astray and leading astray, to which one cannot afford to give free reign. One is not to be limited merely to casting them out of the synagogue, but is to kill them, and in so doing to think oneself especially pious. What the church later practiced during the crusades against the Mohammedans and Albigenses and other "heretical" groups they experienced at a very early time in their own body, without of course learning from that experience. They also were convinced that they rendered a pious service to God by persecuting the "unbelievers." Christians were the non-conformists *par excellence* in antiquity and they had to pay for that.

■ **3** The world thereby shows that it has not known either the Father or Jesus. God is not directly knowable, nor is the one whom he has sent. It is always possible to see here merely a representative of a human lack of understanding, one that violates the sacred tradition. One perceives this attack on the tradition as very dangerous and inexcusable because one lives out of the tradition. If it falls into the twilight zone, into the realm of the dubious, it becomes uncertain, and then the basis of existence is in danger of disappearing, and man falls into the abyss. What the young Christian movement must have experienced was thus a strain of self-defense. John does not of course say that; he only wants to prevent the time of difficulty from disconcerting Christians and causing them to despair.

■ **4** Jesus told them ahead of time that these things would come to pass; they have not therefore befallen the disciples unexpectedly. The Evangelist views that as a help and a comfort. But he never goes so far as to say that God so wills it—the contradiction of verse 2 would be too much. Of course, Jesus did not say that originally either (and thus at the beginning of Jesus' activity as John depicts it), because Jesus himself was with his own. There were attacks at that time also, of course, but they were directed only at Jesus himself.

■ **5** Now, however, he is going away, and the time of difficulty is precisely now since he is no longer present with his own. But it is not clear to the disciples what his departure means; they do not ask: where are you going? If one recalls 13:36, where Peter asks, "Lord, where are you going?", one is of course confronted with a discrepancy. However, the context in the earlier passage is different. The real question was: why could the disciples not follow Jesus, follow him on his path to martyrdom? The answer that is only hinted at is that they were not up to it; only later would Peter be able to follow the same course to his own passion. In the present passage, however, this is the way John sees the situation:

■ **6** Jesus forsakes the disciples at the very moment when they need him most, and that is incomprehensible. And because it is so difficult to understand, it evokes only pain and does not permit the thought to arise that this separation may have its divine meaning.

■ **7** However, it is better for the disciples—and this is the surprising thing—for Jesus' earthly existence to come now to an end: unless he goes away, the "helper," the spirit, cannot come. When he departs, however, he will send the spirit. The disciples therefore need the spirit, to a certain degree, more than they need Jesus.

For those who come to this passage from the letters of Paul or the Synoptics, it is astounding that the death of Jesus is not understood as a sacrifice, by means of which sinful man is reconciled to God. It has long been noted that while the concept of sin appears sixteen times in the Fourth Gospel, it nevertheless does not play a significant role. In 1:29 a traditional formula has been taken over (Jesus is the lamb that takes away the sins of the world); this expresses that Jesus is the redeemer in language that is already obsolete for the Evangelist. But how he is the redeemer we are not told in this expression, namely, that he has been divinely sent, and in him the sovereign, the Father, is made present.

Sin is mentioned four times in 8:21–34. But sin here consists in the fact that men do not acknowledge Jesus as the one sent by the Father: that basically is the only sin known to John: to be blind when God shows himself.

In 8:46, reference is made to the sinlessness of Jesus, which eliminates any reason for the hostility to him.

In 9:34, the Pharisees call the man healed of his blindness a sinner because he confesses Jesus—in this case the reality is therefore turned upside down.

It is made clear in 15:22–24 that there can only be sin where there is revelation (and man closes himself up to it).

There remain only the four references in chapters 16, 19, and 20, which will be discussed presently.

John is nevertheless not so far removed from the Synoptics as these references might make it appear. In their own way, the synoptic words of institution (of the Lord's Supper) make it clear that Jesus' death makes God newly accessible, and John says precisely that more emphatically and expressly: prior to Jesus there was no access to God. Mark 14:24 speaks of the new covenant in Jesus' blood, which is poured out for many: it is pre-supposed that a covenant cannot be entered into without a covenantal sacrifice and that Jesus' blood must there-fore be poured out. This is mentioned only in John 19:34—by way of addition—and this is probably not the Evanglist speaking. But John recognizes only a single sin, namely, that man does not know that Jesus was sent by God; he is also acquainted with only one means of removing this sin, namely, the spirit poured out by Jesus (v 7). To those who receive this gift Jesus, and thus the Father also, come clearly into view; this in turn makes possible a new relationship to God, the new covenant, the "way," or whatever it is called in various Christian traditions. As a consequence, the term "to know" appears in John fifty-six times (the most of the four evangelists) and the verb "to believe" ninety-eight times (again the most frequent of any of the gospels), while the nouns "faith" ($\pi\acute{\iota}\sigma\tau\iota\varsigma$) and "knowledge" ($\gamma\nu\hat{\omega}\sigma\iota\varsigma$) are missing. The preponderance of "to believe" over "to know" indicates that it is not rational knowledge that is involved, not a judgment reached by virtue of "reason." But John means that our eyes have to be opened and that we cannot open them ourselves so that we see God in his love for us.

■ **8–11** These verses speak in a curious way of what the spirit has to do: the spirit is to convince the world of its sin, namely, that it does not believe in Jesus; of the righteousness of Jesus, namely, that he goes to the Father and so is recognized as justified by the highest authority; and of the judgment that has already been executed over the ruler of this world.

■ **12** Verse 12 connects up very well with verse 7: Jesus, who tarries on earth, still has many things to say to the disciples, but they are not yet able to bear them. What these "many" things are is naturally left unmentioned. In any case, it cannot refer to the coming persecution; for he has already spoken to them about that. But perhaps verse 12 is conceived only as preparation for verse 13a.

■ **13a** The spirit of truth will lead the disciples into all truth. It is clearly presupposed in the first half of this verse that what the spirit will teach will go beyond the message of the earthly Jesus; one could perhaps say: it will go as far beyond the message of the earthly Jesus as the Evangelist's corrections and additions go beyond the tradition dictated to him by his source. The Evangelist is clearly aware that there is a break between what the earthly Jesus said and did and the message of the spirit. In his own way Mark was also aware of this break and gave expression to it—as well as he was able. The expectation of the end, which still lay, for Mark, in an indeterminate future as a cosmic event, was radicalized by John in such a way that chronological time was eliminated and with it the transformation of the world expected by Mark and the first Christians.

■ **13b–15** These verses now endeavor to eradicate again the discontinuity between the spirit as advocate and the earthly Jesus. Yet not only that, but the emphasis is here put on the earthly Jesus: the spirit has nothing of his own to say, but has only to express what he has heard and—surprisingly—to make the future known. It is clear that this leads away from the preceding train of thought, since for it the future as something predicted beforehand plays no role. It makes better sense to say that the spirit will glorify Jesus, obtain what belongs to him and declare it. In that way the continuity is preserved without turning the spirit into a mere imitator. The spirit will be the executor of Jesus' will—in any case the verse may be so interpreted—who brings the true glory of Jesus to light: Jesus was not merely a miracle worker, but opened the way to the Father.

■ **15** Verse 15 does not, however, fit well into this context. The verse gives evidence of the difficulty in combining two different conceptions: the spirit is sent by the Father and proclaims his eschatological will; the spirit also proclaims Jesus' message, since everything that the Father possesses also belongs to Jesus. For the Evangelist those conceptions are merely alternative expressions of the same truth. But not everyone is as ready as Bultmann to attribute to the Evangelist the way in which a word is explained here; for Bultmann, it is a characteristic of the Evangelist to insert such elaborations into a pre-existing text.

However that matter is decided, a definitive result of the review remains: in spite of continuity, there exists a distinction between the earthly Jesus and the post-Easter spirit, and the real message is first proclaimed by the spirit. In any case, the church, in fact, took the Easter message and not the preaching of Jesus of Nazareth as the basis of its own proclamation and teaching. And perhaps one may say that it is precisely the Fourth Gospel that confirms the church in that move.

■ **16** A new segment begins with verse 16, which discusses another aspect of the departure of Jesus in elaborate detail.

■ **16–19** Verses 16–19 form a subsection, in which the phrases, "a little while," "see no more," and "see again" play the central role. The disciples are depicted as completely dense in this connection: they simply do not understand what the words in verse 16 mean, "A little while, and you will see me no more; again a little while, and you will see me." But the sentence, "I go to the Father," has all of a sudden become enigmatic also; it was used in 14:28 and did not evoke a question there. Jesus knew what was on the lips of the disciples before they knew themselves and responds in an unexpected way. Earlier it appeared to be a settled matter that Jesus would return to the invisible Father, from whom he went out, and that that would turn out to be a blessing for the disciples: they could now receive the spirit. But now his departure and return have become a mystery.

■ **20ff.** Verses 20ff. seek to cast light on this mystery. Jesus' departure will fill the world with joy and cause the disciples dismay and lamentation. One might suppose that the permanent situation of the disciples after Good Friday is being described. But it is very difficult to carry this interpretation out. For the figure of the woman in travail in verse 21, which is then applied to the disciples in verse 22, speaks rather of the singular situation between Good Friday and Easter (or Pentecost). The disciples now find themselves forsaken in their sorrow by Jesus' death; but that will be replaced by joy evoked by the return of Jesus (as spirit, although that is not expressly said). Yet this situation will not be repeated. At all events, the Evangelist is convinced that the spirit will abide with the disciples for all time, εἰς τὸν αἰῶνα (14:16). An analogy could only be found in the situation of those Christians who find it distressing that Jesus, whose story is told so vividly and consolingly by the tradition, is no longer present, and who have not or not yet experienced the spirit which replaces him according to the tradition and perhaps even surpasses him (the spirit in which he returns). Yet that is a modern construction by means of which one ought not ingeniously to reinterpret this passage, to give it some general application. While the distress of the forsaken disciples is therefore contrasted here with their joy at the return of the Lord (in the spirit),[1] verses 23f. introduce something new.

■ **23f.** Verses 23f. are connected to the preceding by the theme word "joy." It appears as though the verb ἐρωτᾶν here means "ask, request," and not "question," and thereby evidently eases the transition to a new theme. In any case, on the day of Jesus' return every need on the part of the disciples will be met. That much is clear however one translates ἐρωτᾶν. Verse 23 introduces something new: the prayer in the name of Jesus which the disciples had not heretofore known (cf. v 24).

■ **24** Verse 24 promises that their prayer will be granted, that their joy will be full—one asks for what one does not yet possess, and if one receives that, joy is complete. It is certain that a prayer in the name of Jesus was only gradually adopted. It is a different question, however, whether a Christianity of the spirit practiced by those disciples to whom the paraclete had come included such a prayer in its practices. The theme, "prayer in the name of Jesus," is introduced for the first time in 14:14, and then quite surprisingly. Although it is omitted there not merely by the witnesses X λ 565 *al* b sy^{sc} Nonnus and some Vulgate manuscripts, one could imagine that a gloss had crept into the text, especially since it is quite isolated. On the other hand, it could also be a correction, since it was objectionable for the disciples to perform greater works than Jesus himself. This theme is taken up again in verse 26.

■ **25** Before returning to the theme, verse 25 emphasizes that up to this point Jesus has spoken to them in figures; that means, rather: in enigmatic words, veiled sayings, so that the disciples have not understood. The time is coming, however, when this veil will be lifted and Jesus (through the spirit) will no longer speak, as it were, in ciphers, but plainly.

■ **26** Following these words, it is asserted, as though it were new, that the disciples will then "pray in the name of Jesus"; this is introduced by the phrase, "in that day," which appeared earlier in verse 23. However, that is again curiously weakened: Jesus does not mean that he will petition the Father on their behalf, so that he stands between them and the Father (and yet that is actually the case in prayers made in Jesus' name).

■ **27** Verse 27 explains: the Father himself loves them and—one expects the sentence to continue—thus fulfills their prayers. But the sentence continues along a different line: the Father loves the disciples because they have believed that Jesus came from the Father. That is actually the Johannine definition of faith.

■ **28** This definition is undergirded by verse 28. Jesus himself formulates the critical definition: he has come from the Father and has come into the world; he is again leaving the world and returning to the Father.

---

1   Moreover, verse 22 says at its conclusion that this joy
     is final and no one can take it from them; it thus
     concurs with 14:16.

■ **29** The disciples have no difficulty understanding that since it is expressed unenigmatically.

■ **30** They testify immediately to their faith in Jesus' omniscence: he needs no one to question him—this time ἐρωτᾶν means "question" and not "request." The verb ἐρωτᾶν appears twenty-six times in the Gospel of John. Twelve times it has the meaning common in Koine, "request."[2] Of these, 4:47, 19:31 and 19:38 pretty certainly belong to tradition; 17:9, 17:15 and 17:21 likewise certainly belong to the language of the Evangelist, as does 18:21. The two meanings may thus not be assigned to tradition and the Evangelist, respectively. In chapter 9, ἐρωτᾶν means "question" in a segment taken from the tradition, and in 16:5 Jesus uses the term with this meaning in a speech created by the Evangelist. One must therefore reject any attempt to draw conclusions regarding the origin of a verse, whether from tradition or the composition of the Evangelist, on the basis of this distinction in usage.

■ **31f.** To return to verse 31: Jesus contradicts their assurances that they believe with the prediction of their imminent dispersion. If it is the case that Jesus is united with the Father, then his disciples will have tribulation in the world. But they should be comforted: that is not the final word to be said on the matter. This applies to every generation of disciples. The spirit is not here represented as a comforter.

■ **33** Verse 33 does not connect up entirely lucidly: to what does "I have said this to you" refer? That Jesus will not be forsaken by the Father: courage is promised to his disciples with this assurance.

The world is described as darkness in the Gospel of John, as the blackness of a metaphycial abyss. The prince of this world is not God, but the evil one. God is remote from man. It is a world remote from God that is suggested in the Gospel of John with a few strokes of the pen, a world of sin and inner bondage: it is only Jesus, however, who sets his own free (8:32, 36). One can scarcely assess the forlornness, into which the Gospel of John sees humankind as having sunk, too seriously, if one wants to seize the jubilation with which he greets the appearance of Jesus Christ. In Jesus Christ the undreamed of has indeed occurred: the remote God has draw near man in grace. The interdict under which man and his life lay is broken. With Jesus joy breaks into existence (15:11, 16:20–24, 17:13), and a joy not of a past, earthly sort, but true and complete joy, the kind that comes with peace (14:27).

---

2   Bultmann, *John*, 200 n. 3 [148 n. 2].

39. The "High Priestly" Prayer

Bibliography

Agourides, Savas C.
"The 'High Priestly Prayer' of John." *SE* 4 = TU 102 (Berlin: Akademie-Verlag, 1968) 137–43.

Appold, Mark L.
"Christ Alive! Church Alive! Reflections on the Prayer of Jesus in John 17." *CurTM* 5 (1978) 365–73.

Appold, Mark L.
The Oneness Motif in the Fourth Gospel. Motif Analysis and Exegetical Probe into the Theology of John, WUNT 2, 1 (Tübingen: Mohr-Siebeck, 1976).

Battaglia, Oscar
"Preghiera sacerdotale ed innologia ermetica (Giov 17—*CH.* 1,31–32 e 13,18–20." *RivB* 17 (1969) 209–32.

Becker, Jürgen
"Aufbau, Schichtung und theologiegeschichtliche Stellung des Gebets in Joh. 17." *ZNW* 60 (1969) 56–83.

Bobrinskoy, Boris
"Die theologischen Grundlagen des gemeinsamen Gebets für die Einheit." *Una sancta* 22 (1967) 25–37.

Bornkamm, Günther
"Zur Interpretation des Johannesevangeliums. Eine Auseinandersetzung mit E. Käsemanns Schrift 'Jesu letzter Wille nach Johannes 17.'" *EvT* 28 (1968) 8–25.

Bornkamm, Günther
"Die eucharistische Rede im Johannesevangelium." *ZNW* 47 (1956) 161–69. In his *Geschichte und Glauben,* part 2. *Gesammelte Aufsätze,* vol. 4. BEvT 48 (Munich: Chr. Kaiser Verlag, 1971) 51–64.

Cadier, Jean
"The Unity of the Church. An Exposition of John 17." *Int* 11 (1957) 166–76.

Conybeare, Frederick C.
"John XVII. 23–24 [according to Marutha]." *HTR* 17 (1924) 188–89.

Cranny, Titus F.
John 17: As we are one; an exposition and interpretation of the seventeenth chapter of St. John's Gospel of Our Lord, containing His prayer for unity of all His followers (Garrison, NY: Unity Apostolate, 1965).

Delorme, Jean
"Sacerdoce du Christ et ministère (A propos de Jean 17). Sémantique et théologie biblique." *RSR* 62 (1974) 199–219.

Ellwein, Eduard
"Das hohepriesterliche Gebet (Joh 17) in der Auslegung Luthers." In *Die Leibhaftigkeit des Wortes. Theologische und seelsorgerliche Studien und Beiträge als Festgabe für Adolf Köberle zum 60. Geburtstag,* ed. O. Michel and Ulrich Mann (Hamburg: Furche-

Verlag, 1958) 91–106.

Feuillet, André

The Priesthood of Christ and His Ministers, tr. Michael
J. O'Connell (Garden City, NY: Doubleday, 1975)
= *Le sacerdoce du Christ et de ses ministres d'après la
prière sacerdotale du quatrième évangile et plusieurs
données parallèles du Nouveau Testament* (Paris:
Editions de Paris, 1972).

Fürst, Walther

"Die Einheit der Kirche nach Joh 17." *Deutsches
Pfarrerblatt* 64 (1964) 81–86.

George, Augustin

"L'heure de Jean XVII." *RB* 61 (1954) 392–97.

Giblet, Jean

"Sanctifie-les dans la vérité (Jean 17,1–26)." *BVC*
19 (1957) 58–73.

Huby, Joseph

"Un double problème de critique textuelle et
d'interprétation: Saint Jean 17,11–12." *RSR* 27
(1937) 408–21.

Käsemann, Ernst

Jesu letzter Wille nach Johannes 17 (Tübingen: Mohr-
Siebeck, 1966, ³1971, ⁴1980).

Keppler, Paul Wilhelm von

*Unseres Herrn Trost. Erklärung der Abschiedsreden
und des Hohepriesterlichen Gebetes Jesu (Joh c. 14–17)*
(Freiburg: Herder, 1887, ³1914).

Lauretin, André

"We'attah—*καὶ νῦν.* Formule caractéristique des
textes juridiques et liturgiques (à propos de Jean
17,5)." *Bib* 45 (1964) 168–97, 413–32.

Lloyd-Jones, David Martyn

*The Basis of Christian Unity. An Exposition of John 17
and Ephesians 4* (London: Inter-Varsity Press,
1962; Grand Rapids: Wm. B. Eerdmans, 1963).

Luck, Ulrich

"Die kirchliche Einheit als Problem des Johannesevangeliums." *Wort und Dienst* 10 (1969) 51–67.

Malatesta, Edward

"The Literary Structure of John 17." *Bib* 52 (1971)
190–214.

Marzotto, Damiano

L'unità degli uomini nel vangelo di Giovanni, Supplementi alla Rivista Biblica 9 (Brescia: Paideia,
1977).

Michel, Otto

"Das Gebet des scheidenden Erlösers." *ZST* 18
(1941) 521–34.

Michel, Otto

"Die Fürbitte des Erlösers: Joh 17,20–26." *Evangelische Missionszeitschrift* 2 (1941) 353–60.

Minear, Paul S.

"Evangelism, Ecumenism and John Seventeen."
TToday 35 (1978) 5–13.

Minear, Paul S.

"John 17,1–11." *Int* 32 (1978) 175–79.

Morrison, Clinton D.

"Mission and Ethic. An Interpretation of John 17."
Int 19 (1965) 259–273.

Newman, Barclay M.

"The Case of the Eclectic and the Neglected ἐκ of
John 17." *BT* 29 (1978) 339–41.

Radermakers, J.

"La prière de Jésus. Jn 17." *AsSeign* 29 (1973) 48–
86.

Randall, John F.

"The Theme of Unity in John 17:20–23." *ETL* 41
(1965) 373–94.

Riedl, Johannes

"Die Funktion der Kirche nach Johannes. 'Vater,
wie du mich in die Welt gesandt hast, so habe ich
auch sie in die Welt gesandt' (Joh 17,18)." *BK* 28
(1973) 12–14.

Rigaux, Beda

"Die Jünger in Joh 17." *Tübinger theologische
Quartalschrift* 150 (1970) 202–13.

Ritt, Hubert

Das Gebet zum Vater. Zur Interpretation von Joh 17,
Forschung zur Bibel 36 (Würzburg: Echter Verlag,
1979).

Smyth-Florentin, F.

"Jésus veut associer ses disciples à son amour: Jn
17,24–26." *AsSeign* 96 (1967) 40–48.

Schnackenburg, Rudolf

"Strukturanalyse von Joh 17." *BZ* 17 (1973) 67–
78, 196–202.

Stachel, Günter

"Die Einheit in Christus. Eine Katechese über Joh
17,20–23." *Katechetische Blätter* 90 (1965) 313–20.

Steinmeyer, Franz Karl Ludwig

Das hohepriesterliche Gebet Jesu Christi (Berlin:
Wiegandt, 1886).

Thüsing, Wilhelm

*Herrlichkeit und Einheit. Eine Auslegung des Hohe-
priesterlichen Gebetes Jesu (Johannes 17),* Die Welt
der Bibel 14 (Düsseldorf: Patmos-Verlag, 1962).

Thüsing, Wilhelm

*Die Erhöhung und Verherrlichung Jesu im Johannes-
evangelium.* NTAbh 21, 1–2 (Münster: Aschendorff, 1960, ²1970).

Villain, Maurice

"Those Who Believe. A Meditation on John 17."
One in Christ 6 (1970) 140–45, 547–53.

17

1 When Jesus had spoken these words, he lifted up his eyes to heaven and said, "Father, the hour has come; glorify thy Son that the Son may glorify thee, 2/ since thou hast given him power over all flesh, so that he might give eternal life to all whom thou hast given him. 3/ And this is eternal life, that they know thee the only true God, and Jesus Christ whom thou hast sent. 4/ I glorified thee on earth, having accomplished the work which thou gavest me to do; 5/ and now, Father, glorify thou me in they own presence with the glory which I had with thee before the world was made. 6/ I have manifested thy name to the men whom thou gavest me out of the world; thine they were, and thou gavest them to me, and they have kept thy word. 7/ Now they know that everything that thou hast given me is from thee; 8/ for I have given them the words which thou gavest me, and they have received them and know in truth that I came from thee; and they have believed that thou didst send me. 9/ I am praying for them; I am not praying for the world but for those whom thou hast given me, for they are thine; 10/ all mine are thine, and thine are mine, and I am glorified in them. 11/ And now I am no more in the world, but they are in the world, and I am coming to thee. Holy Father, keep them in thy name which thou hast given me, that they may be one, even as we are one. 12/ While I was with them, I kept them in thy name which thou hast given me; I have guarded them, and none of them is lost but the son of perdition, that the scripture might be fulfilled. 13/ But now I am coming to thee; and these things I speak in the world, that they may have my joy fulfilled in themselves. 14/ I have given them thy word; and the world has hated them because they are not of the world, even as I am not of the world. 15/ I do not pray that thou shouldst take them out of the world, but that thou shouldst keep them from the evil one. 16/ They are not of the world, even as I am not of the world. 17/ Consecrate them in the truth; thy word is truth. 18/ As thou didst send me into the world, so I have sent them into the world. 19/ And for their sake I consecrate myself, that they also may be consecrated in truth. 20/ I do not pray for these only, but also for those who are to believe in me through their word, 21/ that they may all be one; even as thou, Father, art in me, and I in thee, that they also may be in us, so that the world may believe that thou hast sent me. 22/ The glory which thou hast given me I have given to them, that they may be one even as we are one, 23/ I in them and thou in

me, that they may become perfectly one,
so that the world may know that thou
hast sent me and hast loved them even
as thou hast loved me. 24/ Father, I
desire that they also, whom thou hast
given me, may be with me where I am, to
behold my glory which thou hast given
me in thy love for me before the foundation of the world. 25/ O righteous
Father, the world has not known thee,
but I have known thee; and these know
that thou hast sent me. 26/ I made
known to them thy name, and I will make
it known, that the love with which thou
hast loved me may be in them, and I in
them."

Introduction

A new section begins here, set off only by the first three
words; the locality is not indicated, any more than it is in
chapters 15 and 16. That Jesus lifts up his eyes to heaven
gives external expression to the fact that he speaks to
God, while earlier he was speaking to Jews (as far as
chapter 10) and to his disciples. The use of "Father" to
address God emphasizes the unique relationship "the
son" sustains to the Father. The text refers only to a
"speaking" ($\epsilon i\pi\epsilon\hat{\iota}\nu$), not to a "praying" ($\pi\rho o\sigma\epsilon\acute{u}\chi\epsilon\sigma\theta\alpha\iota$),
although chapter 17 has been designated "the high
priestly prayer" since David Chytraeus (1531–1600).
This farewell prayer (the few sentences that Jesus will
exchange with Pilate are an entirely separate matter) is so
fundamentally different from all other farewell discourses (e.g., that of Paul in Miletus) that comparison is
really impossible. That owes to the fact that Jesus'
position and situation is unique. The "hour"—the one
that is held steadily in view throughout the Gospel—has
come. Yet that is also by way of anticipation, strictly
speaking. This discourse could not, however, have been
given on the cross at the hour of death. The words, "it is
finished," in 19:30, nevertheless repeat an important
theme from this chapter. The Evangelist has framed this
speech (as one filled with the spirit) and put it on the lips
of Jesus, without having a source. Although it is conceived as a real prayer,[1] it is nevertheless also intended
for the reader, as are other literary farewell discourses
(e.g., the *Testaments of the 12 Patriarchs*); light is cast on
several usages by this connection. "The hour" is actually
Jesus' transition from this world to the glory he had with

the Father before the world was made (vv 5, 24). As such
a "passing over" ($\mu\epsilon\tau\alpha\beta\hat{\eta}\nu\alpha\iota$; vv 5, 24), it looks back to the
past and peers into the future, which is even occasionally
spoken of as though it were already past (vv 4, 11).

■ **1** Verse 1 begins a segment with the theme "glorify"
($\delta o\xi\acute{a}\zeta\omega$), which is a note struck repeatedly in the discourse. It is interrupted, of course, by verses 2f. The
prayer, "glorify thy son," refers in the first instance to
being raised up on the cross, which now confronts Jesus,
and which is simultaneously and here preeminently
exaltation to the Father. The reader is not surprised, as a
consequence, that Jesus is actually praying for his own
death (but cf. 12:27). Jesus does not of course pray for
death as such, but for the completion of his work (cf.
19:30), with which he, crowning his work of salvation,
glorifies the Father. To this extent, the glorification of
the son by the Father and the glorification of the Father
by the son are one and the same thing.

■ **2** "Just as" ($\kappa\alpha\theta\acute{\omega}s$) expresses the connection between
Jesus' authorization to bestow eternal life and his glorifi-
cation. The words, "all flesh" ($\pi\acute{a}\sigma\eta s \sigma\alpha\rho\kappa\acute{o}s$, כָּל בָּשָׂר) has
a correlative expression in 3:35, "has given all things into
his hand," and in 13:3, "had given all things into his
hands." It is nevertheless hyperbole: it exaggerates the
reality. The continuation, "to all whom thou hast given
him," shows that only a selection is intended. The
expression, "all flesh," only appears here in John. The
Evangelist believes that Jesus only gives salvation to the
elect; he does not conceal the fact that faith is not everyone's cup of tea. He does not, however, trace this fact
back to the resistance of many men to the message, but

---

1   Contrary to Käsemann, *The Testament of Jesus.*

150

sees in it the will of the Father. This dualism is not pursued; the reference to the divine will does not give us any insight into the question. The willingness to let the question rest can be interpreted as a reflection of the fact that the community, from which the Fourth Gospel stems, was a small minority, a sect, and that this sect was satisfied to think that it was of the elect, like the community at Qumran. But at that time the Christian faith, as it was embraced by almost the whole of the West, was also not a power governing all men, but was alive and vibrant only in a minority. The question arises again whether it is at all correct to make the total realization of God's will the norm of Christianity. The elect are not chosen simply because they are perfect, but because the Father has adopted them. Bultmann's attempt to save the specific sense of "all flesh" for the Evangelist by claiming that Jesus also executes judgment,[2] disturbs the context, where the subject is limited to salvation. John says nothing about a final redemption of all men, although he uses the traditional saying about the lamb that takes away the sin of the world (1:29).

The construction of verse 2 creates difficulties. The "case without grammatical construction," "everything that you have given him," is placed first and later taken up by a pronoun in another case and number, namely, "to them" ($a\dot{v}\tau o\hat{i}s$).[3] Several interpreters see a Semitism in this construction; but the same construction is also found in colloquial Greek. Here it has the ring of the elegant and solemn. The word "everything" ($\pi\hat{a}v$) is attracted to the following relative clause, $\delta\ \delta\acute{\epsilon}\delta\omega\kappa\alpha s\ \kappa\tau\lambda.$, as is customary in such cases. A literal rendering is impossible in either German or English. The hyperbolic expression is chosen to make the power of Jesus even greater (cf. v 24). The earthly work of Jesus here becomes the basis of the prayer for the requested glorification.

■ **3** Verse 3 explains what eternal life consists of: it consists in knowing the one, true God[4] and the one he has sent. The use of Jesus Christ—this expression appears in the Gospel of John only in 1:17 in addition to the present passage—corresponds to ritualistic style. Part of the price the author must pay for this style is having Jesus speak of himself in the third person. Since the Father is now visible in Jesus (14:9), the Father can be

spoken of only in connection with Jesus. The Evangelist thus combines the supreme authority of Jesus with the oneness of God. "God is God and Mohammed is his prophet" is only an apparent parallel. For Jesus is not a prophet, but "the son." Knowledge is not intended as an intellectual act, but as the beginning of man's life dedication and his union with God (and Jesus).

■ **4** Verse 4 does not refer to a "glorification" that will come in the future in Jesus' death on the cross, but to a "glorification" that belongs already to the past, namely, to the works of Jesus on earth. We thus already have an echo of "It is finished" ($\tau\epsilon\tau\acute{\epsilon}\lambda\epsilon\sigma\tau\alpha\iota$) in 19:30 in "having accomplished" ($\tau\epsilon\lambda\epsilon\iota\acute{\omega}\sigma\alpha s$): Jesus has glorified God on earth by fulfilling in word and deed the task given to him. In this statement the author does not take into consideration that the meaning and proclamation of the earthly life has been disclosed only by the spirit, and thus that Jesus' pre-Easter work on earth was not at all comprehensible before his death—or so the Evangelist sees it. But since at this hour the difference between past and future is almost entirely obliterated and the two interpenetrate one another, it is possible for the Evangelist to interchange the two perspectives. It is the fundamental unity of the work of Jesus that finally makes this comprehensive view possible. The time of salvation for the Evangelist begins here and now, to the extent that Jesus' message finds faith; thanks to the presence of the spirit, the Evangelist did not know of that "nasty ditch," of which Lessing once spoke.

■ **5** Verse 5 resumes the prayer of verse 1 again, but in so doing passes from the past to the expected future. However, there is a difference between "glorify thy son" and "glorify me": the glory now does not appear in the completion of the salvific work of Jesus; what is involved is the glory that Jesus possessed before the foundation of the world in the presence of God (this glory will be mentioned again in v 24). In this connection, the Evangelist of course makes use of a formula that is also found in paganism: "Sovereign mistress Isis . . . glorify me, as I

---

2   *John,* 492f. [376].
3   Cf. BDF §466.
4   Strathmann, *Das Evangelium nach Johannes,* 224:

"Jesus Christ is the end of the history of religion. And God is the end or the impossibility of any Christian hero cult."

have glorified the name of thy son Horus."[5] Bultmann sees a mythological expression in this usage, which the Evangelist has used without understanding it mythologically.[6] But the Evangelist has not given the reader the clue that makes it possible for him or her to understand it mythologically. Nor does he speak of an "eschatological" event; that is the result only of the transformation of the Johannine text into an existential interpretation. It is dubious, however, whether the "dehistoricizing" that is the result corresponds to an expansion of the "now" that is referred to in the Gospel of John. That basically depends on the eternity of the Son of God. In spite of Käsemann, one can ask whether the request for that glory that he once had does not presuppose that he did not again possess it, and therefore was not a "god walking about on earth." The sojourn of Jesus on earth does not then mean merely an irrelevant change in scene, but a forfeiture of that pre-worldly existence that he once possessed. On the other hand, he has glorified the Father precisely because of this sacrifice and thereby also glorified himself; his self-abasement is therefore a glorification, which was unknown to the one who has yet to suffer humiliation.

■ **6** Verse 6 returns to the completed work of Jesus: he has "revealed the name of God to those" whom God gave him out of the world. The words, "they were thine" ($\sigma o \grave{\iota}$ $\mathring{\eta}\sigma\alpha\nu$), are reminiscent of certain Valentinian expressions, according to which only those "spiritual by nature" ($\phi\acute{\upsilon}\sigma\epsilon\iota$) were saved. To say that they have kept the word of God does not refer to some knowledge of the catechism or bible, but to obedience in life that attests their continuing union with God. It is striking how strongly the Evangelist emphasizes the fact that the Father only gives those obedient to him (those he has determined to be obedient) to the son. That was especially invigorating for the Evangelist's colleagues in the faith. The riddle of predestination is never mentioned by name in the Gospel of John. The Evangelist would not have known it from any sort of tradition, but from bitter experience with those over whom the word had been poured without leaving a trace, the word that illuminated the whole of life for him.

■ **7f.** The theology of the Gospel of John is essentially a theology of the word. That of course also became the theology of many gnostics; it is not surprising, for that reason, that some scholars have turned the Evangelist into a gnostic phenomenon. But the gnostic revealer said to the gnostic: your quintessence is basically divine, and it is sufficient to hold fast to this faith in oneself over against a conflicting world. On the other hand, believers in the Johannine community have been taken from their fallen state in the world by means of a rebirth from above, a rebirth that causes them to pass from death to life (3:5f., 5:24), no thanks to their original creation. Jesus has given to them the word that he was given—in a certain sense he is only the mediator, much like an envoy can appear as a mediator between a sovereign and his opposite. They have accepted this word, though it was not established by proofs, that is, they have really believed that this man standing in front of them was sent by the Father. This way of putting it is genuinely Johannine. Since for the Evangelist the deeds of Jesus—however marvelous they may still be—are only pointers to something entirely different, which does not itself come into view as such, and are not legitimating miracles, faith for him is anything but self-evident; rather, it is something tremendous. That Jesus was God's messenger could really only be believed in the face of appearances. A "teacher," but without the proper rabbinic education, without, as it were, the necessary final examination and credentials, attested only by a couple of miracles, the evidential value of which was contested, and finally betrayed by a very close follower and ignominiously put to death—such a teacher was a peculiar emissary of God. That he had come from God and had again returned to God makes sense, on the other hand, only if the God who sent him thought and acted differently than one assumed, judging by the customary image of God. The cross, or to put it even more plainly and crassly, the gallows, affected not only Jesus, but also him who sent Jesus. This tragic event is veiled for us by a tradition 2,000 years old, which all but blotted out the scandal. Today when so many again take offense at Jesus' claim, this scandal has again become visible and the Gospel of John has thereby again become unexpectedly relevant. The Evangelist understood that and conse-

---

5   P. Mag VII = P. London 121.502ff.
6   *John*, 491–97 [375–80].

quently did everything he could to accentuate again and again this objectionable alliance with the Father: it is actually the basis on which the entire faith of the Evangelist rests: only in Jesus, here and only here, does the heaven touch the earth, so to speak, and once again not with consoling palpability. The Evangelist clings, in fact, only to the word (to which Jesus' deeds belong as *verba visibilia*).

■ **9** Verse 9 introduces a new section: the prayer of petition for the community. It is once again made clear that the κόσμος, the world, is not included in this prayer; it includes only those given to the son by the Father. Luther once referred to the Gospel of John as the "tender . . . central gospel." Yet it is anything but tender; in a certain sense it is very harsh and inexorable. For it presents a new puzzle: why direct this "devotion of oneself," this unbounded humility, only to the chosen and not to the entire world? One can make the answer easy by pointing to gnostic dualism, which has certainly influenced the Gospel of John. But history of religions parallels really require not only that one comprehend the religious phenomenon to be investigated, but also its counterparts. And it is by no means claimed that the same motives stand behind possible identical expressions. Gnosticism gives the material world up as lost from the outset, as the battleground of evil spirits and the home of injustice and violence. Life is only bearable for Gnostics if a world of light exists somewhere else, where things go not as they go on earth but as they ought to go. The community of the Gospel of John also suffers under its existence in this world. For it, too, the "world" is bad. But that community is persuaded that the community itself is really no better than the others. Anthropology is not the key to the whole, human decision—however it is understood—is not the decisive thing. One does not thank himself or herself for a privileged position; one owes it to divine compassion. One experiences this compassion in the coming of the divine message. That apparently agrees exactly with gnostic theology. But this message is not encountered in a mythical person, it is not brought by an emissary who only makes a flying visit, for whom the appearance on earth is merely a change in locale; it is encounterd in a real human life, one that

ended on the gallows. The "Father" who ventures into the world in his emissary in such an entirely different form turns out on account of the cross to be someone quite different than the gnostic king of light. He chose a group of men who can boast of nothing that gave them a claim to be chosen. They are not delivered from the world on account of their election, any more than Jesus is spared the cross. As a consequence, Jesus prays for them in connection with his departure—for those God gave him for his own, but not for the world. His own "know" that everything that belongs to Jesus, his deeds, his works, belongs to God, and precisely for that reason is Jesus glorified by them. Only he who so completely sacrifices himself to God reflects the whole glory of the Father's love: that is expounded, or at least indicated, once more in the following verse.

■ **10** Verse 10 discloses how intimate the fellowship between Jesus and the Father is, so intimate that the boundaries between "mine" and "thine" here appear to lose their function. That was intolerable for a Jewish-Christian reader, and for that reason it was not a happy idea when the Gospel of John was called "a missionary tract for Israel."[7] Jesus is glorified in his own, insofar as the chosen believe in Jesus and live in this faith. Jesus' possibilities on earth are limited by the fact that they, and only they, have been given to him.

■ **11** Statements that have different temporal bearings formally are interwoven in this verse. "I am no more in the world, but they are in the world" is suitable only when Jesus' separation from his own already lies behind him in his exaltation; "and I am coming to thee" actually describes the process by which this separation takes place. Bauer sees the matter differently: he sees a prolepsis in the words "I am coming to thee" (κἀγὼ πρὸς σὲ ἔρχομαι), the perspective of which determines the preceding "And now I am no more etc." (οὐκέτι κτλ.).[8] The Father can be called "holy" in his distinction from the world. To guard Christians in the world, the Father is asked that they may all be one. The author does not have in mind the absorption of Christianity into the world, any more than he is thinking of a mystical sense of the unity of all Christians. The accord of God and the believer indicates a renunciation of the world. Unfortunately, we

7   Bornhäuser, *Das Johannesevangelium. Eine Missions-schrift für Israel*, BFCT 2, Sammlung wissenschaftlicher Monographien 15 (Gütersloh: C. Bertelsmann, 1928).

8   Bauer, *Das Johannesevangelium*, 204.

lack any concrete information regarding how this turning away from the world was carried out practically. Some think of a sect-like fellowship closing itself off from the world, an association that is aware of its exceptional position, but at the same time knows how strongly it is threatened. That need not be taken to mean that this fellowship lives spatially apart from the "great world"; it could also exist as a kind of underground in the midst of a large city, without being noticed generally or taken seriously.

■ 12 Jesus has previously guarded his own (note the backward glance in "While I was with them," ἤμην). That seems to presuppose that Jesus has to be spatially present in order to protect Christians from the world. Such a notion would factually assume only a very small circle held together by the presence of the master and "kept in the name of the Father." The word "name" here implies something like "being," but is understood as a energy field. But now this fellowship is threatened with annihilation with the departure of Jesus, while up to this point he was able to protect all but one. The name of the one who has been lost is not mentioned; he appears to be subject to *deletio memoria* ("obliteration of memory") and to be remembered only as the anonymous "son of perdition" (i.e., fallen into perdition, damnation). Nevertheless, even he has not come to ruin on account of Jesus, but because scripture[9] has indicated that God has willed it so.[10]

■ 13 The perspective of the speaker changes again: Jesus is still in the world; but he is about to depart. His prayer of petition is intended to give to his disciples, whose forsakenness is dawning, the complete joy that he himself has in fellowship with the Father. It follows from the certainty they have in being chosen and belonging to him. That is anything but a matter of course, as the following shows.

■ 14 Their situation has not improved by virtue of the fact that they have preserved and accepted the message of Jesus; on the contrary, they have attracted the hatred of the world. This is one of those passages in the Gospel of John that betrays how little this community was loved in its environment. Precisely because they were conscious of their distance from the world, of their peculiarity—

an awareness which they probably also precipitated in their environment—were they hated; but it was precisely this oppressed and oppressing situation that they shared with Jesus, who also did not belong to the world.

■ 15 It would appear that Jesus is asking the Father to take his own out of the world. But that is just what he does not want to do. His own people are to remain within the world and open to its dangers. Jesus asks only that God guard them from the evil one, that they not be drawn into the ways of the world and its decadence.

This picture reminds some of the gnostic Gospel of Thomas. In the Gospel of Thomas the world is felt to be a constant threat, a predator, which is perpetually crouching in ambush, ready to spring. The community in which the Gospel of John arose was not alienated from the world in the sense that there were no longer relations between it and the world, in the sense that it lived in total isolation. Yet it no doubt had the duty of being perpetually watchful. The solemnity of the mode of speech again prevents us from gathering more than hints about particulars, since such language abstracts away from the concrete.

■ 16 Verse 16 affirms once again that these Christians are no more of the world than is Jesus. Yet one should not take this as simply a statement of fact on the part of the Evangelist, but should perceive it as an indirect admonition of which this community stood in need. That is made amply clear in the following.

■ 17 Verse 17 contains the prayer that they may be kept "holy" (ἅγιοι) in their fellowship with God. Chrysostom's interpretation betrays a later period of rival doctrinal opinions in its second part: "Make them holy through the gift of the spirit and by right doctrine."[11] Bauer refers verse 17 to Ps 119 (120):142: "and thy law is true" ("word," λόγος instead of "law," νόμος is a *lapsus calami* ("slip of the pen"), according to Bauer; the Hebrew text correctly has תוֹרָתְךָ אֱמֶת).[12]

■ 18 That Jesus sends the disciples into the world, like the Father sent him, has a double meaning. On the one hand, they are now the bearers of the message, of the word, as was Jesus earlier (cf. 20:21). On the other hand, they thereby come to occupy the position vis-à-vis the world that Jesus had: it turns on them whether the

---

9   Ps 109:7f.
10   Cf. Acts 1:20.
11   *Hom.* 82.1, tom. VIII 483d = *Cat.* 373.20.

12   Bauer, *Das Johannesevangelium*, 205.

hearers are won over and saved or not. The responsibility, but also the fatefulness, of the individual Christian becomes apparent.

The synoptic saying, "I send you into the world as sheep among wolves" (Matt 10:16/ Luke 10:3) belongs to an entirely different context.

■ **19** In verse 19, the word "to sanctify" (ἁγιάζειν) is taken up again from verse 17 but in a different sense: Jesus consecrates himself as a sacrifice for his own. But what does that imply for the disciples, who are now "to be sanctified in truth" (ἡγιασμένοι ἐν ἀληθείᾳ)? Through Jesus have they become "truly consecrated as divine chattels," an idea that Bauer entertains?[13] However, he seems to prefer another interpretation: "By returning home Jesus fills himself with heavenly essence, just as he raised himself again from the dead" (cf. 10:36).[14]

Yet verse 19 expressly emphasizes that Jesus sacrifices himself for his own, so that they may belong to this new reality. "To sanctify" (ἁγιάζειν) is used as a technical term of sacrificial discourse, although the author is not thinking of Jesus' death as a sacrifice or a surrogate. Yet the Evangelist has to use such expressions in order to make it clear, at some risk, that the meaning intended is veiled. Jesus sacrifices himself in order that he may draw them into the circle of selfless love—but not by magic—which is alone capable of continuing his work after his death. "Consecrate" (ἁγιάζειν) properly means "to consecrate something or someone to God," to place exclusively in the service of God. In some such sense, the real disciples of Jesus must live exclusively in the service of God. Understood as a legal demand, this demand kills, like all laws understood in an absolute and unlimited sense. But here the situation is that the disciples are made capable of such love only from the inside out, not on the basis of a mechanical sacrifice. God is not a mathematician who knows how to add and subtract. Because the disciples constantly lag behind the demand to love is the admonition necessary "to abide in the love of Jesus." Man can only hearken to the voice of love as experienced and not contradict it.

■ **20f.** A new section begins with these verses: to the believers of the first generation was added the larger group of those who came to faith through the preaching of the first believers. The community is to be a missionary community, and it would be a contradiction of its essence were it to stop growing. But these new Christians must also be integrated into a unified group. The Evangelist is probably speaking here of his own time, which historically was already far removed from the time of Jesus. This community, too, is to grow into that unity that binds the Father, Jesus, and the first disciples together. The Johannine community also had some history behind it, which it dare not deny. We know very little about it, only as much as these hints reveal. But one thing is clear: the unity and unanimity of Christians ought to convince the world that Jesus is really he whom the Father has sent.

■ **22** Jesus has not retained the glory that the Father has given him, but has passed it on to his own: the knowledge of his Father, so that they may be unified by faith. There were Christians who thought they could live for God only in solitude, only in isolation from others. But for John—who may have been an isolated thinker—the community, in which the unity of the Father with the son was reflected, was indispensable.

■ **23** The departing Jesus prays repeatedly for the unity of his own, a unity that ought to convince the "world" (κόσμος) that God has sent him and that God loves Christians as much as he loves "the son."

■ **24** As in verse 2, "whom you have given me" is anticipated and then resumed by "and those" (κἀκεῖνοι). Jesus prays to the Father to permit Jesus' own people to tarry with him where he is in glory, so that they may see the glory that God gave him before the creation of the world. Will Jesus have admirers whose admiration will enhance and increase his glory? No, the Christ who is about to die means by that that believers will participate in his glory, on which no one can look without himself being affected.

■ **25f.** The Father is called "righteous" in conduct toward the world and toward believers. How he conducts himself toward the world remains a mystery for us. But we know how he behaved with respect to Jesus: he sent Jesus to rescue us, and Jesus carried out this assignment, even to the point of dying on the cross. He will carry out this assignment even further through his disciples, so that

---

13 *Das Johannesevangelium*, 205.
14 *Das Johannesevangelium*, 205; cf. the excursus on 2:22, 49.

the love that he had experienced from the Father may pass over to them and he will abide in them in this love. These verses thus bring together once more the prayer of Jesus, whose death is imminent, and the situation in which he and his own people find themselves: this God is unknown to the world; he is no god to the people of the world. This raises the question for us: in a society that is today shot through with the lust for profit and power, whether this God is not also unknown to us, and therefore really not a god. Since the Christian God is the sole god in the Western tradition who is acknowledged as God, one wonders whether a world does not really exist after the death of God, there where God is no longer acknowledged in the Johannine sense, there where the cross has become an antiquated and purely poetic symbol. But it is a further question whether Nietzsche was not right when he has his madman express his horror about the fact that we do not know what we have conjured up and brought about by killing God. And whether, consequently, the malaise, the widespread dissatisfaction, is not an indictment of Christians, that the world can no longer acknowledge in Christians and in their behavior that Jesus was sent by the Father. If, however, Jesus alone has spoken the word of God, which his own people are to reproduce, not as parrots, but with living voices, and if this word has fallen dumb, then, in the face of a silent God, we really live in a world that has become meaningless, a world that gains no meaning from the repetition of a Christian tradition, for which life and death are rewarding. The Evangelist still has as his point of departure the conviction that Jesus and his own know about the mystery of this God, who has made his son the king of kings only in that Jesus died on the gibbet in defenseless love. This name, unknown to us, Jesus has made known and will continue to make known, so that the love of God will not die out when Jesus quits the earth. With this outlook, with this petition, the "high priestly prayer" comes to an end, the prayer of him who is prepared to die for this love.

Overview

Chapter 17 has its share of peculiarities. That was sensed long ago. Theodore of Mopsuestia and Chrysostom were agreed that it was not a real prayer, but only took the form of one, which the first was inclined to regard as a prophecy, and which the second was inclined to regard as a dialogue to encourage the disciples. Loisy was of course the first to interpret the prayer as unnecessary and designed only for the disciples and readers.[15] M. F. Wiles points to 11:42 and leaves open the question whether an element of unreality or docetism shows up here.[16] In so doing, he anticipates an idea of Käsemann: "Rather, his majestic 'I desire' dominates the whole chapter,"[17] "as God going about on the earth."[18] Further, the more innocent assertion of Käsemann that chapter 17, which of course does not mention the paraclete, is a summary of the Johannine discourses,[19] was anticipated by Barrett as early as 1955.[20] Yet between those earlier judgments of Theodore and Chrysostom and modern critical considerations lay times in which chapter 17 had the force of the true testimony of John the son of Zebedee and the beloved disciple with regard to the words of his master, and Cornelius a Lapide (1567–1637) praised it as Jesus' "swan-song, full of charm, life, and inspiration." Zahn's commentary of 1908, which is of course an anachronism, holds that the prayer was spoken aloud for the consolation and encouragement of the disciples.[21] In 1913, the history of religions movement made an impressive incursion into the interpretation of the Fourth Gospel in Bousset's *Kyrios Christos*,[22] followed by Wetter in his *Sohn Gottes*,[23] in which he points to the *Corpus Hermeticum*. But more apposite are Dodd's references to *Poimandres*: "Your man wishes to share holiness with you, just as you gave him all authority" (ὁ σὸς ἄνθρωπος συναγιάζειν σοι βούλεται, καθὼς παρέδωκας αὐτῷ τὴν πᾶσαν ἐξουσίαν), prior to which there appears: "receive spiritual sacrifices" (δέξαι λογικὰς θυσίας).[24] Barrett quotes Philo, "the one true God" (τὸν ἕνα καὶ ἀληθινὸν θεόν) as a parallel.[25] With *Did.* 9 and 10 in view,

---

15 Loisy, *Le quatrième évangile*, 798–818.
16 *The Spiritual Gospel. The Interpretation of the Fourth Gospel in the Early Church* (Cambridge: The University Press, 1960) 145f.
17 *The Testament of Jesus*, 5.
18 *The Testament of Jesus*, 8f.
19 *The Testament of Jesus*, 3.
20 *John*, 500.

21 *Das Evangelium des Johannes*, 604.
22 *Kyrios Christos: A History of the Belief in Christ from the Beginnings of Christianity ot Irenaeus*, tr. John E. Steely (Nashville: Abingdon, 1970) 211–44.
23 *Der Sohn Gottes*, 129ff.
24 1: 31f.; Dodd, *Interpretation of the Fourth Gospel*, 420.
25 Philo, *De spec. leg.* 1.332 (LCL): Barrett, *John*, 504.

Loisy has designated chapter 17 as a special eucharistic prayer of a prophet that was placed in the *mouth* of Jesus.[26] But one need not be a critical theologian like Loisy to perceive the eucharistic strains in chapter 17; that is demonstrated by Cullmann[27] and W. Wilkens,[28] who conceive this discourse as a eucharistic prayer, without paying attention to the problem of the doctrine of the sacraments in the Fourth Gospel. G. Bornkamm has also joined in this eucharistic chorus,[29] for which he has earned the deserved opposition of J. L. Martyn.[30]

So much for probes into exegesis, old and new. Often questions are contested that scarcely arise any longer: what conclusion may one draw from the expression in verse 1, "lifting up his eyes to heaven"? Does Jesus pray in the open, or is he already in the "upper room," as Loisy asserts?[31] The earlier confidence that here the son of Zebedee—perhaps the first disciple?—was drawing on his own exact memory gradually gave way to the view that a Christian of the second or even third generation was at work, although Noack[32] and others again hoped to find the first written version of the oral tradition in the Gospel of John, on a par with or even exceeding that of Mark. Nor has apology in the old sense died out. The strange "I desire" ($\theta\epsilon\lambda\omega$) in verse 24 loses its edge by the suggestion that Jesus always shares the will of the Father. According to Barret, the ordinary language of prayer breaks down here because Jesus is speaking, so to speak, within the Godhead.[33] The "hour" ($\omega\rho\alpha$) has occasionally been interpreted—as does Lightfoot[34]—as referring only to the hour of glorification, and a feature of the Johannine theology has thereby been excessively accentuated. Barrett has of course already emphasized the paradoxical intertwining of the death and glorification that plays such a dominate role in Bultmann's interpretation of the Gospel of John.[35]

The real turn in the exegesis of John came when the traditon of Johannine authorship was abandoned, and it then was possible to view the author quite differently as one writing to his readers and having Jesus speak on the authority of the spirit; it was not yet possible for Jesus to speak like that within the confines of his earthly existence (16:12). It then followed, almost by itself, that Jesus lifting up his eyes to heaven in 17:1 was not a spatial indication, but a gesture that introduces the prayer. But the question becomes still more pressing: what kind of a prayer is it, really? The distinction is occasionally made between verses 1–5, where Jesus prays for himself, and verses 6–19 and 20–26, where he prays for the disciples and the whole of Christianity that is to come, although one occasionally sets off verses 24–26 as a special conclusion to the third part which just precedes (vv 20–23), as does Strathmann, for example.[36]

But what was this chapter as a whole? Does it provide a testament, a retrospective view of achievements, a model for future Christians, a prophecy, an admonition, and a promise? The real difficulties arise from the fact that the composition of the Evangelist is interwoven in a peculiar way with the prayer of the departing Jesus. In regard to this question, let us take the judgment of modern "critical" theology that this chapter is a composition of the author. The passion, the "hour" when Jesus departs from this life and from his own, follows immediately on this discourse. It is at least a task of this chapter to prepare the reader for this hour. Not, of course, by telling the reader how Jesus wrestled with this hour (and everything that went before and was to follow) and how he was finally reconciled to it. That would be a modern point of view and a perspective that Jesus rejects in 12:27f. as a temptation: "Father, what shall I say? 'Save me from this hour?' No, for this purpose I have come to

26 *Le quatrième évangile,* 798.
27 *Early Christian Worship,* tr. A. S. Todd and J. B. Torrance, SBT 10 (Chicago: Regnery, 1953) 110.
28 *Die Entstehungsgeschichte des vierten Evangeliums* (Zollikon: Evangelischer Verlag, 1958) 156.
29 "Die eucharistische Rede im Johannesevangelium," *ZNW* 47 (1956) 161–69.
30 J. Louis Martyn, *History and Theology in the Fourth Gospel* (Nashville: Abingdon, 1968, ²1979) 146f. n. 219.
31 *Le quatrième évangile,* 798.
32 Cf. B. Noack, *Zur johanneischen Tradition. Beiträge zur*

Kritik an der literarkritischen Analyse des vierten Evangeliums (Copenhagen: Rosenkilde og Bagger, 1954).
33 *John,* 514.
34 *St. John's Gospel,* 297.
35 *John,* 501f.
36 *Das Evangelium nach Johannes,* 223.

this hour. Father, glorify thy name." In this passage, the only positive answer to the temptation is the "yes" to the knowledge that the hour has come, and the request that the Father glorify his name. Some interpreters have allowed themselves to be misled by the view that this passage does not expressly refer to Jesus' death, and are of the opinion that the hour is really nothing but Jesus' exaltation to the Father. But then Jesus' earthly life becomes merely a sojourn in a foreign land, that is now coming to an end, and the "hour" becomes the moment when Jesus, perhaps still giddy like a butterfly from the earth's pull, swings into eternity. But that would be a fundamental misunderstanding. It is not said, to be sure, that this hour is the death on the cross, that now draws near. The wholly dark side of the redemption, the struggle with the world, which now brings Jesus under its sway, in all its violence, in the garden across the Kidron, in the long struggle of Pilate with the Jews, and in the long hours on the cross—all this has here been overcome. One could say that the scene of the prayer is being played already in an eternity where time is no longer in effect. In that connection, it is correct that this is the hour of departure, the "crossing over" ($\mu\epsilon\tau\alpha\beta\hat{\eta}\nu\alpha\iota$), out of the world to the Father, and that past and present flow together in that movement. The Christ still prays in the circle of the disciples, and yet that already lies behind him, together with the future in which the disciples' proclamation will penetrate beyond Jewish boundaries (vv 20–26). The "already" and the "not yet" interchange with each other, because the author's point of view lies way beyond Easter, beyond the reception of the spirit, and, paradoxically, because the backward glance in the discourse of Jesus is more historically authentic than is the vision of the future.

A special emphasis is placed on the unity that embraces the Father, the son, and the son's own: Christians belong to the Father, who is therefore able to give them to the son, and the son has revealed the name of the Father— another term for which is "the words" ($\tau\grave{\alpha}$ $\acute{\rho}\acute{\eta}\mu\alpha\tau\alpha$)—and the disciples and the later generations have accepted that name (words) and kept it. Everything is firmly joined together. That is so emphatically said that one is tempted to ask to what extent it actually occurred. Is the unity of the Johannine community really so free of all uncertainty and is the "son of perdition" the only one who falls outside this unity (because scripture or the effective will

of God causes it to happen), or is Judas only the hint of a possibility, in the end, that is repeated again and again? Verse 23 speaks of the goal that the world will know and acknowledge the sending of Jesus, so that something like a "restoration of all things" ($\mathring{\alpha}\pi o\kappa\alpha\tau\acute{\alpha}\sigma\tau\alpha\sigma\iota\varsigma$ $\pi\acute{\alpha}\nu\tau\omega\nu$) appears to crop up. But verse 25 admits the hatred of the world that is directed to Jesus and his own, who alone possess knowledge and are encircled by love. The lines of demarcation among verses 1–5 (others prefer to say vv 1–8), 9–19, and the remainder are in reality not so evident as it might appear; the unity of the passage prevails by far.

It is not said that Jesus' completion of the task assigned him is something like a kind of justification. The idea that Jesus must justify himself is absurd in the context of Johannine theology. It is rather a matter of a report of a victory at the conclusion of a battle that he has survived, comparable to the expression "it is finished" ($\tau\epsilon\tau\acute{\epsilon}\lambda\epsilon\sigma\tau\alpha\iota$) in 19:30. That indicates how difficult it is to put the prayer in one of the possible categories, and thus uncertainty persists for us in this regard. There goes together with this the fact that the language of the prayer is satisfied with a few expressions that are repeated constantly, and whose sense thus readily shifts.

John 17, the so-called high priestly prayer, can and must be viewed and considered from various perspectives. In form it is primarily a prayer of the son to the Father: after speaking earlier with his disciples, he now speaks only to his Father. But this prayer becomes part of the tradition: it therefore has signficance not only for God, but also for the community. It is simultaneously a review and a preview; it depicts the work that Jesus has completed, and prepares for what is to come. It is a farewell discourse, which thus reminds some of Paul's farewell speech in Miletus. But Jesus has really already departed when he speaks these words (v 11). It is the completion of the revelation, a consolation, and an admonition, all in one; it is both petition and intercession.

The Evangelist consciously used the form of a prayer. There is no mention of a historical tradition. In a certain sense, this prayer replaces that in Gethsemane. That indicates the almost frightening freedom of the Evangelist. But it is also observable in details. When Jesus says that he has glorified the Father on earth, that is no different than saying, as he does in verse 6, that he has made the name of the Father known. In this case, an expression from the history of ancient religion—the hidden name of God is made known—is given a new meaning. To reveal the name of God now means: to reveal God's being, that is, his will, his disposition, and to reveal them to the elect. For God is for only a select number of chosen, of those called; that one of these, Judas, was lost is no failure of Jesus, but the fulfillment of scripture (v 12). Accordingly, Jesus does not pray for the world (v 9); if this faith in Jesus also spreads over the entire world (v 20), it will only do so by individuals coming to faith everywhere. It is only in this sense that it can be said that the "world" will believe that God has sent Jesus (v 21).

It is a question whether other expressions were not also taken out of the tradition and then recoined. God has given Jesus power "over all flesh"; but the "all" that God gave him is nevertheless only a selection: those people that God really gave to Jesus. "Eternal life," according to verse 3, does not consist in an earthly existence being extended beyond death, but in the knowledge of God and Jesus (who are not to be separated from each other) and thus of the true reality. The elect now really know that Jesus "has come" from the Father (v 8). This expression, which sounds purely gnostic, is also revised; it does not refer to a primeval fall of the soul, but refers to the fact that human beings have their home with God, are united with him. That can also of course be understood in a gnostic sense, but it must not be: John was not alone in believing that we do not have permanent states in this life. Knowledge of God and Jesus is eternal life, consequently, because it frees man inwardly from the world and makes him certain of where he belongs. Jesus has come only "to accomplish this work" (v 4) or to give men the words of God (v 8). By making the true God "visible" in himself, he has glorified God, because he has represented him in his true being. The question now is whether the passion of Jesus can be understood in connection with the revelation of the Father. That is the case then if Jesus' death on the cross is the completion of his incarnation or his sending, and if, therefore, in this event the Father draws near the chosen ones, who alone can see that connection. Nothing is said about a vicarious atonement; the word "sin" is never used.

So long as Jesus remained with his disciples, he guarded them; one expects this continuation: now God himself might look after them and keep them. That is actually said in verse 15. But prior to that, there is a sudden mention of the fulfilling joy, which had already been referred to in 15:11. That joy does not consist in the experience of sensation, in particular emotions, in any kind of gladdening experiences, but in a person holding fast to the word of God, together with its content: Jesus has come from God.

40. Arrest, Trial, Denial

Bibliography

A. Passion Narrative (General)

Baumeister, Theofried
"Der Tod Jesu und die Leidensnachfolge des Jüngers nach dem Johannesevangelium und dem ersten Johannesbrief." *Wissenschaft und Weisheit* 40 (1977) 81–99.

Beutler, Johannes
"Die 'Juden' und der Tod Jesu im Johannesevangelium." In *Exodus und Kreuz im ökumenischen Dialog zwischen Juden und Christen. Diskussionsbeiträge für Religionsunterricht und Erwachsenenbildung,* ed. H. H. Henrix and M. Stöhr. Aachener Beiträge zu Pastoral- und Bildungsfragen 8 (Aachen: Einhard-Verlag, 1978) 75–93.

Billings, J. S.
"Judas Iscariot in the Fourth Gospel." *ExpTim* 51 (1939/1940) 156–57.

Bligh, John
The Sign of the Cross. The Passion and Resurrection of Jesus according to St. John (Slough: St. Paul Publications, 1975).

Borgen, Peder
"John and the Synoptics in the Passion Narrative." *NTS* 5 (1958/1959) 246–59.

Brown, Raymond Edward
"The Passion According to John: Chapter 18 and 19." *Worship* 49 (1975) 126–34.

Buse, Ivor
"St. John and the Passion Narratives of St. Matthew and St. Luke." *NTS* 7 (1960/1961) 65–76.

Buse, Ivor
"St. John and the Marcan Passion Narrative." *NTS* 4 (1957/1958) 215–19.

Curtis, K. Peter G.
"Three Points of Contact Between Matthew and John in the Burial and Resurrection Narratives." *JTS*, n.s., 23 (1972) 440–44.

Dauer, Anton
Die Passionsgeschichte im Johannesevangelium. Eine traditionsgeschichtliche und theologische Untersuchung zu Joh 18,1–19,30, SANT 30 (Munich: Kösel, 1972).

Delling, Gerhard
Der Kreuzestod Jesu in der urchristlichen Verkündigung (Göttingen: Vandenhoeck & Ruprecht, 1972), esp. 98–116.

Dibelius, Martin
"Die alttestamentlichen Motive in der Leidensgeschichte des Petrus- und des Johannesevangeliums." In his *Botschaft und Geschichte. Gesammelte Aufsätze* 1 (Tübingen: Mohr-Siebeck, 1953) 221–47.

Dietrich, Suzanne de
  L'heure de l'élévation, à l'écoute de saint Jean (Neuchâtel: Delachaux & Niestlé, 1966).

Evans, Christopher Francis
  The Passion of Christ (London: SCM Press, 1977) 50–66.

Fenton, Joseph C.
  The Passion According to John (London: S. P. C. K., 1961).

Goguel, Maurice
  Les sources du récit johannique de la passion (Paris: G. Fischbacher, 1910).

Haenchen, Ernst
  "Historie und Geschichte in den johanneischen Passionsberichten." In his *Die Bibel und Wir. Gesammelte Aufsätze* 2 (Tübingen: Mohr-Siebeck, 1968) 182–207 = "History and Interpretation in the Johannine Passion Narrative." *Int* 24 (1970) 198–219.

Harvey, A. E.
  Jesus on Trial. A Study in the Fourth Gospel (London: S. P. C. K., 1976).

Howard, J. K.
  "Passover and Eucharist in the Fourth Gospel." *SJT* 20 (1967) 329–37.

Jaubert, Annie
  "The Calendar of Qumran and the Passion-Narrative in John." In *John and Qumran*, ed. J. H. Charlesworth (London: Chapman, 1972) 62–75.

Kittel, Gerhard
  "Ὑψωθῆναι = gekreuzigt werden." *ZNW* 35 (1936) 282–85.

Klein, Hans
  "Die lukanisch-johanneische Passionstradition." *ZNW* 67 (1976) 155–86.

Kretschmar, Georg
  "Kreuz und Auferstehung Jesu Christi. Das Zeugnis der Heiligen Stätten." *Erbe und Auftrag* 54 (1978) 423–31; 55 (1979) 12–26.

Leistner, Reinhold
  Antijudaismus im Johannesevangelium? Darstellung des Problems in der neueren Auslegungsgeschichte und Untersuchung der Leidensgeschichte, Theologie und Wirklichkeit 3 (Bern: H. Lang; Frankfurt: P. Lang, 1974).

Lindars, Barnabas
  "The Passion in the Fourth Gospel." In *God's Christ and His People. Studies in Honour of Nils Alstrup Dahl*, ed. Jacob Jervell and Wayne A. Meeks (Oslo: Universitetsforlaget, 1977) 71–86.

Müller, Ulrich B.
  "Die Bedeutung des Kreuzestodes Jesu im Johannesevangelium. Erwägungen zur Kreuzestheologie im Neuen Testament." *KD* 21 (1975) 49–71.

Nicholson, Godfrey C.
  "Lifting up, Return Above and Cruxifixion. The Death of Jesus in the Johannine Redaction." Dissertation, Vanderbilt University, 1978.

Osten-Sacken, Peter von der
  "Leistung und Grenze der johanneischen Kreuzestheologie." *EvT* 36 (1976) 154–76.

Osty, Emile
  "Les points de contact entre le récit de la passion dans saint Luc et saint Jean." *RSR* 39 (1951) 146–54.

Potterie, Ignace de la
  "La passion selon S. Jean." *AsSeign* 21 (1969) 21–34.

Riaud, J.
  "La gloire et la royauté de Jésus dans la Passion selon saint Jean." *BVC* 56 (1964) 28–44.

Richter, Georg
  "Die Deutung des Kreuzestodes Jesu in der Leidensgeschichte des Johannesevangeliums." *BibLeb* 9 (1968) 21–36.

Senft, Christophe
  "L'évangile de Jean et la théologie de la croix." *Bulletin du Centre Protestant d'Etudes* 30 (1978) 31–37.

Schelkle, Karl Hermann
  "Die Leidensgeschichte Jesu nach Johannes. Motiv- und formgeschichtliche Betrachtung." In his *Wort und Schrift. Beiträge zur Auslegung und Auslegungsgeschichte des Neuen Testaments* (Düsseldorf: Patmos-Verlag, 1966) 76–80.

Schirmer, Dietrich
  Rechtsgeschichtliche Untersuchungen zum Johannes-Evangelium (Berlin: Erlangen, 1964).

Stanley, David Michael
  "The Passion according to St. John." *Worship* 33 (1959) 210–30.

Talvero, S.
  "Problemática de la unidad en Jn. 18–20." *Salmanticensis* 19 (1972) 513–75.

Tosatto, G.
  "La passione di Cristo in S. Giovanni." *Parole di Vita* 15 (1970) 377–88.

Weise, Manfred
  "Passionswoche und Epiphaniewoche im Johannes-Evangelium. Ihre Bedeutung für Komposition und Konzeption des vierten Evangeliums." *KD* 12 (1966) 48–62.

Zeller, Dieter
  Die Passion nach Johannes. Sechs Wortgottesdienste für die Sonntage vor Ostern (Stuttgart: Katholisches Bibelwerk, 1969).

B.   John 18:1–27

Bartina, Sebastián
  "'Yo soy Yahweh.' Nota exegética a Io 18,4–8." *Estudios ecclesiásticos* 32 (1958) 403–26.

Bleek, Friedrich
  "Baur's Ansicht über den Grund der johanneischen Darstellung von dem Verhör Jesu vor dem Hannas." In his *Beiträge zur Einleitung und Auslegung der heiligen Schrift*. Vol. 1, *Beiträge zur Evangelien-Kritik* (Berlin: G. Reimer, 1846) 166.

Chevallier, Max-Alain
"La comparution de Jésus devant Hanne et devant Caïphe (Jean 18,12–14 et 19–24)." In *Neues Testament und Geschichte. Historisches Geschehen und Deutung im Neuen Testament. Oscar Cullmann zum 70. Geburtstag*, ed. H. Baltensweiler and B. Reicke (Zurich: Theologischer Verlag; Tübingen: Mohr-Siebeck, 1972) 179–85.

Church, W. Randolph
"The Dislocations in the Eighteenth Chapter of John." *JBL* 49 (1930) 375–83.

Corssen, Peter
"Die Abschiedsreden Jesu in dem vierten Evangelium." *ZNW* 8 (1907) 125–42.

Daube, David
"Three Notes having to do with Johanan ben Zaccai." *JTS*, n.s., 11 (1960) 53–62.

Doeve, Jan Willem
"Die Gefangennahme Jesu in Gethsemane." *SE* 1 = TU 73 (Berlin: Akademie-Verlag, 1959) 458–80.

Fortna, Robert Tomson
"Jesus and Peter at the High Priest's House: A Test Case for the Question of the Relation Between Mark's and John's Gospels." *NTS* 24 (1977/1978) 371–83.

Gibson, John Monro
"The Gethsemane of the Fourth Gospel." *ExpTim* 30 (1918/1919) 76–79.

Goguel, Maurice
"Did Peter deny his Lord? A Conjecture." *HTR* 25 (1932) 1–28.

Hingston, James H.
"John 18.5,6." *ExpTim* 32 (1920/1921) 232.

Klein, Günter
"Die Verleugnung des Petrus. Eine traditionsgeschichtliche Untersuchung." *ZTK* 58 (1961) 285–328.

Krieger, Norbert
"Der Knecht des Hohenpriesters." *NovT* 2 (1957) 73–74.

Laurentin, André
"We'attah—καὶ νῦν, Formule caractéristique des textes juridiques et liturgiques (à propos de Jean 17,5)." *Bib* 45 (1964) 168–97, 413–32.

Linnemann, Eta
"Die Verleugnung des Petrus." *ZTK* 63 (1966) 1–32.

Mahoney, Aidan
"A New Look at an Old Problem (John 18,12–14, 19–24)." *CBQ* 27 (1965) 137–44.

Masson, Charles
"Le reniement de Pierre. Quelques aspects de la formation d'une tradition." *RHPR* 37 (1957) 24–35.

Mein, P.
"A Note on John 18.6." *ExpTim* 65 (1953/1954) 286–87.

Neirynck, Frans
"The 'Other Disciple' in Jn 18,15–16." *ETL* 51 (1975) 113–41.

Richter, Georg
"Die Gefangennahme Jesu nach dem Johannesevangelium (18,1–12)." *BibLeb* 10 (1969) 26–39.

Sabbe, M.
"The Arrest of Jesus in Jn 18,1–11 and its Relation to the Synoptic Gospels. A Critical Evaluation of A. Dauer's Hypothesis." In *L'Evangile de Jean. Sources, rédaction, théologie*, ed. M. de Jonge. BETL 44 (Gembloux: Duculot; Louvain: University Press, 1977) 203–34.

Schille, Gottfried
"Das Leiden des Herrn. Die evanglische Passionstradition und ihr 'Sitz im Leben.'" *ZTK* 52 (1955) 161–205.

Schneider, Johannes
"Zur Komposition von Joh 18,12–27: Kaiphas und Hannas." *ZNW* 48 (1957) 111–19.

Valentin, Patrick
"Les comparutions de Jésus devant le Sanhédrin." *RSR* 59 (1971) 230–36.

Winter, Paul
On the Trial of Jesus, Studia Judaica, Forschungen zur Wissenschaft des Judentums 1 (Berlin: Walter de Gruyter, 1961).

Winter, Paul
"Marginal Notes on the Trial of Jesus, II." *ZNW* 50 (1959) 221–51.

18

1 When Jesus had spoken these words, he went forth with his disciples across the Kidron valley, where there was a garden, which he and his disciples entered. 2/ Now Judas, who betrayed him, also knew the place; for Jesus often met there with his disciples. 3/ So Judas, procuring a band of soldiers and some officers from the chief priests and the Pharisees, went there with lanterns and torches and weapons. 4/ Then Jesus, knowing all that was to befall him, came forward and said to them, "Whom do you

seek?" 5/ They answered him, "Jesus of Nazareth." Jesus said to them, "I am he." Judas, who betrayed him, was standing with them. 6/ When he said to them, "I am he," they drew back and fell to the ground. 7/ Again he asked them, "Whom do you seek?" And they said, "Jesus of Nazareth." 8/ Jesus answered, "I told you that I am he; so, if you seek me, let these men go." 9/ This was to fulfill the word which he had spoken, "Of those whom thou gavest me I lost not one." 10/ Then Simon Peter, having a sword, drew it and struck the high priest's slave and cut off his right ear. The slave's name was Malchus. 11/ Jesus said to Peter, "Put your sword into its sheath; shall I not drink the cup which the Father has given me?" 12/ So the band of soldiers and their captain and the officers of the Jews seized Jesus and bound him. 13/ First they led him to Annas; for he was the father-in-law of Caiaphas, who was high priest that year. 14/ It was Caiaphas who had given counsel to the Jews that it was expedient that one man should die for the people. 15/ Simon Peter followed Jesus, and so did another disciple. As this disciple was known to the high priest, he entered the court of the high priest along with Jesus, 16/ while Peter stood outside at the door. So the other disciple, who was known to the high priest, went out and spoke to the maid who kept the door, and brought Peter in. 17/ The maid who kept the door said to Peter, "Are not you also one of this man's disciples?" He said, "I am not." 18/ Now the servants and officers had made a charcoal fire, because it was cold, and they were standing and warming themselves; Peter also was with them, standing and warming himself. 19/ The high priest then questioned Jesus about his disciples and his teaching. 20/ Jesus answered him, "I have spoken openly to the world; I have always taught in synagogues and in the temple, where all Jews come together; I have said nothing secretly. 21/ Why do you ask me? Ask those who have heard me, what I said to them; they know what I said." 22/ When he had said this, one of the officers standing by struck Jesus with his hand, saying, "Is that how you answer the high priest?" 23/ Jesus answered him, "If I have spoken wrongly, bear witness to the wrong; but if I have spoken rightly, why do you strike me?" 24/ Annas then sent him bound to Caiaphas the high priest. 25/ Now Simon Peter was standing and warming himself. They said to him, "Are not you also one of his disciples?" He denied it and said, "I am not." 26/ One of the servants of the high priest, a kinsman of the man whose ear Peter had cut off, asked, "Did I not see you in the garden with him?" 27/ Peter again denied it; and at once the cock crowed.

Introduction

In accordance with the picture the narrator paints of the scene, in 14:31 Jesus gets up from the meal with his disciples, and either stands there or departs from there while he is speaking the words reproduced in chapters 15–17. Whether that strikes us as improbable is not important. The narrator had no other way of allowing Jesus to speak once more to his disciples or to address God in prayer prior to his arrest. He now turns to the passion narrative that came down to him in the tradition, a version that is not identical with Mark: the Gethsemane story is not narrated, although it is anticipated in 12:27f.

■ 1 It is tempting to join the words of verse 1 to 14:31 ("Rise, let us go hence"; cf. Mark 14:42, Matt 26:46). In order to make that possible, some scholars have rearranged the farewell discourses in such a way that 18:1ff. follows on 14:31. Bultmann, for example, places chapter 17 after 13:30, and has chapters 15, 16, and 14 follow after that.[1] Incomparably better than swirling the farewell discourses together in that way is the proposal of Corssen:[2] the supplementer, who knew the synoptic tradition, did not want to do without the words, "Rise, let us go hence" (ἐγείρεσθε, ἄγωμεν ἐντεῦθεν). He couldn't insert them after chapter 17 because 18:1–4 blocked the way. He therefore gave them an emergency location in 14:31. The Evangelist couldn't make use of these words because the scene in Gethsemane, which they introduce in the Markan tradition, contradicted his christology. His source had probably already forgotten that tradition or eliminated it. Jesus thus leaves the dining room where the last supper took place with his disciples and goes to a garden across the Kidron.[3] That means: not only is the name Gethsemane, which is also lacking in Luke, not used, but neither is the entire Gethsemane story. Only in 12:27 do we hear a weak echo (see the commentary on this verse).

■ 2 Verse 2 assumes: Judas surmises where Jesus will go after the meal; he had departed himself in 13:30. Wohlenberg's conjecture is pure fantasy: Judas and his "band" went first of all to Mark's house, where the meal had taken place, and there he learned that Jesus had already departed with his disciples; only then did he seek out "Gethsemane."[4] There is no support for this conjecture in the way the Gospel of John represents things. It is already reported in Luke 21:37 that Jesus withdrew each night to the Mount of Olives. John gives a correlative piece of information in this passage, which of course has reference to a garden: Jesus often gathered there with his disciples. This explains how Judas was acquainted with the place.

■ 3 This verse surprisingly makes Judas the subject of the following arrest scene. He "gets" a cohort—as though the Roman garrison in Jerusalem, together with its tribunes, were subordinate to a Jewish civilian—and some "officers" of the chief priests and the Pharisees. That these two groups entered into private service for a quasi-military operation is out of the question. The narrator had perhaps heard something about the temple police; they were of course subordinate only to the high priest and to the "captain,"[5] but not to the lay movement.[6] This Roman-Jewish company (it would have been around 800 men) was armed and provided with torches and lanterns, so that Jesus and his disciples could not hide in the darkness of the night (however, there was a full moon). Such a military column, bespeckled with lights, would have been visible from quite a distance and would have permitted those who sought to flee plenty of time. Dodd would like to reduce the cohort to a maniple (a subdivision of a cohort), and thus a battalion to a company, and he takes the "lights" to be a wise precau-

1   *John*, 490ff. [374ff.].
2   "Die Abschiedsreden Jesu in dem vierten Evangelium," *ZNW* 8 (1907) 125–42.
3   The garden is not mentioned in the Markan tradition; cf. Dodd, *Tradition*, 67.
4   *Der Evangelium nach Markus* (Leipzig: A. Deichert, 1910) 350f.
5   Acts 5:26: στρατηγός.
6   Cf. Foerster, *Neutestamentliche Zeitgeschichte* (Hamburg: Furche, 1968) 127ff.; Billerbeck 2: 494–519; 4,1: 334–52.

tion (one may be permitted to register a doubt about this wisdom).[7] But these precautions are without consequence, since Jesus, in John's view, did not consider fleeing.

Some investigators have conjectured that, since the entire Roman garrison in Jerusalem marched out to make this arrest, the high priests arranged the whole undertaking in advance with Pilate. He gave his consent to the "apprehension of the rebel." This conjecture led to the further question: did Jesus awaken political expectations that would make Pilate's interference more understandable? Did such expectations exist also in the intimate circle of disciples, without Jesus having decisively and clearly dispelled such expectations? We will go into this matter subsequently.[8]

■ 4 Jesus is omniscient. He knows what is now about to befall him; he knows that the "hour" announced long since has finally struck. With this knowledge he goes out (out of the garden?) to the column led by Judas and asks: "Whom do you seek?" Jesus of course knows very well whom they seek; if he asks nevertheless, two things are thereby achieved: first, the demonstration of his power described in verses 5f. thus becomes possible; and, second, the request of Jesus narrated in verse 8, that they let the disciples go, is prepared for. The question of Jesus is thus entirely comprehensible from a literary point of view.

■ 5 To the response given: Jesus the Nazorean (the reader will have understood that in the sense of Jesus of Nazareth), he speaks only two words: "I am he" ($\dot{\epsilon}\gamma\dot{\omega}$ $\epsilon\dot{\iota}\mu\iota$). That is not only the simple statement that he is the person they are seeking; it is simultaneously the revelatory formula of the divine man. This second feature is what produces the following effect.

The information that Judas was standing by contrasts with his description in verse 3: here he is no longer the leader, but merely the one who directed them to the place, who is no longer needed. No further mention is made of him.

■ 6 Verse 6 depicts the unexpected effect of the two words of Jesus: the huge enemy force draws back and falls to the ground. That shows how helpless they are against Jesus. It is self-evident that in this account there is

no room for the ignominious kiss of Judas (Matt 26:48–49). Where does John get the tradition that he reproduces here? Ultimately, no doubt, Christian scribalism once again took OT references from the suffering pious tradition and referred them to Jesus' passion. Two Psalms provided the material: first, Ps 27(26):2: "When evildoers assail me, . . . then my oppressors become weak and fall" (LXX: $\ddot{\epsilon}\pi\epsilon\sigma\alpha\nu$ [$\chi\alpha\mu\alpha\dot{\iota}$]; John: $\ddot{\epsilon}\pi\epsilon\sigma\alpha\nu$ $\chi\alpha\mu\alpha\dot{\iota}$); the second is Ps 35(34):4: "Those who plot evil against me shall fall back" (LXX: $\dot{\alpha}\pi\sigma\sigma\tau\rho\alpha\phi\dot{\eta}\tau\omega\sigma\alpha\nu$ $\epsilon\dot{\iota}s$ $\tau\dot{\alpha}$ $\dot{\sigma}\pi\dot{\iota}\sigma\omega$; John: $\dot{\alpha}\pi\dot{\eta}\lambda\theta\alpha\nu$ $\epsilon\dot{\iota}s$ $\tau\dot{\alpha}$ $\dot{\sigma}\pi\dot{\iota}\sigma\omega$). It becomes evident here why the participation of the Roman cohort in the tradition he made use of was so welcome to the narrator: the magnitude of the hostile powers was unheard of but they nevertheless had to bow to Jesus' word. The passion narrative again derives its color from the OT. It would be absurd to attempt to discover the documentary report of an eyewitness in this passage, or to inquire how the narrator arrived at this fantastic account. The testimony of scripture provides the originator of this tradition with an authority that by far exceeds any human source of information. The description of how everybody, even Judas and the cohort, were lying on the ground attests the faith of the community that told this story. They are not making up stories, but are convinced that they are truly reproducing the OT witness.

■ 7–9 But Jesus' enemies could not continue lying on the ground once their powerlessness had been demonstrated. The history of salvation must continue and Jesus has to be taken into custody. The narrator therefore has Jesus ask once again whom they seek. When they respond, "Jesus, the Nazorean," Jesus makes use of their statement in making an obvious request: if they seek only him, they can let the disciples go. The second theme that was mentioned earlier (in v 4) is thereby introduced: the disciples are allowed to go free. Unlike Mark 14:50, they do not flee, but leave unhindered. Jesus' saying in 17:12 is thus fulfilled: "Of those whom thou gavest me I lost not one."

■ 10f. These verses do not really go with verse 9. But the scene with Peter in 18:25 is prepared for in this way. In addition, Jesus' response to Peter explains his own behavior. In Mark 14:47, Matt 26:51, and Luke 22:49–

7   *Tradition*, 73f.
8   See on 18:33.

51, the aggressive follower of Jesus is nameless, as is the one struck; that does not owe, as one well-intentioned apologetic has conjectured, to the desire to protect Peter from prosecution by the authorities. Rather, the later the legend the more it is informed by the most exact detail. So it is here. Matthew and Luke have already expanded the account. According to Luke, Jesus restores his ear; according to Matthew, Jesus points to the fact that he could have God send him more than twelve legions of angels to help him—but how then are the predictions of the passion and God's will revealed in them to be fulfilled? In the Gospel of John it is Peter who attacks with his sword, and the slave of the high priest is called Malchus. It was this scene that inspired Thornton Wilder to create an unforgetable three-minute act.

Since a high priest who has lost an ear is unfit for service, and the slave stands for his master, Daube has conjectured that the injury done to Malchus was intended to make the high priest indirectly incapable of continuing his service.[9] That is cutting things a bit too fine, especially since Peter could not have known during the tumult in the dark with whom he was struggling. Luke (22:50) is the only one to relate that it was the right ear that was involved. The more precise designation, "right ear," follows the model, the "right hand" (which is more valuable than the left).[10] Matthew subsequently introduces the saying about the twelve legions and only in 26:54 does he mention that the scriptures must be fulfilled. John provides this tradition in a very different form in 18:11: Jesus must yet drink from the cup (of death) the Father has extended to him. Mark (14:48), Matthew (26:55), and Luke (22:52) have transmitted a saying of Jesus with unessential variations: Jesus deplores the fact that they have come out against him as against a robber, with swords and clubs (the temple police carried clubs). That is fortunately missing in the Gospel of John. Following the violent attack by one of the disciples, that would have been wholly out of place. Here one can see clearly how much trouble the surprising and apparently unexpected arrest of Jesus caused the early community. In view of the armed opposition of a follower, it may be conjectured that a figurative saying of Jesus was misinterpreted as an invitation to active opposition (cf. Lk 22:36). The first segment is thus brought to an end: the arrest of Jesus.

■ 12 Verse 12 begins a further subsection that extends, first, to verse 18, and is concluded in verses 25–27. The persons taking part in the arrest are once again enumerated: the cohort, the tribune, and the "officers of the Jews." The Jews take the place here of the high priests and Pharisees mentioned in verse 3, as though they were authorities resident in Jerusalem. The mention of the tribune has disturbed some scholars. For he really had to bring his prisoner to Pilate. B. Weiss was satisfied with this explanation: "The σπεῖρα [band of soldiers] and their captain are mentioned together because they both have to be present until he is delivered over. The arrest itself is performed by the officers alone."[11] Wellhausen ingeniously concludes: "The Roman cohort under a Roman captain, which undertook the arrest, could only be commanded by Pilate," in any case only in version A as conjectured by Wellhausen. Only in the later version B was Jesus taken immediately to the high priest Annas.[12] From the mention of the "robbers" (λῃσταί) and the Johannine report that Jesus was crucified along with two revolutionaries, Winter concludes that the Roman soldiers and the temple police cooperated in the arrest.[13] Pilate was informed in advance.[14] Winter invokes Goguel in this connection: ". . . the authors of the Gospels have corrected an ancient tradition in which the Romans alone intervened."[15] Since the Gospels passed the responsibility more and more to the Jews, the mention of the Roman soldiers in the Gospel of John (which thus runs counter to the general trend) could be taken to support Winter. But it seems to us that, beyond the historical problem, the literary question has not been given sufficient attention by him (see the Overview). That the tribune took the prisoner to the high priest

---

9   "Three Notes Having To Do With Johanan ben Zaccai," *JTS* 11 (1960) 59–61.

10   It would not be easy for a righthanded person to cut off the right ear of an opponent.

11   *Das Johannesevangelium*, 565.

12   *Das Evangelium Johannis*, 105 and 106.

13   *On the Trial of Jesus*, 48–50.

14   *On the Trial of Jesus*, 47.

15   "Juifs et Romains dans l'histoire de la Passion," *RHR* 62 (1910) 165–82, 295–322, esp. 181.

Annas suggests that, in the narrator's mind, the Jews and not Rome bear the responsibility for the death of Jesus on the cross, although the Jews could not condemn Jesus.

■ **13f.** These verses create a problem, however, by the way in which they account for the appearance before Annas: he was the father-in-law of Caiaphas, who held the office of high priest that year. The narrator appears to assume that the office of high priest was held only for a year at a time. In 11:49 he also expressly says that Caiaphas was the high priest that year. Verse 14 is a reference to that passage, according to which Caiaphas avers that it is better that one man should die for the people than that the whole nation should perish (11:49f.). This is also the meaning of the abbreviated version in 18:14.

■ **15** This verse produces a great surprise. Mark 14:54 reports that Peter followed the Lord and the troops who had taken Jesus prisoner from afar and had entered the court of the high priest, sat down with the servants, and warmed himself at the fire. Matt 26:58 leaves the fire out: Peter sits with the guards to watch the end. Mark and Matthew interrupt the scene with Peter at this point.

Luke, on the other hand, carries the story to its conclusion without interruption (22:54ff.). The maid who shows up in 22:56 is also new with him; she gets a good look at Peter in the light of the fire and then says to his face: "You were also with him." We are not told how a maid of the high priest could have such intimate knowledge of Peter. Perhaps she was introduced so that it was not always one of the servants who casts suspicion on Peter. In any case, it might be a "novelistic" feature when the third "accuser" concludes from the fact that Peter speaks like a Galilean that he also belongs to Jesus' circle. It is likewise unrealistic that Peter sits there quietly during this interval, without one of the servants becoming suspicious, just as it is unrealistic that Jesus (Where is he actually? In the courtyard?) should turn and give Peter a significant glance, following the third denial, just as the cock crows. Edwards conjectures that the "cock-crow" was not actually the crowing of a rooster (who can be heard crowing all through the night), but the Roman signal trumpet, the *buccina*.[16] Exegetes often go peculiar ways. This was necessary, we are told, so that a realistic

story, told by eyewitnesses, emerges from a miracle tale. The mocking of Jesus that follows in Luke does not have a firm location in the synoptic tradition. In Mark 14:65 and Matt 26:67f., it follows the condemnation by the Sanhedrin. The christological interpretation of Isa 50:6 has probably provided the material for this feature. The scene in John 18:22f. is derived from that material (see below).

The introduction of that "other disciple" creates considerable difficulties. It must first of all be explained how it was possible for him to go with Jesus unhindered into the court of the high priest. There is no mention of a guard at the gate in the Synoptics. The Gospel of John alone knows of that guard. The guard presents no problem for the "other disciple," since he was "known to the high priest." Interpreters endeavored from an early time to tone these assertions down. The paraphrase of the Fourth Gospel in hexameters—it was ascribed to Nonnos of Panopolis (in upper Egypt), who was alive around 400 CE and who wrote *Dionysiaca;* he must have been a Christian of course—interprets the expression, "the other disciple," as someone who was known as a purveyor of fish from the Sea of Gennesaret to the servants of the high priest. But the expression "known to the high priest" ($\gamma\nu\omega\sigma\tau\grave{o}\varsigma$ $\tau\hat{\omega}$ $\mathring{\alpha}\rho\chi\iota\epsilon\rho\epsilon\hat{\iota}$, as it is found in 18:15) implies still more. Perhaps the characterization of the "other disciple" as the "beloved disciple" (as found in 20:2) is omitted here because this designation comports poorly with the position of someone known to the high priest. Since Peter did not enjoy such privilege, he has to remain outside. That causes the superiority of the "other disciple" over Peter to come fully into view.

■ **16** Only through the "other disciple" was it possible at all for Peter to get into the courtyard. For the other disciple (who is actually identical with the beloved disciple) comes back, speaks with the maid who is guarding the door, and himself leads Peter into the courtyard. He then disappears from the story. He has only taken from Peter the honor of being the only one to follow Jesus into the courtyard of the high priest; besides, he was not accused by anyone and so tempted to betray Jesus. His recommendation did not help Peter. The maid, with whom he spoke on Peter's behalf, brought

---

16   Used to signal changes in the watch. Edwards, *John,* 139.

Peter under suspicion, in spite of his recommendation. Not only does the fact that this episode of the "other disciple" is unknown to the Synoptics speak against it, but so does its continuation.

■ **17** If the "other disciple," who is known to the high priest, has spoken with the maid who guards the gate and has led Peter into the courtyard, it is incomprehensible that she now says to Peter who has been so well certified: "Are not you also one of this man's disciples?" The attempt has been made to explain this "also," in part, by saying that the maid knew that the "other disciple" belonged to Jesus' disciples. In that case, his recommendation of Peter wouldn't be worth a plugged nickel. However, the moment one strikes the words in verse 15 that follow "Simon Peter," together with the whole of verse 16, everything falls into place. The "maid" ($\pi\alpha\iota$-$\delta\acute{\iota}\sigma\kappa\eta$), who already appears in the Lukan tradition, belongs, of course, to this later insertion also.[17] As soon as the maid is no longer called "the doorkeeper," she is the first one to bring Peter under suspicion, as in the Lukan tradition, and to induce him to make his denial. The introduction of the "other disciple" is thus easily understood: it belongs among those passages in which Peter is excelled by another disciple, namely, the one Jesus loved.

■ **18** Thanks to Peter's denial, this incident, the question of the maid, has no further consequences. Peter can now join the slaves and "officers," who have just taken Jesus into custody and who have now made a charcoal fire in the cold night, in order to keep warm. With this, the first part of the denial story comes to an end. The action is now given a new setting in the interior of the palace. For, no one expected the high priest to hold Jesus' hearing in the courtyard in the cold.

■ **19** The high priest now interrogates the prisoner. It would be ill-considered to reproach the narrator for not having reported how Jesus was taken to the high priest. The criticism that Wellhausen and Schwartz have practiced on the Gospel of John is frequently based on such pedantic objections. They overlook the fact that there is a way of narrating that does not concern itself with details of this sort (Luke often proceeds in that way in Acts), which rather leaves it to the reader to recognize

a new scene as such and to imagine the details. We do not learn who was present at the interrogation of Jesus, apart from the officer mentioned in verse 22. Some exegetes assume that the council was present. But did they march along with him when he was sent to Caiaphas (in v 24)? One ought not always to presuppose the sketch of events that the Synoptics have in mind. The Sanhedrin is mentioned in the Gospel of John only in 11:47, and there the expression could even mean "meeting of the council." In the Johannine account, matters never come to a decree of the Sanhedrin. The narrator probably had an entirely different scene in mind: a room in the gloomy palace, perhaps illuminated by a fireplace and a few torches. The old high priest is sitting on a chair. The prisoner stands before him. One or the other of the officers is present; but only those are mentioned whose words and deeds are reported. Witnesses of his blasphemy are not called, and the high priest does not attempt to worm a confession out of Jesus respecting his messiahship. He is concerned primarily with information: disciples? Teaching? One is perhaps reminded of the famous scene in Dostoyevsky's novel, *The Brothers Karamazov,* where Jesus, who has returned, stands before the Grand Inquisitor. In both instances, the princes of the church are the enemy of true faith and regard Jesus as a heretic. And Ivan Karamazov in Dostoyevsky depicts the Grand Inquisitor as an apostate and as one who secretly regards Jesus as a failure, even though he does not reveal it: he and his church "have corrected Thy work and have founded it on miracle, mystery and authority."[18] The church is not with Jesus, but with the evil one, who tempted Jesus: the church has freed man from the burden of his or her own decisions and has taken the sword of Caesar. Nor will the high priest give up his power, even though there is little left to him. Moreover, he wants to know nothing of that freedom that only Jesus can give. But he has nothing further to say, and sends Jesus to another high priest, and that one again to another one, who really possesses earthly power (although not unlimited), to Pilate. Dostoyevsky's Grand Inquisitor is much more modern: what he reproaches Jesus for is that he cannot or will not give earthly bread to the poor, but feeds the poor only with bread from

---

17 The addition of "doorkeeper," $\theta\nu\rho\omega\rho\acute{o}\varsigma$, looks strange alongside "the maid," $\dot{\eta}\ \pi\alpha\iota\delta\acute{\iota}\sigma\kappa\eta$.

18 *The Brothers Karamazov,* tr. Constance Garnett (New York: The Modern Library, 1950) 305.

heaven, and thus does not solve the social question. But in "correcting" Jesus without disclosing it, the Grand Inquisitor betrays a bad conscience. The high priest in the Gospel of John does not recognize that he must bring peace to his own disturbed conscience. He regards Jesus as a rebel who aspires to the power, which he himself will not give up, although he must borrow it from Pilate in an emergency. Annas and even Caiaphas are uncomplicated men; only in 11:50 does it not appear so, when Caiaphas is aware of Jesus' innocence. But there he does not speak on his own behalf, but out of prophetic insight, which is given to the high priest at this moment (like a gift that goes with the office). The problem with which Dostoyevsky's Grand Inquisitor struggles is foreign to the Jewish high priest of the Gospel of John.

■ **20f.** But Jesus does not hand over the information requested. He points to the fact that he has spoken openly to the world, that he has always taught in the synagogue and temple, where all Jews gather together. He has not transmitted secret teaching (does this refer to the secret teaching of gnostics?). Both questions are thus answered: one can learn of his teaching from any of his auditors. It is of course assumed that they agree with his teaching, the teaching presented in the Gospel of John; it therefore need not be made explicit at this point.

■ **22f.** Cf. the scene in Acts 23:2ff.: in Acts Paul uses a lame excuse, which grieves his interpreters. Jesus, on the other hand, remains bold and undaunted, having been reprimanded and struck by one of the officers. If I have spoken wrongly, he replies, bear witness to the wrong; if not, why do you strike me?

■ **24** The high priest does not participate in this conversation; the scene remains open, and the secret victor is Jesus. That he is sent bound to Caiaphas is a clandestine admission of weakness on the part of his opponent. Apparently the narrator knew nothing of a trial of Jesus before a Jewish court (the Jerusalem Sanhedrin). For the Synoptics, on the other hand, the verdict is made by this court: he is guilty of blasphemy and therefore worthy of death.

■ **25–27** These verses bring the story of the denial of Jesus by Peter to a close. As he is warming himself at the fire, Peter is asked whether he does not also belong to Jesus' disciples. When Peter had denied it, a third accusation follows immediately: someone related to Malchus thinks he saw him in the garden. Since "Malchus" is a legendary figure, one sees how the legend here sends out fresh tentacles. Peter repeats his denial and immediately the cock crows. The whole is narrated laconically and unsentimentally. One seeks for a sentence like, "and he wept bitterly," here in vain. There is little room for emotion in the Fourth Gospel.

Overview

Martin Dibelius has asserted: "The Passion story is narrated by all four evangelists with a striking agreement never attained elsewhere. Even John, who deals freely enough with the facts reported by tradition, binds himself to this tradition in the highest degree when describing the Passion."[19] This assertion requires correction at two points. First, it is not the case that the fourth Evangelist binds himself in the highest degree to the tradition employed by the Synoptics. His version deviates from that of the Synoptics to a surprising degree, even in the present pericope and in the next one. True, two hearings before the high priest are still indicated, but the Sanhedrin is not involved at all. Moreover, the Evangelist makes no effort to provide the content of these hearings. What is said in the hearing before Annas provides no new content. But the version in the Fourth Gospel does involve something that is of the highest importance: with the elimination of the Sanhedrin, the decision is taken out of the hands of the Jews. In all versions of the Synoptics, Jesus is sentenced prior to his appearance before Pilate. Not so here. The fact that, in the synoptic accounts, Jesus admits to the Jews that he is the messiah is also connected with this difference. However, in the Fourth Gospel, by contrast, these hearings and even the admission of messiahship are permitted to sink into oblivion. On the other hand, the narrator is eloquent when he comes to the scene of "Jesus before Pilate." Here and only here does it become clear to the reader which verdict is involved.

We have thereby touched on the second question we have to ask Dibelius: to what extent are the deviations of the fourth Evangelist the free creations of the narrator?

19 *From Tradition to Gospel,* tr. Bertram Lee Woolf (New York: Charles Scribner's Sons, n.d.) 179.

There are examples that demonstrate that the fourth Evangelist freely follows to its end a course that others before him have only set out upon.

Whether John knew the Lukan tradition, in which Jesus restores the ear of Malchus, we do not know. In any case, he did not intend to relate a miracle that is basically humane. The thing that is alone important is that Jesus bows to the will of the Father and drinks the cup that the Father gives him. The denial of Peter is related, to be sure, but without having Jesus turn and look at Peter. Jesus is already separated from his disciples, and there is no beloved disciple at his side in the hour of the great decision. But that is also not necessary. That he stands in intimate union with the Father is demonstrated when his opponents fall to the ground before him prior to the arrest. They lie there a moment before him, entirely still, as though the film on which events are recorded stops on a particular frame. The reader has time to allow this picture to sink in, and he will not forget it during the arrest and the shadowy hearings that are to follow. This miracle story is of course later material, presumably taken over by the Evangelist.

How shall we assess the disappearance of the synoptic tradition regarding the meeting of the Sanhedrin? Was Winter correct when he aspired to find bedrock here? Perhaps matters are quite different than this explanation, so plausible at first, makes them out to be. In Luke the emphasis shifts from the Jewish legal processes to the behavior of the Roman governor. In Luke 23:4, Pilate first rules that Jesus is innocent. That occurs a second time in Luke 23:14f. (where a similar ruling on the part of Herod is indicated). In Luke 23:22, finally, Pilate proposes to release Jesus as guiltless (although after scourging).

The other synoptic writers (Matthew and Mark) have first of all endeavored to emphasize the responsibility of the Jews for the crucifixion of Jesus. But then it became more important for a strengthened Christian movement to have a benevolent disposition on the part of Rome.

At that point, Jewish responsibility was not contested; on the contrary, only because the Jews had pressed unrelentingly were the benevolent Romans unable, in the end, to do anything other than permit Jesus to be crucified. What we have, therefore, in Luke and John is not the oldest form of the tradition, but the most recent.

It has proved to be much more difficult in recent generations to decide what historical and theological significance the denial of Peter possesses. Earlier it was taken to be self-evident that Peter had related the triple denial as an eyewitness. Critical scholarship began to doubt this view more and more in the twentieth century. In 1903 Loisy wrote: "The narrative contains what is necessary to show the fulfillment of prophecy [John 13:38]. It is less a matter of 'Peter's' error as such, than of the providential fact that takes place through him."[20] But the whole account stems from a redactor. Bultmann hands down the verdict in brief: "The story of Peter is itself legendary and literary."[21] Goguel prefers to let stand a small historical remnant: Jesus reprimanded Peter for his pretension and foresaw the possibility of defection.[22] With that in mind, this defection was reported as *vaticinium ex eventu* ("prediction after the event"), "because what Jesus had predicted must come to pass." In 1933, Dibelius expressed the view that the denial of Peter was "felt in some way to be the presupposition of the Easter appearances."[23]

We now skip a few decades. The attempts at explanation become ever bolder and more surprising. Schille deduces from the *Epistula Apostolorum* that the tradition of the last night of Jesus got its form from the observance of an early Easter celebration—at the grave of Jesus?—which was interrupted in the morning by the cock-crow.[24] How simple, by comparison, is Winter's explanation that we have before us a post-Easter summons to confession in the face of persecution: confess like Jesus; do not deny like Peter.[25] Grundmann once again sticks very close to the conservative explanation: since Peter's hope in Jesus has collapsed and he no longer

20 *Le quatrième évangile,* 819–49.

21 *History of the Synoptic Tradition,* 269.

22 "Did Peter Deny His Lord? A Conjecture," *HTR* 25 (1932) 27.

23 *From Tradition to Gospel,* tr. Bertram Lee Woolf (New York: Charles Scribner's Sons, n.d.) 215.

24 "Das Leiden des Herrn. Die evangelische Passions- tradition und ihr 'Sitz im Leben.'" *ZTK* 52 (1955)

161–205.

25 "Marginal Notes on the Trial of Jesus, II," *ZNW* 50 (1959) 221–51.

believes in him, Peter renounces him.[26] Yet it is questionable whether the text intends to express Peter's real conviction through his denial.

Klein sets out on an entirely new course in 1961.[27] Peter was a member, successively, of the circle of the twelve, the apostolic group, the "stylites," and finally went his own way. This triple change in position (and change in theological fronts?) shows a tactical nimbleness to conform flexibly to each alteration in the constellation of power, and this awakened "fierce resentment" in opposing circles and was then projected back into the time before Easter as a triple denial of Jesus.[28]

Now this picture of the career of Peter Klein reconstructed first of all from Acts and the letters of Paul; he did not thereby elicit general agreement by any means. We are unable to perceive anything of a "fierce resentment" on the part of the community against hypothetical changes in theological (?) fronts. Finally, the alleged projection of Peter's post-Easter career back into the holy week—and Klein cannot make do without that— does nothing to strengthen our confidence in this "study in psychological interpretation." Linnemann has therefore proposed another denial tradition, after a general discussion of specific points:[29] "In faith the disciples discovered that their behavior during the passion was the denial of faith" and they "expressed it as taking umbrage at Jesus."[30] Linnemann explains that a tradition of Peter's denial could then arise, although the denial of Peter was not a historical fact,[31] because the offense the disciples took is not distinguished qualitatively from Peter's denial, but has the same relationship to it as the general to the specific. That this concretion is attached to the person of Peter results from "the literary reflection of his position of eminence in the community."[32] The tripling of the denial is a stylistic feature; it expresses "the totality and inescapability of this event."[33]

Jesus predicted[34] the denial of Peter in all four canonical gospels.[35] The basic presuppositions of exegetes play an especially large role in how they make use of these two pericopes. Whoever holds the view, as Grundmann does, that the second gospel is the work of John Mark will be inclined to find an echo of Peter's own story in the account of Peter. Whoever believes in Schweitzer's theory of "consistent eschatology" will be given to the view that there are two layers: (l) Jesus' arrest was the beginning, for the disciples, of the messianic tribulations. Jesus was certain that these tribulations would affect only him. The flight of the disciples—which brought the tribulations in relation to them all—is not then a contradiction. (2) The later community no longer held that expectation. For it, Jesus' arrest and the flight of the disciples were only a stumbling block alleviated by prophecy.

Modern critical scholarship is faced with this question: shall we take as our point of departure the text as a representation that reproduces the facts exactly, or must we take the story of the denial as an independent unity, or may we combine it with information from other NT writings, as Klein does? This literary question precedes the historical question. We will begin with the prediction of the denial, but we will not derive from that material a judgment regarding the origin of the denial story. It is necessary in this process to keep all four gospels in view, as well as the Pauline letters.

According to Mark 14:27, Jesus tells the disciples beforehand that they will all take offense at him, and he bases this prediction on a quotation from Zech 13:7. The scattering of the sheep of which Zech 13:7 speaks is interpreted to refer to the flight of the disciples, and this again is understood as a falling away of the disciples, as the loss of faith. It seems to us that the post-Easter community is speaking here; this community interprets not its own real or imagined experience out of OT texts, but also attributes these interpretations to Jesus. The scattering of the sheep can only refer to the group of disciples as a whole, and not to a particular disciple.

It is a different matter in 14:29. A particular story apparently begins here, in which Peter himself is sepa-

26   *Das Evangelium nach Markus,* THKNT 2 (Berlin: Evangelische Verlagsanstalt, 1959, [7]1977) 418.

27   "Die Verleugnung des Petrus," 285–328.

28   "Die Verleugnung des Petrus," 324.

29   "Die Verleugnung des Petrus," 1–32.

30   "Die Verleugnung des Petrus," 32.

31   "Die Verleugnung des Petrus," 21.

32   "Die Verleugnung des Petrus," 22.

33   "Die Verleugnung des Petrus," 21.

34   Mark 14:26–31, Matt 26:30–35, Luke 22:31–34, John 13:36–38.

35   Mark 14:54, 66–72, Matt 26:58, 69–75, Luke 22:54b–62, John 18:15, 25–27.

rated from the other disciples: if the other disciples also fall, he will certainly not. At this point, Jesus tells him that before the cock crows, he will deny him three times. Peter contests that; he would rather die than deny him. Yet the special position of Peter is immediately withdrawn by the concluding words: "And they all said the same." A contradiction thus comes to light: if all the disciples behave like Peter, then it does not square for Jesus to predict that Peter alone will deny him thrice. Granted that Jesus derived his own future from his interpretation of an OT passage; granted further that Peter contested that this interpretation applied to his own behavior; it is then said to the one who denied this interpretation of the OT prophecy that it will be fulfilled precisely in him in the immediate future. It then remains dubious whether we can attribute to Jesus such an interpretation of an OT passage with reference to his own destiny, namely, that he would be abandoned by everyone. It could also be the case that the community understood its own failure in the hour when Jesus was taken into custody as something prophesied by the prophet Zechariah. In that case, the community's failure was the fulfillment of a prophecy, the divine pre-determination of its destiny, which no one can escape. But this was made concrete in the destiny of a particular person (from whom one ought at least to expect such behavior): Peter of all people became the victim of temptation—no fewer than three times. That it is Peter who is chosen as the model of this kind of behavior is suggested by the fact that only he was asked whether he belonged to Jesus or not; the other disciples who also fled were not. It ought not thereby to be asserted that it was in this way and no other that the story of Peter took its rise. It is rather only to be made clear how such a tradition could have taken shape, alongside other possibilities. Some earlier interpreters have assumed that Jesus behaved like a Christian biblical scholar: he saw his destiny foretold in the OT, and an artist could sketch a picture of that picture in which Jesus is reading and reflecting on a book lying on his lap. But did Jesus really relate himself to the OT in that way?

In Luke 22:31f. another tradition appears:[36] Jesus reveals to Simon that Satan has asked for the disciples that he might sift them, like a farmer sifts the chaff from the wheat. But Jesus prayed for Peter that his faith may not fail. That seems to imply in the first instance that Peter will be the only one on whom the satanic temptation will not be able to get a hold. But Jesus' remark goes further: when Peter has turned again, he is to strengthen his brethren. In response to this, Peter only confirms his willingness to face death, and to this assertion on the part of Peter, Jesus replies with the prediction that Peter will deny his Lord three times before the cock crows. It is questionable whether the word ἐπιστρέψας ("turn again") can be understood to mean that the contradiction between denial and faith disappears: first denial, and then faith as at first. When Peter explains, in response to the questions and accusations of the maid and the slaves, that he does not belong to Jesus, that does not necessarily express the innermost conviction of Peter, but is a white lie in an emergency, by means of which he attempts to get out of the spot he is in, in order to learn how things are going to go with Jesus. Formally, it is of course a denial, but he does not run out of the courtyard, but seeks to make it possible to stay longer. The "intense seriousness" with which Klein finds the confession to be completely mistaken with respect to Jesus has no place in the Lukan account.

The Johannine parallel in 13:36–38 is problematic insofar as it does not connect up with verse 34, but with verse 33 (see the commentary on these verses). The context of verses 36 and 37 is clarified when ones accepts the view that Peter has comprehended that Jesus is to be martyred. Only he does not appreciate why he himself is not now also able to suffer martyrdom. Yet he thinks that he is prepared to give his life for Jesus. Jesus answers— not ironically, but with the limitless superiority of the Son of God, who knows about the denial that is to come: Peter will deny him three times before the cock crows. This version is stylistically the most balanced of all. That goes together with the fact that in the Fourth Gospel there is no flight of the disciples and thus no prediction and interpretation of this flight either. Jesus procures their free departure (18:8). The quotation from Zechariah, consequently, does not apply.

When one surveys the four canonical reports

---

36   Scholars have frequently debated this passage
      without coming to a concensus.

(Matthew differs from Mark only in non-essentials), the result is: two traditions have come together, which have had different origins and which do not fit together without gaps. The first is derived from Zechariah 13:7 to the effect that all the disciples will take offense at Jesus, that is, they will not only be separated from him physically. The second concerns only Peter: of him a triple denial is predicted. The denial is therefore simultaneously prepared for and blunted by the prediction. The two pieces of tradition are combined in Mark/Matthew when Peter protests the prophecy which concerns all the disciples. As a result, he comes to know what will befall him and him alone.

The story of the denial itself is temporally and spatially connected with the account of Jesus' hearing. This gives rise to a difficulty: Mark and Matthew have Peter follow Jesus, who has been taken into custody, from afar and enter the courtyard of the high priest (whose situation we cannot determine precisely; the narrator has given us no hints that Annas and Caiaphas are in the same building, but question Jesus in different rooms). At this point, they interrupt the story of Peter and introduce the portentous scene where Jesus is given a hearing. After Jesus is condemned and beaten, the story of Peter is resumed. Only in Luke is the story of Peter told without interruption. John interrupts the story of Peter, which is enlarged by the introduction of the "other disciple," with the hearing before Annas. In the design of the scene, he thereby continues on the course taken by Mark and Matthew.

John, on the other hand, is distinguished from the three Synoptics in that, in his account, the first temptation to deny Jesus takes place as soon as Peter enters the courtyard of the high priest; the instrument is the maid, who functions as gatekeeper. In the Synoptics, Peter has no difficulty getting into the courtyard. The preparation for the Johannine modification is the maid that appears in Luke 22:56 (although she is not a gatekeeper); Mark and Matthew do not mention her. In Luke she interacts with Peter by the fire, where he is warming himself with the officers. That the maid is given the night watch at the gate is made necessary in John by the addition of the scene with the "other disciple." Since the "other disciple" goes into the courtyard with Jesus unhindered, while Peter has to remain outside, he evidences a superiority already with respect to Peter. This superiority is sustained when the "other disciple" returns, speaks with the gatekeeper, and then conducts Peter into the courtyard. But it is precisely at this point that the welding together of these two traditions does not succeed: if the "other disciple" has already conducted Peter into the courtyard—that is the case, according to verse 16—the female gatekeeper cannot interrogate Peter as she does in verse 17. Edwards endeavors to represent the question of the gatekeeper as harmlessly as possible: "You are not really one of this man's followers, are you?" To this Peter responds with an equally harmless, "On, no," which assures his access to the courtyard.[37] Edwards treats the further questions and answers in a similar way. The grave aspects of this denial are in danger of disappearing, on this reading; but those aspects are explicit in verses 25 and 26.

Klein has shown that the denial story is unbelievable, when viewed realistically,[38] and Linnemann rightly agrees with him.[39] For, were Peter the first to come under suspicion as a member of Jesus' group, he would not then have gotten away with a simple verbal denial. "Only an unrestrained psychological fantasy is able to find it plausible" that he can still leave the courtyard unhindered after the three incriminating questions.[40] The tripling of the denial is a literary device. Does it lead back to a simpler version lying behind the present account? Neither Klein nor Linnemann has detected such a possibility. It is therefore a question whether this literary depiction does not first arise in order to represent concretely the traditon of the offense or defection of the disciples (which appears to be affirmed by Zech 13:7). Combining "deny" with the "falling away, taking offense" of the quotation permits the matter to be illustrated in this way. To the "denial" there belongs of course a trial-like situation, in which it is determined whether the one being interrogated avows that he is loyal to Jesus or denies that he belongs in his group. This situation is created by the scene in the courtyard.

The reader of the gospels is repeatedly told that God determined the entire passion event from the outset and

37   Edwards, *John,* 138.
38   Klein, "Die Verleugnung des Petrus," 307f.
39   "Die Verleugnung des Petrus," 7.
40   Klein, "Die Verleugnung des Petrus," 307.

that Jesus knew about it ahead of time and predicted it. That reflects the bewilderment of the young community in reaction to the fact of the surprising arrest and execution of Jesus and the return of the disciples to Galilee. It is precisely this steady flow of prophecy that indirectly attests the extent to which the catastrophe took them by surprise. Of course, once must also consider: the disciples first came to their belief in Jesus as the messiah after Easter. That puts their failure in another light. The gospels therefore represent a later view of things on this point. It was more difficult for them to account for the actions of the disciples. The quotation from Zechariah must be reinterpreted to a great extent—for our sensibilities. In so doing, the guilt of the disciples appears to be greater and more incomprehensible.

Linnemann writes: "In faith the disciples experienced their conduct during the passion as the denial of faith."[41] What is right about that assertion comes out only when one says, to be more precise, "post-Easter faith" rather than "faith." This makes it clear why the judgment regarding the conduct of the disciples becomes more pointed here. That the later gospels correct the earlier ones in a variety of ways permits us to see that we do not have a documentary report before us and that we cannot gain one by weaving the various gospels together for apologetic purposes. The gospels are not concerned here either with exact history, but with the interpretation of the events of the passion in the language of their time. That man—even the man of faith—is not himself secure is of course true.[42] But if Linnemann then goes on to say: "The shocking experience of the self not being secure in itself longs to come to expression,"[43] there is buried in this formulation—thanks to our theological language à la mode—a further fragment of unnecessary psychology. The event of Good Friday was the real tragedy, the real shocking experience, with which one had and has to come to terms.

---

41 Linnemann, "Die Verleugnung des Petrus," 32.
42 Linnemann, "Die Verleugnung des Petrus," 32.
43 Linnemann, "Die Verleugnung des Petrus," 44.

41. Jesus Before Pilate

Bibliography

Allen, J. E.
"Why Pilate?" In *The Trial of Jesus. Cambridge Studies in honour of C. F. D. Moule*, ed. E. Bammel. SBT 13 (Naperville, IL: Allenson, 1970) 78–83.

Bajsíc, Alois
"Pilatus, Jesus und Barabbas." *Bib* 48 (1967) 7–28.

Bammel, Ernst
"Φίλος τοῦ καίσαρος (Joh 19,12)." *TLZ* 77 (1952) 205–10.

Blank, Josef
"Die Verhandlung vor Pilatus: Joh 18,28–19,16 im Lichte der johanneischen Theologie." *BZ* 3 (1959) 60–81.

Boismard, Marie-Emile
"La royauté universelle du Christ: Jn 18,33–37." *AsSeign* 65 (1973) 36–46.

Bonsirven, Joseph
"Hora Talmudica. La notation chronologique de Jean 19,14 aurait-elle un sens symbolique?" *Bib* 33 (1952) 511–15.

Campenhausen, Hans F. von
"Zum Verständnis von Joh 19,11." In his *Aus der Frühzeit des Christentums. Studien zur Kirchengeschichte des ersten und zweiten Jahrhunderts* (Tübingen: Mohr-Siebeck, 1963) 125–34.

Corssen, Peter
"Ἐκάθισεν ἐπὶ Βήματος." *ZNW* 15 (1914) 338–40.

Escande, J.
"Jésus devant Pilate: Jean 18,28–19,16." *Foi et vie* 73 (1974) 66–82.

Haenchen, Ernst
"Jesus vor Pilatus (Joh 18,28–19,15). Zur Methode der Auslegung." In his *Gott und Mensch. Gesammelte Aufsätze* 1 (Tübingen: Mohr-Siebeck, 1965) 144–56.

Hahn, Ferdinand
"Der Prozess Jesu nach dem Johannesevangelium. Eine redaktionsgeschichtliche Untersuchung." EKKNT Vorarbeiten 2 (Neukirchen-Vluyn: Neukirchener-Verlag; Cologne: Benziger, 1970) 23–96.

Hart, H. St. J.
"The Crown of Thorns in John 19,2–5." *JTS*, n.s., 3 (1952) 66–75.

Herranz Marco, Mariano
"Un problema de crítica histórica en el relato de la Pasión: la liberación de Barrabás." *EstBib* 30 (1971) 137–60.

Jaubert, Annie
"La comparution devant Pilate selon Jean. Jean 18,28–19,16." *Foi et vie* 73 (1974) 3–12.

Juechen, Aurel von
Jesus und Pilatus. Eine Untersuchung über das Verhältnis von Gottesreich und Weltreich im Anschluss

an Johannes 18, v. 28–19, v. 16, Theologische Existenz Heute 76 (Munich: Evangelischer Verlag A. Lempp, 1941; reprint Munich: Chr. Kaiser Verlag, 1980).

Kurfess, A.
"'Εκάθισεν ἐπὶ Βήματος (Joh 19,13)." *Bib* 34 (1953) 271.

Merkel, Johannes
"Die Begnadigung am Passahfeste." *ZNW* 6 (1905) 293–316.

Merlier, Octave
"Σὺ λέγεις ὅτι Βασιλεύς εἰμι." *Revue des études grecques* 46 (1933) 204–9.

Mollat, Donatien
"Jésus devant Pilate (Jean 18,28–38)." *BVC* 39 (1961) 23–31.

Mulder, H.
"John 18,28 and the Date of the Cruxification." In *Miscellanea Neotestamentica* 2, ed. T. Baarda, A. F. J. Klijn, and W. C. van Unnik. NovTSup 48 (Leiden: E. J. Brill, 1978) 87–107.

O'Rourke, John J.
"Two Notes on St. John's Gospel." *CBQ* 25 (1963) 124–28.

Potterie, Ignace de la
"Jésus roi et juge d'après Jn 19,13: ἐκάθισεν ἐπὶ Βήματος." *Bib* 41 (1960) 217–47.

Pujol, L.
"'In loco qui dicitur *Lithostrotos.*'" *VD* 15 (1935) 180–86, 204–7, 233–37.

Reich, H.
"Der König mit der Dornenkrone." *Neue Jahrbücher für das klassische Altertum, Geschichte und deutsche Literatur* 13 (1904) 705–33.

Spengler, Oswald
The Decline of the West, 2 vols. Tr. Charles Francis Atkinson (New York: A. A. Knopf, 1926–1928).

Schlier, Heinrich
"Jesus und Pilatus nach dem Johannesevangelium." In his *Die Zeit der Kirche. Exegetische Aufsätze und Vorträge* (Freiburg: Herder, 1956, ⁵1972) 56–74.

Schnackenburg, Rudolf
"Die Ecce-homo-Szene und der Menschensohn." In *Jesus und der Menschensohn. Für Anton Vögtle,* ed. R. Pesch and R. Schnackenburg (Freiburg: Herder,

1975) 371–86.

Schreiber, Johannes
"Das Schweigen Jesu." In *Theologie und Unterricht. Über die Repräsentanz des Christlichen in der Schule* [Festschrift H. Stock], ed. H. Wegenast (Gütersloh: Gerd Mohn, 1969) 79–87.

Schwank, Benedikt
"Was ist Wahrheit?" *Erbe und Auftrag* 47 (1971) 487–96.

Tabachovitz, David
"Ein paar Beobachtungen zum spätgriechischen Sprachgebrauch." *ErJb* 44 (1946) 296–305.

Taylor, Vincent
The Gospel According to St. Mark (London: Macmillan, ²1966).

Twomey, J. J.
"Barabbas was a Robber." *Scr* 8 (1956) 115–19.

Vincent, L.-H.
"Le Lithostrotos évangélique." *RB* 59 (1952) 513–30.

Wead, David W.
"We have a Law." *NovT* 11 (1969) 185–89.

Vollmer, Hans
Jesus und das Sacaeenopfer. Religionsgeschichtliche Streiflichter (Giessen: A. Töpelmann, 1905).

Vollmer, Hans
"Nochmals: Jesus und das Sacaeenopfer." *ZNW* 8 (1907) 320–21.

Wendland, Paul
"Jesus als Saturnalienkönig." *Hermes* 33 (1898) 175–79.

Windisch, Hans
"Der johanneische Erzählungsstil." In ΕΥΧΑΡΙΣ-ΤΗΡΙΟΝ; *Studien zur Religion und Literatur des Alten und Neuen Testaments Hermann Gunkel zum 60. Geburtstage, dem 23 Mai 1922, dargebracht von seinen Schülern und Freunden,* ed. Hans Schmidt. FRLANT, n.s., 19 (Göttingen: Vandenhoeck & Ruprecht, 1923) 174–213.

18

28 Then they led Jesus from the house of Caiaphas to the praetorium. It was early. They themselves did not enter the praetorium, so that they might no be defiled, but might eat the passover. 29/ So Pilate went out to them and said, "What accusation do you bring against this man?" 30/ They answered him, "If this man were not an evil-doer, we would not have handed him over." 31/ Pilate said to them, "Take him yourselves and judge him by your own law." The Jews said to him, "It is not lawful for us to put any man to death." 32/ This was to fulfill the word which Jesus had spoken to show by what death he was to die. [a] 33/ Pilate entered the praetorium again and called Jesus, and said to him, "Are you the King of the Jews?" 34/ Jesus answered, "Do you say this of your own accord, or did others say it to you about me?" 35/ Pilate answered, "Am I a Jew? Your own nation and the chief priests have handed you over to me; what have you done?" 36/ Jesus answered, "My kingship is not of this world; if my kingship were of this world, my servants would fight, that I might not be handed over to the Jews; but my kingship is not from the world." 37/ Pilate said to him, "So you are a king?" Jesus answered, "You say that I am a king. For this I was born, and for this I have come into the world, to bear witness to the truth. Every one who is of the truth hears my voice." 38/ Pilate said to him, "What is truth?" After he had said this, he went out to the Jews again, and told them, "I find no crime in him. 39/ But you have a custom that I should release one man for you at the Passover; will you have me release for you the King of the Jews?" 40/ They cried out again, "Not this man, but Barabbas!" Now Barabbas was a robber.

19   Then Pilate took Jesus and scourged him. 2/ And the soldiers plaited a crown of thorns, and put it on his head, and arrayed him in a purple robe; 3/ they came up to him, saying, "Hail, King of the Jews!" and struck him with their hands. 4/ Pilate went out again, and said to them, "Behold, I am bringing him out to you, that you may know that I find no crime in him." 5/ So Jesus came out, wearing the crown of thorns and the purple robe. Pilate said to them, "Here is the man!" 6/ When the chief priests and the officers saw him, they cried out, "Crucify him, crucify him!" Pilate said to them, "Take him yourselves and crucify him, for I find no crime in him." 7/ The Jews answered him, "We have a law, and by that law he ought to die, because he has made himself the Son of God." 8/ When Pilate heard these words, he was the more afraid; 9/ he entered the praetorium again and said to Jesus, "Where are you from?" But Jesus gave no answer. 10/ Pilate therefore said to him, "You will not speak to me? Do you not know that I have power to release you, and power to crucify you?" 11/ Jesus answered him, "You would have no power over me unless it had been given you from above; therefore he who delivered me to you has the greater sin." 12/ Upon this Pilate sought to release him, but the Jews cried out, "If you release

this man, you are not Caesar's friend; every one who makes himself a king sets himself against Caesar." 13/ When Pilate heard these words, he brought Jesus out and sat him down on the judgment seat at a place called The Pavement, in Hebrew, Gabbatha. 14/ Now it was the day of Preparation for the Passover; it was about the sixth hour. He said to the Jews, "Here is your King!" 15/ They cried out, "Away with him, away with him, crucify him!" Pilate said to them, "Shall I crucify your King?" The chief priests answered, "We have no king but Caesar." 16a/ Then he handed him over to them to be crucified.

■ 28 Who is the leading figure in this pericope? "The Jews" are constantly referred to; only verses 18:35 and 19:6–15 mention the high priests. The narrator says nothing (and knows nothing) of the content of the hearing before Caiaphas. Where Pilate was staying is a matter of controversy.[1] The most frequent conjecture is the earlier palace of Herod; according to Dalman, it lay in the northwest corner of the upper city.[2] The tower of Antonia (located in the northwest corner of the outer court of the temple) has also been considered, of course, by some interpreters. The temporal notice, early in the morning, has no symbolic significance: it was a part of the tradition beginning with Mark 15:1. Verse 28b attempts to account for the fact that the Jews remained outside: pagan houses made them Levitically unclean for seven days.[3] "To eat the passover" means to participate in the passover meal. Jesus was crucified on the fourteenth of Nisan, according to Johannine chronology; one ate the paschal lamb on the late afternoon and evening of that day.[4]

■ 29 Pilate comes out because the Jews do not go into his palace. This mode of depiction is to the credit of the narrator, who is preparing to play out the action on two stages.[5] The question of Pilate makes it appear that he is not yet precisely informed. The narrator stretches the action out and thereby increases the tension.[6]

■ 30 The Jews do not give a precise answer. The commentators detect petulance in their answer, for the most part.[7] But the narrator probably does not want to end the action too quickly. Hearers and readers are to remark how the catastrophe—a catastrophe really only for the Jews—unfolds slowly. The catchword, "to hand down, hand over" ($\pi\alpha\rho\alpha\delta\iota\delta\acute{o}\nu\alpha\iota$: cf. vv 35, 36, 19:11, 16), which appears here for the first time, has the effect of a clock sounding the death knell.

■ 31 Since Pilate has learned nothing exact about the guilt of Jesus, he suggests that the Jews take him and judge him in accordance with Jewish law; at that time they did indeed possess a limited power of judgment. But the answer of Pilate shows, at the same time, that the "Johannine Pilate" is not eager to undertake the trial. The Jews now maintain that they have no power to pass the death sentence or to carry it out. In his well-known book on the Jews in the Roman empire, J. Juster has contested the view of John,[8] and in his commentary Barret has followed Juster.[9] J. Jeremias,[10] comes to

1   Bultmann, *John*, 651 n. 2 [503f. n. 2].
2   *Sacred Sites and Ways*, 335–42.
3   Billerbeck, 2: 838f.
4   Cf. 1 Cor 5:7.
5   Cf. Dodd, *Tradition*, 96f.
6   On questions of composition, see the Overview.
7   Bauer, *Das Johannesevangelium*, 215; Strathmann, *Das Evangelium nach Johannes*, 234; Barrett, *John*, 533.
8   J. Juster, *Les Juifs dans l'Empire romain; leur condition juridique, économique, et sociale* (Paris: P. Geuthner, 1914).
9   *John*, 533–35.
10 "Zum Geschichtlichkeit des Verhörs Jesu vor dem Hohen Rat," *ZNW* 43 (1950/1951) 145–50; also in his *Abba. Studien zur neutestamentlichen Theologie und Zeitgeschichte* (Göttingen: Vandenhoeck & Ruprecht, 1966) 139–44.

Juster's aid and critically demolishes the parade of witnesses to the contrary: (1) it was a special legal right of Jews to kill pagans who enter the inner court of the temple; (2) the burning of a priest's daughter who was taken in adultery took place under Agrippa I, when Jews had an unlimited power of judgment; (3) the high priest Ananus the younger was deposed because he had James, the brother of Jesus, stoned, along with some other Christians, during the absence of the governor.[11]

The stoning of Stephen, contrary to Jeremias, is not to be traced back to a special license granted to the Jews, but was vigilante justice pure and simple.[12] Verse 31 has thus not been historically contradicted up to the present time. In the context, this verse has the aim of informing the reader that the Jews have only one purpose: to put Jesus to death, and since that is not possible directly, they will do so indirectly, via Pilate.

■ **32** The word that Jesus spoke which is being fulfilled here is found in John 12:32f.

According to Bultmann, verse 32 is a redactional addition.[13] It is a play on 3:14, where Jesus spoke of his "lifting up." But what does this verse mean? Does it mean that the Jews cannot kill anyone, with the result that Jesus' word is fulfilled? Or does it mean that the demand of the Jews was successful, so that the word of Jesus might be fulfilled? Presumably it means the latter. In the context, it has the effect of a tacit agreement that reminds the reader that everything occurs in accordance with what Jesus had foretold.

■ **33** "He entered therefore" ($\epsilon i \sigma \hat{\eta} \lambda \theta \epsilon \nu$ $o \hat{v} \nu$) corresponds to the "he went out" ($\epsilon \xi \hat{\eta} \lambda \theta \epsilon \nu$ $o \hat{v} \nu$) of verse 29. The action on the double stage begins; this is a peculiarity of the Johannine way of depicting the action. Contrary to Dodd,[14] it is not a matter of reminding the reader constantly that the pressure of the priests is unrelenting, while Pilate runs hither and yon, "like a hunted hare." This understanding of the Johannine Pilate is entirely mistaken;[15] Pilate calls Jesus in and asks him whether he is the "king of the Jews." This phrase runs through the whole of the passion narrative, from Mark to the Gospel of John. It might stem from earlier tradition. Here it serves simultaneously to introduce the theme of the messianic claim of Jesus and to depict him as rebel and counter-king, who challenges the Roman caesar.

■ **34** Jesus answers with a counter-question: does Pilate speak out of his own knowledge or on the basis of information provided him by the Jews? If the second is the case, then Pilate does not understand the meaning of the expression.

■ **35** Many commentators have detected the Roman contempt for "oriental vassals"[16] or for "the subject races"[17] in Pilate's reply. But the narrator is not suggesting such a sense of superiority here (19:9 is a remark in a different context). Pilate's reply implies that he is here obviously reproducing Jewish intelligence ("handed down," $\pi \alpha \rho \alpha \delta \iota \delta \acute{o} \nu \alpha \iota$).[18] That had not been said unequivocally up to this point, but is now incidentally announced to the reader. Pilate now interrogates Jesus about the acts with regard to which he is accused: at what is the Jewish accusation (never precisely formulated) aimed? Put differently, what does the phrase, "king of the Jews," imply?

■ **36** Jesus—that is, the Evangelist—answers: "My kingship is not of this world." Here it becomes evident that the expression proffered by the tradition did not suit the Evangelist. He did indeed take it over, but reinterpreted it. Jesus first of all bases his claim on the fact that he would have used force to prevent his deliverance to the Jews, were his kingship an earthly one (the act of Peter in 18:10 is forgotten, as is the whole process of handing him over to the Romans). Christianity, as the Evangelist understands it, is not a political movement and therefore makes no use of political means.

■ **37** Pilate had correctly understood: did Jesus not therefore contest that he was a king? What kind of a king was he? Jesus then reminds Pilate that it was Pilate, not he, who first used the designation. It now becomes clear in what sense Jesus (or the Evangelist) makes use of the

---

11   Jos. *Ant.* 20.200ff.
12   Cf. Acts 26:10, where Paul allegedly always votes for the death sentence in the trials of Christians. Was special authority granted for all these trials postulated by Luke?
13   *John,* 653 [505].
14   *Tradition,* 97.
15   See further the Overview.

16   Hirsch, *Das vierte Evangelium,* 405.
17   Edwards, *John,* 141.
18   See above on v 30.

expression: Jesus' kingdom consists in this, that he came to bear witness to the truth. In Jesus the "truth" presents itself to men in incarnate form (14:6). Whoever is of the truth belongs to the kingdom of truth; the one to whom God has granted new existence hears his voice. If Pilate belonged to this kingdom, then he would understand Jesus.

■ **38** The counter-question of Pilate shows that he is not one of these elect, or he would not now ask what truth is. It has customarily been said that Pilate is a skeptic. Thus, for example, Bernhard Weiss writes: "The question is intended to be skeptical (Schanz). From the point of view that one cannot really find the truth, he can look down on the enthusiast (who is nevertheless quite innocent) with a certain derogatory, half mocking (de Wette), half indulgent (Meyer) pity—a dreamer that has bet everything on this phantom."[19] Loisy ascribes only the skepticism of a politician to Pilate: "One had better not expose oneself to unpleasant experiences" for the sake of a truth that one cannot locate with precision; "but it is also not a crime to go in quest of it."[20] Hirsch correctly deepens the truth question posed by Pilate: "The author means: Pilate knows of no truth that convicts man from within, . . . that is, he is not a skeptic in the usual sense. . . . That means, first, that Pilate is a genuine pagan, who knows God only as an undisclosed power of destiny. . . . It means, further, that only the positive power is present, the one that proclaims itself through palpable effects."[21] O. Spengler views the question of Pilate as the only saying in the NT that has good credentials. To this question it is not the tongue that responds, but the silent presence of Jesus with the other question that is finally decisive for religion: "What is reality? For Pilate that is everything; for Jesus it is nothing. My kingdom is not of this world—that is the final word, from which nothing may be permitted to detract. . . . Politics or religion: here there is an either/or and no real accommodation."[22] We may bring this series to an end with Bultmann's interpretation: "The question should not be psychologically

interpreted. . . . For John such [philosophical] skepticism is not open to discussion. . . . He [Pilate] takes the point of view that the state is not interested in the question about the "truth" (ἀλήθεια)—about the reality of God, or as perhaps it ought to be expressed in Pilate's way of thinking, about reality in the radical sense."[23]

However, the Johannine Jesus has already explained in 14:6 that he himself is the truth. If Pilate now asks, when face to face with this truth, the truth that stands before him, "What is truth?", it is clear that Pilate does not belong among those whom "the Father has given to Jesus." Pilate again goes out to the Jews with the conviction that this man is no revolutionary; for him Jesus is "innocent with respect to the (Jewish) charge."

■ **39f.** He therefore wants to release him. And yet he must somehow compensate the Jews. They must not lose face. He therefore invokes an (allegedly existing) prescriptive law, according to which he releases a prisoner to the Jews at Passover. He is ready to release the "king of the Jews": in that case, Jesus would not be acquited; he would receive a pardon. But the Jews do not want to accept this offer. They do not want Jesus; they want Barabbas. "Now Barabbas was a robber." That makes it clear how things stand with the Jews.

■ **19:1–3** So Pilate appears to have failed in his attempt to set Jesus free. But he doesn't give up. The verses that follow are to be understood from that perspective. There is a tradition according to which the soldiers ridicule the condemned Jesus and abuse him: Mark 15:16–20, Matt 27:27–31. The Evangelist has worked this tradition in here, prior to Jesus' condemnation: he understands this tradition, like that of the scourging, in such a way that Pilate follows a fixed plan: Jesus arraigned and arrayed in this way is designed to awaken the pity of the Jews.

The attempt has been made to find a historical kernel in this scene. Vincent Taylor recalls the mocking of the Jewish king, Agrippa I, in Alexandria.[24] H. Reich had sought to follow a similar line prior to Taylor.[25] Cumont and P. Wendland[26] are reminded of the Saturnalia or of

19 B. Weiss, *Das Johannesevangelium*, 580.
20 Loisy, *Le quatrième évangile*, 842–71.
21 Hirsch, *Das vierte Evangelium*, 416.
22 O. Spengler, *The Decline of the West*, 2 vols., tr. Charles Francis Atkinson (New York: A. A. Knopf, 1926–1928) 2: 216.
23 Bultmann, *John*, 656 and n. 2 [507 and n. 8].
24 Philo, *Flacc.* 6.36–39: *The Gospel According to St. Mark* (London: Macmillan & Co., 1953) 646–48.
25 "Der König mit der Dornenkrone," *Neue Jahrbücher für das klassische Altertum, Geschichte und deutsche Literatur* 13 (1904) 705–33.
26 "Jesus als Saturnalienkönig," *Hermes* 33 (1898) 175–79.

the Persian festival of the Sacaea. Plutarch's story of the mocking of a Roman citizen by a group of pirates provides even fewer parallels.[27] Isaiah (50:6) has provided a model for the persecution of the pious who suffer, which is hardly without influence on this story. The synoptic parallel to this story, according to which Jesus is mocked in the Sanhedrin following his condemnation, is found in Mark 14:65, Matt 26:67f., Luke 22: 63ff. There the influence of Isaiah 50:6 is much more clearly in evidence. Whether John knew this OT tradition is unknown to us. But he could not make use of it, since he knew nothing of a Jewish condemnation of Jesus. Whoever wants to insist that this scene is historical is faced with the question: where did the soldiers get a purple robe? Mark has the scarlet robe of the lictor in mind. According to Luke 23:11, Herod sent Jesus back to Pilate in a magnificent robe, after he and the soldiers had mocked him; that may be a secondary version.[28] In Matt 27:29, the mocking is extended still further; the reed (= scepter) is new. The crown of thorns is probably understood by the Evangelist (insofar as mocking by soldiers is involved) as scoffing by means of the pseudo-insignia of a king, and thus not as an instrument of torture (by means of a crown made from the spiney acanthus), but as a crown made from the date palm (Phoenix dactylifera), which is meant to imitate the halo.[29]

■ 4 Verse 4 appears to contain a logical error: if Pilate regards Jesus as guiltless, why did he have him scourged and permit him to be mocked? But the Evangelist has the intention of having Pilate present Jesus in just such a pitiable way, as becomes evident in verse 5.

■ 5 Jesus appears on the threshold of the praetorium wearing the crown of thorns and the purple robe. Now it will emerge whether Pilate has calculated correctly. He points to the pitiable picture, which does not exhibit a "noble countenance," but presents blood-smeared and swollen features. The Johannine description is here brutally realistic, and to this realism Pilate says: "Look, here is the man!" Luther's translation: "See, what a man!"

is in danger of misleading the modern reader. Pilate does not wish to represent Jesus as something to be admired. But neither does Dodd do justice to the text when he finds here a contemptuous expression, which he represents with, "Look! the fellow!" (which means something like, "There is the bloke!").[30] This man is no dangerous revolutionary, but a poor, powerless sufferer, for whom his worst enemies should have compassion.

■ 6 However, the calculations of Pilate do not work out. It is precisely the appearance of the humiliated and bruised figure that incites his enemies—the chief priests and their officers—even more and causes them to cry out, "Crucify! Crucify!" In view of this miscalculation, Pilate seems to lose his nerve. For, although the Jews themselves have already explained that they cannot put anyone to death (18:31), Pilate now says to them: "Take him yourselves and crucify him." In order to get out of this difficulty, the comment of Lightfoot offers this bit of information: the words could not have the same sense as they do in 18:31, except so far as it is an attempt to escape the responsibility.[31] One must view it as a "petulant refusal" to condemn the prisoner. Bultmann interprets similarly: "I do not give my consent to crucify Jesus; if you want his crucifixion, then you must undertake it yourselves! That is, Pilate refuses the demand of the Jews with wrathful irony."[32] Barrett thinks that if Pilate had spoken these words, he must have done so as a taunt; they were probably intended to attribute the responsibility for the death of Jesus to the Jews rather than to the Romans.[33]

However, we do not have the report of an eyewitness. We must therefore first ask what the Evangelist intends to have Pilate say. Has he not used these words in order to prepare for the next Jewish assertion (v 7) and Pilate's response (v 8)?

■ 7 The Jews do not respond directly to the unreasonable demand of the governor, but appeal to the law, in accordance with which Jesus must die, for—and this is the decisive thing in this context—he has made himself

27 Plutarch, *Pomp.* 24.
28 Cf. Grundmann, *Das Evangelium nach Lukas,* THKNT 3 (Berlin: Evangelische Verlagsanstalt, ²1961) 425.
29 See *TDNT* 7: 629–33, with full literature given by Grundmann; also his commentary on Matthew, *Das Evangelium nach Matthäus,* THKNT 1 (Berlin: Evangelische Verlagsanstalt, 1968) 556f.
30 Dodd, *Interpretation of the Fourth Gospel,* 437; Edwards, *John,* shares this view, 144.
31 Lightfoot, *St. John's Gospel,* 313.
32 Bultmann, *John,* 659 [510].
33 Barrett, *John,* 541.

the Son of God. Thus, the decisive thing is no longer the political significance of the messianic claim; rather, the theological offense taken at Jesus' assertion of filial relation to God has now become perceptible as the basis of the Jewish hostility that calls for his death. (It is evident that we are here in the midst of a post-Easter discussion between Jews and Christians.) But precisely this Jewish argument has an unexpected effect on Pilate (as he is represented in the Gospel of John).

■ **8** The procurator was uncomfortable with this whole trial from the beginning. His uneasiness grew when he recognized the innocence of Jesus. But he now becomes anxious in a much worse way: if Jesus is not only politically innocent, but if he really is a divine being clothed in the form of a man, might one not get caught in indescribable guilt by making the wrong move against him? As a heathen, Pilate can know no more; he is very close to the Christian truth, without being able, however, to grasp it.

■ **9** He therefore questions Jesus directly—after hurrying back into the praetorium: "Where are you from?" That means: are you a heavenly being, a god? Wetter recalls a passage in the life of Apollonius of Tyana, of which Philostratus is the author.[34] In this passage, the Roman official Tigellinus takes Apollonius aside—after he has performed a miracle—and asks him who he is. Apollonius immediately names his father and his homeland and says that he does not want to be "something great" (that is a favorite expression among gnostics for "God"). Finally, however, "he seemed to Tigellinus to be divine and beyond human possibility (δαιμόνιά τε εἶναι πρόσω ἀνθρώπου), and as one who takes care not to fight with a god, Tigellinus says: 'Go wherever you want, for you are too powerful to be controlled by me.'"[35]

To the question of Pilate Jesus is silent. The motif of silence has been introduced into the passion tradition from Isaiah 53:7 (cf. Mark 15:5, Luke 23:9). In John, it acquires a fresh sense: the divine does not manifest itself directly. For, the divine is not a mundane object with specific attributes, with respect to which one can make inquiries. If Pilate does not come to faith himself, an answer of Jesus would confirm him in his pagan conviction that God is directly accessible, like a thing within the

world. Whoever does not acknowledge Jesus by devoting himself faithfully to him, for that one God is inaccessible—in spite of all the best intentions in the world on the part of the questioner.

■ **10** The silence of Jesus is incomprehensible for Pilate and exasperates him. He put his question with the best of intentions—why does Jesus not condescend to give him an answer on the crucial point? He therefore flies into a rage and invokes his power: it lies within his authority to determine whether Jesus is set free or is crucified. He is just such a powerful man: Bultmann understands the word "power" (ἐξουσία) as "legitimated power, authority, right."[36] This conception goes together with Bultmann's interpretation of verse 11.

■ **11** Jesus' response dumbfounds Pilate: "You would have no power over me unless it had been given to you from above; therefore he who delivered me to you has the greater sin" (παραδιδόναι: delivered me over). Bultmann interprets this verse as follows: the authority of the state is not derived from the world, but has its basis in God. The "power, authority" (ἐξουσία) of Pilate comes from God, however he may wield it. But in order to be able to perform his office with impartiality vis-à-vis the seduction of the world, he ought to be aware of that. "His attention is thereby called expressly to his responsibility before God. . . . The state executes . . . its acts without personal interest; if it acts impartially, there can be no question of 'sin' (ἁμαρτία) on the part of the state." But if it is corrupted by the world, . . . "the form of the law can at least be observed and thus the authority of the law recognized, so that the one unjustly condemned has to conform to the law. . . . [The state] can succumb to the world; but its motives are never identical with those of the world. . . . Pilate has no personal interest in the death of Jesus; he does not persecute him with the hatred of the Jews, who have delivered Jesus over to him. . . . Their sin is doubled, so to speak, because, in addition to their hatred of Jesus, they have misused the state for their own purposes."[37]

This doctrine of the state, which Bultmann has derived from the Fourth Gospel, is not as self-evident to us as it was to him. He naively presupposes the (modern) concept of "the state." But there was no abstract entity

---

34 Wetter, *Der Sohn Gottes,* 90f. The passage in Philostratus is *Vita Apoll.* 4.44.

35 The translation of Philostratus follows the author's

interpretation of the text.

36 *John,* 662 n. 1 [512 n. 6].

37 Bultmann, *John,* [512f.]; the ET lacks the bulk of this

called "the state" for the Evangelist; he knew only the *Imperium Romanum.* To be sure, Paul develops a doctrine of the existing authorities in Romans 13, to which Christians are to subordinate themselves. Luke certainly does his best in the Acts of the Apostles to represent the the relation of Christians to the Roman authorities as good, indeed, as good even to the Asiarchs (built into the imperial cult).[38] Is it along one of these lines that Jesus is thinking when he tells Pilate that he has received his authority from God? And he adds that Pilate's sin is not as great as that of those who delivered him over. Nevertheless, Pilate is burdened with sin. John faces the fact that Pilate finally abandons Jesus to the Jews. For the Evangelist, the Jews undoubtedly bear the real guilt since they delivered Jesus to Pilate. But God has assigned Pilate a difficult, thankless role, that netted him only a sentence in the creed: *crucifixus sub Pontio Pilato.* It is not merely the weakness of Pilate that causes him to capitulate to the Jews in the end (although that also plays a role); in the last analysis, it is the will of God on which every attempt of this Roman to release Jesus comes to grief.

■ **12** Pilate therefore commits a sin when he condemns Jesus to the cross—Jesus told him that and Pilate appears to have understood it. He therefore attempts once more, in spite of all the setbacks, to effect Jesus' release. The Evangelist was aware that in so doing he was simultaneously negating Israel's claim to be the chosen people, although the historical Pilate was not aware of that. But that does not concern us for the time being.

Scholars have reproached the narrator, in part, because he does not tell us where the Jews learned of Pilate's intentions, and does not make Pilate's sudden reappearance before the praetorium plausible (this owes, in part, to the separation into sources). But the Evangelist does not permit himself to waste words here on such incidentals when everything is proceeding to its conclusion at a dizzying pace. We may therefore assume that the Jews on the outside learned of Pilate's decision on the inside to free Jesus. Now they play their strongest trump: if Pilate releases this "king," he sets himself against Caesar in Rome (who would have been called "king" [βασιλεύς] in the Orient). Pilate possessed the title, *amicus*

Caesaris ("friend of Caesar"). It is doubtful that the narrator knew that. But when Pilate gives Jesus his freedom, he is no "friend of Caesar." For, whoever makes himself out to be king is an enemy of the Roman "king," an enemy of Caesar.

■ **13–15** The decision cannot be postponed longer. Pilate does not have many options. There is really only one way left open to him to save Jesus: if he shows the Jews that they have nothing to adduce against Jesus' kingship in accordance with their own logic, they will have to drop their charges. They themselves claim to have their own king, the messiah. Are they going to reject him? In order to demonstrate that, Pilate has Jesus brought out and sets this one who has been beaten and humiliated on his own seat of judgment. Jesus is now sitting there, on the throne of the king. The Evangelist indicates that it is in this moment that the judgment is rendered by giving the precise place and time: the place is the λιθόστρωτον, "paved with stone" (in Hebrew presumably "Gabbatha," which perhaps means "height, hill"); the time is twelve o'clock noon, on the day of preparation before the Passover. The hearing has now lasted six hours. "Look, here is your king," says Pilate. He is that, of course, only by virtue of Christian conviction. But the Jews cry out: "Crucify! Crucify!" Pilate asks them expressly and emphatically: "Shall I crucify your king?" And now comes the reply of the chief priests, stubborn and blind: "We have no king but Caesar." Israel abandons its claim to be the people of the messiah. Israel wants to be a nation among other nations in the Roman empire. Its special role has been played out, its hour of grace has slipped away. This is the price at which the chief priests have achieved their goal.

■ **16a** Pilate throws in the towel. He gives his permission for Jesus to be crucified. Not by the Jews themselves, but by Roman soldiers: they understand the matter. Pilate has "delivered him over" (παρέδωκεν) to death. The death knell sounds for the last time.

Overview

Earlier exegetes make the following assumptions: the events took place as they are represented. In that case, the question is justified: why do the Jews or Pilate act like

passage.
38 Cf. Haenchen, *Acts of the Apostles,* 574 n. 1, 578.

they do? To this question easy answers were given, like these: "The Jews were incited," or "Pilate was worried." In so doing, the fact was overlooked that we do not have a documentary film before us that was recorded by a hidden camera. Rather, the text provides the picture that is presented to us by the narrator (sometimes an editor also). In so doing, he reworked traditional material from an earlier period to varying degrees, and he was influenced by the views that he grew up within his own community. However, he did not simply reproduce the tradition. Rather, he also actively creates, occasionally to a high degree, in understanding the past and making it understood.

That, fortunately, may not only be asserted for our pericope, but may also be demonstrated. The secluded exchange between Jesus and Pilate was not set down in stenographic notes, recorded, nor were minutes taken of it. Ideas like that proposed by Edwards, whether John, the son of Zebedee, could not have procured transcripts of the trial from Procula (a legendary figure, based on Matt 27:19, invented as Pilate's wife), deserve to be mentioned only as curiosities.[39]

What unites the picture the Gospel of John paints of this event—a picture that is otherwise entirely unique—with the other gospels is this conviction: the question of who Jesus was, in relation to his claim, dominated his trial: was he the messiah, the "king of the Jews," "the witness to the truth," or the one designated by whatever title used by the Christian community to account for his significance?

All that is only to say: the old maxim of Vincentius of Lerinum (died before 450 CE), "what has been believed always, everywhere, and by everybody," is simply a form of self-deception, if it is intended to say more than what has just been said. One needs only to read the four gospels with open eyes to see how radically the hearing before Pilate has suffered modification—modification in a clearly defined direction, in a clearly recognizable trend. In the case of Mark (and Matthew, who follows him fairly faithfully on the whole), the trial culminates in a great scene before the Sanhedrin. The Jews first endeavor to prove Jesus' guilt there by means of false witnesses (his saying about destroying the temple). But

Jesus responds with silence, as Isa 53:7 had prophesied. Subsequently, however, Jesus solemnly confesses his station as "the Christ, the Son of the Blessed," and his return, as Daniel prophesied. This is what concerned Christians above all.

That goes together with the messianic secret theory of Mark. According to this theory, Jesus kept silent during his earthly life regarding his real identity, apart from a self-disclosure to the twelve and another to the three chief disciples, and he enjoined his disciples to keep silent about it as well. It is therefore of the greatest importance that he finally confess his true identity publicly before the Sanhedrin.

The messianic secret theory of Mark makes allowance for the difference between the sayings of Jesus prior to Easter and the expressions of the community subsequent to Easter. Matthew and Luke, however, have already abandoned this messianic secret theory. They presume, rather, that Jesus made himself known as the Son of man during his life. The recognition scene before the Sanhedrin thereby loses its significance. Something else takes its place in the foreground of the story.

In the scene with Pilate, 23:1–5, Luke has brought together everything out of the synoptic traditon that could fuel political objections to Jesus and lets the Jews present them as charges to Pilate. Luke has evidently taken into account the Jewish polemic of his own time in so doing: the Jews cast suspicion on the Christian community vis-à-vis the Romans as a revolutionary sect, which honors Christ as king and thereby opposes him to Caesar. In this assertion of a "political form of Christianity" we are not confronted with the bedrock of the tradition, as Winter and others allege, but with Jewish polemic towards the end of the first century CE. In the Acts of the Apostles, Luke has therefore attempted, not without good reason, to emphasize Paul's good understanding with Roman officials everywhere. As a part of this picture, Luke has Pilate affirm the innocence of Jesus three times (23:4, 14, 22).

A very difficult task devolved upon the later evangelists in this connection, as one can see. On the one hand, Jesus was condemned by a Roman official, in accordance with Roman law, to a form of Roman punishment,

39 *John*, 141.

crucifixion. On the other hand, they had to attempt to show that this same official did not prove to be hostile to Jesus at all, but finally approved the crucifixion only against his will under Jewish pressure. Matthew 27:24 provides the the most graphic expression of this point when it has Pilate wash his hands before the multitude and pronounce the words: "I am innocent of the death of this guiltless man."

The Johannine version of the scene with Pilate is far superior to that of Matthew and Luke. That of course contradicts what Wellhausen has written about this scene: "The 'hearing' before Pilate is not a hearing and yet it is one, although in content, not in form. It does not admit of open proceedings, but takes place only with the two present within the praetorium. The Jews remain outside and learn only through Pilate something of the status of the trial of the accused. To this end, Pilate must constantly run back and forth between the two parties, first into the praetorium, and then back outside. No one can find his way in this confusion."[40]

In reality, however, the narrator has succeeded in creating a fine composition. One senses that already in the external structure of the passage. It is basically quite simple, contrary to Wellhausen. The whole may be divided into three parts. The introduction (18:28–32) depicts the delivery of Jesus over to Pilate by the Jews. The central section (18:33–19:11), in four subsections (18:33–38a, 18:38b–40, 19:1–3, 19:4–11), describes the transactions between Pilate and Jesus and the Jews. This central section makes the transition to the grand closing scene (19:12–16a): Pilate must deliver Jesus up by Jewish demand.

These three segments of course contain some of the "aporias in the Fourth Gospel" that Schwartz so painstakingly and fruitlessly investigated.[41] Everytime he hoped he had finally found an extended segment of material that hung together, he also discovered discrepancies in that segment; it was as though the text fell to pieces in his critical hands. That goes together with the fact that he, like Wellhausen, scrutinized the narrator very closely to see whether he left out a single comma, and where that appeared to be the case, one of the redactors (who multiply like rabbits) must have inter-

vened and, by means of an addition or an omission or an alteration, have corrupted the underlying source, which was historically reliable. And so everything is a jumble. Nevertheless, there stands behind the seeming confusion of the Gospel of John a compositional unity that is well grounded.

First of all, let us consider the first segment of the narrative. The Jews appear with their prisoner before the praetorium, and Pilate immediately comes out like a good citizen in response to a knock on his door. But we must not underestimate the narrator. He simplifies and in this way creates a scene that leaves its impression on every reader. Perhaps a court record had been made of the reception of this delegation by the *Praefectus Judaeae* (which was probably the official title of Pilate).[42] Nevertheless, the narrator either did not know or ignored this transcript. He does not give the Jews a chance, at first, to lay their concerns before Pilate, so that Pilate would have to settle the question of their accusation ($\kappa\alpha\tau\eta\gamma o\rho\iota\alpha$). The Jews apparently shy away from a precise response—because they are angry or excited, as some interpreters think. It comes to light, in connection with Pilate's second pronouncement (v 31), that the Jews are demanding the death sentence against Jesus. If the reader pays close attention to the text, one gains the impression that no charge was really expressed by the Jews at all: they treat the praefect like he was really only the instrument of their will. To use a figure from hunting: the Jews are the beaters, who scare up the game, and Pilate is to be the hunter who makes the kill. However, Pilate does not immediately accommodate himself to this role. He intends, as the central segment will make clear, to determine for himself what the facts of the case are. Of course, there is still more involved. The narrator reserves the accusation implied in the title, "king of the Jews," for the central part of the story. The central segment of the account, and the first part as well, thus have thematic continuity and form a unit that is rounded off. The first segment functions then as a preliminary scene, which nevertheless prepares the way for the two-stage technique that commences in 18:33. Finally, it is made clear in this first section: the narrator is not interested in presenting the hearing before Pilate in fast

40 Wellhausen, *Das Evangelium Johannis*, 83f.
41 "Aporien," 2: 355–57.
42 Dodd, *Interpretation of the Fourth Gospel*, 96 n. 1, with bibliography.

motion (contrast the hearing before the chief priests). On the contrary, the narrator takes time, when he chooses, lots of time, and the reader is thus permitted to sense how slowly the event unfolds, the event whose end all Christians know well, but which takes place here, in a certain sense, "like it really happened." No other evangelist so depicts this story. As a consequence, the story that is narrated in the Gospel of John is new and tension-filled and revelatory.

The main segment of the story is characterized by the double-stage technique. One could take this interchange of scenes—between the scene in the foreground, with Pilate and the hostile and noisy crowd, and the one in quiet of the palace, with the praefect and the bound and silent figure—as a narrative strategy pure and simple, which no one had of course employed before. But it is prompted by internal considerations. Jesus had labored over the Jews in the first twelve chapters, in vain, as 12:37–42 lamentably and accusingly confirms. What is prophesied in Isaiah 53:1 and 6:10, in those important forecasts of doom for a deluded Jewish people, is realized in this passage. As a consequence, Jesus now has nothing more to say to the Jews. But with Pilate it is a different matter. Jesus' conversation with him has not yet been broken off; indeed, it has not yet begun. The narrator thus gives expression to something he wants to say unconditionally to his readers.

The central section of the story is dominated by the theme, "Jesus, king of the Jews." This expression can bear quite different meanings. In the mouth of the Jews, it says that Jesus is a political messiah by design and as such is an enemy of Caesar, and it is in this sense that they report the matter to Pilate (as is shown by 18:33–35). As understood in the Christian community, however, this phrase refers to Jesus as the judge at the end of time, as prophesied in Daniel 7:13. In the third place, it has a special meaning as used by John: it came to him without that special meaning, of course; he had to reinterpret it. That takes place in the saying of Jesus, "My kingdom is not of this world." The Christian faith does not aspire to worldly power. It is not political. The fact that Jesus falls into the hands of the Jews without the opposition of his followers is proof enough of that. But when Jesus nevertheless speaks of his kingdom, what does he mean, positively, by that? At this point, the narrator faces a grave problem. How is the mystery of

Christ's lordship to be communicated to Pilate without giving up the claim of the message of Christ on the faith of the hearer? To what extent is Christianity not "from here"? Jesus has come into the world, so Pilate is told, in order to bear witness for the truth. Whoever is of truth hears his voice. "What is meant by this truth?" asks Pilate. One could substitute the word "God" for the Johannine conception of truth. Jesus calls himself the way, the truth, and the life (14:6). The extent to which he is the way is indicated by the continuation: "And no one comes to the Father, except by me." Because faith can catch sight of the invisible Father in Jesus (14:7), he and the Father are "one," just as the original and the copy are identical to each other. But that one is of the truth who is born from above (3:3), who is from among those given to Jesus by the Father (6:37, 39, 17:2–6). As the narrator sees him, Pilate lives prior to that great awakening that faith brings with it. The possibility of another, new existence (in the midst of this life) is an idea foreign to him. Jesus is also an alien to him. Nevertheless, he understands this much after all: this man who stands before him is not a revolutionary who wants to overthrow Ceasar. He therefore goes out to the Jews and tells them openly that he regards Jesus as innocent. But if he thus takes the part of Jesus in this way, he nevertheless does not want to offend the Jews. As praefect, he must also get along with them. He therefore recommends, on the basis of an alleged legal custom, to release Jesus by way of amnesty. That is to go halfway; its character as a halfway measure is betrayed by virtue of the fact that Pilate keeps referring to Jesus as "the king of the Jews." In using such half measures, Pilate becomes more and more entangled in difficulties connected with his mediating role. The Jews do indeed accept his offer of amnesty, but the amnesty does not go to Jesus, but to the robber, Barabbas. It thereby not only becomes clear who the Jews are (and the world represented by them, which does not find Barabbas to be such a terrible fellow), but also to which company Pilate belongs. He reluctantly continues this capitulation to the Jews. His further attempt to demonstrate to the Jews, *ad oculos,* that "that man there" is no rebel, by having him beaten by the soldiers and outrageously decked out, likewise falls flat. The Jews have now tasted blood and want the object of their hatred totally annihilated. Pilate resists this demand, but in vain. He is like a fish in a net, which desperately wants to be free and feels that its free space grows ever smaller. And precisely at this point the accusation of the Jews hits him (from a literary point of view: a retarding moment): Jesus' claim to be the Son of God. Suppose that is true? Now he is not only fearful that he will permit an innocent man to hang on a cross, but also that he will commit a sin against (a) god. The narrator is aware that Pilate, as he understands him, is in a borderline situation, from which he cannot emerge without sinning.

The third section (19:12–16a) contains difficulties of various kinds. Verse 12a states that Pilate tells the Jews that he wants to release Jesus; Pilate has therefore again gone back outside. Verse 12b then concurs with this understanding: the Jews react violently to the announcement of Pilate. They now trot out their heaviest artillery: they interpret the messianic claim of Jesus ("king of the Jews") to be political, and they accuse the praefect of befriending an enemy of Caesar. In this situation, Pilate now does something completely unexpected. The Greek text is not unambiguous, to be sure, since it orginally had no punctuation. It runs: Πιλᾶτος . . . ἤγαγεν ἔξω τὸν Ἰησοῦν καὶ ἐκάθισεν ἐπὶ βήματος (literally: "Pilate . . . leads Jesus outside and sits [subject indeterminate] on the judgment seat"). The comma that is placed after "Jesus" (Ἰησοῦν) in the modern text corresponds to the customary interpretation of this passage: Pilate sits on the judgment seat himself. This understanding can appeal to the traditional procedure, in accordance with which the Roman judge sat down on the "judgment seat" (βῆμα) at the beginning of the trial. Since the trial had already begun in 18:33 in our passage, it is assumed that 19:13 implies that Pilate took the judgment seat prior to handing down a verdict. But that does not suit the situation: Pilate continues to negotiate with the Jews, and he never delivers a judgment, a guilty verdict, with respect to Jesus, since he is convinced that Jesus is innocent. And this is by no means a normal procedure that the narrator is describing.

Now the word "seat" (ἐκάθισεν) can also be used in a transitive, causative sense. It then has another meaning, the one presumed in the commentary above: "When Pilate heard these words, he lead Jesus out and sat (him) on the judgment seat."[43] We can, in fact, establish that this version existed in early Christianity and show how it arose.

In Justin, *Apology* 1.35.6, it is said of the Jews: "As the prophet said, 'They placed him in mockery on the judgment seat and said, Judge us.'"[44] The words, "as the prophet said," point to an OT passage understood in this way. It was discovered long ago: it is Isaiah 58:2, with the wording: "They ask of me righteous judgment" (LXX: αἰτοῦσίν με νῦν κρίσιν δικαίαν). That that passage is the one intended is shown by the parallel in the *Gospel of Peter* (2:7): "And they put upon him a purple robe and set him on the judgment seat and said, 'Judge righteously, O King of Israel.'"[45] The Gospel of John knew and corrected this tradition: it was not the Jews who put Jesus on the judgment seat (they had no right to do that), but Pilate himself.

John has thus created one of the best and most profound scenes in his gospel, a scene filled with complicated double meanings. Pilate did not believe that Jesus was a political pretender to the throne (a political messiah); but neither did he understand that Jesus was the true king (witness to the truth). The pitiful figure with the mock insignia was intended to show the Jews that Jesus cannot have had the aspirations to the kingship that the Jews claimed he had. Nevertheless, for the narrator the scene shows that the true king sits where he belongs, on the seat of judgment, and Pilate himself has installed him there. Yet is it so certain that Pilate is completely untouched by the "truth," by the Christian truth, for which Jesus is really the true king? Otherwise, how can he say to the Jews—who want to have nothing to do with king Jesus: "Shall I crucify your king?" The words and deeds of Pilate (as the narrator depicts them) hover between two meanings, between yes and no. Only to the extent that it is suggested that Jesus is the true king, do the Jews reject their status as the people of the messiah by reproaching Pilate for having suggested it.

One further word on this, the most dramatic scene in

43 Corssen, "Ἐκάθισεν ἐπὶ βήματος," *ZNW* 15 (1914) 338–40 and Loisy, *Le quatrième évangile*, 865ff., saw this earlier.

44 Tr. E. R. Hardy, *LCC*, vol. 1, *Early Christian Fathers*, 264.

45 *NTApoc* 1: 184.

the Gospel of John.[46] It may appear as though the Jews, who put Pilate under pressure, and Pilate, who resists them, are the real actors in this drama, and that Jesus is only an object, with reference to which the two parties propose to make decisions, but in different ways. But it only appears to be so. In truth, the silent prisoner, who speaks only when meeting alone with Pilate, is the fixed point around which everything turns. He is not the one who is judged; it is the Jews who obtain his death by obstinacy. Pilate is not the judge, but Jesus, and that by virtue of the fact he is not recognized and acknowledged.

Jesus is silent, to be sure, since leaving the praetorium for the last time (19:13). But he speaks in silence, by sitting on the seat of judgment with his mock crown and purple mantle. Of course, this speaking is of a special sort. It is impossible, in human categories, to perceive him saying with unmoving lips, "It is I." Jesus, the earthly Jesus, is not directly accessible in the Fourth Gospel. He is the *Christus absconditus* (the hidden Christ), especially in this scene. Only by virtue of the spirit, after Easter, will he become the *Christus revelatus* (the Christ revealed).

---

46 Cf. Windisch, "Die johanneische Erzählungsstil," in ΕΥΧΑΡΙΣΤΗΡΙΟΝ. *Studien zur Religion und Literatur des Alten und Neuen Testaments Hermann Gunkel zum 60. Geburtstage, dem 23 Mai 1922, dargebracht von seinen Schülern und Freunden,* ed. Hans Schmidt. FRLANT, n.s., 19 (Göttingen: Vandenhoeck & Ruprecht, 1923) 202–4.

42. Passion and Burial

Bibliography

Aubineau, Michel
"La tunique sans couture du Christ. Exégèse patristique de Jean 19,13–24." In *Kyriakon. Festschrift Johannes Quasten*, ed. P. Granfield and J. A. Jungmann, 2 vols. (Münster: Aschendorff, 1970) 100–127.

Bampfylde, Gillian
"Jn XIX. 28, a Case for a Different Translation." *NovT* 11 (1969) 247–60.

Barton, George A.
"A Bone of him shall not be Broken, John 19,36." *JBL* 49 (1930) 13–19.

Broer, Ingo
Die Urgemeinde und das leere Grab Jesu. Eine Analyse der Grablegungsgeschichte im Neuen Testament, SANT 31 (Munich: Kösel, 1972), esp. 201–49.

Dalman, Gustaf Hermann
Jesus-Jeshua: Studies in the Gospels, tr. Paul P. Levertoff (London: S. P. C. K., 1929; New York: KTAV, 1971).

Dauer, Anton
"Das Wort des Gekreuzigten an seine Mutter und den 'Jünger, den er liebte.' Eine traditionsgeschichtliche und theologische Untersuchung zu Joh 19,25–27." *BZ* 11 (1967) 222–39; 12 (1968) 80–93.

Dechent, Hermann
"Zur Auslegung der Stelle Joh 19,35." *TSK* 72 (1899) 446–67.

Dunlop, Laurence
"The Pierced Side. Focal Point of Johannine Theology." *Bible Today* 86 (1976) 960–65.

Feuillet, André
"L'heure de la femme (Jn 16,21) et l'heure de la Mère de Jésus (Jn 19,25–27)." *Bib* 47 (1966) 169–84, 361–80, 557–73.

Feuillet, André
L'heure de la mère de Jésus. Etude de théologie johannique (Franjeux-Prouille, 1969).

Fitzmyer, Joseph A.
"Crucifixion in Ancient Palestine, Qumran Literature, and the New Testament." *CBQ* 40 (1978) 493–513.

Fohrer, Georg
"Begräbnis." *BHH* 1 (Göttingen, 1962) 212.

Forbes, R. J.
"Mumie." *BHH* 2 (Göttingen, 1964) 1247–49.

Ford, J. Massingberd
"'Mingled Blood' from the Side of Christ. (John xix. 34)." *NTS* 15 (1968/1969) 337–38.

Hengel, Martin
"Mors turpissima crucis. Die Kreuzigung in der Antiken Welt und die 'Torheit' des 'Wortes vom Kreuz.'" In *Rechtfertigung. Festschrift für Ernst Käse-*

mann zum 70. Geburtstag, ed. J. Friedrich, W. Pöhlmann, and P. Stuhlmacher (Tübingen: Mohr-Siebeck; Göttingen: Vandenhoeck & Ruprecht, 1976) 125–84.

Kennard, J. Spencer, Jr.
"The Burial of Jesus." *JBL* 74 (1955) 227–38.

Koehler, Theodore
"The Sacramental Theory in Joh 19,1–27." *University of Dayton Review* 5 (1968) 49–58.

Koehler, Theodore
"Les principales interprétations traditionnelles de Jn 19,25–27 pendant les douze premiers siècles." *Etudes Mariales* 26 (1968) 119–55.

Langbrandtner, Wolfgang
Weltferner Gott oder Gott der Liebe? Der Ketzerstreit in der johanneischen Kirche. Eine exegetisch-religions-geschichtliche Untersuchung mit Berücksichtigung der koptisch-gnostischen Texte aus Nag-Hammadi, Beiträge zur biblischen Exegese und Theologie 6 (Frankfurt: P. Lang, 1977), esp. 33–35.

Langkammer, Hugolinus
"Christ's 'Last Will and Testament' (Jn 19,26.27) in the Interpretation of the Fathers of the Church and the Scholastics." *Antonianum* 43 (1968) 9–109.

Ljungvik, Herman
"Aus der Sprache des Neuen Testaments. Einige Fälle von Ellipse oder Brachylogie." *ErJb* 66 (1968) 24–51.

Meyer, Eduard
"Sinn und Tendenz der Schlussszene am Kreuz im Johannesevangelium." SPAW.PH (1924) 157–62.

Michaels, J. Ramsey
"The Centurion's Confession and the Spear Thrust." *CBQ* 29 (1967) 102–9.

Morretto, Giovanni
"Giov. 19,28: La sete di Cristo in croce." *RivB* 15 (1967) 249–74.

Nestle, Eberhard
"Zum Ysop bei Johannes, Josephus und Philo." *ZNW* 14 (1913) 263–65.

Potterie, Ignace de la
"Das Wort Jesu 'Siehe, deine Mutter' und die Annahme der Mutter durch den Jünger (Joh 19,27b)." In *Neues Testament und Kirche. Für Rudolf Schnackenburg,* ed. J. Gnilka (Freiburg: Herder, 1974) 191–219.

Richter, Georg
"Blut und Wasser aus der durchbohrten Seite Jesu." In his *Studien zum Johannesevangelium,* ed. Josef Hainz. BU 13 (Regensburg: F. Pustet, 1977) 120–42.

Sava, A. F.
"The Wound in the Side of Christ." *CBQ* 19 (1957) 343–46.

Seynaeve, Jaak
"Les citations scripturaires en Jn 19,36–37: Une preuve en faveur de la typologie de l'Agneau Pascal?" *Revue Africaine de Théologie* 1 (1977) 67–76.

Schürmann, Heinz
"Jesu letzte Weisung: Joh 19,26–27a." In his *Ursprung und Gestalt. Erörterungen und Besinnungen zum Neuen Testament,* Kommentare und Beiträge zum Alten und Neuen Testament (Düsseldorf: Patmos-Verlag, 1970) 13–28.

Schweizer, Eduard
"Das johanneische Zeugnis vom Herrenmahl." *EvT* 12 (1952/53) 341–63.

Tabachovitz, David
"Ein paar Beobachtungen zum spätgriechischen Sprachgebrauch." *ErJB* 44 (1946) 296–305.

Thyen, Hartwig
"Aus der Literatur zum Johannesevangelium." *TRu* 44 (1979) 97–134, esp. 118–27.

Wilkinson, John
"The Incident of the 'Blood and Water' in John 19,34." *SJT* 28 (1975) 149–72.

Zeitlin, Solomon
"The Date of the Crucifixion according to the Fourth Gospel." *JBL* 51 (1932) 263–71.

19

16b So they took Jesus, **17/** and he went out, bearing his own cross, to the place called the place of a skull, which is called in Hebrew Golgotha. **18/** There they crucified him, and with him two others, one on either side, and Jesus between them. **19/** Pilate also wrote a title and put it on the cross; it read, "Jesus of Nazareth, the King of the Jews." **20/** Many of the Jews read this title, for the place where Jesus was crucified was near the city; and it was written in Hebrew, in Latin, and in Greek. **21/** The chief priests of the Jews then said to Pilate, "Do not write, 'The King of the Jews,' but, 'This man said, I am King of the Jews.'" **22/** Pilate answered, "What I have written I have written." **23/** When the soldiers had crucified Jesus they took his garments

and made four parts, one for each soldier.
But his tunic was without seam, woven
from the top to bottom; 24/ so they said
to one another, "Let us not tear it, but
cast lots for it to see whose it shall be."
This was to fulfill the scripture, "They
parted my garments among them, and for
my clothing they cast lots." ª 25/ So the
soldiers did this; but standing by the
cross of Jesus were his mother, and his
mother's sister, Mary the wife of Clopas,
and Mary Magdalene. 26/ When Jesus
saw his mother, and the disciple whom
he loved standing near, he said to his
mother, "Woman, behold your son!" 27/
Then he said to the disciple, "Behold your
mother!" And from that hour the disciple
took her to his own home. 28/ After this
Jesus, knowing that all was now finished, said (to fulfill the scripture), "I
thirst." 29/ A bowl full of sour wine stood
there; so they put a sponge full of the
wine on hyssop and held it to his mouth.
30/ When Jesus had received the wine,
he said, "It is finished"; and he bowed his
head and gave up his spirit. 31/ Since it
was the day of Preparation, in order to
prevent the bodies from remaining on the
cross on the sabbath (for the sabbath
was a high day), the Jews asked Pilate
that their legs might be broken, and that
they might be taken away. 32/ So the
soldiers came and broke the legs of the
first, and of the other who had been crucified with him; 33/ but when they came
to Jesus and saw that he was already
dead, they did not break his legs. 34/ But
one of the soldiers pierced his side with
spear, and at once there came out blood
and water. 35/ He who saw it has borne
witness–his testimony is true, and he
knows that he tells the truth–that you
also may believe. 36/ For these things
took place that the scripture might be
fulfilled, "Not a bone of him shall be
broken." 37/ And again another scripture
says, "They shall look on him whom they
have pierced." 38/ After this Joseph of
Arimathea, who was a disciple of Jesus,
but secretly, for fear of the Jews, asked
Pilate that he might take away the body
of Jesus; and Pilate gave him leave. So
he came and took his body. 39/ Nicodemus also, who had at first come to him
by night, came bringing a mixture of
myrrh and aloes, about a hundred
pounds' weight. 40/ They took the body
of Jesus, and bound it in linen cloths with
the spices, as is the burial custom of the
Jews. 41/ Now in the place where he
was crucified there was a garden, and in
the garden a new tomb where no one had
ever been laid. 42/ So because of the
Jewish day of Preparation, as the tomb
was close at hand, they laid Jesus there.

■ **16b, 17** The Jews are grammatically the subject of "they took" (παρέλαβον). But in accordance with the sense, they are the subject only to the extent that Pilate yields to Jewish demands. The Roman soldiers carry out the crucifixion (v 23).[1] But Jesus immediately again becomes the real subject of the action: not dejected, he carries his own cross, that is, the cross bar (*patibulum*, a fork-shaped gibbet), which was then fastened to the stem of the cross that had been driven into the ground. Compare Plutarch: "Every evildoer carries his own cross."[2] This probably accounts for the variant in φ: ἐπέθηκαν αὐτῷ τὸν σταυρόν ("They placed the cross on him"). The emphasis in verse 17 prompts the supposition that the narrator knew and rejected another tradition, according to which Jesus broke down under the burden and Simon of Cyrene had to carry his cross (cf. Mark 15:21). Jesus can only be the model for discipleship (cf. Mark 8:34) if he himself bore his cross. Beginning with Origen, apologetic motives caused the synoptic and the Johannine accounts to be harmonized: verse 17 depicts the situation as Jesus leaves the praetorium (or the city); Mark 15:21, on the other hand, depicts what happened along the way. John tells us nothing of the mourners and the women who accompanied the procession (cf. Luke 23:27–31). To the extent that the passage in Luke pictures Jesus as unshaken, it functions like a prelude to the Johannine account. Only in the Gospel of John are the Jewish people as a whole hostile to Jesus. Golgotha (Aramaic: golgoltha) is "the place of the skull," as in Mark 15:22 and Matt 27:33 (Luke 23:33 differs: τὸν τόπον τὸν καλούμενον Κρανίον, "the place called Skull"): The name was probably suggested by the appearance;[3] it was a small hill, which already bore the stems of several crosses driven into the ground.

■ **18** "Where they crucified him": a subordinate clause relates this brutal act of violence and it thereby removes the terrible weight it later possessed in the mysticism of the passion. We are not told, because unimportant, who the two were who were crucified on his right and his left.

Later their names were presumed to be known.[4] According to John 20:25, Jesus was nailed to the cross and not merely tied (through which death was likewise precipitated, only much more slowly, by the lack of circulation): the nails did not pierce the palms of the hands, since they could not carry the weight of the body but would tear; they were put through the wrists instead. But the Evangelist does not mention that. He does not wish to depict the agony of Jesus, like Albrecht Dürer, but wants to portray the one on the cross who is still king.

■ **19** The motif of the so-called *titulus* appears in verse 19; the title indicated the crime of the criminal in each case. But this inscription, which Pilate had prepared and fixed to the cross, serves to honor Jesus, and runs: "Jesus, the Nazoraean, the king of the Jews." While Mark 15:26 gives only, "The king of the Jews," in Matt 27:37 and Luke 23:38, it is already expanded. The designation of Jesus as a Nazoraean (which all the evangelists have probably derived from Nazareth, without being certain of this meaning; the Jewish Christians were later called Nazoraeans) may derive from older tradition. The use of such a title over the cross is not attested; the examples often cited are not at all relevant.[5] Further, what Billerbeck adduces from the Talmud has nothing to do with the matter.[6] Wettstein cites a title of honor in four languages for the fallen Gordian.[7]

■ **20** The inscription was read by many Jews because the site of the crucifixion (in those days) was close to the city. The inscription is in three languges (not a hint in the Synoptics of this): Aramaic, Latin, Greek. It therefore proclaims the exalted station of the one hanging on the cross to all the world, but not his crime, for which the crucifixion was punishment: the charge against him is not mentioned.

■ **21** John is the sole evangelist who takes note of this particular and therefore has the chief priests protest: instead of "the king of the Jews," it must read "he said: I am the king of the Jews." It is possible that the emphasis on the exalted station of Jesus as the king of the Jews

---

1   Bauer, *Das Johannesevangelium*, 221.
2   *Sera num.* 9, p. 554a.
3   Barrett, *John*, 548.
4   Cf. Klostermann, *Markus*, 165.
5   Suetonius, *Caligula* 32; *Domitian* 10; Dio Cassius 54.8; Eusebius, *H. E.* 5.1.44.
6   Billerbeck, 1: 1038: *Sanh.* 6.1 and 11.4.
7   Wettstein, *Novum Testamentum Graecum*, 1: 954.

goes back to early Jewish Christianity.

■ **22** The response of Pilate is laconic, as befits an educated Roman: *Quod scripsi, scripsi* ("what is written, is written"). Stauffer's reflections on why Pilate, a minion of Sejanus, was only moments earlier complaisant with the Jews and now treats them brusquely, has no support in John.

■ **23f.** With verses 23f., the story returns to the soldiers: to those on guard around the cross go the clothes of the crucified as booty. Also, of course, the clothes of the two crucified with Jesus; but John makes no mention of that. The two crucified with Jesus play no role in John, unlike in Luke 23:39–43. The scene itself, the division of the clothes and the casting of lots for "the tunic without seams," is derived from Ps 22:18(19). In that passage the clothes of the innocent sufferer, who is regarded by his enemies as dead already, are confiscated. Ps 22:18(19) contains so-called *parallelismus membrorum*: the same situation is expressed by two statements that differ only slightly: "They divide my garments among them, and for my raiment they cast lots." That was interpreted, in the Christian tradition, as the description of two discrete events: each of the four soldiers on guard receives a fourth of Jesus' clothing. But his (seamless) tunic they are not willing to destroy, so they cast lots for it. The narrator could have had no premonition that it would become a highly valued relic. Early Christians read the Psalms of suffering as predictions and detailed descriptions of the passion of Christ (only the suitable verses were utilized) and narrated the passion story in accordance with them.

■ **25–27** Verses 25–27 provide a scene unknown to the Synoptics. Correspondingly, we find nothing of the mocking words and gestures of those passing by (Mark 15:29f.) in the Gospel of John, nothing of the mockery of the chief priest (Mark 15:31, 32a), and nothing of the scorn of the two crucified with him (Mark 15:32b). The account of the three-hour period of darkness (15:33) is omitted as well. The passion story in the Gospel of John exhibits nothing of the hatred and bitter irony of the world related by Mark, nothing of the enmity of the environment tormenting the crucified. Insead of this isolation, Jesus savours the proximity of those close to him: the mother of Jesus, his mother's sister, the wife of Clopas, and Mary Magdalene stand around the cross. This makes possible the injunction reported in verse 26: when he saw his mother and the disciple whom he loved standing by, he said to the mother, "Mother, behold your son!" The corresponding injunction follows for the disciple, "Behold your mother." What that means is indicated in verse 27: "From that hour the disciple took her to his own home": he has taken over the care for Jesus' mother. According to Acts 1:14, it was of course the brothers of Jesus who lived with his mother. But the tradition being followed here still regards the brothers of Jesus as unbelievers (cf. 7:5). The redactor of this scene has followed Johannine usage in that he has Jesus address his mother as "woman" (cf. 2:4). Of course, this is simultaneously the final honor Jesus paid to the beloved disciple in this account: he takes Jesus' place as an earthly son. Bultmann thinks that Mary here represents Jewish Christianity, while the beloved disciple stands for Gentile Christianity.[8] But there is nothing in the story that points to such a symbolic meaning for these figures.

■ **28f.** These verses again refer to the fulfillment of scripture. But we do not find "I thirst" ($\delta\iota\psi\hat{\omega}$) either in the Psalms of lament or elsewhere in the OT. Ps 22:15a (16a) ("My strength is dried up like a potsherd, and my tongue cleaves to my jaws") and Ps 69:3(4) ("I am weary with crying; my throat is parched") do indeed contain the thirst motif, but expressed differently and in a different context. Bauer has pointed to Ps 69:21(22): "They gave me poison for food, and for my thirst they gave me vinegar to drink."[9] The noun $\delta\iota\psi a$ ("thirst") at least appears here, but the passage suits the synoptic context, but not the Johannine. We may conjecture that the words "(to fulfill scripture) . . ." (v 27) to "he said" (v 30) were inserted by the redactor in order not to miss an important feature of the synoptic account. In particular, the clause "to fulfill the scripture" does not go with the preceding remark of Jesus, "When Jesus knew that all was now finished"—if everything is finished, there is nothing left to follow. Holding a sponge filled with vinegar up to Jesus' mouth does not conform to the Johannine picture of the death of Jesus, to which elements of affliction and agony are alien and in which there remain only the victorious overcoming and

---

8   *John*, 673 [521].
9   *Das Johannesevangelium*, 224.

consummation.

Since the stem of a hyssop plant is thin and not very long, J. Camarius has conjectured ὑσσῷ (ὑσσός, "javelin, short spear"; Latin, *pilum*) for ὑσσώσῳ, as appears already in the manuscript 476*. The one being crucifed did not hang there high above the crowd, as it is represented in many paintings; rather, his feet were close to the ground. The use of hyssop in connection with the Passover has also been suggested,[10] and a play on Jesus as the true paschal lamb conjectured. But allusions of this sort were alien to the soldier in question and to the redactor, as were the symbolic personifications mentioned earlier. Proposed personifications of this sort go back, in the last analysis, to Gnosticism; for example, the Samaritan woman at the well was interpreted as representing the pneumatic.

■ **30** Edwards conjectures that what John the son of Zebedee (!) really heard at that time were the words: "It's all over." But later, when meditating on it, he conceived the notion that the real sense of the words were the majestic, "It is finished."[11] This conjecture is part of the price the English Canon must pay for wanting to make a highly realistic eyewitness report out of the Fourth Gospel.

In connection with Jesus' words, the poorly preserved passage in LXX Job 19:26f. has been suggested because the form συντετέλεσται (cf. τετέλεσται, "it is finished") appears there. But it would be better to mention Job 13:1, where the words εἰς τέλος ἠγάπησεν αὐτούς (=τούς ἰδίους) appear.[12] The love that is mentioned there was brought to its fulfillment on the cross.

"He bowed his head" (κλίνας τὴν κεφαλὴν) implies: he bows his head as in sleep.[13]

■ **31** This verse opens the second part of this section. It works extensively with more recent tradition. The reference to the day of preparation (cf. v 42) does not have the significance that is emphasized here, namely, that it points forward to the sabbath that is rapidly approaching.

Early Judaism did not practice crucifixion as a form of punishment, although one who had been stoned for blasphemy against God would probably have been hanged on a tree. But the corpse would not have been permitted to hang on the tree overnight, but would have been buried on the same day.[14] Billerbeck goes on to say: "One waited with him [the one executed] until it became dark, then the criminal would be hanged and then (immediately) taken down; if one were to leave him overnight, one transgressed . . . a commandment; for it says, 'His corpse is not to be left overnight on the tree.'"[15] According to the Gospel of John, the approaching sabbath is also the first day of the festival and therefore especially holy.

The *crurifragium,* in which the legs are crushed, is taken only in the *Gospel of Peter* (4:14) as a part of the crucifixion, and is intended to hasten death. It is related in that passage that the penitent murderer did not have his legs broken, so that he might suffer longer.[16] In the Gospel of John, on the other hand, the *crurifragium* appears to be an exception, requested by the Jews because of the approaching sabbath. "The Jews" here act like officials, who negotiate with Pilate to get him to carry out their requests. Verse 31 does not imply that the Jews themselves took the body of Jesus down; nor do they break the legs of those crucified. One should not draw dubious conclusions from the brevity of the narrative. That Pilate accedes to their request is not said in what follows, but it is presupposed.

■ **32** Verse 32 can be reconciled with verse 18 only if the soldiers approached the row of three crosses from the

10 Dalman, *Jesus-Jeshua* (Leipzig: J. C. Hinrichs, 1922; Darmstadt: Wissenschaftliche Buchgesellschaft, 1967) 187f. [not in the English translation].
11 Edwards, *John*, 158.
12 An English translation: "He loved them (his own) to the end."
13 Cf. the parallels given in Bauer, *Das Johannesevangelium*, 224f.
14 *Sanh.* 6.4 on Deut 21:22f., quoted by Billerbeck, 1: 1012.
15 Billerbeck, 1: 1048. On this point, cf. Josephus, *BJ* 4.317: The Idumeans "actually went so far in their impiety as to cast out the corpses without burial, although the Jews are so careful about funeral rites that even malefactors who have been sentenced to crucifixion are taken down and buried before sunset." Translated by H. St. J. Thackeray, LCL.
16 *NTApoc* 1: 184: "And they were wroth with him and commanded that his legs should not be broken, so that he might die in torments."

right and from the left (in the event they formed a row). Breaking the legs produces strong fresh hemorrhaging. Moreover, the feet could no longer bear the weight of the body; the entire weight of the body now pulls on the arms.[17] That makes the lack of circulation fatal.

■ **33** Since they find Jesus already dead, he is spared having his legs broken. Kennard claims of course that that is only an awkward attempt to picture Jesus as the true paschal lamb, which, according to Exod 12:46 and Num 9:12, is not to have a bone broken.[18] Jesus suffered the same fate as those crucified with him. But verse 33 is not dependent on the two OT passages mentioned. Rather, Ps 34:20 shows that this expression was referred to the suffering innocent: "Not one of his bones is to be broken." The passage in the Gospel of John understands Jesus as the suffering innocent one and therefore attributes this feature to him. The real sense of this late tradition might be: God's promised protection rests on Jesus. The course of his life is still guided by divine providence even in death.

■ **34** A procedure connected with execution that is not attested elsewhere in that period is depicted in verse 34. The assertion that the spear-thrust belongs to the execution ritual does not make any sense.[19] The spear-thrust into the heart—for that is what $\tau\grave{\eta}\nu$ $\pi\lambda\epsilon\upsilon\rho\grave{\alpha}\nu$ $\ddot{\epsilon}\nu\upsilon\xi\epsilon\nu$ probably means—would then have had to have been carried out on those crucified with Jesus as well, while the action is intended to fulfill a saying that is relevant to Jesus alone. The Synoptics are not aware of this tradition, which is a product of a young Christian scribalism. This story, which is derived from Zech 12:10, becomes, in turn, the point of departure for the statement: "At once there came out blood and water." The usual interpretation, which is the right one, takes the terms as references to the sacraments of baptism and the Lord's Supper, which acquire their efficacy from the death of Jesus. Schweizer sees an allusion to the sacraments in verses 34b, 35, which bear witness to the reality of the crucifixion.[20] That turns matters upside down. Since the

circulation of the blood had ceased in someone who was already dead, the event is conceivable only as a miracle.

■ **35** For this event the testimony of an anonymous eyewitness is introduced in verse 35, a witness who is known as a reliable witness and who has spoken with the full knowledge of the import of what he says. Here the disciple whom Jesus loved is called upon to give his testimony.

The alleged parallel in 1 John 5:6 is directed against Gnosticism and asserts that Jesus came not only "by water," but also "by blood." "This evidently contradicts the gnosticizing view that the heavenly Christ descended into Jesus at his baptism, and then abandoned Jesus again before his death," as Bultmann puts it.[21] The Johannine passion narrative does not refer to bloodshed.

The manuscripts e vg^fuld do not contain this verse: that is not enough, however, to omit the verse from the text. The words $\alpha\mathring{\upsilon}\tauo\mathring{\upsilon}$ $\mathring{\epsilon}\sigma\tau\iota\nu$ are reversed in $\mathfrak{P}^{66}$ $\aleph$ 570 *al*; evidently someone wants to move $\alpha\mathring{\upsilon}\tauo\mathring{\upsilon}$ ("his") closer to $\mu\alpha\rho\tau\upsilon\rho\acute{\iota}\alpha$ ("testimony"). Further, the words "and blood and water came out" were probably added along with verse 35.

■ **36f.** The two OT passages that were taken to have been fulfilled are mentioned in these verses: Ps 34:21 and Zech 12:10. We have already spoken of Ps 34.[22] The text of Zech 12:10 is corrupt. The LXX text reads: $\mathring{\epsilon}\pi\iota\beta\lambda\acute{\epsilon}\psi o\nu\tau\alpha\iota$ $\pi\rho\acute{o}\varsigma$ $\mu\epsilon$ $\mathring{\alpha}\nu\theta'$ $\mathring{\omega}\nu$ $\kappa\alpha\tau\omega\rho\chi\acute{\eta}\sigma\alpha\nu\tauo$ ("they shall look upon me whom they have treated spitefully"); here the correct דָּקָר has been exchanged for the similar looking רָקַד. The text in verse 36 does not follow the LXX; but it has also avoided the impossible אֵל of the Hebrew text. Perhaps Jewish-Christian scribalism was at work here.

All of this has little to do with the Evangelist's own theology. On the other hand, the wound in the side is an absolutely necessary presupposition for the story of Thomas (20:25, 27). That Jesus was protected from one type of wound, but not from the other, was not felt to be an intolerable contradiction. An eschatological event was

---

17 Cf. Kennard, "The Burial of Jesus," 227–38.

18 "The Burial of Jesus," 228f.

19 Kennard, "The Burial of Jesus," 229.

20 E. Schweizer, "Das Johanneische Zeugnis vom Herrenmahl," *EvT* 12 (1952/1953) 348–63.

21 *The Johannine Epistles*, 80.

22 Cf. verse 33.

taken to be forecast in the passage in Zechariah: the enemies of Jesus will have to face him whom they pierced at the final judgment.

■ **38** Verse 38 contains an older tradition and actually connects up with verse 30. Joseph of Arimathea, who was a secret disciple of Jesus (out of fear of the Jews), asked Pilate that he might take the body of Jesus down; the request was granted. The essay of Kennard, cited above, indicates how many questions lurk here. Had Jesus been condemned by Pilate for the crime of *laesae majestatis* (treason), it is doubtful whether it would have been legally permissible to turn the body over at all. Kennard is of the opinion that Joseph paid a large bribe to Pilate;[23] the information provided by Mark 15:45 would then have been only the official version. The narrower circle of disciples (if it had not been altogether destroyed) could not have asked for the body; the women were likewise not possible candidates. It had to have been a carefree and influential person who took the risk on himself. Thus, it is not improbable that a person otherwise anonymous in the gospels undertook the friendly responsibility of burial. When he went to Pilate—according to Kennard, he went at dusk, just as all the Jews were at the Passover meal—[24] is a question for which the text does not supply an answer; the narrative indicates only the most important lines of the story and eliminates unenlightening detail, of which scarcely anything more was known, in any case.

■ **39** Verse 39 may be a legendary expansion of the text; the Synoptics are not aware of Nicodemus and his help with the burial. He is introduced with an allusion to 3:1f. He is also thought of as a secret disciple of Jesus. Only in this way is the account comprehensible that he appeared with a hundred liters of myrrh and aloes. How it came about that he had prepared this gift in advance is again one of those small details that the text does not address.

■ **40** Verse 40 describes how the body of Jesus is wrapped in bandages, between which the spices (ἀρώματα) were placed, and indicates that these were Jewish burial customs. The bandages are essential for the narrative at a later point, in 20:6f. Billerbeck overlooks the fact that the text says nothing here of anointing the body with oil—a body that would already be decaying after a few hours—and that the rabbinic texts say nothing about adding spices to oil.[25] It is especially important, however, that, according to Billerbeck, the practice of embalming the body was not common among the Jews. "The embalming of Jacob and Joseph (Gen 50:2, 26) reflects Egyptian customs."[26] In general, it would not have made any sense to undertake the burial in the way described here.[27] The gases connected with decomposition would have caused the body to explode. Real embalming procedure assumes that the innards are treated, which could be undertaken only by professionals, and which was very offensive to the Jews.

The author of this verse was not acquainted with Jewish burial customs, nor did he know much about embalming.

■ **41f.** Cf. Mark 15:42–47: when Joseph asked Pilate for the body of Jesus, Pilate would have first of all have made inquiries of the officer on watch—who must have been summoned for this purpose in the first place—whether Jesus were really already dead, and then given the body to Joseph. Joseph took the body from the cross, wrapped it in a linen shroud, placed it in a tomb hewn out of rock, and secured the tomb with a stone at the opening. There is no mention in the Markan account of bandages and, correlatively, no mention either of the arrangement of the bandages and handkerchief, which a hasty removal of the body of Jesus precludes. The apologetic attempt to do away with the tensions between Mark and John by accepting the view that Joseph cut the linen shroud up into bandages is to be rejected out of hand. More emphasis is placed on haste in the Markan report, haste prompted by the approach of the sabbath, although "buying a linen shroud" (ἀγοράσας σινδόνα, Mark 15:46) does not comport with that haste. The Johannine account overlooks the question of when the necessary bandages were acquired. The "garden"—it cannot be the same one mentioned in 18:1—belongs to a later tradition. How Mary Magdalene learned the location of the garden is not indicated.

The narrator presumably was not acquainted with the Synoptics, but knew only a passion story that had been enriched with new elements, in relation to Mark, by a scribal exegesis.

---

23   "The Burial of Jesus," 238.
24   "The Burial of Jesus," 230.
25   Billerbeck, 2: 53.

26   G. Fohrer, *BHH* 1: 212.
27   Cf. the article, "Mumie" by Forbes, *BHH* 2: 1247–49.

Overview

About the end of the nineteenth century, how one could still exploit the text for edificatory purposes is shown especially well by the third edition of Godet's commentary on John that appeared in 1885.[28] Godet is so honest that he disdains the pseudo-scientific explanation of the emergence of blood and water so popular at that time: "In our opinion, there remains only one explanation, namely, that this mysterious fact took place outside the customary laws of physiology and belongs in the context of an exceptional body that has not been affected by sin and is on the way to its resurrection without having to suffer decomposition."[29] Rather than decay, Jesus' body has already begun the resurrection! Godet likes to combine a psychologizing of the account with this supernaturalism, for example, in connection with verses 36f.: "In order to have a feeling for what John felt in the moment he is here depicting, one must imagine a Jew who is well acquainted with the OT and think of how he viewed the soldiers who appeared to break the legs of the three persons being executed. What is going on with the body of the messiah, who is still more holy than the paschal lamb?"[30] On verse 39, Godet says: "When Nicodemus saw the crucified Lord he was certainly reminded of the image of the brazen serpent that Jesus conjured up before his eyes" (3:14).[31]

The short work of Wellhausen, *Das Evangelium Johannis,* published in 1908, exhibits the marked change in the direction of scholarship that had set in in the meantime. He claims, relevant to 19:38–41: "There is no way to get around the incompatibility of the two reports. . . . It can be asserted, in favor of the second [verses 38–42] that it is an indispensable element of the narrative." Nevertheless, he repudiates it: the conclusion of the first report is cut off and Joseph and Nicodemus added.[32] The question of sources is thus pointedly posed for this section.

The entire first section, verses 16b–30, is entirely independent of the Synoptics, as details repeatedly demonstrate. This is made evident, in the first instance, by the fact that the scene with Simon of Cyrene is lacking: Jesus carries his own cross. This feature sets the tone for the entire segment: the passion—in spite of crucifixion and death—is no longer what Mark constantly drives home to his readers. The name Golgotha is taken over, and the two crucified with Jesus are mentioned, but not as robbers ($\lambda\eta\sigma\tau\alpha\dot{\iota}$); they are indispensable on account of verses 31–37. The title is expanded with the phrase "the Nazoraean" ($\dot{o}$ $N\alpha\zeta\omega\rho\alpha\hat{\iota}os$)—in accordance with a Jewish-Christian tradition? It is made clear to the reader that the title does not indicate the charge against Jesus ($\alpha\dot{\iota}\tau\dot{\iota}a$), but his exalted station, which the community—the early Jewish-Christian community?—claimed for him. That the inscription is written not only in the local language, but was also to be formulated in the two universal languages, Greek and Latin, announces the proclamation of the message of Christ to the whole world, although, for the time being, only many Jews know it. Verses 20f. are an accretion to an older text; verses 23f. likewise point to an advanced form of the tradition: the interpretation of Ps 22:19b in relation to the seamless tunic appears here for the first time. Godet holds that this tunic was "undoubtedly" a gift to Jesus on the part of the women accompanying him.[33] But perhaps we have here a play on the tunic ($\chi\iota\tau\acute{\omega}\nu$) worn by the high priest, of which Josephus writes: "The high-priest . . . puts on a tunic of blue material. This too reaches to the feet. . . . But this tunic is not composed of two pieces, to be stitched at the shoulders and at the sides: it is one long woven cloth, with a slit for the neck, parted not crosswise but lengthwise from the breast to a point in the middle of the back."[34] That could (but need not) point to an underlying Jewish-Christian tradition, which would have already attributed the office of high priest to Jesus. But our text no longer permits us to perceive such a connection.

A new scene begins with verse 25; this scene is not only unknown to the Synoptics, it is even impossible as they

28 The third German edition appeared in 1890, the English translation in 1883.
29 Godet, *John,* 3: 275.
30 Godet, *John,* 3: 279.
31 Godet, *John,* 3: 281.
32 *Das Evangelium Johannis,* 90.
33 Godet, *John,* 3: 266.
34 Josephus, *Ant.* 3.159ff. Wettstein, *Novum Testamentum Graecum,* 1: 954f. refers to this passage and to Exod 28:31–34, 39:20–24.

represent matters. They report only that women watch how Jesus was crucifed from afar. Among the women, the three Marys are named in Matt 27:56, while no names are given in Luke 23:49. In Mark 15:40, Mary Magdalene stands first, and Jesus' mother is replaced by Salome. The Synoptics never mention the disciple whom Jesus loved. The Synoptics likewise do not know the word from the cross, "I thirst" (διψῶ). Luke is silent about a drink for Jesus; Mark 15:23 relates that Jesus was offered a spiced wine, which he rejected; according to Matt 27:34, the wine is mixed with gall (Ps 69:22!), and when Jesus had tasted it, he refused to drink. John 19:30, on the other hand, implies that Jesus tasted the vinegar before he died. Verse 30 is remotely reminiscent of Luke 23:46b: "He breathed his last" (ἐξέπνευσεν). The loud cry reported by all three Synoptics does not appear in the Gospel of John: it does not fit into the narrator's notion of the death of Jesus. But more important than all these differences is the fact that the Gospel of John produces an entirely new general picture of the passion. The passion of Jesus recedes in the Gospel of John to such an extent that one can comprehend Käsemann's assertion: "The one who walks on earth as a stranger, as the messenger sent by the Father, the one who passes through death without turmoil and with jubilation, because he has been called back to the realm of freedom, has fulfilled his mission, as his last word from the cross indicates."[35] Incarnation and passion mark a change in locale for Käsemann and thus in the range of his manifestation. But exegesis thereby exceeds its boundaries, for the statement, "The word became flesh" (ὁ λόγος σάρξ ἐγένετο) is fundamentally emptied of its meaning. When Jesus really dies, that is not only a change in locale.

But Käsemann has called attention to a problem that the harmonizing apologetic of earlier times had not seen and could not see: the historicity and thus the development of the account of the passion. It develops from Mark, through Luke, to John, in the sense that exaltation comes more and more to the front. All three Synoptics are in agreement in not describing the bodily suffering of Jesus during the crucifixion. They permit the reader a glimpse into the inner passion, into its depths. For Mark, the passion of Jesus consists, in the last analysis, in Jesus'

complete forsakenness, in his total rejection. The first thing that this Evangelist narrates about the crucifixion is the dividing of Jesus' clothing (including his sandals, girdle, and covering for his head). People were stoned naked; they were presumably also crucified naked. Everything by way of earthly goods that Jesus possessed—and that was not much—was taken from him. He was treated as though he were already dead; the soldiers divide his legacy among them. That this man, who is now possessionless and defenseless, is designated the king of the Jews sounds like a mean taunt. For companions, there remain to him only the criminals. Mark certainly does not regard the "robbers" (λῃσταί) as national freedom fighters or as partisans. We no longer sense how gruesome the following mocking scene really is: the words are too familiar to us, and the gestures of those shaking their heads in derision are alien to us. The taunts ring out for the one who will allegedly destroy the temple and in three days restore it: Save yourself! Come down from the cross! After the passersby come the chief priest and the scribes, those who represent established religion. They mock him who had helped others and who is now himself helpless: You, the anointed king of Israel, please step down from the cross—if you do that, we will believe in you! He has no more to do with these representatives of his ancestral religion; he is totally ostracized by them. Whom does he have left? The two crucified with him share his agony. But that does not prevent them from mocking him: neither do they wish to be his companions in death. Jesus has nothing more to expect of humankind. They have all abandoned him. And now comes the great darkness. That darkness blankets the entire world, as though it were no longer there. Now Jesus is with God alone. But is God there? When it had again become light, after three hours of darkness, Jesus cries out: "My God, My God, why hast thou forsaken me?" Psalm 22 begins in this way. Most interpreters think Jesus is quoting the Psalm, which ends with the certainty of an indestructible unity with God. In that case, Jesus' words would be an expression of his unbroken trust in God. But did Mark understand the words in this way? Why then does he not have Jesus speak of his trust in God? What the Evangelist intends to say

---

35 *The Testament of Jesus,* 20.

here is something even more bleak than anything that has gone before: his God, the God of Jesus, has forsaken him. The passion of Jesus reaches its crest with this Godforsakenness. What now follows is like a satyr play following the tragedy. Nothing, of course, relieves the tension; but it makes the mockery sound like a bad joke. Did the man on the cross perhaps call on Elijah, the helper in distress? Good, we will wait to see whether he helps him. So that he will have the strength to wait, they take a sponge, soak it in the cheap wine vinegar of the soldiers, put it on a reed, and hold it to his mouth. But Jesus cries out and dies.

This picture of the death of Jesus could mislead the reader. Mark therefore elaborates with the remark about the rending of the curtain of the temple. By entering into the uttermost extremity of a death removed from God, on our behalf, Jesus has again opened the way for us to God. When that is not comprehended by any of the Jews standing by, then the pagan centurion on watch has to say it: "Truly, this man was the Son of God."

The palette from which Mark takes the colors for this picture offers only a black that steadily deepens. With this medium Mark has produced the most audacious sketch of the event of the crucifixion that the NT contains.

It was so harsh and appalling that it was immediately modified. Luke has sketched out a new picture: it becomes brighter in spite of the darkness of death. In Luke, Simon of Cyrene still carries the cross of Jesus. But he carries it "behind Jesus," as the first in a long line of those who will carry their cross like Jesus. How little Luke wishes to depict Jesus as downcast is shown by the episode of the weeping daughters of Jerusalem. They should not weep for him, but for themselves and their children—Luke was convinced that the destruction of Jerusalem in 70 CE was punishment for the crucifixion. He relates the act of the crucifixion very briefly, as well as the crucifixion of the two criminals to the right and left of Jesus. Without being aware of it, they have now fulfilled the prophecy of Isa 53:12 (which Luke had already mentioned in 22:37): "And he was reckoned with transgressors." Jesus' request for forgiveness for them because they know not what they do, in 23:34, is missing in the oldest manuscripts. One sees here how the portrayal of Jesus in Luke is expanded in accordance with its sense. The division of Jesus' clothing receives no empha-

sis in Luke. The people do not mock: they only stand by and watch. Of course, the "rulers" (ἄρχοντες), the leading citizens, know better and so mock the presumed messiah for all they are worth. The soldiers follow them and offer vinegar; the Elijah scene into which the vinegar is inserted in Mark would have been incomprehensible to Luke's readers. The inscription over the cross is mentioned, as though in passing, with the words, "There was also an inscription" (ἦν δὲ καὶ ἐπιγραφή). But now something very significant takes place: no longer do both criminals rail at him, but only the one. The other comes to faith in the one dying on the cross next to him and asks him to remember him when he comes into his kingdom. In response, he receives the promise: "Truly, I say to you, today you will be with me in Paradise." It is the *Christus de cruce regnans* ("the Christ reigning from the cross") that Luke so depicts. The one who came to believe in him first and his Lord will enter Paradise that very day together: the end of the agony is near. The darkness and the rending of the temple curtain become events that are ominous threats to the Jews. And finally, instead of the outcry to the absent God, we hear Jesus praying a verse outloud from Ps 31:6: "Father, into Thy hands I commend my spirit." That was the evening prayer prayed by every pious Jews before going to sleep: death has become a sleep for Jesus.

The suffering Jesus is to be seen in Luke's account as the secret victor. Of course, he must still pass through the dark vale. But beyond there already shines the bright splendor of Paradise.

The job of depicting the passion of Jesus has been assigned, in the Fourth Gospel, to the hearing scene before Pilate and the story of the burial. The death of Jesus, on the other hand, is free of all the mockery and agony reported in connection with it by the other gospels, although it remains a death; jubilation is nowhere mentioned. This remarkable modification of the picture is achieved by what is left out and by what is taken up. Omitted is Simon of Cyrene. Jesus is not in collapse. He does not need anyone to carry his cross. He does it himself. The execution of the crucifixion—only in the tradition that becomes audible in John is there reference to nailing the hands (only later do we learn that the feet were also pierced with nails) in 20:25, 27—is mentioned in a subordinate clause, "Where they crucified him," as in the other gospels. There is no place in the Gospel of John for the "street of suffering," the *via dolorosa,* which a later time, passionate by nature and which willingly took suffering on itself, arranged for Jesus' journey to death (the handkerchief of Veronica has not yet appeared in John).

The inscription, on the other hand, half hidden in Luke, becomes apparent to all the world: the whole world must recognize who Jesus is. The memorial to ignominy has become an inscription of honor.

In the case of the division of the clothing, the misunderstanding of *parallelism membrorum* has given rise to the story of the seamless robe, which only the high priest otherwise wears. The Epistle to Hebrews will develop the high priestly office further. At a later time, the seamless robe was also regarded as an allusion to the unity of the church. But John has none of these things in mind.

In contrast to these additions, one must not overlook the omissions, and especially those that give Mark's account its special character: Jesus is no longer ostracized and ridiculed by the world. Passersby no longer make their taunting remarks and gestures to the crucified. The mocking chief priests and scribes are silent. Neither the soldiers nor those crucified with him mock him. The hostile world has disappeared. The story of the darkness that engulfs the world externally is thereby made superfluous. Simultaneously, with the omission of all these features, something else and different is achieved: an unheard of concentration on the Jesus who hangs on the cross. He, and only he, is really there. It almost appears as though the cross were the one and only reality.

But that could lead to misunderstanding, as though Jesus were separated from the world in the gnostic sense, as though he existed in an absolute stillness. That is prevented by the story of the beloved disciple and the mother of Jesus, which were deliberately placed here. Jesus cares for those close to him, and he is not foresaken by them, even in death.

That he says, "I thirst" (only on account of an OT prophecy), has been inserted by an alien hand. The only thing that has to be said is rather the phrase (not derived from the OT), "It is finished," that hovers over the cross and the life of Jesus like a true inscription.

The second section of our story treats the burial of Jesus. It will repay us, before we set out the proper perspective on the problems, to cite an exegete who published his commentary on John a generation ago, F. Büchsel.[36] He was convinced that it was John, the son of Zebedee, the beloved disciple, who was here reporting as an eyewitness. "Verses 31–37 are without parallels in the Synoptics," he asserts first of all.[37] But that does not shake his confidence in the "Johannine version." Because according to Deut 21:23 someone was hanged causes the land to be defiled if he is left over night, and in view of the sabbath that begins at sundown, the Jews ask Pilate to take the crucified down from the cross. They are "to be killed quickly by shattering their legs, which is also known elsewhere as a painful but quick means of putting to death. That is superfluous in the case of Jesus. The soldiers confirm that he is dead and are satisfied to stab him with a spear, which, in the event of an error on their part, makes resuscitation impossible. . . . The words of John about the emergence of blood and water probably imply nothing more than he is really dead and was a man like other men."[38]

This remarkably sensible explanation presupposes that here John, the son of Zebedee, intends to supplement the synoptic account. As soon as one rejects this presupposition—what would have prompted the synoptic writers to pass over this material?—an entirely different solution presents itself: this passage is a prime example of how early Christian exegesis worked creatively with the passion story. Primitive Christian biblical erudition interpreted passages from the Psalms that refer to the suffering innocent to refer to Jesus in many cases. And that is what happened here: Ps 34:21 is referred to Jesus. It was thus prophesied of him, "Not a bone of him shall be broken." In that case, the possibility must have existed for someone to want to break the legs of Jesus. Breaking the legs with a club was otherwise, of course, an independent form of punishment, especially in the case of slaves who had run away and were caught. If that is threatened in our story, the reason for it only could be that Jesus' death had to hurried—and naturally that of the two crucified with him—because the beginning of the sabbath was at hand. And so it came about that the Jews requested that Pilate take this step, who, in turn,

---

36   *Das Evangelium nach Johannes,* ²1935.
37   *Das Evangelium nach Johannes,* 174.
38   *Das Evangelium nach Johannes,* 174.

gave the requisite command. However, when the soldiers came to Jesus, he was already dead, and crushing his legs was unnecessary. With this ingenious reconstruction was combined a second: Zech 12:10, a verse that has been uncertainly transmitted, was also taken to refer to the passion of Jesus. This verse was taken to mean that he must have been "pierced." That was connected with the story preceding by having a soldier stab him in the (left) side. This was not "a part of the execution ritual," as one piece of modern erudition taking its flight of fancy supposes.[39] Nor is it attested as such elsewhere. The wound in the side, along with the nail marks in his hands, now became, in the tradition transmitted by the Gospel of John, an important and definite mark of the resurrected Christ and his identification with the "historical" Jesus (John 20:20, 25, 27).

But the attempt to gain new edifying ground was not brought to a close with that. That is shown by the fact that verse 36 does not connect with verse 35, but with "pierced" ($\H{\epsilon}\nu\upsilon\xi\epsilon\nu$) in verse 34, and that in Rev 1:7 the verse from Zechariah can be quoted without reference to blood and water. The tradition that blood and water poured out following the spear thrust is not derived from the OT. One could not therefore point to such a passage, but had to appeal to the testimony of someone who had seen it. He remains anonymous, but can only be the disciple who stood by the cross, according to later Johannine tradition. In any case, in 21:24, he is only designated as the one who bears witness to these things. That means, as Bultmann has already seen,[40] that the redactor has here introduced his theology of the sacraments: baptism and the Lord's Supper obtain their power from Jesus' death on the cross.[41]

Büchsel's explanation that the spear thrust only demonstrates that Jesus is really dead[42] overlooks the fact that it is superfluous following verse 31. The second thing that the spear thrust is taken to demonstrate, namely, that Jesus was a man like other men, is not cognizant of the fact that the effect of the spear thrust is just the opposite. Büchsel was not thinking of something different than what Kennard was considering: when did the Jews ask Pilate to take Jesus down from the cross? Only when the sabbath drew near and Jesus was already dead? That would have been too late. For Pilate was not at hand. He is available on a moment's notice only in the narrative. Was it therefore already early in the morning, following the announcement of the judgment, as Kennard thinks?[43] In that case, verse 31 has been inserted in the wrong place. It is so unnecessary for a spear thrust to follow after verse 30 that Kennard makes it a part of the execution ritual, and it would then be executed on those crucified with Jesus as well. In that case, breaking their legs would have been pointless. The narrator does not think of all these problems. He is only happy to be able to show that God's providence looks over Jesus even after his death.

Verses 38–40 are reminiscent of the synoptic tradition. The comment on individual verses has indicated how many problems are connected with this passage. The appearance of Nicodemus with one hundred liters of myrrh and aloes to embalm Jesus has been explained by ingenuous interpreters, like Büchsel, as evidence of his high regard for Jesus.[44] But Büchsel hastens to add that the text does not say that the entire amount was used. If Jesus' body had been wrapped in this way, the women could not of course have come later to anoint him. That explains why 20:1 does not indicate why Mary comes to the tomb. Moreover, the text says nothing about to whom the tomb belongs. It is difficult to believe that Joseph would have made use of a strange grave. Was it therefore his own? But would he have located it next to a place of execution, of all places? To what ends "realistic investigators" go when faced with such questions becomes clear again in the case of Kennard: he reckons with a double burial of Jesus; the watch set at the grave mentioned by Matthew was bribed by Joseph, just as he bribed Pilate. In this respect, the Jews were correct in

---

39 Kennard, "The Burial of Jesus," 229.

40 *John*, 677f. [525].

41 Cf. 3:5 and 6:51–58.

42 Wettstein, *Novum Testamentum Graecum*, 1: 956f., attests that in the ancient world a wound in the heart was considered absolutely fatal.

43 "The Burial of Jesus," 228.

44 *Das Evangelium des Johannes*, 175.

their assertion that the disciples "stole" the body of Jesus.[45]

John 19:31–37 and 38–42 stem from different traditions, which do not comport with each other. The uses of the verb "to take away, remove" ($a\H{\i}\rho\epsilon\iota\nu$) in verses 31 and 38 do square with each other. The two accounts, as they lie before us, are late; the Markan account might be considerably older. One does not do the Johannine story of the descent from the cross and the entombment justice if one endeavors to prove that one or the other of the details is historical. It is designed to persuade the believer that God's gracious plan, conceived long ago, is being fulfilled here, and that Jesus, in spite of everything, received an honorable burial and not the ignominious end of a law breaker.

---

45 "The Burial of Jesus," 238.

43. The Appearances of Jesus and the First Conclusion

Bibliography

A. Easter Appearances

Alsup, John E.
The Post-Resurrection Appearance Stories of the Gospel Tradition. A history-of-tradition analysis with Text-Synopsis, Calwer Theologische Monographien 5 (Stuttgart: Calwer Verlag, 1975).

Bacon, Benjamin Wisner
"Immortality in the Fourth Gospel." In *Religion and the Future Life. The Development of the Belief in Life after Death* ed. E. H. Sneath (New York: Fleming H. Revell, 1922) 259–94.

Ballenstedt, Heinrich Christian
"Jesus überraschet seine Schüler bey verschlossenen Thüren und macht sie amtsfähig. Joh 20,19–23." In his *Philo und Johannes; oder, Neue philosophisch-kritische Untersuchung des Logos beym Johannes nach dem Philo, nebst einer Erklärung und Uebersetzung des ersten Briefes Johannes aus der geweiheten Sprache der Hierophanten,* 3 vols. (Braunschweig: F. B. Culemann, 1802); *oder, Fortgesetzte Anwendung des Philo zur Interpretation der Johanneischen Schriften; mit besonderer Hinsicht auf die Frage: ob Johannes der Verfasser der ihm zugeschriebenen Bücher seyn könne?* (Göttingen: H. Dieterich, 1812) 142–48.

Becker, Jürgen
Auferstehung der Toten im Urchristentum, SBS 82 (Stuttgart: Katholisches Bibelwerk, 1976) 117–48.

Bligh, John
The Sign of the Cross. The Passion and Resurrection of Jesus according to St. John (Slough: St. Paul Publications, 1975).

Curtis, K. Peter G.
"Three Points of Contact Between Matthew and John in the Burial and Resurrection Narratives." *JTS,* n.s., 23 (1972) 440–44.

Dodd, Charles Harold
"The Appearance of the Risen Christ." In *Studies in the Gospels. Essays in Memory of R. H. Lightfoot,* ed. D. E. Wineham (Oxford: Blackwell, 1967) 9–35.

Duparc, L. H.
"Le premier signe de la Résurrection chez saint Jean. Jean 20,7." *BVC* 86 (1969) 70–77.

Feuillet, André
"Les christophanies pascales du quatrième évangile sont-elles des signes?" *NRT* 97 (1975) 577–92.

Finegan, Jack
Die Überlieferung der Leidens- und Auferstehungsgeschichte Jesu, BZNW 15 (Giessen: A. Töpelmann, 1934), esp. 93–97.

Fuller, Reginald Horace
The Formation of the Resurrection Narratives (New York: Macmillan, 1971).

Grass, H.
Ostergeschehen und Osterberichte (Göttingen: Vandenhoeck & Ruprecht, ²1962), esp. 51–85.

Hoffmann, Paul
"Auferstehung." In *Theologische Realenzyklopädie*, ed. Gerhard Krause and Gerhard Müller (Berlin: Walter de Gruyter, 1979) 4: 478–513.

Kegel, Günter
Auferstehung Jesu—Auferstehung der Toten. Eine traditionsgeschichtliche Untersuchung zum Neuen Testament (Gütersloh: Gerd Mohn, 1970).

McNamara, Martin
"The Ascension and the Exaltation of Christ in the Fourth Gospel." *Scr* 19 (1967) 65–73.

Mees, Michael
"Erhöhung und Verherrlichung Jesu im Johannes-evangelium nach dem Zeugnis neutestamentlicher Papyri." *BZ* 18 (1974) 32–44.

Michaelis, Wilhelm
Die Erscheinungen des Auferstandenen (Basel: H. Majer, 1944).

Michel, Otto
"Ein johanneischer Osterbericht." In *Studien zum Neuen Testament und zur Patristik. Erich Klostermann zum 90. Geburtstag dargebracht*, TU 77 (Berlin: Akademie-Verlag, 1961) 35–42.

Moule, Handley Clarr Flyn
Jesus and the Resurrection. Expository Studies on St. John XX. XXI (London: Seeley, 1893).

Nebe, August
Die Auferstehungsgeschichte unsers Herrn Jesu Christi nach den vier Evangelien ausgelegt (Wiesbaden: Niedner; Philadelphia: Schäfer & Koradi, 1882), esp. 48–108, 179–338.

Perrin, Norman
The Resurrection According to Matthew, Mark, and Luke (Philadelphia: Fortress Press, 1977).

Riggenbach, Eduard
"Die Quellen der Auferstehungsgeschichte, mit besonderer Berücksichtigung des Schauplatzes der Erscheinungen." In *Aus Schrift und Geschichte; Theologische Abhandlungen und Skizzen Herrn Prof. D. Conrad von Orelli zur Feier seiner 25-jährigen Lehr-tätigkeit in Basel von Freunden und Schülern gewidmet* (Basel: R. Reich, 1898) 109–53.

Schwank, Benedikt
"Die Ostererscheinungen des Johannesevange-liums und die Post-mortem-Erscheinungen der Parapsychologie." *Erbe und Auftrag* 44 (1968) 36–53.

Thüsing, Wilhelm
Die Erhöhung und Verherrlichung Jesu im Johannes-evangelium, NTAbh 21, 1–2 (Münster: Aschen-dorf, 1960, ²1970).

Wetter, Gillis Petersson
"Religionsgeschichtliche Studien zu dem vierten Evangelium mit Ausgangspunkt 'Verherrli-chung.'" *Religionswissenschaft* 2 (1918) 32–113.

B.   John 20:1–31

Aland, Kurt
Studien zur Überlieferung des Neuen Testaments und seines Textes, Arbeiten zur Neutestamentlichen Textforschung 2 (Berlin: Walter de Gruyter, 1967).

Becquet, G.
"Le Christ ressuscité transfère sa mission à la communauté des croyants (Jn 20,19–31)." *Esprit et vie* 80 (1970) 193–96.

Benoit, Pierre
"Marie-Madeleine et les Disciples au Tombeau selon Joh 20,1–18." *Judentum, Urchristentum, Kirche. Festschrift für Joachim Jeremias*, ed. W. Eltester (Berlin: A. Töpelmann, 1960) 141–52.

Bode, Edward Lynn
The First Easter Morning. The Gospel Accounts of the Women's Visit to the Tomb of Jesus, AnBib 45 (Rome: Pontifical Biblical Institute, 1970).

Burney, D. F.
The Aramaic Origin of the Fourth Gospel (London: Clarendon Press, 1922).

Cadbury, Henry Joel
"The Meaning of John 20:23, Matthew 16:19 and Matthew 18:18." *JBL* 58 (1939) 251–54.

Charpentier, E.
"Jour de pâques: Le tombeau vide (Jn 20.1–9)." *Esprit et vie* 79 (1969) 262–66.

Colwell, Ernest Cadman
The Greek of the Fourth Gospel. A Study of its Arama-isms in the Light of Hellenistic Greek (Chicago: University of Chicago Press, 1931).

Crome, Friedrich Gottlieb
"Ueber Lk 1,1–4 und Joh 20,30–31." *TSK* 2 (1829) 754–66.

Cook, J. I.
"Joh 20,19–23—An Exegesis." *Reformed Review* (Holland, MI, 1967) 2–10.

Curtis, K. Peter G.
"Luke xxiv,12 and John xx,3–10." *JTS*, n.s., 22 (1971) 512–15.

Dalman, Gustaf Hermann
Grammatik des Jüdisch-Palästinischen Aramäisch nach den Idiomen des palästinischen Talmud des Onkelos-targum und Prophetentargum und des Jerusalemischen Targum (Leipzig: J. C. Hinrichs, 1894, ²1905; Darmstadt: Wissenschaftliche Buchgesellschaft, 1960).

Dauer, Anton
"Die Herkunft der Tomasperikope Joh 20,24–29." In *Biblische Randbemerkungen. Schülerfestschrift für Rudolf Schnackenburg zum 60. Geburtstag*, ed. H. Merklein and J. Lange (Würzburg: Echter Verlag, 1974) 56–76.

Dayton, Wilber T.
"The Greek Perfect Tense in Relation to Jn 20,23." Dissertation, Chicago, 1953.

Dupont, Liliane et al.
"Recherche sur la structure de Jean 20." *Bib* 54 (1973) 482–98.

Erdozain, Luis
La función del signo en la fe según el cuarto evangelio (Rome: Pontifical Biblical Institute, 1968).

Feuillet, André
"La communication de l'Esprit-saint aux Apôtres (Jn, XX 19–23) et le ministère sacerdotale de la réconciliation des hommes avec Dieu." *Esprit et vie* 82 (1972) 2–7.

Feuillet, André
"L'apparition du Christ à Marie-Madeleine *Jean 20,11–18*. Comparison avec l'apparition aux disciples d'Emmaüs *Luc 24,13–35.*" *Esprit et vie* 88 (1978) 193–204, 209–23.

Fowler, David C.
"The Meaning of 'Touch Me Not' in John 20,17." *EvQ* 47 (1975) 16–25.

Fuller, Reginald Horace
"John 20,19–23." *Int* 32 (1978) 180–84.

Ghiberti, Giuseppe
I racconti pasquali del cap. 20 di Giovanni confrontati con le altre tradizioni neotestamentarie, Studi Biblici 19 (Brescia: Paideia, 1972).

Ghiberti, Giuseppe
"Gv 20 nell' esegesi contemporanea." *Studia Patavina* 20 (1973) 293–337.

Ghiberti, Giuseppe
"'Abbiamo veduto il Signore.' Struttura e messaggio dei racconti pasquali in S. Giovanni." *Parole di Vita* 15 (1970) 389–414.

Groenewald, E. P.
"The Christological meaning of John 20:31." *Neot* 2 (1968) 131–40.

Harnack, Adolf von
New Testament Studies. Vol. 3, *The Acts of the Apostles,* tr. J. R. Wilkinson (New York: G. P. Putnam's Sons; London: Williams & Norgate, 1909) = *Die Apostelgeschichte* (Leipzig: J. C. Hinrichs, 1908).

Hartmann, Gert
"Die Osterberichte in Joh 20 im Zusammenhang der Theologie des Johannesevangeliums." Dissertation, Kiel, 1963.

Hartmann, Gert
"Die Vorlage der Osterberichte in Joh 20." *ZNW* 55 (1964) 197–220.

Kierkegaard, Sören
Die Tagebücher, ed. and tr. Hayo Gerdes (Düsseldorf: E. Diederich, 1962) 104.

Kruijf, Theo C. de
"'Hold the Faith' or, 'Come to Believe'? A Note on John 20,31." *Bijdragen. Tijdschrift voor philosophie en theologie* 36 (1975) 439–49.

Langbrandtner, Wolfgang
Weltferner Gott oder Gott der Liebe? Der Ketzerstreit in der johanneischen Kirche. Eine exegetisch-religions-geschichtliche Untersuchung mit Berücksichtigung der koptisch-gnostischen Texte aus Nag-Hammadi, Beiträge zur biblischen Exegese und Theologie 6 (Frankfurt: P. Lang, 1977), esp. 35–38.

Lee, G. M.
"Presbyters and Apostles." *ZNW* 62 (1971) 122.

Lindars, Barnabas
"The Composition of John xx." *NTS* 7 (1960/1961) 142–47.

Mahoney, Robert
Two Disciples at the Tomb. The Background and Message of John 20,1–10, Theologie und Wirklichkeit 6 (Bern: H. Lang; Frankfurt: P. Lang, 1974).

Mantey, Julius Robert
"The Mistranslation of the Perfect Tense in John 20:23, Mt 16:19 and Mt 18:18." *JBL* 58 (1939) 243–49.

Márquez, M.
"El Espíritu Santo, principio de la nueva creación, en función de la misión apostólica en Jn 20,21–22." *Semana bíblica Española* 26 (1969) 121–48.

Minear, Paul S.
"'We don't know where . . .' John 20,2." *Int* 30 (1976) 125–39.

Mollat, Donatien
"La découverte du tombeau vide Jn 20,1–9." *AsSeign* 21 (1969) 90–100.

Neirynck, Frans
"PARAKYPSAS BLEPEI. Lc 24,12 et Jn 20,5." *ETL* 53 (1977) 113–62.

Neirynck, Frans
"*Apēlthen pros heauton.* Lc 24,12 et Jn 10,10." *ETL* 54 (1978) 104–118.

Neirynck, Frans
"Les Femmes au Tombeau. Etude de la rédaction Matthéenne (Matt. xxviii.1–10)." *NTS* 15 (1968/1969) 168–90.

Niccacci, Alviero
"La fede nel Gesù storico e la fede nel Cristo risorto. (Gv 1,19–51//20,1–29)." *Antonianum* 53 (1978) 423–442.

Osborne, Basil
"A Folded Napkin in an Empty Tomb: John 11:44 and 20:7 Again." *HeyJ* 14 (1973) 437–40.

Pereira, Francis
"Maria Magdalena apud sepulcrum (Jo 20,1–18)." *VD* 47 (1969) 1–21.

Perles, Felix
"Noch einmal Mt 8,22, Lk 9,60 sowie Joh 20,17." *ZNW* 25 (1926) 286–87.

Pflugk, Ulrich
"Die Geschichte vom ungläubigen Thomas in der Auslegung der Kirche von den Anfängen bis zur Mitte des 16. Jahrhunderts." Dissertation, Hamburg, 1966.

Prete, Benedetto
"Beati coloro che non vedono e credono (Giov. 20,29)." *BeO* (1967) 97–114.

Richter, Georg
"Der Vater und Gott Jesu und seiner Brüder in Joh 20,17. Ein Beitrag zur Christologie des Johannes-

evangeliums." In his *Studien zum Johannes-evangelium*, ed. Josef Hainz. BU 13 (Regensburg: F. Pustet, 1977) 266–80.

Salvoni, Fausto
"The So-Called Jesus Resurrection Proof (John 20:7)." *Restoration Quarterly* 22 (1979) 72–76.

Suggit, J.
"The Eucharistic Significance of John 20.19–29." *Journal of Theology of South Africa* 16 (1976) 52–59.

Suriano, T.
"Doubting Thomas: An Invitation to Belief." *Bible Today* 53 (1971) 309–15.

Thyen, Hartwig
Studien zur Sündenvergebung im Neuen Testament und seinen alttestamentlichen und jüdischen Voraussetzungen, FRLANT 96 (Göttingen: Vandenhoeck & Ruprecht, 1970), esp. 243–51.

Thyen, Hartwig
"Aus der Literatur zum Johannesevangelium." *TRu* 39 (1974) 1–69, 222–52, 289–330; 42 (1977) 211–70; 43 (1978) 328–59; 44 (1979) 97–134, esp.: 3: 224–26, 232–34, 261–69; 4: 341, 352; 5: 127–28.

Violet, Bruno
"Ein Versuch zu Joh 20,17." *ZNW* 24 (1925) 78–80.

Vaganay, Léon
"La finale du quatrième Evangile." *RB* 45 (1936) 512–28.

20

1 Now on the first day of the week Mary Magdalene came to the tomb early, while it was still dark, and saw that the stone had been taken away from the tomb. 2/ So she ran, and went to Simon Peter and the other disciple, the one whom Jesus loved, and said to them, "They have taken the Lord out of the tomb, and we do not know where they have laid him." 3/ Peter then came out with the other disciples, and they went toward the tomb. 4/ They both ran, but the other disciple outran Peter and reached the tomb first; 5/ and stooping to look in, he saw the linen cloths lying there, but he did not go in. 6/ Then Simon Peter came, following him, and he went into the tomb; he saw the linen cloths lying, 7/ and the napkin, which had been on his head, not lying with the linen cloths but rolled up in a place by itself. 8/ Then the other disciple, who reached the tomb first, also went in, and saw and believed; 9/ for as yet they did not know the scripture, that he must rise from the dead. 10/ Then the disciples went back to their homes. 11/ But Mary stood weeping outside the tomb, and as she wept she stooped to look into the tomb; 12/ and she saw two angels in white, sitting where the body of Jesus had lain, one at the head and one at the feet. 13/ They said to her, "Woman, why are you weeping?" She said to them, "Because they have taken away my Lord, and I do not know where they have laid him." 14/ Saying this, she turned round and saw Jesus standing, but she did not know that it was Jesus. 15/ Jesus said to her, "Woman, why are you weeping? Whom do you seek?" Supposing him to be the gardener, she said to him, "Sir, if you have carried him away, tell me where you have laid him, and I will take him away." 16/ Jesus said to her, "Mary."

She turned and said to him in Hebrew, "Rabboni!" (which means Teacher). 17/ Jesus said to her, "Do not hold me, for I have not yet ascended to the Father; but go to my brethren and say to them, 'I am ascending to my Father and your Father, to my God and your God.'" 18/ Mary Magdalene went and said to the disciples, "I have seen the Lord"; and she told them that he had said these things to her. 19/ On the evening of that day, the first day of the week, the doors being shut where the disciples were, for fear of the Jews, Jesus came and stood among them and said to them "Peace be with you." 20/ When he had said this, he showed them his hands and his side. Then the disciples were glad when they saw the Lord. 21/ Jesus said to them again, "Peace be with you. As the Father has sent me, even so I send you." 22/ And when he had said this, he breathed on them, and said to them, "Receive the Holy Spirit. 23/ If you forgive the sins of any, they are forgiven; if you retain the sins of any, they are retained." 24/ Now Thomas, one of the twelve, called the Twin, was not with them when Jesus came. 25/ So the other disciples told him, "We have seen the Lord." But he said to them, "Unless I see in his hands the print of the nails, and place my finger in the mark of the nails, and place my hand in his side, I will not believe." 26/ Eight days later, his disciples were again in the house, and Thomas was with them. The doors were shut, but Jesus came and stood among them, and said, "Peace be with you." 27/ Then he said to Thomas, "Put your finger here, and see my hands; and put out your hand, and place it in my side; do not be faithless, but believing." 28/ Thomas answered him, "My Lord and my God!" 29/ Jesus said to him, "Have you believed because you have seen me? Blessed are those who have not seen and yet believe."

30 Now Jesus did many other signs in the presence of the disciples, which are not written in this book; 31/ but these are written that you may believe that Jesus is the Christ, the Son of God, and that believing you may have life in his name.

■ 1 Early in the morning on Easter Sunday (cf. Luke 24:1), Mary Magdalene went to the tomb. She alone is left of all the women in the synoptic tradition (three in Mark 16:1, two in Matt 28:1, more than three in Luke 24:1; cf. Luke 8:2f. and 24:10). Although it is still dark, she can see that the stone has been removed from the door.

■ 2 An insertion begins with verse 2: without examining matters more closely, she hurries away to Peter and to the "other disciple whom Jesus loved"—they are together in Jerusalem (contrary to 16:32)—and she says to them: "They have taken the Lord (τὸν κύριον perhaps corresponds to τὸν κύριόν μου in v 13) away and we do not know where they have laid him." It is difficult to determine whether this "we" is a trace of the synoptic tradition known to the redactor (= several women), or an oriental manner of speaking,[1] which also has a counterpart in Greek.[2] That Mary says the same thing in verses 13 and 15, without satisfying herself more closely, goes together with the fact that the redactor does not grant Mary the prerogative of having seen the empty tomb first.

■ 3 In response to the alarming report of Mary ("then, therefore," οὖν, as in vv 6, 8, 10f., 19f., 30), Peter and the "other disciple whom Jesus loved" went out (out of the house, or a Semitism?) and ran to the tomb (cf. Luke 24:12). This verse, which is lacking in D a b e l r¹, is not an insertion in John 20, as has been assumed: it was omitted because it contradicted Luke 24:24, according to which several disciples went to the tomb. For that reason, Luke 24:12 now began to be recognized as the original text.[3] Luke 24:12, 24 could have been the thing that prompted the redactor to introduce the "disciple whom Jesus loved" (ἐφίλει) into the account alongside Peter, and even to have the former excel the latter.

■ 4f. Since the "other disciple" ran faster than Peter, he reached the tomb first and, stooping, looked in and was the first to see lying there the bandages in which Joseph of Arimathea and Nicodemus had wrapped the body of Jesus. But the redactor does not allow this disciple to enter the tomb as yet.

■ 6 And thus he can allow Peter to be the first to go into the tomb (here he probably fastens onto a tradition). Peter now also sees the linen cloths lying there (cf. John 19:40); but this look does not convey anything important to him.

■ 7 And Peter also sees the napkin that had been placed on the face of the dead man, neatly folded up and laid aside. Bandages and "napkin, handkerchief" (σουδάριον) demonstrate that the theft of the body by the disciples is not involved. The redactor evidently knows the legend

mentioned in Matt 27:64, 28:13–15, *Gospel of Peter*, 5. 30, Justin, *Dial.* 108.2, Tertullian, *Spec.* 30, *Apol.* 23.

■ 8 Now for the first time the "other disciple" also enters the tomb and sees what Peter had seen. In his case, however, what he sees causes him to believe in the resurrection. In this way, it is possible for the redactor, on the one hand, to give Peter the honor of being the first to enter the tomb, and, on the other, to represent the "other disciple" (who was the first to arrive outside the tomb) as being the first to come to faith in the resurrection. That he does not say anything about Peter having this faith makes it clear that the other disciple alone returned home from the empty tomb as a believer.

■ 9 Verse 9 gives the reason it was necessary for the disciples to see the empty tomb, the bandages, and the like, in order to come to faith: they did not yet know that the scripture foretold the resurrection of Jesus. Acts 2:25–28 refers to Ps 16:8–11 (cf. Acts 13:35). There is thus no reason to omit this verse as a later addition, or to think that Peter also became a believer. The lack of knowledge of the scripture makes both points comprehensible: one disciple becomes a believer, the other doesn't. But that the "other disciple" becomes a believer once again shows that he is superior to Peter.

■ 10 The insertion comes to a close with this verse (cf. on v 2): the two disciples return to their homes. Mary Magdalene cannot share the faith of the "other disciple" because otherwise the continuation of the story about the disconsolate and weeping woman would become senseless.

■ 11 This verse does not go well with what precedes: Mary, who had not participated in the footrace of the two disciples, suddenly appears at the tomb, weeping. This situation returns to that of verse 1. It is uncertain what the tradition that the redactor adapted for his insertion looked like. Bultmann regards the episode of the angels, introduced with verse 11, as original: "It corresponds to the type found in Mark 16:5–7."[4] The Evangelist (!) eliminated the original conclusion to the

1   Dalman, *Grammatik des jüdisch-palästinensischen Aramäisch* (Leipzig: J. C. Hinrichs, 1894, ²1905; Darmstadt: Wissenschaftliche Buchgesellschaft, 1960) 265f.

2   Colwell, *The Greek of the Fourth Gospel. A Study of its Aramaisms in the Light of Hellenistic Greek* (Chicago: University of Chicago Press, 1931) 111f.

3   Haenchen, *Acts*, 58f.; Aland, *Studien zur Überlieferung des Neuen Testaments und seines Textes,* Arbeiten zur Neutestamentlichen Textforschung 2 (Berlin: Walter de Gruyter, 1967) 157.

4   *John*, 682 [529].

story of Mary (acceptance of the message by the disciples), Bultmann conjectures, and replaced it with verses 14–18. But it is unlikely that the Evangelist was at work at this point, and in the way that Bultmann supposes. The moment one no longer ascribes the account of the footrace to the Evangelist, but attributes it to the redactor, one will also credit the redactor with the features that approximate the synoptic tradition (i.e., the mention of the angel), but will pinpoint the message of the Evangelist in the encounter between Mary and Jesus. The awkwardness of the continuation, "and as she wept" ($\dot{\omega}s$ $o\tilde{\upsilon}\nu$ $\check{\epsilon}\kappa\lambda\alpha\iota\epsilon\nu$), permits us to recognize how difficult it was to work the activity of Mary into the account. That she stoops down to look into the tomb—it appears to be a burial chamber—"within which the real grave is found as a trough or as a bench,"[5] is reminiscent of verse 5. Bultmann thinks that it is possible that motifs from the story of Mary are employed in verses 3ff.[6] But actually only "to stoop down" ($\pi\alpha\rho\dot{\epsilon}\kappa\upsilon\psi\epsilon\nu$) comes into consideration, and this term leads to an entirely different sequence than in verses 3ff.

■ **12** Mary sees two angels in white garments sitting in the tomb—to the surprise of many readers and scholars like Wellhausen–[7] one at the head, and one at the foot of the place where Jesus' body had been laid. The one angel in Mark 16:5, like the one in Matt 28:5, and the "two men in dazzling apparel" in Luke 24:4, have the collective task of interpreting the fact of the empty grave and giving instructions for the communication of Jesus' resurrection to the disciples. Since the disciple whom Jesus loved is said to have come to faith on his own, however, the two angels could not yet become visible to him and to Peter. But because an encounter between Mary and Jesus himself is to follow in verses 14ff., the angels cannot play the role of interpreting angels, as they do in the Synoptics. The reason they are introduced at all is because the redactor, who was presumably familiar with the synoptic tradition, mentions them because they are part of that tradition.

■ **13** The attempt to assign some further role to the angels leads to the question they pose to Mary: "Woman, why are you weeping?" To this Mary can respond only with her earlier complaint: they have taken Jesus' body

away, and she does not know where. The angels are unable to respond to this; otherwise they would rob Jesus' conversation with Mary of its content. Consequently, the action has to take a new turn at this point.

■ **14** The fresh turn comes when Mary, who had been looking into the burial chamber up to this point, looks around and thus into the open and sees Jesus standing there, whom she does not recognize. This motif—the risen Jesus is unrecognizable (cf. Luke 24:16, John 21:4)—is designed to show that the risen Jesus is not accessible like he once was.

■ **15** Jesus now directs the question of the angels to Mary, but asks further whom she seeks. She mistakes him for the gardener—according to 19:41 the tomb was located in a garden—and asks him where he had taken the body, in the event he was the one who did; she wants to take the body away. This picture is not realistic: how is the woman to take the body away (it is presumably already decaying) and where has she prepared a grave? But the narrator has not asked himself these questions, since what they presuppose does not fit the story: Jesus is risen!

■ **16** Jesus responds to this with a single word: he names only her (Aramaic) name. At that she turns around. The word $\sigma\tau\rho\alpha\phi\epsilon\hat{\iota}\sigma\alpha$ ("turning") appears now to be meaningless in view of $\dot{\epsilon}\sigma\tau\rho\dot{\alpha}\phi\eta$ ("she turned") in verse 14; it is perhaps a scribal error. But for reasons of rhythm, one hesitates to dispense with it. Was the redactor thinking only of a turning of the head in verse 14, and now there follows a turning of the entire body? Mary answers in Aramaic, and also with a single word: "Rabboni!" The meaning assigned to it is "Teacher!" The form "Rabboni" contradicts the form used in the *Targum Onkelos*, רַבּוֹנִי. But Black holds that the pronunciation in the *Targum Onkelos* probably reflects a literary language that was never spoken; the form $\dot{\rho}\alpha\beta\beta\upsilon\upsilon\iota$ ("Rabbouni") preserved in verse 16 and Mark 10:51 appears to reflect precisely the real pronunciation in the time of Jesus, according to recent finds.[8]

■ **17** Jesus' answer has given rise to various interpretations. Inspired by C. F. Burney and G. R. Driver, B. Violet attempted to demonstrate that an Aramaic word is involved, with the sense "attach oneself to a person" (from the stem *dabaq*), which may also mean "follow."

---

5   Bultmann, *John*, 684 n. 6 [530 n. 6], in dependence on Dalman, *Sacred Sites and Ways*, 371ff.

6   *John*, 682 [528].

7   *Das Evangelium Johannis*, 92.

8   Black, *An Aramaic Approach*, 21. On this point, cf. the Overview.

The actual sense of the passage would then be: "Follow me."[9] But the saying known in its Latin translation as *noli me tangere* would not in that case be explained. For if Jesus now ascends to the Father—and what else could be involved?—how is the woman supposed to be able to follow him there? The conjecture of Perles, to substitute πτόου ("to desire passionately") for ἅπτου ("touch"), deserves no more than a mere mention.[10] Barrett takes πτόου meaning "fear not" into consideration as an explanation only as a last possibility, if no other offers itself.[11] In Matt 28:9, the women who are meeting the resurrected Jesus approach him and touch (ἐκράτησαν) his feet. Our narrator possibly wants to exclude something of this kind: the risen Lord must not be worshiped with the customary form of the greeting (*proskunein*: to prostrate oneself before).[12] The real difficulty lies in the fact that there is no intermediate state between the one who is already resurrected and his existence with the Father—at least, if one does not conceive the resurrection as a return to a mundane state (cf. the story of the raising of Lazarus). The tradition that is repeated here is still trapped by a naive form of conceptualization (today often taken as the only really orthodox position): it is conceived as an alteration within the mundane realm, as is the ascent to the Father. The Evangelist makes use of this tradition on account of its vividness, but attempts, at the same time, to correct it. That becomes clear in our passage, but even more in verse 29.

The words "not yet" (οὔπω κτλ.) are intended to make it possible for Thomas to touch Jesus later on. But it is far from the Evangelist's mind to ascribe to the risen Jesus a kind of intermediate state, in which he still goes about on earth like he did before his death (cf. Acts 1), or returns to earth again as though some spatial distance separated God and the world (vv 14, 26). In reality, the Evangelist presupposes a demythized concept of the resurrection, in which Jesus returns as a spirit. Mary appears to encounter Jesus in a state in which the transition from his earthly form to a state of spirituality has not yet taken place (this is told in reliance on a crude tradition); the Evangelist also felt this state, which is impossible to our way of thinking, to be inappropriate. For that reason, he cuts short a further conversation with Mary in which he has Jesus ask Mary to tell the disciples that he will return to the Father. By giving this order, Jesus takes on the role, so to speak, that belongs to *angelus interpres* in the angel tradition. The distinction between "my Father" and "your Father" and between "my God" and "your God" has sometimes been interpreted to mean that Jesus intends to emphasize how different his relationship to God is compared with that of the disciples. But that is to miss the intention of the Evangelist. He really intends to say that the God of Jesus is now also the God of the disciples, that the Father of Jesus is the same as the Father of the disciples. The distinction in relationship to God between Jesus and the disciples has been abolished and not continued, as will be repeated in verses 21f. in another form.

■ **18** Mary carries out this order: she does not mention the angels, but reports only her encounter with Jesus and his command, which is understandably not quoted again word for word. Nor is it reported how the disciples behave in response to this message. That is reserved for the next scene, which, in a certain sense, only confirms what Jesus had already instructed Mary to say to them. But the significance of the resurrection of Jesus for the disciples becomes much clearer there.

■ **19** A new scene opens with this verse, and extends as far as verse 23. After Jesus has first appeared to Mary alone, who is therefore the first to have seen the resurrected Jesus, he now comes to the disciples themselves. They have gathered together behind closed doors, "for fear of the Jews." This expression is to be explained on the grounds that the Jews are not regarded here as a people, but as community hostile to Christians, from which the disciples (who are also of course Jews by birth) are to be basically distinguished. At the same time, this is an indication of the relationship of Jews and Christians towards the end of the first century CE. As someone resurrected, Jesus is no longer subject to mundane limitations: that is illustrated by his arrival through closed doors. He greets his disciples with the peace greeting. "Peace" here has the meaning of Hebrew "shalom," that encompasses everything meant by "health, salvation."

■ **20** Verse 20 may have been inserted by the redactor:

---

9   "Ein Versuch zu Joh 20,17," *ZNW* 24 (1925) 78–80.
10 "Noch einmal Mt 8,22, Lk 9,60, sowie Joh 20,17," *ZNW* 25 (1926) 286–87.

11 *John*, 565.
12 Bultmann, *John*, 687 and n. 2 [532 n. 6], also takes this position.

the account of the wounds in his side is found only in 19:34 and is there to be regarded as a later addition. The appearance of Jesus fills the disciples with joy (however, cf. the version in Matt 28:17, which deviates from this). As the resurrected one, he is called here "the Lord" (ὁ κύριος) and wherever he is spoken of in the third person.

■ **21** In order to get the story interrupted by verse 20 going again, the redactor has Jesus repeat the peace greeting. There follows the statement that comes from the hand of the Evangelist (cf. 17:18), which is here enunciated directly as the commission: "As the Father has sent me, even so I send you." The disciples—and not just the twelve or an elite group or spiritual leaders— enter into the office and position of Jesus. On their words hang the decision whether the hearers will find the way to the Father or miss it. Power and service are joined.

■ **22** Just as God once breathed his spirit into man in the creation story (Gen 2:7), so Jesus now does so with the words: "Receive the Holy Spirit." At this point Easter and Pentecost fall together. What, in the belief of the Evangelist, was not yet possible for Jesus during his earthly life he now dispenses to his disciples: the spirit, which will lead them into all truth and will disclose to them the message of Christ as the truth. Of course, they will all learn about the limitations that were indicated earlier in 17:9, 24: the Father has not given all human-kind to Jesus and his disciples.

■ **23** That the community has the power and the right to forgive and not to forgive sins is asserted in a different form in Matt 16:19 and 18:19. That does not belong to the Johannine message. In the Johannine view of things, it does not depend on the will of man whether one will be numbered among the disciples. No one can perceive, on his or her own, the word of Jesus and his message as God's admonition; whether one hears it as such depends on the will of the Father. We therefore have to do, in this verse, with one of those additions of the redactor, who constantly demonstrates that he is familiar with the synoptic tradition.

■ **24** In intention this verse is the counterpart of Luke 24:36–43: the tradition that is incorporated here attempts to overcome the doubt that grew stronger—no doubt, as the result of the death of the first witnesses.

Luke and the source of the Evangelist propose to vanquish this doubt by showing that such a doubt had already bestirred itself among the disciples and is refuted by Jesus himself. If one examines the matter more closely, it becomes clear that the Thomas scene does not really go with what precedes: for, the commissioning of the disciples and their endowment with the spirit applies to all the disciples. In Matt 28:17, those doubting are not mentioned by name. John 20:29 shows how the Evangelist has added his correction to this tradition.

■ **25** Thomas receives what was only accessible to the second generation and the generations to follow and what, in the view of the Evangelist, was the only thing Jesus gave to the first disciples: the word. For, there is no verifying experience (miracle!) by which we can be convinced of God's reality with objective certainty.

■ **26** But now the unexpected happens: on the next Sunday the disciples are again gathered—behind closed doors—and Jesus again appears in their midst and greets them as before. Now it must be indicated whether and how Thomas came to faith. Kierkegaard wrote in 1837: "If Christ is to come in order to dwell in me, that has to transpire in accordance with the heading of the gospel for the day in the calendar: 'Christ enters through closed doors.'"[13] That applies not only to Kierkegaard.

■ **27** Jesus offers Thomas the opportunity he had requested: he may convince himself by visual inspection and touching that Jesus has really been resurrected, of course with the added admonition: "Do not be faithless, but believing." We are not told whether the narrator thinks of the wounds of Jesus as having been healed in the meantime. In any case, the scars will prove the identity of the risen with the earthly Jesus.

■ **28** The answer of Thomas suggests that he did not make use of the opportunity he requested to verify the resurrection, but joins in the confession of the church without it: "My Lord and my God." Since the Father is visible in Jesus for those who believe, in the view of the Evangelist, the Thomas story appears to concur entirely with the theology of the Evangelist. But that is not the case, as verse 29 shows.

■ **29** Verse 29 evidently provides the Evangelist's correction of this faith: "You have believed me because you

---

13   *Die Tagebücher*, ed. and tr. Hayo Gerdes (Düsseldorf: E. Diederich, 1962) A II 730.

have seen me. Blessed are those who have not seen and yet believe." Bultmann objects: "Does not the reproach of Thomas apply to all the other disciples as well? All of them indeed, like Mary Magdalene, believed only when they saw; and this applies also to the two mentioned in vv 3–8, who indeed were convinced not through the appearance of the Risen Lord but through the sight of the empty grave. Thomas demanded no other proof than Jesus had freely offered the others (v 20). Then does the blessing extol those born later, because they have this precedence over the first disciples, in that they believe without seeing, and precisely on the basis of the disciples' word? That can hardly be possible."[14]

Bultmann answers this question in the following way: "Rather the doubt of Thomas is representative of the common attitude of men, who cannot believe without seeing miracles (4.48). As the miracle is a concession to the weakness of man, so is the appearance of the Risen Jesus a concession to the weakness of the disciples. . . . Fundamentally it ought not to be the sight of the Risen Lord that first moves the disciples to believe 'the word that Jesus spoke' (2.22), for this word alone should have the power to convince them."[15] There seems to us to be a mixture of the true and the false. John does not say that Peter came to belief in the tomb when he saw the linen cloths, etc., and that contradicts the Evangelist's attempt to exhibit the superiority of that "other disciple" with respect to Peter. Further, it apparently overlooks the fact that, in the view of the Evangelist (7:39b), the disciples did not perceive the Father in Jesus (14:8f.) in the period when they were eyewitnesses of the earthly Jesus. Yet Thomas now requests that he not only be granted sight, but says that he wants to touch the wounds of Jesus. Touching in those days was the surest means of ascertaining the reality of some phenomenon. In this respect, the request of Thomas stands out from what was granted to all eyewitnesses. Moreover, we have already indicated that verse 20 was inserted by the redactor. On the other hand, Bultmann is right in pointing out that these Easter stories do not quite fit the theology of the Evangelist: they are all derived from earlier tradition, not of course from the earliest.[16] In fact, for the Evangelist, the true Christians are those of a later generation, who never saw the earthly nor the risen Jesus, but only knew the message that had been transmitted to them, with respect to which they came to faith. As a consequence, they, and not Thomas, are blessed. The faith of Thomas attempts to verify God like a thing present within the world. By not blessing this faith, the Evangelist is correcting the conception of faith handed down in the tradition. He thereby also rejects as imperfect that tradition which attempts to overcome doubt by palpable proof of the visible, as in Luke 24:36–43.

■ **30f.** Verses 30f. probably formed the conclusion to the "gospel" from which the Evangelist selected, omitted things, and which he supplemented and improved. Not all of the deeds of Jesus are recorded in this book—for the source that means: not all the miracles; for the Evangelist it means: not all the pointers—but only some of them. But the selection that the book contains ought to lead to faith in the Son of God. The Evangelist himself had used this old "gospel" with all its miracle stories. He had understood it in an entirely different sense, to be sure, than its author, but he believed firmly—one ought not to doubt that—that Jesus had really performed all these great miracles. In this respect, it was not difficult for him to take over these miracle stories (nor the passion narrative either). These miracles were proofs that Jesus was the Son of God for his predecessor. He hoped, as a result, that its reiteration would also awaken faith in Jesus among persons beyond the eyewitnesses. It was of course incomprehensible that so great a demonstration of power had not converted the entire Jewish people. They must have been stiff-necked not to acknowledge their own king (19:15).

The Evangelist agreed with his predecessor that the Jews were alienated from and hostile to God. But he understood the word σημεῖα, which the author had interpreted as "miracle," in the sense of "sign, pointer, allusion," a meaning the word σημεῖα can also have. That permitted him to see the relation of man to God and of human possibilities vis-à-vis God in an entirely new light. God the "Father" is not accessible to humankind: no one has ever seen God. He is therefore only made known by the revelation of him who had tarried at the bosom of the unseen Father. But this revealer, this one sent by

---

14 Bultmann, *John*, 696 [539].
15 *John*, 696 [539].
16 Cf. the discussion in the Overview.

God, did not find faith in his earthly activity. That is a fact that the reader of the Gospel of John readily overlooks. Not only the Jews, but also the disciples, are uncomprehending up to the passion; they do not understand that the Father can be seen in Jesus. Only the resurrected one can pour out the spirit on them (20:22), which will cause them to know Jesus truly and thus to turn them into those sent by Jesus, just as he was sent by the Father.

Overview

Sixty years ago the voices of critical and uncritical scholars could still be heard side by side. In his commentary on John, Zahn saw nothing difficult in chapter 20.[17] The "we know" ($o\emph{i}\delta\alpha\mu\epsilon\nu$) of verse 2 shows that other women had also gone to the tomb and had seen more than Mary Magadene had,[18] but only Mary Magdalene had run to the house where Peter and the disciple whom Jesus loved lived. This disciple, who was John, the son of Zebedee, did not mention that Peter had also become a believer "because . . . he recalled the powerful shift in mood that he had experienced in that moment."[19] One can clearly see how the psychology which Zahn imports at this point causes a problem to disappear. The Evangelist, so we read further, by no means "thought of" the risen Jesus as "afflicted permanently with scars," although Zahn does not notice that he shatters the evidential power of his argument by so doing.[20] "The breath breathed out of the mouth of Jesus into the disciples does not penetrate them internally, . . . but touches them only externally";[21] this has nothing to do with the sending of the paraclete, with the pouring out of the spirit on Pentecost. In this manner the text is interpreted in accordance with ecclesiastical tradition and dogma.

Wellhausen's little book, *Das Evangelium Johannis*, appeared in the same year, 1908; this book was loaded with critical dynamite, including a critical examination of chapter 20.[22] Verse 2b, "they have taken the Lord out of the tomb and we do not know where they have laid him,"

anticipates an assertion that occurs at the right point only in verse 11, for it is only then that "Mary Magdalene peered into the grave." The form "we know" ($o\emph{i}\delta\alpha\mu\epsilon\nu$) therefore perhaps appears because the redactor was thinking of the synoptic account where several women come to the tomb. The redactor inserted verses 2–10. Jesus' expression, "I have not yet ascended to the Father" seems to have as it point of departure "that Jesus appeared to the disciples only after his ascension and that therefore the touching of him by Thomas took place only afterwards."[23]

More recently, so cautious and reserved a scholar as C. H. Dodd has attempted to show that the Evangelist first formed the presentation of this chapter out of a series of oral traditions, in which non-synoptic elements deserve careful treatment.[24] In fact, the various traditions in this chapter regarding the empty grave and the appearances of Jesus can be combined into a unified picture only with considerable effort (whether only individual oral traditions were involved is another question). But we understand this composition only when we recognize what its development and modification have produced and in what, nevertheless, its unity consists.

The oldest tradition that we possess on the subject is quoted for us by Paul in 1 Cor 15:1–8. He says explicitly that he took this tradition over and that he passes it on as a matter of first importance. When examined closely, it falls into two distinct parts. Verses 3f. state that "Christ died for our sins in accordance with the scriptures, that he was buried, that he was raised on the third day in accordance with the scriptures." The first and the third claims are supported explicitly by references to the OT. We do not learn which passage or passages provide this evidence.

How did Paul conceive the resurrection of Christ as expressed in this passage? According to 1 Cor 15:20–23, Paul appears to have thought of the resurrection of Christians (who had already died at the time of the parousia) as analogous to that of Christ. The resurrection

17 *Das Evangelium des Johannes*, 672–89.
18 *Das Evangelium des Johannes*, 673.
19 *Das Evangelium des Johannes*, 674.
20 *Das Evangelium des Johannes*, 678.
21 *Das Evangelium des Johannes*, 679.
22 *Das Evangelium Johannis*, 91–95.
23 *Das Evangelium Johannis*, 93.
24 *Tradition*, 140–51.

of Christians is described in 1 Cor 15:52 and 1 Thess 4:15–17: it is not the decomposed body that will be made living again (as is presumed in the story of Lazarus). Rather, simultaneous with the resurrection a transformation takes place—flesh and blood cannot inherit the kingdom of God (1 Cor 15:20). Christians receive a new, different kind of "spiritual" body, in which they will be taken up to meet the Lord in the air. If Paul conceived Jesus' resurrection in a way corresponding to this event, that would then imply: on the third day Christ received such a "spiritual body" ($\sigma\hat{\omega}\mu\alpha$ $\pi\nu\epsilon\nu\mu\alpha\tau\iota\kappa\acute{o}\nu$) and is thus taken up to God, leaving behind him an empty grave.[25] But Paul says nothing about an empty grave, since, for him, the decisive thing was the resurrected Lord, the "Lord of glory" ($\kappa\acute{\nu}\rho\iota\sigma$ $\tau\hat{\eta}\varsigma$ $\delta\acute{o}\xi\eta\varsigma$), whom he has seen.

That brings us to the second part of the tradition Paul is citing, 1 Cor 15:5–7. In this part it is stated (connected grammatically to the preceding with "and that"): "and that he appeared to Cephas, then to the Twelve. Then he appeared to more than five hundred brethren at one time, most of whom are still alive, though some have fallen asleep. Then he appeared to James, then to all the apostles." He is no longer speaking of the witness of scripture, but of what the series of witnesses named have seen. They are mentioned in chronological order. That Paul himself is included in verse 6b is all but certain on formal grounds. It is a matter for conjecture whether there resonates the expectation, in this connection, that these eyewitnesses would not die prior to the parousia. But it is very likely that Paul added verse 6b in order to show that there were many, many more witnesses to whom appearances had occurred and who could vouch for what they had seen. Harnack, who was always quite happy to advance hypotheses, also advanced three conjectures in this connection, and owing to the reputation he enjoyed, they received undeserved approbation.[26] In the first place, he believed that Acts 2 and 5:17–42 are doublets, blocks of material that are intrusive and objectionable within chapters 2–5.[27]

Secondly: the enthusiasm of the first believers, "the 5,000, which probably means 500," grew into ecstasy at the return of the persecuted apostles;[28] that may have been "the real, historical Pentecost"! The sleight-of-hand by which he divides the 5,000 by ten by a mere "probably," allows him to find here the appearance to the 500 brethren at one time in 1 Cor 15:6a, although Luke never intimates such a thing. Finally, he conjectures that the apostles left Jerusalem after twelve years and James took over the leadership of the community. "It was perhaps only after his death, however, that the legends arose that Jesus had appeared to him first. . . ."[29] We can exclude the possibility that Paul (who, moreover, was with Peter for fourteen days in Jersusalem three years after his conversion and during this period also conversed with James, the Lord's brother, as we learn from Gal 1:18f.) communicated so recent a tradition to the Corinthians, one he himself had just received.

Paul added his own vision of Christ as the sixth to the list of five transmitted to him (1 Cor 15:8). That makes sense only if it were of the same type, that is, if it were a matter, in each instance, of the Christ who had already been exalted to God making his appearance. Put differently, between the resurrection of Jesus on the third day, confirmed by the reference to scripture, and his exaltation to God's right hand, there were not the forty days there were in Acts, during which Jesus was indeed raised, but stayed on earth for a time and ate and drank with the apostles (Acts 10:41). There is an evident shift in outlook in this passage, which presumably arose in the community when those who had been witnesses of the resurrection died off. The confession that Paul transmits in 1 Cor 15:3–5 disappeared with surprising speed from the consciousness of the Christian community. The formula, "the Lord has risen indeed and has appeared to Peter," appears only in Luke 24:34, awkwardly inserted into the account of the disciples on the road to Emmaus.

Why do we not have other early witnesses for this original Christian Easter tradition? An answer is sug-

---

25 H. Grass, *Ostergeschehen und Osterberichte* (Göttingen: Vandenhoeck & Ruprecht, [2]1962) 185, interprets differently.

26 He advanced these conjectures in his *Acts of the Apostles*, vol. 3 of his *New Testament Studies*.

27 *Acts of the Apostles*, 142.

28 *Acts of the Apostles*, 146.

29 *Acts of the Apostles*, 127.

gested by the emphasis on the doubt respecting the reality of the resurrection in the gospels of Matthew, Luke, and John. In Matt 28:17, we are told only that some of the disciples doubted when they saw Jesus on the mountain in Galilee. The Evangelist trumps this doubt by means of the majestic pronouncement of Jesus: "All authority has been given to me in heaven and on earth" (Matt 28:18). The doubt proves to be more tenacious in Luke 24:36ff. Here the disciples think that they have seen a ghost—for this Luke thoughtfully uses the term "spirit" ($\pi\nu\epsilon\hat{\upsilon}\mu\alpha$). When Jesus shows them his hands and his feet and asks them to touch him—a spirit does not have flesh and blood like he has—that does not settle the matter: they still have doubts. Only when Jesus eats a piece of fish in front of them (24:41–43) are their doubts quelled. In John 20:24–28, Thomas requests not only to see the nail marks, but also to touch the nail holes and the wound in his side; otherwise he will not believe. Only when he is given this palpable proof of the reality of the resurrection does he erupt in the confession: "My Lord and my God" (20:28).

The basis of the doubt, as becomes especially apparent from Luke 24, is that one could throw suspicion on the appearance of the resurrected Jesus as a mere "vision," or, put in modern terms, as a mere subjective sensory perception; the resurrection could and was suspected of having been just such a thing. It was a matter, therefore, of describing the reality of the appearances so that this doubt was eliminated. As a consequence, we find a description in Luke 24:41–43 of the conduct of the resurrected Jesus which would have sounded blasphemous to Paul. The Fourth Gospel expresses its critique of the story of Thomas and the faith of Thomas in John 20:29.

There was also a second opportunity to protect the reality of the resurrection from doubts. This second possibility is provided by the (later) account of the women finding the tomb empty. When the disciples found the empty tomb, that was not yet fatal for their doubt—the Jews had indeed claimed, as Matthew relates, that the disciples had stolen the body and so caused the grave to be empty. Moreover, people were at first convinced that the disciples were scattered following the arrest of Jesus and had returned to Galilee—John 21 is, of course, a distorted echo of this tradition. Joseph of Arimathea had no reason to go looking for the tomb that

belonged to him on Easter morning. There thus remain only the women who had accompanied Jesus; the anointing of the body could function as their motive. When they found the tomb empty, the doctrine of the resurrection on the third day was no longer confirmed by an uncertain scripture reference alone, but by the eyewitness testimony of the women, who had presumably watched the burial from a distance.

It immediately becomes apparent, nevertheless, that the women finding an empty tomb was not enough: the empty tomb admitted of various explanations, as John 20:13 demonstrates. The fact of the empty tomb therefore requires interpretation. This task demands an *angelus interpres* or two of them. But could it have ended there? Did not this piece of news have to be communicated to the disciples? This form of the tradition is shown by Mark 16:1–7. In this passage, the women receive instructions to tell the disciples that Jesus has risen and goes before them into Galilee, where they will see him. The tradition of the empty tomb and the women is connected in this way with that of the disciples. But weren't the disciples still in Jerusalem? Or how could the women reach them? Mark has avoided this difficulty by having the women remain silent out of fear and having them say nothing to anyone. This also explains why the tradition of the women, which was truly late, had not been known earlier.

These events have been complicated in Matthew by virtue of the fact that he inserts the legend of the guard at the tomb. The guards block the entrance to the tomb. But the appearance of the angel, who opens the tomb, puts the guards out of action, and permits the women to learn the good news. While they are on their way to the disciples, they meet Jesus himself and can verify his reality for themselves when they grasp his feet in the customary greeting ($\pi\rho o\sigma\kappa\upsilon\nu\epsilon\hat{\iota}\nu$). Jesus repeats the instructions given to them earlier by the angels, who then see Jesus on the mountain in Galilee.

In Luke 24:1–12, a rather large number of women are permitted to discover the empty tomb at first, and to be instructed by two angels, but were not subsequently believed by the disciples. Only Peter runs to the tomb (v 12), sees the linen cloths, and returns wondering what had happened. According to verse 24, which is again derived from another tradition (the Emmaus disciples), even some of the disciples went to the tomb and found it as the women had described it, but without meeting Jesus. The dénouement then brings Jesus himself, who suddenly appears in their midst.

The Fourth Gospel originally used another variant of the tradition of the empty tomb. It has been obscured by the redactor, who inserts the footrace of the disciples. It probably had the following shape: Mary Magdalene went alone to the tomb and found it empty. Jesus, whom she takes for the gardener, asks the weeping woman whom she seeks. She asks him to turn the body over to her, in the event he has taken it away. But instead of a corpse, she now sees the living Jesus. Jesus speaks only a single, Aramaic word to her: her name, "Miriam." She likewise answers with a single, Aramaic word: "Rabbouni" ("My master"). She is then given the task of telling the disciples that Jesus now goes to his and their Father and God.

This entire account is preparation, in the mind of the Evangelist, for the coming of Jesus to the disciples, in spite of the closed doors. The redactor has also introduced a synoptic feature into the account (vv 20, 21a, as far as the greeting, "Peace be with you"). Verse 23, known from the Synoptics, probably also goes back to him. The account of the Evangelist is of utmost simplicity, which nevertheless indicates the essentials. Jesus gives them the greeting of peace, bestows the spirit on them by breathing into them as God breathed into Adam at the creation, and turns them into those sent of God, just as he has been sent by God.

The word *ecclesia,* which primitive Christianity used to designate both the individual church and the church as a whole, does not appear in the Gospel of John any more than it does in Mark. But also the circle of the twelve, which plays such an important role in the Synoptics, has all but lost its significance for John. Judas the betrayer is designated by the traditonal term in 6:71, as is the disciple Thomas in 20:24: one of the twelve. Further, Jesus mentions at the end of chapter 6 what has not been told earlier, namely, that he had chosen the twelve. But when Peter answers the question about whether they will forsake Jesus with a passionate confession of faith in Jesus, Jesus responds: "Did I not chose you, the twelve? And one of you is a devil. He spoke of Judas the son of Simon Iscariot, for he, one of the twelve, was to betray him" (6:70f.). It cannot be said that this context is adequate to put the twelve in a clear light. But there is something else that is even more important: when the

risen Jesus comes to the disciples and pours out the spirit on them, the twelve are not mentioned, but "the disciples are." That is no accident. The saying of Jesus: "As the Father sent me, so I send you" makes all the disciples into apostles, turns them into ones that are sent in the sense just indicated. What is expressed by the doctrine of the priesthood of all believers is very strongly emphasized in this passage: there is a *successio apostolica,* but all believers belong to that succession. John uses the word apostle only once, in 13:16: "A servant is not greater than his master; nor is he who is sent [i.e., an apostle] greater than he who sent him." This word is again spoken to the disciples, whose feet Jesus had washed at the last supper. The modern reader usually thinks of the twelve in connection with this scene. But John says nothing of the kind; he again speaks only generally of "the disciples." Nor does John mention the church as an institution. What is important to him is genuine discipleship, the true follower. The genuine, however, now gains a significance that exceeds that which is the right of an institution: he now stands before those of his time as a fully authorized emissary, just as Jesus did in his generation. And, just as Jesus became salvation and judgment, by means of his word, for his hearers, so the disciples now have the same function vis-á-vis their hearers. The disciple is the one sent, of course, because he has been sent by Jesus himself; in other words, the spirit with which the disciple is endowed and which leads him or her into all truth, has been poured out by the exalted Lord. We see in the fourth Evangelist what kind of power can be conferred on one in this process. For, the fourth Evangelist wrote his gospel afresh for his own time as just such a disciple, and in it he has had to say things which the disciples who went around with Jesus had still not comprehended.

This is not to say, by any means, that there were not, in the time of John, distinctions like those we know from the letters of Paul, distinctions among specific gifts and offices, like apostle, prophet, teacher, deacon, and many others. But for John that was not the most important issue. What was critical for him was the Lord whom God had sent and who, in turn, sends all Christians. It is not surprising that, when the institutional church became secularized, the "spiritual church" of John inspired Christians as the ideal in relation to which the church was to be reformed. But this "spiritual church" was not suited as a reform program of an institution. As John represents him, the Christ looks at the individual and says to him or her, as he did to Peter (21:22), "You, follow me!"

The Evangelist thereby finds a concrete form for what cannot really be represented concretely: the sending of the spirit, the paraclete.

What is the upshot of this development? The Easter story has retained the meaning, "The Lord is really risen." Yet, in so doing, it has become more diverse and more unified. More diverse: there is no more agreement about the names and number of women who play a part, than there is about the number and words of the angel(s). Further, whether the women met Jesus himself and whether and with what success the disciples got the message, is variously reported. On the other hand, one thing is clear: the Easter story is concentrated increasingly on Jerusalem. For, that is where the tomb was, that is where the women were, and in some accounts the disciples also. The representation of the risen Jesus becomes more mundane, more palpable, out of concern that he could fade away into a "spirit."

The fourth Evangelist follows a different course. He understood the Easter tradition as a cipher for the coming of the spirit. But in so doing he does not deal adequately with the folk tradition. His picture of the risen one, which suffers from the tension between literalness and what he really intends to say, was painted over in traditional style and thereby becomes quite a puzzle, entirely apart from the victory of the beloved disciple who competes with Peter. Only the one who becomes immersed in the text of the Gospel of John, both lovingly and critically, can still discern the original contours and colors of this painting.

44. The Epilogue

Bibliography

Ackroyd, Peter R.
"The 153 Fishes in John XXI.11—A Further Note." *JTS*, n.s., 10 (1959) 94.

Agourides, Savas C.
"The Purpose of John 21." In *Studies in the History and Text of the New Testament in honor of Kenneth Willis Clark, Ph.D*, ed. B. L. Daniels and M. J. Suggs. Studies and Documents 29 (Salt Lake City, UT: University of Utah Press, 1967) 127–32.

Arvedson, Tomas
"Några notiser till tva nytestamentliga perikoper." *SEÅ* 21 (1956) 27–29.

Bacon, Benjamin Wisner
"The Motivation of John 21,15–25." *JBL* 50 (1931) 71–80.

Bauer, Johannes Baptist
"'Oves meae' quaenam sunt? (Jo. 21,15ff. et 10,16)." *VD* 32 (1954) 321–24.

Bleek, Friedrich
"Gegen Baur's Annahme, dass mit Joh 21 auch Kap. 20,30.31 später Anhang sei." In his *Beiträge zur Einleitung und Auslegung der heiligen Schrift.* Vol. 1, *Beiträge zur Evangelien-Kritik* (Berlin: G. Reimer, 1846) 179–81.

Boice, James Montgomery
Witness and Revelation in the Gospel of John, Contemporary Evangelical Perspectives (Grand Rapids: Zondervan, 1970).

Boismard, Marie-Emile
"Le chapitre XXI de saint Jean: essai de critique littéraire." *RB* 54 (1947) 473–501.

Burton, Henry
"The Breakfast on the Shore." *Expositor,* 5th ser. (1895) 456–72.

Camaldolese, Thomas Matus
"The First and the Last Encounter (Joh 1 and cap. 21)." *Bible Today* 42 (1969) 2893–97.

Cassien, Bishop
"John xxi." *NTS* 3 (1956/1957) 132–36.

Chapman, John
"We Know that his Testimony is True." *JTS* 31 (1929/1930) 379–87.

Cross, John A.
"On St. John XXI,15–17." *Expositor,* 4th ser., 7 (1893) 312–20.

Dodd, Charles Harold
"Note on John xxi.24." *JTS*, n.s., 4 (1953) 212–13.

Eberhardt, Max
Ev. Joh c. 21. Ein exegetischer Versuch als Beitrag zur johanneischen Frage (Leipzig: Verlag der Dürr'schen Buchhandlung, 1897).

Edwards, Hubert Edwin
The Disciple who Wrote these Things. A New Inquiry into the Origins and Historical Value of the Gospel

according to St. John (London: J. Clarke, 1953).

Emerton, John Adney
"Some New Testament Notes." *JTS*, n.s., 11 (1960) 329–36.

Emerton, John Adney
"The 153 fishes in John XXI,23–25." *Theology* 20 (1930) 229.

Gaechter, Paul
"Das dreifache 'Weide meine Lämmer'!" *ZKT* 69 (1947) 328–44.

Gils, Felix
"Pierre et la foi au Christ ressuscité." *ETL* 38 (1962) 5–43.

Ghiberti, Giuseppe
"Mission e primato de Pietro sec. Gv 21." *Atti della settimana biblica* 13 (1967) 167–214.

Glombitza, Otto
"Petrus—der Freund Jesu. Überlegungen zu Joh xxi, 15ff." *NovT* 6 (1963) 277–85.

Grant, Robert M.
"One-Hundred-Fifty-Three Large Fishes." *HTR* 42 (1949) 273–75.

Grimm, Wilibald
"Ueber Evangelium Joh 21,22f." *ZWT* 18 (1875) 270–78.

Grosheide, F. W.
"Jn 21,24 en de Canon." *Gereformeerd theologisch tijdschrift* 53 (1953) 117–18.

Gwynn, John
"On the external Evidence alleged against the Genuineness of St. John XXI,25." *Hermanthena* 19 (1893) 368–84.

Handschke, Johann Carl Lebrecht
De authentia cap. XXI ev. Johannei, e sola orationis indole, indicanda (Leipzig: J. F. Glueck, 1818).

Hilgenfeld, Adolf
"Die Rätselzahl Joh 21.11." *ZWT* 41 (1898) 480.

Horn, Karl
Abfassungszeit, Geschichtlichkeit und Zweck von Evangelium des Johannes, Kap. 21. Ein Beitrag zur johanneischen Frage (Leipzig: A. Deichert, 1904).

Jonge, Marinus de
"The Beloved Disciple and the Date of the Gospel of John." In *Text and Interpretation. Studies in the New Testament presented to Matthew Black*, ed. E. Best and R. McL. Wilson (New York and London: Cambridge University Press, 1979) 99–114.

Klöpper, Albert
"Das 21. Capitel des 4. Evangeliums." *ZWT* 42 (1899) 337–81.

Kohlbrügge, Hermann Friedrich
Der Herr der Erde. Eine Auslegung von Johannes 21 (Berlin: Furche-Verlag, 1937).

Kruse, Heinz
"Magni Pisces Centum Quinquaginta Tres (Jo 21,11)." *VD* 38 (1960) 129–48.

Lee, G. M.
"Joh xxi,20–23." *JTS*, n.s., 1 (1950) 62–63.

Lorenzen, Thorwald
"Johannes 21." Dissertation, Zurich, 1970.

Lorenzen, Thorwald
Der Lieblingsjünger im Johannesevangelium. Eine redaktionsgeschichtliche Studie, SBS 55 (Stuttgart: Katholisches Bibelwerk, 1971).

Losada, Diego A.
"El relato de la pesca milagrosa." *RB* 40 (1978) 17–26.

Marrow, Stanley B.
John 21—An Essay in Johannine Ecclesiology (Rome: Gregorian University, 1968).

McEleney, Neil J.
"153 Great Fishes (John 21,11)—Gematriacal Atbash." *Bib* 58 (1977) 411–17.

Pesch, Rudolf
Der reiche Fischfang. Lk 5,1–11 / Jo 21,1–14. Wundergeschichte-Berufungserzählung-Erscheinungsbericht, Kommentare und Beiträge zum Alten und Neuen Testament (Düsseldorf: Patmos-Verlag, 1969)

Peterson, Erik
"Zeuge der Wahrheit." In his *Theologische Traktate* (Munich: Kösel, 1951) 165–224.

Reim, Günter
"Johannes 21—Ein Anhang?" In *Studies in New Testament Language and Text. Essays in Honour of George D. Kilpatrick on the Occasion of his sixty-fifth Birthday*, ed. J. K. Elliott. NovTSup 44 (Leiden: E. J. Brill, 1976) 330–37.

Rissi, Mathias
"Voll grosser Fische, 153, Joh 21,1–14." *TZ* 35 (1979) 73–89.

Romeo, Joseph A.
"Gematria and John 21:11—The Children of God." *JBL* 97 (1978) 263–64.

Scott, John A.
"The Words for 'Love' in John 21,25ff." *The Classical Weekly* 39 (1945/1946) 71–72; 40 (1946/1947) 60–61.

Shaw, Alan
"The Breakfast by the Shore and the Mary Magdalene Encounter as Eucharistic Narratives." *JTS*, n.s., 25 (1974) 12–26.

Shaw, Alan
"Image and Symbol in John 21." *ExpTim* 86 (1975) 311.

Sheehan, John F. X.
"Feed my Lambs." *Scr* 16 (1964) 21–27.

Smalley, Stephen S.
"The Sign in John xxi." *NTS* 20 (1973/1974) 275–88.

Solages, Bruno de and J. M. Vacherot
"Le Chapitre XXI de Jean est-il de la même plume que le reste de l'Evangile?" *BLE* 80 (1979) 96–101.

Sortino, Placido M. de
"La vocazione di Pietro secondo la tradizione sinottica e secondo S. Giovanni." *Atti della settimana biblica* 19 (1966) 27–57.

Scheffer, H.-L.

Examen critique et exégétique du XXI. Chap. de l'évangile selon S. Jean (Strassburg: F. G. Levrault, 1839).

Thomas, W. H. Griffith

"The Purpose of the Fourth Gospel: John 21." *BSac* 125 (1968) 254–62.

Thompson, J. M.

"Is John XXI an Appendix?" *Expositor*, 8th ser., 10 (1915) 139–47.

Thyen, Hartwig

"Entwicklung innerhalb der johanneischen Theologie und Kirche im Spiegel von Joh 21 und der Lieblingsjüngertexte des Evangeliums." In *L'Evangile de Jean. Sources, rédaction, théologie*, ed. M. de Jonge. BETL 44 (Gembloux: Duculot; Louvain: University Press, 1977) 259–99.

Vermeil, Frank

Etude sur le 21. chapitre de l'évangile selon S. Jean (Strassbourg: Berger-Levrault, 1861).

Weber, Michael

Authentia capitis ultimi evangelii Johannis hujusque evangelii totius et primae Joh. Epistolae, argumentorum internorum usu, vindicata, Miscellaneous dissertations 119 (Halle: Fr. Ruff, 1823).

21

1   After this Jesus revealed himself again to the disciples by the Sea of Tiberias; and he revealed himself in this way. 2/ Simon Peter, Thomas called the Twin, Nathanael of Cana in Galilee, the sons of Zebedee, and two others of his disciples were together. 3/ Simon Peter said to them, "I am going fishing." They said to him, "We will go with you." They went out and got into the boat; but that night they caught nothing. 4/ Just as day was breaking, Jesus stood on the beach; yet the disciples did not know that it was Jesus. 5/ Jesus said to them, "Children, have you any fish?" They answered him, "No." 6/ He said to them, "Cast the net on the right side of the boat, and you will find some." So they cast it, and now they were not able to haul it in, for the quantity of fish. 7/ That disciple whom Jesus loved said to Peter, "It is the Lord!" When Simon Peter heard that it was the Lord, he put on his clothes, for he was stripped for work, and sprang into the sea. 8/ But the other disciples came in the boat, dragging the net full of fish, for they were not far from the land, but about a hundred yards off. 9/ When they got on land, they saw a charcoal fire there, with fish lying on it, and bread. 10/ Jesus said to them, "Bring some of the fish that you have just caught." 11/ So Simon Peter went aboard and hauled the net ashore, full of large fish, a hundred and fifty-three of them; and although there were so many, the net was not torn. 12/ Jesus said to them, "Come and have breakfast." Now none of the disciples dared ask him, "Who are you?" They knew it was the Lord. 13/ Jesus came and took the bread and gave it to them, and so with the fish. 14/ This was now the third time Jesus was revealed to the disciples after he was raised from the dead. 15/ When they had finished breakfast, Jesus

said to Simon Peter, "Simon, son of John, do you love me more than these?" He said to him, "Yes, Lord; you know that I love you." He said to him, "Feed my lambs." 16/ A second time he said to him, "Simon, son of John, do you love me?" He said to him, "Yes, Lord; you know that I love you." He said to him, "Tend my sheep." 17/ He said to him the third time, "Simon, son of John, do you love me?" Peter was grieved because he said to him a third time, "Do you love me?" And he said to him, "Lord, you know everything; you know that I love you." Jesus said to him, "Feed my sheep. 18/ Truly, truly, I say to you, when you were young, you girded yourself and walked where you would; but when you are old, you will stretch out your hands, and another will gird you and carry you where you do not wish to go." 19/ (This he said to show by what death he was to glorify God.) And after this, he said to him, "Follow me." 20/ Peter turned and saw following them the disciple whom Jesus loved, who had lain close to his breast at the supper and had said, "Lord, who is it that is going to betray you?" 21/ When Peter saw him, he said to Jesus, "Lord, what about this man?" 22/ Jesus said to him, "If it is my will that he remain until I come, what is that to you? Follow me!" 23/ The saying spread abroad among the brethren that the disciple was not to die; yet Jesus did not say to him that he was not to die, but, "If it is my will that he remain until I come, what is that to you?"

24 This is the disciple who is bearing witness to these things, and who has written these things; and we know that his testimony is true. 25/ But there are also many things which Jesus did; were every one of them to be written, I suppose that the world itself could not contain the books that would be written.

■ 1 "After this" (μετὰ ταῦτα) is again used as a transitional phrase.[1] But it does not connect up with 20:30f. Since Jesus reveals himself here for the third time (v 14), 21:2 actually connects up with 20:29. The two preceding appearances are narrated in 20:19–23 and 20:20, 24–29. The appearance to Mary Magdalene in 20:1–10 is not taken into consideration; strictly speaking, Jesus did not appear to the disciples there either. That fact that in the very first of all his appearances the risen Jesus presented himself to a woman may have played a role in this enumeration. Mary Magdalene, who played a significant role in Christian Gnosticism, also experienced opposition in that connection; that is proved by logion 114 in the

1   Cf. 3:22, 5:1, 6:1, 7:1; μετὰ τοῦτο, 2:12.

Gospel of Thomas.[2] The redactor who added chapter 21 to the Fourth Gospel took care not to obliterate the text that lay before him; he preferred to settle for internal tension. So also here: the two appearances of 20:19–23 and 20:24–29 take place in Jerusalem, but the third takes place at the Sea of Galilee. This difference becomes especially striking when 20:30f. intervenes. With respect to content, it is surprising that the disciples return to their old vocation as fishermen in chapter 21, as though such decisive events as the outpouring of the spirit and the mission charge had not preceded. Bultmann has conjectured, consequently, that Jesus' appearance early in the morning at the Sea of Galilee was the first resurrection story to be told.[3] It functions here, of course, as the beginning of a longer and more important composition.

The words "he revealed himself" (ἐφανέρωσεν ἑαυτόν) exhibit a somewhat different usage than do the other uses of φανεροῦν in John.[4] Because the text could be misunderstood in the sense that Jesus revealed himself earlier at this same location, some manuscripts have altered the text: ℵ syᵖ move the critical word "again" (πάλιν) to a position before "himself" (ἑαυτόν); D goes still further and places it before "he revealed himself" (ἐφανέρωσεν); finally, G al syˢ sa simply leave πάλιν out. In accordance with the sense, ἑαυτόν ("himself") is to be supplied with the second ἐφανέρωσεν ("he revealed"); the first "he revealed himself" (ἐφανέρωσεν ἑαυτόν) was so far removed by all the qualifiers coming between that the redactor decided to give the readers some help: he repeated the verb.

It is surprising that Jesus does not reveal himself with an "It is I," as he does, for example, in Mark 6:50b, but rather by the miracle of the superabundant catch of fish; but in so doing, the author opened up the possibility of introducing the so-called beloved disciple in verse 7.[5] It is also thought that there is certain resemblance between this story and the story of the disciples on the road to Emmaus (Luke 24:16–31a); that Jesus appears unrecog-

nized in 21:4 is not enough to confirm the conjecture that our story was once so structured that Jesus was recognized in the breaking of bread and then disappeared.

■ **2** This verse lists the seven participating disciples. It is not surprising that the group of twelve is not mentioned, unlike 20:24: it is really only a story about Peter (and, according to v 14, also about the beloved disciple). In addition to Peter, the others mentioned by name are Thomas, Nathaniel, and for the first and last time in the Gospel of John, "the sons of Zebedee." It almost appears as if the author reveals the incognito of the beloved disciple in this passage. But this appearance is deceptive: he could also belong to the two unnamed disciples.

■ **3** In order to make the fishing scene vivid, the account begins with Peter's remark. But he cannot manage the boat and the drag-net alone. Since the other disciples declare themselves ready to take part in the fishing expedition, this difficulty is surmounted. The entire group of disciples leaves the house—it is evening (cf. the end of v 3)—in which they were staying ("they went out," ἐξῆλθον), and board the ship. For "ship" the word πλοῖον is used here and in verse 6, but the word πλοιάριον ("little ship"; popular in spoken Koine Greek) in verse 8, which does not mean "little ship" in spite of its diminutive form. The verb πιάζω is used elsewhere in the Gospel of John for attempts to "seize" Jesus;[6] but here it designates a catch of fish. The preparation for the following story is now complete.

■ **4** The actual self-revelation of Jesus begins early in the morning. That the disciples had once again come to land is by no means "of course," as Bultmann thinks.[7] Hirsch takes offense (without justification, of course) at the "perfectly absurd self-proclamation of the risen Jesus by calling loudly with a voice that resounds over perhaps one hundred meters of water."[8] But the author does not say that Jesus calls; he simply has Jesus "say." Neither the author nor the reader will have reflected on how loudly one must call to be heard across one hundred meters of

2   Cf. Haenchen, *Die Botschaft des Thomasevangeliums,* 69.

3   Bultmann, *John,* 705 and n. 5 [546]. Cf. the book of E. Hirsch, *Die Auferstehungsgeschichten und der christliche Glaube* (Tübingen: J. C. B. Mohr, 1940) 11–26, 65–98. It is unfortunate that this book has been forgotten.

4   Cf. John 1:33, 2:11, 3:21, 7:4, 9:3, 17:6.

5   See the Excursus on the Beloved Disciple.

6   Cf. 7:30, 32, 44, 8:20, 10:39, 11:57.

7   *John,* 707 [548].

8   Hirsch, *Studien,* 180.

water. Jesus appears on the beach in the morning, following the alleged efforts of the disciples during the night, but still unrecognized. It is reminiscent of Luke 24:16 that the disciples do not recognize him. In that passage, it is explained that the non-recognition owes to the fact that "their eyes were kept from seeing." Only when Jesus then broke bread with them at the (evening) meal were their eyes opened—and at this moment he disappears in front of them (Luke 24:31). It has been proposed that the Johannine story also once ended in a similar way.[9] Of course, this story would then have been unusable for the author of this chapter.

■ **5** Jesus now asks the disciples, whom he addresses as "children" (παιδία)—as a still unrecognized master, of course—whether they have anything to eat. The word προσφάγιον really means "relish" (eaten with bread). Since this "relish" consisted mostly of fish, it came to have the meaning of ὀψάριον, the hellenistic diminutive form of ὄψον, "fish," that is, "food." The "no" of the disciples reminds the reader that the fishing expedition has not been successful up to this point. This is again reminiscent of Luke 5:1–11. The author of this chapter might at least have been acquainted with the Gospel of Luke.

■ **6** In response, Jesus instructs them to cast the net on the right side of the ship, the propitious side; then they will "find some." Presupposed here is Jesus' omniscience: he knows where the fish are to be found.[10] His question in verse 5 was only the preparation for his surprisingly successful advice: the disciples were not able to haul the net into the ship on account of the quantity of fish. Since, according to verse 11, there were only 153 fish, they must have been unusually large and heavy. The number of fish has presumably come into the text in connection with the special scene with Peter in verses 10f. In that case, the story would originally have been closer to the parallel story in Luke 5:6f. Another item supports this view.

■ **7** In the parallel passage in Luke, Peter specifically recognizes that he is standing before a supernatural being as a result of the marvelous boon of the catch. In John, on the other hand, the recognition that the one providing the blessed counsel is "the Lord" is attributed to the beloved disciple. That is reminiscent of 20:8,

where the beloved disciple becomes a believer when he sees the bandages and the handkerchief, although he does not express his belief to Peter. In chapter 21, he shares his conviction with Peter: "It is the Lord," but he remains glued to the spot and does not seem to have communicated his conviction to the other disciples. By contrast, the remark of the beloved disciple to Peter elicits an unusual reaction: Peter puts on his clothes and girds himself about (the term γυμνός need not mean "naked," but clad only in a shirt) and throws himself into the sea—no doubt to get as quickly as possible to the shore and to Jesus. But nothing is narrated of his reaching the shore and of his meeting with Jesus. Not until verse 11 is there mention of the "going aboard" of Peter (ἀναβαίνειν), and his meeting with Jesus is shifted to verses 15–17. If Peter was fishing "naked" (γυμνός), then the same thing is to be assumed for the other disciples; that they put their clothes on before the landing is not mentioned as something unessential. The present text presents the problem that Peter put on his clothes before jumping into the sea to swim to shore. The author apparently wants to show how much the observation of the beloved disciple affected Peter and how ardently Peter longed to be with Jesus. Yet that is said only between the lines. Thus one is tempted to understand the word διεζώσατο ("to put on one's clothes") in verse 7 as preparation for the ἐζώννυες ("gird oneself about") in verse 18. Apparently the author was fond of such clandestine allusions and references.[11]

■ **8** There is no further mention of the swimming Peter in verse 8, only of the other disciples. They do not jump into the water like Peter, but simply steer to the nearby shore, dragging the fish. They were not a hundred meters from the shore, as we now learn.

■ **9** In verse 9 we are told that they are surprised by a new marvel: a charcoal fire was burning on land, and bread and fish were there. The textual tradition, however, has κειμένην; but for a fire to "lie" does not make good sense. But if one considers that καιομένην, "burning," was at that time pronounced like κεομένην, then the difference between κειμένην and κεομένην disappears, especially since the omicron was often written especially small. Now since the old Latin manuscripts up to b and f read *incensos*

---

9   Cf. the comments on vv 1 and 12.
10   Cf. 1:47–50.
11   See on verse 9.

$= \kappa\alpha\iota o\mu\acute{\epsilon}\nu\eta\nu$, $\kappa\epsilon\iota\mu\acute{\epsilon}\nu\eta\nu$ is a very old scribal error.

But what does the charcoal fire signify here? In 18:18, we are told that the servants and officers in the courtyard of the high priest had lighted a charcoal fire on account of the cold, at which Peter had warmed himself—during the denial scene! The mention of $\dot{\alpha}\nu\theta\rho\alpha\kappa\acute{\iota}\alpha$ ("charcoal fire") in verse 9 suggests that the author intends to remind the reader of the earlier scene, which forms the background of verses 15–17.

■ **10** This verse has Jesus order them to bring some of the fish they had just caught. But it is neither related that these fish are to be cleaned and prepared for the fire, nor is it apparent why they are required in view of the fish already present. That leads to the suggestion that the author has attempted to unify two different stories. The one treats of a mysteriously prepared meal on the shore (cf. Mark 6:34ff.), at which, however, Jesus is only the host, not a table guest. The other tells of a miraculous catch of fish; it is reminiscent of Luke 5:1–11. Even the diction speaks for this hypothesis: the fish miraculously procured by Jesus on the shore are called $\dot{o}\psi\acute{\alpha}\rho\iota o\nu$ in verses 9 and 13; for the fish taken in the miraculous catch, however, the term $\dot{\epsilon}\chi\theta\acute{\nu}s$ is used in verses 6, 8, and 11. Verse 10, which struggles to connect the two stories, speaks only of $\dot{o}\psi\acute{\alpha}\rho\iota o\nu$ and thus obscures the distinction. Two different miracles have in fact been combined, in each of which fish play a role. Of course, verse 10 is not only in this sense a transitional and connective verse, but also prepares for the surprising action of verse 11 at the same time.

■ **11** The word $\dot{\alpha}\nu\acute{\epsilon}\beta\eta$ (literally, "went up") in verse 11 is puzzling: does it mean that Peter, who long ago must have come to shore, boards the ship again and unties the net that was secured there, so that he can draw it to land; or does Peter, who had already jumped into the water in verse 7, only now reach land, untie the net with the fish in it, and bring it to shore? Of course, Peter could have jumped into the sea in order to get to land and Jesus more quickly. That might exclude the second meaning of $\dot{\alpha}\nu\acute{\epsilon}\beta\eta$ suggested above. But the situation is not entirely simple. But one can clear away some of the underbrush by assuming that the two stories of the "beloved disciple" and Peter, as well as the story of Peter

and the net bursting with fish, already combined in a secondary fashion, were put together with a story of a miraculous catch of fish and with a further account of a marvelous meal by the sea. Accordingly, we would first of all have to ignore verse 7 and the word $\ddot{\alpha}\lambda\lambda o\iota$ ("other") in verses 8, 10, and 11. But that, of course, does not explain everything. That Peter pulls the net with the 153 large fish ashore by himself, without tearing it (cf. Luke 5:6), presents great difficulties for comprehension.

According to Edwards, one is not to interpret the number 153 allegorically; Peter counted the fish as an experienced fisherman, in order to give each partner what was coming to him.[12] But the text does not state that Peter counted the fish; Peter is not the author of the Fourth Gospel and therefore did not note the number of fish in this account. Why then does the author of chapter 21 mention the number of fish? And why should 153 fish of the kind found in the Sea of Galilee threaten to break the net?

It contributes nothing to our understanding to say that 153 is the triangular number of 17: $1 + 2 + 3 + 4 \ldots + 17 = 153$. The earliest assistance we have is the suggestion of Jerome: older authors, for example, Oppianus Cilix, assert with respect to $\dot{\alpha}\lambda\iota\epsilon\nu\tau\iota\kappa\acute{\alpha}$ ("species of fish") that there are 153 kinds of fish. Since in the Synoptics Peter is a fisherman and is promised by Jesus that he will become a fisher of men, as is related in Mark 1:16, Matt 4:19, and Luke 5:10 (although the Gospel of John knows nothing of this promise), the author of chapter 21 or the tradition he is reflecting could have indicated that Peter, the fisher of men, successfully operated the net of the church, and in so doing believers from all the peoples of the earth were won to the faith.[13] Bultmann's objection, "for it would then be reasonable to look for the 153 not only among the fishes but also among men," does not take into account that in this allegory it is precisely men who are symbolized by fish.[14] But one can grant to Bultmann that it is not a question of a pure or consistent allegory, since Peter appears in both the text to be interpreted and in the text as interpreted. The author does not intend to point to a physical tour de force on the part of Peter; rather, he is obliquely suggesting his spiritual proficiency in the administration of the church.

---

12 *The Disciple Who wrote these Things. A New Inquiry into the Origins and Historical Value of the Gospel according to St. John* (London: J. Clarke, 1953) 180.

13 Jerome, *In Ezechielen*, 47.12.

14 Bultmann, *John*, 709 n. 2 [549 n. 1].

■ **12** With verse 12 the action of verse 8 is taken up again: Jesus invites the disciples to breakfast. A remark about the inner disposition of the disciples curiously follows the invitation: none of them dared to ask Jesus (for "ask" ἐξετάζω rather than ἐρωτάω, which is customary in the Gospel of John): "Who are you?" Their unwillingness to ask is based on their knowledge that they knew he was the Lord. But if they really knew that, it would have been unnecessary to ask. The statement that "they dared not ask him" makes sense, rather, if the disciples did not know that, but yet would like it confirmed out of his own mouth. According to Bultmann, "this is intended to describe the peculiar feeling that befalls the disciples in the presence of the Risen Jesus: . . . it is not he, whom they hitherto have known, and yet it is he!"[15] This is said in the text. On the other hand, 4:27 has been cited by way of explanation. In that case, the meaning would be: the awe of the disciples in the face of the Lord—whom they recognized—was so great that they did not dare direct a question to him. But that in itself does not completely eliminate the inconsistency in the passage. Not a single word is spoken by any of the disciples in this scene—other than the word spoken by the beloved disciple to Peter. Jesus' invitation in verse 12 has the effect of an ingredient in a cultic scene, during which only the divinity speaks.

■ **13** Verse 13, according to Bultmann, supplanted the original conclusion, which related the lifting of the ban that had lain on the disciples. Bultmann conjectures further that the original conclusion contained an act of homage on the part of the disciples and their call to be "fishers of men."[16] The present story might have the meaning that Jesus established fellowship with the disciples by dispensing the eucharistic meal,[17] which, for the author, forms the basis for the following conversation of Jesus with Peter.

"Jesus comes" appears to assume that Jesus was not standing before the charcoal fire, but was on the beach at the point where the disciples had come ashore.

▣ **14** Verse 14 emphasizes once more, by way of conclusion, that this is the third time that the risen Jesus had revealed himself to the disciples. This form of the assertion is distinguished from that employed in verse 1 stylistically : in verse 1, φανερόω ("reveal") is used in the active voice, either with an expressed ἑαυτόν ("himself") or with one to be supplied; while in verse 14 the third person singular passive is used (although in the same sense). The character of verse 14 indicates that it is the conclusion of a scene. The author of chapter 21 has probably taken it over as such, since a dialogue between Jesus and Peter is reported in the balance of the story.

■ **15** This highly stylized dialogue opens with verse 15. In the first half of the verse, the form "Simon Peter," customary in the Gospel of John, is used. By contrast, Jesus addresses the disciple through verse 17 as "Simon, son of John." The first of the three questions to Peter is: "Do you love me more (than these)?" There is nothing Peter has said in the Gospel of John to which Jesus can be alluding, although there is in Matt 26:33. In that passage, Peter says to Jesus: "Though they all fall away because of you, I will never fall away." The tradition being utilized in John 21:15–17 appears to be acquainted with the tradition employed in Matt 16:17. Peter does not maintain the claim he once made, but invokes Jesus' own knowledge that Peter loves him. In response, Jesus confers the highest task on him: "Feed my sheep." It would thus appear that Peter has been forgiven for once denying Jesus.

■ **16** To our surprise, Jesus' question is repeated once more—but without the words "more (than these)?" Peter again replies: "Lord, you know that I love you!" Once again he receives the commission: "Feed my sheep." Only the words for "feed" and "sheep" are expressed in different ways: for "feed," the terms βόσκε and ποίμαινε appear; for "sheep," the terms ἀρνία and πρόβατα. If one uses a and b to designate the first pair of terms, and the second pair with c and d, the scheme of the three expressions can then be indicated as: a–c; b–c; a–d (although the dimuntive form προβάτια appears at d). Jesus' commission is therefore never expressed in the same words. One can see that the diction is carried out with considerable artistry: every form of schematic repetition is avoided. And the word for "love" is also varied: there is a transition from ἀγαπᾶν to φιλεῖν.

■ **17** Verse 17 reports that Peter was grieved at the third repetition of the question; it appears as though Jesus does

15   *John*, 709f. [549].
16   *John*, 704f. [545].
17   Cf. 6:11.

225

not exact assurances from him each time and that he thereby rescinds his commission on each occasion. It is clear that the author is not realistically depicting an event, but is representing it in a sacral style: the threefold denial of Peter at an earlier time corresponds to a threefold vow taken now and to a commission thrice repeated. Bultmann indeed concedes that verses 15–17 stem from an old tradition.[18] But he contests that verses 15–17 are intended to rehabilitate Peter after his denial, although the author of chapter 21 so understood it. The passage taken by itself provides no hint of a relationship to the denial story. "Surely the denial and the repentance of Peter ought to have found mention! And nothing like an absolution is expressed in the statement of Jesus."[19] But this objection does not do justice to the characteristic features of the story. It is not private in character and is not meant to portray Peter's soul—only in the words "Peter was grieved" is there anything like a hint of the emotive background in the entire story. But just this note makes it possible to break off Jesus' questioning. It is not merely a private scene, but a public, ritual scene, the threefold character of which is conceived as a counterpart to the threefold denial of Peter. For this reason, Peter does not say, "Lord, I deeply repent that I denied you three times," and Jesus does not reply, "Good, then all is forgiven you." It has to do, rather, with the fact that Peter forfeited his prerogative to lead the community of Jesus by his threefold denial. Now, however, he is again expressly acknowledged as that leader. Peter is not thereby acknowledged as bishop of Rome, but as the leader of the Jerusalem community, which was orphaned by Jesus' death.

■ **18, 19a** Verse 18, which is elucidated by verse 19a, has been the object of considerable interpretive effort, although interpreters have not come to agreement on it. Verse 19 speaks of a martyrdom, by means of which Peter "will glorify God." That would be understandable as an expression of the language of Christian edification. But in that case, the interpretation must take verse 18

into account as well. This verse is an enigma that calls for illumination in view of the explanation indicated in verse 19. We thus encounter the problem that verse 18 refers to contrasting circumstances. It is characterized by pairs of words or phrases: (a) "young"/"old"; (b) "gird yourself" / "be girded by another"; (c) "go where you want" / "carry you where you do not want to go." An additional expression occurs only in the second group: "stretch out your hands." Bultmann and others aver that a proverb lies behind verse 18, that could have gone something like this: "In youth a man is free to go where he will; in old age a man must let himself be taken where he does not will."[20] The helplessness of the aged is thus being described: the hands are outstretched groping for support or someone to lead. We do not regard the reconstruction of this proverb, supposedly lying behind the expression in verse 18, as fortunate. Nothing is said about the aged having to grope, and why someone leading would take a helpless old person somewhere he or she did not want to go is incomprehensible.

"Taking someone where he or she does not want to go" refers to the grave. The combination of old age and death is not uncommon. "To bring, carry" is closer to the intended sense than "lead." If one presupposes this interpretation of the proverb, then it becomes more readily comprehensible that the author selected just this proverb to suggest martyrdom. What then is the situation with the phrases "gird yourself" and "be girded," which were probably not originally included in the proverb? The author introduced these phrases to indicate crucifixion as the kind of martyrdom Peter would suffer; the same thing applies to the outstretched hands. The second expression is found in ancient, non-Christian literature, in examples quoted by Wettstein.[21]

(a) Epictetus: ἐκτείνας σεαυτὸν ὡς οἱ ἐσταυρωμένοι, "stretching yourselves out as those crucified";[22]

(b) Artemidorus, the interpreter of dreams, says with respect to a dream: εἰ δέ τις ὑψηλὸς ἐπί τινος ὀρχεῖτο, εἰς φόβον καὶ δέος πεσεῖται, κακοῦργος δὲ ὢν σταυρωθήσεται,

18 *John*, 713 [552].
19 *John*, 712 [551].
20 *John*, 713 [552].
21 Wettstein, *Novum Testamentum Graecum*, vol. 1 (Amsterdam: Dommerian, 1752; Graz: Akademische Druck- und Verlagsanstalt, 1962) 964f.
22 Epictetus, 3. 26.

διὰ τὸ ὕψος καὶ τὴν τῶν χειρῶν ἔκτασιν ("If anyone should leap up high [upon something], he will fall into fear and anxiety, and being a criminal, he shall be crucified, because of the height and the outstretched hands");[23]

(c) Plautus, *Carbonaria: Patibulum* (the crossbar of the cross) *feram per urbem, deinde affigor cruci:* "I will carry the crossbar through the city and then make it fast to the cross" (to the stake that was already driven into the ground at the place of execution);

(d) Plautus, *miles glor.: Credo ego istoc extemplo tibi esse eundum actutum extra portam, dispessis manibus* (with outstretched hands) *patibulum cum habetis* ("You'll soon have to trudge out beyond the gate in that attitude, I take it—arms outspread, with your gibbet on your shoulders").[24]

Bauer refers also to Tertullian:[25] *tunc Petrus ab altero cingitur, cum cruci adstringitur* ("Then is Peter girt by another, when he is made fast to the cross"), and gives the right interpretation, in my judgment, of verse 18: "The criminal has to carry *the patibulum* ('the crossbar') to the place of execution with outstretched arms bound to the beam."[26] Bauer refers, further, to H. Fulda, who shows that this is the Roman custom in contrast to the oriental.[27]

The words "where you do not want to go" are not intended to refer to Peter as a man who is fearful of death; they belong to the expression for death taken over from the proverb.

Peter girded himself in verse 7 (put on his clothes); the situation in which someone else would "gird him" still lies ahead. The author has chosen this word and the action of Peter (who "girds" his long outer garment, since otherwise it would have hindered him as he swam) and therefore replaced the word "bind" (δήσει), already inappropriate in verse 7, with ζώσει in verse 18. To say that ζώννυμι does not really mean "bind" itself is not a valid argument;[28] it gains this meaning through the context. Verse 18 might therefore be translated: "Truly, truly, I say to you: as a young man you gird yourself [put your clothes on] and go wherever you want; as an old man, however, you will stretch your hands out and another will 'gird you' and take you where you do not want to go." What in fact is a remarkable relationship between the two tenses is to be explained by the fact that the young man is viewed from the perspective of the old man, and the old man from the point of view of the young man.

■ **19b** Verse 19b is again a transition to what follows, in that the author uses "follow" in a double sense. The term hovers here between the spatial meaning, "to go behind someone," and the figurative sense, "to imitate," in this context, to follow as a martyr. Of course one must not ask where the risen one goes and Peter follows in the spatial sense. For, Jesus already has his martyrdom on the cross behind him. One must not, therefore, completely eliminate the spatial sense of "follow"; if the spatial sense is not also included in the term, the next conversation between Peter and Jesus is emptied of its meaning.

■ **20** Peter turns around himself and sees the beloved disciple following—in the spatial sense—who was not enjoined to do so. The reader is thereby reminded once more of the scene in which he is first mentioned (13:23ff.): at the last supper, he lay (leaning backwards) on the breast of Jesus and asked who the betrayer would be. Mary (Magdalene) is likewise depicted in 11:2 as that Mary who had anointed the Lord with oil and wiped his feet with her hair— although the scene does not take place until 12:3. Similarly, in 12:1 Lazarus is identified as the one Jesus earlier raised from the dead (11:43f.). In 19:39, correlatively, Nicodemus, who comes to bury Jesus, is characterized as the one who has earlier come to Jesus by night (3:1ff.), and Judas Iscariot is identified as "the betrayer" once and for all. It is as though all of these figures in the sacred tradition were once and for all connected with the special situations in which they made a particular impression on the mind. The concurrence of a feature like this with the earlier examples does not add up to much for the "authenticity" of chapter 21.

23 Artemidorus, 1: 76.
24 *Miles glor.* 2.4.7, tr. Paul Nixon, LCL 3.161.
25 *Scorp.* cap. 15 (from the year 211 CE) ANF 3: 648.
26 *Das Johannesevangelium*, 238.
27 *Das Johannesevangelium*, 239, with reference to H. Fulda, *Das Kreuz und die Kreuzigung* (1878), 119f., 137f., 219.
28 Bultmann, *John*, 713 n. 7 [552 n. 6].

■ **21** Verse 21 now picks up the action afresh (οὖν, "now, therefore," as always in the narrative sections of the Gospel of John): when Peter, in turning around, sees the beloved disciple following (of whom no martyrdom has been foretold), he asks Jesus what will happen to this disciple. Inasmuch as "to follow" has a profound sense, as well as "to follow in martyrdom," and the beloved disciple is prepared to follow, it is not unnatural for Peter to ask the Lord, in view of this uncertainty, what has been allotted to that other disciple, with respect to whom it has been determined that he is not "to follow" but who nevertheless now follows.

■ **22** Jesus answers sharply: "If it is my will that he remain (live) until I come (again), what is that to you? Concern yourself with your own destiny and follow me" (to martyrdom).

Jesus' "coming" can here only mean his return from heaven, as Paul (1 Cor 15:21–28; 1 Thess 4:13–17), primitive Christianity (Acts 1:11), and the book of Revelation conceived it. Chapter 21 therefore presupposes that apocalyptic drama, a parousia, that the Fourth Gospel relocates in the moment of faith's conception; chapter 21 thus abandons the special theology of this Gospel, just as happens in earlier passages, in an especially striking way, for example, in 5:27–29. But the harshness of the answer put in the mouth of Jesus by the narrator obscures the predicament in which he finds himself in this passage. For he, too, basically regards the glorification of God through martyrdom as far superior to any other kind of death. Moreover, the knowledge that Jesus did not speak of fact, but only of eventuality or potentiality (v 23) is anything but convincing.

■ **23** Verse 23 quits the scene and speaks of a rumor that had spread among all Christians (who are only here called "brethren"): that disciple will still be living at the time of the parousia. We now have a polemic directed against this alleged misunderstanding of what Jesus had said: Jesus had certainly not promised that that disciple would not die, but had only spoken of that possibility without commitment. The polemic of verse 23 makes sense only if that disciple (who was certainly not merely a symbolic figure) no longer "remained," but had died. His death cannot have taken place too far in the past; for

otherwise the false notion that he would be spared death would have collapsed and would no longer have required contradiction. It is all but impossible to conclude from this verse that that disciple was still living and that his (eventual) death is spoken of only by way of prevention, so to speak, so that verse 23 could even still be ascribed to him.

■ **24** This verse now betrays why the narrator of chapter 21 had such a great interest in this disciple (and his destiny): that disciple, whom the redactor of the Gospel invokes, the last surviving eyewitness, whose testimony is true, as the "we" which is not more precisely defined knows, has even written this Gospel himself. The narrator overrides the limits which he had observed up to this point with the words "and who has written these things" (καὶ ὁ γράψας ταῦτα): the beloved disciple is not only the witness who has been invoked; he is even the author of the Gospel itself.

■ **25** A new concluding verse has now become necessary; the chapter and the Gospel could not end with verse 24. The author of chapter 21, who is the redactor of the whole Gospel at the same time, has therefore taken 20:30f. as a model. But he has discredited this new conclusion by a grotesque exaggeration: Jesus had done so many other things that there would be no room in the world for all the books were all that to be recorded. In view of this authorial lapse, B. Weiss resorts to this bit of intelligence: "That is certainly hyperbole, which is not, however, at all improbable, 'particularly for a man who was not well acquainted with books' (Ewald), and which is very likely explicable on the basis of the enthusiasm with which he looked back over a rich life."[29] On the other hand, Wikenhauser is correct in pointing to comparable exaggerations on the part of other authors in antiquity, for example, on the part of Philo, where he concludes with these words: "But since if one should wish to tell in full all the praises of equality and her offspring justice the time will fail him, be his life of the longest, it seems better to me to content myself with what has been said. . . ."[30] The interpretation of B. Weiss is thereby refuted: a rhetoric loved by ancient authors is the dominant factor in verse 24, rather than the clumsiness of a man "who was not well acquainted with books." Strathmann

---

29   B. Weiss, *Das Johannes-Evangeliums*, 634.
30   Wikenhauser, *Das Evangelium nach Johannes*, 353.
     The passage from Philo is found in *De Spec. leg.*

4.238, tr. F. H. Colson, LCL, 1939.

has taken quite a different course in saving the Evangelist: "The editors who become evident in verse 24" have taken the two scenes in chapter 21, which lay before them only as narrative material, and "appended them" to the work of the revered disciple "and in this way saved it for the furture community."[31] The tensions in chapter 21, for which Strathmann had a sharp eye, are not to be charged to the author of the Gospel, but only to the editors.

Overview

The twenty-first chapter of the Gospel of John poses an especially difficult puzzle. If one reads chapter 20 through to the end, one is then convinced that 20:30f. form a good conclusion. And yet the story continues— but in what a curious way! The disciples are no longer in Jerusalem; we find them again on the Sea of Galilee, although we are not told how they came to be in this new situation. Apparently they have entered once again into their old jobs as fishermen. Peter appears—in strong contrast to chapters 1–20—to set the tone. To our surprise the disciple Nathaniel, from Cana, has rejoined the group; we have heard nothing of him since chapter 1. Thomas is present, as are the two sons of Zebedee, about whom John has been steadily silent up to this point. Their names, James and John, are of course not mentioned. In addition, there are two further, unnamed disciples. One of this group of seven must be the "beloved disciple," according to verses 7 and 20, but the two unnamed disciples make it impossible for us to determine his name. If the disciples in chapter 20:21f. have been sent by Jesus himself, as the Father sent him, and if they have received their appointment as missionaries, they seem to have forgotten. Nothing is said of a group of twelve: there are only seven on the scene. The difficulty is thereby overcome that arose from the exclusion of Judas from their circle. It almost appears as though they have returned to the pre-Easter period.

Such a break in the composition as comes to light here ought not really to be credited to the Evangelist. Nevertheless, two highly regarded exegetes like A. Schlatter and W. Bauer, who represent very different schools of thought, and who were otherwise seldom in the same camp, agree in attributing chapter 21 to the Evangelist. Schlatter argues for this conclusion in 1930 as follows: "The assignment of the new narrative to another author is impossible, however, because the linguistic habits of the author are continued without alteration."[32] Bauer seconds this judgment: "So far as stance, tone, and word preference are concerned, nothing distinguishes chapter 21 from the other chapters"; he then adds as a further argument: "There is nothing in the history of the text to suggest that the Fourth Gospel ever existed without chapter 21. . . . Also, awkwardness in handling his sources, which leads to vague scenes, strikes us again and again and we meet it again [in chap. 21]. . . . We will therefore do well to reject the view that various hands are involved. One and the same person wrote the entire book. Not at one sitting . . . The last thing he undertook in connection with his book . . . was the addition of chapter 21."[33] We have thus set out everything that can be adduced in favor of the view that the Evangelist also wrote chapter 21. But these proofs are not conclusive.

The view that chapter 21 stems from the author of chapters 1–20 has been all but given up by modern scholarship. The principal piece of evidence against it is provided by 20:21f: it does not makes sense to expect the Evangelist to have the disciples return to Galilee to their own vocation as fishermen after the outpouring of the spirit and their commissioning. To this internal argument may be added an external, linguistic argument: it is precisely linguistic peculiarities of the inconspicuous sort and which therefore elude imitation that distinguish chapter 21 from the rest of the Gospel, as Bultmann has rightly emphasized.[34] There is the causative ἀπό in verse 6 ("for the quantity of fish"), the partitive ἀπό instead of ἐκ in verse 2 ("from Cana"), ἰσχύω for δύναμαι ("be able") in verse 6, ἐξετάζω for ἐρωτᾶν ("ask") in verse 12, ὑπάγω with the infintive in verse 3 ("I am going fishing"), ἀδελφοί for μαθηταί ("brethren" for "disciples") in verse 23, to name only a few. That new words appear, occasioned by the particular situation, and which appear elsewhere in the NT, in part, is not a compelling counterargument.[35] If, on the other hand, one refers to the many points of agreement between chapters 1–20 and 21, one should also observe the judgment of Hirsch:

31   *Das Evangelium nach Johannes*, 258.
32   *Der Evangelist Johannes*, 363.
33   W. Bauer, *Das Johannesevangelium*, 235.
34   *John*, 700f. [542].
35   This is Bultmann's position also, *John*, 700f. [542f.].

the Johannine style is easily imitated. John employs only a small vocabulary, and his noticeable stylistic peculiarities (like asyndeton, parataxis, frequent οὖν, "therefore, then," the sentence initial position of the verb) are mostly an inconspicuous part of spoken Koine Greek.[36]

This poses the question for us: why was chapter 21 added to the Gospel? Was the purpose not to omit some stories that had not yet been incorporated into the Gospel of John? In view of 20:30, such a "purposeless" addition is improbable; chapter 21 was therefore composed with a conscious purpose in mind (as will be shown) and was not a written source that has been complicated by a redactor. A close analysis and interpretation of the text is of course required to confirm this judgment.

Chapter 21 is divided into two scenes, broadly speaking, namely, verses 1–14 and 15–23; verses 24f. form a brief new concluding segment.

The first scene provides a new self-revelation of the risen Christ, in which the expression ἐφανέρωσεν (ἑαυτόν), "revealed himself," used differently elsewhere in the Gospel of John, is striking. The disciples are suddenly in Galilee and have gone back to their old trade. Of the seven men who are together on the "Sea of Tiberias," from the Synoptics we know only Simon Peter, Thomas, and the two "sons of Zebedee," mentioned here for the first time in the Gospel of John, but whose names are of course not given. From the Gospel of John itself (1:45), we know Nathanael, about whom we have heard nothing for a long time. For the first time we learn that he comes from Cana. We are not told how he came to be a fisherman. In addition to these five, there are "two other disciples." They make the identification of the "disciple whom Jesus loved" impossible; this disciple, according to verse 7, also belongs to the group. There is good reason why the author has not named him as a member of the group: only in this way is his secret preserved, and the redactor does not have the slightest reason to reveal it.

Peter explains in verse 3 that he is going fishing; the others join him. A single disciple could hardly have managed the boat and the drag-net alone. But this question and others —may one conclude from verse 4 that it is evening, and from verse 5 that the disciples have nothing more to eat?—bring us basically to the problem:

may one interpret the "story" at all as a realistic account? Earlier that was taken for granted among exegetes; today one does well to treat such assertions circumspectly. The author is more concerned with a chiaroscuro, an interplay of black and white, in which what is real and what is symbolic is not distinguished for us. Consequently, he does not tell us why Peter went fishing, and has the others join in without giving a word of explanation about why this act was necessary. Peter, however, is depicted as the leader of the group of disciples, but, of course, in an unemphatic way.

The story reminds us, in the first place, of the account of the miraculous catch of fish in Luke 5, which does not, however, take place at dawn, as it does in 21:4. This is the means for combining another story of a miraculous meal by the sea in chapter 21. Jesus stands, unrecognized, on the shore in the morning twilight and "says" to the disciples: "Children, have you any fish?" Bultmann states: "The disciples of course have come to land again."[37] But that is not at all realistic. If Jesus tells them to cast the net on the right side of the boat, and if they are then about 200 cubits from land, then they are still on the sea and not on land. Then, of course, Hirsch appears to have reason to make fun of "the curious self-revelation of the risen Jesus."[38] But neither Hirsch nor Bultmann have observed that this text has not been created as a realistic description of an event. "Of course"—to use Bultmann's expression—the narrative does not have Jesus call out. Also, when the disciples do not take offense at the form of address, "children," and when the advice of an unknown person is followed without hesitation, that is striking only if one assumes the intention to depict an event realistically. The question of Jesus whether they have anything to eat permits the narrator to connect the story of the incognito figure of Jesus, who invites the disciples to a meal, with the tradition of a miraculous catch of fish. We thus have before us a literary composite, which, however, stands in the service of a thoroughly thought through theological composition, as we will show.

When the disciples answer Jesus' question about food negatively, he has them simply cast the net there where they are, but on the right side of the boat, the favorable

---

36 Hirsch, "Stilkritik und Literaranalyse im vierten Evangelium," *ZNW* 43 (1950/1951) 129–43.

37 *John*, 707 [548].

38 *Studien*, 180.

side, and immediately the net is full of fish. At this point, following the completion of the miracle, the narrator can introduce the "beloved disciple" (if this expression is permitted), who says to Peter: "It is the Lord!" Why he has him speak to Peter in particular has the same basis: in this way he can create a scene which calls to mind the footrace between the two disciples to the tomb. The beloved disciple is the first to recognize the risen Jesus. But he doesn't act on that knowledge. In 20:5, he does not go into the tomb himself, but leaves that to Peter (only later does he also enter the tomb). Peter reacts emotionally in our story to the remark of the beloved disciple. Nevertheless, he dresses himself decently before he jumps into the water. We will speak later of the reason he first "girds himself." It is not said that Peter comes to Jesus, and Bultmann finds fault with that.[39] But the author does not have the form of the fisherman climbing out of the water dripping wet in mind; he is concerned to move the narrative along, and he willingly tolerates a certain amount of obscurity, both here and subsequently, as part of the price. So he has the disciples steer the boat to shore, dragging the net full of fish behind.

This forms the transition from the story of the miraculous catch of fish to the account of the mysterious meal: a charcoal fire burns on the beach, on which fish is cooking; bread is at hand. But Jesus does not invite the disciples immediately to the meal, but first tells them to bring some of the fish they had caught. Bultmann is reproachful of this confusion, especially because these fish are not even prepared and eaten.[40] But this does not concern the author. Rather, he uses Jesus' request as a compositional medium. It permits him finally to bring Peter into the action: Peter alone pulls the net with the 153 huge fish to shore. Nothing is said of Peter counting the fish as the senior fisherman (as the English commentator Edwards thinks).[41] It is obvious that symbolism comes into play here. For, if it is emphasized that the net is not torn in spite of the number of fish, then there is no adequate realistic explanation for that: whales do not live in the Sea of Galilee. Jerome reports that, according to ancient views, there were 153 kinds of fish. In that case, these 153 fish represent all the people of the world that the net of the church encompasses, without having its

unity broken. These fish were obviously not cooked and eaten! Instead, Jesus invites the disciples to a meal (v 12). That the disciples dare not ask him, "Who are you?" shows that originally in this meal story—as in that of the disciples on the road to Emmaus—Jesus came to the disciples incognito. Only in the eucharist was he recognized and "their eyes were opened" ($αὐτῶν διηνοίχθησαν οἱ ὀφθαλμοί$), to use the language of Luke 24:31. But the author could not make use of this tradition in its old form. For the beloved disiciple had already recognized the Lord and also made it known. That explains the brief sentence awkwardly appended to verse 12 (looked at from the literary point of view): "They knew it was the Lord."

The author does not depict a course of action that develops in a straight line, although he strives for that as much as possible. The whole that he achieves is created by combining certain elements and motifs of various origins into a single literary composition. But it is not a scene that is viewed realistically: the net with the fish is a net full of fish that is drawn from the water to the shore, as well as the church with all its people and encompassing unity. Peter is the fisherman trudging along on land (v 11, $ἀνέβη$, "he went on board"), and yet also the apostle to whom the leadership of the church has been entrusted. That is not only expressed in symbolic form, but later stated plainly. This is one of those elements that connects the first story in chapter 21 with the second, and about which there is still more to be said.

The unity of the first story, as an account of the revelation of Jesus incognitio at the Sea of Galilee, is maintained of course only with some effort; it functions simultaneously as the introduction to a further narrative, and it is on the second that the real emphasis lies. The second narrative is itself again divided into three parts. The first subdivision contains the thrice repeated question of Jesus to Peter: "Simon, son of John, do you love me?", the thrice repeated affirmative answer to this question, and the commissioning of Peter told three times. This course of action portrayed in liturgical solemnity threatens to crystallize in monotony. It is therefore enlivened by means of larger and smaller

---

39   *John*, 703 [544].
40   *John*, 703 [544].
41   Edwards, *John*, 180.

distinctions. Jesus' first question specifically is: "Do you love me more than these" (love me)? This question does not correspond to John 13:37 ("I will lay down my life for you"), but to the reassurance of Peter in Mark 14:29: "Even though they all fall away, I will not."[42] The author of chapter 21 knows Mark as well as Matthew. When Peter meekly answers, "Lord, you know I love you," Jesus' question loses its edge. Now he asks: "Do you love me?" Peter's answers persists in its decisiveness: "You know that I love you," Peter explains repeatedly. On the third occasion, however, the human element breaks through the rigidity of the solemn cadence: Peter was grieved, and then he answers: "Lord, you know everything. You know that I love you" (v 17).

The threefold denial of Peter gains its positive counterpart in this scene with its threefold confession and commission—that is not to be contested. It would be more than incongruous were the narrator now to report Peter's repentance. Bultmann calls attention to the threefold repetition in cultic or magical-juristic usage and Mephistopholes' remark in Faust: "You must say it three times."[43] The solemnity of ritual of course predominates in chapter 21.[44] It is self-evident that the commission of the Lord to the disciple who had denied him three times cannot be well represented in conversational tone. Finally, it is not a small matter to be entrusted with the leadership of the church, and in Matt 16:17f. it is also expressed with corresponding solemnity.

The two related concepts used in John 21, "to feed, pasture" and "sheep," are so varied that no one of the three sayings of Jesus corresponds word for word to any of the other two:

βόσκε τὰ ἀρνία μου, "feed my lambs"
ποίμαινε τὰ προβάτιά μου, "tend my sheep"
βόσκε τὰ προβάτιά μου, "feed my sheep."

It therefore cannot admit of doubt, in all probability, that we have here a composition that is carefully weighed and that in this form, which is thought through in detail, it is entirely comparable with Matt 16:17f.: it is a com-

mission and authorization in which Peter is entrusted with the highest task in Christendom. It is not surprising that only in the symbolic scene in verse 11 is Peter depicted as a fisher of men, while here he is depicted as the good shepherd: it was simply not possible to coin a saying involving the figure of the fisherman, corresponding to the imperative of verses 15–17, and it was certainly not possible to repeat it three times with variation.

There follows immediately upon Peter's commissioning the announcement of his martyrdom, with the solemn affirmation, "truly, truly" (ἀμὴν, ἀμὴν), which nevertheless forms a second scene. May one say that Peter, in the judgment of the author, was honored by martyrdom—and precisely this martyrdom? The remark of Jesus in verse 18 is not to be misinterpreted in the sense that Peter will cling to life and be drug to the cross against his will. However, Bultmann is undoubtedly correct in his conjecture that the author is here making use of a proverb regarding humankind: "When a man is young, he goes where he wants; when he gets old, he is led where he does not wish to go (scil. to the grave)."[45] This proverb is transposed into the second person and made to refer to martyrdom—admittedly somewhat forcibly—by means of the phrase, "be girded about." It is related in verse 7 that Peter girded himself about. That is no more accidental than is the mention of the charcoal fire, the ἀνθρακία, in verse 9, about which the reader has heard in connection with Peter's denial in 18:18. That also probably belongs among those inconspicuous literary devices by means of which the author seeks to give his composition a somewhat tighter sequence and unity. The objection of Bultmann that "gird" does not mean "fetter" is of course correct.[46] But the author nevertheless has in mind an allusion to the martyrdom of Peter: the criminal must stretch out his arms, so that they can be fettered to the crossbeam of the cross—those to be crucified were often not nailed but fettered to the cross: the agony then lasts longer. When this crossbeam

42 Bultmann, *John*, 711 n. 4 [551 n. 1].
43 Bultmann, *John*, 712 n. 3 [551 n. 5]. Goethe, *Faust*,
    1: 1532.
44 Cf. 13:38 and chap. 18.
45 Bultmann, *John*, 713 [552]. For further discussion,
    cf. the author's remarks on verses 18,19a above.
46 *John*, 713f. n. 7 [552 n. 6].

is heaved up, one is taken "where he does not want to go."

The author has not only narrated this prediction of martyrdom for its own sake. He is preparing, at the same time, for something different, namely, a corresponding word about the fate of the beloved disciple. Literarily speaking, he succeeds in making the connection only imperfectly, at least so far as our sensibilities are concerned. He has the Lord say to Peter: "Follow me!" This saying has a double meaning, as Bultmann shows.[47] It means following Jesus in his martyrdom on the cross and it also means following after him now, literally. It is only this second sense that permits the further connection— admittedly still difficult—with the following action: Peter turns around and inquires about the fate of the beloved disciple. However, the word ἀκολουθοῦντα ("following") in verse 20 can refer only to following literally, spatially after Jesus (the scene is not really imaginable). The word is lacking even in ℵ* (together with the following ὅς, "who," of course) and in W and ff². That does not prove, however, that it did not appear in the oldest text. It could of course be a very old gloss. That Peter looks around is not to be explained psychologically. Rather, we once again are confronted with a literary device, by means of which—in addition to the appended question, "What about this man"— the author joins on the discussion about the beloved disciple. It makes good literary sense that the mention of the beloved disciple in verse 20 calls to mind the scene during the last supper in 13:23, while his mention in verse 7 does not: in verse 7, the action is annoyingly interrupted. In verse 20, on the other hand, the special love this disciple enjoyed from Jesus is emphasized. It does make literary sense that this mention calls to mind the scene at the last supper and not the footrace between the two disciples in 20:3ff. or the mention of the beloved disciple in 19:26: in the last (19:26), Peter appears only indirectly—that is, in his absence; the footrace could not readily be introduced at this point. The author could not very well say: "This disciple is the one who once ran faster than Peter!" Because the beloved disciple enjoyed Jesus' special love, the reader could expect that the Lord has determined a special destiny for him.

Peter provokes the answer of Jesus in verse 22 with the question, which is not to be interpreted psychologically any more than is Jesus' answer, "What is that to you?" It would thereby be completely misunderstood. Peter is neither curious nor envious, nor does Jesus give him a sharp reprimand in verse 22. The author is probably wavering between two things. On the one hand, in accordance with early Christian thinking, a disciple so highly placed ought to honor God with a martyr's death; "to remain" does not rank higher by any means, as Bultmann thinks—[48] it may then be that the disciple will really remain alive until the parousia.[49] In the second place, the ground was evidently being laid for the conviction that that disciple whom the author had in view, if he were speaking of the beloved disciple, would not die prior to the parousia (and naturally not afterwards, either). And yet he had now gone to his rest, and entirely peaceably at that! The response of Jesus to Peter's question now meets this difficulty, without making a definite assertion: "If it is my will that he remain until I come, . . ." It is quite clear that the author is not thinking merely of a symbolic person, but of a particular disciple, who died at an extremely old age—to the general consternation. For, while in Paul's day it appeared certain that the overwhelming number of Christians would experience the parousia, and while it could still be said in Mark 9:1: "There are some standing here who will not taste death before they see the kingdom of God come with power," this disciple was evidently the last supporting pillar of the imminent expectation that the parousia would yet come in his lifetime. The author uses the occasion to take the sting out of this disappointment: Jesus had not really promised anything in particular at all! Incidentally, that does not imply that this disciple died immediately preceding the conception of chapter 21 and the publication of the Gospel of John, although it cannot have been too long a time since his death. For, this disciple is now represented as the guarantee of the Jesus tradition and, finally, even as the author of the Gospel of John. The author has no occasion to discuss how far his authorship extends into chapters 1–20 of the Gospel.

What does this story, which was undoubtedly very

47 *John,* 714 [553].
48 *John,* 716 [554f.].
49 Cf. 1 Thess 4:15.

deliberately composed, and to which the whole chapter leads up, really intend to say to the reader? It is concerned with two persons: Simon Peter and the beloved disciple. Peter receives something like the promise or the concession of the leadership of the church—that is clear and is rather widely recognized by scholars. But why does the text assure the reader of this point? Does it involve something that has been under dispute? Why must the Fourth Gospel of all documents rehabilitate Peter in its conclusion and extend recognition to him so solemnly? Is it perhaps because earlier in this Gospel the beloved disciple always relegates Peter to second place? It was not Peter but the other disciple who lay on the breast of the Lord and was permitted to inquire after the name of the betrayer. It was not Peter who stood by the cross and received the mother of Jesus as his mother, so that he took the place of Jesus as son, but the beloved disciple. It is not Peter who comes first to the tomb and who first believes in the risen Lord, but the beloved disciple. And in 21:7 it is not Peter who first recognizes the Lord, but the beloved disciple. We then have to say: in view of the way in which Peter is depicted in the Fourth Gospel, it really became necessary that he should

be appreciated at least once. A problem persists here, of course, as it does in connection with Matt 16:17f.: what does the acknowledgement of Peter as the one who tends the sheep of the Lord mean in view of the fact that he was already dead and no Roman bishop had yet laid claim to the continuation of the primacy of Peter?

But whatever this recognition of Peter meant, which was further amplified by the honor attached to his martyrdom, it made the position of the beloved disciple dubious. What remains for him and for his Gospel? Is he to take over the leadership of the church after the death of Peter? There is no hint of this. Nor does the text imply, contrary to Bultmann, "that the authority assigned to Peter has passed over to him."[50] Rather, one thing only is promised to him: he is the guarantee for the Fourth Gospel, which would otherwise never have been taken up into the canon. Indeed, the beloved disciple allegedly wrote this gospel himself. He is the guarantee of the right doctrine promulgated by this gospel.

---

50 *John*, 717 [555].

Excursus:
The Beloved Disciple

Bibliography

Broomfield, Gerald Welele
"The Beloved Disciple." In his *John, Peter and the Fourth Gospel* (New York: Macmillan; London: S. P. C. K., 1934) 146–61.

Brown, Raymond, E.
The Community of the Beloved Disciple (New York: Paulist, 1979).

Bruns, J. Edgar
"Ananda: The Fourth Evangelist's Model for the 'Disciple whom Jesus Loved'?" *SR* 3 (1973) 236–43.

Colson, Jean
L'énigme du disciple que Jésus aimait, Theologie historique 10 (Paris: Beauchesne, 1969).

Draper, H. Mudie
"The Disciple whom Jesus Loved." *ExpTim* 32 (1920/1921) 428–29.

Edwards, Hubert Edwin
The Disciple who Wrote these Things. A New Inquiry into the Origins and Historical Value of the Gospel according to St. John (London: J. Clarke, 1953).

Filson, Floyd V.
"Who was the Beloved Disciple?" *JBL* 68 (1949) 83–88.

Garvie, Alfred E.
The Beloved Disciple (London: Hodder & Stoughton, 1922).

Griffith, B. J.
"The Disciple whom Jesus Loved." *ExpTim* 32 (1920/1921) 379–81.

Hawkin, David J.
"The Function of the Beloved-Disciple-Motif in the Johannine Redaction." *Laval théologique et philosophique* 33 (1977) 135–50.

Hoernle, Edward Selwyn
The Record of the Beloved Disciple together with the Gospel of St. Philip: being a reconstruction of the sources of the Fourth Gospel (Oxford: Blackwell, 1931).

Johnson, Lewis
"Who Was the Beloved Disciple?" *ExpTim* 77 (1966) 157–58.

Johnson, Lewis
"The Beloved Disciple—A Reply." *ExpTim* 77 (1966) 380.

Johnson, N. E.
"The Beloved Disciple and the Fourth Gospel." *CQR* 167 (1966) 278–91.

Jonge, Marinus de
"The Beloved Disciple and the Date of the Gospel of John." In *Text and Interpretation. Studies in the New Testament presented to Matthew Black,* ed. E. Best and R. McL. Wilson (New York and London: Cambridge University Press, 1979) 99–114.

Kilpatrick, George Dunbar

"What John Tells About John." In *Studies in John Presented to Professor J. N. Sevenster on the Occasion of his Seventieth Birthday* (Leiden: E. J. Brill, 1970) 75–87.

Kragerud, Alo

Der Lieblingsjünger im Johannesevangelium (Oslo: Universitätsverlag, 1959).

Lee, G. M.

"Eusebius, H. E. 3,39.4." *Bib* 53 (1972) 412.

Lewis, Frank Warburton

"The Disciple whom Jesus Loved." *ExpTim* 33 (1921/22) 42.

Lofthouse, William Frederick

The Disciple whom Jesus Loved (London: Epworth, 1934).

Lorenzen, Thorwald

Der Lieblingsjünger im Johannesevangelium. Eine redaktionsgeschichtlicher Studie, SBS 55 (Stuttgart: Katholisches Bibelwerk, 1971).

Minear, Paul S.

"The Beloved Disciple in the Gospel of John. Some Clues and Conjectures." *NovT* 19 (1977) 105–23.

Morris, Leon

"The Tradition that John the Apostle was Martyred Early." In his *Studies in the Fourth Gospel* (Grand Rapids: Wm. B. Eerdmans, 1969) 280–83.

Morris, Leon

"Was the Author of the Fourth Gospel an Eyewitness?" In his *Studies in the Fourth Gospel* (Grand Rapids: Wm. B. Eerdmans, 1969) 139–214.

O'Grady, John F.

"The Role of the Beloved Disciple." *BTB* 9 (1979) 58–65.

Porter, J. R.

"Who was the Beloved Disciple?" *ExpTim* 77 (1966) 213–14.

Rigg, H.

"Was Lazarus 'the Beloved Disciple'?" *ExpTim* 33 (1921/1922) 232–34.

Rogers, Donald G.

"Who Was the Beloved Disciple?" *ExpTim* 77 (1966) 214.

Roloff, Jürgen

"Der johanneische 'Lieblingsjünger' und der Lehrer der Gerechtigkeit." *NTS* 15 (1968/1969) 129–51.

Russell, Ralph

"The Beloved Disciple and the Resurrection." *Scr* 8 (1956) 57–62.

Solages, Bruno de

"Jean, fils de Zébédée et l'énigme du disciple que Jésus aimait." *BLE* 73 (1972) 41–50.

Schnackenburg, Rudolf

"Der Jünger, den Jesus liebte." In EKKNT Vorarbeiten 2 (Neukirchen-Vluyn: Neukirchener-Verlag; Cologne: Benziger, 1970) 97–117.

Titus, Eric L.

"The Identity of the Beloved Disciple." *JBL* 69 (1950) 323–28.

Chapter 21 indicates how the redactor proposes to understand the figure of the beloved disciple.[1] It is by no means easy for us to flesh out this notion. The synoptic tradition knows nothing of a "beloved disciple"; if the Synoptics were to confer this title of honor upon any of the twelve, only one man would come under consideration: Peter. However, from the outset, the redactor of the Fourth Gospel conceived and depicted the figure of the beloved disciple in direct contrast to Peter.

The "beloved disciple" is mentioned for the first time in 13:23–26. In that passage Peter has to ask the beloved disciple to inquire of Jesus who was to betray him—without the answer readily given by Jesus having any consequences. But for the redactor it was not only important that the "beloved disciple" had inquired about who would betray Jesus, but also that he had lain on Jesus' breast at the last supper. The reader is reminded of both of these things in 21:20, when the "beloved disciple" is characterized once again. In 18:15f., where the "beloved disciple" puts in another appearance, he actually provides Peter with the possibility of getting into the courtyard of the high priest.

The most remarkable appearance of the "beloved disciple" occurs in 19:26f. Although nothing is said about Peter here, we learn that the "beloved disciple" stands by the cross with the mother of Jesus and is charged with her care: from now on he shall be her son and, in this respect, become Jesus' successor, so to speak, in his human relation to Mary.

Only the "beloved disciple," and not Peter, comes to faith when confronted with the empty tomb (20:8). And he alone recognizes the Lord as the stranger by the sea (21:7). Lastly, we learn in 21:24 that this disciple is he who bears witness to "these things"—and even the author of "these things," which most likely means the Fourth Gospel, according to the present text. On the basis of 21:24, it also seems probable that the eyewitness of the crucifixion mentioned in 19:35 was the "beloved

---

1   The voice of the redactor has more often been audible in the earlier sections of this gospel than one is willing to admit today.

disciple." Only for one of these scenes, namely, the account of the footrace of the disciples, is there anything like a point of contact with the synoptic tradition, in this case, with Luke 24:12, 24.

Finally, it could also be mentioned that Peter and John appear together in Acts 3:1, 3, 4:13, 19, 8:14–25, although John gives the impression of being only the "shadow" of Peter. Further, Paul designates James, the brother of the Lord, and Peter and John as pillars of the Jerusalem church in Gal 2:9. There is no mention, however, of a beloved disciple in either Acts or by Paul.

It remains to be considered, moreover, that the popular expression, "beloved disciple," does not correspond literally to the Greek wording. In the Greek text it is rather "the disciple whom Jesus loved." That says more than the expression "beloved disciple." "Beloved disciple" can refer to a disciple that Jesus loved more than the other disciples. "The disciple whom Jesus loved," on the other hand, suggests the notion that Jesus' love applies only to this one disciple. The synoptic gospels are unaware of such an exceptional standing of one of the disciples; but it is also alien to the christology of the Fourth Gospel. For, only when the risen Lord breathes the spirit into his disciples (7:39b, 20:21f.) will true faith become possible.

Where then did the redactor get the inspiration for the notion of a disciple whom Jesus loved? Perhaps two things worked together to produce the idea. The first may have been 11:3. In this passage, the two sisters Mary and Martha send the message to Jesus: "Lord, look, he whom you love [φιλεῖς] is ill." Of course, in the context, this merely implies that Lazarus, like his sisters, belongs among Jesus' friends.[2] But the word ἀγαπᾶν ("love") is used in 11:5 instead of φιλεῖν (which of course has the same meaning), and the result is the sentence: "Now Jesus loved ... Lazarus" (ἠγάπα δὲ ὁ Ἰησοῦς ... τὸν Λάζαρον). Consequently, Kreyenbühl and Eisler took Lazarus to be the "beloved disciple" (he could of course have taken the name John after his resurrection ...). The Evangelist did not intend that in chapter 11, and neither did the redactor. Nevertheless, the redactor derived the possibility from these passages that among the disciples there was one whom Jesus loved. There

naturally went with this the view that such a disciple understood the Lord particularly well and was the best possible witness for a gospel.

Now there lived a disciple—probably until the last decade of the first century CE—who had been acquainted, in his youth, with both Jesus and the circle of apostles. Chronologically, that is quite conceivable: if this disciple were about twenty years old around the year 30 CE and lived to be eighty years old, he would have lived until the year 90 CE. Under these circumstances, it would not be surprising that belief arose in the community in which he lived that this disciple would not die until the Lord returned. That is not to say that the Evangelist regarded him as the "beloved disciple." The coalescence of the long-lived with the beloved disciple is better attributed to the one who repeatedly depicts the beloved disciple as superior, that is: the redactor. On the other hand, it is quite possible that everything this disciple passed on as recollections of his youth was taken as absolutely reliable. This disciple had an extraordinary authority at his disposal.

The redactor was in need of just such authority for the gospel he had come across and which he wanted to introduce into his community alongside the writings already regarded as canonical. No disciple was better suited as an authoritative source than the beloved disciple. Moreover, it is unnecessary for this elderly disciple to lay claim to being the witness for the special message of a gospel. It would be completely satisfactory if he had taught the same thing, on one or more points, as the written gospel.[3] On the other hand, we need not assume that this elderly disciple went by the name of John—for then the redactor could hardly have allowed him to remain anonymous. And, in the end, it was much better that way. Perhaps it was still remembered that John, the son of Zebedee, had suffered a martyr's death; Mark 10:35–40 presumes that. Moreover, the advanced age of John was not completely uncontested, as Mark 10:35–40 and Matt 20:22–23 suggest and Luke 9:54 confirms. On the other hand, an anonymous disciple of Jesus whom he loved could not have been so attacked and criticized. Nevertheless, his authority, which surpassed that of Peter, had to be illustrated for the reader

---

2   Cf. 11:11: "Our friend Lazarus has fallen asleep."
3   Perhaps just such a case lies before us in 19:35.

in concrete examples. Luke 24:12, 24 could have offered the occasion for such an example to be inserted. We would then have to understand all those interpolations about which we have spoken in this commentary as just such illustrations, which exemplify the superiority of this disciple, in one way or another, even over Peter.

Of course, the references of the Fourth Gospel to the disciple whom Jesus loved involve certain difficulties. For one thing, the polemic directed against Peter, although it does not concern doctrinal differences, impeded the acceptance of the Fourth Gospel in those communities in which Peter was the preeminent figure in the apostolic circle and the shepherd of the church. This could be taken into account if it were related, at the end of the Gospel, that Peter was commissioned to fill this office and if the honor of his (generally acknowledged) martyrdom were expressly attributed to him.

There is the further difficulty that the long-lived disciple had finally died and had not experienced the parousia (still outstanding). This difficulty could be eliminated by portraying this conviction of the community as a misunderstanding of a real saying of Jesus: Jesus spoke of this disciple "remaining" only as a possibility. The reader then had to be given a hint about how this misunderstanding of a saying of Jesus came about.

Further, the Fourth Gospel contains some things that the redactor did not want to transmit with the authority of his special disciple because he himself did not regard them as unambiguously correct. A few revisions therefore had to be effected in the Fourth Gospel, or, better yet, some additions: the sacraments of baptism (3:5) and the Lord's Supper (6:51–58) must be mentioned, and futuristic eschatology indicated along with the realized form (5:27–30, 6:39f., 44, 54, 21:22f.). Along with that goes the eschatological judgment (according to ethical norms), which cannot be omitted (3:19–21, 12:48). And so the major objections to which the Fourth Gospel, with its peculiarties, would have given rise are cleared away at once.

The phrase, "the one writing these things" (καὶ ὁ γράψας ταῦτα), of course, seems to us to be an early addition that precipitates insurmountable difficulties and makes the following reference to this disciple's testimony seem odd ("We know that his testimony is true," καὶ οἴδαμεν κτλ.). The divergence of the textual witnesses with regard to these words could be taken as an indication that this is a later addition.

It is therefore unnecessary to understand the passages involving the "beloved disciple" prior to chapter 21 as symbolic, as Bultmann does (this disciple stands for Gentile Christianity, while Peter and Mary represent Jewish Christianity) and to assume another meaning for the "beloved disciple" in chapter 21.

In this we are not contesting that the Gospel of John also has something to say about Gentile Christians: they are mentioned in 10:16 and 12:20ff. But not in the sense that they and the Jewish Christians are represented, by individual persons, like the "beloved disciple," or Peter, or Mary, as the case may be. From this point of view, there is no reason, consequently, to adopt Bultmann's interpretation of the "beloved disciple" as a symbol of Gentile Christians. But the conclusion at which Kragerud arrives, namely, that Peter represents the ecclesiastical office, while the "beloved disciple" represents the apostolic itinerant prophet, is not to be recommended.[4] The Evangelist had no more interest in ecclesiastical officials than he did in an order of Christian itinerant prophets. It is correct that the redactor acknowledged Peter to be the shepherd of the sheep; but that does not imply that he was interested in a class of Christian prophets—if there were one in his day. Rather, 21:24 discloses why the editor of the Gospel of John manifests such a great interest in this disciple and his fate: that disciple upon whom the redactor calls as the witness and author of the Gospel of John, the last living eyewitness, whose testimony is true, the "beloved disciple," has died. Although the disciple whom Jesus loved may have fallen asleep, he gives warrant for orthodox doctrine and continues to speak to the brethren from the pages of his book: this, he says, is the gospel.

---

4   Kragerud, *Der Lieblingsjünger im Johannesevangelium* (Oslo: Universitätsverlag, 1959).

Appendix
Bibliography
Indices

Appendix

Ernst Haenchen
and His Commentary on John:
Biographical Notes and Sketches
of His Johannine Theology[1]

Ernst Haenchen's commentary on John, which had been anticipated by many colleagues,[2] appeared in 1980 and was based on materials in his literary estate. As editor I received the very kind invitation from *Analecta Lovaniensia Biblica et Orientalia* to record the story of its creation and editing and to append a brief sketch of the deceased author's life. Frau Margit Haenchen graciously made her husband's papers available to me, so that I could draw on biographical notes and letters and documents written in his own hand in creating this sketch.

This essay is divided into four parts in accordance with its aims. The first part provides a sketch of the author's life; the second relates the story of the editing of his commentary; the third is a sketch of the theological position of Ernst Haenchen, in particular of his debates with Rudolf Bultmann and Ernst Käsemann. The final section takes up a request made by my revered deceased teacher to continue his work and so sets out some problematic aspects of Johannine research insofar as they are of special interest to me at the moment.

1.   Ernst Haenchen, 1894–1975

Ernst Haenchen was born on 10 December 1894 in Czarnikau, in what was then the Prussian province of Posnania, as the third and youngest child of Karl Haenchen, who was a royal Prussian district secretary, and his wife Elfriede, whose maiden name was Kubsch. Ernst lost his father when he was three years old, and the family moved to Breslau. There he attended the parish school for four years, until the family moved to Berlin in 1904. Beginning Easter 1905, he attended the royal Joachimthalische Gymnasium located there; he pursued his course of study until he took the *Abitur* (exams), from the fourth class on as an alumnus. In the biographical sketch he prepared for his first pastor's examination, he wrote about his time in the *Gymnasium*: "Learning was easy for me. I was especially happy when studying ancient languages, so that my relatives expected that I would

study classical philology, like my brother, who was older than me by eleven years. During the *Untersekunda*, there arose for the first time, so far as I remember, doubt about the religious views I had received from the church, through instruction, and in the home of my parents: the worldview provided by astronomy threatened, at that time, to rob me of faith in the heaven above the earth and also of faith in God." However, his engagement with the Old Testament prophets disclosed another world to him that did not yield a physical system. When he was in the upper classes, the wish to study theology took firmer shape, although doubts still came to him during this period: "How is the omniscience of God related to the freedom of humankind?" But these doubts did not alter his resolution to study theology. As a consequence, he matriculated in 1914 in the Friedrich Wilhelm University in Berlin, after he had passed his *Abitur* (exams) *primus omnium*. The resolution of the Old Testament into sagas and myths in the lectures of Gressmann and Graf Baudissin and the history of the rise of dogma as depicted by Adolf von Harnack brought him the first difficulties. "What room is there for God when everything is shown to be contingent upon its historical, political, ecumenical, and ideological position within history?" His first philological labors over the basic texts of Christianity, the bible, and the texts of the ecumenical councils, initially helped him over these questions, under the tutelage of Martin Dibelius.

But then the First World War broke out. Since he had not been put in school in Breslau until he was seven years old on account of his unstable health, so now he was also rejected as a volunteer for the war on the same grounds. Thus it became possible for him to continue his studies in Heidelberg in the spring of 1915 and to attend the lectures of Martin Dibelius. Then on 21 May 1915 he received his induction orders. He was faced with "a duty gladly performed." After a short period on the Eastern front, his company was transferred to Serbia, where he experienced baptism by fire in the crossing of the Save. Shortly thereafter, on 22 October 1915, he was severely wounded for the first time. He was able to convalesce in the garrison of Landsberg, and was able, through the lecture notes of a friend,[3] to do a

---

1   Appeared originally as Ulrich Busse, "Ernst Haenchen und sein Johanneskommentar: Biographische Notizen und Skizzen zu seiner johanneischen Theologie," *ETL* 57; ALBO 6,5 (Louvain: Peeters, 1981) 125–43.

2   See James M. Robinson and Helmut Koester, *Trajectories Through Early Christianity* (Philadelphia: Fortress Press, 1971) 236f. n. 11; H. Thyen in *TRu* 42 (1977)

212, 227, 242.

3   The lecture notes from Dibelius' lectures on John have been preserved. It is planned to publish them when Frau Haenchen has transposed them from the shorthand used by students belonging to the Tübingen Stift.

little theological work. However, in August 1917 he reported back to the field and was sent to Riga and Volhynia. Following a short officer's training course, he was promoted to the rank of Lieutenant in the reserve. A short time later, in September 1917, he was sent to France. During the summer offensive he was wounded for the third time on the seventh of July 1918.[4] He lost his right leg.

After eleven operations, he was able only in August 1919 to leave the Lazarett in Berlin. Immediately, however, he began again to attend lectures and to take up his studies. The writings of A. Schweitzer, which he read during this period, now showed him—renewing questions he had raised during his first two semesters in Berlin—that the history of religions method basically only pushed questions back rather than resolved them. Jesus, who was now stripped of his messianic claims (by W. Wrede), now stood in stark, pronounced contrast to the veneration of the Son of God by the primitive church and Paul, although not so clearly as in the work of Wrede. Even the demonstration of influences from the mystery religions on Paul's conception of salvation could not alter the case that Christianity after Jesus very quickly basically distinguished itself from Jesus himself. Even all the other history of religions parallels so abundantly collected from hellenistic texts by R. Reitzenstein and M. Dibelius, among others, could explain the "new" doctrine of Paul, only in a very unsatisfactory way, because a certain parallelism in some expressions was not enough to account for the richness of Paul's thought. It likewise remains striking that Paul, who was given to hellenistic culture, had no more lasting effect on the ancient church. Haenchen thus posed the question for himself whether Paul's doctrine might be the direct continuation of the message of Jesus, whether there might be some connection between the eschatological claim of Jesus and the veneration of the kyrios in the Pauline churches (W. Bousset), which bridged the "nasty ditch" between the historical Jesus and the Christ of faith. This was a question for Ernst Haenchen not only in the purely scientific, completely objective sense, but also an existential question: could he personally accept as truth that the message of Jesus and that of Paul were internally connected, i.e., that the invitation articulated in their messages also applied to him. The acceptance and affirmation of this invitation gave him the strength, in spite of very poor health, which also brought him a life of suffering from neuritis, to finish his studies for his first

theological degree. He sat for the examination before the Berlin Consistory on 8–11 July 1922.

He then left Berlin and continued his studies in Tübingen (winter semester 1922/23 to the summer semester 1925) with the serious aim of making the New Testament his field of concentration. When he perceived, as he had to, that a degree and habilitation with W. Heitmüller would consume too much time in relation to his age, he threw himself into an honors essay on the subject: "Die Aufstellungen und Verhandlungen über den Urfall seit Julius Müller sind darzustellen und zu beurteilen" ("A Presentation and Evaluation of the Hypotheses and Discussion of the Primal Fall Since Julius Müller"). After submitting his essay, he took a position, on 1 November 1925, as Vicar in the service of the Evangelical Church of the old Prussian Union. When his Vicarate came to an end on 1 August 1926, he became a private assistant to K. Heim in Tübingen. Since a position as an assistant was to be authorized only in the following fiscal year, Ernst Haenchen received, in addition to his veteran's disability pension (RM 30), 50 RM from K. Heim and a daily lunch as compensation. There were two reasons for the auspicious unfolding of his academic career, although it was also a very difficult time financially: (1) Shortly after the beginning of his teaching vicarship in Friedeberg (Neumark), he received the news from Tübingen that his essay had been awarded the prize. His essay was then accepted as a thesis. Thus Ernst Haenchen was awarded a doctor's degree in theology on 15 January 1926 *summa cum laude*. Very soon thereafter he took the second theological examinations in Berlin (10–13 April 1926). (2) The second reason Haenchen entered in upon an academic career was his interest in the natural sciences and technology. Already in his student days Haenchen had come to the aid of a longtime friend who was troubled by the causal, mechanical worldview. "The attacks of the modern natural sciences on the Christian faith" led him as a matter of course to K. Heim and dogmatic theology. For, in addition to the biblical writings, the writings of K. Heim, especially his *Glaubensgewissheit* ("Certainty of Faith"), and his *Leitfaden der Dogmatik* ("Leitmotifs of Theology"), were his companions and helpers in this battle. It was a question for Haenchen, "whether the gospel was still in force today, whether therefore the dogmas of the gospel contained propositions that were outdated or had become meaningless, as well as whether the New Testament was an entity belonging to the past, in fact, whether one

---

4   A second wound received in 1917 was light.

could discover a living God whom one could preach to one's own age."

In the course of this year, which proved to be decisive for his academic history, Ernst Haenchen met Ernst Käsemann. The latter came as a student in his fifth semester from Marburg to Tübingen; in Marburg he had heard the first course of lectures by Rudolf Bultmann on the Gospel of John. He came to Tübingen to write an honors essay on the theme, "The Present State of the Johannine Question" (1928). The two of them discussed all the problems attendant on the Gospel of John on an almost daily basis during the semester, and continued their discussions by letter during holidays. In this intensive way Ernst Haenchen became knowledgeable of and conversant with Bultmann's interpretation of the Fourth Gospel, which was still completely unknown at that time, and with Gogarten's systemic theology. The two men also read Fichte's *Anweisung zum seligen Leben (Instruction for the Blessed Life)*, by way of contrast. And thus arose a lifelong friendship between the two, although in their views of the Gospel of John they differed substantively on some major points.

Haenchen used the period as assistant to K. Heim to write his *Habilitationsschrift*, "Die Frage nach der Gewissheit beim jungen Augustin" ("The Question of Certainty in the Early Augustine"). It was accepted by the faculty in the early autumn of 1927, and soon thereafter he received the *venia legendi* for systematic theology (12 December 1927). In his trial lecture in the context of the *Habilitations* process, he treated the theme, "Die Sündenlehre der neueren spekulativen Theologie" ("The Doctrine of Sin in More Recent Speculative Theology"), and in his inaugural lecture on 12 February 1928, he discussed the theme, "Symbol und Offenbarung in der neuesten Theologie" ("Symbol and Revelation in the Most Recent Theology"). However, the strain of the year just past had so weakened the body of the young *Privatdozent* that, as a consequence of his war injuries, following a haematemesis, he fell seriously ill with tuberculosis during the last days of February. As a consequence, he could not continue his teaching, but had to convalesce in Davos, Switzerland for two long years. But during this period his engagement to Marguerite Fahrenberger, the daughter of the local evangelical pastor, gave him renewed strength and courage to resume his teaching duties in Tübingen in the summer semester of 1930, on a trial basis (initially with a lingering pneumothorax). A year later they were married. His teaching was very quickly successful with students: he attempted to make students acquainted with the dialectical theology of Gogarten and Thurneysen, K. Barth and Brunner, as well as that of R. Bultmann; he expressed difficult trains of thought simply, used no unnecessary strange terms,

and in every case avoided the flood of words that obscured the essential in a problem. This success got him on the short list for the chair in systematic theology at Giessen. His competitor was P. Brunner. Haenchen received the call and took up his teaching duties at the University of Giessen beginning in the summer semester of 1933.

The year 1933 marked a profound turning-point in German history. The time of national socialism brought a period of temptation and trial to Ernst Haenchen. He had been given a Prussian education, and, as a highly decorated participant in the war (Iron Cross first and second class), who had put his youth and his health on the line for the "Fatherland," he had served and suffered for the Weimar Republic, first as a student—he had financed his education in large part by tutoring—and then as an Assistant, and finally as a *Privatdozent* and as a disabled person. The promise of the "Great German *Reich*" and the German Christians to win many who had drifted away back to the church must have sounded alluring to him, especially since he had become acquainted with Emanuel Hirsch in Freudenstadt in 1931 and had come to respect him. He very quickly became active in church politics when he, as Dean, demanded the resignation of *Reichs* Bishop Ludwig Müller in the name of the Giessen faculty; the same demand was simultaneously made of the Bishop of the Nassau-Hessischen *Landeskirche*. In 1936 he was appointed to the council of the German Evangelical Church under the leadership of General Superintendent Zoellner. At that time this commission consisted of Professors Stählin (Münster), Odenwald (Heidelberg), Althaus (Erlangen), Elert (Erlangen), Gogarten (Göttingen), Brunstäd (Rostock), Bornkamm (Leipzig), Schniewind (Kiel), Petersmann (Breslau), Lilje (Berlin), Goeters (Münster), among others. His political engagement did not go discernibly beyond this appointment, which was no doubt important from the point of view of church politics. In 1939 he received the call to the University of Münster, where he was able to teach in peace for only one semester.

The Second World War then broke out. The war prompted the almost complete dissolution of the faculty because both students and colleagues were inducted into the military. During this period, in addition to the discipline of dogmatic theology, Haenchen placed emphasis on his teaching in the ethical domain. As early as the winter semester of 1933/34, he had given a two-hour course on the letter to the Romans, and soon thereafter a similar course of lectures on Galatians. As already indicated, the outbreak of WW II brought with it the dispersal of his colleagues, and Ernst Haenchen—almost by himself now—endeavored to maintain a course of studies. He now lectred on subjects that the few remaining students (mostly wounded) "wanted" him to lecture on. Münster soon came within range of enemy bombers. He was compelled, as a consequence, to carry on instruction in the cellar of a University building, the *Fürstenberghaus*. The University was closed for good following the summer semester of 1944. Ernst Haenchen's health had once again deteriorated during this period to the extent that he was forced to return to Davos to convalesce; his convalescence was arranged by his Swiss relatives. Only a Nestle Greek New Testament accompanied him on this trip, a book that came inadvertently and unnoticed across the border into Switzerland, in spite of edict that forbade the importation of anything printed in Germany. The Nestle text was to pave the way for him to begin a second academic career as an exegete during his long years in Davos.

Haenchen's convalesence in Davos was to have lasted only four weeks. The situation at that time, however, caused it to stretch into four long years. But it was during this period that Haenchen laid the basis for a second, more fruitful era of productivity. Without any secondary literature whatever, he attempted, with only the Greek text at hand, to interpret the New Testament of itself, which had taken on special interest for him during his reading. He thus made preparations for what were to be his major works: the commentary on Acts (KEK), his commentary on Mark and the synoptic parallels (*Der Weg Jesu*), his interpretation of the Corinthian letters (unpublished), as well as three volumes of essays on the Gospel of John (unpublished in part). Yet the absence of any secondary literature proved to be a singular stroke of luck. Encouraged and supported by W. Michaelis of Bern, he took the basic premise of all historical-critical interpretation to heart and became "a reader of the author." He thereby simultaneously anticipated a methodological principle of redaction criticism, which dominates the second half of this century. And so his essay on Matthew 23[5] can rightly be termed "an early, paradigmatic example of redaction-critical work,"[6] although Haenchen himself preferred the term "composition criticism." Nineteen forty-six, the year in which he was offered retirement as Professor of Systematic Theology at his own initiative, for reasons of health, was also the year

in which he finished the first edition of his commentary on Acts. Only afterwards did he work in the secondary literature, which W. Michaelis had originally placed at his disposal; later, after his return to Münster in 1948, he had his own library at hand, as well as the library of the University and faculty. With great tenacity of purpose, he began to adjust his library to his new goals. Works in systematic theology were replaced, one by one, by exegetical titles. The reworking of his text was to last ten more years, until finally the Acts commentary appeared in 1956. It went through four new editions in five years and the seventh was, at the time, in preparation under the direction of Haenchen himself. To the surprise of the author, the sale of the commentary exceeded even that of Bultmann's commentary on John, and made Haenchen famous overnight,[7] if not world famous, since an English publisher did not forego the opportunity to bring out this great tome in English translation. Haenchen's success as an exegete was anticipated in 1954, on the occasion of his sixtieth birthday, when the evangelical theological faculty of the University of Mainz did him the honor of conferring on him a Doctor of Theology *honoris causa* "in recognition of service in the field of systematic theology as well as of New Testament theology."

Haenchen's efforts to communicate theological insights of a broader range intelligibly, and yet communicate them with the authority of a scholar whose situation of necessity is "ivory tower," are demonstrated pre-eminently in his interpretation of the Gospel of Mark and its canonical parallels. That work appeared in its second edition already in 1968. He gave the title, *Der Weg Jesu* (The Path of Jesus), to his work on Mark, but for him it applied not only to the Gospel of Mark, but also to his work on John. For, in his judgment, the Gospel of John, written from a post-Easter perspective, in the power of the spirit, depicts the entire life of Jesus as the revelation and realization of the love of God.[8] From John's perspective, the entire life of Jesus was the completion of a journey that led to Jerusalem and death, which simultaneously signified his exaltation.

In addition to work that grew out of his period of preparation in Davos, as Professor emeritus, he undertook, in 1949, at the request of the faculty, an

5   *ZTK* 48 (1951) 38–63.

6   J. Lange, *Das Matthäus-Evangelium,* Wege der Forschung 525 (Darmstadt: Wissenschaftliche Buchgesellschaft, 1980) 25.

7   The impression the appearance of the commentary made on students at the time is described graphically by R. Smend, *ZTK* 72 (1975) 304–307.

8   Cf. Haenchen, "Der Vater," 72.

advanced course in Greek, and, until he reached pension age in 1959, he lectured each semester on topics that now claimed his entire attention. In the summer semester of 1956, he announced a two-hour course on "the newly discovered 'Gospel of Truth' and the New Testament"; in the winter semester of 1957/58, he gave a course on "Problems of the Gospel of John." The selection of topics made it evident how his interests were now finally recognized as related to a specific sphere of problems, interests that had claimed his attention earlier as a student and assistant, viz., the gospel of John and its history-of-religions proximity to Gnosticism, as R. Bultmann and others had averred. Since he was fluent in Coptic (in addition to eleven other foreign languages), the discoveries at Nag Hammadi fascinated him to such an extent that he became one of the first translators of texts from the Nag Hammadi library (from Coptic into German). His translation of the Gospel of Thomas[9] has become the *textus receptus* in the German language realm since its adoption in the *Synopsis Quattuor Evangeliorum* by K. Aland. Haenchen labored up to the day of his death, 30 April 1975, almost daily for eight hours, as his health permitted, on "preparations" for his commentary on John. To his commentary he desired to bring the mature fruit of his long study of Johannine problems and the most diverse attempts at their resolution in the scholarly literature, without neglecting to lay out a solution of his own or to point the way to one, which, in his opinion, best led to an entirely convincing goal. Unfortunately, it was not permitted to him to complete this great goal he had envisaged for this ancient document. It has been left for his students, friends, and especially his wife to form a commentary text out of a mountain of manuscripts, a text that best corresponded to his aim.

2. The Commentary on John

The true extent of Haenchen's "preparations" for a commentary on John became evident only after his death. Frau Haenchen arranged the manuscripts in accordance with the degree to which the paper had turned yellow, the kinds of paper, and the type of writing, so that one could determine the age of the individual pieces of "preparation" with a high degree of probability. The author possessed some characteristic mannerisms that helped the editor subsequently find his way around in the sea of papers, many of which also contained writing on the reverse side. After a year of strenuous sorting, Frau Haenchen was able to produce six huge organizers filled with "preparatory material" and a lecture notebook of her husband, which he used in giving a lecture on the Gospel of John.[10] The materials had been collected out of the cellar, manuscript cabinets, pigeonholes in his desk, and hiding places in and behind books in his library. The seeking and finding of these manuscripts confirms in its way a saying about Ernst Haenchen: he is undoubtedly "the greatest *Verleger*."[11] The manuscripts permitted themselves to be sorted, at first glance, into four successive stages of development. The oldest stage contained fully formed materials for a sketch of the commentary, which was probably composed beginning in 1954, although some materials may be earlier, since they could go back to his time in Davos. But this question can no longer be clearly resolved, because the oldest manuscript was written on an electric typewriter, to judge by the type, which was purchased in 1954.[12] Ernest Haenchen had an affinity for typewriters of all kinds, but especially for the electric typewriter. In his office one could admire the development of the German typewriter for the last few decades. Each time a typewriter that appeared to be better came on the market or came to his attention, one could be sure that he would try it out and then acquire one.[13] His peculiar disposition now enabled us to date his work in relation to the production date of the various typewriters on which he did his work; this was made easier by virtue of the fact that his failing eyesight prompted him gradually to increase the size of the type he used. The sifting of the materials thus yielded the following results for the commentary:

---

9   *Die Botschaft des Thomas-Evangeliums* (Berlin: A. Töpelmann, 1961).

10 According to information provided by E. Käsemann, the lecture must have been held at the outbreak of WW II in Münster.

11 *Verleger* means both to publish and to mislay.—Translator

12 This machine was given to the author by Ernst Haenchen so that he could write his doctoral dissertation with it and thus "bring him luck."

13 In addition to his predelection for modern office equipment, he also liked to have several radios around him, each of which was tuned to a particular domestic or foreign station. Thus, he was able at any time to receive reports from all over the world. It was regularly the case that he was better informed about the day's events than was the author.

	A	B	C	D
§1	A	B	C	
§2	A	B	C	D
§3	A	B		
§4	A		C	D
§5	A		C	D
§6.1	A	B		D
§6.2		B	C	D
§6.3			C	
§6.4			C	
1:1–18	A	B	C	
1:19–28	A	B	C	D
1:29–34	A		C	D
1:35–51	A		C	
2:1–11	A	B	C	D
2:12	A			
2:13–22		B	C	D
2:23–25	A	B		
3:1–21	A			D
3:22–36	A			
4:1–42	A	B	C	D
4:43–54	A		C	
5:1–30	A	B	C	D
5:31–47	A		C	
6:1–15	A		C	D(1–13)
6:16–25	A		C	D(14–25)
6:26–51a			C	
6:51b–59			C	
6:60–71	A			
7:1–13		B	C	
7:14–52	A	B	C	
8:12–59	A			
9:1–41	A	B		
10:1–42	A			
11:1–44	A	B	C	D
11:45–54			C	D
12:1–8	A			
12:9–11	A			
12:12–19	A	B		
12:20–36		B		
12:36b–50	A			
13:1–38	A	B		
14:1–31	A			
15:1–17	A			
15:18–26	A			
16:1–33	A			
17:1–26	A	B	C	
18:1–27			C	D
18:29–19:16a		B(19:40)	C	D
19:16b–41				D
20:1–31	A		C	
21:1–25	A		C	

In addition to the "preparatory work," there were also sketches which he had earlier sent to well-known friends and colleagues. Thus, J. M. Robinson of Claremont sent back his copy of a commentary on John which proved to be almost identical with the C version. Further, in the literary remains of Georg Richter, who was to prepare a commentary on John for the *Regensburger Neuen Testament* and who died much too young in the same year as Ernst Haenchen, a sketch was discovered, which however covered only the first five chapters of John. In addition, there were many special publications of the author on the Gospel of John and Gnosticism that had appeared in various periodicals, *Festschriften*, and lexica, as well as his commentary on Mark, which often went into matters in the Gospel of John; there were his numerous reviews in the fields related to John, and, last but not least, his collected essays. From this mass of materials a final version of the commentary had to be constructed, a version that fully reflected the development of the thinking of the author and demonstrated that he was a pathfinder in research on the Gospel of John in a post-Bultmannian and critical (but by no means apologetic) sense; at the same time, the final version had to offer the reader a complete commentary on John. This difficult task had to take into account the fact that all the versions were aimed at different levels of readership, although in their various forms they followed one methodological and theoretical conception, for the most part. In one instance, the author strove for the form of the *Handbuch zum Neuen Testament* (A), since Haenchen's commentary was originally to have replaced or supplemented the one created by W. Bauer. In another form, Haenchen was expounding the Gospel for a wider audience (B), as he has attempted to do in his commentary on Mark, *Der Weg Jesu*. Another form was obligated to his commentary on Acts (C). Since this form was retained in the latest revision (D), it seemed logical to select this form as the final one. All earlier versions thus had to be reworked so as to correspond to the form of Haenchen's commentary on Acts. At the same time, all Haenchen's notes were taken up or worked into the text, in order to be able to reserve the footnote region for remarks of the editor. Matters were difficult only where an older version for a particular pericope existed, e.g., perhaps only version B. In such cases, it was necessary to attempt to fill out the text and achieve the final form of the exposition with the help of essays, reviews, and his commentary on Mark. This procedure was successful for some passages. Unfortunately, it was not possible to shape the sections on the farewell discourses, chapters 14–16, in this way, since the material at hand was not sufficient for this purpose, although Haenchen had repeatedly assured the editor that "he had written enough on the farewell discourses."[14] In this way it was laid down as a principle that the point of departure for the commentary was to be the most recent edition, and only when necessary was the editor to fall back on earlier versions.

Two examples will serve to exemplify the viability as well as the difficulties of the principles adopted. The final version of John 6:26–59, the famous "discourse on bread," is constructed relatively simply, since it appeared among Haenchen's papers in a single (C) version, deviating only insignificantly from the Robinson text. However, there was attached to this fully worked out manuscript a further essay which was an exposition of John 6:25–71 under the title, "Jesus in Capernaum," without reference to the disjunction in verses 59f. Yet this interpretation broke off in the middle of verse 34; a continuation could not be found among the manuscripts Haenchen left behind. Moreover, the essay itself appeared to involve a discrepancy, since the interpretation of verse 30 contradicted that of verse 27. This observation made it easier to omit the trilateral, most likely unfortunate exegetical attempt from consideration. In checking the translation of the original Greek text, separately appended, which had to be supplemented, in verses 32 and 45, with a missing clause, it turned out that the author must have made the translation at the same time as the essay I had discarded as editor. For, here also John 6:25–71 was translated as one piece, but under the caption, "Jesus' Discourse in Capernaum and Its Consequence." The C-version, on the other hand, carried the title, "Jesus, the True Bread of Life" (John 6:26–51a), and the text provided by Robinson (6:26–59) read, "Jesus' Discourse on the True Bread from Heaven." Since the Overview takes verses 51b–59 as its point of departure, it seemed appropriate to choose the more comprehensive rubric and to form no special subdivision for these verses, which, according to the consensus of critical scholarship, were added by the redactor. At the same time, one paragraph of the introduction that preceded was omitted, because it anticipated the result of the exegesis.[15] Following this decision, the C-version was compared with the Robinson text for all possible deviations; they were fortunately few in number. All citations, furthermore, were checked and proofed, since the author occasionally quoted freely. Finally, the bibliography could be compiled on the basis of my own research: a selection of literature was made for each pericope for the period 1800 to the present.[16] The section was thereby made ready for the press and could be dictated.

The second example consists of the interpretation of John 4:1–42, which was available in all four versions. Thus, the most recent version—written on a Gabriele 5000—was determinative for this section of the commentary. In this case, only verses 19 and 20, which were treated together in the most recent version, were separated, with the help of older materials. At the same time, there was discovered in the old version A a reconstruction of the original form of the dialogue, which was added to the Overview. It could be documented in this manner that Ernst Haenchen earnestly sought in his early work to resolve literary-critical source questions, like his predecessors in this realm, Julius Wellhausen and Eduard Schwartz.[17] However, in the course of his work, it became dubious to Haenchen that an exact reconstruction was possible, without thereby throwing the acquired judgment overboard that the final version of the Gospel of John with chapter 21, like the Synoptics, had a longer history that had to be

---

14 Perhaps in a second edition a way will be found to rectify the deficiency.

15 The text of the omitted paragraph runs: "The great discourse that begins here and extends finally to the end of chapter six is concerned now with the significance of the 'sign' of the multiplication of loaves, at least in the first section. The text is often opaque and shows evidence of later expansions, without which of course the Gospel would not have become known. The feeding of the 5,000 (the reality of which the Evangelist did not doubt) is itself something that remains within the context of the mundane world; Jesus creates earthly bread, of course in an extraordinary way, that satiates hungry persons. But this event, in which Jesus produces such bread that satisfies human beings, is a sign, an allusion to something different, which is there to be seen. Whoever sees only the mundane occurrence of the multiplication of the loaves has not seen the sign at all, viz., the allusion to Jesus as the bread of life, and as the bread of life he always satiates people and leads forever."

16 I am grateful to Gilbert Van Belle, Löwen, for valuable suggestions. The scholarly literature has been further supplemented for the English translation.

17 Also see the Overview to John 11.

taken into consideration in any interpretation of the work. Only so can the diverging theological assertions in this Gospel be cogently explained, after a fashion. When the final version was assembled, which contained the steps already described, a separate manuscript in a late hand was also worked into the Overview, a discussion in which Haenchen was debating with the work of B. Olsson.[18] This was done in order not to permit the final fruits of the author's reading and his critical response to be lost. It also demonstrates that Ernst Haenchen was fully participant in the exegetical discussion of the Gospel of John shortly before his death just prior to his eighty-first birthday.

A text-critical edition of all the works of Ernst Haenchen on the Gospel of John would certainly produce still further valuable suggestions that would exceed the selection made here of necessity. My preeminent aim was to keep twenty-five years of research on the Gospel of John from being lost and to gain a true hearing once more for the weighty voice of an esteemed teacher. Much of value from the first drafts could not be included in the final version of the commmentary because it had to be kept within the economic range of its readers.

3. Johannine Exegesis

Ernst Haenchen gained his theological conceptions as well as his literary-critical ideas of source, identifiable only in outline, in conversation above all with Bultmann's interpretation of the Gospel of John. He set out his point of departure for his theological reflections already in his programmatic essay, "Der Vater, der mich gesandt hat" (1963). His divergent opinion with respect to Bultmann's interpretation was further detailed in his essay, "Das Johannesevangelium und sein Kommentar" (1964).

For Rudolf Bultmann the Johannine Jesus was the revealer who, 'out of his oneness with God,'[19] as one sent alone into the world with the pure *that* (*Dass*) of his *coming*, makes possible the true existence of man in the moment of the decision for faith. For, this eschatological now of the revelation (= the sending) and of faith permits the indwelling of God in man and opens up for the one who decides for the long expected revealer an eternal future life, but for the one who does not so decide there is judgment. "John . . . in his Gospel presents only the fact (*Das Dass*) of the Revelation without describing its content (*ihr Was*)."[20] Jesus reveals "as the Revealer of God . . . *nothing but that he is the Revealer.*"[21] Bultmann accordingly interprets the Gospel of John in a radically anthropological way under the point of view of an existential faith-decision for or against the presence of God in the history, in the fact of the *coming* of Jesus. Accordingly, the tender of salvation by God is not confined to Jesus' Jewish contemporaries; rather, eschatological salvation repeatedly occurs as the history of Jesus, that is, in the history of Christian missionary preaching that takes Jesus as its reference. This message of Jesus' *coming* is the comprehensive formula for the sending of Jesus, for his becoming flesh and his earthly works, for his death and resurrection, for the parousia and the outpouring of the spirit on the church.

For Ernst Haenchen, it was a matter of supplementing or destroying Johannine theology for Bultmann to confirm, in the original text, the close existential management of both christological and eschatological sayings in the Gospel of John by means of historical criticism. For Haenchen, the modern concept of revelation employed by Bultmann was far from acceptable.[22] If the word "revealer" does not appear in the Gospel of John (except, perhaps, at John 17:6),[23] how can this concept be selected as the key notion for the interpretation of John? As in the first epistle of John, the Gospel also champions the thesis that God dwells in a light that is inaccessible to knowledge, from whom, however, the Son as one sent has brought a message. The Evangelist conceives the position of Jesus as positively subordinistic. All activity proceeds from the Father, who sent his son into the world. It is precisely the first two verses of the prologue, which Bultmann offers as evidence that the revealer is identical with God, that prove him wrong. For, as in the case of Philo and Origen, for the Gospel of John, too, there exists a distinction between "God" (ὁ θεός) and "divine" (θεός). "That contains a christology of the subordination of the son, albeit still covertly. It is precisely for this reason that the believer sees the Father in the son: the son does not speak his own words, he does not do his own

---

18 *Structure and Meaning in the Fourth Gospel. A Text-Linguistic Analysis of John 2:1–11 and 4:1–42*, tr. Jean Gray. ConBNT 6 (Lund: C. W. K. Gleerup, 1974).

19 *New Testament Theology*, 2: 62.

20 Bultmann, *Theology of the New Testament*, 2: 66.

21 Bultmann, *Theology of the New Testament*, 2:66.

22 Cf. "Das Johannesevangelium und sein Kommentar," 218.

23 See the Commentary on 14:21.

works, he does not effect his own will, but subordinates himself entirely to the words, work, and will of the Father."[24] The son, therefore, is only "one" with the Father to this extent (cf. John 10:29f. with 14:28), and the two are not "of one" because Jesus does what the Father does.[25] Jesus remains constantly subordinate to the Father in the Gospel of John. Otherwise, in the so-called "high priestly prayer" Jesus would be conducting a monologue. Even the expression ἐγώ εἰμι ("I am") speaks of Jesus as he whom the Father has sent. "In the last analysis, therefore, the Father is also the true subject of the 'I am' sayings."[26]

If the "refined concept of revelation in the twentieth century"[27] is not adequate to the task, then the question of the content, of the "what" of the message of the Johannine Jesus is posed anew. As whom does the son now reveal the Father? "John saw the earthly life of Jesus as the revelation and the realization of God's love."[28] He depicts that trenchantly in the footwashing scene (John 13:1–30). "Jesus' act in washing feet—denoting his self-abnegation to the extent of death—is his salvific act of revelation. One cannot enter into fellowship with him and thereby with the "Father" whom he has revealed if one is not prepared for this same act of self-abnegation. Everything turns on this kind of existence, which alone makes unity with the Father and the son possible."[29] Insofar as Jesus himself fulfills this self-abnegating love in an ignominious death is he the bread of life, the light of the world, the true shepherd, and the true vine.

Further, the oft repeated thesis of Bultmann that Jesus' revelation or sending consists in the pure communication of the faith-demanding assertion "that he is the revealer whom the Father has sent leads to error, for Ernst Haenchen. "For, the capitulation of the [supply: perceiving—author] reason, which ought to occur in view of the identity asserted between two absolutely diverse entities [supply: Father and son—author], would lead to Nihilism, but not to faith in the forgiveness of sins and trust in a new future provided by God, which cannot arise without a pronouncement about a gracious God. For, according to Bultmann's own presupposition, God is unknown to man prior to his revelation to man, and

thus an *x*. Accordingly, Jesus' statement (the one John provides according to Bultmann) is reduced from "I am God" to "I am *x*." Since, however, this *x* must not be filled with content (by a forbidden assertion about the "how" of God), it remains a "nothing."[30] But in this way faith would be transmitted as an arbitrary acceptance of the "how" of God. For this reason, it is indispensable to give the Johannine concept of God some content. For the Johannine tradition it is the love of God, which has been manifested in the incarnation and works of Jesus, to the extent of his self-sacrifice in a singular death. On this basis, Haenchen also opposes a constriction of the sending of Jesus to "the moment of his coming." Rather, in the Gospel of John, from a post-Easter, spirit-filled perspective, a Jesus story is sketched out in which three years of public works have revealed and realized the love of God. Thus, in the Gospel, there is a compelling presentation of "the earthly life of Jesus as the word of the Father's love spoken and enacted by Jesus to and for those believing," . . . "which, however, can be only be understood in the light of the resurrection, in the sending of the spirit by the risen one, and which belongs to those enabled to come to faith by this same spirit."[31]

In this same context, Haenchen is also forced to negate Bultmann's thesis that the Evangelist remodelled a gnostic cosmological dualism into an anthropological dualism of decision in his revelation discourses. Quite apart from the fact that dualism is not an unambiguous gnostic phenomenon, but is also at home in wisdom, many Johannine texts speak against such an interpretation. "Anthropology is not the key to the whole, human decision—however it is understood—is not the decisive thing. One does not thank himself or herself [supply: as a Christian—author] for a privileged position; one owes it to divine compassion. One experiences this compassion in the coming of the divine message. That apparently agrees exactly with gnostic theology. But this message is not encountered in a mythical person, it is not brought by an emissary who only makes a flying visit, for whom the appearance on earth is merely a change in locale; it is encountered in a real human life, one that ended on the gallows. The 'Father' who ven-

---

24 Commentary on John 1:1: 111.

25 See the Commentary on John 10:31.

26 Haenchen, "Das Johannesevangelium und sein Kommentar," 221f.; cf. the Commentary on John 1:1 and 10:8.

27 Haenchen, "Das Johannesevangelium und sein Kommentar," 218.

28 Haenchen, "Der Vater," 72.

29 Commentary on John 13:1–30: 114.

30 Haenchen, "Das Johannesevangelium und sein Kommentar," 121 n. 37; cf. the Commentary on 14:21.

31 Haenchen, "Das Johannesevangelium und sein Kommentar," 230.

tures into the world in his emissary in such an entirely different form turns out on account of the cross to be someone quite different than the gnostic king of light. He chose a group of men who can boast of nothing that gave them a claim to be chosen."[32] Ernst Haenchen would prefer to speak of a kind of anthropological "determinism"[33] in the Gospel of John only with the proviso that some texts reflect precisely the experience of the Johannine community (but cf. also Mark 14:14–20: "the message of Jesus: no matter how persuasively and scintillatingly it is presented, it still seizes some while leaving others cold. For one it is the word of God; for the other, it is merely a human word that is not convincing."[34] God himself has revealed himself in Jesus as the Father who accepts the world in love, on the Evangelist's view (John 3:16f., 4:42, 6:33, 8:12, 9:5, 17:21, 23).

In addition to his conversation with R. Bultmann, his criticial relation to the position of Ernst Käsemann helped him to sharpen his own position.[35] He was unable to discern a "naive docetism" in the Gospel of John. He also rejected the formulation that Jesus was represented in the Gospel as "a god striding over the earth," an expression that Käsemann had taken from liberal theology (Baldensperger), as not justified by the text. On Haenchen's view, Jesus' journey to the cross reveals that love is the content of the sending of the son. He actually "executed" the commission of God on the cross (John 19:30). The redactional reworking of the text attempts, above all, to guard the Gospel against the docetic error, into which the Evangelist himself had not yet fallen, by emphasizing the reality of Jesus' death (19:34f.) and resurrection (20:20, 25, 27), and by making the sacrament more realistically palpable (6:51–59).[36] Even John 17 must not be misunderstood, from the perspective of the Evangelist, in this sense. "Some interpreters have allowed themselves to be misled by the view that this passage does not expressly refer to Jesus' death, and are of the opinion that the hour is really nothing but Jesus' exaltation to the Father. But then Jesus' earthly life becomes merely a sojourn in a foreign land, that is now coming to an end, and the 'hour' becomes the moment when Jesus, perhaps still giddy like a butterfly from the earth's pull, swings into eternity. But that would be a fundamental mis-

understanding. It is not said, to be sure, that this hour is the death on the cross, that now draws near. . . . One could say that the scene of the prayer is being played already in eternity where time is no longer in effect. . . . The 'already' and the 'not yet' interchange with each other, because the author's point of view lies way beyond Easter, beyond the reception of the spirit."[37]

Haenchen also rejected the other thesis of Käsemann, viz., the alleged "docetic" traits of the Johannine miracle stories. He held that these stories had their origin in putative theos-aner legends. The Evangelist was able to take these traditions over because he was convinced of the actuality of the miracles.[38] Yet he did not view—contrary to his source—the miracles of Jesus as proofs of his divinity, but as signs, as pointers to something entirely different. This something different, however, had as its goal the same goal as Jesus' path, viz., death.[39] The true glory of Jesus is only revealed specifically in his death. Johannine theology remains true to the representation of Jesus' life in the synoptic tradition: only first in or after the scandalous criminal's death suffered by Jesus was his true essence and destiny revealed. "The earthly life of Jesus is important to him [the Evangelist] because it eliminates the danger that the experience of the spirit [on the part of post-Easter Christians] will turn out to be a subjective dream. And yet the Evangelist does not simply reproduce the historical past. . . . He rather has the historical Jesus interpret the practical knowledge of the spirit and thus takes the historical Jesus up into the new reality of the spirit."[40] In this way, the passion of Jesus does not represent the kind of problem for Haenchen that it does for Ernst Käsemann; rather, in that passion . . . the path of Jesus, from a historical perspective, reaches its macabre depth, yet from a soteriological point of view it achieves its absolute salvific goal.

A further problem for Haenchen was the history of the tradition underlying the Gospel of John: he did not bring his view to a logical conclusion, but he had it constantly in view and knew that it was a problem to be taken seriously by further research. Bultmann's commentary on John was the most recent impetus for thinking through the question afresh.

---

32 Commentary on John 17:9.
33 He had no use for dogmatic concepts in the exegetical realm.
34 Commentary on John 6:40.
35 Cf. Ernst Käsemann, "Ketzer und Zeuge. Zum johanneischen Verfasserproblem," in: *Exegetische Versuche und Besinnungen* 1 (Göttingen: Vandenhoeck & Ruprecht, 1967) 168–187; "The Structure and

Purpose of the Prologue to John's Gospel," in: *New Testament Questions*: 138–167; *The Testament of Jesus.*
36 Commentary on John 6:52.
37 Commentary, Overview on John 17: 158.
38 Commentary, Overview on 6:26–59: 300f.
39 Commentary, Overview on John 17:1–26: 159.
40 Commentary on John 14:25f.

Bultmann reckoned with a signs-source, a compendium of revelatory discourses connected with the baptismal sect, and an independent passion narrative as distinctive materials, which the Evangelist collected and arranged in a single gospel. This gospel may later have been supplemented once more by an "ecclesiastical redactor" and chapter 21 added, and altogether reworked for ecclesiastical use. Beyond that, Bultmann reckoned with an erroneous rearrangement on the part of the redactor, who, for example, reversed the order of chapters 5 and 6. He explained the disorder on the basis that the redactor no longer knew the original order of the text, because it had earlier been destroyed by external circumstances.[41] Thus he saw himself compelled to reconstitute the text on his part as well (or as poorly) as he could.

Since this account of the origin of the Gospel of John appeared extremely dubious to Ernst Haenchen, he gladly reverted to the knowledge of those old masters of source criticism, Julius Wellhausen and Eduard Schwartz. Both had already attempted, at the turn of the century, to separate out from each other the putative documents used by the author. However, according to the unanimous opinion of the scholarly world, their effort was a failure. No one seriously attempted subsequently to work their knowledge into a new source model. It was therefore a matter of avoiding their mistakes and yet holding to their thesis: "A gospel as extensive as the Gospel of John cannot have been written without the use of some sources."[42] If, in his "preparatory work," Haenchen took as his basic hypothesis that the textual basis of the Gospel consisted of a non-canonical "miracle gospel," a signs-source, which contained more than miracle stories the author had recast with the help of his pneumatic christology and eschatology, so his literary-critical interests shifted with the progress of his work. He now no longer proposed to reconstruct the oldest textual layer, but refrained from this task and attempted to ascertain the relationship between Evangelist and redactor more closely. And so in the commentary itself, he regularly poses the source question, but does not recommend a final solution in relation to the history of research, which is loaded with partition theories. He made do with three levels in the text:

(1) The final redaction, which is responsible for chapter 21 and which repeatedly advocates, among other things, a futuristic eschatology and a pronounced doctrine of the sacraments; this final editing also urgently demands brotherly love as a consequence of the sending Jesus, and attempts to establish the Johannine catechetical tradition with the help of the paraclete and the "beloved disciple." This makes it possible to fix the place of this literary stratum in the history of theology. The redactor appears to be waging war against a gnosticising docetism within the Johannine community, as is the author of 1 John.

(2) The Evangelist formed his gospel out of various traditonal materials, among others, out of individual putative miracle stories and an independent passion narrative. His aim is not to provide a true picture of Jesus' past, "but he proposes to plead the cause of Jesus himself by having Jesus say what the Evangelist takes to be the truth—in his consciousness of possessing the Spirit."[43] His place in the history of theology, as well as his sociological home, is an underground conventicle of pneumatic Christians, who "caught sight of the sole important thing, the thing that gave meaning to life, in the present encounter with the message of Jesus."[44]

(3) The Evangelist has also made use of traditions—as already indicated—but whether that includes a non-canonical signs-sources, as many conjecture, Haenchen became increasingly dubious as time went by.

In spite of his healthy skepticism with respect to hazardous source theories, Ernst Haenchen did not shift to the contrary thesis that the Fourth Gospel was a unity on the basis of stylistic and linguistic grounds. For him, the language and style of the Gospel of John represented spoken Koine Greek of a community still possibily influenced by Jewish Christians in the region of Asia Minor. The redactor easily imitated the colloquial language with its profuse use of substantives and small vocabulary. He therefore viewed the attempt "to introduce 'objective' characteristics of the language of the Gospel of John as arguments against partition into sources" as a failure.[45]

41 Cf. the Commentary, Introduction, §4: Disorder and Rearrangement.
42 Commentary, Introduction, §6: Sources, Composition, Style, and Author: 74.
43 Commentary on John 6:26.
44 Commentary on John 6:26–59, Overview: 299.
45 Commentary, Introduction, §5: The Language of the Gospel of John: 66.

4. The Work Continues

This last section can be given the same title as the last section of Haenchen's introduction to his commentary on Acts: "The Work Continues."[46] In the introduction to his work, Haenchen requests that even the reader understand his work as an attempt "that requires a correlative degree of reflection and forbearance on his or her part."[47] The author of these lines cannot hide the fact that precisely the mixture of literary and redaction criticism, together with theological penetration in the discipline of critical thought, inspired him to seize the central theme and with its help probe the problematic of the Gospel of John and its message.

As an example, we may once again have recourse to the "discourse on bread" in John 6:26–59. For Haenchen, verses 51b–59 constituted a redactional interpolation, which had already been fitted out with secondary additions (vv 27, 39, 40, 44). "While the Evangelist sees the present of the exalted one in the word of the proclamation (kerygma), that does not satisfy the redactor. He has not grasped that Jesus made the Father present in his word and deed and that the preaching of the disciples continues that making present of the Father—they thus proclaim that in which the Father was and is to be seen. This 'is' occurs, however, only in the word."

"The redactor, on the other hand, wants more 'palpability'; he wants what the sacrament appears to provide. His doctrine of the sacrament, however, is not easy to comprehend. His basic presupposition is that the exalted one has taken his humanity with him into heaven, so to speak. Contact with him depends on that humanity. . . . The believing Christian acquires communion with the humanity of Jesus—so the redactor appears to intend his doctrine of the eucharist: the Christian literally takes that humanity into himself and thus Jesus also. That is a complete misunderstanding on the part of the Evangelist: the humanity of Jesus is important for him only because it makes possible the 'becoming visible' of the invisible Father—in suggestive deeds and words. . . ."

"For the redactor, on the other hand, much more weight lay on the palpability of the connection with Jesus in the present. For him the reality of the connection of the believer with his heavenly savior is alone important because this believer no longer understood himself as 'spirit,' but as a person of flesh and blood. . . . It becomes evident on the basis of the letters of Ignatius why such weight was placed on the tangibility of the eating and drinking of the resurrected Christ: only in this way did one guard against the gnostic heresy that Jesus' body was only an apparition. Gnosticism held the view it did because for it an incarnation already signified an entry into the sinful world. For Christians, on the other hand, such a doctrine was unacceptable, because on this view Jesus would be only an appearance, a phantom, which was not a revelation of the Father."[48] The isolation of redactional elements succeeds, in this case, only in developing a theological contrast between the Evangelist and the redactor.

This process prompts the question whether it really makes sense when the redactor, in spite of his theological opposition to statements in the text, takes precisely these statements over and reworks and supplements them in accordance with his own purpose. What links nevertheless make that possible for him? It is understandable only when the redactional reworking goes beyond what has hitherto been accepted and also takes up theological aspects that are the Evangelist's own. The understanding of the sacraments thus acquires a different relative position. Following a suggestion of Bornkamm[49] and Thyen,[50] the redactional interpolation could begin with verse 47. For, verses 47–51a repeat kernel statements of the alleged discourse on bread that are important to the redactor, and they remain important for him since verse 58 returns to them once again. From this point of view, verse 33 is also secondary, at least verse 33b, since this verse anticipates the answer to the question in verse 34, to which the original trajectory of the dialogue was directed. Verse 33, moreover, is close to verses 50f., 58 in content. Likewise, it is hardly every contested anymore that verses 39f., with their futuristic eschatology, are redactional additions. Further, there appears in these verses a motif on whose account verse 40 is constructed as an analogue to verse 39. The motif "seeing and believing" (cf. John 20) has already been appended in verse 30 as a question to the original "What work do you perform?" and stands in tension

46   *Acts of the Apostles*, 116–132.
47   Commentary: 1.
48   Commentary on John 6:26–59: 298f.
49   "Die eucharistische Rede im Johannesevangelium," *ZNW* 47 (1956) 161–169.
50   "Aus der Literatur zum Johannesevangelium," *TRu* 43 (1978) 328–359; 44 (1979) 97–118.

with it. Only verse 36 then remains problematical. The motif shows up here in a somewhat altered form, and the verse appears to participate in the anticipation of verse 41. One could therefore conclude that the verse belongs to the source and prompted the redactor to work this motif, which appeared important to him (cf. John 20:29), in at other points in the passage. Yet this motif was already introduced in verses 29f., so that an additional suggestion was unnecessary. Be that as it may, it appears that in the final version of the discourse on bread the redactor worked in not only the ideas about futuristic eschatology and the sacraments, but also the motif of the descent of the one who is the bread of life for the salvation of the world and the motif of "seeing and believing," the latter having been taken over from the source. This observation, in my judgment, permits the contrast between two opposing theological positions in the discourse to appear improbable. Rather, the redactor corrects his source circumspectly, pointedly, and by nuancing, and gives it a final apologetic twist. Finally, it is best explained, as a matter of fact, as presenting an antidocetic front.

Has Ernst Haenchen—like many others before him—correctly characterized docetism as an aporia in early ecclesiastical christology (and not as an intrusion of gnosis into the christology of the church)? Is the "phantom body" really the heart of this doctrine? Apart from the fact that docetism is found outside of Gnosticism also,[51] in the struggle within the church over docetism the central question, in my opinion, is whether Jesus, who has returned to God and who already prior to the creation lay on the bosom of the Father, really become man or, as a heavenly being, did he merely become an epiphany by putting on flesh (cf. the concept σαρκοφόρος ["wear flesh"] Ign. *Smyr.* 5.2). According to graeco-hellenistic thought, a divine being can never be a genuine element of the world. Such a being only appears to be a part of the world. The question of the "historical Jesus" is thus posed for the first time in the history of Christian theology; the saving faith of Christians and the redemption of the world hangs on Jesus' history and message. In as much as the redactor now not only coarsens the understanding of the sacraments and connects them with the eating and drinking of the flesh and blood of Jesus, but also connects them with the motif of "seeing and believing" as well as with the concept of Jesus' descent into the world, in receiving the sacraments, all Christians testify that Jesus, as true man, has created a life-giving relationship with

God for all those who believe. Since Christians eat and drink the body and blood of Jesus as signs of faith, they receive eternal life (v 56), because the promise is connected therewith that Jesus will raise them on the last day. Thus, the common primitive Christian meal sacrament is employed antidocetically and functions apologetically.

The pointing character of the miracle in the understanding of the Evangelist, correctly emphasized by Ernst Haenchen, is likewise accepted by the redactor and deliberately taken over. The comments in John 20:29–31 support this view. John 20:30–31 does not form a conclusion to a "miracles gospel" that the Evangelist allowed to stand as something displaced or which he inserted, but with these intervening verses (John 20:29–31; interpreted as such already by Johann Cocceius [1603–1669]) he comments on the significance of the resurrection stories for his post-Easter readers in the acute situation of a controversy over docetism. He can therefore permit an additional Easter story to follow in chapter 21 without contradiction. He reckons it consciously as the third appearance story (John 21:14); it thereby becomes clear which epiphany stories were added by him to the original Easter story of the Evangelist (20:1, 11–17). All of them emphasize the palpability of the resurrected Jesus. There is no further mention of an apparition, as in Luke 24:37.

Ernst Haenchen affirmed the thesis, generally accepted since P. Gardner-Smith, that there was no literary dependence between the Gospel of John and the Synoptics. At the same time, he emphasized that the Christian tradition was transmitted orally as well as in written form for a long time, until the time of the Church Fathers and the Nag Hammadi texts. It is for this reason that some narrative segments, of which a relationship to synoptic parallels cannot be denied, are transmitted in the Johannine tradition in another form. But it is also possible that, although there was no literary dependence between individual synoptic gospels and particular strata in the Gospel of John (or was there?), there was nevertheless a theological interchange of ideas. In the scholarly literature there is constant reference to the proximity of Luke 24 to John 20. Haenchen himself believed that there was theological borrowing on the part of the Evangelist from the Markan tradition. That calls for a review of an old question.

In the same context, it must also be asked whether there is not a greater degree of relationship between the Gospel of John and 1 John than has genrally been

---

51   Cf. Gen 18 with Philo, *De Abr.* 22.107, 113; 23.118; 24.119; Josephus, *Ant.* 1.11.2 and Tob 12:19).

conceded for a long time now. Since the redactor uses the same argumentative weapons against docetism as does the author of 1 John, the two could be one and the same person or could stem from the same school. In any case, 1 John offers a better key by far to an understanding of the redactional reworking of the Fourth Gospel than do some excursions into the history of hellenistic-Jewish religion.

For Ernst Haenchen the message of the Evangelist was evidence of a special Christian development on the edge of the Christianity of "the great church"; this special development—in some respects proximate to Gnosticism—led an isolated life of its own. But is this opinion, shared also by Ernst Käsemann, really well founded? It is at least possible that exactly the reverse is the case. The Johannine tradition then represents the faith and experience of normal, pneumatic Christianity in Asia Minor and Syria during the waning years of the first century. This form of Christianity has its basis in those Christian enthusiasts who made life difficult for Paul and whose followers were in the majority among Antiochian

Christians in the time of Ignatius. The language and style of the Gospel of John provides persuasive evidence for this view. John lacks a significant diction of its own. Further, the formative drive of a literate author struggling with the gospel form is frequently sorely lacking. The impression is not so easily dismissed that Paul, Mark, Matthew, and Luke are real exceptional phenomena, by contrast. Was it not perhaps necessary for the redactor to come first in order to overcome some of the one-sided statements of the Evangelist? For, only so could the last canonical gospel be of equal rank with the others or even exceed them, viewed from the perspective of the effect of each on history.

The inquiries here directed at research, deliberately formulated thetically, are designed to demonstrate that the labors of Ernst Haenchen centered on the Gospel of John—labors that lasted for decades—have certainly not solved all the problems, yet they point the way, in this arena of NT studies where debate is so vigorous, to a larger consensus to which we may aspire.

Universität Duisburg
Ulrich Busse

Bibliography

1. General and Reference

Aland, Kurt
Studien zur Überlieferung des Neuen Testaments und seines Textes, Arbeiten zur Neutestamentlichen Textforschung 2 (Berlin: Walter de Gruyter, 1967).

Aland, Kurt, ed.
Synopsis of the Four Gospels: Greek English Edition of the Synopsis Quattuor Evangeliorum (United Bible Societies, ³1979).

Baly, Denis
The Geography of the Bible, rev. ed. (New York: Harper & Row, 1974).

Bardenhewer, O., et al.
Bibliothek der Kirchenväter (Munich: Kösel, 1911–1930).

Bauer, Walter
A Greek-English Lexicon of the New Testament and Other Early Christian Literature, tr. and adapted by William F. Arndt and F. Wilbur Gingrich. Second edition, revised and augmented by F. Wilbur Gingrich and Frederick W. Danker (Chicago and London: University of Chicago Press, 1979) = *Griechisch-Deutsches Wörterbuch zu den Schriften des Neuen Testaments und der übrigen urchristlichen Literatur* (Berlin: A. Töpelmann, ⁴1952, ⁵1958).

Bauer, Walter
Orthodoxy and Heresy in Earliest Christianity, ed. Robert A. Kraft and Gerhard Krodel (Philadelphia: Fortress Press, 1971).

Bengel, Johann Albrecht
Gnomen of the New Testament, tr. Charlton T. Lewis and Marvin R. Vincent (Philadelphia: Perkinpine & Higgins, 1864) 2:782–822; reprinted as *New Testament Word Studies* (Grand Rapids: Kregel, 1971) = *Gnomon Novi Testamenti* (Stuttgart: Steinkopf, 1860).

Beyer, K.
Semitische Syntax im Neuen Testament. Vol. 1, part 1: *Satzlehre,* SUNT 1 (Göttingen: Vandenhoeck & Ruprecht, ²1968).

Bihlmeyer, Karl
Die apostolischen Väter. Vol. 1, *Didache, Barnabas, Klemens I und II, Ignatius, Polykarp, Papias, Quadratus, Diognetbrief,* SAQ, 2, 1 (Tübingen: Mohr-Siebeck, 1924).

Black, Matthew
An Aramaic Approach to the Gospels and Acts (Oxford: Clarendon Press, ²1954).

Blass, F., A. Debrunner, and R. W. Funk
A Greek Grammar of the New Testament (Chicago: University of Chicago Press, 1961).

Braun, Herbert
"Qumran und das Neue Testament. Ein Bericht über 10 Jahre Forschung (1950–1959)." *TRu* 28 (1962) 56–61.

Brown, Raymond E.
Peter in the New Testament: A Collaborative Assessment by Protestant and Roman Catholic Scholars (Minneapolis: Augsburg; New York: Paulist, 1973).

Bruyne, Donatien de
Die ältesten Evangelien-Prologe und die Bildung des Neuen Evangelienprologe, SPAW.PH 24 (Berlin: G. Reimer, 1928).

Bultmann, Rudolf
History of the Synoptic Tradition, tr. John Marsh (New York: Harper & Row, 1963).

Bultmann, Rudolf
Theology of the New Testament, vol 2. Tr. Kendrick Grobel (London: SCM Press, 1955).

Cadbury, Henry J.
The Making of the Luke-Acts (London: S. P. C. K., 1968).

Charles, Robert Henry, ed.
The Apocrypha and Pseudepigrapha of the Old Testament in English, with Introductions and Critical and Explanatory Notes to the Several Books, 2 vols. Vol. 1, *Apocrypha;* Vol. 2, *Pseudepigrapha* (Oxford: Clarendon Press, 1913).

Colpe, Carsten
Die religionsgeschichtliche Schule. Darstellung und Kritik ihres Bildes vom gnostischen Erlösermythos, FRLANT, n.s., 60 (Göttingen: Vandenhoeck & Ruprecht, 1961).

Cramer, John Anthony, ed.
Catenae graecorum patrum in Novum Testamentum, 8 vols. Vol. 2, *Catenae in evangelia s. Lucae et s. Johannis* (Oxford, 1838–1944; reprint Hildesheim: G. Olms, 1967).

Cross, F. L., ed. and tr.
The Jung Codex: A Newly Recovered Gnostic Papyrus. Three Studies by H. C. Puech, G. Quispel and W. C. van Unnik (London: A. R. Mowbray, 1955).

Dalman, Gustaf
Sacred Sites and Ways: Studies in the Topography of the Gospels, tr. Paul P. Levertoff (London: S. P. C. K.; New York: Macmillan, 1935).

Dalman, Gustaf Hermann
Grammatik des jüdisch-palästinensischen Aramäisch (Leipzig: J. C. Hinrichs, 1894, ²1905; Darmstadt: Wissenschaftliche Buchgesellschaft, 1960).

Dibelius, Martin
From Tradition to Gospel, tr. Bertram Lee Woolf (New York: Charles Scribner's Sons, n.d.).

Dibelius, Martin and Conzelmann, Hans
The Pastoral Epistles: A Commentary on the Pastoral Epistles, ed. Helmut Koester; tr. Philip Buttolph and Adela Yarbro. Hermeneia—A Critical-Historical Commentary on the Bible (Philadelphia: Fortress Press, 1972) = *Die Pastoralbriefe,* ed.

Günther Bornkamm. HNT 13 (Tübingen: Mohr-Siebeck, ⁴1966).

Dungan, David L. and Cartlidge, David R.
Documents for the Study of the Gospels (Cleveland: Collins, 1980).

Eisler, Robert
Ἰησοῦς βασιλεὺς οὐ βασιλεύσας. *Die messianische Unabhängigkeits Bewegung vom Auftreten Johannes des Täufers bis zum untergang Jakobs des Gerechten, nach der neuerschlossenen Eroberung von Jerusalem des Flavius Josephus und den christlichen Quellen*, 2 vols. (Heidelberg: Carl Winter, 1929–1930).

Ewald, Heinrich
Geschichte des Volkes Israel, 7 vols. Vol. 7, *Die Geschichte der Ausgänge des Volkes Israel und des nachapostolischen Zeitalters* (Göttingen: Dieterich, ³1864–1868).

Foakes-Jackson, F. J. and Kirsopp Lake, eds.,
The Beginnings of Christianity, 5 vols. (Grand Rapids: Baker Book House, 1979).

Foerster, Werner
Die Gnosis. Vol. 1, *Zuegnisse der Kirchenväter. Unter Mitwirkung von E. Haenchen und M Krause eingeleitet, übersetzt und erläutert*, ed. C. Andresen. Die Bibliothek der Alten Welt, Reihe Antike und Christentum (Zurich and Stuttgart: Artemis, 1969); Vol. 2, *Koptische und Mandäische Quellen, eingeleitet, übersetzt und erläutert von M. Krause, K. Rudolph, mit Registern zu Bd. I und II* (Zurich and Stuttgart: Artemis, 1971).

Foerster, Werner
Neutestamentliche Zeitgeschichte (Hamburg: Furche, 1968).

Frickel, J.
Die "Apophasis Megale" in Hyppolyt's Refutatio (VI 9–18): Eine Paraphrase zur Apophasis Simons, Orientalia Christiana Analecta 182 (Rome: Pontifical Institute of Oriental Studies, 1968).

Gaffron, Hans-Georg
"Studien zum koptischen Philippusevangelium unter unter besonderer Berücksichtigung der Sakramente," Dissertation, Bonn, 1969.

Galling, Kurt, ed.
Religion in Geschichte und Gegenwart, ed. Kurt Galling (Tübingen: Mohr-Siebeck, ²1927–1932; ³1957–1962).

Gärtner, B. E.
The Theology of the Gospel according to Thomas, tr. Eric J. Sharpe (New York: Harper & Brothers, 1961).

Giversen, S.
Apocryphon Johannis: The Coptic Text of the Apocryphon Johannis in the Nag Hammadi Codex II with Translation, Introduction and Commentary, Acta Theological Danica 5 (Copenhagen: Prostant apud Munksgaard, 1963).

Giversen, S.
Sanhedens Evangelium. De Gnostiske Håndskrifter fra Nildaden, Theologiske studier, Raekke 2, Nr. 2 (Copenhagen: G. E. C. Gads Forlag, 1957).

Goodspeed, Edgar J.
Die älteste Apologeten; Texte mit kurzen Einleitungen (Göttingen: Vandenhoeck & Ruprecht, 1914).

Grant, Robert M.
Gnosticism. A Sourcebook of Heretical Writings from the Early Christian Period (New York: Harper & Brothers, 1961).

Grese, W. C.
Corpus Hermeticum XIII and Early Christian Literature, Studia ad Corpus Hellenisticum Novi Testamenti 5 (Leiden: E. J. Brill, 1979).

Groebel, Kendrick
The Gospel of Truth. A Valentinian Meditation on the Gospel; Translation from the Coptic and Commentary (Nashville: Abingdon Press; London: A. & C. Black, 1960).

Grundmann, Walter
Das Evangelium nach Lukas, THKNT 3 (Berlin: Evangelische Verlagsanstalt, ²1961).

Grundmann, Walter
Das Evangelium nach Matthäus, THKNT 1 (Berlin: Evangelische Verlagsanstalt, 1968).

Grundmann, Walter
Das Evangelium nach Markus, THKNT 2 (Berlin: Evangelische Verlagsanstalt, 1959, ⁷1977).

Guillaumont, A. et al.
The Gospel According to Thomas. Coptic Text Established and Translated (Leiden: E. J. Brill; London: Collins; New York: Harper & Brothers, 1959).

Haardt, R.
Die Gnosis. Wesen und Zeugnisse (Salzburg: O. Müller, 1967).

Haenchen, Ernst
Die Botschaft des Thomas-Evangeliums, Theologische Bibliothek Töpelmann 6 (Berlin: A. Töpelmann, 1961).

Haenchen, Ernst
The Acts of the Apostles: A Commentary (Philadelphia: Westminster Press, 1971) = *Die Apostelgeschichte*, KEK (Göttingen: Vandenhoeck & Ruprecht, ¹⁴1965).

Hatch, Edwin and Henry A. Redpath, compilers
A Concordance to the Septuagint and the Other Greek Versions of the Old Testament (Including the Apocryphal Books), 2 vols. (Graz-Austra: Akademische Druck- und Verlagsanstalt, 1954).

Hausrath, Adolf
Neutestamentliche Zeitgeschichte (Heidelberg: Bassermann, ²1874).

Hirsch, Emmanuel
Frühgeschichte des Evangeliums. Vol. 1, *Das Werden des Markus-Evangeliums* (Tübingen: Mohr-Siebeck, 1941).

Hirsch, Emmanuel
Geschichte der neueren evangelischen Theologie (Gütersloh: Gerd Mohn, 1960–1964).

Hirsch, Emmanuel
Die Auferstehungsgeschichten und der christliche Glaube

(Tübingen: Mohr-Siebeck, 1940).

Jastrow, Marcus
  A Dictionary of the Targumim, the Talmud Babli and Yerushalmi, and the Midrashic Literature, 2 vols. (New York: Pardes Publishing House, 1950).

Jeremias, Joachim
  Jerusalem in the Time of Jesus. An Investigation into Economic and Social Conditions during the New Testament Period (Philadelphia: Fortress Press, 1969) = *Jerusalem zur Zeit Jesu* (Göttingen: Vandenhoeck & Ruprecht, ³1962).

Jeremias, Joachim
  Jesus als Weltvollender, BFCT 33, 4 (Gütersloh: C. Bertelsmann, 1930).

Jeremias, Joachim
  The Eucharistic Words of Jesus, tr. A. Ehrhardt (New York: Macmillan, 1955).

Jonas, Hans
  The Gnostic Religion. The Message of the Alien God and the Beginnings of Christianity (Boston: Beacon Press, 1958, ²1963).

Jonas, Hans
  Gnosis und spätantiker Geist, 2 vols. Vol. 1, *Die Mythologische Gnosis,* FRLANT, n.s., 33 (Göttingen: Vandenhoeck & Ruprecht, 1934); Vol. 2, *Von der Mythologie zur mystischen Philosophie,* FRLANT, n.s., 45 (Göttingen: Vandenhoeck & Ruprecht, 1954).

Josephus, Flavius
  Opera Recognovit, 6 vols. ed. Benedict Niese (Berlin: Weidmann, 1888–1995).

Jülicher, Adolf
  Itala. Das Neue Testament in altlateinischer Überlieferung, ed. A. Jülicher, W. Matzkow and K. Aland. Vol. 4, *Johannes-Evangelium* (Berlin: Walter de Gruyter, 1963).

Juster, J.
  Les Juifs dans l'Empire romain. Leur condition juridique, économique, et sociale (Paris: P. Geuthner, 1914).

K. Elliger and W. Rudolph, ed.
  Biblical Hebraica, textum masoreticum curavit H. P. Rüger (Stuttgart: Bibelstiftung, 1977).

Kasser, Rudolphe, ed.
  Papyrus Bodmer III: Evangile de Jean et Genèse I–IV, 2 en bohaïrique, Corpus Scriptorum Christianorum Orientalium 194–195 = Scriptores Coptici 27–28 (Louvain, 1958).

Kittel, G. and G. Friedrich
  Theological Dictionary of the New Testament, 10 vols., tr. Geoffrey W. Bromiley (Grand Rapids: Wm. B. Eerdmans, 1964–1976).

Koester, Helmut
  Introduction to the New Testament. Vol. 1, *History Culture, and Religion in the Hellenistic Age;* Vol. 2, *History and Literature of Early Christianity,* Foundations & Facets (Philadelphia: Fortress Press; Berlin and New York: Walter de Gruyter, 1982).

Krause, M and P. Labib
  Die Drei Versionen des Apokryphon des Johannes im koptischen Museum zu Alt-Kairo, Abhandlungen des Deutschen Archäologischen Instituts Kairo, Koptische Reihe, Band 1 (Wiesbaden: Otto Harrossowitz, 1962).

Kroll, Josef
  Die Lehren des Hermes Trismegistos (Munster: Aschendorff, 1914).

Kümmel, Werner Georg
  Introduction to the New Testament, tr. Howard C. Kee (Nashville: Abingdon Press, 1975).

Lake, Kirsopp, ed.
  Eusebius. The Ecclesiastical History; With an English Translation, 2 vols. LCL (London: Wm. Heinemann, 1926–1932).

Lake, Kirsopp, ed.
  The Apostolic Fathers; With an English Translation, 2 vols. LCL (Cambridge: Harvard University Press, 1952).

Lampe, G. W. H.
  A Patristic Greek Lexicon. With Addenda and Corrigenda (Oxford: Clarendon Press, 1968).

Lawlor, H. J. and J. E. Oulton, tr.
  Eusebius, *The Ecclesiastical History and The Martyrs of Palestine,* 2 vols. (London: S. P. C. K., 1927–1928).

Layton, Bentley
  The Gnostic Treatise on Resurrection From Nag Hammadi, Harvard Dissertations in Religion 12 (Missoula: Scholars Press, 1979).

Leipoldt, J. and H.-M. Schenke
  Koptisch-gnostische Schriften aus den Papyrus-Codices von Nag Hammadi, TF 20 (Hamburg-Bergstedt: Herbert Reich-Evangelishcer Verlag, 1960).

Lidzbarski, Mark, ed.
  Das Johannesbuch der Mandäer, 2 vols. in 1 (Giessen: A. Töpelmann, 1905–1915).

Lidzbarski, Mark, ed. and tr.
  Ginza; Der Schatz oder das Große Buch der Mandäer, Quellen der Religionsgeschichte 13 (Göttingen: Vandenhoeck & Ruprecht; Leipzig: J. C. Hinrichs, 1925).

Lidzbarski, Mark, tr.
  Mandäische Liturgien, Abhandlungen der königlichen Gesellschaft der Wissenschaften zu Göttingen, Philologisch-historische Klasse, 17/1 (Berlin: Weidmann, 1920).

Lietzmann, Hans
  Der Weltheiland (Bonn: Markus and Webers Verlag, 1909).

Lietzmann, Hans
  A History of the Early Church, 4 vols., tr. Bertram Lee Woolf (Cleveland and New York: World Publishing Co., 1961).

Lohmeyer, Ernst
  Das Evangelium des Markus, übersezt und erklärt, KEK 1,2 (Göttingen: Vandenhoeck & Ruprecht, 1932, ¹⁶1963).

Maier, Johann
  Die Texte vom Toten Meer, 2 vols. Vol. 1, *Übersetzung;* Vol. 2, *Anmerkungen* (Munich: E. Reinhardt, 1960).

Malatesta, Edward
   St. John's Gospel: 1920–1965, AnBib 32 (Rome: Pontifical Biblical Institute, 1967).

Martin, Victor and Rudolphe Kasser, eds.
   Papyrus Bodmer XIV–XV. Evangile de Luc et Jean [Luc chap. 3–24; Jean chap. 1–15] (Cologny-Geneva: Bibliotheca Bodmeriana, 1961).

Martin, Victor, ed.
   Papyrus Bodmer II: Evangile de Jean chap. 1–14 (Cologny-Geneva: Bibliotheca Bodmeriana, 1956).

Martin, Victor, ed.
   Papyrus Bodmer II, Supplément. Evangile de Jean, chap. 14–21 (Cologny-Geneva: Bibliotheca Bodmeriana, 1958).

Mayser, Edwin
   Grammatik der griechischen Papyri aus der Ptolemäerzeit, 2 vols. (Leipzig/Berlin: 1904–1934).

Ménard, J.-E.
   L'Evangile de Vérité. Rétroversion grecque et commentaire (Paris: Letouzey & Ané, 1962).

Ménard, J.-E.
   L'Evangile selon Philippe. Introduction—texte—traduction—commentaire (Paris: Letouzey & Ané, 1967).

Metzger, Bruce M.
   The Text of the New Testament: Its Transmission, Corruption, and Restoration (New York and London: Oxford University Press, 1964).

Metzger, Bruce M., ed.
   Index to Periodical Literature on Christ and the Gospels (Grand Rapids: Wm. B. Eerdmans, 1962).

Michaelis, Wilhelm
   Einleitung in das Neue Testament. Die Entstehung, Sammlung und Überlieferung der Schriften des Neuen Testaments (Bern: B. Haller, ²1954).

Migne, Jacques-Paul, ed.
   Patrologiae Cursus Completus. Series Graeca, 161 vols in 167 (Paris: Lutetiae Parisiorum, 1857–1903).

Moda, Aldo
   "Quarto Vangelo: 1966–1972. Una selezione bibliografica." *RivB* 22 (1974) 53–86.

Moda, Aldo
   "Rassegna di lavori cattolici su San Giovanni dal 1950 al 1960." *RivB* 10 (1962) 64–91.

Morgenthaler, Robert
   Statistik des Neutestamentlichen Wortschatzes (Zurich and Frankfurt: Gotthelf-Verlag, 1958).

Moulton, J. H., F. W. Howard, and N. Turner
   A Grammar of New Testament Greek, 4 vols. (Edinburgh: T. & T. Clark, 1906–1976) 2: 205–83.

Moulton, W. F. and A. S. Geden
   A Concordance to the Greek Testament according to the Texts of Westcott and Hort, Tischendorf, and the English Revisers (Edinburgh: T & T Clark, 1957).

Nestle Eberhard and Erwin Nestle
   Novum Testamentum Graece; apparatum criticum recensuerunt, rev. and expanded by Kurt Aland and Barbara Aland (Stuttgart: Deutsche Bibelstiftung, ²⁶1979).

Nestle, Eberhard
   Einführung in das Griechische Neue Testament, ed. Ernst von Dobschütz (Göttingen: Vandenhoeck & Ruprecht, ⁴1923).

Nock, A. D. and A. J. Festugière,
   Corpus Hermeticum, 4 vols. (Paris: Les Belles Lettres, 1945–1954).

Pallis, Alexander
   Notes on St. Mark and St. Matthew (London: Oxford University Press, 1932).

Philo
   Philo; With an English Translation, ed. F. H. Colson and G. H. Whitaker, et al. 10 vols., 2 supplements. LCL (London: Wm. Heinemann, 1929–1964).

Plumley, J. Martin
   An Introductory Coptic Grammar (Sahidic Dialect) (London: Home & van Thal, 1948).

Quispel, G.
   Makarius, das Thomasevangelium und das Lied von der Perle, NovTSup 15 (Leiden: E. J. Brill, 1967).

Radermacher, L.
   Neutestamentliche Grammatik. Das Griechisch des Neuen Testaments im Zusammenhang mit der Volkssprache dargestellt, HNT 1 (Tübingen: Mohr-Siebeck, ²1925).

Rahlfs, Alfred, ed.
   Septuaginta; id est vetus testamentum graece iuxta LXX interpretes, 9th ed. (Stuttgart: Bibelstiftung, n.d.).

Reitzenstein, R., and H. H. Schaeder
   Studien zum antiken Synkretismus aus Iran und Griechenland (Leipzig: B. G. Teubner, 1926; reprint Darmstadt: Wissenschaftliche Buchgesellschaft, 1965).

Reitzenstein, Richard
   Poimandres. Studien zur griechisch-ägyptischen und frühchristlichen Literatur (Leipzig: B. G. Teubner, 1904; reprint Stuttgart: B. G. Teubner, 1966).

Reitzenstein, Richard
   Das mandäische Buch des Herrn der Größe und die Evangelien, SHAW.PH 12 (Heidelberg: Carl Winter, 1919).

Reitzenstein, Richard
   Die Göttin Psyche in der hellenistischen und frühchristlichen Literatur, SHAW.PH 10 (Heidelberg: Carl Winter, 1917).

Reitzenstein, Richard
   Das iranische Erlösungsmysterium (Bonn: A Marcus & E. Weber, 1921).

Reitzenstein, Richard
   Die Vorgeschichte der christlichen Taufe (Leipzig: B. G. Teubner, 1929).

Riessler, Paul, ed. and tr.
   Altjüdisches Schrifttum ausserhald ber Bibel (Augsburg: Dr. Benno Filser Verlag, 1928).

Roberts, Alexander and James Donaldson, eds.
   The Ante-Nicene Fathers: The Writings of the Fathers down to A. D. 325, 10 vols. (Buffalo: Christian Literature Publishing Co., 1885–97; reprint

Grand Rapids: Wm. B. Eerdmans, 1951–56).

Robinson, James M., ed.
The Nag Hammadi Library in English (New York: Harper & Row, 1977).

Robinson, James M., ed.
The Future of Our Religions Past. Essays in Honour of Rudolph Bultmann, tr. Charles E. Carlston and Robert P. Scharlemann (New York: Harper & Row, 1971) = *Zeit und Geschichte. Dankesgabe an Rudolf Bultmann zum 80. Geburtstag im Auftrage der Alten Marburger und in Zusammenarbeit mit Hartwig Thyen,* ed. E. Dinkler (Tübingen: Mohr-Siebeck, 1964).

Rudolph, Kurt
Die Mandäer, 2 vols. Vol. 1, *Prolegomena: Das Mandäerproblem,* FRLANT, n.s., 56; Vol. 2, *Der Kult,* FRLANT, n.s., 57 (Göttingen: Vandenhoeck & Ruprecht, 1960–1961).

Rudolph, Kurt
Die Gnosis. Wesen und Geschichte einer spätantiken Religion (Göttingen: Vandenhoeck & Ruprecht, 1977).

Schlatter, Adolf
Der Evangelist Matthäus: Seine Sprache, seine Zeit, seine Selbständigkeit (Stuttgart: Calwer Verlag, [1929] ⁶1963).

Scholem, Gershom Gerhard
Major Trends in Jewish Mysticism (New York: Schocken, 1946).

Schwartz, Eduard, ed.
Eusebius Kirchengeschichte, Kleine Ausgabe (Leipzig: J. C. Hinrichs, ²1914).

Schweitzer, Albert
The Quest of the Historical Jesus: A Critical Study of its Progress from Reimarus to Wrede, tr. W. Montgomery (New York: Macmillan, 1961) = *Geschichte der Leben-Jesu-Forschung* (Tübingen: Mohr-Siebeck, 1906, ⁶1951).

Schweitzer, Albert
The Mysticism of Paul the Apostle, tr. William Montgomery (London: A. and C. Black, ²1953) = *Die Mystik des Apostels Paulus* (Tübingen: Mohr-Siebeck, 1930, ³1981).

Schwertner, Siegfried
International Abbreviations for Theology and Related Subjects (New York and Berlin: Walter de Grutyer, 1974).

Scott, W. and A. S. Ferguson
Hermetica. The Ancient Greek and Latin Writings Which Contain Religious and Philosophic Teachings Ascribed to Hermes Trismegistos, 4 vols. (Oxford: Clarendon Press, 1924–1936).

Spengler, Oswald
The Decline of the West, 2 vols. Tr. Charles Francis Atkinson (New York: A. A. Knopf, 1926–1928).

Steyer, G.
Handbuch für das Studium des neutestamentlichen Griechisch. Vol. 2, *Satzlehre des neutestamentlichen Griechisch* (Gütersloh: Gerd Mohn, ² 1975).

Streeter, Burnett Hillmann
The Four Gospels. A Study of Origins, Treating of the Manuscript Tradition, Sources, Authorship, and Dates (London: Macmillan, 1924).

Taylor, Vincent
The Gospel According to St. Mark (London: Macmillan, ²1966).

Thackeray, H. St. J. and Ralph Marcus
Josephus; With an English Translation, 9 vols. LCL (London: Wm. Heinemann, 1926–1965).

Thackeray, H. St. John
Josephus. The Man and the Historian (New York: KTAV Publishing House, 1967).

Till, W. C.
Das Evangelium nach Philippos, Patristische Texte und Studien 2 (Berlin: Walter de Gruyter, 1963).

Till, W. C.
Die gnostischen Schriften des koptischen Papyrus Berolinensis 8502, TU 60 (Berlin: Akademie-Verlag, 1955).

Till, Walter C.
Koptische Grammatik (Saïdischer Dialekt). Mit Bibliographie, Lesestücke und Worterverzeichmissen, 2nd improved edition (Leipzig: VEB Verlag Enzyklopädie, 1961).

Wellhausen, Julius
Das Evangelium Marci (1905, ²1909).

Wendland, Paul
Die urchristlichen Literaturformen, HNT 1, 3 (Tübingen: Mohr-Siebeck, 1912).

Westcott, B. F. and F. J. A. Hort
The New Testament in the Original Greek, 2 vols. (Cambridge and London: Macmillan, 1890–1896).

Wettstein, J. J.
Novum Testamentum Graecum editionis receptae cum Lectionibus variantibus . . . necnon commentario pleniore . . . opera studio Joannis Jacobi Wetstenii, 2 vols. (Amsterdam, 1751, 1752).

Wilson, R. McL.
The Gnostic Problem. A Study of the Relations between Hellenistic Judaism and the Gnostic Heresy (London: A. R. Mowbray, 1958, 1964).

Wilson, R. McL.
Gnosis and the New Testament (Philadelphia: Fortress Press; Oxford: Blackwell, 1968).

Wilson, R. McL.
Studies in the Gospel of Thomas (London: A. R. Mowbray, 1960).

Wilson, R. McL.
The Gospel of Philip. Translated from the Coptic Text with an Introduction and Commentary (New York and Evanston: Harper & Row; London: A. R. Mowbray, 1962).

Wilson, R. McL., ed.
New Testament Apocrypha. Vol. 1: *Gospels and Related Writings,* tr. A. J. B. Higgins, George Ogg, Richard E. Taylor, and R. McL. Wilson; Vol. 2: *Writings Related to the Apostles; Apocalypses and Related Subjects,* tr. Ernest Best, David Hill, George

Ogg, G. C. Stead, and R. McL. Wilson (Philadelphia: Westminster Press, 1963–1964).

Windisch, Hans
Der zweite Korintherbrief, ed. G. Strecker, KEK 6 (Göttingen: Vandenhoeck & Ruprecht, 1970).

Wohlenberg, G.
Das Evangelium des Markus, KNT 2 (Leipzig: A. Deichert, 1910) 55.

Wrede, William
The Messianic Secret, tr. J. C. G. Greig. The Library of Theological Translations (Greenwood, SC: Attic Press, 1971).

Zahn, Theodor
Geschichte des neutestamentlichen Kanons 2 (Leipzig: A. Deichert, 1890–1892).

2. Commentaries

Barclay, William
The Gospel of John, rev. ed., 2 vols. The Daily Study Bible Series (Philadelphia: Westminster Press, 1975).

Barrett, Charles Kingsley
The Gospel According to St. John. An Introduction with Commentary and Notes on the Greek Text (Philadelphia: Westminster Press, ²1978).

Bauer, Bruno
Kritik der evangelischen Geschichte des Johannes (Bremen: C. Schünemann, 1840).

Bauer, Bruno
Kritik der evangelischen Geschichte der Synoptiker, 2 vols. (Leipzig: O. Wigand, ²1846).

Bauer, Walter
Das Johannesevangelium, HNT 6 (Tübingen: Mohr-Siebeck, ³1933).

Baumgarten-Crusius, Ldw. Fr. Otto
Theologische Auslegung der Johanneischen Schriften. 2 vols. (Jena: F. Luden, 1843–1845).

Bäumlein, W. F. L.
Kommentar über das Evangelium des Johannes (Stuttgart: Metzler, 1863).

Baur, Ferdinand Christian
Kritische Untersuchungen über die kanonischen Evangelien, ihr Verhältniß zu einander, ihren Charakter und Ursprung (Tübingen: L. F. Fues, 1847).

Becker, Jürgen
Das Evangelium nach Johannes. Vol. 1, *Kapitel 1–10,* Ökumenischer Taschenbuchkommentar zum Neuen Testament 4/1; Güersloher Taschenbücher Siebenstern 505 (Gütersloh: Gerd Mohn, 1979); Vol. 2, *Kapitel 11–21,* Ökumenischer Taschenbuchkommentar zum Neuen Testament 4/2; Güersloher Taschenbücher Siebenstern 506 (Gütersloh: Gerd Mohn, 1979; Würzburg: Echter-Verlag, 1981).

Belser, Johannes Evangelist
Das evangelium des heiligen Johannes, übersetzt und erklärt (Freiburg: Herder, 1905).

Bernard, John Henry
A Critical and Exegetical Commentary on the Gospel according to St. John, 2 vols., ed. A. H. McNeile (New York: Charles Scribner's Sons, 1929).

Blank, Josef
Das Evangelium nach Johannes, 2 vols. Geistliche Schriftlesung, Erläuterungen zum Neuen Testament (Düsseldorf: Patmos-Verlag, 1977).

Boehmer, Julius
Das Johannesvangelium nach Aufbau und Grundgedanken (Eisleben: A. Klöppel, 1928).

Boice, James Montgomery
The Gospel of John (Grand Rapids: Zondervan, 1979).

Boismard, M. E. and Lamouille, A.
Synopse des quatres Evangiles en français. Vol. 1, *L'Evangile de Jean* (Paris: Edition du Cerf, 1977).

Bouyer, L.
The Fourth Gospel, tr. Patrick Byrne (Westminster, MD: Newman Press; Athlone, Ireland: St. Paul Publications, 1964) = *Le quatrième Evangile— Introduction et commentaire* (Tournai: Casterman, ²1955).

Braun, François-Marie
L'Evangile selon Saint Jean, La Sainte Bible 10 (Paris, Letouzy & Ané, 1946).

Brown, Raymond E.
The Gospel According to John. Introduction, Translation, and Notes, 2 vols. Vol. 1, *i–xii,* AB 29 (Garden City: Doubleday, 1966); Vol. 2, *xiii–xxi,* AB 29A (Garden City: Doubleday, 1970).

Büchsel, Friedrich
Das Evangelium nach Johannes, NTD 4 (Göttingen: Vandenhoeck & Ruprecht, ²1935).

Bultmann, Rudolf
The Gospel of John: A Commentary, tr. G. R. Beasley-Murray (Oxford: B. Blackwell, 1971) = *Das Evangelium des Johannes,* KEK 2 (Göttingen: Vandenhoeck & Ruprecht, ¹⁰1968).

Bussche, Henri van den
Het Vierde Evangelie. Het Boek der tekens, 3 vols. Vol. 1, *Verklaring van Jo 1–4* (Tielt/Den Haag: Lannoo, 1959); Vol. 2, *Verklaring van Jo 5–12* (Tielt/Den Haag: Lannoo, 1960); Vol. 3, *Verklaring van Jo 18–21* (Tielt/Den Haag: Lannoo, 1960).

Calmes, Theodore
L'Evangile selon saint Jean (Paris: V. Lecoffre, 1904).

Charnwood, G. R. B.
According to St. John (London: Hodder & Stoughton, 1926).

Delafosse, Henri
Le quatrième évangile. Traduction nouvelle avec introduction, notes et commentaire (Paris: Rieder, 1925).

Edwards, R. A.
The Gospel According to St. John (London: Eyre & Spottiswoode, 1954).

Ewald, Heinrich
Die Johanneischen Schriften, übersetzt und erklärt, 2 vols. (Göttingen: Dieterich, 1861).

259

Fenton, Joseph C.
The Gospel according to John in the Revised Standard Version (New York and Oxford: Oxford University Press, 1970).

Gaebelein, A. C.
The Gospel of John (New York: Our Hope Publications Office, 1925).

Godet, F.
Commentary on the Gospel of John, 3 vols., tr. M. D. Cusin (Edinburgh: T. & T. Clark, 1883).

Goguel, Maurice
Le quatrième Evangile (Paris: Leroux, 1923).

Grant, F. C.
The Gospel and Epistles of John, Harper's Annotated Bibles Series (New York: Harper, 1956).

Grundmann, Walter
Das Evangelium nach Johannes, THKNT, ed. E. Fascher (Berlin-Ost: Evangelischer Verlaganstalt, 1968).

Guthrie, D.
"John." In *The New Bible Commentary Revised*, ed. D. Guthrie et al. (Grand Rapids: Wm. B. Eerdmans, 1970) 926–67.

Hase, Carl Alfr.
Vom Evangelium des Johannes. Eine Rede an die Gemeinde (Leipzig: Breitkopf & Härtel, 1866).

Heitmüller, W.
Das Evangelium des Johannes (Göttingen, 1908) 685–861.

Hendriksen, W.
Exposition of the Gospel according to John, 2 vols. (Grand Rapids: Baker Book House, 1953).

Hengstenberg, Ernst Wilhelm
Commentary on the Gospel of St. John, 2 vols. (Edinburgh: T. & T. Clark, 1879) = *Das Evangelium des heiligen Johannes erläutert*, 3 vols. (Berlin: G. Schlawitz, 1861–1863).

Hilgenfeld, A.
Die Evangelien, nach ihrer Entstehung und geschichtlichen Bedeutung (Leipzig: Hirzel, 1854) 227–349.

Hirsch, Emmanuel
Das vierte Evangelium in seiner ursprünglichen Gestalt verdeutscht und erklärt (Tübingen: Mohr-Siebeck, 1936).

Hobbs, Herschel H.
An Exposition of the Gospel of John (Grand Rapids: Baker Book House, 1968).

Holland, H. S.
The Fourth Gospel, ed. W. Richmond (London: Murray, 1923).

Holtzmann, Heinrich Julius
Das Evangelium des Johannes, rev. Walter Bauer. HKNT 4 (Tübingen: Mohr-Siebeck, ³l908).

Holtzmann, O.
Das Johannesevangelium, untersucht und erklärt (Darmstadt: Waitz, 1887).

Hoskyns, Edwin Clement
The Fourth Gospel, ed. F. N. Davey (London: Faber, 1940, ²1947).

Howard, W. F. and Arthur John Gossip
"The Gospel According to St. John." IB 7 (New York and Nashville: Abingdon Press, 1952).

Huby, J., A. Valensin, and A. Durand
The Gospel according to St. Luke. The Gospel according to St. John, tr. J. J. Heenan (Milwaukee: Bruce, 1957).

Hunter, A. M.
The Gospel According to John, Cambridge Bible Commentary: New English Bible (London and New York: Cambridge University Press, 1965).

Jacquier
Lesécrits johanniques, Histoire des livres du Nouveau Testament 4 (Paris: V. Lecoffre, 1908).

Kealy, S. P.
That You May Believe. The Gospel According to John (Slough, UK: St. Paul Publications, 1978).

Keil, Carl Friedrich
Commentar über das Evangelium des Johannes (Leipzig: Dörffling & Franke, 1881).

Klee, Heinrich
Commentar über das Evangelium nach Johannes (Mainz: Kupferberg, 1829).

Kögel, Julius
Das Evangelium des Johannes, Schriftverständnis des Neuen Testaments 2 (Gütersloh: C. Bertelsmann, 1918).

Kühnöl, C. G. (alias Kuinöls)
Commentarius in libros NT historicos. Vol. 3, *Commentarius in Ev. Joh.* (1825).

Kysar, Robert
John: The Maverick Gospel (Atlanta: John Knox, 1976).

Lagrange, M. Marie-Joseph
L'évangile selon S. Jean, Etudes bibliques (Paris: J. Gabalda, ²1925, ⁸1947).

Lampe, F. A.
Commentarius analytico-exegeticus in Evangelium secundum Joannem, 3 vols. (Amsterdam, 1724–1726).

Lange, J. P.
Das Evangelium nach Johannes, Die Heilige Schrift des Neuen Testaments 4 (Bielefeld: Belhagen & Klasing, 1860, ⁴1880).

Lightfoot, R. H.
St. John's Gospel. A Commentary, ed. C. F. Evans (Oxford: Clarendon Press; London: Cumberlege, 1956).

Lindars, Barnabas
The Gospel of John, New Century Bible (Greenwood, SC: Attic Press, 1972).

Loisy, Alfred
Le quatrième évangile (Paris: A. Picard & Fils, 1903, ²1921).

Lücke, Fr.
Commentar über das Evangelium des Johannes, 2 vols. (Bern: Weber, 1820–1824, ²1833–1834, ³1840–1843).

Luthardt, Christian Ernst

*Das johanneische Evangelium nach seiner Eigentüm-
lichkeit geschildert un erklärt.* 2 vols. (Nuremberg:
Geiger, 1852–1853, ²1875–1876).

Luthardt, Christian Ernst and Otto Zöckler

*Das Evangelium nach Johannes und die Apostel-
geschichte,* Kurzgefaßter Kommentar zu den
Heiligen Schriften Alten und Neuen Testaments 2
(München: C. H. Beck, 1886, ²1894).

MacGregor, George Hogarth Carnaby

The Gospel of John (london: Hodder & Stoughton,
1928).

McPolin, James

John, New Testament Message 6 (Wilmington, DE:
Glazier, 1979).

MacRae, George W.

*Invitation to John. A Commentary on the Gospel of John
with Complete Text from The Jerusalem Bible* Garden
City, NY: Doubleday, 1978).

Maier, A.

Commentar über das Evangelium des Johannes, 2 vols.
(Freiburg: Herder, 1843, 1845).

Manson, W.

*The Incarnate Glory. An Expository Study of the Gospel
according to St. John* (London: J. Clarke, 1923).

Marsh, J.

The Gospel of St. John, The Pelican Gospel
Commentaries (Baltimore: Penguin, 1968).

Meyer, F. B.

*The Gospel of John. The Life and Light of Man, Love to
the Uttermost,* Lakeland Series Reprint (London:
Oliphants, 1970).

Meyer, H. A. W.

Handbuch Über das Evangelium des Johannes, KEK 2
(Göttingen: Vandenhöck & Ruprecht, 1834,
²1852, ³1856, ⁴1862, ⁵1869).

Moe, Olaf

Johannesevangeliet, Innledet og Fortolket (Oslo:
Aschehoug, 1938).

Molla, C. F.

Le quatrième évangile (Geneva: Labor & Fides,
1977).

Morgan, G. C.

The Gospel According to John (London, 1909).

Morris, Leon

*The Gospel According to St. John. The English Text with
Introduction, Exposition and Notes,* The New Inter-
national Commentary on the New Testament
(Grand Rapids: Wm. B. Eerdmans, 1971).

Neill, S.

The Gospel according to St. John (Cambridge:
Cambridge University Press, 1930).

Odeberg, Hugo

*The Fourth Gospel. Interpreted in its Relation to
Contemporaneous Religious Currents in Palestine and
in the Hellenistic-Oriental World* (Uppsala: Almqvist
& Wiksells, 1929; reprint Amsterdam: B. R.
Grüner; Chicago: Argonaut, 1968).

Olshausen, Herm.

*Biblischer Commentar über sämmtliche Schriften des
Neuen Testament.* Vol. 2, *Das Evangelium Johannes,
die Leidensgeschichte und Apostelgeschichte enthaltend*
(Königsberg: Unzer, 1830, 1832, ²1834, ³1838,
⁴1861).

Oporin, J.

In clave Ev. S. Johannis (Göttingen, 1742).

Overbeck, F.

*Das Johannes-Evangelium. Studien zur Kritik seiner
Erforschung,* ed. Carl A. Bernoulli (Tübingen:
Mohr-Siebeck, 1911).

Pallis, A.

Notes on St. John and the Apocalypse (Oxford: Oxford
University Press, 1926).

Paulus, Heinrich Eberhard Gottlob

Commentar über das Evangelium des Johannes. In his
*Philologisch-kritischer und historischer Commentar über
das Neue Testament, in welchem der Griechische Text
. . .* (Lübeck: J. F. Bohn, 1804).

Perkins, P.

*The Gospel According to St. John. A Theological
Commentary,* Herald Scriptural Library (Chicago:
Franciscan Herald Press, 1978).

Prete, Benedetto

Vangelo secondo Giovanni (Mailand, 1965).

Reuss, Joseph, ed.

*Johannes-Kommentare aus der griechischen Kirche. Aus
Katenenhandschriften gesammelt und herausgegeben,*
TU 89 (Berlin: Akademie-Verlag, 1966).

Richardson, Alan

The Gospel According to St. John, Torch Bible
Commentary (London: SCM Press, 1959).

Robinson, B. W.

The Gospel of John. A Handbook for Christian Teachers
(New York: Macmillan, 1925).

Russel, R.

St. John, A New Catholic Commentary on Holy
Scripture (London, 1969).

Sanders, J. N.

A Commentary on the Gospel according to St. John, ed.
B. Mastin. Harper's New Testament Commentaries (New York and Evanston, IL: Harper,
1969).

Schlatter, Adolf

*Der Evangelist Johannes. Wie er spricht, denkt und
glaubt. Ein Kommentar zum 4. Evangelium* (Stuttgart:
Calwer Vereinsbuchhandlung, 1930).

Schnackenburg, Rudolf

The Gospel According to St. John, 3 vols. Vol. 1,
Introduction and Commentary on Chapters 1–4, tr.
Kevin Smyth (New York: Seabury Press, 1980) =
Das Johannesevangelium, part 1. HTKNT 4,1
(Freiburg: Herder, 1965); Vol. 2, *Commentary on
Chapters 5–12,* tr. Cecily Hastings, Francis
McDonagh, David Smith, and Richard Foley (New
York: Seabury Press, 1980) = *Das Johannes-
evangelium,* part 2. HTKNT 4,2 (Freiburg:
Herder, 1971); Vol. 3, *Commentary on Chapters 13–
21,* tr. David Smith and G. A. Kon (New York:

Crossroad, 1982) = *Das Johannesevangelium*, part 3. HTKNT 4,3 (Freiburg: Herder, 1975).

Schneider, J.
Das Evangelium nach Johannes, THKNT, Sonderband (Berlin: Evangelische Verlaganstalt, 1976).

Scholten, J. H.
Das Evangelium nach Johannes. Kritisch-historische Untersuchung, tr. H. Lang (Berlin: G. Reimer, 1867).

Schulz, Siegfried
Das Evangelium nach Johannes, NTD 4 (Göttingen: Vandenhoeck & Ruprecht, [12]1972).

Semler, Jh. Sem.
Paraphrasis evangelii Johannis, cum notis et Cantabrig. Codicis Latino (Halle: Schwetschke & Sohn, 1771, 1772).

Smith, D. Moody, Jr.
John, Proclamation Commentaries: New Testament Witnesses for Teaching (Philadelphia: Fortress Press, 1976).

Spörri, G.
Das Evangelium nach Johannes, 2 vols. (Zurich: Zwingli Verlag, 1950).

Strachan, R. H.
The Fourth Gospel. Its Significance and Environment (London: SCM Press, [3]1946).

Strathmann, H.
Das Evangelium nach Johannes, NTD 4 (Göttingen: Vandenhoeck & Ruprecht, [11]1968).

Swain, L.
The Gospel According to St. John, New Testament for Spiritual Reading 4 (London: Sheen & Ward, 1978).

Tasker, R. V. G.
The Gospel According to St. John, Tyndale New Testament Commentaries (Grand Rapids: Wm. B. Eerdmans, 1971).

Temple, W.
Readings in St. John's Gospel, 2 vols. Vol. 1, *Chapters 1–12* (London: Macmillan, 1939); Vol. 2, *Chapters 13–21* (London: Macmillan, 1940).

Tenney, Merrill C.
John, the Gospel of Belief. An Analytic Study of the Text (Grand Rapids: Wm. B. Eerdmans, 1948).

Tholuck, Augustus
Commentary on the Gospel of John, tr. Charles P. Krauth (Philadelphia: Smith, English & Co., 1859) = *Commentar zu dem Evangelium Johannis* (Hamburg: F. Perthes, 1827; Gotha: F. A. Perthes, [7]1857).

Tillmann, Fritz
Das Johannesevangelium, übersetz und erklärt (Bonn: Peter Hanstein, 1914, 4th improved ed., 1931).

Tittmann, Karl Christian
Meletemata sacra sive Commentarius crit.—exeg.— dogmaticus in Evangelium Joannis (Leipzig: Weidmann, 1816).

Titus, E. L.
The Message of the Fourth Gospel (Nashville: Abingdon Press, 1957).

Vawter, Bruce
The Gospel According to John, Jerome Bible Commentary 2 (Englewood Cliffs, NJ: Prentice Hall, 1968) 414–66; *Johannine Theology*, Jerome Bible Commentary 2 (Englewood Cliffs, NJ: Prentice Hall, 1968) 828–39.

Wahle, G. F.
Das Evangelium nach Johannes (Gotha: F. A. Perthes, 1888).

Weiss, Bernhard
Das Johannesevangelium als einheitliches Werk. Geschichtlich erklärt (Berlin: Trowitzsch & Sohn, 1912).

Weiss, Bernhard
Das Johannes-Evangelium, KEK 2 (Göttingen: Vandenhoeck & Ruprecht, 1834, [9]1902).

Weiss, Josef
Die Schriften des Neuen Testaments. Vol, 1, *Die drei älteren Evangelien. Die Apostelgeschichte* (Göttingen: Vandenhoeck & Ruprecht, [2]1907).

Wellhausen, Julius
Das Evangelium Johannis (Berlin: G. Reimer, 1908).

Westcott, B. F.
The Gospel According to St. John, The Authorized Version with Introduction and Notes and a new Introduction by Adam Fox (London: J. Clarke, 1958).

Wette, William Martin Leberecht de
Kurze Erklärung des Evangeliums und der Briefe Johannis, ed. B. Brückner. Kurzgefaßtes exegetisches Handbuch zum Neuen Testament 1,3 (Leipzig: Weidmann, [4]1852).

Wikenhauser, A.
Das Evangelium nach Johannes, RNT 4 (Regensburg: F. Pustet, [2]1957).

Wright, C. J.
The Meaning and Message of the Fourth Gospel (London: Hodder, 1933).

Zahn, Theodor
Das Evangelium des Johannes ausgelegt (Leipzig: A. Deichert, [6]1921).

3. Studies

Aalem, S.
"'Truth' a key word in St. John's Gospel." *SE* 2 = TU 87 (Berlin: Akademie-Verlag, 1964) 3–24.

Aall, Anathon
Der Logos. Geschichte seiner Entwickelung in der griechischen Philosophie und der christlichen Literatur, 2 vols. Vol. 1, *Geschichte der Logosidee in der griechischen Philosophie*; Vol. 2, *Geschichte der Logosidee in der christlichen Literatur* (Leipzig: O. R. Reisland, 1896 and 1899).

Abbot, Ezra
"The Authorship of the Fourth Gospel." In his *The Authorship of the Fourth Gospel and Other Critical Essays Selected from the Published Papers* (Boston: G. H. Ellis, 1888) 9–112.

Abbott, Edwin Abbott
Johannine Grammar (London: A. & C. Black, 1906; reprint Farnborough, England: Gregg International Publishers, 1968).

Abbott, Edwin Abbott
Johannine Vocabulary (London: A. & C. Black, 1905). Reprinted as part one of his *Johannine Grammar* (Farnborough, England: Gregg International Publishers, 1968).

Abelson, J.
The Immanence of God in Rabbinical Literature (London, 1912; reprint New York: Herman Press, 1969).

Abramowski, R.
"Der Christus der Salomooden." *ZNW* 35 (1936) 44–69.

Achtemeier, Elizabeth R.
"Jesus Christ, the Light of the World. The Biblical Understanding of Light and Darkness." *Int* 17 (1963) 439–49.

Ackermann, J. S.
"The Rabbinic Interpretation of Psalm 82 and the Gospel of John: John 10:34." *HTR* 59 (1966) 186–91.

Ackroyd, Peter R.
"The 153 Fishes in John XXI.11—A Further Note." *JTS*, n.s., 10 (1959) 94.

Aebert, B.
"Die Eschatologie des Johannesevangeliums." Dissertation (Breslau: Teildruck Würzburg, 1936).

Agnew, F.
"Vocatio primorum discipulorum in traditione synoptica." *VD* 46 (1968) 129–47.

Agourides, Savas C.
"The 'High Priestly Prayer' of John." *SE* 4 = TU 102 (Berlin: Akademie-Verlag, 1968) 137–43.

Agourides, Savas C.
"The Purpose of John 21." In *Studies in the History and Text of the New Testament in honor of Kenneth Willis Clark, Ph.D*, ed. B. L. Daniels and M. J. Suggs. Studies and Documents 29 (Salt Lake City, UT: University of Utah Press, 1967) 127–32.

Aland, Kurt
"Eine Untersuchung zu Joh 1,3.4. Über die Bedeutung eines Punktes." *ZNW* 59 (1968) 174–209.

Aland, Kurt
Die Stellung der Kinder in der frühen christlichen Gemeinde und ihre Taufe, Theologische Existenz Heute, n.s., 138 (Munich: Chr. Kaiser Verlag, 1967).

Albright, William Foxwell
"The Ephraim of the Old and New Testament." *JPOS* 3 (1923) 36–40.

Alegre Santamaria, X.
"El concepto de salvacion en las Oda de Salomon." Contribución al estudio de una soteriologia gnostizante y sus posibles relaciones con el cuarto evengelio. Dissertation, Münster, 1978.

Aletti, J.-N.

"Le discours sur le pain de vie (Jean 6). Problèmes de composition et fonction des citations de l'Ancien Testament." *RSR* 62 (1974) 169–97.

Alfaro, Juan I.
"La mariología del Cuarto Evangelio. Ensayo de teología bíblica." *RivB* 41 (1979) 193–209.

Allen, E. L.
"The Jewish Christian Church in the Fourth Gospel." *JBL* 74 (1955) 88–92.

Allen, J. E.
"Why Pilate?" In *The Trial of Jesus. Cambridge Studies in honour of C. F. D. Moule*, ed. E. Bammel. SBT 13 (Naperville, IL: Allenson, 1970) 78–83.

Allen, Willoughby C.
"St. John vii. 37, 38." *ExpTim* 34 (1922/1923) 329–30.

Allis, Oswald T.
"The Alleged Aramaic Origin of the Fourth Gospel." *Princeton Theological Review* 26 (1928) 531–72.

Alsup, John E.
The Post-Resurrection Appearance Stories of the Gospel Tradition. A history-of-tradition analysis with Text-Synopsis, Calwer Theologische Monographien 5 (Stuttgart: Calwer Verlag, 1975).

Amadon, Grace
"The Johannine-Synoptic Argument." *ATR* 26 (1944) 107–15.

Amerding, Carl
"The Marriage in Cana." *BSac* 118 (1961) 320–26.

Ammon, Christoph Friedrich von
Progr. de prologi Johannis Evangelistae fontibus et sensu (Göttingen, 1800).

Ammon, Christoph Friedrich von
Docetur Johannem Evangelii auctorem ab editore huius libri fuisse diversum (Erlangen, 1811).

Andersen, Axel
"Zu Joh 6,51bff." *ZNW* 9 (1908) 163f.

Andrews, Mary E.
"Pioneer Work on the Gospel of John." *JBL* 59 (1940) 181–92.

Anne-Etienne, Sr.
"Une lecture communautaire de la Bible." *Foi et vie* 77 (1978) 79–86.

Anonymous
"Noch ein Versuch über das Wandeln Jesu auf dem Meere nach Mt 14,24–33; Mk 6,45–51 und Joh 6,16–21." *Magazin für Religionsphilosophie, Exegese und Kirchengeschichte* 12 (1802) 310–33.

Anonymous
Die Evangelienfrage im Allgemeinen und die Johannesfrage insbesondere (Zurich, 1858).

Anonymous (M. S. K.)
"Gedanken über die Vorliebe zum Ev. Johannis." *Neues theologisches Journal* 10 (1802) 1–33.

Appel, Heinrich
Die Echtheit des Johannesevangeliums mit besonderer Berücksichtigung der neuesten kritischen Forschungen (Leipzig: A. Deichert, 1915).

Appold, Mark L.
"Christ Alive! Church Alive! Reflections on the Prayer of Jesus in John 17." *CurTM* 5 (1978) 365–73.

Appold, Mark L.
The Oneness Motif in the Fourth Gospel. Motif Analysis and Exegetical Probe into the Theology of John, WUNT 2, 1 (Tübingen: Mohr-Siebeck, 1976).

Arai, Sasagu
Early Christianity and Gnosticism (Tokyo, 1971).

Argyle, A. W.
"A Note on John 4:35." *ExpTim* 82 (1971) 247–48.

Arichea, D. C.
"Translating 'believe' in the Gospel of John." *BT* 30 (1979) 205–9.

Arvedson, Tomas
"Några notiser till tva nytestamentliga perikoper." *SEÅ* 21 (1956) 27–29.

Asbeck, M. d'
"La ponctuation des versets 3 et 4 du Prologue du quatrième Evangile et la doctrine du Logos." In *Congrès d'histoire du Christianisme: Jubilé Alfred Loisy,* ed. P.-L. Couchoud (Paris: Les éditions Rieder, 1928) 220–28.

Ashbey, G.
"Lamb of God." *Journal of Theology for Southern Africa* 21 (1977) 63–65; 25 (1978) 62–65.

Atal, Dosithée
Structure et signification des cinq premiers versets de l'hymne johannique au Logos, Recherches africaines de théologie 3 (Louvain: Nauwelaerts, 1973).

Atal, Dosithée
"Die Wahrheit wird euch freimachen." In *Biblische Randbemerkungen. Schülerfestschrift für Rudolf Schnackenburg zum 60. Geburtstag,* ed. H. Merklein and J. Lange (Würzburg: Echter Verlag, 1974) 283–99.

Aubineau, Michel
"La tunique sans couture du Christ. Exégèse patristique de Jean 19,13–24." In *Kyriakon. Festschrift Johannes Quasten,* ed. P. Granfield and J. A. Jungmann, 2 vols. (Münster: Aschendorff, 1970) 100–127.

Ausejo, Serafín de
"Es un himno a Cristo el prólogo de San Juan." *EstBib* 15 (1956) 223–77, 381–427.

Baaren, Theodorus Van
Some Reflections on the Symbolism of Light and Darkness, in honor of Harald Biezais (Stockholm, 1979) 237–41.

Bacchiocchi, Samuele
"John 5:17: Negation or Clarification of the Sabbath?" *AUSS* 19 (1981) 3–19.

Bächli, Otto
"'Was habe ich mit Dir zu schaffen?' Eine formelhafte Frage im A. T. und N. T." *TZ* 33 (1977) 69–80.

Bacon, Benjamin Wisner
"Pauline Elements in the Fourth Gospel. I: A Study of John i–iv." *ATR* 11 (1928/1929) 199–223.

Bacon, Benjamin Wisner
"Pauline Elements in the Fourth Gospel. II: Parables of the Shepherd." *ATR* 11 (1928/1929) 305–20.

Bacon, Benjamin Wisner
"History and Dogma." *HibJ* 28 (1929/1930) 112–23.

Bacon, Benjamin Wisner
"'Native Place' in John." *Expositor,* 8th ser., 23 (1922) 41–46.

Bacon, Benjamin Wisner
"The Sacrament of the Footwashing." *ExpTim* 43 (1931/1932) 218–21.

Bacon, Benjamin Wisner
"'In my Father's house are many mansions' John 14,2." *ExpTim* 43 (1931/1932) 477–78.

Bacon, Benjamin Wisner
"Displacement of John 14." *JBL* 13 (1894) 64–76.

Bacon, Benjamin Wisner
"The 'Other' Comforter." *Expositor,* 8th ser., 14 (1917) 273–82.

Bacon, Benjamin Wisner
"Immortality in the Fourth Gospel." In *Religion and the Future Life. The Development of the Belief in Life after Death* ed. E. H. Sneath (New York: Fleming H. Revell, 1922) 259–94.

Bacon, Benjamin Wisner
"The Motivation of John 21,15–25." *JBL* 50 (1931) 71–80.

Bacon, Benjamin Wisner
The Fourth Gospel in Research and Debate (New Haven: Yale University Press, ²1918).

Bacon, Benjamin Wisner
"The 'Defense' of the Fourth Gospel." *HibJ* 6 (1907/1908) 118–41.

Bacon, Benjamin Wisner
"The Elder John, Papias, Irenaeus, Eusebius and the Syriac Translator." *JBL* 27 (1908) 1–23.

Bacon, Benjamin Wisner
"External Evidence." In his *The Gospel of the Hellenists* (New York: Holt, 1933) 7–51.

Bacon, Benjamin Wisner
"Date and Habitat of the Elders of Papias." *ZNW* 12 (1911) 176–87.

Bacon, Benjamin Wisner
"Papias." In the *New Schaff-Herzog Encyclopedia of Religious Knowledge* (Grand Rapids: Baker Book House, 1959) 8: 336–40.

Bacon, Benjamin Wisner
"The Johannine Problem." *The Independent* 57 (1904) 736–37.

Bacon, Benjamin Wisner
"An Emendation of the Papias Fragment." *JBL* 17 (1898) 176–83.

Bacon, Benjamin Wisner
"Marcion, Papias and 'The Elders.'" *JTS* 23 (1921/1922) 134–60.

Bacon, Benjamin Wisner
"The Anti-Marcionite Prologue to John." *JBL* 49 (1930) 43–54.

Bacon, Benjamin Wisner
"The Mythical 'Elder John' of Ephesus." *HibJ* 29 (1931) 312–26.

Bacon, Benjamin Wisner
"John and the Pseudo-John." *ZNW* 31 (1932) 132–50.

Bacon, Benjamin Wisner
"The Elder of Ephesus and the Elder John." *HibJ* 26 (1927) 112–34.

Bacon, Benjamin Wisner
"The Elder John in Jerusalem." *ZNW* 26 (1927) 187–202.

Bacon, Benjamin Wisner
"Recent Aspects of the Johannine Problem: I. The External Evidence." *HibJ* 1 (1902/1903) 510–31; 2 (1903/1904) 323–46; 3 (1904/1905) 353–75.

Bacon, Benjamin Wisner
"Tatian's Rearrangement of the Fourth Gospel." *AJT* 4 (1900) 770–95.

Bacon, Benjamin Wisner
"John and the Synoptists." In his *The Gospel of the Hellenists* (New York: Holt, 1933) 111–19.

Bacon, Benjamin Wisner
"Lucan versus Johannine Chronology." *Expositor,* 7th ser., 3 (1907) 206–20.

Bacon, Benjamin Wisner
"Sources and Method of the Fourth Evangelist." *HibJ* 25 (1926) 115–30.

Bacon, Benjamin Wisner
The Gospel of the Hellenists (New York: Holt, 1933).

Bailey, John Amadee
The Traditions Common to the Gospels of Luke and John, NovTSup 7 (Leiden: E. J. Brill, 1963).

Bajsíc, Alois
"Pilatus, Jesus und Barabbas." *Bib* 48 (1967) 7–28.

Baker, John Austin
"The 'Institution' Narratives and the Christian Eucharist." In *Thinking about the Eucharist. Essays by Members of the Archibishop's Commission on Christian Doctrine,* with a preface by Ian T. Ramsey (London: SCM Press, 1972) 38–58.

Balagué, Miguel
"San Juan y los Sinópticos." *CB* 12 (1955) 347–52.

Baldensperger, Wilhelm
Der Prolog des vierten Evangeliums. Sein polemisch-apologetischer Zweck (Tübingen: Mohr-Siebeck, 1898).

Baldi, D.
"Betania in Transgiordania." *Terra Santa* 22 (1947) 44–48.

Balembo, Buetubela
"Jean 3,8: L'Esprit-Saint ou le vent naturel?" *Revue Africaine de Théologie* 4 (1980) 55–64.

Ball, C. J.
"Had the Fourth Gospel an Aramaic Archetype?" *ExpTim* 21 (1909/1910) 91–93.

Ballenstedt, Heinrich Christian
Philo und Johannes; oder, Neue philosophisch-kritische Untersuchung des Logos beym Johannes nach dem Philo, nebst einer Erklärung und Uebersetzung des ersten Briefes Johannes aus der geweihten Sprache der Hierophanten, 3 vols. (Braunschweig: F. B. Culemann, 1802).

Ballenstedt, Heinrich Christian
Philo und Johannes; oder, Fortgesetzte Anwendung des Philo zur Interpretation der Johanneischen Schriften; mit besonderer Hinsicht auf die Frage: ob Johannes der Verfasser der ihm zugeschriebenen Bücher seyn könne? (Göttingen: H. Dieterich, 1812).

Baltensweiler, H.
"Wunder und Glaube im Neuen Testament." *TZ* 23 (1967) 241–56.

Bammel, Ernst
"The Baptist in Early Christian Tradition." *NTS* 18 (1971/1972) 95–128.

Bammel, Ernst
"'John did no miracle': John 10, 41." In *Miracles. Cambridge Studies in their Philosophy and History,* ed. C. F. D. Moule. (London: A. R. Mowbray, 1965) 197–202.

Bammel, Ernst
"Joh 11,45–47." In *The Trial of Jesus. Cambridge Studies in honour of C. F. D. Moule,* ed. E. Bammel. SBT 13 (Naperville, IL: Allenson, 1970) 11–40.

Bammel, Ernst
"Jesus und der Paraklet in Joh 16." In *Christ and Spirit in the New Testament* [Festschrift C. F. D. Moule], ed. B. Lindars and S. S. Smalley (New York: Cambridge University Press, 1973) 199–217.

Bammel, Ernst
"Φίλος τοῦ καίσαρος (Joh 19,12)." *TLZ* 77 (1952) 205–10.

Bampfylde, Gillian
"Jn XIX. 28, a Case for a Different Translation." *NovT* 11 (1969) 247–60.

Barclay, William
"Great Themes of the New Testament—John 1,1–14." *ExpTim* 70 (1958) 78–82; (1959) 114–17.

Barker, Margaret
"Caiaphas' Words in Jn 11,50 refer to Messiah be Joseph." In *The Trial of Jesus. Cambridge Studies in honour of C. F. D. Moule,* ed. E. Bammel. SBT 13 (Naperville, IL: Allenson, 1970) 41–46.

Barksdale, J. O.
"Victory of Light. II: Joh 12,20–36." *Japanese Christian Quarterly* 28 (1962) 48–54.

Baron, M.
"La progression des confessions de foi dans les dialogues de saint Jean." *BVC* 82 (1968) 32–44.

Barrett, Charles Kingsley
The Gospel of John and Judaism, tr. D. M. Smith (London: S. P. C. K.; Philadelphia: Fortress Press, 1975) = *Das Johannesevangelium und das Judentum* (Stuttgart: W. Kohlhammer, 1970).

Barrett, Charles Kingsley
"Zweck des vierten Evangeliums." *ZST* 22 (1953) 257–73.

Barrett, Charles Kingsley
"The Dialectical Theology of St. John." In his *New Testament Essays* (London: S. P. C. K., 1972) 49–69.

Barrett, Charles Kingsley
"The Prologue of St. John's Gospel." In his *New Testament Essays* (London: S. P. C. K., 1972) 27–48.

Barrett, Charles Kingsley
"Κατέλαβεν in John 1,5." *ExpTim* 53 (1941/1942) 297.

Barrett, Charles Kingsley
"The Lamb of God." *NTS* 1 (1954/1955) 210–18.

Barrett, Charles Kingsley
"Das Fleisch des Menschensohns (Joh 6,53)." In *Jesus und der Menschensohn. Für Anton Vögtle,* ed. R. Pesch and R. Schnackenburg (Freiburg: Herder, 1975) 342–54.

Barrett, Charles Kingsley
"Paradox and Dualism." In his *Essays on John* (London: S. P. C. K., 1982) 98–115.

Barrett, Charles Kingsley
"Unsolved New Testament Problems—The Place of Eschatology in the Fourth Gospel." *ExpTim* 59 (1947/1948) 302–5.

Barrett, Charles Kingsley
"John and the Synoptic Gospels." *ExpTim* 85 (1973/1974) 228–33.

Barrett, Charles Kingsley
"'The Father is Greater than I' (Joh 14,28): Subordinationist Christology in the New Testament." In *Neues Testament und Kirche. Für Rudolf Schnackenburg,* ed. J. Gnilka (Freiburg: Herder, 1974) 144–59.

Barrett, Charles Kingsley
"The Holy Spirit in the Fourth Gospel." *JTS,* n.s., 1 (1950) 1–15.

Barrett, Charles Kingsley
"The Theological Vocabulary of the Fourth Gospel and of the 'Gospel of Truth.'" In *Current Issues in New Testament Interpretation. Essays in honor of Otto A. Piper,* ed. W. Klassen and G. F. Snyder (New York: Harper, 1962) 210–23, 297–98.

Barrosse, Thomas
"The Seven Days of the New Creation in St. John's Gospel." *CBQ* 21 (1959) 507–16.

Barrosse, Thomas
"Some Aspects of Love and Faith in St. John." In *Readings in Biblical Morality.* ed. C. L. Salm (Englewood Cliffs, NJ: Prentice Hall, 1967) 137–41.

Barth, C. H. W.
"Nähere Beleuchtung des 6. Kapitels des Ev. Johannes." *Magazin für christliche Prediger* 2.1 (1824) 43–63.

Barth, C. H. W.
"Ueber den Menschenmörder von Anfang—eine exegetische Studie zu Joh 8 v. 44." *Magazin für christliche Prediger* 2, 2 (1824) 35–69.

Barth, Carola
Die Interpretation des Neuen Testamentes in der valentinianischen Gnosis, TU, 3rd ser., 7,3 (Leipzig: J. C. Hinrichs, 1911).

Bartholomew, Gilbert Leinbach
"An Early Christian Sermon-Drama: John 8,31–59." Dissertation, Union Theological Seminary, 1974.

Bartina, Sebastián
"'Yo soy Yahweh.' Nota exegética a Io 18,4–8." *Estudios ecclesiásticos* 32 (1958) 403–26.

Bartlet, J. Vernon
"Papias' Exposition; Its Date and Contents." In *Amicitiae Corolla, A Volume of Essays presented to James Rendel Harris,* ed. H. G. Wood (London: University of London Press, 1933) 15–44.

Bartlett, W.
"The Coming of the Holy Ghost according to the Fourth Gospel." *ExpTim* 37 (1925/1926) 72–75.

Barton, George A.
"The Origin of the Discrepancy between the Synoptists and the Fourth Gospel as to the Date and Character of Christ's Last Supper with his Disciples." *JBL* 43 (1924) 28–31.

Barton, George A.
"A Bone of him shall not be Broken, John 19,36." *JBL* 49 (1930) 13–19.

Battaglia, Oscar
"Preghiera sacerdotale ed innologia ermetica (Giov 17—CH. 1,31–32 e 13,18–20." *RivB* 17 (1969) 209–32.

Bauer, Bruno
Kritik der paulinischen Briefe (Berlin: G. Hempel, 1852; Aalen: Scientia, 1972).

Bauer, Bruno
Christus und die Cäsaren. Der Ursprung des Christentums aus dem römischen Griechenthum (Berlin: E. Grosser, 1877; Hildesheim: G. Olms, 1968).

Bauer, Johannes Baptist
"Πῶς in der griechischen Bibel." *NovT* 2 (1958) 81–91.

Bauer, Johannes Baptist
"Drei Cruces." *BZ* 9 (1965) 84–91.

Bauer, Johannes Baptist
"'Oves meae' quaenam sunt? (Jo. 21,15ff. et 10,16)." *VD* 32 (1954) 321–24.

Bauer, Walter
"Johannesevangelium und Johannesbriefe." *TRu,* n.s., 1 (1929) 135–60.

Baumann, Emile
"Zur Hochzeit geladen." *PJ* 4 (1908) 67–76.

Baumbach, Günter
"Die Funktion der Gemeinde in der Welt in johanneischer Sicht." *Zeichen der Zeit* 21 (1971) 161–67.

Baumbach, Günter
"Gemeinde und Welt im Johannes-Evangelium." *Kairos* 14 (1972) 121–36.

Baumbach, Günther
Qumran und das Johannes-Evangelium. Eine ver-

gleichende Untersuchung der dualistichen Aussagen der Ordensregel von Qumrān und des Johannes-Evangeliums mit Berücksichtigung der spätjüdischen Apokalypsen, Aufsätze und Vorträge zur Theologie und Religionswissenschaft 6 (Berlin: Evangelische Verlaganstalt, 1958).

Baumeister, Theofried
"Der Tod Jesu und die Leidensnachfolge des Jüngers nach dem Johannesevangelium und dem ersten Johannesbrief." *Wissenschaft und Weisheit* 40 (1977) 81–99.

Baur, Ferdinand Christian
"Zur johanneischen Frage: 1) Über Justin den Märtyrer gegen Luthardt; 2) Über den Passahstreit gegen Steitz." *Theologische Jahrbücher* 16 (Tübingen, 1857) 209–57.

Baur, Ferdinand Christian
"Die johanneische Frage und ihre neuesten Beantwortungen durch Luthardt, Delitzsch, Brückner, Hase." *Theologische Jahrbücher* 13 (Tübingen, 1854) 196–287.

Baur, Ferdinand Christian
"Die johanneischen Briefe. Ein Beitrag zur Geschichte des Kanons." *Theologische Jahrbücher* 7 (Tübingen, 1848) 293–337.

Baur, Ferdinand Christian
Das manichäische Religionssystem nach den Quellen neu untersucht und entwickelt (Tübingen: C. F. Osiander, 1831; Hildesheim: G. Olms, 1973).

Baur, Ferdinand Christian
Die christliche Gnosis; oder, die christliche Religionsphilosophie in ihrer geschichtlichen Entwicklung (Tübingen: C. F. Osiander, 1835; Darmstadt: Wissenschaftliche Buchgesellschaft, 1967).

Baur, Ferdinand Christian
"Das Verhältnis des ersten johanneischen Briefs zum johanneischen Evangelium." *Theologische Jahrbücher* 16 (Tübingen, 1857) 315–31.

Baur, Ferdinand Christian
"Das johanneische Evangelium und die Passafeier des zweiten Jahrhunderts." *Theologische Jahrbücher* 7 (Tübingen, 1848) 264–86.

Baur, Ferdinand Christian
"Kritische Studien über den Begriff der Gnosis." *TSK* 10 (1837) 511–79.

Baur, Ferdinand Christian
"Das Wesen des Montanismus nach den neuesten Forschungen." *Theologische Jahrbücher* 10 (Tübingen, 1851) 538–94.

Baur, Ferdinand Christian
"Ueber die Composition und den Charakter des johanneischen Evangeliums." *Theologische Jahrbücher* 3 (Tübingen, 1844) 1–191, 397–475, 615–700.

Beasley-Murray, George R.
"The Eschatology of the Fourth Gospel." *EvQ* 18 (1946) 97–108.

Beauvery, Robert
"Accueillir le dessein d'amour que Dieu révèle en Jésus (Jn 3,14–21)." *Esprit et vie* 80 (1970) 113–16.

Beauvery, Robert
"Le fils de Joseph! Manna descendue du ciel? Jn 6,41–52." *AsSeign* 50 (1974) 43–49.

Beauvery, Robert
"Voulez-vous partir, vous aussi? Jn 6,60–69." *AsSeign* 52 (1974) 44–51.

Beauvery, Robert
"Jésus élevé attire les hommes à lui." *Esprit et vie* 80 (1970) 117–19.

Beauvery, Robert
"Evangiles et homélies. Présentation exégétique des Evangiles de Dimanche [Jn 14,1–12; 14,15–21; Mc 13,33–37]." *Esprit et vie* 79 (1969) 287–91, 317–19, 633–36.

Beauvery, Robert
"La mission des disciples: demeurer dans l'amour par l'obéissance (Jn 15, 9–17)." *Esprit et vie* 80 (1970) 273–75.

Beauvery, Robert
"Les disciples, communauté à laquelle Jésus donne vie (Jn 15,1–8)." *Esprit et vie* 80 (1970) 242–45.

Beck, Dr.
"Ueber Joh 14,1.2." *TSK* 4 (1831) 130–34.

Beck, Magnus M.
Die Ewigkeit hat schon begonnen. Perspektiven johanneischer Weltschau (Frankfurt: Verlag Josef Knecht, 1965).

Becker, Heinz
Die Reden des Johannesevangeliums und der Stil der gnostischen Offenbarungsreden, FRLANT, n.s., 50 (Göttingen: Vandenhoeck & Ruprecht, 1956).

Becker, Jürgen
"Auferstehung und Leben im Johannesevangelium." In his *Auferstehung der Toten im Urchristentum*, SBS 82 (Stuttgart: Katholisches Bibelwerk, 1976) 117–48.

Becker, Jürgen
"Beobachtungen zum Dualismus im Johannesevangelium." *ZNW* 65 (1974) 71–87.

Becker, Jürgen
"Joh 3,1–21 als Reflex johanneischer Schuldiskussion." In *Das Wort und die Wörter. Festschrift Gerhard Friedrich zum 65. Geburtstag*, ed H. Balz and S. Schulz (Stuttgart: W. Kohlhammer, 1973) 85–95.

Becker, Jürgen
Das Heil Gottes. Heils- und Sündenbegriffe in den Qumrantexten und im Neuen Testament. SUNT 3 (Göttingen: Vandenhoeck & Ruprecht, 1964) 217–37.

Becker, Jürgen
"Die Abschiedsreden Jesu im Johannesevangelium." *ZNW* 61 (1970) 215–46.

Becker, Jürgen
"Aufbau, Schichtung und theologiegeschichtliche Stellung des Gebets in Johannes 17." *ZNW* 60 (1969) 56–83.

Becker, Jürgen
"Wunder und Christologie. Zum literarkritischen und christologischen Problem der Wunder im Johannesevangelium." *NTS* 16 (1969/1970) 130–48.

Becker, Jürgen
"Aus der Literatur zum Joannesevangelium (1978–1980)." *TRu*, n.s., 47 (1982) 279–301.

Becker, Ulrich
Jesus und die Ehebrecherin. Untersuchungen zur Text- und Überlieferungsgeschichte von Joh. 7,53–8,11, BZNW 28 (Berlin: A. Töpelmann, 1963).

Becquet, G.
"Jésus, Bon Pasteur, donne vie à une nouvelle communauté (Jn 10,11–18)." *Esprit et vie* 80 (1970) 242–43.

Becquet, G.
"Le Christ ressuscité transfère sa mission à la communauté des croyants (Jn 20,19–31)." *Esprit et vie* 80 (1970) 193–96.

Behler, Gerhard Maria
Die Abschiedsworte des Herrn: Joh 13–17 (Salzburg: O. Müller, 1962).

Behm, Johannes
"Der gegenwärtige Stand der Erforschung des Johannesevangeliums." *TLZ* 73 (1948) 21–30.

Behm, Johannes
"Die johanneische Christologie als Abschluss der Christologie des Neuen Testaments." *NKZ* 41 (1930) 577–601.

Bell, H. Idris
"Search the Scriptures" [Joh 5,39]. *ZNW* 37 (1938) 10–13.

Belle, Gilbert Van
De Sèmeia-bron in het vierde Evangelie. Ontstaan en groei van hypothese, Studiorum Novi Testamenti Auxilia 10 (Louvain: University Press, 1975).

Belleville, Linda L.
"Born of Water and Spirit: John 3:5." *Trinity Journal* (1981) 125–41.

Benoit, Pierre
"Découvertes archéologiques autour de la piscine de Béthesda." In *Jerusalem through the Ages*, ed. P. W. Lapp (Jerusalem: Israel Exploration Society, 1968) 48–57.

Benoit, Pierre
"Marie-Madeleine et les Disciples au Tombeau selon Joh 20,1–18." *Judentum, Urchristentum, Kirche. Festschrift für Joachim Jeremias*, ed. W. Eltester (Berlin: A. Töpelmann, 1960) 141–52.

Berger, Klaus
"Zu 'Das Wort ward Fleisch' Joh I,14a." *NovT* 16 (1974) 161–66.

Bergh van Eysinga, G. A. van den
"Zum richtigen Verständnis des johanneischen Prologs." *Protestantische Monatshefte* 13 (1909) 143–50.

Bergmeier, Roland
Glaube als Gabe nach Johannes. Religions- und theologiegeschichtliche Studien zum prädestinatianischen Dualismus im vierten Evangelium, BWANT 112 (Stuttgart: W. Kohlhammer, 1980).

Bergmeier, Roland
"Studien zum religionsgeschichtlichen Ort des prädestinatianischen Dualismus in der johanneischen Literatur." Dissertation, Heidelberg, 1974.

Bergmeier, Roland
"Glaube als Werk? Die 'Werke Gottes' in Damaskusschrift II, 14–15 und Johannes 6, 28–29." *RevQ* 6 (1967) 253–60.

Bernard, Jacques
"La guérsion de Bethesda. Harmoniques judéo-hellénistiques d'un récit de miracle un jour de sabbat (suite et fin)." *MScRel* 33 (1976) 3–34.

Bernard, Jacques
"Jean V et le Jésus de l'histoire." Dissertation, Université de Lille III, 1978.

Bernard, Jacques
"Témoignage pour Jésus-Christ: Jean 5:31–47." *MScRel* 36 (1979) 3–55.

Bernard, John Henry
"Die Traditionen über den Tod des Zebedäussohnes Johannes." In *Johannes und sein Evangelium*, ed. K. H. Rengstorf (Darmstadt: Wissenschaftliche Buchgesellschaft, 1973) 273–90.

Berrouard, M.-F.
"La multiplication des pains et le discours du pain de vie (*Jean*, 6)." *Lumière et vie* 18 (1969) 63–75.

Berrouard, M.-F.
"Le Paraclète, défenseur du Christ devant la conscience du croyant (Jn 16,8–11)." *RSPT* 33 (1949) 361–89.

Bert, Georg
Das Evangelium des Johannes. Versuch einer Lösing seines Grundproblems (Gütersloh: C. Bertelsmann, 1922).

Bertling, D.
"Eine Transposition im Evangelium Johannis." *TSK* 53 (1880) 351–53.

Bertram, G.
"Ev Joh 14,9 und das gnostische Christusbild." *Akten des Internationalen Kongresses, Christ. Arch.* 7 (Berlin: Civitas Vaticanum, 1969) 379–89.

Besser, W. F.
"Über Joh 2, 4." *TSK* 18 (1845) 416–25.

Betz, Otto
"Das Problem des Wunders bei Flavius Josephus im Vergleich zum Wunderproblem bei den Rabbinen und im Johannesevangelium." In *Josephus Studien. Untersuchungen zu Josephus, dem antiken Judentum und das Neuen Testament. Otto Michel zum 70. Geburtstag gewidmet*, ed. O. Betz, K. Elliger and M. Hengel (Göttingen: Vandenhoeck & Ruprecht, 1974) 23–44.

Betz, Otto
"Kann denn aus Nazareth etwas Gutes kommen?" In *Wort und Geschichte* [Festschrift for K. Elliger],

ed. H. Gese and H. P. Rüger (Neukirchen: Neukirchener Verlag, 1973) 6–16.

Betz, Otto
Der Paraklet. Fürsprecher im häretischen Spätjudentum, im Johannes-Evangelium und in den neu gefundenen gnostischen Schriften, AGSU 2 (Leiden: E. J. Brill, 1963).

Beutler, Johannes
"Glaube und Zeugnis im Johannesevangelium." *Bijdragen* 34 (1973) 60–68.

Beutler, Johannes
"'Und das Wort ist Fleisch geworden. . . .' Zur Menschwerdung nach dem Johannesprolog." *Geist und Leben* 46 (1973) 7–16.

Beutler, Johannes
Martyria. Traditionsgeschichtliche Untersuchungen zum Zeugnisthema bei Johannes, Frankfurter theologische Studien 10 (Frankfurt: Verlag Josef Knecht, 1972).

Beutler, Johannes
"Die 'Juden' und der Tod Jesu im Johannesevangelium." In *Exodus und Kreuz im ökumenischen Dialog zwischen Juden und Christen. Diskussionsbeiträge für Religionsunterricht und Erwachsenenbildung,* ed. H. H. Henrix and M. Stöhr. Aachener Beiträge zu Pastoral- und Bildungsfragen 8 (Aachen: Einhard-Verlag, 1978) 75–93.

Beutler, Johannes
"Psalm 42/43 im Johannesevangelium." *NTS* 25 (1978/1979) 33–57.

Bevan, T. W.
"The Four Anointings." *ExpTim* 39 (1927/1928) 137–39.

Beyschlag, Willibald
Zur johanneischen Frage. Beiträge zur Würdigung des vierten Evangeliums gegenüber den Angriffen der Kritischen Schule (Gotha: F. A. Perthes, 1876) and *TSK* 47 (1874) 607–723; 48 (1875) 235–87, 413–79.

Bietenhard, Hans
Die himmlische Welt im Urchristentum und Spätjudentum, WUNT 2 (Tübingen: Mohr-Siebeck, 1951).

Billerbeck, Paul
"On John 3:21." 2: 429.

Billerbeck, Paul
"Zu Mt 1,18" and "zu Mt 9,15." 1: 500–17.

Billings, J. S.
"Judas Iscariot in the Fourth Gospel." *ExpTim* 51 (1939/1940) 156–57.

Bindemann, E.
"Ueber die von Justinus dem Märtyrer gebrauchten Evangelien." *TSK* 15 (1842) 355–482.

Birdsall, J. Neville
The Bodmer Papyrus of the Gospel of John (London: Tyndale Press, 1960).

Birdsall, J. Neville
"The Text of the Fourth Gospel: Some Current Questions." *EvQ* 29 (1957) 195–205.

Bishop, Eric F. F.
"'He that Eateth Bread with me hath Lifted up his Heel against me': —Jn xiii. 18 (Ps xli. 9)." *ExpTim* 70 (1958/1959) 331–32.

Bjerkelund, Carl J.
"En tradisjons- og redaksjonshistorik analyse av perikopene om tempelrendelsen." *NorTT* 69 (1968) 206–16.

Black, Matthew
"Does an Aramaic Tradition Underlie John i. 16?" *JTS* (1941) 69–70.

Black, Matthew
An Aramaic Approach to the Gospels and Acts (Oxford: Clarendon Press, 1946, ²1954).

Blakeway, C. E.
"Behold the Lamb of God." *ExpTim* 31 (1919/1920) 364–65.

Blank, Josef
"Der johanneische Warheits-Begriff." *BZ* 7 (1963) 164–73.

Blank, Josef
"Das Johannesevangelium. Der Prolog: Joh 1,1–18." *BibLeb* 7 (1966) 28–39, 112–27.

Blank, Josef
Krisis. Untersuchungen zur johanneischen Christologie und Eschatologie (Freiburg: Lambertus-Verlag, 1964).

Blank, Josef
"Die Gegenwartseschatologie des Johannesevangeliums." In *Vom Messias zum Christus. Die Fülle der Zeit in religionsgeschichtlicher und theologischer Sicht,* ed. K. Schubert (Vienna: Herder, 1964) 279–313.

Blank, Josef
"Die johanneische Brotrede. Einführung: Brotvermehrung und Seewandel Jesu: Jo 6,1–21." *BibLeb* 7 (1966) 193–207.

Blank, Josef
"'Ich bin das Lebensbrot' Jo 6,22–50." *BibLeb* 7 (1966) 255–70.

Blank, Josef
"Predigtmeditationen: Joh 8, 48–59." In his *Schriftauslegung in Theorie und Praxis,* Biblische Handbibliothek 5 (Munich: Kösel, 1969) 207–20.

Blank, Josef
"Das Wort, der Geist und die Gemeinde (Joh 14,23–31)." *Am Tische des Wortes* 3 (1965) 28–44.

Blank, Josef
"Predigtmeditationen: Joh 14,23–31." In his *Schriftauslegung in Theorie und Praxis,* Biblische Handbibliothek 5 (Munich: Kösel, 1969) 188–206.

Blank, Josef
"Die Verhandlung vor Pilatus: Joh 18,28–19,16 im Lichte der johanneischen Theologie." *BZ* 3 (1959) 60–81.

Blauert, H.
"Die Bedeutung der Zeit in der johanneischen Theologie." Dissertation, Tübingen, 1953.

Bleek, Friedrich

"Beschränkung der Anforderung an die wörtliche Treue in der Wiedergabe der längeren Reden und Unterredungen im Johannesevangelium." In his *Beiträge zur Einleitung und Auslegung der heiligen Schrift*, 1: 240–44.

Bleek, Friedrich

"Verhältniss der johanneischen Darstellung zur synoptischen in der Erzählung vom Wandeln Jesu auf dem Meere." In his *Beiträge zur Einleitung und Auslegung der heiligen Schrift*, 1: 102–5.

Bleek, Friedrich

"Ueber Joh 7,8, die richtige Lesart (. . .) und den Sinn." In his *Beiträge zur Einleitung und Auslegung der heiligen Schrift*, 1: 105–7.

Bleek, Friedrich

"Der Verfasser des vierten Evangeliums beweist durch seine Bekanntschaft mit dem AT sich als einen Juden und Palästinenser. . . ." In his *Beiträge zur Einleitung und Auslegung der heiligen Schrift*, 1: 244–57.

Bleek, Friedrich

"Auslassung der Auferweckung des Lazarus bei den Synoptikern." In his *Beiträge zur Einleitung und Auslegung der heiligen Schrift*, 1: 100–101.

Bleek, Friedrich

"Ueber den Monathstag des Todes Christi und des letzten Abendmahles mit seinen Jüngern und die in der Beziehung zwischen Johannes und den Synoptikern stattfindende Differenz." In his *Beiträge zur Einleitung und Auslegung der heiligen Schrift*, 1: 107–56.

Bleek, Friedrich

"Ueber Joh 14,31 als Beweis der Authentie der johanneischen Reden." In his *Beiträge zur Einleitung und Auslegung der heiligen Schrift*, 1: 236–39.

Bleek, Friedrich

"Baur's Ansicht über den Grund der johanneischen Darstellung von dem Verhör Jesu vor dem Hannas." In his *Beiträge zur Einleitung und Auslegung der heiligen Schrift*, 1: 166.

Bleek, Friedrich

"Gegen Baur's Annahme, dass mit Joh 21 auch Kap. 20,30.31 später Anhang sei." In his *Beiträge zur Einleitung und Auslegung der heiligen Schrift*, 1: 179–81.

Bleek, Friedrich

Beiträge zur Einleitung und Auslegung der heiligen Schrift. Vol. 1, *Beiträge zur Evangelien-Kritik* (Berlin: G. Reimer, 1846).

Bleek, Friedrich

"Die Zeugnisse und Erscheinungen in der Kirche während des zweiten Jahrhunderts führen entschieden darauf, dass das Johannes-Evangelium schon wenigstens seit dem Anfange dieses Jahrhunderts in der Kirche bekannt und anerkannt war." In his *Beiträge zur Einleitung und Auslegung der heiligen Schrift*, 1: 200–226.

Bleek, Friedrich

"Ueber die Spuren in den Synoptischen Evangelien, welche für die johanneische Darstellung des äusseren Verlaufes der evangelischen Geschichte, . . . zeugen." In his *Beiträge zur Einleitung und Auslegung der heiligen Schrift*, 1: 92–99.

Bleibtreu, Walther

"Evang. Joh. 16, 23, 24." *NKZ* 22 (1911) 958–62.

Blenkinsopp, J.

"The Quenching of Thirst: Reflections on the Utterance in the Temple, Jn 7, 37–39." *Scr* 12 (1950) 39–48.

Blenkinsopp, J.

"John 7, 37–39: Another Note on a Notorious Crux." *NTS* 6 (1959/1960) 95–98.

Bligh, John

"Four Studies in St. John, II: Nicodemus." *HeyJ* 8 (1967) 40–51.

Bligh, John

"Jesus in Samaria [Jn 4:1–42]." *HeyJ* 3 (1962) 329–46.

Bligh, John

"Jesus in Jerusalem [Jn 5]." *HeyJ* 4 (1963) 115–34.

Bligh, John

"Jesus in Galilee." *HeyJ* 5 (1964) 3–26.

Bligh, John

"Four Studies in St. John, I: The Man Born Blind." *HeyJ* 7 (1966) 129–44.

Bligh, John

The Sign of the Cross. The Passion and Resurrection of Jesus according to St. John (Slough: St. Paul Publications, 1975).

Blindley, T. H.

"Jn 7, 37–38." *Expositor*, 8th ser., 20 (1920) 443–47.

Blinzler, Josef

"Die Strafe für Ehebruch in Bibel und Halacha. Zur Auslegung von Joh VIII, 5." *NTS* 4 (1957/1958) 32–47.

Blinzler, Josef

Johannes und die Synoptiker, ein Forschungsbericht (Stuttgart: Katholisches Bibelwerk, 1965).

Blinzler, Josef

"Zum Geschichtsrahmen des Johannesevangeliums." In his *Aus der Welt und Umwelt des Neuen Testaments. Gesammelte Aufsätze* 1, SBB (Stuttgart: Katholisches Bibelwerk, 1969) 94–107.

Bludau, Augustinus

Die ersten Gegner der Johannesschriften, BibS(F) 22, 1–2 (Freiburg: Herder, 1925).

Blumenthal, M.

"Die Eigenart des johanneischen Erzählungsstiles." *TSK* 106 (1934/1935) 204–12.

Bobrinskoy, Boris

"Die theologischen Grundlagen des gemeinsamen Gebets für die Einheit." *Una sancta* 22 (1967) 25–37.

Boccali, Giovanni

"Spirito e vita (Gv 6,63)." *Parole di vita* 13 (1968) 118–31.

Boccali, Giovanni
"Un maschal evangelico e la sua applicazione [Gv 6,63]." *BeO* 10 (1968) 53–58.

Böcher, Otto
"Wasser und Geist." In *Verborum Veritas. Festschrift für Gustav Stählin zum 70. Geburtstag*, ed. O. Böcher and K. Haacker (Wuppertal: F. A. Brockhaus, 1970) 197–209.

Böcher, Otto
Der johanneische Dualismus im Zusammenhang des nachbiblischen Judentums (Gütersloh: Gerd Mohn, 1965).

Bockel, Pierre
Le verbe au présent. Le message de Saint Jean l'Evangéliste (Paris: Fayard, 1978).

Bode, Edward Lynn
The First Easter Morning. The Gospel Accounts of the Women's Visit to the Tomb of Jesus, AnBib 45 (Rome: Pontifical Biblical Institute, 1970).

Boers, Hendrikus
"Discourse Structure and Macro-Structure in the Interpretation of Text: John 4:1–42 as an Example." SBLASP (Chico, CA: Scholars Press, 1980) 159ff.

Bogaert, M.
"Jn 1,19–28." *AsSeign* 5 (1966) 41–54.

Bogaert, P.-M.
"Quelques ouvrages récents sur l'Evangile de saint Jean." *BVC* 102 (1971) 80–82.

Bogart, John
Orthodox and Heretical Perfectionism in the Johannine Community as Evident in the First Epistle of John, SBLDS 33 (Missoula: Scholars Press, 1977).

Bogart, John
"Recent Johannic Studies." *ATR* 60 (1978) 80–87.

Böhmer, Wilhelm
"Das Fusswaschen Christi, nach seiner sacramentlichen Würde dargestellt." *TSK* 23 (1850) 829–42.

Boice, James Montgomery
Witness and Revelation in the Gospel of John, Contemporary Evangelical Perspectives (Grand Rapids: Zondervan, 1970).

Boismard, Marie-Emile
Le Prologue de S. Jean, LD 11 (Paris: Editions du Cerf, 1953).

Boismard, Marie-Emile
"'Dans le sein du Père.' (Jn. I, 18)." *RB* 59 (1952) 23–39.

Boismard, Marie-Emile
"La première semaine du ministère de Jésus selon S. Jean." *VSpir* 94 (1956) 593–603.

Boismard, Marie-Emile
Du baptême à Cana, LD 18 (Paris: Editions du Cerf, 1956) 133–59.

Boismard, Marie-Emile
"Aenon, près de Salem: *Jean*, III,23." *RB* 80 (1973) 218–29.

Boismard, Marie-Emile
"Les traditions johanniques concernant le Baptiste." *RB* 70 (1963) 5–42.

Boismard, Marie-Emile
"L'amie de l'époux (Jo. III,29)." In *A la rencontre de Dieu. Mémorial Albert Gelin*, Bibliothèque de la faculté Catholique de Théologie à Lyon 8 (Le Puy/Paris: Xavier Mappus, 1961) 289–95.

Boismard, Marie-Emile
"Saint Luc et la rédaction du quatrième évangile (Jn iv, 46–54)." *RB* 69 (1962) 185–211.

Boismard, Marie-Emile
"Guérison du fils d'un fonctionnaire royal." *AsSeign* 75 (1965) 26–37.

Boismard, Marie-Emile
"L'évolution du thème eschatologique dans les traditions johanniques." *RB* 68 (1961) 507–24.

Boismard, Marie-Emile
"A propos de Jean V,39. Essai de critique textuelle." *RB* 55 (1948) 5–34.

Boismard, Marie-Emile
"De son ventre couleront des fleuves d'eau (Jn 7,38)." *RB* 65 (1958) 523–46.

Boismard, Marie-Emile
"Les citations targumiques du quatrième évangile." *RB* 66 (1959) 374–78.

Boismard, Marie-Emile
"Jésus, le prophète par excellence, d'après Jean 10,24–39." In *Neues Testament und Kirche. Für Rudolf Schnackenburg*, ed. J. Gnilka (Freiburg: Herder, 1974) 160–71.

Boismard, Marie-Emile
"Le caractère adventice de Jn 12,45–50." *Sacra pagina* 2 (1959) 189–92.

Boismard, Marie-Emile
"Le lavement des pieds (*Jn*, XIII, 1–17)." *RB* 71 (1964) 5–24.

Boismard, Marie-Emile
"La royauté universelle du Christ: Jn 18,33–37." *AsSeign* 65 (1973) 36–46.

Boismard, Marie-Emile
"Le chapitre XXI de saint Jean: essai de critique littéraire." *RB* 54 (1947) 473–501.

Boismard, Marie-Emile
"Lectio brevior, potior." *RB* 58 (1951) 161–68.

Boismard, Marie-Emile
"Problèmes de critique textuelle concernant le quatrième évangile." *RB* 60 (1953) 341–71.

Boismard, Marie-Emile
"Le papyrus Bodmer II." *RB* 64 (1957) 363–98.

Boismard, Marie-Emile
"Un procédé rédactionnel dans le quatrième évangile: la Wiederaufnahme." In *L'Evangile de Jean. Sources, rédaction, théologie*, ed. M. de Jonge. BETL 44 (Gembloux: Duculot; Louvain: University Press, 1977) 235–41.

Boismard, Marie-Emile
"Saint Luc et la rédaction du quatrième évangile (Jn iv, 46–54)." *RB* 69 (1962) 185–211.

Boismard, Marie-Emile
"La royauté du Christ dans le quatrième évangile."

Lumière et vie 11 (1962) 43–63.

Boismard, Marie-Emile
"Jesus the Savior According to St. John." In *Word and Mystery. Biblical Essays on the Person and Mission of Christ*, ed. L. J. O'Donovan, S.J. (Glen Rock, NJ, and London: Newman, 1968) 69–85.

Boismard, Marie-Emile
"Jesus, sauveur, d'après saint Jean." *Lumière et vie* 15 (1954) 103–22.

Bojorge, Horacio
"La entrada en la tierra prometida y la entrada en el Reino. El trasfondo teológico del diálogo de Jesús con Nicodemo (Jn 3)." *RevistB* 41 (1979) 172–86.

Bonneau, N. R.
"The Woman at the Well: John 4 and Genesis 24." *Bible Today* 67 (1973) 1252–59.

Bonner, Campbell
"Traces of Thaumaturgic Technique in the Miracles." *HTR* 20 (1927) 171–81.

Bonsack, Bernard
"Syntaktische Überlegungen zu Joh 1,9–10." In *Studies in New Testament Language and Text. Essays in Honour of George D. Kilpatrick on the Occasion of his Sixty-fifth Birthday*, ed. J. K. Elliott. NovTSup 44 (Leiden: E. J. Brill, 1976) 52–79.

Bonsirven, Joseph
"Hora Talmudica. La notation chronologique de Jean 19,14 aurait-elle un sens symbolique?" *Bib* 33 (1952) 511–15.

Bonsirven, Joseph
"Les aramaïsmes de S. Jean l'évangéliste?" *Bib* 30 (1949) 405–32.

Booth, K. N.
"The Self-Proclamation of Jesus in St. John's Gospel." *Colloquium* 7 (1975) 36–47.

Borgen, Peder
"Observations on the Targumic Character of the Prologue of John." *NTS* 16 (1969/1970) 288–95.

Borgen, Peder
"Logos was the True Light. Contributions to the Interpretation of the Prologue of John." *NovT* 14 (1972) 115–30. In Swedish: "Logos war det sanne lys. Momenter til tolkning av Johannesprologen." *SEÅ* 35 (1970) 79–95.

Borgen, Peder
Bread from Heaven. An Exegetical Study of the Concept of Manna in the Gospel of John and the Writings of Philo, NovTSup 10 (Leiden: E. J. Brill, 1965).

Borgen, Peder
"Observations on the Midrashic Character of John 6." *ZNW* 54 (1963) 232–40.

Borgen, Peder
"The Unity of the Discourse in John 6." *ZNW* 50 (1959) 277–78.

Borgen, Peder
"The Use of Tradition in John 12.44–50." *NTS* 26 (1979/1980) 18–35.

Borgen, Peder
"God's Agent in the Fourth Gospel." In *Religions in Antiquity. Essays in Memory of E. R. Goodenough*, ed. J. Neusner (Leiden: E. J. Brill, 1968) 137–47.

Borgen, Peder
"John and the Synoptics in the Passion Narrative." *NTS* 5 (1958/1959) 246–59.

Borgen, Peder
"Some Jewish Exegetical Traditions as Background for Son of Man Sayings in John's Gospel (Jn 3, 13–14 and context)." In *L'Evangile de Jean. Sources, rédaction, théologie*, ed. M. de Jonge. BETL 44 (Gembloux: Duculot; Louvain: University Press, 1977) 243–58.

Borig, Rainer
Der wahre Weinstock. Untersuchungen zu Jo 15,1–10, SANT 16 (Munich: Kösel, 1967).

Boring, M. Eugene
"The Influence of Christian Prophecy on the Johannine Portrayal of the Paraclete and Jesus." *NTS* 25 (1978/1979) 113–23.

Bormann, Karl
"Die Ideen-und Logoslehre Philons von Alexandrien." Dissertation, Köln, 1955.

Bornhäuser, Karl Bernard
"Jesus und die Ehebrecherin. Zum Verständnisse des Perikope Joh 8,1–11." *NKZ* 37 (1926) 353–63.

Bornhäuser, Karl Bernard
"Meister, wer hat gesündigt, dieser oder seine Eltern, dass er ist blind geboren?: Joh. 9, 2." *NKZ* 38 (1927) 433–37.

Bornhäuser, Karl Bernard
Das Johannesevangelium, eine Missionsschrift für Israel (Gütersloh: C. Bertelsmann, 1928).

Bornkamm, Günther
"Das Johannesevangelium und die johanneische Briefe." In his *Bibel, das neue Testament. Eine Einführung in seine Schriften im Rahmen der Geschichte des Urchristentums*, Themen der Theologie 9 (Stuttgart and Berlin: Kreuz-Verlag, 1971) 149–63.

Bornkamm, Günther
"Die eucharistische Rede im Johannes-Evangelium." *ZNW* 47 (1956) 161–69. In his *Geschichte und Glauben*, part 1. *Gesammelte Aufsätze*, vol. 3. BEvT 48 (Munich: Chr. Kaiser Verlag, 1968) 60–67.

Bornkamm, Günther
"Vorjohanneische oder nachjohanneische Bearbeitung in der eucharistischen Rede Joh 6?" In his *Geschichte und Glauben*, part 2. *Gesammelte Aufsätze*, vol. 4. BEvT 53 (Munich: Chr. Kaiser Verlag, 1971) 51–64.

Bornkamm, Günther
"Joh 7, 10–18: Eine Meditation." *Wissenschaft und Praxis in Kirche und Gesellschaft* 59 (1970) 108–13.

Bornkamm, Günther
"Die Heilung des Blindgeborenen (Joh 9)." In his *Geschichte und Glaube*, part 2. *Gesammelte Aufsätze*, vol. 4. BEvT 53 (Munich: Chr. Kaiser Verlag, 1971) 65–72.

Bornkamm, Günther
"Die Zeit des Geistes. Ein johanneisches Wort und seine Geschichte." In his *Geschichte und Glauben*, part 1. *Gesammelte Aufsätze*, vol. 3. BEvT 48 (Munich: Chr. Kaiser Verlag, 1971) 90–103.

Bornkamm, Günther
"Zur Interpretation des Johannesevangeliums." *EvT* 28 (1968) 8–25.

Bornkamm, Günther
"Der Paraklet im Johannesevangelium." In his *Geschichte und Glauben*, part 1. *Gesammelte Aufsätze*, vol 3. BEvT 48 (Munich: Chr. Kaiser Verlag, 1968) 68–89.

Bornkamm, Günther
"Zur Interpretation des Johannesevangeliums. Eine Auseinandersetzung mit E. Käsemanns Schrift 'Jesu letzter Wille nach Johannes 17.'" *EvT* 28 (1968) 8–25.

Borsch, Frederick Hauk
The Christian and Gnostic Son of Man, SBT, 2nd ser., 14 (Naperville, IL: Allenson, 1970).

Botha, F. J.
"The Jews in the Fourth Gospel [Afrikaans]." *Theologia evangelica* 2 (1969) 40–45.

Bourke, Myles M.
"The Miracles Stories of the Gospels." *DunR* 12 (1972) 21–34.

Bousset, Wilhelm
"Johannesevangelium." *RGG*[1] 3 (1912) 608–36.

Bousset, Wilhelm
Jüdisch-christlicher Schulbetrieb in Alexandria und Rom. Literarische Untersuchungen zu Philo und Clemens von Alexandria, Justin und Irenäus, FRLANT, n.s., 6 (Göttingen: Vandenhoeck & Ruprecht, 1915; Hildesheim and New York: G. Olms, 1975).

Bousset, Wilhelm
"Ist das vierte Evangelium eine literarische Einheit?" *TRu* 12 (1909) 1–12, 39–64.

Bousset, Wilhelm
"Der Verfasser des Johannesevangeliums." *TRu* 8 (1905) 225–44, 277–95.

Bousset, Wilhelm
Kyrios Christos. A History of the Belief in Christ from the Beginnings of Christianity to Irenaeus, tr. John E. Steely (Nashville: Abingdon Press, 1970) = *Kyrios Christos. Geschichte des Christusglaubens von den Anfängen des Christentums bis Irenaeus* (Göttingen: Vandenhoeck & Ruprecht, [5]1965).

Bowen, Clayton R.
"Love in the Fourth Gospel." *JR* 13 (1933) 39–49.

Bowen, Clayton R.
"The Fourth Gospel as Dramatic Material." *JBL* 49 (1930) 292–305.

Bowker, J. W.
"The Origin and Purpose of St. John's Gospel." *NTS* 11 (1964/1965) 398–408.

Bowman, John
"Early Samaritan Eschatology." *JJS* 6 (1955) 63–72.

Bowman, John
"Samaritan Studies." *BJRL* 40 (1957/1958) 298–329.

Bowman, John
"The Identity and Date of the Unnamed Feast of John 5,1." In *Near Eastern Studies in Honor of William Foxwell Albright*, ed. Hans Goedicke (Baltimore: Johns Hopkins University Press, 1971) 43–56.

Bowman, John
The Fourth Gospel and the Jews. A Study in R. Akiba, Esther and the Gospel of John, PTMS 8 (Pittsburgh: Pickwick, 1975).

Bowman, John
"The Fourth Gospel and the Samaritans." *BJRL* 40 (1957/1958) 298–329.

Boxel, Piet van
"Die präexistente Doxa Jesu im Johannesevangelium." *Bijdragen* 34 (1973) 268–81.

Boxel, Piet van
"Glaube und Liebe. Die Aktualität des johanneischen Jüngermodells." *Geist und Leben* 48 (1975) 18–28.

Boyd, W. J. Peter
"The Ascension according to St. John. Chapters 14–17 not pre-passion but post-resurrection." *Theology* 70 (1967) 207–11.

Boyle, John L.
"The Last Discourse (Jn 13,31–16,33) and Prayer (Jn 17): Some Observations on Their Unity and Development." *Bib* 56 (1975) 210–22.

Brandenburger, Egon
"Joh 4,31–38: Exegese und Anregungen zur Meditation und Predigt." *Kirche im Dorf* 22 (1971) 203–9.

Bratcher, Robert G.
"'The Jews' in the Gospel of John." *BT* 26 (1975) 401–9.

Braun, François-Marie
"L'arrière-fond judaïque du quatrième évangile et la communauté de l'alliance." *RB* 62 (1955) 5–44.

Braun, François-Marie
La mère des fidèles (Paris: Casterman, [2]1954) 47–74.

Braun, François-Marie
"L'expulsion des vendeurs du Temple (Mt. xxi, 12–17, 23–27; Mc. xi, 15–19, 27–33; Lc xix, 45–xx, 8; Jo. ii, 13–22)." *RB* 38 (1929) 178–200.

Braun, François-Marie
"In spiritu et veritate." *RevThom* 52 (1952) 245–74.

Braun, François-Marie
"'La vie d'en haut' (Jo. III,1–15)." *RSPT* 40 (1956) 3–24.

Braun, François-Marie
"Avoir soif et boire: Jn 4,10–14; 7,37–39." In *Mélanges bibliques en hommage au R. P. Béda Rigaux*, ed. A. Descamps and A. De Halleux (Gembloux: Duculot, 1970) 247–58.

Braun, François-Marie
"Quatre 'signes' johanniques de l'unité chrétienne." *NTS* 9 (1962/1963).

Braun, François-Marie
"Le baptême d'après le quatrième Evangile." *RevThom* 48 (1948) 347–93.

Braun, François-Marie
"L'eucharistie selon saint Jean." *RevThom* 70 (1970) 5–29.

Braun, François-Marie
"Le lavement des pieds et la réponse de Jésus à Saint Pierre (Jean XIII,4–10)." *RB* 44 (1935) 22–33.

Braun, François-Marie
"Apostolique et pneumatique selon saint Jean." *RevThom* 71 (1971) 451–62.

Braun, François-Marie
"Où en est l'étude du quatrième évangile?" *ETL* 32 (1956) 535–46.

Braun, François-Marie
"La foi selon saint Jean." *RevThom* 69 (1969) 357–77.

Braun, François-Marie
"La 'lettre de Barnabé' et l'évangile de Saint Jean (Simples réflexions)." *NTS* 4 (1957/1958) 119–24.

Braun, François-Marie
Jean le théologien et son evangile dans l'église ancienne (Paris: J. Gabalda, 1959).

Braun, François-Marie
"La reduction du pluriel au singulier dans l'évangile et la première lettre de Jean." *NTS* 24 (1977/1978) 40–67.

Braun, François-Marie
"La seigneurie du Christ dans le monde, selon saint Jean." *RevThom* 67 (1967) 357–86.

Braun, Herbert
"Das Stirb und Werde in der Antike und im NT." In *Libertas Christiana, Friedrich Delekat* zum *fünfundsechzigsten Geburtstag,* ed. W. Matthias and E. Wolf. BEvT 26 (Munich: Chr. Kaiser Verlag, 1967) 9–29.

Braun, Herbert
"Entscheidende Motive in den Berichten über die Taufe Jesu von Markus bis Justin." In his *Gesammelte Studien zum Neuen Testament und seiner Umwelt* (Tübingen: Mohr-Siebeck, 1967) 168–72.

Braun, Herbert
"Joh 15,1–8." *Göttinger Predigtmeditationen* 23 (1968/1969) 290–93.

Bream, Howard N.
"No Need to be Asked Questions. A Study of John 16,30." In *Search the Scriptures. New Testament Studies in Honor of Raymond T. Stamm,* ed. J. M. Myers, O. Reimherr and H. N. Bream. Gettysburg Theological Studies 3 (Leiden: E. J. Brill, 1969) 49–74.

Bréhier, Emile
Les idées philosophiques et religieuses de Philon d'Alexandrie. (Paris: A. Picard & Fils, 1907; Librairie philosophique J. Vrin, ²1925).

Bretschneider, Karl Gottlieb
Probabilia de Evangelii et Epistolarum Joannis Apostoli indole et origine eruditorum iudiciis modeste subiecit (Leipzig: J. A. Barth, 1820).

Bretschneider, Karl Gottlieb
"Einige Bemerkungen zu dem Aufsatze des Herrn D. Goldhorn (...) über das Schweigen des johanneischen Evangeliums von dem Seelenkampfe Jesu in Gethsemane." *Magazin für christliche Prediger* 2,2 (1824) 153–74.

Briggs, Charles A.
New Light on the Life of Jesus (New York: Charles Scribner's Sons, 1904) 140–58.

Brinkmann, B.
"Zur Frage der ursprünglichen Ordnung im Johannesevangelium." *Greg* 20 (1939) 55–82.

Brodie, Louis T.
"Creative Rewriting: Key to a New Methodology." In *SBL 1978 Seminar Papers* 2, SBLASP 14 (Missoula: Scholars Press, 1978) 261–67.

Broer, Ingo
Die Urgemeinde und das leere Grab Jesu. Eine Analyse der Grablegungsgeschichte im Neuen Testament, SANT 31 (Munich: Kösel, 1972).

Bromboszoz, Theophil
Die Einheit des Johannesevangeliums (Kattowitz, 1927).

Brooks, O. S.
"The Johannine Eucharist. Another Interpretation." *JBL* 82 (1963) 293–300.

Broome, Edwin C.
"The Sources of the Fourth Gospel." *JBL* 63 (1944) 107–21.

Broomfield, George Welele
"The Fourth Evangelist and the Synoptic Tradition." In his *John, Peter and the Fourth Gospel* (New York: Macmillan; London: S. P. C. K., 1934) 82–107.

Broomfield, George Welele
"John and Luke." In his *John, Peter and the Fourth Gospel* (New York: Macmillan; London: S. P. C. K., 1934) 108–45.

Broomfield, Gerald Welele
"The Beloved Disciple." In his *John, Peter and the Fourth Gospel* (New York: Macmillan; London: S. P. C. K., 1934) 146–61.

Bröse, Ernst
"Noch einmal: der Teich Bethesda." *TSK* 76 (1903) 153–56.

Brown, F. J.
"Displacement in the Fourth Gospel." *ExpTim* 57 (1945/1946) 217–20.

Brown, Raymond E.
"The Kerygma of the Gospel According to John. The Johannine View of Jesus in Modern Studies." *Int* 21 (1967) 387–400.

Brown, Raymond E.
"The 'Mother of Jesus' in the Fourth Gospel." In

L'Evangile de Jean. Sources, rédaction, théologie, ed. M. de Jonge. BETL 44 (Gembloux: Duculot; Louvain: University Press, 1977) 307–10.

Brown, Raymond E.
"The Problem of Historicity in John." *CBQ* 24 (1962) 1–14.

Brown, Raymond E.
"The Eucharist and Baptism in John." Proceedings of the Society of Catholic College Teachers of Sacred Doctrine 8 (1962) 14–37. In his *New Testament Essays* (Milwaukee: Bruce, 1965) 77–95.

Brown, Raymond E.
"The Johannine Sacramentary Reconsidered." *TS* 23 (1962) 183–206. In his *New Testament Essays* (Milwaukee: Bruce, 1965) 51–76.

Brown, Raymond E.
"Gospel of John." *Catholic Encyclopedia* 7 (New York: Catholic Encyclopedia Press, 1967) 1080–88.

Brown, Raymond E.
"The Fourth Gospel in Modern Research." *Bible Today* 52 (1965) 1302–10.

Brown, Raymond E.
"Roles of Woman in the Fourth Gospel." *TS* 36 (1975) 688–99.

Brown, Raymond E.
New Testament Essays (Milwaukee: Bruce, 1965).

Brown, Raymond E.
"The Relationship to the Fourth Gospel Shared by the Author of 1 John and by his Opponents." In *Text and Interpretation. Studies in the New Testament presented to Matthew Black,* ed. E. Best and R. McL. Wilson (New York and London: Cambridge University Press, 1979) 57–68.

Brown, Raymond E.
"The Qumran Scrolls and the Johannine Gospel and Epistles." In *The Scrolls and the New Testament,* ed. K. Stendahl (New York: Harper & Brothers, 1957) 183–207.

Brown, Raymond E.
"John and the Synoptic Gospels." In his *New Testament Essays* (Milwaukee: Bruce, 1965) 192–213.

Brown, Raymond E.
"The Paraclete in the Fourth Gospel." *NTS* 13 (1966/1967) 113–32.

Brown, Raymond E.
"The 'Paraclete' in the Light of Modern Research." *SE* 4 = TU 102 (Berlin: Akademie-Verlag, 1968) 158–65.

Brown, Raymond E.
"'Other Sheep not of this Fold': The Johannine Perspective on Christian Diversity in the Late First Century." *JBL* 97 (1978) 5–22.

Brown, Raymond E.
The Community of the Beloved Disciple (New York: Paulist, 1979).

Brown, Raymond E.
"Johannine Ecclesiology—The Community's Origins." *Int* 31 (1977) 379–93.

Brown, Raymond E.
"The Passion According to John: Chapter 18 and 19." *Worship* 49 (1975) 126–34.

Brown, Schuyler
"From Burney to Black. The Fourth Gospel and the Aramaic Question." *CBQ* 26 (1964) 323–39.

Bruce, F. F.
"'It is they that bear witness to me.'" In his *The Time is Fulfilled. Five Aspects of the Fulfilment of the Old Testament in the New* (Grand Rapids: Wm. B. Eerdmans, 1978) 33–53.

Bruce, F. F.
"St. John at Ephesus." *BJRL* 60 (1978) 339–61.

Brun, Lyder
"'Floder av levende vand,' (Joh 7, 37–39)." *NorTT* 29 (1928) 71–79.

Brun, Lyder
"Die Gottesschau des johanneischen Christus." *Symbolae Osloenses* 5 (1927) 1–22.

Bruns, J. Edgar
"The Discourse on the Good Shepherd and the Rite of Ordination." *AER* 149 (1963) 386–91.

Bruns, J. Edgar
"A Note on Jn 12,3." *CBQ* 28 (1966) 219–22.

Bruns, J. Edgar
"A Note on John 16:33 and 1 John 2:13–14." *JBL* 86 (1967) 451–53.

Bruns, J. Edgar
"The Fourth Gospel: Present Trends of Analysis." *Bible Today* 59 (1972) 699–703.

Bruns, J. Edgar
The Art and Thought of John (New York: Herder & Herder, 1969).

Bruns, J. Edgar
"Ananda: The Fourth Evangelist's Model for the 'Disciple whom Jesus Loved'?" *SR* 3 (1973) 236–43.

Bruns, J. Edgar
"John Mark: A Riddle Within the Johannine Enigma." *Scr* 15 (1963) 88–92.

Bruns, J. Edgar
"The Confusion between John and John Mark in Antiquity." *Scr* 17 (1965) 23–26.

Bruyne, Donatien De
"Les plus anciens prologues latins des évangiles." *RBén* 40 (1928) 193–214.

Buchanan, George Wesley
"The Samaritan Origin of the Gospel of John." In *Religions in Antiquity. Essays in Honor of E. R. Goodenough,* ed. J. Neusner. Studies in the History of Religions 14 (Leiden: E. J. Brill, 1968) 149–75.

Büchsel, Friedrich
"Mandäer und Johannesjünger." *ZNW* 26 (1927) 219–30.

Büchsel, Friedrich
"Κρίνω." *TDNT* 3: 933–41.

Büchsel, Friedrich
Der Geist Gottes im Neuen Testament (Gütersloh: C. Bertelsmann, 1926) 485–511.

Büchsel, Friedrich
Johannes und der hellenistische Synkretismus, BFCT 2; Sammlung wissenschaftlicher Monographien 16 (Gütersloh: C. Bertelsmann, 1928).

Büchsel, Friedrich
"Johannes und die Synoptiker." *ZST* 4 (1927) 240–65.

Büchsel, Friedrich
"Die Stelle des Johannesevangeliums in einer Theologie des Neuen Testaments." *TBl* (1937) 301–6.

Bühner, Jan-A.
"Zur Form, Tradition und Bedeutung der ἦλθον - Sprüche." In *Das Institutum Judaicum der Universität Tübingen* (Tübingen, 1971/1972) 45–68.

Bühner, Jan-A.
Der Gesandte und sein Weg im vierten Evangelium. Die kultur- und religionsgeschichtlichen Grundlagen der johanneischen Sendungschristologie sowie ihre traditionsgeschichtliche Entwicklung, WUNT 2, 2 (Tübingen: Mohr-Siebeck, 1977).

Bull, Robert J.
"An Archaeological Context for Understanding John 4:20." *BA* 38 (1975) 54–59.

Bultmann, Rudolf
"Johanneische Schriften und Gnosis." In his *Exegetica. Aufsätze zur Erforschung des Neuen Testaments*, ed. E. Dinkler (Tübingen: Mohr-Siebeck, 1967) 230–54.

Bultmann, Rudolf
"Untersuchungen zum Johannesevangelium." *ZNW* 29 (1930) 169–92. In his *Exegetica: Aufsätze zur Erforschung des Neuen Testaments*, ed. Erich Dinkler (Tübingen: Mohr-Siebeck, 1967) 124–97.

Bultmann, Rudolf
"Zur Geschichte der Lichtsymbolik im Altertum." In his *Exegetica. Aufsätze zur Erforschung des Neuen Testaments*, ed. E. Dinkler (Tübingen: Mohr-Siebeck, 1967) 323–55.

Bultmann, Rudolf
"Die Eschatologie des Johannes-Evangelium." *Zwischen den Zeiten* 6 (1928) 4–22.

Bultmann, Rudolf
"Urchristliche Religion." *ARW* 24 (1926) 83–164.

Bultmann, Rudolf
"Johannesevangelium." *RGG*[3] 3 (1959) 840–50.

Bultmann, Rudolf
"Hirschs Auslegung des Johannes-Evangeliums." *EvT* 4 (1937) 115–42.

Bultmann, Rudolf
"Zur johanneischen Tradition." *TLZ* 60 (1955) 524.

Bultmann, Rudolf
"The Concept of the Word of God in the New Testament." In his *Faith and Understanding* 1, ed. Robert W. Funk; tr. Louise Pettibone Smith (London: SCM Press, 1969) 286–312 = "Der Begriff des Wortes Gottes im Neuen Testament." In his *Glauben und Verstehen: Gesammelte Aufsätze* 1

(Tübingen: Mohr-Siebeck, [6]1966) 268–93.

Bultmann, Rudolf
Jesus and the Word, tr. Louise Pettibone Smith and Erminie Huntress Lantero (New York: Charles Scribner's Sons, 1958).

Bultmann, Rudolf
"Der religionsgeschichtliche Hintergrund des Prologs zum Johannes-Evangelium." In his *Exegetica: Aufsätze zur Erforschung des Neuen Testaments,* ed. Erich Dinkler (Tübingen: Mohr-Siebeck, 1967) 10–35.

Bultmann, Rudolf
"Die Bedeutung der neuerschlossenen mandäischen und manichäischen Quellen für das Verständnis des Johannesevangeliums." *ZNW* 24 (1925) 100–146. In his *Exegetica: Aufsätze zur Erforschung des Neuen Testaments,* ed. Erich Dinkler (Tübingen: Mohr-Siebeck, 1967) 55–104.

Bultmann, Rudolf
"Das Johannesevangelium in der newesten Forschung." *Christliche Welt* 41 (1927) 502–11.

Burch, Vacher
The Structure and Message of St. John's Gospel (London: M. Hopkinson, 1928).

Burchard, C.
"Εἰ nach einem Ausdruck des Wissens oder Nichtwissens Joh 9:25, Act 19:2, I Cor 1:16, 7:16." *ZNW* 52 (1961) 73–82.

Burghardt, Walter J.
"Did Saint Ignatius of Antioch Know the Fourth Gospel?" *TS* 1 (1940) 1–26, 130–56.

Burney, Charles Fox
The Aramaic Origin of the Fourth Gospel (London: Clarendon Press, 1922).

Burney, Charles Fox
"Our Lord's Old Testament Reference in Joh 7, 37–38." *Expositor,* 8th ser., 20 (1920) 385–88.

Burney, Charles Fox
"The Aramaic Equivalent of ἐκ τῆς κοιλίας in Jn 7, 38." *JTS* 24 (1922/1923) 79–80.

Burrows, Millar
"The Johannine Prologue as Aramaic Verse." *JBL* 45 (1926) 57–69.

Burrows, Millar
"The Original Language of the Gospel of John." *JBL* 49 (1930) 95–139.

Burton, Henry
"The Breakfast on the Shore." *Expositor,* 5th ser. (1895) 456–72.

Buse, Ivor
"St. John and 'The First Synoptic Pericope.'" *NovT* 3 (1959) 57–61.

Buse, Ivor
"The Cleansing of the Temple in the Synoptics and in John." *ExpTim* 70 (1958/1959) 22–24.

Buse, Ivor
"John v, 8 and the Johannine-Marcan Relationship." *NTS* 1 (1954/1955) 134–36.

Buse, Ivor
"St. John and 'The First Synoptic Pericope.'" *NovT* 3 (1959) 57–61.

Buse, Ivor
"St. John and the Marcan Passion Narrative." *NTS* 4 (1957/1958) 215–19.

Buse, Ivor
"St. John and the Passion Narratives of St. Matthew and St. Luke." *NTS* 7 (1960/1961) 65–76.

Bussche, Henri van den
"De tout être la parole était la vie. Jean 1, 1–5." *BVC* 69 (1966) 57–65.

Bussche, Henri van den
"Il était dans le monde." *BVC* 81 (1968) 19–25.

Bussche, Henri van den
"Het wijnwonder te Cana (Joh 2,1–11)." *Collationes Gandavenses* 2 (1952) 113–253.

Bussche, Henri van den
"Le Signe du Temple (Jean 2, 13–22)." *BVC* 20 (1957/1958) 92–100.

Bussche, Henri van den
"Les paroles de Dieu: Jean 3, 22–36." *BVC* 55 (1964) 23–28.

Bussche, Henri van den
"Guérison d'un paralytique à Jerusalem le jour du sabbat. Jean 5, 1–18." *BVC* 61 (1965) 18–28.

Bussche, Henri van den
"Jésus, l'unique source d'eau vive, Jn 7, 37–39." *BVC* 65 (1965) 17–23.

Bussche, Henri van den
"Leurs écritures et Son enseignement. Jean 7, 14–36." *BVC* 72 (1966) 21–30.

Bussche, Henri van den
"Si le grain de blé ne tombe pas en terre (Jn 12,20–39)." *BVC* 5 (1954) 53–67.

Bussche, Henri van den
Le discours d'adieu de Jésus; commentaire des chapitres 13 à 17 de l'évangile selon saint Jean, tr. C. Charlier and P. Goidts (Tournai: Casterman, 1959) = *Jesus' woorden bij het Afscheidsmaal; verklaring van de hoofdstukken 13–17 van het Sint-Jansevangelie* (Den Haag: Lannoo, Tielt, 1957).

Bussche, Henri van den
"Nu is de Mensensoon verheerlijkt (Joh 13,31–38)." *Collationes Gandavenses* 3 (1953) 97–105.

Bussche, Henri van den
"La vigne et ses fruits (Jn 15, 1–8)." *BVC* 26 (1959) 12–18.

Bussche, Henri van den
"Die Kirche im vierten Evangelium." In *Von Christus zur Kirche. Charisma und Amt im Urchristentum* (Freiburg: Herder, 1966) 79–107.

Busse, Ulrich
Die Wunder des Propheten Jesus. Die Rezeption, Komposition und Interpretation der Wundertradition im Evangelium des Lukas, Forschung zur Bibel 24 (Stuttgart: Katholisches Bibelwerk, 1977 ²1979).

Busse, Ulrich and Anton May
"Das Weinwunder von Kana (Joh 2, 1–11).

Erneute Analyse eines 'erratischen Blocks.'" *Biblische Notizen* 12 (1980) 35–61.

Buttmann, Alexander
Review of "Über den Gebrauch des Pronomen ἐκεῖνος im vierten Evangelium," by Georg Eduard Steitz. *TSK* 33 (1860) 505–36.

Buzy, Denis
"Béthanie au-delà du Jourdain." *RSR* 21 (1931) 444–62.

Cadbury, Henry Joel
"The Meaning of John 20:23, Matthew 16:19 and Matthew 18:18." *JBL* 58 (1939) 251–54.

Cadier, Jean
"The Unity of the Church. An Exposition of John 17." *Int* 11 (1957) 166–76.

Cadman, William Healey
"The Raising of Lazarus." *SE* 1 = TU 73 (Berlin: Akademie-Verlag, 1959) 423–34.

Cadman, William Healey
The Open Heaven. The Revelation of God in the Johannine Sayings of Jesus, ed. G. B. Caird (New York: Herder & Herder, 1969).

Cahill, Peter Joseph
"The Johannine *Logos* as Center." *CBQ* 38 (1976) 54–72.

Cahill, Peter Joseph
"Narrative Art in John IV." *Religious Studies Bulletin* 2 (1982) 41–48.

Caird, George B.
"The Glory of God in the Fourth Gospel. An Exercise in Biblical Semantics." *NTS* 15 (1968/1969) 265–77.

Caird, George B.
"Judgment and Salvation. An Exposition of John 12,31–32." *CJT* 2 (1956) 231–37.

Calmes, T.
La formazione dei Vangeli: a questione sinottica e il Vangelo di S. Giovanni (Rome: Desclée, 1923).

Camaldolese, Thomas Matus
"The First and the Last Encounter (Joh 1 and cap. 21)." *Bible Today* 42 (1969) 2893–97.

Cambe, Michel
"Jésus baptise et cesse de baptiser en Judée (Jean 3,22–4,3)." *ETR* 53 (1978) 97–102.

Camerlynck, A.
"La question johannique." *RHE* 1 (1900) 201–11, 419–29, 633–44.

Campenhausen, Hans von
"Zum Verständnis von Joh 19,11." In his *Aus der Frühzeit des Christentums. Studien zur Kirchengeschichte des ersten und zweiten Jahrhunderts* (Tübingen: Mohr-Siebeck, 1963) 125–34.

Campenhausen, Hans von
"Zur Perikope von der Ehebrecherin (Joh 7,53–8,11)." *ZNW* 68 (1977) 164–75.

Campenhausen, Hans von
"Zur Auslegung von Joh 13,6–10." *ZNW* 33 (1934) 259–71.

Cantwell, L.
"Immortal Longings in Sermone Humili. A Study of John 4,5–26." *SJT* 36 (1983) 73–86.

Capdevila i Montaner, V.-M.
"Les caractéristiques de la caritat en Saint Jean." *Estudios Franciscanos* 78 (1977) 413–54.

Carey, G. L.
"The Lamb of God and Atonement Theories." *TynBul* 32 (1981) 97–122.

Carmichael, C. M.
"Marriage and the Samaritan Woman." *NTS* 26 (1979/1980) 332–46.

Carmichael, J.
Leben und Tod des Jesus von Nazareth (Munich: Szczesny Verlag, ²1965).

Carmody, J.
"The 'Death of God' and John 14–17." *Bible Today* 30 (1967) 2082–90.

Carnegie, D. R.
"Kerygma in the Fourth Gospel." *Vox Evangelica* 7 (1971) 39–74.

Carpenter, J. W.
"Water Baptism." *Restoration Quarterly* 54 (1957) 59–66.

Carpenter, Joseph Estlin
The Johannine Writings. A Study of the Apocalypse and the Foruth Gospel (New York: Houghton & Mifflin, 1927).

Carroll, Kenneth L.
"The Fourth Gospel and the Exclusion of Christians from the Synagogues." *BJRL* 40 (1957/1958) 19–32.

Carson, Dan A.
"The Function of the Paraclete in John 16:7–11." *JBL* 98 (1979) 547–66.

Carson, Dan A.
"Current Source Criticism of the Fourth Gospel: Some Methodological Questions." *JBL* 97 (1978) 411–29.

Casey, Robert P.
"Professor Goodenough and the Fourth Gospel." *JBL* 64 (1945) 535–42.

Cassel, P.
Die Hochzeit von Kana, theologisch und historisch in Symbol, Kunst und Legende ausgelegt. Mit einer Einleitung in das Evangelium Johannis (Berlin: F. Schulze's Verlag, 1883).

Cassem, N. H.
"A Grammatical and Contextual Inventory of the Use of κόσμος in the Johannine Corpus with some Implications for a Johannine Cosmic Theology." *NTS* 19 (1972/1973) 81–91.

Cassien, Bishop
"Kirche oder Reich Gottes? Zur johanneischen Eschatologie." In *Extremis* 6–8 (1939) 186–202.

Cassien, Bishop
Le Pentecôte johannique (Paris: Editeurs Réunis, 1939).

Cassien, Bishop
"John xxi." *NTS* 3 (1956/1957) 132–36.

Cassien, Bishop
"The Interrelation of the Gospels Mt—Lk—Jn." *SE* 1 = TU 73 (Berlin: Akademie-Verlag, 1959) 129–47.

Cerfaux, Lucien
"Les miracles, signes messianiques de Jésus et oeuvres de Dieu selon l'évangile de S. Jean." In *L'attente du Messie*, ed. L. Cerfaux et al. (Paris: Desclée de Brouwer, 1954) 131–38.

Cerfaux, Lucien
"La charité fraternelle et le retour du Christ (Jn 13,33–38)." *ETL* 24 (1948) 321–32.

Cerfaux, Lucien
"L'évangile de Jean et 'le logion johannique' des Synoptiques." In his *Recueil Lucien Cerfaux. Etudes d'exégèse et d'histoire religieuse de Monseigneur Cerfaux réunies à l'occasion de son soixante-dixième anniversaire*, vol. 3. Supplement, BETL 18 (Gembloux: Duculot, 1962) 161–74.

Ceroke, Christian P.
"The Problem of Ambiguity in John 2, 4." *CBQ* 21 (1959) 316–40.

Chapman, John
"We Know that his Testimony is True." *JTS* 31 (1929/1930) 379–87.

Chappuis, Jean-Marc
"Jesus and the Samaritan Woman. The Variable Geometry of Communication." *Ecumenical Review* 34 (1982) 8–34.

Charlesworth, James H.
"Qumran, John and the Odes of Solomon." In *John and Qumran*, ed. J. H. Charlesworth (London: Chapman, 1972) 107–36.

Charlesworth, James H.
"A Critical Comparison of the Dualism in 1 QS 3,13–4,26 and the 'Dualism' Contained in the Gospel of John." In *John and Qumran*, ed. J. H. Charlesworth (London: Chapman, 1972) 76–106.

Charlesworth, James H. and R. Alan Culpepper
"The Odes of Solomon and the Gospel of John." *CBQ* 35 (1973) 298–322.

Charlier, Célestin
"La présence dans l'absence (Jn 12,31–14,31)." *BVC* 2 (1953) 61–75.

Charlier, Jean-Pierre
"La notion de signe (*sēmeion*) dans le IVe Evangile." *RSPT* 43 (1959) 434–48.

Charlier, Jean-Pierre
Le signe de Cana. Essai de théologie johannique (Brussels: La Pensée Catholique, 1959).

Charlier, Jean-Pierre
"La multiplication des pains." *AsSeign* 32 (1967) 31–45.

Charlier, Jean-Pierre
"L'exégèse johannique d'un précepte légal: Jean 8, 17." *RB* 67 (1960) 503–15.

Charpentier, E.
"Jour de pâques: Le tombeau vide (Jn 20.1–9)."

Esprit et vie 79 (1969) 262–66.

Chastand, Gédéon

L'Apôtre Jean et le quatrième évangile. Etude de critique et d'histoire (Paris: G. Fischbacher, 1888).

Chazel

"Essai d'interpretation de jean v,26–30." *Revue de théologie et de questions religieuses* 2 (1893) 199–210, 295–305.

Chevallier, Max-Alain

"La comparution de Jésus devant Hanne et devant Caïphe (Jean 18,12–14 et 19–24)." In *Neues Testament und Geschichte. Historisches Geschehen und Deutung im Neuen Testament. Oscar Cullmann zum 70. Geburtstag,* ed. H. Baltensweiler and B. Reicke (Zurich: Theologischer Verlag; Tübingen: Mohr-Siebeck, 1972) 179–85.

Christensen, C. R.

"John's Christology and the 'Gospel of Truth.'" *Gordon Review* 10 (1966) 23–31.

Christie, W. M.

"Did Christ Eat the Passover with his Disciples? or, The Synoptics *versus* John's Gospel." *ExpTim* 43 (1931/1932) 515–19.

Church, W. Randolph

"The Dislocations in the Eighteenth Chapter of John." *JBL* 49 (1930) 375–83.

Cignelli, Lino

"Giovanni 14,28 nell'esegesi di S. Ireneo." *Studii Biblici Franciscani Liber Annuus* 27 (1977) 173–96.

Cipriani, Settimio

"Dio è amore. La dottrina della carità in San Giovanni." *Scuola Cattolica* 94 (1966) 214–31.

Cipriani, Settimio

"La confessione di Pietro in Giov 6,69–71 e suoi rapporti con quella dei Sinottici." In *San Pietro. Atti della XIX settimana Biblica, Associazione Biblica Italiana* (Brescia: Paideia, 1967) 93–111.

Clark, Albert Curtis

The Primitive Text of the Gospels and Acts (Oxford: Clarendon Press, 1914).

Clark, G. H.

The Johannine Logos, An International Library of Philosophy and Theology, Biblical and Theological Studies (Nutley, NJ: Presbyterian & Reformed, 1972).

Clavier, Henri

"Notes sur un mot-clef du johannisme et de la sotériologie biblique, ἱλασμός." *NovT* 10 (1968) 287–304.

Clavier, Henri

"La structure du quatrième évangile." *RHPR* 35 (1955) 174–95.

Clemen, Carl Christian

Die Entstehung des Johannesevangeliums (Halle: M. Niemeyer, 1912).

Cludius, H. H.

Uransichten des Christenthums nebst Untersuchungen über einige Bücher des Neuen Testaments (Altona: Hammerich, 1808).

Coetzee, J. C.

"Christ and the Prince of this World in the Gospel and the Epistles of St. John." *Neot* 2 (1968) 104–21.

Coetzee, J. C.

"Life (eternal life) in John's Writings and the Qumran Scrolls." *Neot* 6 (1972) 48–66.

Cohn, Leopold

"Zur Lehre vom Logos bei Philo." In *Judaica. Festschrift zu Hermann Cohens siebzigstem Geburtstag* (Berlin: Bruno Cassirer, 1912) 303–31.

Coleman, B. W.

"The Woman Taken in Adultery. Studies in Texts: John 7, 53–8, 11." *Theology* 73 (1970) 409–10.

Collantes, Justo

"Un Commentario gnostico a Io I, 3." *Estudios ecclesiásticos* 27 (1953) 65–83.

Collins, Adela Yarbro

"Crisis and Community in the Gospel of John." *CurTM* 7 (1980) 196–204.

Collins, Raymond F.

"The Oldest Commentary on the Fourth Gospel." *Bible Today* 98 (1978) 1769–75.

Collins, Raymond F.

"Cana (Jn. 2:1–12)—The First of His Signs or the Key to His Signs?" *ITQ* 47 (1980) 79–95.

Collins, Raymond F.

"The Search for Jesus. Reflections on the Fourth Gospel." *Laval Théologique et Philosophique* 34 (1978) 27–48.

Collins, T. A.

"Changing Style in Johannine Studies." [Festschrift M. Gruenthaner] (New York, 1962) 202–25.

Colpe, Carsten

"Heidnische, jüdische und christliche Überlieferung in den Schriften von Nag Hammadi III." JAC 17 (1974) 122.

Colson, Jean

L'énigme du disciple que Jésus aimait, Theologie historique 10 (Paris: Beauchesne, 1969).

Colwell, Ernest Cadman

John Defends the Gospel (New York: Willett, Clark & Co., 1936).

Colwell, Ernest Cadman

The Greek of the Fourth Gospel. A Study of its Aramaisms in the Light of Hellenistic Greek (Chicago: University of Chicago Press, 1931).

Colwell, Ernest Cadman

"The Fourth Gospel and the Struggle for Respectability." *JR* 14 (1934) 286–305.

Comblin, Joseph

Sent from the Father. Meditations on the Fourth Gospel, tr. Carl Kabat (Maryknoll, NY: Orbis Books, 1979).

Comiskey, J. P.

"Rabbi, Who Has Sinned?" *Bible Today* 26 (1966) 1808–14.

Connick, C. Milo

"The Dramatic Character of the Fourth Gospel."

JBL 67 (1948) 159–69.

Conybeare, Frederick C.
"John XVII. 23–24 [according to Marutha]." *HTR* 17 (1924) 188–89.

Conzelmann, H.
Grundriss der Theologie des Neuen Testaments. Einführung in die evangelischen Theologie 2 (Munich: Chr. Kaiser Verlag, 1967) 351–90.

Conzelmann, Hans
"Paulus und die Weisheit." *NTS* 12 (1965/1966) 231–244. In his *Theologie als Schriftauslegung. Aufsätze zum Neuen Testament,* BEvT 65 (Munich: Chr. Kaiser Verlag, 1974) 167–76.

Conzelmann, Hans
"The Mother of Wisdom." In *The Future of our Religious Past. Essays in Honor of Rudolf Bultmann,* tr. Charles E. Carlston and Robert P. Scharlemann (New York: Harper & Row, 1971) = "Die Mutter der Weisheit." In *Zeit und Geschichte. Dankesgabe an Rudolf Bultmann zum 80. Geburtstag im Auftrage der Alten Marburger und in Zusammenarbeit mit Hartwig Thyen,* ed. Erich Dinkler (Tübingen: Mohr-Siebeck, 1964) 225–34. Also in his *Theologie als Schriftauslegung. Aufsätze zum Neuen Testament,* BEvT 65 (Munich: Chr. Kaiser Verlag, 1974) 167–76.

Cook, J. I.
"Joh 20,19–23—An Exegesis." *Reformed Review* (Holland, MI, 1967) 2–10.

Coppens, Joseph
"Les logia johanniques du Fils de l'homme." In *L'Evangile de Jean. Sources, rédaction, théologie,* ed. M. de Jonge. BETL 44 (Gembloux: Duculot; Louvain: University Press, 1977) 311–15.

Coppens, Joseph
"Miscellanées bibliques. Le Fils de l'homme johannique." *ETL* 54 (1978) 126–30.

Corell, Alf
Consummatum est. Eschatology and Church in the Gospel of St. John (London: S. P. C. K., 1958; New York: Macmillan, 1959).

Corssen, Peter
"Die Abschiedsreden Jesu in dem vierten Evangelium." *ZNW* 8 (1907) 125–42.

Corssen, Peter
"Ἐκάθισεν ἐπὶ Βήματος." *ZNW* 15 (1914) 338–40.

Corssen, Peter
Die monarchianischen Prologe zu den vier Evangelien (Leipzig: J. C. Hinrichs, 1896).

Corssen, Peter
"Warum ist das vierte Evangelium für ein Werk des Apostels Johannes erklärt worden?" *ZNW* 2 (1901) 202–27.

Cortés Quirant, J.
"Torrentes de agua viva. ¿Una nueva interpretación de Jn 7, 37–38?" *EstBib* 16 (1957) 279–306.

Cortés, Juan B.
"The Wedding Feast at Cana." *TD* 14 (1966) 14–17.

Cortés, Juan B.
"Yet Another Look at Jn 7, 37–38." *CBQ* 29 (1967) 75–86.

Costa, M.
"Nota sul simbolismo sacramentale del IV Vangelo." *RivBib* 13 (1965) 239–54.

Cothenet, Edouard
"Gestes et actes symboliques du Christ dans le IVᵉ Evangile." In *Gestes et paroles dans les diverses familles liturgiques,* Bibliotheca "Ephemerides Liturgicae" "Subsidia" 14 [Rome] 24 (Rome: Centro Liturgico Vincenzio, 1978) 95–116.

Cottam, Thomas
"At the Feast of Booths." *ExpTim* 48 (1936/1937) 45.

Cottam, Thomas
"Some Displacements in the Fourth Gospel." *ExpTim* 38 (1926/1927) 91–92.

Cottam, Thomas
The Fourth Gospel Rearranged (London: Epworth Press, 1956).

Cousar, Charles B.
"John 1:29–42." *Int* 31 (1977) 401–6.

Craddock, F. B.
The Pre-existence of Christ in the New Testment (Nashville and New York: Abingdon Press, 1968).

Craig, Clarence Tucker
"Sacramental Interest in the Fourth Gospel." *JBL* 58 (1939) 31–41.

Cranfield, C. E. B.
"John 1:14: 'became.'" *ExpTim* 93 (1982) 215.

Cranny, Titus F.
John 17: As we are one; an exposition and interpretation of the seventeenth chapter of St. John's Gospel of Our Lord, containing His prayer for unity of all His followers (Garrison, NY: Unity Apostolate, 1965).

Crehan, J. H.
Review of *The Gospel of the Signs,* by R. T. Fortna. *TS* 31 (1970) 757–59.

Creutzig, Hans Erich
"Zur johanneischen Christologie." *NKZ* (*Luthertum*) 49 (1938) 214–22.

Cribbs, F. Lamar
"St. Luke and the Johannine Tradition." *JBL* 90 (1971) 422–50.

Cribbs, F. Lamar
"A Study of the Contacts that Exist between St. Luke and St. John." SBLASP 2 (Missoula: Scholars Press, 1973) 1–93.

Cribbs, F. Lamar
"The Agreements that Exist between Luke and John." SBLASP 1 (Missoula: Scholars Press, 1979) 215–61.

Cribbs, F. Lamar
"The Agreements that Exist between John and Acts." In *Perspectives on Luke-Acts,* ed. C. H. Talbert. Special Studies Series 5 (Danville, VA: Association of Baptist Professors of Religion, 1978) 40–61.

Cribbs, F. Lamar
"A Reassessment of the Date of Origin and the Destination of the Gospel of John." *JBL* 89 (1970) 38–55.

Croatto, J. Severino
"Riletture dell'Esodo nel cap. 6 di San Giovanni." *BeO* 17 (1975) 11–20.

Crome, Friedrich Gottlieb
"Ueber Lucas 1,1–4 und Johannes 20,30.31, nebst einem Zusatz über Johannes 1,1–5, 9–14, 16–18, als Beitrag zur Beantwortung der Frage: unter welchen Umständen sind unsere vier canonischen Evangelien entstanden." *TSK* 2 (1829) 754–66.

Crome, Friedrich Gottlieb
"Ueber Lk 1,1–4 und Joh 20,30–31." *TSK* 2 (1829) 754–66.

Crönert, W.
"Die Überlieferung des Index Academicorum." *Hermes* 38 (1903) 357–405.

Cross, F. L., ed.
Studies in the Fourth Gospel (London: A. R. Mowbray, 1957).

Cross, John A.
"On St. John XXI,15–17." *Expositor,* 4th ser., 7 (1893) 312–20.

Crossan, John Dominic
"It is Written: A Structuralist Analysis of John 6." SBLASP 1 (Missoula: Scholars Press, 1979) 197–214.

Cullmann, Oscar
"Das Rätsel des Johannesevangeliums im Lichte der neuen Handschriftenfunde von Qumran." In his *Vorträge und Aufsätze 1925–1962,* ed. K. Fröhlich (Tübingen: Mohr-Siebeck; Zurich: Zwingli Verlag, 1966) 260–91.

Cullmann, Oscar
"Ὁ ὀπίσω μου ἐρχόμενος." In *In honorem Antonii Fridrichsen sexagenarii,* ConNT 11 (Lund: C. W. K. Gleerup, 1947) 26–32.

Cullmann, Oscar
The Johannine Circle, tr. John Bowden (Philadelphia: Westminster Press, 1976) = *Der johanneische Kreis. Sein Platz im Spätjudentum, in der Jüngerschaft Jesu und im Urchristentum. Zum Ursprung des Johannesevangelium* (Tübingen: Mohr-Siebeck, 1975).

Cullmann, Oscar
"Πέτρα," "Πέτρος, Κηφᾶς." *TDNT* 6: 95–112.

Cullmann, Oscar
"L'opposition contre le temple de Jérusalem, motif commun de la théologie johannique et du monde ambiant." *NTS* 5 (1958/1959) 157–73. In his *Des sources de l'évangile à la formation de la théologie chrétienne* (Neuchâtel: Delachaux & Niestlé, 1969) 25–41.

Cullmann, Oscar
"Samaria and the Origins of the Christian Mission." In his *The Early Church,* ed. A. J. B. Higgins; tr. A. J. B. Higgins and S. Godman (London: SCM Press; Philadelphia: Westminster Press, 1956) 183–92.

Cullmann, Oscar
The Christology of the New Testament, tr. Shirley C. Guthrie and Charles A. M. Hall (Philadelphia: Westminster Press, 1959) = *Die Christologie des Neuen Testaments* (Tübingen: Mohr-Siebeck, 1957 ²1958).

Cullmann, Oscar
"Sabbat und Sonntag nach dem Johannesevangelium: Joh 5,17." In his *Vorträge und Aufsätze 1925–1962,* ed. K. Fröhlich (Tübingen: Mohr-Siebeck; Zurich: Zwingli Verlag, 1966) 187–91.

Cullmann, Oscar
Early Christian Worship, tr. A. S. Todd and J. B. Torrance. SBT 10 (Chicago: Regnery, 1953) = *Urchristentum und Gottesdienst,* ATANT 3 (Zurich: Zwingli Verlag, ²1950).

Cullmann, Oscar
"Von Jesus zum Stephanuskreis und zum Johannesevangelium." In *Jesus und Paulus. Festschrift für Werner Georg Kümmel zum 70. Geburtstag,* ed. E. E. Ellis and E. Grässer (Göttingen: Vandenhoeck & Ruprecht, 1975) 44–56.

Cullmann, Oscar
"A New Approach to the Interpretation of the Fourth Gospel." *ExpTim* 71 (1959/1960) 8–12, 39–43.

Cullmann, Oscar
"Der johanneische Gebrauch doppeldeutiger Ausdrücke als Schlüssel zum Verstädnis des vierten Evangeliums." *TZ* 4 (1948) 360–72. In his *Vorträge und Aufsätze 1925–1962,* ed. K. Fröhlich (Tübingen: Mohr-Siebeck; Zurich: Zwingli Verlag, 1966) 176–86.

Culpepper, R. Alan
"The Pivot of John's Prologue." *NTS* 27 (1980/1981) 1–31.

Culpepper, R. Alan
The Johannine School. An Evaluation of the Johannine-School Hypothesis Based on an Investigation of the Nature of Ancient Schools, SBLDS 26 (Missoula: Scholars Press, 1975).

Curtis, K. Peter G.
"Three Points of Contact Between Matthew and John in the Burial and Resurrection Narratives." *JTS,* n.s., 23 (1972) 440–44.

Curtis, K. Peter G.
"Luke xxiv,12 and John xx,3–10." *JTS,* n.s., 22 (1971) 512–15.

Dagonet, P.
Selon saint Jean une femme de Samarie, Epiphanie (Paris: Editions du Cerf, 1979).

Dahl, Nils Alstrup
"Manndraperen og hans far (Joh 8,44)." *NorTT* 64 (1963) 129–62.

Dahl, Nils Alstrup
"Der Erstgeborene Satans und der Vater des Teufels." In *Apophoreta. Festschrift für Ernst

Haenchen zu seinem siebzigsten Geburtstag am 10.
Dezember 1964, BZNW 30 (Berlin: A. Töpelmann,
1964) 70–84.

Dahl, Nils Alstrup
"The Johannine Church and History." In *Current
Issues in New Testament Interpretation: Essays in honor
of Otto A. Piper,* ed. William Klassen (New York:
Harper & Brothers, 1962) 124–42.

Dahl, Nils Alstrup
*Das Volk Gottes. Eine Untersuchung zum Kirchen-
bewusstsein des Urchristentums,* Skrifter utgitt av det
norske videnskaps-akademi i Oslo—Historisk-
filosofisk klasse 2, 9 (Darmstadt: Wissenschaftliche
Buchgesellschaft, ²1963).

Dalman, Gustaf
The Words of Jesus, tr. D. M. Kay (Edinburgh: T. &
T. Clark, 1902) = *Die Worte Jesu* (Leipzig: J. C.
Hinrichs, 1898, ²1930; reprint Darmstadt: Wissen-
schaftliche Buchgesellschaft, 1965).

Dalman, Gustaf
Jesus-Jeshua: Studies in the Gospels, tr. Paul P.
Levertoff (London: S. P. C. K., 1929; New York:
KTAV, 1971).

Dalman, Gustaf
*Grammatik des Jüdisch-Palästinischen Aramäisch nach
den Idiomen des palästinischen Talmud des Onkelos-
targum und Prophetentargum und des Jerusalemischen
Targum* (Leipzig: J. C. Hinrichs, 1894, ²1905;
Darmstadt: Wissenschaftliche Buchgesellschaft,
1960).

Daniélou, Jean
"Joh 7, 37 et Ezéch 47, 1–11." *SE* 2 = TU 87
(Berlin: Akademie-Verlag, 1964) 158–63.

Daniélou, Jean
Philon d'Alexandrie (Paris: A. Fayard, 1958).

Daube, David
"The 'I am' of the Messianic Presence." In his *The
New Testament and Rabbinic Judaism* (London: Uni-
versity of London, Athlone Press, 1956) 325–29.

Daube, David
"Jesus and the Samaritan Woman: The Meaning of
σνγχράομαι." *JBL* 69 (1950) 137–47 = "Samaritan
Women." In his *The New Testament and Rabbinic
Judaism* (University of London: Athlone Press,
1956) 373–82.

Daube, David
"Three Notes having to do with Johanan ben
Zaccai." *JTS,* n.s., 11 (1960) 53–62.

Dauer, Anton
*Die Passionsgeschichte im Johannesevangelium. Eine
traditionsgeschichtliche und theologische Untersuchung
zu Joh 18,1–19,30,* SANT 30 (Munich: Kösel,
1972).

Dauer, Anton
"Das Wort des Gekreuzigten an seine Mutter und
den 'Jünger, den er liebte.' Eine traditionsgeschichtliche und theologische Untersuchung zu
Joh 19,25–27." *BZ* 11 (1967) 222–39; 12 (1968)
80–93.

Dauer, Anton
"Die Herkunft der Tomasperikope Joh 20,24–29."
In *Biblische Randbemerkungen. Schülerfestschrift für
Rudolf Schnackenburg zum 60. Geburtstag,* ed. H.
Merklein and J. Lange (Würzburg: Echter Verlag,
1974) 56–76.

Dausch, Petrus
*Das Johannesevangelium, seine Echtheit und Glaub-
würdigkeit,* Biblische Zeitfragen 2, 2 (Münster i.W:
Aschendorff, 1909).

Dautzenberg, Gerhard
"Die Geschichte Jesu im Johannesevangelium." In
Gestalt und Anspruch des Neuen Testaments, ed. J.
Schreiner (Würzburg: Echter Verlag, 1969) 229–
48.

Davey, D. M.
"Justin Martyr and the Fourth Gospel." *Scr* 17
(1965) 117–22.

Davey, James Ernest
*The Jesus of St. John. Historical and Christological
Studies in the Fourth Gospel* (London: Lutterworth
Press, 1958).

Davies, John Gordon
"The Primary Meaning of παράκλητος." *JTS,* n.s., 4
(1953) 35–38.

Dayton, Wilber T.
"The Greek Perfect Tense in Relation to Jn
20,23." Dissertation, Chicago, 1953.

Dechent, Hermann
"Zur Auslegung der Stelle Joh 19,35." *TSK* 72
(1899) 446–67.

Deeks, David
"The Prologue of St. John's Gospel." *BTB* 6 (1976)
62–78.

Deeks, David
"The Structure of the Fourth Gospel." *NTS* 15
(1968/1969) 107–29.

Dehn, G.
Jesus und die Samariter. Eine Auslegung von Jo 4,1–12
(Neukirchen: Neukirchener Verlag, 1956).

Deissner, K.
"Die Seelentechnik in der antiken Religion und
Sittlichkeit im Lichte des Evangeliums." In *Von der
Antike zum Christentum, Untersuchungen als Festgabe
für Victor Schultze zum 80. Geburtstag am 13.
Dezember 1931, dargebracht von Greifswalden Kollegen*
(Stettin: Fischer & Schmidt, 1931) 9–21.

Dekker, C.
"Grundschrift und Redaktion im Johannesevangelium." *NTS* 13 (1966/1967) 66–80.

Delff, Heinrich K. H.
*Neue Beiträge zur Kritik und Erklärung des vierten
Evangeliums* (Husum: C. F. Delff, 1890).

Delff, Heinrich K. H.
*Das vierte Evangelium, ein authentischer Bericht über
Jesus von Nazareth, wiederhergestellt, übersetzt und
erklärt* (Husum: C. F. Delff, 1890).

Delling, Gerhard
Der Kreuzestod Jesu in der urchristlichen Verkündigung

(Göttingen: Vandenhoeck & Ruprecht, 1972).

Delling, Gerhard
Wort und Werk Jesu im Johannes-Evangelium (Berlin: Evangelische Verlagsanstalt, 1966).

Delorme, Jean
"Renouveau des Etudes johanniques." *L'ami du clergé* 77 (1967) 367–78.

Delorme, Jean
"Sacerdoce du Christ et ministère (A propos de Jean 17). Sémantique et théologie biblique." *RSR* 62 (1974) 199–219.

Dembowsky, J.
"Das Johannesverständnis des Origenes." Dissertation, Göttingen, 1952.

Demke, Christoph
"Der sogenannte Logos-Hymnus im johanneischen Prolog." *ZNW* 58 (1967) 45–68.

Dequeker, L.
"De bruiloft te Kana (Jo., II 1–11)." *Collectanea Mechliniensia* 52 (1967) 177–93.

Derrett, John Duncan Martin
"Water into Wine." *BZ* 7 (1963) 80–97.

Derrett, John Duncan Martin
"Fresh Light on the Lost Sheep and the Lost Coin." *NTS* 26 (1979/1980) 36–60.

Derrett, John Duncan Martin
"Law in the New Testament: The Story of the Woman Taken in Adultery." *NTS* 10 (1963/1964) 1–26.

Derrett, John Duncan Martin
"The Good Shepherd: St. John's Use of Jewish Halakah and Haggadah." *ST* 27 (1973) 25–50.

Derrett, John Duncan Martin
"The Anointings at Bethany." *SE* 2 = TU 87 (Berlin: Akademie-Verlag, 1964) 174–82.

Derrett, John Duncan Martin
"'Domine, tu mihi lavas pedes?' (Studio su Giovanni 13,1–30)." *BeO* 21 (1979) 13–42.

Dewailly, L.-M.
"La parole parlait à Dieu? [Joh 1:1b–2]." *RTP* 100 (1967) 123–28.

Dewey, Kim E.
"Peter's Denial Reexamined: John's Knowledge of Mark's Gospel." SBLASP 1 (Missoula: Scholars Press, 1979) 109–12.

Dibelius, Martin
"Im Anfang war das ewige Wort. Zu Joh 1,1–18." *BibLeb* 10 (1969) 237–39.

Dibelius, Martin
Die urchristliche Überlieferung von Johannes dem Täufer, FRLANT 15 (Göttingen: Vandenhoeck & Ruprecht, 1911).

Dibelius, Martin
"Die Vorstellung vom göttlichen Licht. Ein Kapitel aus der hellenistischen Religionsgeschichte." *Deutsche Literaturzeitung* 36 (1915) 1469–83.

Dibelius, Martin
"Joh. 15:13: Eine Studie zum Traditionsproblem des Johannesevangeliums." In *Festgabe für Adolf Deissmann zum 60. Geburtstag, 7. November 1926* (Tübingen: Mohr-Siebeck, 1927) 168–86.

Dibelius, Martin
"Die alttestamentlichen Motive in der Leidensgeschichte des Petrus- und des Johannesevangeliums." In his *Botschaft und Geschichte. Gesammelte Aufsätze* 1 (Tübingen: Mohr-Siebeck, 1953) 221–47.

Dibelius, Martin
"Johannesevangelium." *RGG²* 3 (1929) 349–63.

Dibelius, Martin
"Papias." *RGG²* 4: 892–93.

Dibelius, Martin
"The Structure and Literary Character of the Gospels." *HTR* 20 (1927) 151–70.

Dibelius, Martin, ed. and tr.
Der Hirt des Hermas, HNT, Ergänzungsband 4 (Tübingen: Mohr-Siebeck, 1923).

Dieck, C. F.
"Ueber die Geschichte von der Ehebrecherin im Evangelium Johannis vom juristischen Standpunkte." *TSK* 5 (1832) 791–822.

Dieckmann, Hermann
"'Der Sohn des Menschen' im Johannesevangelium." *Scholastik* 2 (1927) 229–47.

Dietrich, Suzanne de
L'heure de l'élévation, à l'écoute de saint Jean (Neuchâtel: Delachaux & Niestlé, 1966).

Díez Merino, Luis
"'Galilea' en el IV Evangelio." *EstBib* 31 (1972) 247–73.

Dillon, John M.
The Middle Platonist. A Study of Platonism, 80 B. C. to A. D. 220 (London: Duckworth, 1977).

Dillon, Richard Joseph
"Wisdom, Tradition and Sacramental Retrospect in the Cana Account (Jn 2,1–11)." *CBQ* 24 (1962) 268–96.

Dinechin, Olivier de
"Καθώς: la similitude dans l'Evangile selon saint Jean." *RSR* 58 (1970) 195–236.

Dinger, Rainer
"Der johanneische Weg zum Verstehen des Glaubens. Eine Aufzeichnung des Gespräches über die Auslegung des Johannesevangeliums zwischen R. Bultmann und seinen Schülern." Dissertation, Tübingen, 1979.

Dinger, Rainer
"Der johanneische Weg zum Verstehen des Glaubens." *TLZ* 104 (1979) 469–71.

Dinkler, Erich
"Das Kana-Wunder. Fragen der wissenschaftlichen Erforschung der Hl. Schrift. Protokoll der Landessynode der Ev. Kirche im Rheinland," (January 1962) 47–61.

Dion, Hyacinthe-M.
"Quelque traits originaux de la conception johannique du Fils de l'Homme." *Sciences ecclésiastiques* 19 (1967) 49–65.

Dion, Hyacinthe-M.

"Quelque traits originaux de la conception johannique du Fils de l'homme." *Sciences ecclésiastiques* 19 (1967) 49–65.

Dix, G. H.

"The Use and Abuse of Papias on the Fourth Gospel." *Theology* 4 (London, 1932) 8–20.

Dix, G. H.

"The Heavenly Wisdom and the Divine Logos in Jewish Apocalyptic." *JTS* 26 (1924/1925) 1–12.

Dobschütz, E. von

"Zum Charakter des vierten Evangeliums." *ZNW* 28 (1929) 161–77.

Dodd, Charles Harold

"The Background of the Fourth Gospel." *BJRL* 19 (1935) 329–43.

Dodd, Charles Harold

"The Prologue to the Fourth Gospel and Christian Worship." In *Studies in the Fourth Gospel*, ed. F. L. Cross (London: A. R. Mowbray, 1957) 9–22.

Dodd, Charles Harold

Review of *Theologisches Wörterbuch zum Neuen Testament, Lieferungen 1–7, JTS* 34 (1933) 280–85.

Dodd, Charles Harold

Historical Tradition in the Fourth Gospel (Cambridge: Cambridge University Press, 1965).

Dodd, Charles Harold

"Une parabole cachée dans le quatrième Evangile [Jn 5:20a]." *RHPR* 42 (1962) 107–15. In his *More New Testament Studies*. (Grand Rapids: Wm. B. Eerdmans, 1968) 30–40.

Dodd, Charles Harold

"Notes from Papyri: Joh 5,5." *JTS* 26 (1924/1925) 77–78.

Dodd, Charles Harold

"The Epistle of John and the Fourth Gospel." *BJRL* 21 (1937) 129–56.

Dodd, Charles Harold

"A l'arrière-plan d'un dialogue Johannique." *RHPR* 1 (1957) 5–17. In his *More New Testament Studies* (Grand Rapids: Wm. B. Eerdmans, 1968) 41–57.

Dodd, Charles Harold

"The Prophecy of Caiaphas: John 11,47–53." In his *More New Testament Studies* (Grand Rapids: Wm. B. Eerdmans, 1968) 58–68.

Dodd, Charles Harold

"The Appearance of the Risen Christ." In *Studies in the Gospels. Essays in Memory of R. H. Lightfoot*, ed. D. E. Wineham (Oxford: Blackwell, 1967) 9–35.

Dodd, Charles Harold

"Note on John xxi.24." *JTS*, n.s., 4 (1953) 212–13.

Dodd, Charles Harold

The Interpretation of the Fourth Gospel (Cambridge: Cambridge University Press, 1953).

Dodd, Charles Harold

"The Portrait of Jesus in John and in the Synoptics." In *Christian History and Interpretation. Studies Presented to John Knox*, ed. W. R. Farmer,

C. F. D. Moule, R. R. Niebuhr (Cambridge: Cambridge University Press, 1967) 183–98.

Dodd, Charles Harold

"Some Johannine 'Herrenworte' with Parallels in the Synoptic Gospels." *NTS* 2 (1955/1956) 75–86.

Doeve, Jan Willem

"Die Gefangennahme Jesu in Gethsemane." *SE* 1 = TU 73 (Berlin: Akademie-Verlag, 1959) 458–80.

Dölger, Franz Josef

"Soter." *PW* 2, 3rd series, 1211–21.

Dörrie, Heinrich

"Der Prolog zum Evangelium nach Johannes im Verständnis der älteren Apologeten." In *Kerygma und Logos. Beiträge zu den geistesgeschichtlichen Beziehungen zwischen Antike und Christentum. Festschrift für Carl Andresen zum 70. Geburtstag*, ed. A. M. Ritter (Göttingen: Vandenhoeck & Ruprecht, 1979) 136–52.

Draper, H. Mudie

"The Disciple whom Jesus Loved." *ExpTim* 32 (1920/1921) 428–29.

Driver, Godfrey Rolles

"The Original Language of the Fourth Gospel." *Jewish Guardian* (1923) 1–8.

Drummond, James

An Inquiry into the Character and Authorship of the Fourth Gospel (London: Williams & Norgate, 1903; New York: Scribners, 1904).

Drumwright, Huber L.

"A Re-evaluation of the Significance of John's Gospel." *Southwestern Journal of Theology* 8 (1965) 7–20.

Dubarle, André-Marie

"Le signe du temple [Jn. 2:19]." *RB* 48 (1939) 21–44.

Dubarle, André-Marie

"Des fleuves d'eau vive (S. Jean VII, 37–39)." *Vivre et penser* 3 = *RB* 52 (1943/1944) 238–41.

Dulière, W. L.

La haute terminologie de la rédaction johannique. Les vocables qu'elle a introduits chez les Gréco-Romains: Le Logos-Verbe, le Paraclet-Esprit-Saint et le Messias-Messie, Collection Latomus 117 (Brussels: Latomus, 1970).

Dunkel, Franz

"Die Berufung der vier ersten Jünger Jesu; der wunderbare Fischfang bei Lk 5 und Joh 21." *Das heilige Land* 73 (1929) 53–59.

Dunkerley, Roderic

"The Sign of the Meal (Jn 6)." *London Quarterly and Holborn Review* 32 (1963) 61–66.

Dunkerley, Roderic

"Lazarus." *NTS* 5 (1958/1959) 321–27.

Dunlop, Laurence

"The Pierced Side. Focal Point of Johannine Theology." *Bible Today* 86 (1976) 960–65.

Dunn, James D. G.

"John VI—An Eucharistic Discourse?" *NTS* 17 (1970/1971) 328–38.

Dunn, James D. G.
"The Washing of Disciples' Feet in John 13:1–20." *ZNW* 61 (1970) 247–52.

Duparc, L. H.
"Le premier signe de la Résurrection chez saint Jean. Jean 20,7." *BVC* 86 (1969) 70–77.

Dupont, Jacques
Essais sur la christologie de saint Jean. Le Christ, parole, lumière et vie, la gloire du Christ (Brugge: Editions de l'Abbaye de Saint-André, 1951).

Dupont, Liliane et al.
"Recherche sur la structure de Jean 20." *Bib* 54 (1973) 482–98.

Duprez, A.
Jésus et les dieux guérisseurs. A propos de Jean V, Cahiers de la Revue Biblique 12 (Paris: J. Gabalda, 1970).

Durand, A. S. O.
"Jean et ses devanciers." *Etudes* 64 (1927) 129–41.

Durand, M. G. de
"Pentecôte johannique et Pentecôte lucanienne chez certains Pères." *BLE* 79 (1978) 97–126.

Dürr, L.
Die Wertung des göttlichen Wortes im Alten Testament und im antiken Orient, zugleich ein Beitrag zur Vorgeschichte des neutestamentlichen Logosbegriffes, MVAG 42,1 (Leipzig: J. C. Hinrichs, 1938).

Dyroff, Adolf
"Zum Prolog des Johannes-Evangeliums." In *Pisciculi; Studien zur Religion und Kultur des Altertums; Franz Joseph Dölger zum sechzigsten Geburtstage dargeboten von Freunden, Verehrern und Schülern* (Münster i.W: Aschendorff, 1939) 89–93.

Easton, Burton Scott
"Bultmann's RQ Source." *JBL* 65 (1946) 143–56.

Eberhardt, Max
Ev. Joh c. 21. Ein exegetischer Versuch als Beitrag zur johanneischen Frage (Leipzig: Verlag der Dürr'schen Buchhandlung, 1897).

Ebrard, Johannes Heinrich August
Das Evangelium Johannis und die neueste Hypothese Über seine Entstehung. Ein Beitrag zur Kritik der Evangelien (Zurich: Meyer & Zeller, 1845).

Eckhardt, Karl August
Der Tod des Johannes als Schlüssel zum Verständnis der johanneischen Schriften (Berlin: Walter de Gruyter, 1961).

Eckle, Wolfgang
Geist und Logos bei Cicero und im Johannesevangelium (Hildesheim: G. Olms, 1978).

Edwards, Hubert Edwin
The Disciple Who Wrote These Things. A New Inquiry into the Origins and Historical Value of the Gospel according to St. John (London: J. Clarke, 1953).

Edwards, Sarah A.
"P75 and B in John: A Study in the History of the Text." Dissertation, Hartford Seminary, 1974.

Egenter, Richard
"Joh 8,31f. im christlichen Lebensbewusstsein." In

Wahrheit und Verkündigung. Festschrift M. Schmaus II, ed. Leo Scheffczyk et al. (Munich: Schöningh, 1967) 1583–605.

Eisler, Robert
"La ponctuation du prologue antimarcionite à l'Evangile selon Jean." *Revue de philologie, de littérature et d'histoire anciennes* 56 (1930) 350–71.

Eisler, Robert
The Messiah Jesus and John the Baptist, ed. A. H. Krappe (London: Methuen, 1930).

Eisler, Robert
"Jesus und die ungetreue Braut [Joh 8,1–11]." *ZNW* 22 (1923) 305–7.

Eisler, Robert
"Zur Fusswaschung am Tage vor dem Passah." *ZNW* 14 (1913) 268–71.

Eisler, Robert
The Enigma of the Fourth Gospel. Its Author and Its Writer (London: Methuen, 1937).

Elliot, James Keith
"John 1,14 and the New Testament's Use of *plērēs*." *BT* 28 (1977) 151–53.

Ellis, Edward Earle
"The Purpose of John's Writings." *Reformed Review* 19 (1965) 9–17.

Ellwein, Eduard
"Das hohepriesterliche Gebet (Joh 17) in der Auslegung Luthers." In *Die Leibhaftigkeit des Wortes. Theologische und seelsorgliche Studien und Beiträge als Festgabe für Adolf Köberle zum 60. Geburtstag*, ed. O. Michel and Ulrich Mann (Hamburg: Furche-Verlag, 1958) 91–106.

Eltester, Walther
"Der Logos und sein Prophet. Fragen zur heutigen Erklärung des johanneischen Prologs." In *Apophoreta. Festschrif für Ernst Haenchen zu seinem siebzigsten Geburtstag am 10. Dezember 1984*, BZNW 30 (Berlin: A. Töpelmann, 1964) 109–34.

Eltester, Walther
Eikon im Neuen Testament, BZNW 23 (Berlin: A. Töpelmann, 1958).

Emerton, John Adney
"Melchizedek and the Gods: Fresh Evidence for the Jewish Background of John X,34–36." *JTS*, n.s., 17 (1966) 399–401.

Emerton, John Adney
"Some New Testament Notes." *JTS*, n.s., 11 (1960) 329–36.

Emerton, John Adney
"The 153 fishes in John XXI,23–25." *Theology* 20 (1930) 229.

Enciso Viana, Jesús
"La vocación de Natanael y el Salmo 24." *EstBib* 19 (1960) 229–36.

Ensfelder, J. T.
"Die Weissagung des Hohenpriesters Kaiphas—ein exegetischer Versuch über Joh XI, 50–51." *Theologische Jahrbücher* 1 (Tübingen, 1842) 792–800.

Ensley, Eugene C.
"Eternity is Now. A Sermon on Joh 14:1–11." *Int* 19 (1965) 295–98.

Enslin, Morton Scott
"The Perfect Tense in the Fourth Gospel." *JBL* 55 (1936) 121–31.

Epp, Eldon Jay
"Wisdom, Torah, Word: The Johannine Prologue and the Purpose of the Fourth Gospel." In *Current Issues in Biblical and Patristic Interpretation. Studies in Honor of Merrill C. Tenney Presented by His Former Students,* ed. Gerald F. Hawthorne (Grand Rapids: Wm. B. Eerdmans, 1974) 128–46.

Eppstein, Victor
"The Historicity of the Gospel Account of the Cleansing of the Temple." *ZNW* 55 (1964) 42–58.

Erdozáin, Luis
La función del signo en la fe según el cuarto evangelio. Estudio crítico exegético de las perícopas Jn IV,46–54 y Jn XX,24–29, AnBib 33 (Rome: Pontifical Biblical Institute, 1963).

Escande, J.
"Jésus devant Pilate: Jean 18,28–19,16." *Foi et vie* 73 (1974) 66–82.

Evans, Christopher Francis
"The Eucharist and Symbolism in the New Testament." In *Thinking about the Eucharist. Essays by Members of the Archibishop's Commission on Christian Doctrine,* with a preface by Ian T. Ramsey (London: SCM Press, 1972) 59–66.

Evans, Christopher Francis
The Passion of Christ (London: SCM Press, 1977) 50–66.

Evanson, Edward
The Dissonance of the Four Generally Received Evangelists, and the Evidence of their Respective Authenticity Examined (Ipswich: G. Jermym, 1792).

Evdokimow, Paul
"Etude sur Jean 13,18–30." *Esprit et Vie* (1950) 201–16.

Ewald, Heinrich
"Ueber die Zweifel an der Abkunft des vierten Evangeliums und der drei Sendschreiben vom Apostel Johannes." *Jahrbücher der biblischen Wissenschaft* 10 (1859/1860) 83–114.

Fagal, Harold E.
"John and the Synoptic Tradition." In *Scripture, Tradition, and Interpretation. Essays Presented to Everett F. Harrison by His Students and Colleagues in Honor of His Seventy-fifth Birthday,* ed, W. W. Gasque and W. S. LaSor (Grand Rapids: Wm. B. Eerdmans, 1978) 127–45.

Farmer, William R.
"The Palm Branches in John 12,13." *JTS,* n.s., 3 (1952) 62–66.

Fascher, Erich
"Christologie und Gnosis im vierten Evangelium." *TLZ* 93 (1968) 721–30.

Fascher, Erich

"'Ich bin die Tür!' Eine Studie zu Joh X, 1–18." *Deutsche Theologie* 79 (1942) 33–57, 118–33.

Fascher, Erich
"Zur Auslegung von Joh X, 17–18." *Deutsche Theologie* 78 (1941) 37–66.

Fascher, Erich
"Johannes 16, 32. Eine Studie zur Geschichte der Schriftauslegung und zur Traditionsgeschichte des Urchristentums." *ZNW* 39 (1940) 171–230.

Fascher, Erich
"Vom Logos des Heraklit und dem Logos des Johannes." In his *Frage und Antwort. Studien zur Theologie und Religionsgeschichte* (Berlin: Evangelische Verlagsanstalt, 1968) 117–33.

Fascher, Erich
"Der Logos-Christus als göttlicher Lehrer bei Clemens von Alexandrien." In *Studien zum Neues Testament und zur Patristik, Erich Klostermann zum 90. Geburtstag dargebracht,* TU 77 (Berlin: Akademie-Verlag, 1961) 193–207.

Faure, Alexander
"Die alttestamentlichen Zitate im 4. Evangelium und die Quellenscheidungshypothese." *ZNW* 21 (1922) 99–121.

Faure, Alexander
"Das 4. Evangelium im muratorischen Fragment." *ZST* 19 (1942) 143–49.

Fee, Gordon D.
"Once More—John 7, 37–39." *ExpTim* 89 (1978) 116–18.

Fee, Gordon D.
"Codex Sinaiticus in the Gospel of John: A Contribution to Methodology in Establishing Textual Relationships." *NTS* 15 (1968/1969) 23–44.

Fee, Gordon D.
Papyrus Bodmer II (P66): Its Textual Relationships and Scribal Characteristics, Studies and Documents 34 (Salt Lake City: University of Utah Press, 1968).

Fee, Gordon D.
"The Text of John in the Jerusalem Bible: A Critique of the Use of Patristic Citations in New Testament Textual Criticism." *JBL* 90 (1971) 163–73.

Fee, Gordon D.
"The Use of the Definite Article with Personal Names in the Gospel of John." *NTS* 17 (1970/1971) 168–83.

Fennema, David A.
"Jesus and the Father in the Fourth Gospel." Dissertation, Duke University, 1978.

Fennema, David A.
"Jesus and God According to John. An Analysis of the Fourth Gospel's Father/Son Christology." Dissertation, Duke University, 1979.

Fensham, F. C.
"*Love* in the Writings of Qumrân and John." *Neot* 6 (1972) 67–77.

Fensham, F. Charles
"I am the Way, the Truth and the Life." *Neot* 2

(1968) 81–88.

Fenton, Joseph C.
The Passion According to John (London: S. P. C. K., 1961).

Fenton, Joseph C.
"Towards an Understanding of John." *SE* 4 = TU 102 (Berlin: Akademie-Verlag, 1968) 28–37.

Ferguson, John
"Philippians, John and the Traditions of Ephesus." *ExpTim* 83 (1971) 85–87.

Ferraro, Giuseppe
"Il senso di *heos arti* nel testo di Gv 5,17." *RivB* 20 (1972) 529–45.

Ferraro, Giuseppe
"Giovanni 6,60–71. Osservazioni sulla struttura letteraria e il valore della pericope nel quarto vangelo." *RivB* 26 (1978) 33–69.

Festugière, A. J.
Observations stylistiques sur l'évangile de S. Jean, Etudes et commentaires 84 (Paris: Klincksieck, 1974).

Feuillet, André
Le mystère de l'amour divin dans la théologie johannique, Etudes bibliques (Paris: J. Gabalda, 1972).

Feuillet, André
Le prologue du quatrième évangile (Paris: Desclée de Brouwer, 1968).

Feuillet, André
Johannine Studies, tr. Thomas E. Crane (Staten Island, NY: Alba House, 1964) 17–37 = *Etudes Johanniques,* Museum Lessianum Section biblique 4 (Paris: Desclée de Brouwer, 1962).

Feuillet, André
"La signification fondamentale du premier miracle de Cana (Jo II, 1–11) et le symbolisme johannique." *RevThom* (1965) 517–35.

Feuillet, André
"L'heure de Jésus et le signe de Cana. Contribution à l'étude de la structure du quatrième évangile." *ETL* 36 (1960) 5–22.

Feuillet, André
"La signification théologique du second miracle de Cana (*Jo.* IV,46–54)." *RSR* 48 (1960) 62–75.

Feuillet, André
"Les thèmes bibliques majeurs du discours sur le pain de vie (Jn 6). Contribution à l'étude des sources de la pensée johannique." *NRT* 82 (1960) 803–22, 918–39, 1040–62.

Feuillet, André
"Note sur la traduction de Jér xxxi 3c." *VT* 12 (1962) 122–24.

Feuillet, André
Le discours sur le pain de vie (Jean, chapitre 6) (Paris: Desclée de Brouwer, 1967).

Feuillet, André
"Les fleuves d'eau vive." In *Parole de Dieu et sacerdoce* [Festschrift J. J. Weber], ed. E. Fischer and L. Bouyer (Paris and New York: Desclée et Cie, 1962) 107–20.

Feuillet, André
The Priesthood of Christ and His Ministers, tr. Michael J. O'Connell (Garden City, NY: Doubleday, 1975) = *Le sacerdoce du Christ et de ses ministres d'après la prière sacerdotale du quatrième évangile et plusieurs données parallèles du Nouveau Testament* (Paris: Editions de Paris, 1972).

Feuillet, André
"L'heure de la femme (Jn 16,21) et l'heure de la Mère de Jésus (Jn 19,25–27)." *Bib* 47 (1966) 169–84, 361–80, 557–73.

Feuillet, André
L'heure de la mère de Jésus. Etude de théologie johannique (Franjeux-Prouille, 1969).

Feuillet, André
"Les christophanies pascales du quatrième évangile sont-elles des signes?" *NRT* 97 (1975) 577–92.

Feuillet, André
"La communication de l'Esprit-saint aux Apôtres (Jn, XX 19–23) et le ministère sacerdotale de la réconciliation des hommes avec Dieu." *Esprit et vie* 82 (1972) 2–7.

Feuillet, André
"L'apparition du Christ à Marie-Madeleine *Jean 20,11–18.* Comparison avec l'apparition aux disciples d'Emmaüs *Luc 24,13–35.*" *Esprit et vie* 88 (1978) 193–204, 209–23.

Feuillet, André
"Giovanni e i Sinottici." *Studi Cattolici* 13 (1969) 121f.

Feuillet, André
"Les *Ego Eimi* christologiques du quatrième évangile." *RSR* 54 (1966) 5–22, 213–40.

Fiebig, Paul
"Die Fusswaschung [Joh 13:8–10]." *Angelos* 3 (1930) 121–28.

Fiebig, Paul
"Die Mekhilta und das Johannes-Evangelium." *Angelos* 1 (1925) 57–59.

Fiebig, Paul
"Zur Form des Johannesevangeliums." *Der Geisteskampf der Gegenwart* 64 (1928) 126–32.

Filson, Floyd V.
"The Gospel of Life: A Study of the Gospel of John." In *Current Issues in New Testament Interpretation: Essays in honor of Otto A. Piper,* ed. William Klassen and G. F. Snyder (New York: Harper & Brothers, 1962) 111–23.

Filson, Floyd V.
"Who was the Beloved Disciple?" *JBL* 68 (1949) 83–88.

Finegan, Jack
Die Überlieferung der Leidens- und Auferstehungsgeschichte Jesu, BZNW 15 (Giessen: A. Töpelmann, 1934).

Finkel, Abraham
The Pharisees and the Teacher of Nazareth. A Study of their Background, their Halachic and Midrashic Teachings, the Similarities and Differences, AGJU 4

(Leiden: E. J. Brill, 1964).

Fiorenza, Elizabeth Schüssler
"The Quest for the Johannine School. The Apocalypse and the Fourth Gospel." *NTS* 23 (1976/1977) 402–27.

Fischer
"Ueber den Ausdruck *hoi Joudaioi* im Ev. Johannis. Ein Beitrag zur Charakteristik desselben." *Tübinger Zeitschrift für Theologie* 11 (1840) 96–133.

Fischer, Günter
Die himmlischen Wohnungen. Untersuchungen zu Joh 14,2f, Europäische Hochschulschriften, Series 23; Theologie 38 (Bern: H. Lang; Frankfurt: P. Lang, 1975).

Fischer, Karl Martin
"Der johanneische Christus und der gnostische Erlöser. Überlegungen auf Grund von Joh 10." In *Gnosis und Neues Testament. Studien aus Religionswissenschaft und Theologie,* ed. K.-W. Tröger (Gütersloh: Gerd Mohn; Berlin: Evangelische Verlagsanstalt, 1973) 245–67.

Fitch, W. O.
"The Interpretation of St. John 5,6." *SE* 4 = TU 102 (Berlin: Akademie-Verlag, 1968) 194–97.

Fitzmyer, Joseph A.
"Crucifixion in Ancient Palestine, Qumran Literature, and the New Testament." *CBQ* 40 (1978) 493–513.

Flatt, Karl Christian
Dissertatio historico-exegetica qua variae de Antichristis et pseudoprophetis in prima Joannis epistola notatis sententiae modesto examini subjiciuntur (Tübingen, 1809).

Floor, L.
"The Lord and the Holy Spirit in the fourth Gospel." *Neot* 2 (1968) 122–30.

Florival, Ephrem
"'Les siens ne l'ont pas reçu' Jn 1,11. Regard évangélique sur la question juive." *NRT* 89 (1967) 43–66.

Flowers, H. J.
"The Displacement of John 7, 37–44." *Expositor,* 8th ser., 22 (1921) 318–20.

Flowers, H. J.
"Interpolations in the Fourth Gospel." *JBL* 40 (1921) 146–58.

Flowers, H. J.
"Mark as a Source for the Fourth Gospel." *JBL* 46 (1927) 207–36.

Fohrer, Georg
"Begräbnis." *BHH* 1 (Göttingen, 1962) 212.

Fonseca, Almada G. Wollheim de
Quaestio Johannaea (Rome, ³1949).

Forbes, Henry Prentice
The Johannine Literature and the Acts of the Apostles (New York and London: G. P. Putnam's Sons, 1907).

Forbes, R. J.
"Mumie." *BHH* 2 (Göttingen, 1964) 1247–49.

Ford, J. Massingberd
"'Mingled Blood' from the Side of Christ. (John xix. 34)." *NTS* 15 (1968/1969) 337–38.

Formesyn, R.
"Le sèmeion johannique et le sèmeion hellénistique." *ETL* 38 (1962) 856–94.

Fortna, Robert T.
"Theological Use of Locale in the Fourth Gospel." In *Gospel Studies in honor of J. E. Johnson,* ed. M. H. Shepherd, Jr. and E. C. Hobbs. Anglican Theological Review, Supplementary Studies 3 (Evanston, IL, 1974) 58–95.

Fortna, Robert T.
"From Christology to Soteriology. A Redaction-Critical Study of Salvation in the Fourth Gospel." *Int* 27 (1973) 31–47.

Fortna, Robert T.
"Christology in the Fourth Gospel. Redaction-Critical Perspectives." *NTS* 21 (1974/1975) 489–504.

Fortna, Robert T.
"Source and Redaction in the Fourth Gospel's Portrayal of Jesus' Signs." *JBL* 89 (1970) 151–66.

Fortna, Robert T.
The Gospel of Signs. A Reconstruction of the Narrative Source Underlying the Fourth Gospel, NovTSup 11 (New York and London: Cambridge University Press, 1970).

Fortna, Robert T.
"Jesus and Peter at the High Priest's House: A Test Case for the Question of the Relation Between Mark's and John's Gospels." *NTS* 24 (1977/1978) 371–83.

Foston, Hubert M.
"Two Johannine Parentheses." *ExpTim* 32 (1920/1921) 520–23.

Fowler, David C.
"The Meaning of 'Touch Me Not' in John 20,17." *EvQ* 47 (1975) 16–25.

Fowler, R.
"Born of Water and the Spirit (Jn 3:5)." *ExpTim* 82 (1971) 159.

Franke, August Hermann
"Die Anlage des Johannes-Evangeliums." *TSK* 57 (1884) 80–154.

Franke, August Hermann
Das AT bei Johannes. Ein Beitrag zur Erklärung und Beurtheilung der johanneischen Schriften (Göttingen: Vandenhoeck & Ruprecht, 1885).

Freed, Edwin D.
"Some Old Testament Influences on the Prolog of John." In *A Light Unto My Path. Old Testament Studies in Honor of Jacob M. Myers,* ed. H. N. Bream, R. D. Heim, and C. A. Moore. Gettysburg Theological Studies 4 (Philadelphia: Temple University Press, 1974) 145–61.

Freed, Edwin D.
"Theological Prelude to the Prologue of John's Gospel." *SJT* 32 (1979) 257–69.

Freed, Edwin D.
"*Egō Eimi* in John 1:20 and 4:25." *CBQ* 41 (1979) 288–91.

Freed, Edwin D.
"The Son of Man in the Fourth Gospel." *JBL* 86 (1967) 402–9.

Freed, Edwin D.
"The Manner of Worship in John 4,23." In *Search the Scriptures* [Festschrift for R. T. Stamm], ed. J. M. Meyers et al. (Leiden: E. J. Brill, 1969) 33–48.

Freed, Edwin D.
"Jn IV, 51: παῖς or υἱός?." *JTS*, n.s., 16 (1965) 448–49.

Freed, Edwin D.
Old Testament Quotations in the Gospel of John, NovTSup 11 (Leiden: E. J. Brill, 1965).

Freed, Edwin D.
"Did John Write His Gospel Partly to Win Samaritan Converts?" *NovT* 12 (1970) 241–56.

Freed, Edwin D.
"Samaritan Influence in the Gospel of John." *CBQ* 30 (1968) 580–87.

Freed, Edwin D.
"The Entry into Jerusalem in the Gospel of John." *JBL* 80 (1961) 329–38.

Freed, Edwin D.
"Variations in the Language and Thought of John." *ZNW* 55 (1964) 167–97.

Freed, Edwin D. and R. B. Hunt
"Fortna's Signs-Source in John." *JBL* 94 (1975) 563–79.

Frei, W.
"Gnostische Lehre und johanneische Verkündigung." Dissertation, Bern, 1958.

Fridrichsen, Anton
"Bemerkungen zur Fusswaschung Joh 13." *ZNW* 38 (1939) 94–96.

Friedrich, Gerhard
Wer ist Jesus? Die Verkündigung des vierten Evangelisten dargestellt an Johannes 4, 4–42, Biblisches Seminar (Stuttgart: Calwer Verlag, 1967).

Friedrichsen, Anton
"Herdekapitlet Joh 10." *SEÅ* 8 (1943) 30–48.

Frieling, R.
Agape. Die göttliche Liebe im Johannes-Evangelium (Stuttgart: Verlag Urachhaus, 1936).

Frisch, M. J. F.
Vollständige biblische Abhandlung vom Osterlamme überhaupt (Leipzig: Breitkopf, 1758).

Frisque, Jean and Thierry Maertens
"Deuxième dimanche du temps pascal." *Paroisse et liturgie* 47 (1965) 338–50.

Fritsch, Irénée
"'. . . videbitis . . . angelos Dei ascendentes et descendentes super Filium hominis' (Jn 1,51)." *VD* 37 (1959) 3–11.

Fritschel, Theodore Carl
"The Relationship between the Word and the Sacraments in John and in Ignatius." Dissertation, Hamburg, 1962/1963.

Frommann, Georg Karl
Der johanneische Lehrbegriff in seinem Verhältnisse zur gesammten biblisch-christlichen Lehre (Leipzig: Breitkopf & Härtel, 1839).

Frommann, Georg Karl
"Über die Echtheit und Integrität des Evangeliums Johannis, mit besonderer Rücksicht auf Weisse's evangelische Geschichte." *TSK* 13 (1840) 853–930.

Fulco, W. J.
Maranatha. Reflections on the Mystical Theology of John the Evangelist (New York and Toronto: Paulist, 1973).

Fuller, Reginald Horace
"The 'Jews' in the Fourth Gospel." *Dialog* 16 (1977) 31–37.

Fuller, Reginald Horace
The Formation of the Resurrection Narratives (New York: Macmillan, 1971).

Fuller, Reginald Horace
"John 20,19–23." *Int* 32 (1978) 180–84.

Furnish, Victor P.
The Love Command in the New Testament (London: SCM Press, 1973) 132–38.

Fürst, Walther
"Die Einheit der Kirche nach Joh 17." *Deutsches Pfarrerblatt* 64 (1964) 81–86.

Gabler, Johann Philipp
Meletemata in locum Joh 1,29 (Jena, 1808–1811).

Gaechter, Paul
"Strophen im Johannesevangelium." *ZKT* 60 (1936) 99–120, 402–423.

Gaechter, Paul
"Maria in Kana (Jo. 2, 1–11)." *ZKT* 55 (1931) 351–402.

Gaechter, Paul
"Zur Form von Joh 5,19–30." In *Neutestamentliche Aufsätze. Festschrift für Prof. Josef Schmid zum 70. Geburtstag*, ed. J. Blinzler, O. Kuss, F. Mussner (Regensburg: F. Pustet, 1963) 65–68.

Gaechter, Paul
"Der formale Aufbau der Abschiedsrede Jesu." *ZKT* 58 (1934) 155–207.

Gaechter, Paul
"Das dreifache 'Weide meine Lämmer'!" *ZKT* 69 (1947) 328–44.

Gaeta, Giancarlo
Il dialogo con Nicodemo. Per l'interpretazione del capitole terzo dell'evangelo di Giovanni. Studi Biblici 26 (Brescia: Paideia, 1974).

Gaffney, J.
"Believing and Knowing in the Fourth Gospel." *TS* 26 (1965) 215–41.

Gaffron, Hans-Georg
"Studien zum koptischen Philippusevangelium unter besonderer Berücksichtigung der Sakramente." Dissertation, Bonn, 1969.

Galbiati, Enrico
"Esegesi degli Evangeli festivi: La testimonianza die Giovanni Battista (Giov. 1,19–28)." *BeO* 4 (1962) 227–33.

Galbiati, Enrico
"Nota sulla struttura del 'libro dei segni' (*Gv.* 2–4)." *Euntes docete* 25 (1972) 139–44.

Gall, August Freiherr von
Die Herrlichkeit Gottes. Eine biblisch-theologische Untersuchung ausgedehnt über das Alte Testament, die Targume, Apokryphen, Apokalypsen, und das Neue Testament (Giessen: J. Ricker [A. Töpelmann], 1900) 105–9.

Galot, Jean
Etre né de Dieu. Jean 1, 13, AnBib 37 (Rome: Pontifical Biblical Institute, 1979).

Gambino, G.
"Struttura, composizione et analisi letterario-teologica di Gv 6,26–51b." *RivB* 24 (1976) 337–58.

Gardner, Percy
The Ephesian Gospel (London: Williams & Norgate; New York: G. P. Putnam's Sons, 1915).

Gardner-Smith, Percival
"St. John's Knowledge of Matthew." *JTS,* n.s., 4 (1953) 31–35.

Gardner-Smith, Percival
Saint John and the Synoptic Gospels (Cambridge: Cambridge University Press, 1938).

Garofalo, S.
"Preparare la strada al Signore." *RivB* 6 (1958) 131–34.

Gärtner, Bertil
"The Pauline and Johannine Idea of 'to Know God' against Hellenistic Background. The Greek Philosophical Principle 'Like by Like' in Paul and John." *NTS* 14 (1967/1968) 209–31.

Gärtner, Bertil
The Temple and the Community in Qumran and the New Testament. A Comparative Study in the Temple Symbolism of the Qumran Texts and the New Testament, SNTSMS 1 (London: Cambridge University Press, 1965).

Gärtner, Bertil
John 6 and the Jewish Passover, ConNT 17 (Lund: C. W. K. Gleerup; Copenhagen: Ejnar Munskgaard, 1959).

Garvie, Alfred E.
"The Glory in the Fourth Gospel." *Expositor,* 8th ser., 17 (1919) 36–47.

Garvie, Alfred E.
"The Witness in the Fourth Gospel." *Expositor,* 8th ser., 10 (1915) 466–75.

Garvie, Alfred E.
"The Prologue to the Fourth Gospel and the Evangelist's Theological Reflexions." *Expositor,* 8th ser., 10 (1915) 163–72.

Garvie, Alfred E.
"The Evangelist's Experimental Reflexions in the Fourth Gospel." *Exp.,* 8th ser., 10 (1915) 255–64.

Garvie, Alfred E.
The Beloved Disciple (London: Hodder & Stoughton, 1922).

Garvie, Alfred E.
"The Synoptic Echoes and Second-Hand-Reports in the Fourth Gospel." *Expositor,* 8th ser., 10 (1915) 316–26.

Garvie, Alfred E.
"Jesus in the Fourth Gospel." *Expositor,* 8th ser., 17 (1919) 312–20.

Gaugler, Ernst
"Die Bedeutung der Kirche in den johanneischen Schriften." *Internationale Kirchliche Zeitschrift* 14 (1924) 97–117.

Gaugler, Ernst
"Das Christuszeugnis des Johannesevangeliums." In *Christus im Zeugnis der heiligen Schrift und der Kirche,* ed. K. L. Schmidt. BEvT 2 (Munich: Chr. Kaiser Verlag, 1936) 34–69.

Gebhardt, H.
Lehrbegriff der Apocalypse und sein Verhältnis zum Lehrbegriff des Evangeliums und der Episteln des Johannes (1973).

Gebhardt, Hermann
Die Abfassungszeit des Johannesevangeliums (Leipzig: A. Deichert, 1906).

Geoltrain, P.
"Les noces à Cana. Jean 2, 1–12. Analyse des structures narratives." *Foi et vie* 73 (1974) 83–90.

George, Augustin
"Je suis la porte des brebis. Jean 10, 1–10." *BVC* 51 (1963) 18–25.

George, Augustin
"L'évangile Jn 14,23–30: Les venues de Dieu aux croyants." *AsSeign* 51 (1963) 63–71.

George, Augustin
"Jésus, la vigne véritable (Jn 15,1–17)." *Logos* 2 (Tokyo, 1960) 148–67.

George, Augustin
"L'évangile: Les témoins de Jesus devant le monde." *AsSeign* 50 (1966) 30–40.

George, Augustin
"L'Esprit, guide vers la vérité plénière. Jn 16,12–15." *AsSeign* 31 (1973) 40–47.

George, Augustin
"La tâche du Paraclet: Jn 16,5–14." *AsSeign* 47 (1963) 28–36.

George, Augustin
"La nouveauté de pâques: Jn 16,23–30." *AsSeign* 48 (1965) 39–46.

George, Augustin
"L'heure de Jean XVII." *RB* 61 (1954) 392–97.

Gericke, W.
"Zur Entstehung des Johannes-Evangeliums." *TLZ* 90 (1965) 807–20.

Gerritzen, F.
"El lavatorio de los pies (Joh 13,1–17)." *Sinite* 4 (1963) 145–64.

Gersdorf, Christoph Gotthelf
   Beiträge zur Sprachcharakteristik der Schriftsteller des Neuen Testaments. Eine Sammlung meist neuer Bemerkungen (Leipzig: Weidmann, 1816).

Gese, Hartmut
   "Der Johannesprolog." In his *Zur biblischen Theologie. Alttestamentliche Vorträge.* BEvT 78 (Munich: Chr. Kaiser Verlag, 1977) 152–201.

Geyser, A.
   "The Semeion at Cana of the Galilee." In *Studies in John Presented to Professor J. N. Sevenster on the Occasion of his Seventieth Birthday* (Leiden: E. J. Brill, 1970) 12–21.

Ghiberti, Giuseppe
   "Il c[ap] 6 di Giovanni e la presenza dell' Eucarestia nel 4° Vangelo." *Parole di Vita* 14 (1969) 105–25.

Ghiberti, Giuseppe
   "La rivelazione giovannea del Paraclito." In *Lo Spirito Santo nella liturgia della parola* (Treviso: Editrice Trevigiana, 1968) 7–58.

Ghiberti, Giuseppe
   I racconti pasquali del cap. 20 di Giovanni confrontati con le altre tradizioni neotestamentarie, Studi Biblici 19 (Brescia: Paideia, 1972).

Ghiberti, Giuseppe
   "Gv 20 nell' esegesi contemporanea." *Studia Patavina* 20 (1973) 293–337.

Ghiberti, Giuseppe
   "'Abbiamo veduto il Signore.' Struttura e messagio dei racconti pasquali in S. Giovanni." *Parole di Vita* 15 (1970) 389–414.

Ghiberti, Giuseppe
   "Mission e primato de Pietro sec. Gv 21." *Atti della settimana biblica* 13 (1967) 167–214.

Giblet, Jean
   "Développement dans la théologie johannique." In *L'Evangile de Jean. Sources, rédaction, théologie,* ed. M. de Jonge. BETL 44 (Gembloux: Duculot; Louvain: University Press, 1977) 45–72.

Giblet, Jean
   "Aspects of the Truth in the New Testament." *Concilium* 83 (1973) 35–42.

Giblet, Jean
   "Pour rendre témoignage à la lumière (Jean I, 29–34)." *BVC* 16 (1956/1957) 80–86.

Giblet, Jean
   "Le Temple de l'Eternelle Alliance, Joh 2,21s." *Eglise vivante* 9 (1957) 122–25.

Giblet, Jean
   "Le témoignage du Père (Jean 5, 31–47)." *BVC* 12 (1955/1956) 49–59.

Giblet, Jean
   "The Eucharist in St. John's Gospel (John 6)." *Concilium* (GB) 4 (1969) 60–69.

Giblet, Jean
   "Et il y eut la dédicace. Jn 10, 22–39." *BVC* 66 (1965) 17–25.

Giblet, Jean
   "Sanctifie-les dans la vérité (Jean 17,1–26)." *BVC* 19 (1957) 58–73.

Giblin, Charles Homer
   "The Miraculous Crossing of the Sea (Jn 6,16–21)." *NTS* 29 (1983) 96–103.

Gibson, John Monro
   "The Gethsemane of the Fourth Gospel." *ExpTim* 30 (1918/1919) 76–79.

Gieseler, J. K. L.
   "Vermischte Bemerkungen: Zu Joh 6,22." *TSK* 2 (1829) 137–38.

Gieseler, J. K. L.
   "Vermischte Bemerkungen: zu Joh 7,38." *TSK* 2 (1829) 139–41.

Gifford, George
   "'Ἐπὶ τῆς θαλάσσης (Joh 6,19)." *ExpTim* 40 (1928/1929) 236.

Gilchrist, E. J.
   "And I knew him not." *ExpTim* 19 (1907/1908) 379–80.

Gils, Felix
   "Pierre et la foi au Christ ressuscité." *ETL* 38 (1962) 5–43.

Gingrich, Felix Wilbur
   "The Gospel of John and Modern Greek." *Classical Weekly* 38 (1945) 145–82.

Girard, Marc
   "La structure heptapartie du quatrième évangile." *RSR* 5 (1975/1976) 350–59.

Girgensohn, Herbert
   "Worte Jesu an die ecclesia viatorum. Betrachtungen zu Joh 14,1–6." In his *Heilende Kräfte der Seelsorge Aufsätze* (Göttingen: Vandenhoeck & Ruprecht, 1966) 177–84.

Glas, S.
   Philologia Sacra (Amsterdam, 1694; Leipzig: J. F. Gleditschium, ²1705).

Glasson, T. Francis
   "Jn I, 9 and a Rabbinic Tradition." *ZNW* 49 (1958) 288–90.

Glasson, T. Francis
   "A Trace of Xenophon in John i, 3." *NTS* 4 (1957/1958) 208–9.

Glasson, T. Francis
   "John the Baptist in the Fourth Gospel." *ExpTim* 67 (1956) 245–46.

Gleiss, Catharina
   "Beiträge zu der Frage nach der Entstehung und dem Zweck des Johannesevangeliums." *NKZ* 18 (1907) 470–98, 548–91, 632–88.

Gloag, Paton James
   Introduction to the Johannine Writings (London: J. Nisbet, 1891).

Glombitza, Otto
   "Petrus—der Freund Jesu. Überlegungen zu Joh xxi, 15ff." *NovT* 6 (1963) 277–85.

Glusman, Edward F.
   "The Cleansing of the Temple and the Anointing at Bethany: The Order of Events in Mark 11 and

John 11–12." In *SBL 1979 Seminar Papers* 1, SBLASP 16 (Missoula: Scholars Press, 1979) 113–17.

Glusman, Edward F.
"The Shape of Mark and John: A Primitive Gospel Outline." Dissertation, Duke University, 1978.

Glusman, Edward F.
"Criteria for a Study of the Outlines of Mark and John." SBLASP 2 (Missoula: Scholars Press, 1978) 239–49.

Gnilka, Joachim
"Neue katholische Literatur zum Johannes-evangelium." *TRev* 63 (1967) 145–52.

Gnilka, Joachim
"Der historische Jesus als gegenwärtiger Christus im Johannesevangelium." *BibLeb* 7 (1966) 270–78.

Goetz, H.
"Der theologische und anthropologische Heils-universalismus bei Johannes in seiner exegetischen Begründung." Dissertation, 1896.

Goguel, Maurice
Au seuil de l'Evangile Jean-Baptiste (Paris: C. Payot, 1928).

Goguel, Maurice
"Les sources des récits du quatrième évangile sur Jean-Baptiste." *Revue de théologie et de questions religieuses* 21 (1911) 12–44.

Goguel, Maurice
The Eucharist from the Beginning to the Time of Justin Martyr, tr. Charles Porter Coffin (Evanston, IL, 1933) = *L'Eucharistie des origines jusqu'à Justin Martyr* (Paris: G. Fischbacher, 1910).

Goguel, Maurice
"La venue de Jésus à Jérusalem pour la fête des tabernacles (Joh 7)." *RHR* 83 (1921) 123–62.

Goguel, Maurice
Les sources du récit johannique de la passion (Paris: G. Fischbacher, 1910).

Goguel, Maurice
"Did Peter deny his Lord? A Conjecture." *HTR* 25 (1932) 1–28.

Goguel, Maurice
"La formation de la tradtion johannique d'après B. W. Bacon." *RHPR* 14 (1934) 415–39.

Goguel, Maurice
"Juifs et Romains dans l'histoire de la Passion." *RHR* 62 (1910) 165–82, 295–322.

Goldberg, A. M.
Untersuchungen über die Vorstellung von der Schekhinah in der frühen rabbinischen Literatur—Talmud und Midrash, Studia Judaica 5 (Berlin: Walter de Gruyter, 1969).

Gollwitzer, Helmut
"Ausser Christus kein Heil? Joh 14,6." In *Anti-judaismus im Neuen Testament? Exegetische und systematische Beiträge*, ed. W. P. Eckert, N. P. Levinson, M. Stöhr. Abhandlungen zum christlich-jüdischen Dialog 2 (Munich: Chr. Kaiser Verlag, 1967) 171–94.

Goodenough, Erwin Ramsdell
"John a Primitive Gospel." *JBL* 64 (1945) 145–82.

Goodenough, Erwin Ramsdell
By Light, Light. The Mystic Gospel of Hellenistic Judaism (New Haven: Yale University Press, 1935 ²1969).

Goodwin, Charles
"How did John Treat his Sources?" *JBL* 73 (1954) 61–75.

Goppelt, Leonhard
"Das neutestamentliche Zeugnis von der Wahrheit nach dem Johannesevangelium." In *Was ist Wahrheit?* ed. H. R. Müller-Schwefe (Göttingen, 1965) 80–93.

Goppelt, Leonhard
"Taufe und neues Leben nach Joh. 3 und Röm 6." *Stimme der Orthodoxie* 4 (1970) 51–53; 5 (1970) 36–41.

Gourbillon, J.-G.
"La parabole du serpent d'Airain et la 'lacune' du Ch. III de l'évangile selon s. Jean." *RB* 51 (1942) 213–26.

Grady, L. A.
"Martin Buber and the Gospel of St. John." *Thought* 53 (1978) 283–91.

Graf, Eduard
"Bemerkung über Joh 13, 1–4." *TSK* 40 (1867) 714–48.

Graf, J.
"Nikodemus (Joh. 3,1–21)." *Tübinger theologische Quartalschrift* 132 (1952) 62–86.

Granger, F.
"The Semitic Element in the Fourth Gospel." *Expositor*, 8th ser., 11 (1916) 349–71.

Granskou, David M.
"Structure and Theology in the Fourth Gospel." Dissertation, Princeton, 1960.

Grant, Frederick C.
"Was the Author of John Dependent upon the Gospel of Luke?" *JBL* 56 (1937) 285–307.

Grant, Robert M.
"The Fourth Gospel and the Church." *HTR* 35 (1942) 95–116.

Grant, Robert M.
"One-Hundred-Fifty-Three Large Fishes." *HTR* 42 (1949) 273–75.

Grant, Robert M.
"The Oldest Gospel Prologues." *ATR* 23 (1941) 231–45.

Grant, Robert M.
"The Origin of the Fourth Gospel." *JBL* 69 (1950) 305–22.

Grass, H.
Ostergeschehen und Osterberichte (Göttingen: Vandenhoeck & Ruprecht, ²1962).

Grässer, Erich
"Die Juden als Teufelssöhne nach Joh 8, 37–47." In *Antijudaismus im Neuen Testament? Exegetische und systematische Beiträge*, ed. W. P. Eckert et al.

Abhandlung zum christlich-jüdischen Dialog 2 (Munich: Chr. Kaiser Verlag, 1967) 157–70.

Grässer, Erich
"Die Antijüdische Polemik im Johannesevangelium." *NTS* 11 (1964/1965) 74–90.

Grassi, Joseph A.
"The Wedding at Cana (John II 1–11): A Pentecostal Meditation?" *NovT* 14 (1972) 131–36.

Grau, R. F.
Entwicklungsgeschichte des neutestamentlichen Schriftthums, 2 vols. (Gütersloh, 1871) 2: 369–472.

Grayston, Kenneth
"Jesus and the Church in St. John's Gospel." *London Quarterly and Holborn Review* 35 (1967) 106–15.

Green, Humphrey C.
"The Composition of St. John's Prologue." *ExpTim* 66 (1954/1955) 291–94.

Green-Armytage, Adrian Howell North
John Who Saw. A Layman's Essay on the Author of the Fourth Gospel (London: Faber & Faber, 1952).

Greiff-Marienburg, A.
"Platons Weltseele und das Johannesevangelium." *ZKT* 52 (1928) 519–31.

Grelot, Pierre
"Le problème de la foi dans le quatrième évangile." *BVC* 52 (1963) 61–71.

Grelot, Pierre
"'De son ventre couleront des fleuves d'eau.' La citation scripturaire de Jean 7,38." *RB* 66 (1959) 369–74.

Grelot, Pierre
"A propos de Jean 7,38." *RB* 67 (1960) 224–25.

Grelot, Pierre
"Jn VII, 38: Eau du rocher ou source du temple?" *RB* 70 (1963) 43–51.

Grensted, L. W.
"I Cor. x. 9; John i. 22." *ExpTim* 35 (1923/1924) 331.

Grether, O.
Name und Wort Gottes im Alten Testament (Giessen: A. Töpelmann, 1934).

Griffith, B. J.
"The Disciple whom Jesus Loved." *ExpTim* 32 (1920/1921) 379–81.

Grill, Julius
Untersuchungen über die Entstehung des vierten Evangeliums, 2 vols. (Tübingen: Mohr-Siebeck, 1902–1923).

Grimm, Carl Ludwig Wilibald
"Johannes der Apostel und Evangelist." In *Allgemeine Enzyklopädie der Wissenschaften und Künste* 2, section 12.

Grimm, Carl Ludwig Wilibald
"Ueber den ersten Brief des Johannes und sein Verhältnis zum vierten Evangelium." *TSK* 22 (1849) 269–303, ep. 287–89.

Grimm, Carl Ludwig Wilibald
De joanneae christologiae indole paulinae comparatae (Leipzig: Lehnholdiana libraria, 1833).

Grimm, Carl Ludwig Wilibald
"Ueber Evangelium Joh 21,22f." *ZWT* 18 (1875) 270–78.

Grimm, Carl Ludwig Wilibald
"Ueber das Evangelium und den ersten Brief des Johannes als Werke eines und desselben Verfassers." *TSK* 20 (1847) 171–87.

Grimm, Werner
"Das Opfer eines Menschen. Eine Auslegung von Joh 11,47–53." In *Israel hat dennoch Gott zum Trost. Festschrift für Schalom Ben-Chorin*, ed. G. Müller (Trier: Paulinus-Verlag, 1978) 61–82.

Grimm, Werner
"Die Preisgabe eines Menschen zur Rettung des Volkes (Joh 11,50)." In *Josephus Studien. Untersuchungen zu Josephus, dem antiken Judentum und dem Neuen Testament. Otto Michel zum 70. Geburtstag gewidmet*, ed. O. Betz, K. Haacker, and M. Hengel (Göttingen: Vandenhoeck & Ruprecht, 1974) 133–46.

Groenewald, E. P.
"The Christological meaning of John 20:31." *Neot* 2 (1968) 131–40.

Groos, Dr.
"Der Begriff der κρίσις bei Johannes, exegetisch entwickelt, ein Beitrag zur neutestamentlichen Lehre vom Gericht." *TSK* 41 (1868) 244–73.

Grosheide, F. W.
"Jn 21,24 en de Canon." *Gereformeerd theologisch tijdschrift* 53 (1953) 117–18.

Grossouw, William K.
"Ich bin die Auferstehung und das Leben. Glaubst du das?" *Schrift* 9 (1970) 98–102.

Grossouw, William K.
"A Note on John xiii 1–3." *NovT* 8 (1966) 124–31.

Groussouw, William K.
"Three Books on the Fourth Gospel." *NT* 1 (1956) 36–46.

Grubb, Edward
"The Word Made Flesh." Notes on the Johannine Gospel and Epistles (London: SCM Press, 1920).

Grundmann, Walter
"Das Wort von Jesu Freunden (Joh 15,13–16) und das Herrenmahl." *NovT* 3 (1959) 62–69.

Grundmann, Walter
"Verständnis und Bewegung des Glaubens im Johannes-Evangelium." *KD* 6 (1960) 131–54.

Grundmann, Walter
Zeugnis und Gestalt des Johannes-Evangeliums. Eine Studie zur denkerischen und gestalterischen Leistung des vierten Evangelisten, Arbeiten zur Theologie 7 (Stuttgart: Calwer Verlag, 1961).

Gryglewicz, Feliks
"Die Aussagen Jesu und ihre Rolle in Joh 5,16–30." *Studien zum Neuen Testament und seiner Umwelt* 5 (1980) 5–17.

Gryglewicz, Feliks
"Die Pharisäer und die Johanneskirche." In *Prob-*

leme der Forschung, ed. A. Fuchs. Studien zum
Neuen Testament und seiner Umwelt A, 3
(Vienna and Munich: Verlag Herold, 1978) 144–
58.

Guilding, A.
*The Fourth Gospel and Jewish Worship. A Study of the
Relation of St. John's Gospel to the Ancient Jewish
Lectionary System* (Oxford: Clarendon Press, 1960).

Guitton, J.
L'évangile dans la vie (Paris, 1977).

Gümbel, Ludwig
*Das Johannes-Evangelium, eine Ergänzung des Lukas-
Evangeliums: exegetische Studie* (Speyer a.R: Verlag
der Buchhandlung Nimtz, 1911).

Gumlich, Fr.
"Die Räthsel der Erweckung Lazari." *TSK* 35
(1862) 65–110.

Gundry, Robert H.
"In my Father's House are Many *Monai* (John
14:2)." *ZNW* 58 (1967) 68–72.

Guthrie, Donald
"The Importance of Signs in the Fourth Gospel."
Vox evangelica 5 (1967) 72–83.

Gwynn, John
"On the external Evidence alleged against the
Genuineness of St. John XXI,25." *Hermanthena* 19
(1893) 368–84.

Gyllenberg, Rafael
"Intåget i Jerusalem och Johannesevangeliets." *SEÅ*
41/42 (1976/1977) 81–86.

Gyllenberg, Rafael
"Anschauliches und Unanschauliches im vierten
Evangelium." *Studia Theologica Lundensia* 21 (1967)
83–109.

Haacker, Klaus
*Die Stiftung des Heils. Untersuchungen zur Strukturen
der johanneischen Theologie*, Arbeiten zur Theologie
1, 47 (Stuttgart: Calwer Verlag, 1972).

Haacker, Klaus
"Eine formgeschichtliche Beobachtung zu Joh 1,3
fin." *BZ* 12 (1968) 119–21.

Haacker, Klaus
"Jesus und die Kirche nach Johannes." *TZ* 29
(1973) 179–201.

Hadidan, Yervant H.
"Philonism in the Fourth Gospel." In *The Macdonald Presentation Volume, a Tribute to Duncan Black
Macdonald, consisting of articles by his former students,
presented to him on his seventieth birthday, April 9,
1933* (Princeton: Princeton University Press,
1933) 211–22.

Hadjuk, A.
"'Ego-eimi' bei Jesus und seine Messianität."
Communio viatorum 6 (1963) 55–60.

Haenchen, Ernst
Review of *The Spiritual Gospel*, by M. F. Wiles. *TLZ*
86 (1961) 505–6.

Haenchen, Ernst
Review of *Historical Tradition in the Fourth Gospel*,
by Charles Harold Dodd. *TLZ* 93 (1968) 346–48.

Haenchen, Ernst
Review of *The Composition and Order of the Fourth
Gospel*, by D. Moody Smith, Jr. *TLZ* 91 (1966)
508–10.

Haenchen, Ernst
Review of *Origenes: Das Evangelium nach Johannes*,
ed. R. Gögler. *TLZ* 87 (1962) 604–5.

Haenchen, Ernst
Review of *Zeugnis und Gestalt des Johannes-Evangeliums*, by Walter Grundmann. *TLZ* 87 (1962)
930.

Haenchen, Ernst
Review of *Das Heilsgeschehen im Johannesevangelium*,
by T. Müller. *TLZ* 88 (1963) 116–18.

Haenchen, Ernst
Review of *Das Johannesevangelium*, by R.
Schnackenburg. *TLZ* 93 (1968) 427–29.

Haenchen, Ernst
Review of *De Resurrectione. Gnomon* 36 (1964) 359–
63.

Haenchen, Ernst
Review of *The Fourth Gospel and Jewish Worship*, by
A. Guilding. *TLZ* 86 (1961) 670–72.

Haenchen, Ernst
"Aus der Literatur zum Johannes-Evangelium."
TRu 23 (1955) 295–335.

Haenchen, Ernst
"Gnosis und NT." *RGG*³ (1958) 2: 1652–56.

Haenchen, Ernst
"Probleme des johanneischen 'Prologs.'" *ZTK* 60
(1963) 305–34. In his *Gott und Mensch*, 114–43.

Haenchen, Ernst
"Das Johannesevangelium und sein Kommentar."
TLZ 89 (1964) 881–98. In his *Die Bibel und Wir*,
206–34.

Haenchen, Ernst
"Probleme des johanneischen 'Prologs.'" In his *Gott
und Mensch*, 135–38.

Haenchen, Ernst
"Petrus-Probleme." *NTS* 7 (1960/1961) 187–97.
In his *Gott und Mensch*, 55–67.

Haenchen, Ernst
*Der Weg Jesu. Eine Erklärung des Markus-Evange-
liums und der kanonischen Parallelen* (Berlin: Walter
de Gruyter, ²1966).

Haenchen, Ernst
"Johanneische Probleme." *ZTK* 56 (1959) 19–54.
Also in his *Gott und Mensch*, 78–113.

Haenchen, Ernst
"Literatur zum Codex Jung." *TRu* 30 (1964) 39–
82.

Haenchen, Ernst
"Zum Text der Apostelgeschichte." In his *Gott und
Mensch*, 172–205.

Haenchen, Ernst
"Historie und Geschichte in den johanneischen
Passionsberichten." In his *Die Bibel und Wir*, 182–
207 = "History and Interpretation in the

Johannine Passion Narrative." *Int* 24 (1970) 198–219.

Haenchen, Ernst
Die Bibel und Wir. Gesammelte Aufsätze 2 (Tübingen: Mohr-Siebeck, 1968).

Haenchen, Ernst
"Jesus vor Pilatus (Joh 18,28–19,15). Zur Methode der Auslegung." In his *Gott und Mensch*, 144–56.

Haenchen, Ernst
Review of *Der johanneische Dualismus im Zusammenhang des nachbiblischen Judentums*, by Otto Böcher. *TLZ* 91 (1966) 584.

Haenchen, Ernst
"Statistische Erforschung des Neuen Testaments." *TLZ* 87 (1962) 487–98.

Haenchen, Ernst
"Der Vater, der mich gesandt hat." *NTS* 9 (1962/1963) 208–16. In his *Gott und Mensch*, 68–77.

Haenchen, Ernst
Gott und Mensch. Gesammelte Aufsätze 1 (Tübingen: Mohr-Siebeck, 1965).

Haenchen, Ernst
"Vom Wandel des Jesusbildes in der frühen Gemeinde." In *Verborum Veritas. Festschrift für Gustav Stählin zum 70. Geburtstag*, ed. O. Böcher and K. Hacker (Wuppertal: F. A. Brockhaus, 1970) 3–14.

Haenchen, Ernst
"Aufbau und Theologie des Poimandres." In his *Gott und Mensch. Gesammelte Aufsätze* 1 (Tübingen: Mohr-Siebeck, 1965) 335–77.

Haenchen, Ernst
"Spruch 68 des Thomasevangeliums." *Le Muséon* 75 (1962) 19–29.

Haenchen, Ernst
"Das Buch Baruch." In his *Gott und Mensch*, 299–334.

Haenchen, Ernst
"Neuere Literatur zu den Johannesbriefen." TRu, n.s., 26 (1960) 1–13, 267–91.

Haenchen, Ernst
"Literatur zum Thomasevangelium." *TRu*, n.s., 27 (1961) 146–78, 306–38.

Haenchen, Ernst
"Neutestamentliche und gnostische Evangelien." In *Christentum und Gnosis*, ed. Walther Eltester. BZNW 37 (Berlin: A. Töpelmann, 1969) 19–45.

Haenchen, Ernst
"Gab es eine vorchristliche Gnosis?" *ZTK* 49 (1952) 316–49.

Haenchen, Ernst
Review of *Das Heilsgeschehen im Johannesevangelium*, by T. Müller. *TLZ* 88 (1963) 116–18.

Haenchen, Ernst
Review of *De resurrectione (Epistula ad Rheginum): Codex Jung F. XXIIʳ–F. XXVᵛ*, by M. Malinine. *Gnomen* 36 (1964) 350–63.

Hagner, D. A.
"The Vision of God in Philo and John. A Comparative Study." *Journal of the Evangelical Theological Society* 14 (1971) 81–93.

Hahn, Ferdinand
"Beobachtungen zu Joh 1,18.34." In *Studies in New Testament Language and Text. Essays in Honour of George D. Kilpatrick on the Occasion of his Sixty-fifth Birthday*, ed. J. K. Elliott. NovTSup 44 (Leiden: E. J. Brill, 1976) 24–37.

Hahn, Ferdinand
"Die Jüngerberufung Joh 1,35–51." In *Neues Testament und Kirche. Für Rudolf Schnackenburg*, ed. J. Gnilka (Freiburg: Herder, 1974) 172–90.

Hahn, Ferdinand
"Sehen und Glauben im Johannesevangelium." In *Neues Testament und Geschichte. Historisches Geschehen und Deutung im Neuen Testament. Oscar Cullmann zum 70. Geburtstag*, ed. H. Baltensweiler and B. Reicke (Zurich: Theologischer Verlag; Tübingen: Mohr-Siebeck, 1972) 125–41.

Hahn, Ferdinand
Christologische Hoheitstitel. Ihre Geschichte im Frühen Christentum, FRLANT 83 (Göttingen: Vandenhoeck & Ruprecht, 1963) 112–25.

Hahn, Ferdinand
"Die Worte vom lebendigen Wasser im Johannesevangelium. Eigenart und Vorgeschichte von Joh 4,10.13f; 6,35; 7,37–39." In *God's Christ and His People. Studies in honor of Nils A. Dahl*, ed. Jacob Jervell and Wayne A. Meeks (Oslo: Universitetsforlaget, 1977) 51–70.

Hahn, Ferdinand
"Das Heil kommt von den Juden." In *Wort und Wirklichkeit. Studien zur Afrikanistik und Orientalistik. Eugen Ludwig Rapp zum 70. Geburtstag*. Vol. 1, *Geschichte und Religionswissenschaft-Bibliographie*, ed. B. Benzing, O. Böcher, and G. Mayer (Meisenheim am Glan: Anton Hain, 1976) 67–84.

Hahn, Ferdinand
"Die Hirtenrede in Joh 10." In *Theologia Crucis—Signum Crucis. Festschrift für Erich Dinkler zum 70. Geburtstag*, ed. C. Andresen and G. Klein (Tübingen: Mohr-Siebeck, 1979) 185–200.

Hahn, Ferdinand
"Der Prozess Jesu nach dem Johannesevangelium. Eine redaktionsgeschichtliche Untersuchung." EKKNT Vorarbeiten 2 (Neukirchen-Vluyn: Neukirchener-Verlag; Cologne: Benziger, 1970) 23–96.

Hall, David R.
"The Meaning of *synchraomai* in John 4:9." *ExpTim* 83 (1971/1972) 56–57.

Hambly, W. F.
"Creation and Gospel. A Brief Comparison of Gen 1,1–2,4 and Joh 1,1–2, 12." *SE* 5 = TU 103 (Berlin: Akademie-Verlag, 1968) 69–74.

Hamerton-Kelly, Robert G.
Pre-existence, Wisdom, and the Son of Man. A Study of the Idea of Pre-existence in the New Testament, SNTSMS 21 (New York: Cambridge University

Press, 1973).

Hammer, J.
"Eine klare Stellung zu Joh 14,31b." *Bibel und Kirche* 14 (1959) 33–40.

Hamp, Vinzenz
Der Begriff "Wort" in den aramäischen Bibelübersetzungen. Ein exegetischer Beitrag zur HypostasenFrage und zur Geschichte der Logos-Spekulationen (Munich: Neuer Filser-Verlag, 1938).

Handschke, Johann Carl Lebrecht
De authentia cap. XXI ev. Johannei, e sola orationis indole, indicanda (Leipzig: J. F. Glueck, 1818).

Hanhart, Karel
"'About the Tenth Hour' . . . on Nisam 15 (Jn 1:35–40)." In *L'Evangile de Jean. Sources, rédaction, théologie,* ed. M. de Jonge. BETL 44 (Gembloux: Duculot; Louvain: University Press, 1977) 335–46.

Hanhart, Karel
"The Structure of John 1,35–4,54." In *Studies in John Presented to Professor J. N. Sevenster on the Occasion of his Seventieth Birthday* (Leiden: E. J. Brill, 1970) 22–46.

Hanson, Anthony
"John's Citation of Psalm 82. John 10:33–6." *NTS* 11 (1964/1965) 158–62.

Hanson, Anthony
"John's Citation of Psalm 82 Reconsidered." *NTS* 13 (1966/1967) 363–67.

Hanson, Anthony A.
"The Jesus of the Fourth Gospel." *New Divinity* 5 (1974) 20–24.

Hanson, Anthony T.
"John 1,14–18 and Exodus 34." *NTS* 23 (1976/1977) 90–101.

Haring, N. M.
"Historical Notes on the Interpretation of John 13:10." *CBQ* 13 (1951) 355–80.

Harnack, Adolf von
"Ich bin gekommen. Die Ausdrücklichen Selbstzeugnisse Jesu über den Zweck seiner Sendung und seines Kommens." *ZTK* 22 (1912) 1–30.

Harnack, Adolf von
"Über das Verhältnis des Prologs des vierten Evangeliums zum ganzen Werk." *ZTK* 2 (1892) 189–231.

Harnack, Adolf von
New Testament Studies. Vol. 2, *The Sayings of Jesus, the Source of Matthew and St. Luke,* tr. J. R. Wilkinson (New York: G. P. Putnam's Sons; London: Williams & Norgate, 1908) = *Beiträge zur Einleitung in das Neue Testament.* Vol. 2, *Sprüche und Reden Jesu. Die zweite Quelle des Matthäus und Lukas* (Leipzig: J. C. Hinrichs, 1907).

Harnack, Adolf von
New Testament Studies. Vol. 3, *The Acts of the Apostles,* tr. J. R. Wilkinson (New York: G. P. Putnam's Sons; London: Williams & Norgate, 1909) = *Die Apostelgeschichte* (Leipzig: J. C. Hinrichs, 1908).

Harnack, Adolf von
"Zum Johannesevangelium." In his *Erforschtes und Erlebtes* (Giessen: A. Töpelmann, 1923) 36–43.

Harnack, Adolf von
Die ältesten Evangelien-Prologe und die Bildung des Neuen Testaments, SPAW.PH 24 (Berlin: G. Reimer, 1928) 320–41.

Harnack, Adolf von
"Zur Textkritik und Christologie der Schriften des Johannes. Zugleich ein Beitrag zur Würdigung der ältesten lateinischen Überlieferung und der Vulgata." SPAW 5,2 (Berlin: G. Reimer, 1915) 534–73.

Harnack, Adolf von
"Das 'Wir' in den johanneischen Schriften." SPAW.PH 31 (Berlin: G. Reimer, 1923) 96–113.

Harner, P. B.
The "I Am" of the Fourth Gospel. A Study in Johannine Usage and Thought, Facet Books, Biblical Series 26 (Philadelphia: Fortress Press, 1971).

Harris, J. Rendel
"Athena, Sophia, and the Logos." *BJRL* 7 (1922/1923) 56–72.

Harris, J. Rendel
"The Origin of the Prologue to St. John's Gospel." *Expositor,* 8th ser., 12 (1916) 147–60, 161–70, 314–20, 388–400, 415–26.

Harris, J. Rendel
"Stoic Origin of the Fourth Gospel." *BJRL* 6 (1921/1922) 439–51.

Harris, Richard
"Rivers of Living Water (Jn 7,38)." *Expositor,* 8th ser., 20 (1920) 196–202.

Harrison, Everett F.
"A Study of John 1:14." In *Unity and Diversity in New Testament Theology. Essays in Honor of George E. Ladd,* ed. R. A. Guelich (Grand Rapids: Wm. B. Eerdmans, 1978) 23–36.

Harrison, Everett F.
"The Christology of the Fourth Gospel in the Relation to the Synoptics." *BSac* 116 (1959) 303–9.

Harsch, H. and G. Voss, eds.
Versuche mehrdimensionaler Schriftauslegung. Part 2, *Gesprächsmodell: Joh 2,1–11* (Stuttgart: Katholisches Bibelwerk; Munich: Chr. Kaiser Verlag, 1972) 72–140.

Hart, H. St. J.
"The Crown of Thorns in John 19,2–5." *JTS,* n.s., 3 (1952) 66–75.

Hartke, Wilhelm
Vier urchristliche Parteien und ihre Vereinigung zur Apostolischen Kirche, I and II, Deutsche Akademie der Wissenschaften zu Berlin, Schriften der Sektion für Altertumswissenschaft 24 (Berlin: Akademie-Verlag, 1961).

Hartmann, Gert
"Die Osterberichte in Joh 20 im Zusammenhang der Theologie des Johannesevangeliums." Dissertation, Kiel, 1963.

Hartmann, Gert
"Die Vorlage der Osterberichte in Joh 20." *ZNW* 55 (1964) 197–220.

Harvey, A. E.
Jesus on Trial. A Study in the Fourth Gospel (London: S. P. C. K., 1976).

Hatch, William H. P.
"An Allusion to the Destruction of Jerusalem in the Fourth Gospel." *Expositor,* 8th ser., 17 (1919) 194–97.

Hatch, William H. P.
"The Meaning of John 16,8–11." *HTR* 14 (1921) 103–5.

Hauck, Friedrich
"Καθαρός." *TDNT* 3: 425–26.

Hauck, Friedrich
"Κόπος" and "Κοπιάω." *TDNT* 3: 827–30.

Hauck, Friedrich
"Καρπός." *TDNT* 3: 614–16.

Hauff, Karl Victor
Die Authentie und der hohe Werth des Evangeliums Johannis (Nuremberg, 1831).

Hauff, Pfarrer
"Einige Bemerkungen über die Abhandlung von D. v. Baur über die Composition und den Charakter des johanneischen Evangeliums." *TSK* 19 (1846) 550–629.

Haupt, Erich
Die alttestamentlichen Citate in den vier Evangelien erörtert (Colberg: C. Jancke, 1871).

Hauret, Charles
Les Adieux du Seigneur (Jean XIII–XVII). Charte de vie apostolique (Paris: J. Gabalda, 1952).

Hawkin, David J.
"Orthodoxy and Heresy in John 10,1–21 and 15,1–17." *EvQ* 47 (1975) 208–13.

Hawkin, David J.
"The Function of the Beloved-Disciple-Motif in the Johannine Redaction." *Laval théologique et philosophique* 33 (1977) 135–50.

Hayes, Doremus Almy
John and his Writings (New York and Cincinnati: The Methodist Book Concern, 1917).

Hayward, C. T. R.
"The Holy Name of the God of Moses and the Prologue of St. John's Gospel." *NTS* 25 (1978/1979) 16–32.

Hayward, Robert
Divine Name and Presence: The Memra (Totowa, NJ: Allanheld, Osmun, 1981).

Hayward, Robert
"Memra and Shekhina: A Short Note." *JJS* 31 (1980) 210–13.

Headlam, Arthur Cayley
The Fourth Gospel as History (Oxford: Blackwell, 1948).

Heard, R. G.
"The Oldest Gospel Prologues." *JTS,* n.s., 6 (1955) 1–16.

Heckel, D. T.
Wahrheit im Johannesevangelium und bei Luther (Helsinki, 1944).

Heer, Josef
"Johanneische Botschaft XI: Der Glaube des Königlichen (Jo 4,43–54)." *Sein und Sendung* 33 (1968) 147–64.

Hegermann, Harald
"'Er kam in sein Eigentum.' Zur Bedeutung des Erdenwirkens Jesu im vierten Evangelium." In *Der Ruf Jesu und die Antwort der Gemeinde. Exegetische Untersuchungen Joachim Jeremias zum 70. Geburtstag gewidmet von seinen Schülern,* ed. E. Lohse et al. (Göttingen: Vandenhoeck & Ruprecht, 1970) 112–31.

Hegermann, Harald
Die Vorstellung vom Schöpfungsmittler im hellenistischen Judentum und Urchristentum, TU 82 (Berlin: Akademie-Verlag, 1961).

Heil, J. P.
Jesus Walking on the Sea. Meaning and Gospel Functions of Matt 14:22–23, Mark 6:45–52 and John 6:15b–21, AnBib 87 (Rome: Pontifical Biblical Institute, 1981).

Heine, R.
"Zur patristischen Auslegung von Joh 2,1–12." *Wiener Studien* 83, n.s., 4 (1970) 189–95.

Heinemann, Isaak
Philons griechische und jüdische Bildung. Kulturvergleichende Untersuchungen zu Philons Darstellung der jüdischen Gesetze (Breslau: M. & H. Marcus, 1932).

Heinisch, Paul
Personifikationen und Hypostasen im AT und Alten Orient, Biblische Zeitfragen 10/12 (Münster: Aschendorff, 1921).

Heinrici, C. F. Georg
Die Hermesmystik und das Neue Testament, Arbeiten zur Religionsgeschichte des Urchristentums 1,1 (Leipzig: J. C. Hinrichs, 1918).

Heinze, M.
Die Lehre vom Logos in der griechischen Philosophie (Oldenburg: F. Schmidt, 1872).

Heise, Jürgen
Bleiben. Menein in den johanneischen Schriften, Hermeneutische Untersuchungen zur Theologie 8 (Tübingen: Mohr-Siebeck, 1967).

Heising, Alkuin
"Exegese und Theologie der alt- und neutestamentlichen Speisewunder." *ZKT* 86 (1964) 80–96.

Heitmüller, Wilhelm
"Zur Johannes-Tradition." *ZNW* 15 (1914) 189–209.

Helderman, J.
"'In ihren Zelten...' Bemerkungen bei Codex 13 Nag Hammadi p. 47: 14–18, im Hinblick auf Joh 1,14." In *Miscellanea neotestamentica* 1, NovTSup 47 (Leiden: E. J. Brill, 1978) 181–211.

Hellwag, Julius
"Die Vorstellung von der Präexistenz Christi in

der ältesten Kirche." *Theologische Jahrbücher* 7 (Tübingen, 1848) 144–61, 227–63.

Hélou, C.

Symbole et langage dans les écrits johanniques: lumière—ténèbres (Paris: Mame, 1980).

Hengel, Martin

Der Sohn Gottes. Die Entstehung der Christologie und die jüdisch-hellenistische Religionsgeschichte (Tübingen: Mohr-Siebeck, 1975).

Hengel, Martin

"Mors turpissima crucis. Die Kreuzigung in der Antiken Welt und die 'Torheit' des 'Wortes vom Kreuz.'" In *Rechfertigung. Festschrift für Ernst Käsemann zum 70. Geburtstag*, ed. J. Friedrich, W. Pöhlmann, and P. Stuhlmacher (Tübingen: Mohr-Siebeck; Göttingen: Vandenhoeck & Ruprecht, 1976) 125–84.

Hengstenberg, E. W.

Ueber den Eingang des Evangeliums St. Johannis (Berlin: Schlawitz, 1859).

Hennecke, Edgar

"Jean 1,3–4 et l'enchaînement du Prologue." In *Congrès d'histoire du Christianisme: Jubilé Alfred Loisy*, ed. P.-L. Couchoud (Paris: Les éditions Rieder, 1928) 207–19.

Hennig, John

"Was ist eigentlich geschehen? Joh 2,11." *ZRGG* 15 (1963) 276–86.

Herder, Johann Gottfried von

Von Gottes Sohn, der Welt Heiland. Nach Johannes Evangelium. Nebst einer Regel der Zusammenstimmung unsrer Evangelien aus ihrer Entstehung und Ordnung (Riga: J. F. Hartnoch, 1797).

Hermann, Rudolf

"Die Prüfungsstunde des Sendungsgehorsams Jesu (Joh 12,20–43[50])." *ZST* 7 (1929/1930) 742–71.

Herranz Marco, Mariano

"Un problema de crítica histórica en el relato de la Pasión: la liberación de Barrabás." *EstBib* 30 (1971) 137–60.

Hickling, C. J. A.

"Attitudes to Judaism in the Fourth Gospel." In *L'Evangile de Jean. Sources, rédaction, théologie*, ed. M. de Jonge. BETL 44 (Gembloux: Duculot; Louvain: University Press, 1977) 347–54.

Hiers, Richard H.

"Purification of the Temple: Preparation for the Kingdom of God [Mk 11:15–17]." *JBL* 90 (1971) 82–90.

Higgins, Angus J. B.

"The Words of Jesus According to St. John." *BJRL* 49 (1966/1967) 363–86.

Hilgenfeld, Adolf

"Der gnostische und der kanonische Johannes über das Leben Jesu." *ZWT* 43 (1900) 1–61.

Hilgenfeld, Adolf

"Das Johannes-Evangelium und die neuesten Schriften von Hofstede de Grot, Keim und Scholten." *ZWT* 11 (1868) 213–31.

Hilgenfeld, Adolf

"Das Johannes-Evangelium und seine gegenwärtigen Auffassungen." *ZWT* 2 (1859) 281–348, 385–448.

Hilgenfeld, Adolf

"Der Passastreit und das Evangelium Johannis." *Theologischer Jahrbücher* 8 (Tübingen, 1849) 209–81.

Hilgenfeld, Adolf

"Der Gnostizismus und das NT." *ZWT* 13 (1870) 233–75.

Hilgenfeld, Adolf

"Der Gnostizismus und die Philosohpumena." *ZWT* 5 (1862) 400–464.

Hilgenfeld, Adolf

"Das neueste Forscher-Paar über das Johannes-Evangelium." *ZWT* 28 (1885) 393–425.

Hilgenfeld, Adolf

Review of *Der Prolog des vierten Evangeliums*, by W. Baldensperger. *ZWT* 42 (1899) 631–33.

Hilgenfeld, Adolf

"Hr. D. Riggenbach und das Johannes-Evangelium." *ZWT* 10 (1867) 179–98.

Hilgenfeld, Adolf

"Der kleinasiatische Johannes und W. Bousset." *ZWT* 48 (1905) 560ff.

Hilgenfeld, Adolf

"Das Johannes-Evangelium und seine neuesten Kritiker." *ZWT* 47 (1904) 21–56.

Hilgenfeld, Adolf

"Das Johannesevangelium und Godet und Luthardt." *ZWT* 23 (1880) 1–31.

Hilgenfeld, Adolf

"Neuer und alter Zweikampf wegen der Johannes-Schriften." *ZWTh* 32 (1889) 330–48.

Hilgenfeld, Adolf

"Ein französischer Apologet des Johannes-Evangeliums." *ZWT* 32 (1889) 129–47.

Hilgenfeld, Adolf

"Das Johannesevangelium und seine gegenwärtigen Auffassungen." *ZWT* 2 (1859) 281–348, 377–448.

Hilgenfeld, Adolf

"Das Johannes-Evangelium alexandrinisch oder gnostisch?" *ZWT* 25 (1882) 388–435.

Hilgenfeld, Adolf

"Die johanneische Theologie und ihre neueste Bearbeitung." *ZWT* 6 (1863) 214–28.

Hilgenfeld, Adolf

"Noch ein Wort über Joh 6,71." *ZWT* 9 (1866) 336.

Hilgenfeld, Adolf

"Der Antijudaïsmus des Johannes-Evangeliums." *ZWT* 36 (1893) 507–17.

Hilgenfeld, Adolf

"Die Rätselzahl Joh 21.11." *ZWT* 41 (1898) 480.

Hilgenfeld, Adolf

"Die neueste Evangelienforschung. I. W. Beyschlag und das Johannesevangelium. II. B.

Weiss und die synoptischen Evangelien." *ZWT* 20 (1877) 1–47.

Hilgenfeld, Adolf
Das Evangelium und die Briefe Johannis, nach ihrem Lehbegriff dargestellt (Halle: C. A. Schwetschke & Sone, 1849).

Hilgenfeld, Adolf
"Noch einmal Johannes in Kleinasien." *ZWT* 16 (1873) 102–11.

Hilgenfeld, Adolf
"Noch einmal: Petrus in Rom und Johannes in Kleinasien." *ZWT* 20 (1877) 486–525.

Hilgenfeld, Adolf
"Petrus in Rom und Johannes in Kleinasien." *ZWT* 15 (1872) 349–83.

Hill, David
"The Request of Zebedee's Sons and the Johannine *doxa*-theme." *NTS* 13 (1966/1967) 281–85.

Hill, David
"The Relevance of the Logos Christology." *ExpTim* 78 (1967) 136–39.

Hillmer, M. R.
"The Gospel of John in the Second Century." Dissertation, Harvard, 1965/1966.

Hindley, J. C.
"Witness in Fourth Gospel." *SJT* 18 (1965) 319–37.

Hingston, James H.
"John 18.5,6." *ExpTim* 32 (1920/1921) 232.

Hirsch, Emanuel
"Stilkritik und Literaranalyse im vierten Evangelium." *ZNW* 43 (1950/1951) 129–43.

Hirsch, Emanuel
Studien zum vierten Evangelium (Tübingen: Mohr-Siebeck, 1936).

Hitchcock, Francis Ryan Montgomery
A Fresh History of the Fourth Gospel (London: S. P. C. K., 1911).

Hoang Dac-Anh, S.
"La liberté par la vérité." *Ang* 55 (1978) 193–211.

Hoare, Frederick Russell
The Original Order and Chapters of St. John's Gospel (London: Burns, Oates & Washbourne, 1944).

Hoare, Frederick Russell
The Gospel According to St. John Arranged in its Conjectural Order (London: Burns, Oates & Washbourne, 1949).

Hobbs, H. H.
"Word Studies in the Gospel of John." *Southwestern Journal of Theology* 8 (1965) 67–79.

Hodges, Zane C.
"Grace after Grace—John 1:16. Part 1 of *Problem Passages in the Gospel of John*." *BSac* 135 (1978) 34–45.

Hodges, Zane C.
"Untrustworthy Believers—Joh 2,23–25." *BSac* 135 (1978) 139–52.

Hodges, Zane C.
"Problem Passages in the Gospel of John, Part 3:

Water and Spirit—John 3:5." *BSac* 135 (1978) 206–20.

Hoernle, Edward Selwyn
The Record of the Beloved Disciple Together with the Gospel of St. Philip. Being a Reconstruction of the Sources of the Fourth Gospel (Oxford: Blackwell, 1931).

Hofbeck, Sebald
Semeion. Der Begriff des "Zeichens" im Johannesevangelium unter Berüchsichtigung seiner Vorgeschichte (Münsterschwarzach: Vier-Türme-Verlag, 1966).

Hoffmann, Gerhard
Das Johannesevangelium als Alterswerk. Eine Psychologie Untersuchung, NTF 4, Evangelienprobleme 1 (Gütersloh: Evangelischer Verlag, 1933).

Hoffmann, Paul
"Auferstehung." In *Theologische Realenzyklopädie*, ed. Gerhard Krause and Gerhard Müller (Berlin: Walter de Gruyter, 1979) 4: 478–513.

Hofius, Otfried
"Erwählung und Bewahrung. Zur Auslegung von Joh. 6,37." *Theologische Beiträge* 8 (1977) 24–29.

Hofius, Otfried
"Die Sammlung der Heiden zur Herde Israels (Joh 10:16, 11:51f.)." *ZNW* 58 (1967) 289–91.

Hofrichter, Peter
Nicht aus Blut, sondern monogen aus Gott geboren. Textkritische, dogmengeschichtliche und exegetische Untersuchung zu Joh 1,13–14, Forschung zur Bibel 31 (Würzburg: Echter Verlag, 1978).

Hofrichter, Peter
"'Egeneto anthropos.' Text und Zusätze im Johannesprolog." *ZNW* 70 (1979) 214–37.

Hofstede de Groot, P.
Basilides am Ausgange des apostolischen Zeitalters als erster Zeuge für Alter und Autorität neutestamentlicher Schriften, insbesondere des Johannesevangeliums, in Verbindung mit anderen Zeugen bis zur Mitte des zweiten Jahrhunderts (Leipzig: J. C. Hinrichs, 1868).

Hogan, M. P.
"The Woman at the Well (Jn 4,1–42)." *Bible Today* 82 (1976) 633–69.

Holst, Robert Arthur
"The Relation of John 12 to the So-called Johannine Book of Glory." Dissertation, Princeton Theological Seminary, 1974.

Holtzmann, Heinrich Julius
Review of *Der johanneische Ursprung des vierten Evangeliums*, by C. E. Luthardt. *ZWT* 18 (1875) 442–52.

Holtzmann, Heinrich Julius
"Zur neuesten Literatur über neutestamentliche Probleme." *ARW* 12 (1909) 382–408, 15 (1912) 513–529.

Holtzmann, Heinrich Julius
"D. F. Strauss und die Evangelienkritik." *Protestantische Kirchenzeitung für das evangelische Deutschland* 11 (1864) 321–330.

Holtzmann, Heinrich Julius

"Hugo Delff und das vierte Evangelium." *ZWT* 36 (1893) 503–7.

Holtzmann, Heinrich Julius
"Ueber das Problem des ersten johanneischen Briefes in seinem Verhältnis zum Evangelium." *Jahrbücher for protestantische Theologie* 7 (1881) 690–712; 8 (1882) 128–52, 316–42, 460–85.

Holtzmann, Heinrich Julius
"Das schriftstellerische Verhältnis des Johannes zu den Synoptikern." *ZWT* 12 (1869) 62–85, 155–78, 446–56.

Holtzmann, Heinrich Julius
"Sakramentliches im Neuen Testament." *ARW* 7 (1904) 58–69.

Holtzmann, Heinrich Julius
"Die Gnosis und das johanneische Evangelium." In *Die Anfänge des Christentums. Beitrage zum Verständnis des Neuen Testaments* (Berlin: A. Haack, 1877) 7: 112–43.

Holtzmann, Heinrich Julius
"Hermas und Johannes." *ZWT* 18 (1875) 40–51.

Holtzmann, Heinrich Julius
"Das Verhältnis des Johannes zu Ignatius und Polykarp." *ZWT* 20 (1877) 187–214.

Holtzmann, Heinrich Julius
"Johannes der Apostel"; "Johannes der Presbyther." In *Bibel-Lexikon. Realwörterbuch zum Handgebrauch für Geistliche und Gemeindeglieder,* ed. Daniel Schenkel (Leipzig: F. A. Brockhaus, 1871) 3: 328–42, 352–60.

Holtzmann, Heinrich Julius
"Papias und Johannes." *ZWT* 23 (1880) 64–77.

Holtzmann, Heinrich Julius
"Barnabas und Johannes." *ZWT* 14 (1871) 336–51.

Holtzmann, Heinrich Julius
"Unordnungen und Umordnungen im vierten Evangelium." *ZNW* 3 (1902) 50–60.

Holtzmann, Heinrich Julius
"Über die Disposition des vierten Evangeliums." *ZWT* 24 (1881) 257–90.

Holtzmann, Heinrich Julius
"Der Logos und der eingeborene Gottessohn im 4. Evangelium." *ZWT* 36 (1893) 385–406.

Holwerda, David Earl
The Holy Spirit and Eschatology in the Gospel of John; A Critique of Rudolf Bultmann's Present Eschatology (Kampen: Kok, 1959).

Holzmeister, Urban
"'Medius vestrum stetit, quem vos nescitis' (Jn I,26)." *VD* 20 (1940) 329–32.

Hönig, Wilhelm
"Die Construktion des vierten Evangeliums." *ZWT* 14 (1871) 535–66.

Hooke, S. H.
"'The Spirit Was Not Yet.'" *NTS* 9 (1962/1963) 372–80.

Hooker, Morna
"John the Baptist and the Johannine Prologue." *NTS* 16 (1969/1970) 354–58.

Hooker, Morna
"The Johannine Prologue and the Messianic Secret." *NTS* 21 (1974/1975) 40–58.

Horn, Karl
Abfassungszeit, Geschichtlichkeit und Zweck von Evangelium des Johannes, Kap. 21. Ein Beitrag zur johanneischen Frage (Leipzig: A. Deichert, 1904).

Hornung, A.
"Nachfolge im Lichte der Apostelberufungen." *Claretianum* 10 (1970) 79–108.

Horst, Georg Konrad
"Lässt sich die Echtheit des Johannes-Evangeliums aus hinlänglichen Gründen bezweifeln, und welches ist der wahrscheinliche Ursprung dieser Schrift?" *Museum für Religionswissenschaft in ihrem ganzen Umfange* 1 (1803) 47–118.

Horst, Georg Konrad
"Ueber einige anscheinende Widersprüche in dem Evangelium des Johannis, in Absicht auf den Logos, oder das Höhere in Christo." *Museum für Religionswissenschaft in ihrem ganzen Umfange* 1 (1803) 20–46.

Horst, J.
Proskynein. Zur Anbetung im Urchristentum nach ihrer religionsgeschichtlichen Eigenart (Gütersloh: C. Bertelsmann, 1932).

Howard, J. K.
"Passover and Eucharist in the Fourth Gospel." *SJT* 20 (1967) 329–37.

Howard, Wilbert Francis
"The Fourth Gospel and Mandaean Gnosticism." *London Quarterly Review* (January, 1927).

Howard, Wilbert Francis
Christianity According to St. John (London: Duckworth, 1943).

Howard, Wilbert Francis
"The Antimarcionite Prologues to the Gospels." *ExpTim* 47 (1936) 534–38.

Howard, Wilbert Francis
The Fourth Gospel in Recent Criticism and Interpretation (London: Epworth Press, ⁴1955).

Howton, John
"The Son of God in the Fourth Gospel." *NTS* 10 (1963/1964) 227–37.

Hoyt, H. A.
"The Explanation of the New Birth." *Grace Journal* (1967) 14–21.

Hruby, Kurt
"Die Trennung von Kirche und Judentum." In *Theologische Berichte 3. Judentum und Kirche: Volk Gottes,* ed. J. Pfammatter and F. Fürger (Zurich and Cologne: Benziger, 1974) 135–56.

Huber, Hugo
Der Begriff der Offenbarung im Johannes-Evangelium. Ein Beitrag zum Verständnis der eigenart des vierten Evangeliums (Göttingen: Vandenhoeck & Ruprecht, 1934).

Huby, Joseph
Le discours de Jésus après la Cène; suivi d'une étude sur

la connaissance de foi dans Saint Jean (Paris: Beauchesne, 1933).

Huby, Joseph
"Un double problème de critique textuelle et d'interprétation: Saint Jean 17,11–12." *RSR* 27 (1937) 408–21.

Huby, Joseph
"De la connaissance de foi dans saint Jean." *RSR* 21 (1931) 385–421.

Hudry-Clergeon, C.
"De Judée en Galilee. Etude de Jean 4,1–45." *NRT* 113 (1981) 818–30.

Hügel, F. von
"Gospel of St. John." *Encyclopedia Brittanica*¹¹ 15: 452–58.

Hulen, Amos B.
"The Call of the Four Disciples in John I." *JBL* 67 (1948) 153–57.

Hunkin, J. W.
"'Pleonastic' ἄρχομαι in the New Testament." *JTS* 25 (1923/1924) 390–402.

Hunt, W. B.
"John's Doctrine of the Spirit." *Southwestern Journal of Theology* 8 (1965) 45–65.

Hunter, A. M.
"Recent Trends in Johannine Studies." *ExpTim* 71 (1959/1960) 164–67, 219–22.

Huppenbauer, H. W.
Der Mensch zwischen zwei Welten. Der Dualismus der Texte von Qumran (Höhle I) und der Damascusfragmente. Ein Beitrag zum Vorgeschichte des Evangeliums, ATANT 34 (Zurich: Zwingli Verlag, 1959).

Hurley, J. M.
"The Paraclete in the Fourth Gospel." *Bible Today* 36 (1968) 2485–88.

Iber, G.
"Überlieferungsgeschichtliche Untersuchung zum Begriff des Menschensohns im Neuen Testament." Dissertation, Heidelberg, 1953.

Ibuki, Yu
Die Wahrheit im Johannesevangelium, BBB 39 (Bonn: Peter Hanstein, 1972).

Ibuki, Yu
"Lobhymnus und Fleischwerdung. Studien über den johanneischen Prolog." *Annual of the Japanese Biblical Institute* 3 (1977) 132–56.

Ibuki, Yu
"Offene Fragen zur Aufnahme des Logoshymnus in das vierte Evangelium." *Annual of the Japanese Biblical Institute* 5 (1979) 105–32.

Ibuki, Yu
"Καὶ τὴν φωνὴν αὐτοῦ ἀκούεις. Gedankenaufbau und Hintergrund des dritten Kapitels des Johannesevangeliums." *Bulletin of Seikei University* 14 (1978) 9–33.

Iersel, B. M. F. van
"Tradition und Redaktion in Joh 1 19–36." *NovT* 5 (1962) 245–67.

Iglesias, Manuel
"Sobre la transcripción 'Hijo de Dios' (Jn 10,36 en P⁴⁵)." *SPap* 8 (1969) 89–96.

Inch, Morris A.
"Apologetic Use of 'Sign' in the Fourth Gospel." *EQ* 42 (1970) 35–43.

Inge, William Ralph
"The Theology of the Fourth Gospel." In *Essays on Some Biblical Questions of Today,* ed. Henry Barclay Swete (London: Macmillan, 1909).

Irigoin, J.
"La composition rythmique du prologue de Jean (I, 1–18)." *RB* 78 (1971) 501–14.

Isaacs, Marie E.
The Concept of Spirit. A Study of Pneuma *in Hellenistic Judaism and its Bearing on the New Testament,* Heythrop Monographs 1 (London: Heythrop College [University of London], 1976).

Jackson, Henry Latimer
The Fourth Gospel and Some Recent German Criticism (Cambridge: Cambridge University Press, 1906).

Jackson, Henry Latimer
The Problem of the Fourth Gospel (Cambridge: Cambridge University Press, 1918).

Jacobi, Bernhard
"Über die Erhöhung des Menschensohnes. Joh 3, 14.15." *TSK* 8 (1835) 7–70.

James, M. R.
"Notes on Apocrypha." *JTS* 7 (1906) 562–68.

Janssens, Yvonne
"Une source gnostique du Prologue?" In *L'Evangile de Jean. Sources, rédaction, théologie,* ed. M. de Jonge. BETL 44 (Gembloux: Duculot; Louvain: University Press, 1977) 355–58.

Jaschke, H. J.
"Das Johannesevangelium und die Gnosis im Zeugnis des Irenäus von Lyon." *MTZ* 29 (1978) 337–76.

Jaubert, Annie
"Une lecture du lavement des pieds au mardi-mercredi saint." *Muséon* 79 (1966) 257–86.

Jaubert, Annie
"L'image de la vigne (Jean 15.)" In *Oikonomia. Heilsgeschichte als Thema der Theologie. Oscar Cullmann zum 65. Geburtstag gewidmet,* ed. Felix Christ (Hamburg: B. Reich, 1967) 93–99.

Jaubert, Annie
"The Calendar of Qumran and the Passion-Narrative in John." In *John and Qumran,* ed. J. H. Charlesworth (London: Chapman, 1972) 62–75.

Jaubert, Annie
"La comparution devant Pilate selon Jean. Jean 18,28–19,16." *Foi et vie* 73 (1974) 3–12.

Jaubert, Annie
Approches de l'Evangile de Jean, Parole de Dieu (Paris: Editions du Seuil, 1976).

Jaubert, Annie
"Solution of the Conflict Between John and the Synoptics." In her *The Date of the Last Supper,* tr. I. Rafferty (Staten Island, NY: Alba House, 1965)

95–101.

Jendorff, B.

Der Logosbegriff. Seine philosophische Grundlegung bei Heraklit von Ephesos und seine theologische Indienstnahme durch Johannes den Evangelisten, Europäische Hochschulschriften, Series 20; Philosophie 19 (Frankfurt and Bern: P. Lang, 1976).

Jeremias, Joachim

Der Prolog des Johannesevangeliums. (Johannes 1,1–18), Calwer Hefte 88 (Stuttgart: Calwer Verlag, 1967).

Jeremias, Joachim

"'Αμνὸς τοῦ Θεοῦ - παῖς Θεοῦ (Jn I:29, 36)." *ZNW* 34 (1935) 117–23.

Jeremias, Joachim

"Die Berufung des Nathanael." *Angelos* 3 (1928) 2–5.

Jeremias, Joachim

The Rediscovery of Bethesda; John 5:2, New Testament Archaeology 1 (Louisville, KY: Southern Baptist Theological Seminary, 1966) = *Die Wiederentdeckung von Bethesda, Joh 5,2.* FRLANT, n.s., 41 (Göttingen: Vandenhoeck & Ruprecht, 1949).

Jeremias, Joachim

"Die Bedeutung des Fundes vom Toten Meer (3 Q 15 bestätigt Jo 5,2)." *Informationsblatt für die Gemeinden der niederdeutschen lutherischen Landeskirchen* 9 (1960) 193–94.

Jeremias, Joachim

"Die Kupferrolle von Qumran und Bethesda." In his *Abba. Studien zur neutestamentlichen Theologie und Zeitgeschichte* (Göttingen: Vandenhoeck & Ruprecht, 1966) 361–64.

Jeremias, Joachim

"Joh 6,51c–58—redaktionell?" *ZNW* 44 (1952/1953) 256–57.

Jeremias, Joachim

"Zur Geschichtlichkeit des Verhörs Jesu vor dem Hohen Rat." *ZNW* 43 (1950/1951) 145–50. Also in his *Abba. Studien zur neutestamentlichen Theologie und Zeitgeschichte* (Göttingen: Vandenhoeck & Ruprecht, 1966) 139–44.

Jeremias, Joachim

"Mc 14,9." *ZNW* 44 (1952/1953) 103–7.

Jeremias, Joachim

"An Unknown Gospel with Johannine Elements (Pap. Egerton 2)." In *New Testament Apocrypha* 1, ed. R. McL. Wilson; tr. A. J. B. Higgins, George Ogg., Richard E. Taylor, and R. McL. Wilson (Philadelphia: Westminster Press, 1963) 94–97 = "Unbekanntes Evangelium mit Johanneischen Einschlägen (Pap. Egerton 2)." In *Neutestamentliche Apokryphen* 1, ed. Edgar Hennecke and Wilhelm Schneemelcher (Tübingen: Mohr-Siebeck, 1959) 58–60.

Jeremias, Joachim

"Johanneische Literarkritik." *TBl* 20 (1941) 33–46.

Jeremias, Joachim

"Zum Logos-Problem." *ZNW* 59 (1968) 82–85.

Jervell, Jacob

"'Er kam in sein Eigentum.' Zu Joh. 1,11." *ST* 10 (1957) 14–27.

Jervell, Jacob

Imago Dei. Gen 1,26f. im Spätjudentum, in der Gnosis und in den Paulinischen Briefen, FRLANT, n.s., 58 (Göttingen: Vandenhoeck & Ruprecht, 1960).

Jocz, Jacob

"Die Juden im Johannesevangelium." *Judaica* 9 (1953) 129–42.

Johansson, Nils

"Parakletoi. Vorstellungen von Fürsprechern für die Menschen vor Gott in der alttestamentlichen Religion, im Spätjudentum und Urchristentum." Dissertation (Lund: C. W. K. Gleerup, 1940).

Johnson, A. F.

"A Stylistic Trait of the Fourth Gospel in the *Pericope Adulterae?*" *Bulletin of the Evangelical Theological Society* 9 (1966) 91–96.

Johnson, A. M.

"The Cultural Context of the Gospel of John." Dissertation, University of Pittsburgh, 1978.

Johnson, Daniel B.

"A Neglected Variant in Gregory 33 (John v,8)." *NTS* 18 (1971/1972) 231–32.

Johnson, Lewis

"Who Was the Beloved Disciple?" *ExpTim* 77 (1966) 157–58.

Johnson, Lewis

"The Beloved Disciple—A Reply." *ExpTim* 77 (1966) 380.

Johnson, N. E.

"The Beloved Disciple and the Fourth Gospel." *CQR* 167 (1966) 278–91.

Johnson, Thomas Floyd

"The Antitheses of the Elders: A Study of the Dualistic Language of the Johannine Epistles." Dissertation, Duke University, 1980 [DissAbstr 80–08189].

Johnston, Edwin D.

"The Johannine Version of the Feedings of the Five Thousand—an Independent Tradition?" *NTS* 8 (1961/1962) 151–54.

Johnston, Edwin D.

"A Reexamination of the Relation of the Fourth Gospel to the Synoptics." Dissertation, Louisville, 1955.

Johnston, George

"The Spirit-Paraclete in the Gospel of John." *Pittsburgh Perspective* 9 (1968) 29–37.

Johnston, George

The Spirit-Paraclete in the Gospel of John, NovTSup 12 (New York and London: Cambridge University Press, 1970).

Jonas, Hans

Gnosis und spätantiker Geist, 2 vols. Vol. 1, *Die Mythologische Gnosis,* FRLANT, n.s., 33 (Göttingen: Vandenhoeck & Ruprecht, 1934); Vol. 2, *Von der*

Mythologie zur mystischen Philosophie, FRLANT, n.s., 45 (Göttingen: Vandenhoeck & Ruprecht, 1954).

Jong, K. H. E. de
"Joh 9, 2 und die Seelenwanderung." *ARW* 7 (1904) 518–19.

Jonge, Heik Jan de
"Caro in spiritum." In *De Geest in het geding. Opstellen aangeboden aan J. A. Oosterbaan ter gelegenheid van zijn afscheid als hoogleraar,* ed. I. B. Horst et al. (Alphen/Rijn: Willinck, 1978) 145–68.

Jonge, Marinus de
"Signs and Works in the Fourth Gospel." In *Miscellanea Neotestamentica,* ed. T. Baarda, A. F. J. Klijn, and W. C. van Unnik, 2 vols. NovTSup 47 and 48 (Leiden: E. J. Brill, 1978) 2: 107–27.

Jonge, Marinus de
"Jesus as Prophet and King in the Fourth Gospel." *ETL* 49 (1973) 160–77.

Jonge, Marinus de
"Nicodemus and Jesus: Some Observations on Misunderstanding and Understanding in the Fourth Gospel." *BJRL* 53 (1971) 337–59.

Jonge, Marinus de
"Son of God and Children of God in the Fourth Gospel." In *Saved by Hope. Essays in Honor of Richard C. Oudersluys,* ed. J. I. Cook (Grand Rapids: Wm. B. Eerdmans, 1978).

Jonge, Marinus de
"The Beloved Disciple and the Date of the Gospel of John." In *Text and Interpretation. Studies in the New Testament presented to Matthew Black,* ed. E. Best and R. McL. Wilson (New York and London: Cambridge University Press, 1979) 99–114.

Jonge, Marinus de
Jesus: Stranger from Heaven and Son of God. Jesus Christ and the Christians in Johannine Perspective, tr. J. E. Steeley. SBLSBS 11 (Missoula: Scholars Press, 1977).

Jonge, Marinus de and Adam Simon van den Woude
"11Q Melchizedek and the New Testament." *NTS* 12 (1965/1966) 301–26.

Jonge, Marinus de and Jan-A. Bühner
"Johanneische studies." *NorTT* 32 (1978) 318–30.

Jörns, K. P.
"Die johanneischen 'Ich-bin'-Worte." *Deutsches Pfarrerblatt* 71 (1971) 741–44, 782–84.

Jost, Wilhelm
"Poimen" Das Bild vom Hirten in der biblischen Überlieferung und seine christologische Bedeutung (Giessen: Kindt, 1939).

Joubert, H. L. N.
"'The Holy One of God' (John 6:69)." *Neot* 2 (1968) 57–69.

Joüon, Paul
"L'Agneau de Dieu (Jean I, 29)." *NRT* 67 (1940–1945) 318–21.

Joüon, Paul
"Notes philologiques sur les évangiles." *RSR* 18 (1928) 358.

Juechen, Aurel von
Jesus und Pilatus. Eine Untersuchung über das Verhältnis von Gottesreich und Weltreich im Anschluss an Johannes 18, v. 28–19, v. 16, Theologische Existenz Heute 76 (Munich: Evangelischer Verlag A. Lempp, 1941; reprint Munich: Chr. Kaiser Verlag, 1980).

Jülicher, Adolf and Erich Fascher
Einleitung in das Neue Testament (Tübingen: Mohr-Siebeck, ⁷1931).

Junker, H.
"Die Auferstehung und das ewige Leben." *Evangelische Erziehung* 16 (1964) 330–33.

Kahn, C. H.
"Stoic Logic and Stoic Logos." *Archiv für Geschichte der Philosophie* 51 (1969) 158–72.

Kalitsunakis, J.
Grammatik der neugriechischen Volkssprache (Berlin: Walter de Gruyter, 1963).

Kallas, J. G.
"John and the Synoptics—A Discussion of Some of the Differences between them." Dissertation, University of Southern California, 1968.

Kammerstätter, J.
"Zur Struktur des Johannesevangeliums." Dissertation, Vienna, 1970.

Kanavalli, P. S.
"The Concept of Logos in the Writings of John and Justin." Dissertation, Munich, 1969.

Käsemann, Ernst
"Der gegenwärtige Stand der johanneischen Frage." *Preisarbeit der Hochwürdigen Evangelisch-Theologischen Fakultät der Universität Tübingen.* 1925.

Käsemann, Ernst
"Zur Johannesinterpretation in England." In his *Exegetische Versuche und Besinnungen* (Göttingen: Vandenhoeck & Ruprecht, 1964) 2: 131–55.

Käsemann, Ernst
The Testament of Jesus: A Study of the Gospel of John in the Light of Chapter 17, tr. Gerhard Krodel (Philadelphia: Fortress Press, 1968) = *Jesu letzter Wille nach Johannes 17* (Tübingen: Mohr-Siebeck, 1966).

Käsemann, Ernst
"Aufbau und Anliegen des johanneischen Prologs." In *Libertas Christiana, Friedrich Delekat zum fünfundsechzigsten Geburtstag,* ed. W. Matthias and E. Wolf. BEvT 26 (Munich: Chr. Kaiser Verlag, 1957) 75–99. Also in Käsemann's *Exegetische Versuche und Besinnungen* (Göttingen: Vandenhoeck & Ruprecht, 1964) 2: 155–80.

Käsemann, Ernst
"Ketzer und Zeuge." *ZTK* 48 (1951) 292–311. In Ernst Käsemann, *Exegetische Versuche und Besinnungen* 1 (Göttingen: Vandenhoeck & Ruprecht, 1960) 168–87.

Kasser, Rudolphe
L'évangile selon S. Jean et les versions coptes de la Bible, Bibliothèque théologique (Neuchâtel: Delachaux &

Niestlé, 1966).

Kassing, Altfrid
"Das Evangelium der Fusswaschung." *Erbe und Auftrag* 36 (1960) 83–93.

Keck, Leander E.
"John the Baptist in Christianized Gnosticism." In *Initiation*, ed. C. J. Bleeker (Leiden: E. J. Brill, 1965) 184–94.

Keferstein, Friedrich
Philos Lehre von den göttlichen Mittelwesen. Zugleich eine kurze Darstellung der Grundzüge des philonischen Systems (Leipzig: W. Jurany, 1846).

Kegel, Günter
Auferstehung Jesu—Auferstehung der Toten. Eine traditionsgeschichtliche Untersuchung zum Neuen Testament (Gütersloh: Gerd Mohn, 1970).

Kehl, M.
"Der Mensch in der Geschichte Gottes. Zum Johannesprolog 6–8." *Geist und Leben* 40 (1967) 404–9.

Kelly, John
"What Did Christ Mean by the Sign of Love?" *African Ecclesiastical Review* 13 (1971) 113–21.

Kemp, I. S.
"'The Light of Men' in the Prologue of John's Gospel." *Indian Journal of Theology* 15 (1966) 154–64.

Kennard, J. Spencer, Jr.
"The Burial of Jesus." *JBL* 74 (1955) 227–38.

Keppler, Paul Wilhelm von
Unseres Herrn Trost. Erklärung der Abschiedsreden und des Hohepriesterlichen Gebetes Jesu (Joh c. 14–17) (Freiburg: Herder, 1887, ³1914).

Kern, Walter
"Der symmetrische Gesamtaufbau von Jo 8, 12–58." *ZKT* 78 (1956) 451–54.

Kiefer, Otto
Die Hirtenrede: Analyse und Deutung von Joh 10, 1–18 (Stuttgart: Katholisches Bibelwerk, 1967).

Kiefer, Otto
"Le seul troupeau et le seul Pasteur: Jésus et les siens, Jn 10, 1–18." *AsSeign* 25 (1969) 46–61.

Kieffer, René
Au delà des recensions? L'évolution de la tradition textuelle dans Jean VI, 52–71, ConBNT 3 (Lund: C. W. K. Gleerup, 1968).

Kierkegaard, Sören
Die Tagebücher, ed. and tr. Hayo Gerdes (Düsseldorf: E. Diederich, 1962) 104.

Kilmartin, Edward J.
"Liturgical Influence on John VI." *CBQ* 22 (1960) 183–91.

Kilmartin, Edward J.
"The Formation of the Bread of Life Discourse (John 6)." *Scr* 12 (1960) 75–78.

Kilpatrick, George Dunbar
"John iv,41: *pleion* or *pleious*?" *NovT* 18 (1976) 131–32.

Kilpatrick, George Dunbar

"John 4:9." *JBL* 87 (1968) 327–28.

Kilpatrick, George Dunbar
"Jn IV,51: παῖς or υἱός?" *JTS*, n.s., 14 (1963) 393.

Kilpatrick, George Dunbar
"Some Notes on Johannine Usage." *BT* 2 (1960) 173–77.

Kilpatrick, George Dunbar
"The Punctuation of John 7, 37–38." *JTS*, n.s., 11 (1960) 340–42.

Kilpatrick, George Dunbar
"What John Tells About John." In *Studies in John Presented to Professor J. N. Sevenster on the Occasion of his Seventhieth Birthday* (Leiden: E. J. Brill, 1970) 75–87.

Kim Pyung-Hak, R.
"Lebendiges Wasser und Sakramentssymbolik." Dissertation, Rome, 1969/1970.

King, J. S.
"The Prologue to the Fourth Gospel: Some Unsolved Problems." *ExpTim* 86 (1975) 372–75.

King, J. S.
"Sychar and Calvary: A Neglected Theory in the Interpretation of the Fourth Gospel [Jn 4]." *Theology* 77 (1974) 417–22.

Kipp, John Lewis
"The Relationship between the Conception of the 'Holy Spirit' and the 'Risen Christ' in the Fourth Gospel." Dissertation, Princeton Theological Seminary, 1964.

Kittel, Gerhard
"Die Wirkungen des christlichen Abendmahls nach dem Neuen Testament." *TSK* 96/97 (1925) 214–37.

Kittel, Gerhard
"῾Υψωθῆναι = gekreuzigt werden." *ZNW* 35 (1936) 282–85.

Kittel, Rudolf
"Zur Eschatologie des Johannesevangeliums." *Deutsches Pfarrerblatt* 65 (1965) 716–20.

Kittlaus, Lloyd R.
"Evidence from Jn 12 that the Author of John knew the Gospel of Mark." In *SBL 1979 Seminar Papers* 1, SBLASP 16 (Missoula: Scholars Press, 1979) 119–22.

Kittlaus, Lloyd R.
"John and Mark: A Methodological Evaluation of N. Perrin's Suggestion." In *SBL 1978 Seminar Papers* 2, SBLASP 15 (Missoula: Scholars Press 1978) 269–79.

Kittlaus, Lloyd R.
"The Fourth Gospel and Mark: John's Use of Markan Redaction and Composition." Dissertation, Chicago, 1978.

Klein, Franz-Norbert
"Die Lichtterminologie bei Philon von Alex. und in den hermetischen Schriften." Dissertation, Leiden, 1962.

Klein, Günter
"'Das wahre Licht scheint schon.' Beobachtungen

zur Zeit- und Geschichtserfahrung einer urchristlichen Schule." *ZTK* 68 (1971) 261–326.

Klein, Günter
"Die Verleugnung des Petrus. Eine traditionsgeschichtliche Untersuchung." *ZTK* 58 (1961)
285–328.

Klein, Hans
"Die lukanisch-johanneische Passionstradition."
ZNW 67 (1976) 155–86.

Kleinknecht, Hermann
"Logos." *TDNT* 4: 77–91.

Kleist, James A.
"A Note on the Greek Text of St. John 12,7."
Classic Journal 21 (1925) 46–48.

Klijn, A. J. F.
"John 14,22 and the Name Judas Thomas." In
*Studies in John. Presented to Professor J. N. Sevenster
on the Occasion of his Seventieth Birthday* (Leiden: E. J.
Brill, 1970) 88–96.

Kling, Prof.
"Zur neuesten apologetischen Literatur." *TSK* 19
(1846) 949–1028.

Klöpper, Albert
"Das 21. Capitel des 4. Evangeliums." *ZWT* 42
(1899) 337–81.

Klos, Herbert
*Die Sakramente im Johannesevangelium. Vorkommen
und Bedeutung von Taufe, Eucharistie und Buße im
vierten Evangelium,* SBS 46 (Stuttgart: Katholisches
Bibelwerk, 1970).

Knight, George A. F.
"Antisemitism in the Fourth Gospel." *Reformed
Theological Review* 27 (1968) 81–88.

Knox, Wilfred L.
"John 13. 1–10." *HTR* 43 (1950) 161–63.

Koehler, Theodore
"The Sacramental Theory in Joh 19,1–27."
University of Dayton Review 5 (1968) 49–58.

Koehler, Theodore
"Les principales interprétations traditionnelles de
Jn 19,25–27 pendant les douze premiers siècles."
Etudes Mariales 26 (1968) 119–55.

Kohlbrügge, Hermann Friedrich
Der Herr der Erde. Eine Auslegung von Johannes 21
(Berlin: Furche-Verlag, 1937).

Köhler, H.
*Von der Welt zum Himmelreich oder die johanneische
Darstellung des Werkes Jesu Christi synoptisch geprüft
und ergänzt* (Halle: M. Niemeyer, 1892).

Kohler, Mere
"Des fleuves d'eau vive. Exégèse de Jean 7, 37–39."
RTP 10 (1960) 188–201.

Kölbing, F. W.
"Biblische Erörterungen: Ueber Joh 13,34.35."
TSK 18 (1845) 685–96.

Kolenkow, Anitra Bingham
"The Changing Patterns: Conflicts and the Necessity of Death: John 2 and 12 and Markan Parallels." In *SBL 1979 Seminar Papers* 1, SBLASP 16

(Missoula: Scholars Press, 1979) 123–25.

Kopp, Klemens
Das Kana des Evangeliums. Palästinahefte des
deutschen Vereins vom Heiligen Lande 28 (Köln:
Bachem, 1940).

Kopp, Klemens
Die heiligen Stätten der Evangelien (Regensburg: F.
Pustet, 1959).

Korteweg, T.
"The Reality of the Invisible. Some Remarks on St.
John 14,8 and Greek Philosophic Tradition." In
Studies in Hellenistic Religions, ed. M. J. Vermaseren.
Etudes préliminaires aux religions orientales dans
l'empire romain 78 (Leiden: E. J. Brill, 1979) 50–
102.

Koschorke, Klaus
"Eine gnostische Paraphrase des johanneischen
Prologs." *VC* 33 (1979) 383–92.

Kossen, H. B.
"Who were the Greeks of John 12,20?" In *Studies in
John Presented to J. N. Sevenster on the Occasion of his
Seventieth Birthday* (Leiden: E. J. Brill, 1970) 97–
110.

Köster, Helmut
"Geschichte und Kultus im Johannesevangelium
und bei Ignatius von Antiochien." *ZTK* 54 (1957)
56–69.

Köster, Helmut
"Dialog und Spruchüberlieferung in den
gnostischen Texten von Nag Hammadi." *EvT* 39
(1979) 532–56.

Köster, Helmut
"Apocryphal and Canonical Gospels." *HTR* 73
(1980) 105–30.

Köster, Helmut
"Gnostic Writings as Witnesses for the Development of the Sayings Tradition." In *The Rediscovery
of Gnosticism,* Vol. 1, *The School of Valentinus,* ed.
Bentley Layton. Studies in the History of Religions
[Supplements to *Numen*] 41 (Leiden: (E. J. Brill,
1980) 238–61.

Köstlin, Karl Reinhold
*Der Lehrbegriff des Evangeliums und der Briefe
Johannis* (Berlin: G. Bethge, 1853).

Kothgasser, Alois M.
"Die Lehr-, Erinnerungs-, Bezeugungs- und Einführungsfunktion des johanneischen Geist-Parakleten gegenüber der Christus-Offenbarung."
Salesianum 33 (1971) 557–98; 34 (1972) 3–51.

Kothgasser, Alois M.
"Das Problem der Dogmenentwicklung und die
Lehrfunktion des johanneischen Parakleten."
Dissertation, Rome, 1968.

Kraeling, Carl H.
John the Baptist (New York and London: Charles
Scribner's Sons, 1951).

Kraeling, Carl H.
"The Fourth Gospel and Contemporary Religious
Thought." *JBL* 49 (1930) 140–59.

Kraft, Heinz
"Untersuchungen zu den Gemeinschafts- und
Lebensformen häretischer christlicher Gnosis des
2. Jahrhunderts." Dissertation, Heidelberg, 1950.

Kragerud, Alo
Der Lieblingsjünger im Johannesevangelium (Oslo:
Universitätsverlag, 1959).

Krebs, Engelbert Gustav Hans
*Der Logos als Heiland im ersten Jahrhundert; ein
religions- und dogmengeschichtlicher Beitrag zur Erlö-
sungslehre. Mit einem Anhang: Poimandres und
Johannes; kritisches Referat über Reitzensteins religionsgeschichtliche Logosstudien* (Freiburg: Herder, 1910).

Kremer, Jacob
"Jesu Verheissung des Geistes—Zur Verankerung
der Aussage von Joh 16,13 im Leben Jesu." In *Die
Kirche des Anfangs. Festschrift für Heinz Schürmann
zum 65. Geburtstag*, ed. R. Schnackenburg, J. Ernst
and J. Wanke. Erfurter Theologische Studien 38
(Leipzig: St. Benno; Freiburg: Herder, 1977) 246–
76.

Krenkel, Max
"Joseph von Arimathäa und Nikodemus." *ZWT* 8
(1865) 438–45.

Kretschmar, Georg
"Kreuz und Auferstehung Jesu Christi. Das
Zeugnis der Heiligen Stätten." *Erbe und Auftrag* 54
(1978) 423–31; 55 (1979) 12–26.

Kreyenbühl, Johannes
*Das Evangelium der Wahrheit. Neue Lösung der
johanneischen Frage*, 2 vols. (Berlin: C. A.
Schwetschke & Sohn, 1900–1905).

Krieger, Norbert
"Fiktive Orte der Johannestaufe." *ZNW* 45 (1954)
121–23.

Krieger, Norbert
"Der Knecht des Hohenpriesters." *NovT* 2 (1957)
73–74.

Kruijf, T. C. de
"The Glory of the Only Son." In *Studies in John.
Presented to Professor J. N. Sevenster on the Occasion of
his Seventieth Birthday* (Leiden: E. J. Brill, 1970)
111–23.

Kruijf, Theo C. de
"Messias Jezus en Jezus Christus." *Theologie en
Pastoraat* 63 (1967) 372–78.

Kruijf, Theo C. de
"'Hold the Faith' or, 'Come to Believe'? A Note on
John 20,31." *Bijdragen. Tijdschrift voor philosophie en
theologie* 36 (1975) 439–49.

Krummacher, E. W.
"Bezieht sich Joh 3,5 auf die heilige Taufe?." *TSK*
31 (1859) 507–11.

Kruse, Heinz
"Magni Pisces Centum Quinquaginta Tres (Jo
21,11)." *VD* 38 (1960) 129–48.

Küchler, Max
*Frühjüdische Weisheitstraditionen. Zum Fortgang
weisheitlichen Denkens im Bereich des frühjüdischen*

Jahweglaubens, OBO 26 (Fribourg: Universitätsverlag; Göttingen: Vandenhoeck & Ruprecht,
1979).

Kugelman, Richard
"The Gospel for Pentecost [John 14:23–31]." *CBQ*
6 (1944) 259–75.

Kuhl, Josef
*Die Sendung Jesu Christi und der Kirche nach dem
Johannesevangelium* (Siegburg: Steyler, 1967).

Kuhli, Horst
"Nathanael—'wahrer Israelit'? Zum angeblich
attributiven Gebrauch von ἀληθῶς in Joh 1,47."
Biblische Notizen 9 (1979) 11–19.

Kuhn, K. H.
"St. John 7, 37–38." *NTS* 4 (1957/1958) 63–65.

Kuhn, Karl G.
"The Two Messiahs of Aaron and Israel." In *The
Scrolls and the New Testament*, ed. K. Stendahl (New
York: Harper & Brothers, 1957) 54–64.

Kühne, W.
"Eine kritische Studie zu Joh 12,7." *TSK* 98/99
(1926) 476–77.

Kümmel, Werner Georg
"Die Eschatologie der Evangelien. Ihre Geschichte
und ihr Sinn." *Theologische Bücherei* 5 (1936) 225–
41.

Kümmel, Werner Georg
*Die Theologie des Neuen Testaments nach seinen
Hauptzeugen Jesu—Paulus—Johannes*, Grundisse
zum NT, NTD Ergänzungsreihe 3 (Göttingen:
Vandenhoeck & Ruprecht, 1969) 227–85.

Kümmel, Werner Georg
*The New Testament: The History of the Investigation of
its Problems*, tr. S. McLean Gilmour and Howard C.
Kee (Nashville: Abingdon Press, 1972) = *Das Neue
Testament; Geschichte der Erforschung seiner Probleme*
(Freiburg: K. Alber, 1958).

Kundsin, Karl
"Zur Diskussion über die Ego-Eimi-Sprüche des
Johannesevangeliums." In [Festschrift J. Köpp]
(Stockholm, 1954) 95–107.

Kundsin, Karl
*Topologische Überlieferungsstück im Johannes-Evange-
lium*, FRLANT, n.s., 22 (Göttingen: Vandenhoeck
& Ruprecht, 1925).

Kundsin, Karl
"Die Wiederkunft Jesu in den Abschiedsreden des
Johannesevangeliums." *ZNW* 33 (1934) 210–15.

Kundsin, Karl
Charakter und Ursprung der johanneischen Reden
(Riga, 1939).

Kunniburgh, E.
"The Johannine 'Son of Man.'" *SE* 4 = TU 102
(Berlin: Akademie-Verlag, 1968) 64–71.

Kurfess, A.
"Ἐκάθισεν ἐπὶ Βήματος (Joh 19,13)." *Bib* 34 (1953)
271.

Kürzinger, Josef
"Papias von Hierapolis: Zu Titel und Art seines

Werkes." *BZ* 23 (1979) 172–86.

Kuyper, Lester J.
"Grace and Truth. An Old Testament Description of God, and its Use in the Johannine Gospel." *Int* 18 (1964) 3–19.

Kuzenzama, K. P. M.
"La préhistoire de l'expression 'pain de vie' (Jn 6,35b.48)." *Revue Africaine de Théologie* 4 (1980) 65–83.

Kypke, Georg David
Observationes sacrae in Novi Foederis libros ex auctoribus potissimum graecis et antiquitatibus, 2 vols. (Breslau: Korn, 1755).

Kysar, Robert
The Fourth Evangelist and his Gospel: An Examination of Contemporary Scholarship (Minneapolis: Augsburg, 1975).

Kysar, Robert
"The Background of the Prologue of the Fourth Gospel. A Critique of Historical Methods." *CJT* 16 (1970) 250–55.

Kysar, Robert
"A Comparison of the Exegetical Presuppositions and Methods of C. H. Dodd and R. Bultmann in the Interpretation of the Prologue of the Fourth Gospel." Dissertation, Northwestern University, 1967.

Kysar, Robert
"Rudolf Bultmann's Interpretation of the Concept of Creation in John 1,3–4. A Study in Exegetical Method." *CBQ* 32 (1970) 77–85.

Kysar, Robert
"Christology and Controversy: The Contributions of the Prologue of the Gospel of John to New Testament Christology and their Historical Setting." *CurTM* 5 (1978) 348–64.

Kysar, Robert
"The Eschatology of the Fourth Gospel—A Correction of Bultmann's Hypothesis." *Perspective* 13 (1972) 23–33.

Kysar, Robert
"Community and Gospel: Vectors in Fourth Gospel Criticism." *Int* 31 (1977) 355–66.

Kysar, Robert
"The Source Analysis of the Fourth Gospel—A Growing Consensus?" *NovT* 15 (1973) 134–52.

Lacan, M. F.
"L'oeuvre du Verbe incarné: le don de la vie." *RSR* 45 (1957) 61–78.

Lacomara, Aelved
"Deuteronomy and the Farewell Discourse (Jn 13:31–16:33)." *CBQ* 36 (1974) 65–84.

Làconi, M.
"La critica letteraria applicata al IV Vangelo." *Ang* 40 (1963) 277–312.

Lagrange, Marie-Joseph
Review of "Les plus anciens prologues latins des Evangiles," by Donatien De Bruyne. *RB* 38 (1929) 115–21.

Lagrange, Marie-Joseph
"Vers le logos de saint Jean." *RB* 32 (1923) 161–84, 321–71.

Lamarche, P.
"Le Prologue de Jean." *RSR* 52 (1964) 497–537.

Langbrandtner, Wolfgang
Weltferner Gott oder Gott der Liebe. Der Ketzerstreit in der johanneischen kirche. Eine exegetisch- religionsgeschichtliche Untersuchung mit Berücksichtigung der koptisch-gnostischen Texte aus Nag-Hammadi, Beiträge zur biblischen Exegese und Theologie 6 (Frankfurt: P. Lang, 1977).

Langkammer, H.
"Zur Herkunft des Logostitels im Johannesprolog." *BZ* 9 (1965) 91–94.

Langkammer, Hugolinus
"Christ's 'Last Will and Testament' (Jn 19,26.27) in the Interpretation of the Fathers of the Church and the Scholastics." *Antonianum* 43 (1968) 9–109.

Larfeld, Wilhelm
Die beiden Johannes von Ephesus, der Apostel und der Presbyter, der Lehrer und der Schüler; ein Beitrag zur Erklärung des Papiasfragmentes bei Eusebius (Munich: C. H. Beck, 1914).

Larfeld, Wilhelm
"Das Zeugnis des Papias über die beiden Johannes von Ephesus." In *Johannes und sein Evangelium,* ed. K. H. Rengstorf (Darmstadt: Wissenschaftliche Buchgesellschaft, 1973) 381–401.

La Roche, S.
"Versuch einer Erklärung der Stelle Joh 14,1.2." *TSK* 3 (1830) 114–18.

Lasic, H.
"Recherches sur la notion de vie chez saint Jean et les influences sur lui." Dissertation, Fribourg, 1970.

Lategan, B. C.
"The truth that sets man free. John 8:31–36." *Neot* 2 (1968) 70–80.

Lattey, Cuthbert
"The Semitisms of the Fourth Gospel." *JTS* 20 (1918/1919) 330–36.

Lattke, Michael
Einheit im Wort. Die spezifische Bedeutung von 'agape,' 'agapan' und 'philein' im Johannesevangelium, SANT 41 (Munich: Kösel, 1975).

Lattke, Michael
"Sammlung durch das Wort. Erlöser, Erlösung, und Erlöste im Johannesevangelium." *BK* 30 (1975) 118–22.

Laurentin, André
"We'attah—καὶ νῦν, Formule caractéristique des textes juridiques et liturgiques (à propos de Jean 17,5)." *Bib* 45 (1964) 168–97, 413–32.

Lazure, N.
"Le lavement des pieds (Jn 13,1–15)." *AsSeign* 38 (1967) 40–50.

Lazure, N.
"Louange au Fils de l'homme et commandement

nouveau. Jn 13,31–33a. 34–35." *AsSeign* 26 (1973) 73–80.

Lazure, N.
Les valeurs morales de la théologie johannique (Evangiles et Epîtres), Etudes bibliques (Paris: J. Gabalda, 1965).

LeDéaut, Roger
"Une aggadah targumique et les 'murmures' de Jean 6." *Bib* 51 (1970) 80–83.

LeFort, Pierre
Les structures de l'église militante selon saint Jean. Etude d'ecclésiologie concrète appliquée au IVe évangile et aux épîtres johanniques, Nouvelle Série Théologique 25 (Geneva: Labor & Fides, 1970).

Leal, Juan
"Exegesis catholica de Agno Dei in ultimis viginti et quinque annis." *VD* 28 (1950) 98–109.

Leal, Juan
"De realitate eucharistia panis vitae." *VD* 31 (1953) 144ff.

Leal, Juan
"Spiritus et caro in Joh 6,64." *VD* 30 (1952) 257ff.

Leaney, Alfred Robert Clare
"The Historical Background and Theological Meaning of the Paraclete." *Duke Divinity School Review* 37 (1972) 146–59.

Leaney, Alfred Robert Clare
"The Johannine Paraclete and the Qumran Scrolls." In *John and Qumran,* ed. J. H. Charlesworth (London: Chapman, 1972) 38–61.

Leanza, Sandro
"Testimonianze della tradizione indiretta su alcuni passi del Nuovo Testamento (Giov VII, 37–38 e altri passi)." *RivB* 15 (1967) 407–18.

Lebram, Jürgen Christian
"Der Aufbau der Areopagrede." *ZNW* 55 (1964) 221–43.

Lebram, Jürgen Christian
"Die Theologie der späten Chokma und des häretischen Judentums." *ZAW* 77 (1965) 202–11.

Lechler, G. V.
Review of *Ueber die Echtheit des johanneischen Evangeliums,* by Niermeyer, Mayer, and Schneider. *TSK* 29 (1856) 867–911.

Lee, Edwin Kenneth
"St. Mark and the Fourth Gospel." *NTS* 3 (1956/1957) 50–58.

Lee, Edwin Kenneth
The Religious Thought of St. John (London: S. P. C. K., 1950).

Lee, Edwin Kenneth
"St. Mark and the Fourth Gospel." *NTS* 3 (1956/1957) 50–58.

Lee, G. M.
"New Testament Gleanings." *Bib* 51 (1970) 235–40.

Lee, G. M.
"John 15,14: 'Ye are my friends.'" *NovT* 15 (1973) 260.

Lee, G. M.
"Presbyters and Apostles." *ZNW* 62 (1971) 122.

Lee, G. M.
"Joh xxi,20–23." *JTS,* n.s., 1 (1950) 62–63.

Lee, G. M.
"Eusebius, H. E. 3,39.4." *Bib* 53 (1972) 412.

Leenhardt, F.-J.
"La structure du chapitre 6 de l'évangile de Jean." *RHPR* 39 (1959) 1–13.

Leenhardt, Franz Johan
"Abraham et la conversion de Saul de Tarse, suivi d'une note sur 'Abraham dans Jean VIII.'" *RHPR* 53 (1973) 331–51.

Legault, André
"An Application of the Form-Critique Method to the Anointings in Galilee (Lk. 7,36–50) and Bethany (Mt. 26,6–13; Mk. 14,3–9; Jn 12,1–8)." *CBQ* 16 (1954) 131–45.

Leidig, E.
"Jesu Gespräch mit der Samariterin." Dissertation, Basel, 1980.

Leipoldt, J.
"Johannesevangelium und Gnosis." In *Neutestamentliche Studien Georg Heinrici zu seinem 70. Geburtstag (14 März 1914) dargebracht von Fachgenossen, Freunden und Schülern,* UNT 6 (Leipzig: J. C. Hinrichs, 1914) 140ff.

Leisegang, Hans
"Logos." PW 13.1 (1926) 1035–81.

Leistner, Reinhold
Antijudaismus im Johannesevangelium? Darstellung des Problems in der neueren Auslegungsgeschichte und Untersuchung der Leidensgeschichte, Theologie und Wirklichkeit 3 (Bern: H. Lang; Frankfurt: P. Lang, 1974).

Lejoly, R.
Annotations pour une étude du papyrus 75, c'est-à-dire du text grec de Jean 1–14, Bodmer XV (Dison: Editions "Concile," 1976).

Lemonnyer, Antoine
"L'onction de Béthanie (Jean 12,1–8)." *RSR* 18 (1928) 105–17.

Lentzen-Deis, Fritzleo
"Das Motiv der 'Himmelsöffnung' in verschiedenen Gattungen der Umweltsliteratur des Neuen Testaments." *Bib* 50 (1969) 301–27.

Léon-Dufour, Xavier
"Le signe du temple selon saint Jean [Jn. 2:13–22]." *RSR* 39 (1951/1952) 155–75.

Léon-Dufour, Xavier
"Le mystère du Pain de Vie (Jean 6)." *RSR* 46 (1958) 481–523.

Léon-Dufour, Xavier
"Père, fais-moi passer sain et sauf à travers cette heure!" In *Neues Testament und Geschichte. Historisches Geschehen und Deutung im Neuen Testament. Oscar Cullman zum 70. Geburtstag,* ed. H. Baltensweiler and B. Reicke (Tübingen: Mohr-Siebeck; Zurich: Theologischer Verlag, 1972) 157–66.

Léon-Dufour, Xavier
"Autour de sémeion johannique." In *Die Kirche des Anfangs. Festschrift für Heinz Schürmann zum 65. Geburtstag*, ed. R. Schnackenburg, J. Ernst and J. Wanke. Erfurter Theologische Studien 38 (Leipzig: St. Benno; Freiburg: Herder, 1970) 363–78.

Léonard, Jeanne-Marie
"Notule sur l'Evangile de Jean. Le récit des noces de Cana et Esaie 25." *ETR* 57 (1982) 119–20.

Léonard, Jeanne-Marie
"2 Rois 4 42–44 et Jean 6 1–13." *ETR* 55 (1980) 265–70.

Leroy, Herbert
"Das Weinwunder in Kana. Ein exegetische Studie zu Jo 2,1–11." *BibLeb* 4 (1963) 168–75.

Leroy, Herbert
"'. . . dass Jesus der Christus, der Sohn Gottes ist.' Eigenart und Herkunft des Johannesevangelium." *BK* 30 (1975) 114–17.

Leroy, Herbert
Rätsel und Mißverständnis. Ein Beitrag zur Formgeschichte des Johannesevangeliums, BBB 30 (Bonn: Peter Hanstein, 1968).

Leroy, Herbert
"Das johanneische Mißverständnis als literarische Form." *BibLeb* 9 (1968) 196–207.

Leroy, Herbert
"Jesusverkündigung im Johannesevangelium." In *Jesus in den Evangelien*, ed. Josef Blinzler et al. (Stuttgart: Katholisches Bibelwerk, 1970) 148–70.

Lewis, Frank Warburton
"A Certain Village—Not Bethany." *ExpTim* 32 (1920/1921) 330.

Lewis, Frank Warburton
"The Disciple whom Jesus Loved." *ExpTim* 33 (1921/22) 42.

Lewis, Frank Warburton
Disarrangements in the Fourth Gospel (Cambridge: Cambridge University Press, 1910).

Lewis, Frank Warburton
"Disarrangements in the Fourth Gospel." *ExpTim* 44 (1932/1933) 382.

Lieske, A.
Die Theologie der Logosmystik bei Origenes, Münsterische Beiträge zur Theologie 22 (Münster i.W: Aschendorff, 1938).

Lieu, Judith M.
"Gnosticism and the Gospel of John." *ExpTim* 90 (1979) 233–37.

Lightfoot, Joseph Barber
"External Evidence for the Authenticity and Genuineness of St. John's Gospel." In his *Biblical Essays* (London: Macmillan, 1904) 47–122.

Lindars, Barnabas
"New Books on John." *Theology* 72 (1969) 153–58.

Lindars, Barnabas
"The Son of Man in the Johannine Christology." In *Christ and Spirit in the New Testament* [Festschrift for C. F. D. Moule], ed. B. Lindars and S. S. Smalley (Cambridge: Cambridge University Press, 1970) 43–60.

Lindars, Barnabas
"Two Parables in John." *NTS* 16 (1969/1970) 318–29.

Lindars, Barnabas
"Word and Sacrament in the Fourth Gospel." *SJT* 29 (1976) 49–64.

Lindars, Barnabas
"Δικαιοσύνη in Jn 16,8 and 10." In *Mélanges bibliques en hommage au R. P. Béda Rigaux*, ed. A. Descamps and A. De Halleux (Gembloux: Duculot, 1970) 275–86.

Lindars, Barnabas
"The Passion in the Fourth Gospel." In *God's Christ and His People. Studies in Honour of Nils Alstrup Dahl*, ed. Jacob Jervell and Wayne A. Meeks (Oslo: Universitetsforlaget, 1977) 71–86.

Lindars, Barnabas
"The Composition of John xx." *NTS* 7 (1960/1961) 142–47.

Lindars, Barnabas
Behind the Fourth Gospel, Studies in Creative Criticism 3 (London: S. P. C. K., 1971).

Lindars, Barnabas
"Traditions Behind the Fourth Gospel." In *L'Evangile de Jean. Sources, rédaction, théologie*, ed. M. de Jonge. BETL 44 (Gembloux: Duculot; Louvain: University Press, 1977) 107–24.

Lindars, Barnabas and Rigaux, Beda
Témoignage de l'évangile de Jean, Pour une histoire de Jésus 5 (Paris: Desclée de Brouwer, 1974).

Lindblom, Johannes
Das ewige Leben. Eine Studie über die Entstehung der religiösen Lebensidee im Neuen Testament (Uppsala: A.-b. Akademiska bokhandeln i kommission, 1914).

Linder, Gottlieb
"Gesetz der Stoffteilung im Johannes-Evangelium." *ZWT* 40 (1897) 444–54; 42 (1899) 32–35.

Lindijer, C. H.
De sacramenten in het Vierde Evangelie (Haarlem: Bohn, 1964).

Linnemann, Eta
"Die Hochzeit zu Kana und Dionysios oder das Unzureichende der Kategorien." *NTS* 20 (1973/1974) 408–18.

Linnemann, Eta
"Jesus und der Täufer." In *Festschrift für Ernst Fuchs*, ed. G. Ebeling et al. (Tübingen: Mohr-Siebeck, 1973) 219–36.

Linnemann, Eta
"Die Verleugnung des Petrus." *ZTK* 63 (1966) 1–32.

Linton, Olaf
"Johannesevangeliet og eskatologien." *SEÅ* 22–23 (1957/1958) 98–110.

Ljungvik, Herman
"Aus der Sprache des Neuen Testaments. Einige Fälle von Ellipse oder Brachylogie." *ErJb* 66 (1968) 24–51.

Lloyd-Jones, David Martyn
The Basis of Christian Unity. An Exposition of John 17 and Ephesians 4 (London: Inter-Varsity Press, 1962; Grand Rapids: Wm. B. Eerdmans, 1963).

Locher, Gottfried W.
"Der Geist als Paraklet. Eine exegetisch-dogmatische Besinnung." *EvT* 26 (1966) 565–79.

Loewe, R.
"'Salvation' is Not for the Jews." *JTS,* n.s., 32 (1981) 341–68.

Loewenich, Walther von
"Johanneisches Denken. Ein Beitrag zur Erkenntnis der johanneischen Eigenart." *TBl* 15 (1936) 260–75.

Loewenich, Walther von
Das Johannesverständnis im zweiten Jahrhundert (Giessen: A. Töpelmann, 1932).

Lofthouse, William Frederick
"The Holy Spirit in the Acts and the Fourth Gospel." *ExpTim* 52 (1940/1941) 334–36.

Lofthouse, William Frederick
The Disciple whom Jesus Loved (London: Epworth, 1934).

Lohfink, Gerhard
"Kein Wunder in Nazareth." *Katechetische Blätter* 102 (1977) 699–700.

Lohmeyer, Ernst
Das Urchristentum. Vol. 1, *Johannes der Täufer* (Göttingen: Vandenhoeck & Ruprecht, 1932) 26–31.

Lohmeyer, Ernst
"Über Aufbau und Gliederung des vierten Evangeliums." *ZNW* 27 (1928) 11–36.

Lohmeyer, Ernst
Christuskult und Kaiserkult, Sammlung gemeinverständlicher Vorträge und Schriften aus dem Gebiet der Theologie und Religionsgeschichte 90 (Tübingen: Mohr-Siebeck, 1919).

Lohmeyer, Ernst
"Die Fusswaschung." *ZNW* 38 (1939) 74–94.

Lohse, Eduard
"Jesu Worte über den Sabbat." In his *Die Einheit des Neuen Testaments. Exegetische Studien zur Theologie des Neuen Testaments* (Göttingen: Vandenhoeck & Ruprecht, 1973) 62–72.

Lohse, Eduard
"Wort und Sakrament im Johannesevangelium." *NTS* 7 (1960/1961) 110–25.

Lohse, Eduard
Grundriss der neutestamentlichen Theologie, Theologische Wissenschaft 5 (Stuttgart: W. Kohlhammer, 1974) 29–34.

Lohse, Wolfram
"Die Fusswaschung (Joh 13,1–20). Eine Geschichte ihrer Deutung." Dissertation, Erlangen, 1966/1967.

Loisy, Alfred
"Le prologue du quatrième évangile." *Revue d'histoire et de littérature religieuses* 1 (1897) 43ff.

Loisy, Alfred
Le mandéisme et les origines chrétiennes (Paris: E. Nourry, 1934).

Loman, Abraham Dirk
Bijdragen ter inleiding op de Johanneische schriften des NTs. Iste stuk: Het getuigenis aangaande Johannes in het Fragment van Muratori (Amsterdam: Loman & Verster, 1865).

Loman, Abraham Dirk
"De bouw van het vierde Evangelie." *TT* 11 (1877) 371–437.

Lona, Horacio E.
Abraham in Johannes 8. Ein Beitrag zur Methodenfrage, Europäische Hochschulschriften, Series 22; Theologie 65 (Bern: H. Lang; Frankfurt: P. Lang, 1976).

Long, A. A., ed.
Problems in Stoicism (London: University of London, The Athlone Press, 1971).

Lorenzen, Thorwald
"Johannes 21." Dissertation, Zurich, 1970.

Lorenzen, Thorwald
Der Lieblingsjünger im Johannesevangelium. Eine redaktionsgeschichtliche Studie, SBS 55 (Stuttgart: Katholisches Bibelwerk, 1971).

Losada, Diego A.
"El relato de la pesca milagrosa." *RB* 40 (1978) 17–26.

Louw, J. P.
"Narrator of the Father—ἐξηγεῖσθαι and Related Terms in the Johannine Christology." *Neot* 2 (1968) 32–40.

Lovelady, E. J.
"The Logos-Concept of John 1,1." *Grace Journal* 4:2 (1963) 15–24.

Lowe, Malcolm
"Who were the *IOUDAIOI*?" *NovT* 18 (1976) 101–30.

Luck, Ulrich
"Die kirchliche Einheit als Problem des Johannesevangeliums." *Wort und Dienst* 10 (1969) 51–67.

Lücke, F.
"Kritik der bisherigen Untersuchungen über die Gnostiker bis auf die neuesten Forschungen darüber." *TZ* 2 (1820) 132–71.

Lussier, E.
God is Love. According to St. John (New York: Alba House, 1977).

Lütgert, Wilhelm
"Die Juden im Johannesevangelium." In *Neutestamentliche Studien Georg Heinrici zu seinem 70. Geburtstag (14 März 1914) dargebracht von Fachgenossen, Freunden und Schülern,* UNT 6 (Leipzig: J. C. Hinrichs, 1914) 147–54.

Lütgert, Wilhelm

Die johanneische Christologie (Gütersloh: C. Bertelsmann, 1899, ² 1916).

Luthardt, Christoph Ernst
""Έργον τοῦ θεοῦ und πίστις in ihrem gegenseitigen Verhältnis nach der Darstellung des johanneischen Evangeliums." *TSK* 25 (1852) 333–74.

Luthardt, Christoph Ernst
Der johanneische Ursprung des vierten Evangeliums (Leipzig: Dörfflung und Franke, 1874).

Luthardt, Christoph Ernst
St. John and the Author of the Fourth Gospel, revised, translated, and the literature much enlarged by Caspar René Gregory (Edinburgh: T. & T. Clark, 1875).

Lützelberger, Ernst Carl Julius
Die kirchliche Tradition über den Apostel Johannes und seine Schriften in ihrer Grundlosigkeit nachgewiesen (Leipzig: F. A. Brockhaus, 1840).

Luzarraga, J.
Oración y missión en el Evangelio de Juan, "Teología-Deusto" 11 (Bilbao: Universidad de Deusto—Mensajero, 1978).

Lyman, M. E.
"Hermetic Religion and the Religion of the Fourth Gospel." *JBL* 49 (1930) 265–76.

Macaulay, W. M.
"The Nature of Christ in Origin's *Commentary on John*." *SJT* 19 (1966) 176–87.

Macdonald, J.
The Theology of the Samaritans, NTL (Philadelphia: Westminster Press, 1965).

McDowell, Edward A.
"The Stuctural Integrity of the Fourth Gospel." *RevExp* 34 (1937) 397–416.

McEleney, Neil J.
"153 Great Fishes (John 21,11)—Gematriacal Atbash." *Bib* 58 (1977) 411–17.

MacGregor, G. H. C., and A. Q. Morton
The Structure of the Fourth Gospel (Edinburgh: Oliver & Boyd, 1961).

MacGregor, George Hogarth Carnaby
"The Eucharist in the Fourth Gospel." *NTS* 9 (1962/1963) 111–19.

MacGregor, George Hogarth Carnaby
"How Far is the Fourth Gospel a Unity?" *Expositor*, 8th ser., 24 (1922) 81–110; 25 (1923) 161–85; 26 (1924) 358–76.

MacGregor, George Hogarth Carnaby
"The Rearrangement of John vii and viii." *ExpTim* 33 (1921/1922) 74–78.

Mack, Burton L.
Logos und Sophia: Untersuchungen zur Weisheitstheologie im hellenistischen Judentum, SUNT 10 (Göttingen: Vandenhoeck & Ruprecht, 1973).

Mackowski, Richard M.
"Scholar's Qanah. A Re-examination of the Evidence in Favor of Khirbet-Qanah." *BZ* 23 (1979) 278–84.

McNamara, Martin

"The Ascension and the Exaltation of Christ in the Fourth Gospel." *Scr* 19 (1967) 65–73.

McNamara, Martin
"*Logos* of the Fourth Gospel and *Memra* of the Palestinian Targum (Ex 12:42)." *ExpTim* 79 (1968) 115–17.

McNaugher, John
"The Witnessing Spirit and the Witnessed Christ." *BSac* 88 (1931) 207–19.

McNeil, Brian
"The Raising of Lazarus." *Downside Review* 92 (1974) 269–75.

McPolin, James
"Bultmanni theoria litteraria et Jo 6,51c–58c." *VD* 44 (1966) 243–58.

McPolin, James
"Holy Spirit in Luke and John." *ITQ* 45 (1978) 117–131.

McPolin, James
"Mission in the Fourth Gospel." *ITQ* 36 (1969) 113–22.

McPolin, James
"The 'Name' of the Father and of the Son in the Johannine Writings." Dissertation, Rome, 1971.

MacRae, George W.
"The Fourth Gospel and *Religionsgeschichte*." *CBQ* 32 (1970) 13–24.

MacRae, George. W.
"The Ego-Proclamation in Gnostic Sources." In *The Trial of Jesus. Cambridge Studies in honour of C. F. D. Moule*, ed. E. Bammel. SBT, 2nd ser., 13 (Naperville, IL: Allenson, 1970) 122–35.

McReynolds, Paul R.
"John 1:18 in Textual Variation and Translation." In *New Testament Textual Criticism. Its Significance for Exegesis. Essays in Honour of Bruce M. Metzger*, ed. E. J. Epp and G. D. Fee (New York and Oxford: Clarendon Press, 1981) 105–18.

Macuch, R.
"Alter und Heimat des Mandäismus nach neuererschlossenen Quellen." *TLZ* 82 (1957) 401–8.

Macuch, R.
"Anfänger der Mandäer." In *Die Araber in der Alten Welt*, ed. F. Altheim and R. Stiehl (Berlin: Walter de Gruyter, 1965) 76–190.

Maerten, T.
"Le troisième dimanche de l'Avent (Jn 1,19–28; Phil 4,4–7)." *Paroisse et liturgie* 44 (1962) 710–16.

Magaß, Walter
"11 Thesen zum Bibelleser- und zum 'Suchen' in der Schrift (Joh 5,39)." *Linguistica Biblica* 47 (1980) 5–20.

Mahoney, Aidan
"A New Look at an Old Problem (John 18,12–14, 19–24)." *CBQ* 27 (1965) 137–44.

Mahoney, Robert
Two Disciples at the Tomb. The Background and Message of John 20,1–10, Theologie und Wirklichkeit 6 (Bern: H. Lang; Frankfurt: P. Lang, 1974).

Malatesta, Edward
"The Literary Structure of John 17." *Bib* 52 (1971) 190–214.

Malina, B. J.
The Palestinien Manna Tradition. The Manna Tradition in the Palestinian Targums and its Relationship to the New Testament Writings, AGSU 7 (Leiden: E. J. Brill, 1968).

Malinine, M. et al., eds.
De resurrectione. Codex Jung. (Zurich and Stuttgart: Rascher Verlag, 1963).

Malmede, Hans Hermann
"Die Lichtsymbolik im Neuen Testament." Dissertation, Bonn, 1960.

Manson, Thomas Walter
"The Pericope de Adultera (Joh 7,53–8,11)." *ZNW* 44 (1952/1953) 255–56.

Manson, William
The Incarnate Glory. An Expository Study of the Gospel According to St. John (London: J. Clarke; Boston: The Pilgrim Press, 1923).

Mantey, Julius Robert
"The Mistranslation of the Perfect Tense in John 20:23, Mt 16:19 and Mt 18:18." *JBL* 58 (1939) 243–49.

Marchesi, G.
"La verità nel Vangelo di San Giovanni." *Civiltà cattolica* 129 (1978) 1: 348–62.

Marrow, Stanley B.
John 21—An Essay in Johannine Ecclesiology (Rome: Gregorian University, 1968).

Marshall, I. Howard
"The Problem of New Testament Exegesis [John 4:1–45]." *Journal of the Evangelical Theological Society* 17 (1974) 67–73.

Martens, R. F.
"The Prologue of the Gospel of John: An Examination of its Origin and Emphasis." Dissertation, Concordia Seminary in Exile, 1974.

Martin, Alain G.
"Le Saint-Esprit et l'Evangile de Jean dans une perspective trinitaire." *Revue réformée* 29 (1978) 141–51.

Martin, James P.
"History and Eschatology in the Lazarus Narrative, John 11.1–44." *SJT* 17 (1964) 332–43.

Martin, James P.
"John 19, 1–10." *Int* 32 (1978) 171–75.

Martin, Josef
Symposion. Die Geschichte einer literarischen Form, Studien zur Geschichte und Kultur des Altertums 17 (Paderborn: F. Schöningh, 1931).

Martin, R. A.
"The Date of the Cleansing of the Temple in Joh 2,13–22." *Indian Journal of Theology* 15 (1966) 52–56.

Martin, Victor and Rudolphe Kasser, eds.
Papyrus Bodmer XIV–XV. Evangile de Luc et Jean [Luc chap. 3–24; Jean chap. 1–15] (Cologny-Geneva: Bibliotheca Bodmeriana, 1961).

Martin, Victor, ed.
Papyrus Bodmer II, Supplément. Evangile de Jean, chap. 14–21 (Cologny-Geneva: Bibliotheca Bodmeriana, 1958).

Martin, Victor, ed.
Papyrus Bodmer II: Evangile de Jean chap. 1–14 (Cologny-Geneva: Bibliotheca Bodmeriana, 1956).

Martyn, James Louis
"We Have Found Elijah." In *Jews, Greeks, and Christians. Religious Cultures in Late Antiquity. Essays in Honor of William David Davies,* ed. Robert Hamerton-Kelly and Robin Scroggs. SJLA 21 (Leiden: E. J. Brill, 1976) 181–219.

Martyn, James Louis
"Clementine Recognitions 1, 33–71, Jewish Christianity and the Fourth Gospel." In *God's Christ and His People. Studies in Honor of Nils A. Dahl,* ed. J. Jervell and Wayne A. Meeks (Oslo: Universitetsforlaget, 1977) 265–95.

Martyn, James Louis
History and Theology in the Fourth Gospel (Nashville: Abingdon Press, 1968, ²1979).

Martyn, James Louis
"Glimpses into the History of the Johannine Community. From its Origin through the Period of its Life in which the Fourth Gospel was Composed." In *L'Evangile de Jean. Sources, rédaction, théologie,* ed. M. de Jonge. BETL 44 (Gembloux: Duculot; Louvain: University Press, 1977) 149–76.

Martyn, James Louis
"Source Criticism and Religionsgeschichte in the Fourth Gospel." In *Jesus and Man's Hope,* ed. G. Buttrick. A Perspective Book (Pittsburgh: Pittsburgh Theological Seminary, 1970) 1: 247–73.

Mary Therese, Sr.
"The Good Shepherd." *Bible Today* 38 (1968) 2657–64.

Marzotto, Damiano
L'unità degli uomini nel vangelo di Giovanni, Supplementi alla Rivista Biblica 9 (Brescia: Paideia, 1977).

Marzotto, Damiano
L'unità degli uomini nel vangelo di Giovanni, Supplementi alla Rivista Biblica 9 (Brescia: Paideia, 1977).

Masson, Charles
"Le prologue du quatrième évangile." *RTP,* n.s. 28 (1940) 297–311.

Masson, Charles
"Pour une traduction nouvelle de Jn I:1b et 2." *RTP* 98 (1965) 376–81.

Masson, Charles
"Le reniement de Pierre. Quelques aspects de la formation d'une tradition." *RHPR* 37 (1957) 24–35.

Mastin, B. A.
"A Neglected Feature of the Christology of the

Fourth Gospel." *NTS* 22 (1975/1976) 32–51.

Matsunaga, Kikuo
"The Galileans in the Fourth Gospel." *Annual of the Japanese Biblical Institute* 2 (1976) 139–58.

Matthaei, Georg Christian Rudolf
Auslegung des Evangeliums Johannis zur Reform der Auslegung desselben (Göttingen: G. Kübler, 1837).

Mattill, A. J., Jr.
"Johannine Communities behind the Fourth Gospel: Georg Richter's Analysis." *TS* 38 (1977) 294–315.

Maurer, Christian
"Steckt hinter Joh 5,17 ein Übersetzungsfehler?" *Wort und Dienst*, n.f., 5 (1957) 130–40.

Maurer, Christian
Ignatius von Antiochien und das Johannesevangelium, ATANT 18 (Zurich: Zwingli Verlag, 1949).

Maurer, Christian
"Der Exklusivanspruch des Christus nach dem Johannesevangelium." In *Studies in John Presented to Professor J. N. Sevenster on the Occasion of his Seventieth Birthday* (Leiden: E. J. Brill, 1970) 143–60.

May, E. E.
Ecce Agnus Dei! A Philological and Exegetical Approach to John 1:29, 36, Studies in Sacred Theology, 2nd ser., 5 (Washington: The Catholic University of America Press, 1947).

Mayeda, Goro
Das Leben-Jesu-Fragment Papyrus Egerton 2 und seine Stellung in der urchristlichen Literaturgeschichte (Bern: P. Haupt, 1946).

Mayer, Georg Karl
Die Aechtheit des Evangeliums nach Johannes (Schaffhausen: F. Hurter, 1854).

Maynard, Arthur H.
"Common Elements in the Outlines of Mark and John." SBLASP 2 (Missoula: Scholars Press, 1978) 251–60.

Meagher, John C.
"John 1:14 and the New Temple." *JBL* 88 (1969) 57–68.

Mealand, David L.
"The Christology of the Fourth Gospel." *SJT* 31 (1978) 449–67.

Meeks, Wayne A.
"The Man from Heaven in Johannine Sectarianism." *JBL* 91 (1972) 44–72.

Meeks, Wayne A.
"Galilee and Judea in the Fourth Gospel." *JBL* 85 (1966) 159–69.

Meeks, Wayne A.
"'Am I a Jew?' Johannine Christology and Judaism." In *Christianity, Judaism and Other Greco-Roman Cults. Studies for Morton Smith at Sixty. Part 1, New Testament,* ed. Jacob Neusner. SJLA 12 (Leiden: E. J. Brill, 1975) 163–86.

Meeks, Wayne A.
"The Divine Agent and his Counterfeit in Philo and the Fourth Gospel." In *Aspects of Religious*

Propaganda in Judaism and Early Christianity. ed. E. Schüssler-Fiorenza. University of Notre Dame Center for the Study of Judaism and Christianity in Antiquity 2 (Notre Dame and London: University of Notre Dame, 1976) 43–67.

Meeks, Wayne A.
"Die Funktion des vom Himmel herabgestiegenen Offenbarers für das Selbstverständnis der johanneischen Gemeinde." In *Zur Soziologie des Urchristentums. Ausgewählte Beiträge zum frühchristlichen Gemeinschaftsleben in seiner gesellschaftlichen Umwelt,* ed. Wayne A. Meeks. TBü 62 (Munich: Chr. Kaiser Verlag, 1979) 245–83 = "The Man from Heaven in Johannine Sectarianism." *JBL* 91 (1972) 44–72.

Meeks, Wayne A.
The Prophet King: Moses Traditions and Johannine Christology (Leiden: E. J. Brill, 1967).

Mees, Michael
"Textverständnis und Varianten in Kap. 5 des Johannesevangeliums bei Epiphanius von Salamis." *Lateranum* 46 (1980) 250–84.

Mees, Michael
"Unterschiedliche Lesarten in Bodmer Papyrus XV (P^{75}) und Codex Vaticanus aus Joh 1–9." *Augustinianum* 9 (1969) 370–79.

Mees, Michael
"Sinn und Bedeutung westlicher Textvarianten in Joh 6." *BZ* 13 (1969) 244–51.

Mees, Michael
"Erhöhung und Verherrlichung Jesu im Johannesevangelium nach dem Zeugnis neutestamentlicher Papyri." *BZ* 18 (1974) 32–44.

Mees, Michael
"Petrus und Johannes nach ausgewählten Varianten von P 66 und S." *BZ* 15 (1971) 238–49.

Mees, Michael
"Lectio brevior im Johannesevangelium und ihre Beziehung zum Urtext." *BZ* 12 (1968) 111–19, 377.

Mehlmann, Johannes
"Propheta a Moyse promissus in Jo 7,52 citatus." *VD* 44 (1966) 79–88.

Mehlmann, John
"Notas sobre Natanael—S Bartolomeus, Joh 1,45–51." *Revista di Cultura Biblica* 5 (1961) 337–42.

Mein, P.
"A Note on John 18.6." *ExpTim* 65 (1953/1954) 286–87.

Meinertz, Max
"Die 'Nacht' im Johannesevangelium." *TQ* 133 (1953) 400–407.

Menard, Jacques-E.
"L'interprétation patristique de Jean VII, 38." *RUO* (1955) 5–25.

Mendner, Siegfried
"Die Tempelreinigung." *ZNW* 47 (1956) 93–112.

Mendner, Siegfried
"Nikodemus." *JBL* 77 (1958) 293–323.

Mendner, Siegfried
"Zum Problem 'Johannes und die Synoptiker.'"
NTS 4 (1957/1958) 282–307.

Menken, Gottfried
Über die eherne Schlange und das symbolische Verhältniß derselben zu der Person und Geschichte Jesu
(Frankfurt, 1812; Bremen: Kaiser, 1828).

Menoud, Philippe-Henri
"'Le fils de Joseph.' Etude sur Jean I, 45 et IV, 42."
RTP 18 (1930) 275–88.

Menoud, Philippe-Henri
L'évangile de Jean d'après les recherches récentes
(Neuchâtel and Paris: Delachaux et Niestlé,
²1947).

Menoud, Phillippe-Henri
"Les travaux de E. Hirsch sur le quatrième
évangile." *RTP* 25 (1937) 132–39.

Menoud, Phillippe-Henri
*L'évangile de Jean. Les études johanniques de
Bultmann à Barrett*, Recherches Bibliques 3
(Brugges, 1958).

Menoud, Phillippe-Henri
"La signification du miracle selon le NT." *RHPR*
28 (1948/1949) 173–92.

Menoud, Phillippe-Henri
"La foi dans l'évangile de Jean." Cahiers bibliques
de Foi et Vie 1 (1936) 27–43.

Menoud, Phillippe-Henri
"L'origingalité de la pensée johannique." *RTP*,
n.s., 28 (1940) 233–61.

Mensinga, J. A.
"Das Johannes-Evangelium und die Synopsis."
ZWT 35 (1892) 98–104.

Mer, J.
"La notion de temoignage dans l'évangile selon S.
Jean." Dissertation, Fribourg, 1970.

Merkel, Johannes
"Die Begnadigung am Passahfeste." *ZNW* 6 (1905)
293–316.

Merli, Dino
"Lo scopo della risurrezione di Lazzaro in Giov.
11,1–44." *BeO* 12 (1970) 59–82.

Merlier, Octave
"Langue et exégèse néotestamentaire: La péricope
de la femme adultère." In Festschrift M. Trianta-
phyllidis (Athens, 1960) 553–61.

Merlier, Octave
"Σὺ λέγεις ὅτι Βασιλεύς εἰμι." *Revue des études
grecques* 46 (1933) 204–9.

Merlier, Octave
Le quatrième évangile (Paris: Presses Universitaires
de France, 1962).

Metzger, Bruce M.
"The Bodmer Papyrus of Luke and John." *ExpTim*
73 (1961/1962) 201–3.

Metzger, H. O.
"Neuere Johannes-Forschung." *VF* 12 (1967) 12–
29.

Meyer, Arnold

"Johanneische Literatur." *TRu* 5 (1902) 316–33,
497–507; 7 (1904) 473–84, 519–31; 9 (1906)
302–11, 340–59, 381–97; 13 (1910) 15–26, 63–
75, 94–100, 151–62; 15 (1912) 239–49, 278–93,
295–305.

Meyer, Arnold
"Die Behandlung der johanneischen Frage im
letzten Jahrzehnt." *TRu* 2 (1899) 255–63, 295–
305, 333–45.

Meyer, Eduard
"Sinn und Tendenz der Schlussszene am Kreuz im
Johannesevangelium." SPAW.PH (1924) 157–62.

Meyer, Heinrich
*Die mandäische Lehre vom göttlichen Gesandten mit
einem Ausblick auf ihr Verhältnis zur johanneischen
Christologie* (Breklum: Jensen, 1929). Partial publi-
cation from "Mandäische und johanneischen
Soteriologie." Dissertation, Kiel, 1929.

Meyer, Paul W.
"John 2:10." *JBL* 86 (1967) 191–97.

Meyer, Paul W.
"The Eschatology of the Fourth Gospel." Dissertation, Union Theological Seminary, 1955.

Meyer, Paul W.
"A Note on John 10:1–18." *JBL* 75 (1956) 232–35.

Michael, J. Hugh
"The Meaning of ἐξηγήσατο in St. John i, 18." *JTS*
22 (1920/1921) 13–16.

Michael, J. Hugh
"The Origin of St. John I.13." *Expositor,* 8th ser.,
16 (1918) 301–20.

Michael, J. Hugh
"The Actual Saying behind St. John vi. 62."
ExpTim 43 (1931/1932) 427–28.

Michaelis, Wilhelm
"Joh 1,51, Gen 28,12 und das Menschensohn-
Problem." *TLZ* 85 (1960) 561–78.

Michaelis, Wilhelm
Die Sakramente im Johannesevangelium (Bern: Buchhandlung der Evangelischen Gesellschaft, 1946).

Michaelis, Wilhelm
"Zur Herkunft des johanneischen Paraklet-Titels."
ConNT 11 (1948) 147–62.

Michaelis, Wilhelm
Die Erscheinungen des Auferstandenen (Basel: H.
Majer, 1944).

Michaels, J. Ramsey
"Origen and the Text of John 1,15." In *New
Testament Textual Criticism. Its Significance for Exe-
gesis. Essays in Honour of Bruce M. Metzger,* ed. E. J.
Epp and G. D. Fee (New York and Oxford:
Clarendon Press, 1981) 87–104.

Michaels, J. Ramsey
"Nathanael under the Fig-tree (Jn 1:48; 4:19)."
ExpTim 78 (1966/1967) 182–83.

Michaels, J. Ramsey
"Alleged Anti-Semitism in the Fourth Gospel."
Gordon Review 11 (1968) 12–24.

Michaels, J. Ramsey

"The Centurion's Confession and the Spear Thrust." *CBQ* 29 (1967) 102–9.

Michaud, Jean-Paul
"Le signe de Cana dans son contexte johannique." *Laval théologique et philosophique* 18 (1962) 239–85.

Michel, M.
"Nicodème ou le non-lieu de la vérité." *RSR* 55 (1981) 227–36.

Michel, Otto
"Der Anfang der Zeichen Jesu." In *Die Leibhaftigkeit des Wortes. Theologische und seelsorgliche Studien und Beiträge als Festgabe für Adolf Köberle zum 60. Geburtstag*, ed. O. Michel and Ulrich Mann (Hamburg: Furche-Verlag, 1958) 15–22.

Michel, Otto
"Das Gebet des scheidenden Erlösers." *ZST* 18 (1941) 521–34.

Michel, Otto
"Die Fürbitte des Erlösers: Joh 17,20–30." *Evangelische Missionszeitschrift* 2 (1940) 353–60.

Michel, Otto
"Ein johanneischer Osterbericht." In *Studien zum Neuen Testament und zur Patristik. Erich Klostermann zum 90. Geburtstag dargebracht*, TU 77 (Berlin: Akademie-Verlag, 1961) 35–42.

Michiels, R.
"De opwekking van Lazarus." *Collationes Brugenses et Gandavenses* 21 (1975) 433–47.

Michl, Johann
"Bemerkungen zu Jo. 2, 4." *Bib* 36 (1955) 492–509.

Michl, Johann
"Der Sinn der Fusswaschung." *Bib* 40 (1959) 697–708.

Middleton, R. D.
"Logos and Shekina in the Fourth Gospel." *JQR* 29 (1938/1939) 101–33.

Miguens, M.
"El Agua y el Espíritu en Jn 7, 37–39." *EstBib* 31 (1972) 369–98.

Miller, E. L.
"Salvation History in the Prologue of John 1,3–4." Dissertation, Basel, 1981.

Miller, E. L.
"The Logos of Heraclitus: Updating the Report." *HTR* 74 (1981) 161–76.

Miller, G.
"The Nature and Purpose of Signs in the Fourth Gospel." Dissertation, Duke University, 1968.

Miller, John Whelan
"The Concept of the Church in the Gospel according to John." Dissertation, Princeton Theological Seminary, 1976.

Minear, Paul S.
"Evangelism, Ecumenism and John Seventeen." *TToday* 35 (1978) 5–13.

Minear, Paul S.
"John 17,1–11." *Int* 32 (1978) 175–79.

Minear, Paul S.
"'We don't know where . . .' John 20,2." *Int* 30 (1976) 125–39.

Minear, Paul S.
"The Beloved Disciple in the Gospel of John. Some Clues and Conjectures." *NovT* 19 (1977) 105–23.

Miranda, Juan Peter
Der Vater, der mich gesandt hat. Religionsgeschichtliche Untersuchungen zu den johanneischen Sendungsformeln. Zugleich ein Beitrag zur johanneischen Christologie und Ekklesiologie, Europäische Hochschulschriften, Series 23; Theologie 7 (Bern: H. Lang; Frankfurt: P. Lang, 1972).

Mitton, C. L.
"Modern Issues in Biblical Studies: The Provenance of the Fourth Gospel." *ExpTim* 71 (1959/1960) 337–40.

Modersohn, E.
"Des Täufers Selbst- und Christuszeugnis (Joh 1,19–24)." *Heilig dem Herrn* 31 (1940) 157–59.

Moe, Olaf
"Spor av Johannes traditionen hos Lukas." *NorTT* 25 (1924) 103–28.

Moeller, H. B.
"Wisdom Motifs and John's Gospel." *Bulletin of the Evangelical Theological Society* 6 (1963) 92–100.

Moffatt, James
"The Lord's Supper in the Fourth Gospel." *Expositor*, 8th ser., 7 (1913) 1–22.

Moffatt, James
New Translation of the Bible Containing the Old and New Testaments (New York and London: Harper & Brothers, 1935).

Mollat, Donatien
"Le chapitre VI⁵ de Saint Jean." *Lumière et vie* 31 (1957) 107–19.

Mollat, Donatien
"L'évangile Jn 8, 45–59: 'Avant qu'Abraham ne fût je suis.'" *AsSeign* 34 (1963) 54–63.

Mollat, Donatien
"La guérsion de l'aveugle-né." *BVC* 23 (1958) 22–31.

Mollat, Donatien
"Le bon pasteur." In *Populus Dei. Studi in onore del Card. Alfredo Ottaviani per il cinquantesimo di sazerdozio: 18.3.1966* (Roma: Christen tipografia offset, 1969) 927–68.

Mollat, Donatien
"Jésus devant Pilate (Jean 18,28–38)." *BVC* 39 (1961) 23–31.

Mollat, Donatien
"La découverte du tombeau vide Jn 20,1–9." *AsSeign* 21 (1969) 90–100.

Mollat, Donatien
Etudes johanniques, Parole de Dieu 19 (Paris: Editions du Seuil, 1979).

Mollat, Donatien
"La foi dans le quatrième évangile." *Lumière et Vie* 22 (1955) 91–107.

Moloney, Francis J.
The Johannine Son of Man, Biblioteca di scienze religiose 14 (Rome: Libreria Ateneo Salesiano, 1976, ²1979).

Moloney, Francis J.
"The Johannine Son of Man." *BTB* 6 (1976) 177–89.

Moloney, Francis J.
"From Cana to Cana (Jn. 2:1–4:54) and the Fourth Evangelist's Concept of Correct (and Incorrect) Faith." *Salesianum* 40 (1978) 817–43.

Moloney, Francis J.
"John 6 and the Celebration of the Eucharist." *Downside Review* 93 (1975) 243–51.

Moloney, Francis J.
"The Fourth Gospel's Presentation of Jesus as 'the Christ' and J. A. T. Robinson's *Redating.*" *Downside Review* 95 (1977) 239–53.

Moloney, Francis J.
"The Johannine Son of Man." *Salesianum* 38 (1976) 71–86.

Mommert, Carl
Aenon und Bethania, die Taufstätten des Täufers (Leipzig: E. Haberland, 1903).

Mondula, N.
La puissance vivificatrice de la chair du Christ selon l'évangile de S. Jean (Rome, 1978).

Montgomery, James Alan
The Origin of the Gospel According to St. John (Philadelphia: The John C. Winston Co., 1923).

Moore, F. J.
"Eating the Flesh and Drinking the Blood: A Reconsideration." *ATR* 48 (1966) 70–75.

Moore, George Foot
"Intermediaries in Jewish Theology: Memra, Shekinah, Metatron." *HTR* 15 (1922) 41–85.

Moore, W. E.
"Sir, We wish to See Jesus—Was this an Occasion of Temptation?" *SJT* 20 (1967) 75–93.

Márquez, M.
"El Espíritu Santo, principio de la nueva creación, en función de la misión apostólica en Jn 20,21–22." *Semana bíblica Española* 26 (1969) 121–48.

Moreton, M. J.
"Feast, Sign and Discourse in Joh 5." *SE* 4 = TU 102 (Berlin: Akademie-Verlag, 1968) 209–13.

Morretto, Giovanni
"Giov. 19,28: La sete di Cristo in croce." *RivB* 15 (1967) 249–74.

Morris, Leon
"On Love in the Fourth Gospel." In *Saved by Hope. Essays in Honor of Richard C. Oudersluys,* ed. J. I. Cook (Grand Rapids: Wm. B. Eerdmans, 1978).

Morris, Leon
Studies in the Fourth Gospel (Grand Rapids: Wm. B. Eerdmans, 1969).

Morris, Leon
"The Tradition that John the Apostle was Martyred Early." In his *Studies in the Fourth Gospel,* 280–83.

Morris, Leon
"Was the Author of the Fourth Gospel an Eyewitness?" In his *Studies in the Fourth Gospel,* 139–214.

Morris, Leon
"A Feature of Johannine Style." In his *Studies in the Fourth Gospel,* 293–310.

Morris, Leon
"The Relationship of the Fourth Gospel to the Synoptics." In his *Studies in the Fourth Gospel,* 15–63.

Morris, Leon
"The Composition of the Fourth Gospel." In *Scripture, Tradition, and Interpretation. Essays presented to Everett F. Harrison by His Students and Colleagues in Honor of His Seventy-fifth Birthday,* ed. W. W. Gasque and W. S. LaSor (Grand Rapids: Wm. B. Eerdmans, 1978) 157–75.

Morrison, Clinton D.
"Mission and Ethic. An Interpretation of John 17." *Int* 19 (1965) 259–73.

Moule, C. F. D.
"A Note on 'Under the Fig-tree' in John i. 48, 50." *JTS,* ns. 5 (1954) 210–11.

Moule, C. F. D.
"A Neglected Factor in the Interpretation of Johannine Eschatology." In *Studies in John Presented to Professor J. N. Sevenster on the Occasion of his Seventieth Birthday* (Leiden: E. J. Brill, 1970) 155–60.

Moule, C. F. D.
"A Note on Didache IX.4." *JTS,* n.s., 6 (1955) 240–43.

Moule, C. F. D.
"The Individualism of the Fourth Gospel." *NovT* 5 (1962) 171–90.

Moule, C. F. D.
"The Meaning of 'Life' in the Gospel and Epistles of St. John. A Study in the Story of Lazarus, John 11:1–44." *Theology* 78 (1975) 114–25.

Moule, Handley Clarr Flyn
Jesus and the Resurrection. Expository Studies on St. John XX. XXI (London: Seeley, 1893).

Moulton, Harold K.
"*Pantas* in John 2:15." *BT* 18 (1967) 126–27.

Mowinckel, Sigmund
"Die Vorstellungen des Spätjudentums vom heiligen Geist als Fürsprecher und der johanneische Paraklet." *ZNW* 32 (1933) 97–130.

Mozley, A. D.
"St. John i. 29." *ExpTim* 26 (1914/1915) 46–47.

Mühl, M.
"Der λόγος ἐνδιάθετος und προφορικος von der älteren Stoa bis zur Synode von Sirmium 351." *Archiv für Begriffsgeschichte* 7 (1962) 7–56.

Mühlenberg, Ekkehard
"Das Problem der Offenbarung in Philo von Alexandrien." *ZNW* 64 (1973) 1–18.

Muilenburg, James
"Literary Form in the Fourth Gospel." *JBL* 51 (1932) 40–53.

Muirhead, Lewis Andrew
The Message of the Fourth Gospel (London: Williams & Norgate, 1925).

Mulder, H.
"John 18,28 and the Date of the Cruxification." In *Miscellanea Neotestamentica* 2, ed. T. Baarda, A. F. J. Klijn, and W. C. van Unnik. NovTSup 48 (Leiden: E. J. Brill, 1978) 87–107.

Müller, Carl
De nonnullis doctrinae gnosticae vestigiis, quae in quarto evangelio inesse feruntur dissertatio (Freiburg: Herder, 1883).

Müller, D. H.
"Das Johannes-Evangelium im Lichte der Strophentheorie." SAWW.PH 160 (Wien: Akademie-Verlag, 1909) 1–60.

Müller, Karlheinz
"Joh 9, 7 und das jüdische Verständnis des Šiloh-Spruches." *BZ* 13 (1969) 251–56.

Müller, Ludolf
"Die Hochzeit zu Kana." In *Glaube, Geist, Geschichte. Festschrift für Ernst Benz zum 60. Geburtstag*, ed. G. Müller and W. Zeller (Leiden: E. J. Brill, 1967) 99–106.

Müller, Ulrich B.
"Die Parakletenvorstellung im Johannesevangelium." *ZTK* 71 (1974) 31–77.

Müller, Ulrich B.
"Die Bedeutung des Kreuzestodes Jesu im Johannesevangelium. Erwägungen zur Kreuzestheologie im Neuen Testament." *KD* 21 (1975) 49–71.

Müller, Ulrich B.
Die Geschichte der Christologie in der johanneischen Gemeinde, SBS 77 (Stuttgart: Katholisches Bibelwerk, 1975).

Mundle, W.
"Das Wahrheitsverständnis des johanneischen Schrifttums." *Lutherischer Rundblick* 16 (1968) 82–94, 161–65.

Munro, Winsome
"The Anointing in Mark 14,3–9 and John 12,1–8." In *SBL 1979 Seminar Papers* 1, SBLASP 16 (Missoula: Scholars Press, 1979) 127–30.

Murray, John Owen Fargnar
Jesus According to St. John (London: Longmans & Co., 1936).

Mussner, Franz
"Johanneische Theologie." *Sacramentum Mundi* 2 (Freiburg, 1968) 957–65.

Mussner, Franz
Petrus und Paulus—Pole der Einheit. Eine Hilfe für die Kirchen. Quaestiones Disputatae 76 (Freiburg: Herder, 1976).

Mussner, Franz
"ZΩH" *Die Anschauung vom "Leben" im vierten Evangelium unter Berücksichtigung der Johannesbriefe. Ein Beitrag zur biblischen Theologie*, Münchener Theologische Studien 1,5 (Munich: Zink, 1952).

Mussner, Franz
"Fusswaschung (Joh 13, 1–17). Versuch einer Deutung." *Geist und Leben* 31 (1958) 25–30.

Mussner, Franz
"Die johanneischen Parakletsprüche und die apostolische Tradition." In his *Praesentia Salutis. Gesammelte Studien zu Fragen und Themen des Neuen Testamentes*, Kommentare und Beiträge zum Alten und Neuen Testament (Düsseldorf: Patmos-Verlag, 1967) 147–58.

Mussner, Franz
"Der Charakter Jesu nach dem Johannesevangelium." *TTZ* 62 (1953) 321–32.

Mussner, Franz
"'Kultische' Aspekte im johanneischen Christusbild." *Liturgisches Jahrbuch* 14 (1964) 185–200. Cf. "Liturgical Aspects of John's Gospel." *Theological Digest* 14 (1966) 18–22. In his *Praesentia Salutis. Gesammelte Studien zu Fragen und Themen des Neuen Testamentes*, Kommentare und Beiträge zum Alten und Neuen Testament (Düsseldorf: Patmos-Verlag, 1967) 133–45.

Nagel, Walter.
"'Die Finsternis hat's nicht begriffen' (Joh 1:5)." *ZNW* 50 (1959) 132–37.

Nägelsbach, Friedrich
"Die Voraussagungen Jesu nach Joh. 14–16 und ihre Folgerungen." *NKZ* 22 (1911) 663–96.

Naish, J. B.
"The Fourth Gospel and the Sacraments." *Expositor*, 8th ser., 23 (1922) 53–68.

Nauck, W.
Die Tradition und der Charakter des ersten Johannesbriefes, WUNT 3 (Tübingen: Mohr-Siebeck, 1957).

Nearon, J. R.
"My Flesh for the World." An Essay in Biblical Theology (Rome, 1973).

Nebe, August
Die Auferstehungsgeschichte unsers Herrn Jesu Christi nach den vier Evangelien ausgelegt (Wiesbaden: Niedner; Philadelphia: Schäfer & Koradi, 1882).

Negoitsa, Athanase and Constantin Daniel
"L'Agneau de Dieu et le Verbe de Dieu (Ad Jo i 29 et 36)." *NovT* 13 (1971) 24–37.

Neirynck, Frans
"John and the Synoptics." In *L'Evangile de Jean. Sources, rédaction, théologie*, ed. M. de Jonge. BETL 44 (Gembloux: Duculot; Louvain: University Press, 1977).

Neirynck, Frans
"The 'Other Disciple' in Jn 18,15–16." *ETL* 51 (1975) 113–41.

Neirynck, Frans
"Apēlthen pros heauton. Lc 24,12 et Jn 10,10." *ETL* 54 (1978) 104–118.

Neirynck, Frans
"Les Femmes au Tombeau. Etude de la rédaction Matthéenne (Matt. xxviii.1–10)." *NTS* 15 (1968/1969) 168–90.

Neirynck, Frans
"*Parakypsas blepei:* Lc 24,12 et Jn 20,5." *ETL* 53 (1977) 113–52.

Neirynck, Frans
"John and the Synoptics." In *L'Evangile de Jean. Sources, rédaction, théologie,* ed. M. de Jonge. BETL 44 (Gembloux: Duculot; Louvain: University Press, 1977) 73–106.

Neirynck, Frans et al.
"L'Evangile de Jean. Examen critique du commentaire de M.-E. Boismard et A. Lamouille." *ETL* 53 (1977) 363–478.

Neirynck, Frans et al.
Jean et les Synoptiques. Examen critique de l'exégèse de M.-E. Boismard, BETL 49 (Louvain: University Press, 1979) 23–39.

Nestle, Eberhard
"Zum Ysop bei Johannes, Josephus und Philo." *ZNW* 14 (1913) 263–65.

Neugebauer, F.
Die Entstehung des Johannesevangeliums. Altes und Neues zur Frage seines historischen Ursprungs, Arbeiten zur Theologie 1, 36 (Stuttgart: Calwer Verlag, 1968).

Neugebauer, Fritz
"Miszelle zu Joh 5,35." *ZNW* 52 (1961) 130.

Nevius, Richard C.
"The Use of the Definitive Article with 'Jesus' in the Fourth Gospel." *NTS* 12 (1965/1966) 81–85.

Newman, Barclay M.
"Some Observations Regarding a Poetic Restructuring of John 1,1–18." *BT* 29 (1978) 206–12.

Newman, Barclay M.
"The Case of the Eclectic and the Neglected ἐκ of John 17." *BT* 29 (1978) 339–41.

Newman, Barclay M., Jr.
"Some Observations Regarding the Argument, Structure, and Literary Characteristics of the Gospel of John." *BT* 26 (1975) 234–39.

Neyrey, Jerome H.
"The Jacob Allusions in John 1:51." *CBQ* 44 (1982) 586–605.

Neyrey, Jerome H.
"John III—A Debate over Johannine Epistemology and Christology." *NovT* 23 (1981) 115–27.

Neyrey, Jerome H.
"Jacob Traditions and the Interpretation of John 4:10–26." *CBQ* 41 (1979) 419–37.

Niccacci, Alviero
"La fede nel Gesù storico e la fede nel Cristo risorto (Gv 1,19–51//20,1–19)." *Antonianum* 53 (1978) 423–42.

Niccacci, Alviero
"Siracide 6,19 e Giovanni 4,36–38." *BeO* 23 (1981) 149–53.

Niccacci, Alviero
"L'unitá litteraria di Gv 13,1–38." *Euntes docet* 29 (1976) 291–323.

Niccacci, Alviero
"Esame letterario di Gv 14." *Euntes docet* 31 (1978) 209–60.

Nicholson, Godfrey C.
"Lifting up, Return Above and Cruxifixion. The Death of Jesus in the Johannine Redaction." Dissertation, Vanderbilt University, 1978.

Nicklin, T.
"A Suggested Dislocation in the Text of St. John xiv–xvi." *ExpTim* 44 (1932/1933) 382–83.

Nicol, W.
The Sēmeia in the Fourth Gospel. Tradition and Redaction, NovTSup 32 (Leiden: E. J. Brill, 1972).

Nicol, W.
"The History of Johannine Research During the Past Century." *Neot* 6 (1972) 8–18.

Niedner, Christian Wilhelm
"De subsistentia τῷ θείῳ λόγῳ apud Philonem Judaeum et Joannem Apostolum tributa." *ZHT* 11 (1849) 337–81.

Niermeyer, Antonie
Bijdragen Aer verdediging van de echtheit der johanneische Schriften (Schoonk: Van Nooten, 1852).

Niermeyer, Antonie
Verhandeling over de echtheit der joh. Schriften (s'Gravenhage, 1852).

Niewalda, P.
Sakramentssymbolik im Johannesevangelium. Eine exegetisch-historische Studie (Limburg: Lahn-Verlag, 1958).

Noack, Bent
Zur johanneischen Tradition. Beiträge zur Kritik an der literarkritischen Analyse des vierten Evangeliums (Copenhagen: Rosenkilde og Bagger, 1954).

Nolloth, Charles Frederick
The Fourth Evangelist. His Place in the Development of Religious Thought (London: J. Murray, 1925).

Norris, J. P.
"On the Chronology of St. John V. and VI." *The Journal of Philology* 3 (1871) 107–12.

Nötscher, F.
Zur theologischen Terminologie der Qumran-Texte. BBB 10 (Bonn: Peter Hanstein, 1956) 112f.

Nunn, Henry Preston Vaughan
"The Fourth Gospel in the Early Church." *EvQ* 16 (1944) 173–91, 294–99.

Nunn, Henry Preston Vaughan
The Authorship of the Fourth Gospel (Windsor: Alden & Blackwell (Eton), 1952).

O. L. in Schlesien
"Nathanael." *ZWT* 16 (1873) 96–102.

Odeberg, Hugo
"Über das Johannesevangelium." *ZST* 16 (1939) 173–88.

Oeder, G. L.
De scopo Evangelii S. Joannis Haeres Cerinthi et Ebionis oppositi adversum F. A. Sampe, liber unus. In quo et Irenaeus atque Calovius contra iniquas criminationes defenduntur (Frankfurt: Schmidt, 1732).

Oehler, W.
Zum Missionscharakter des Johannesevangeliums (Gütersloh: C. Bertelsmann, 1941).

Oehler, W.
Das Johannesevangelium eine Missionsschrift für die Welt der Gemeinde ausgelegt (Gütersloh: C. Bertelsmann, 1936).

Oehler, Wilhelm
Das Wort des Johannes an die Gemeinde: Evangelium Johannis 15–17, Johannes-Briefe und Offenbarung des Johannes (Gütersloh: C. Bertelsmann, 1938).

Oepke, Albrecht
"Das missionarische Christuszeugnis des Johannesevangeliums." *Evangelische Missionszeitschrift* 2 (1941) 4–26.

O'Grady, John F.
"The Good Shepherd and the Vine of the Branches." *BTB* 8 (1978) 86–89.

O'Grady, John F.
Individual and Community in John (Rome: Pontifical Biblical Institute, 1978).

O'Grady, John F.
"Johannine Ecclesiology: A Critical Evaluation." *BTB* 7 (1977) 36–44.

O'Grady, John F.
"Individualism and Johannine Ecclesiology." *BTB* 5 (1975) 227–61.

O'Grady, John F.
"The Role of the Beloved Disciple." *BTB* 9 (1979) 58–65.

Oke, C. Clark
"At the Feast of Booths. A Suggested Rearrangement of John vii–ix." *ExpTim* 47 (1935/1936) 425–27.

Olbricht, Thomas H.
"Its Works Are Evil (John 7:7)." *Restoration Quarterly* 7 (1963) 242–44.

Olivieri, Jean and Marie-Joseph Lagrange
"La conception qui domine le quatrième évangile." *RB* 35 (1926) 382–97.

Olsson, Birger
Structure and Meaning in the Fourth Gospel. A Text-Linguistic Analysis of John 2:1–11 and 4:1–42, tr. Jean Gray. ConBNT 6 (Lund: C. W. K. Gleerup, 1974).

O'Neill, J. C.
"The Prologue to St. John's Gospel." *JTS,* n.s., 20 (1969) 41–52.

O'Neill, J. C.
"The Lamb of God in the Testaments of the Twelve Patriarchs." *JSNT* 2 (1979) 2–30.

Onuki, Takashi
Gemeinde und Welt im Johannesevangelium. Ein Beitrag zur Frage nach der theologischen und pragma-tischen Funktion des johanneischen Dualismus (Stuttgart: W. Kohlhammer, 1983).

Onuki, Takashi
"Die johanneischen Abschiedsreden und die synoptische Tradition—eine traditionskritische und traditionsgeschichtliche Untersuchung." *Annual of the Japanese Biblical Institute* 3 (1977) 157–268.

O'Rourke, John J.
"Two Notes on St. John's Gospel." *CBQ* 25 (1963) 124–28.

O'Rourke, John J.
"*Eis* and *en* in John." *BT* 25 (1974) 139–42.

O'Rourke, John J.
"The Historic Present in the Gospel of John." *JBL* 93 (1974) 585–90.

Osborn, Eric Francis
Justin Martyr, BHT 47 (Tübingen: Mohr-Siebeck, 1973).

Osborne, Basil
"A Folded Napkin in an Empty Tomb: John 11:44 and 20:7 Again." *HeyJ* 14 (1973) 437–40.

Osborne, R. E.
"Pericope adulterae." *CJT* 12 (1966) 281–83.

Osten-Sacken, Peter von der
"Der erste Christ. Johannes der Täufer als Schlüssel zum Prolog des vierten Evangeliums." *Theologia viatorum* 13 (1975/1976) 155–73.

Osten-Sacken, Peter von der
Gott und Belial. Traditionsgeschichtliche Untersuchungen zum Dualismus in den Texten aus Qumran, SUNT 6 (Göttingen: Vandenhoeck & Ruprecht, 1969).

Osten-Sacken, Peter von der
"Leistung und Grenze der johanneischen Kreuzestheologie." *EvT* 36 (1976) 154–76.

Osty, Emile
"Les points de contact entre le récit de la passion dans saint Luc et saint Jean." *RSR* 39 (1951) 146–54.

Overbeck, Franz
"Über zwei neue Ansichten von Zeugnissen des Papias für die Apostelgeschichte und das vierte Evangelium." *ZWT* 10 (1867) 35–74.

Overbeck, T. G.
Neue Versuche über das Evangelium Johannis (Gera: Beckmannsche Buchhandlung, 1784).

Pagels, Elaine H.
The Johannine Gospel in Gnostic Exegesis: Heracleons Commentary on John, SBLMS 17 (Missoula: Scholars Press, 1973).

Pahk, S. S.
"The Meaning of Bread: A Structuralist Analysis of John VI, 1–58." Dissertation, Vanderbilt University, 1980.

Painter, John
John: Witness and Theologian (London: S. P. C. K., 1976).

Painter, John
"Christ and the Church in John 1,45–51." In

L'Evangile de Jean. Sources, rédaction, théologie, ed. M. de Jonge. BETL 44 (Gembloux: Duculot; Louvain: University Press, 1977) 359–62.

Painter, John
"The Church and Israel in the Gospel of John. A Response." *NTS* 25 (1978/1979) 103–12.

Pallis, Alexander
Notes on St. John and the Apocalypse (London: Oxford University Press, 1926).

Pamment, Margaret
"Is There Convincing Evidence of Samaritan Influence on the Fourth Gospel?" *ZNW* 73 (1982) 221–30.

Pancaro, Severino
"A Statistical Approach to the Concept of Time and Eschatology in the Fourth Gospel." *Bib* 50 (1969) 511–24.

Pancaro, Severino
"The Metamorphosis of a Legal Principle in the Fourth Gospel. A Close Look at Jn 7,51." *Bib* 53 (1972) 340–61.

Pancaro, Severino
"The Relationship of the Church to Israel in the Gospel of St John." *NTS* 21 (1974/1975) 396–405.

Pancaro, Severino
"'People of God' in St. John's Gospel?" *NTS* 16 (1969/1970) 114–29.

Paret, O.
Die Überlieferung der Bibel (Stuttgart: Württembergische Bibelanstalt, ⁴1966).

Parker, Pierson
"Bethany beyond Jordan." *JBL* 74 (1955) 257–61.

Parker, Pierson
"John the Son of Zebedee and the Fourth Gospel." *JBL* 81 (1962) 35–43.

Parker, Pierson
"Luke and the Fourth Evangelist." *NTS* 9 (1962/1963) 317–36.

Parker, Pierson
"Two Editions of John." *JBL* 75 (1956) 303–14.

Parkin, V.
"'On the Third Day There Was a Wedding in Cana of Galilee' (John 2.1)." *Irish Biblical Studies* 3 (1981) 134–44.

Pascher, Joseph
"Der Glaube als Mitteilung des Pneumas nach Joh 6,61–65." *Theologische Quartalschrift* 117 (1936) 301–21.

Pass, H. Leonard
The Glory of the Father. A Study in S. John XIII–XVII (London and Oxford: A. R. Mowbray, 1935).

Pastor Piñeiro, Félix-Alejandro
"Comunidad y ministerio en el evangelio joaneo." *Estudios ecclesiásticos* 50 (1975) 323–56.

Pastor Piñeiro, Félix-Alejandro
La ecclesiologia juanea según E. Schweizer, Analecta Gregoriana 168, Series Facultatis Theologicae (Rome: Gregorian University, 1968).

Patrick, Johnstone G.
"The Promise of the Paraclete." *BSac* 127 (1970) 333–45.

Patsch, Hermann
"Der Einzug Jesu in Jerusalem. Ein historischer Versuch." *ZTK* 68 (1971) 1–26.

Paul, Ludwig
"Ueber die Logoslehre bei Justin Martyr. Artikel II." *Jahrbücher für Protestantische Theologie* 17 (1891) 124–48.

Paulus, Heinrich Eberhard Gottlob
Review of *Probabilia . . .*, by Karl Gottlieb Bretschneider. *Heidelberger Jahrbücher der Literatur* 14 (1821) 112–42.

Payot, Christian
"L'interprétation johannique du ministère de Jean-Baptiste." *Foi et vie* 68 (1969) 21–37.

Percy, Ernst
Untersuchungen über den Ursprung der johanneischen Theologie, zugleich ein Beitrag zur Frage nach der Entstehung des Gnostizismus (Lund: C. W. K. Gleerup, 1939).

Pereira, Francis
"Maria Magdalena apud sepulcrum (Jo 20,1–18)." *VD* 47 (1969) 1–21.

Perles, Felix
"Noch einmal Mt 8,22, Lk 9,60 sowie Joh 20,17." *ZNW* 25 (1926) 286–87.

Pernot, M.
"Langue de la Septante." *Revue des études grecques* 42 (1929) 411–25.

Perrin, Norman
The Resurrection According to Matthew, Mark, and Luke (Philadelphia: Fortress Press, 1977).

Perry, Alfred M.
"Is John an Alexandrian Gospel?" *JBL* 62 (1944) 99–106.

Pesch, Rudolf
"Das Weinwunder bei der Hochzeit zu Kana (Joh 2,1–12)." *TGl* 24 (1981) 219–25.

Pesch, Rudolf
"'Ihr müsst von oben geboren werden': Eine Auslegung von Jo 3,1–12." *BibLeb* 7 (1966) 208–19.

Pesch, Rudolf
Der reiche Fischfang. Lk 5,1–11/Jo 21,1–14. Wundergeschichte-Berufungserzählung-Erscheinungsbericht, Kommentare und Beiträge zum Alten und Neuen Testament (Düsseldorf: Patmos-Verlag, 1969)

Peterson, Erik
"Der Gottesfreund—Beiträge zur Geschichte eines religiösen Terminus." *ZKG* 42 (1923) 161–202.

Peterson, Erik
"Zeuge der Wahrheit." In his *Theologische Traktate* (Munich: Kösel, 1951) 165–224.

Pfleiderer, Otto
"Beleuchtung der neuesten Johannes-Hypothesen." *ZWT* 12 (1869) 394–421.

Pfleiderer, Otto
Primitive Christianity. Its Writings and Teachings in

Their Historical Connections, tr. W. Montgomery (New York: G. Putnam's Sons; London: Williams & Norgate, 1906–11) = *Das Urchristentum, seine Schriften und Lehren in geschichtlichen Zusammenhang,* 2 vols. (Berlin: G. Reimer, ²1902).

Pfleiderer, Otto
"Neue Lösungsversuche zur johanneischen Frage." *Protestantische Monatshefte* 5 (1901) 169–82.

Pfleiderer, Otto
"Zur johanneischen Christologie, mit Rücksicht auf W. Beyschlag's 'Christologie des Neuen Testaments.'" *ZWT* 9 (1866) 241–66.

Pflugk, Ulrich
"Die Geschichte vom ungläubigen Thomas in der Auslegung der Kirche von den Anfängen bis zur Mitte des 16. Jahrhunderts." Dissertation, Hamburg, 1966.

Philips, T.
Die Verheissung der heiligen Eucharistie nach Johannes; eine exegetische Studie (Paderborn: F. Schöningh, 1922).

Phillips, Gary
"This is a Hard Saying: Who Can be a Listener to It?" SBLASP 1 (Missoula: Scholars Press, 1979) 185–96.

Pierce, F. X.
"Chapter-Rearrangements in St. John's Gospel." *AER* 102 (1940) 76–82.

Pillai, C. J.
"'Advocate' —Christ's Name for the Holy Spirit." *Bible Today* 30 (1967) 2078–81.

Pinto de Oliveira, C. J.
"Le verbe δίδοναι comme expression des rapports du Père et du Fils dans le quatrième évangile." *RSPT* 49 (1965) 81–104.

Pinto, Basil de
"Word and Wisdom in St. John." *Scr* 19 (1967) 19–27, 107–25.

Plessis, I. J. du
"Christ as the 'Only Begotten.'" *Neot* 2 (1968) 22–31.

Plessis, P. J. du
"Zie het Lam Gods." In *De Knechtsgestalte van Christus. Studies door collega's en oud-leerlingen aangeboden aan Prof. dr. Herman Nicolaas Ridderbos,* ed. H. H. Grosheide et al. (Kampen: Kok, 1978) 120–38.

Pollard, T. E.
"Cosmology and the Prologue of the Fourth Gospel." *VC* 12 (1958) 147–53.

Pollard, T. E.
"The Father-Son and God-Believer Relationship according to St. John." In *L'Evangile de Jean. Sources, rédaction, théologie,* ed. M. de Jonge. BETL 44 (Gembloux: Duculot; Louvain: University Press, 1977) 363–70.

Pollard, T. E.
Johannine Christology and the Early Church, SNTSMS 13 (London and New York: Cambridge University Press, 1970).

Pollard, T. E.
"Logos and Son in Origen, Arius and Athanasios." *Studia Patristica* 2 (1957) 282–87.

Ponthot, J.
"Signification génerale et structure du chapitre VI de S. Jean." *Revue Diocésaine de Tournai* 11 (1956) 414–19.

Porsch, Felix
Pneuma und Wort. Ein exegetischer Beitrag zur Pneumatologie des Johannesevangeliums, Frankfurter Theologische Studien 16 (Frankfurt: Verlag Josef Knecht, 1974).

Porsch, Felix
Anwalt der Glaubenden. Das Wirken des Geistes nach dem Zeugnis des Johannesevangeliums, Geist und Leben (Stuttgart: Katholisches Bibelwerk, 1978).

Porter, C. F.
"An Analysis of the Textual Variations between P⁷⁵ and Codex Vaticanus in the Text of John." In *Studies in the History and Text of the New Testament in Honor of Kenneth Willis Clark, Ph. D,* ed. B. L. Daniels and M. J. Suggs. Studies and Documents 29 (Salt Lake City: University of Utah Press, 1967) 71–80.

Porter, Calvin L.
"John 9.38, 39a: A Liturgical Addition to the Text." *NTS* 13 (1966/1967) 387–94.

Porter, J. R.
"Who was the Beloved Disciple?" *ExpTim* 77 (1966) 213–14.

Potter, R. D.
"Topography and Archaeology in the Fourth Gospel." *SE* 1 = TU 73 (Berlin: Akademie-Verlag, 1959) 329–37.

Potterie, Ignace de la
"La verité in San Giovanni." *RivB* 11 (1963) 3–24.

Potterie, Ignace de la
La verité dans Saint Jean, 2 vols. Vol. 1, *Le Christ et la vérité,* AnBib 73; Vol. 2, *L'Esprit et la vérité,* AnBib 74 (Rome: Pontifical Biblical Institute, 1977).

Potterie, Ignace de la
"De interpunctione et interpretatione versuum Io. 1, 3–4." *VD* 33 (1955) 193–208.

Potterie, Ignace de la
"Ecco l'Agnello di Dio." *BeO* 1 (1959) 161–69.

Potterie, Ignace de la
"L'Exaltation du Fils de l'homme." *Greg* 49 (1968) 460–78.

Potterie, Ignace de la
"Naître de l'eau et naître de l'Esprit. Le texte baptismal de Jn 3,5." *Sciences ecclésiastiques* 14 (1962) 417–43.

Potterie, Ignace de la
"Structura primae partis Evangelii Johannis (capita III et IV)." *VD* 47 (1969) 130–40.

Potterie, Ignace de la
"Ad dialogum Jesu cum Nicodemo (2,23–3,21).

Analysis litteraria." *VD* 47 (1969) 141–50.

Potterie, Ignace de la
"Jesus et Nicodemus: de necessitate generationis ex Spiritu (Jo 3,1–10)." *VD* 47 (1969) 193–214.

Potterie, Ignace de la
"Jesus et Nicodemus: de revelatione Jesu et vera fide in eum (Jo 3,11–21)." *VD* 47 (1969) 257–83.

Potterie, Ignace de la
"L'exaltation du Fils de l'homme (Jn. 12,31–36)." *Greg* 49 (1968) 460–78.

Potterie, Ignace de la
"'Je suis la Voie, la Vérité et la Vie' (Joh 14,6)." *NRT* 88 (1966) 907–42.

Potterie, Ignace de la
"L'Esprit Saint dans l'Evangile de Jean." *NTS* 18 (1971/1972) 448–51.

Potterie, Ignace de la
"Parole et Esprit dans S. Jean." In *L'Evangile de Jean. Sources, rédaction, théologie*, ed. M. de Jonge. BETL 44 (Gembloux: Duculot; Louvain: University Press, 1977) 177–201.

Potterie, Ignace de la
"La passion selon S. Jean." *AsSeign* 21 (1969) 21–34.

Potterie, Ignace de la
"Jésus roi et juge d'après Jn 19,13: ἐκάθισεν ἐπὶ Βήματος." *Bib* 41 (1960) 217–47.

Potterie, Ignace de la
"Das Wort Jesu 'Siehe, deine Mutter' und die Annahme der Mutter durch den Jünger (Joh 19,27b)." In *Neues Testament und Kirche. Für Rudolf Schnackenburg*, ed. J. Gnilka (Freiburg: Herder, 1974) 191–219.

Potterie, Ignace de la
"Structura primae partis Evangelii Johannis (capita III et IV)." *VD* 47 (1969) 130–40.

Power, Albert
"The Original Order of St. John's Gospel." *CBQ* 10 (1948) 399–405.

Power, E.
"Jo. 2. 20 and the Date of the Crucifixion." *Bib* 9 (1928) 257–88.

Preisker, Herbert
"Johannes 2, 4 und 19, 26." *ZNW* 42 (1949) 209–14.

Preisker, Herbert
"Jüdische Apokalyptik und hellenistischer Synkretismus im Johannes-Evangelium dargelegt am Begriff 'Licht.'" *TLZ* 77 (1952) 673–78.

Preisker, Herbert
"Zum Charakter des Johannesevangeliums." In *Luther, Kant, Schleiermacher in ihrer Bedeutung für den Protestantismus. Forschung und Abhandlungen Georg Wobbermin zum 70. Geburtstag (27 Oktober 1939) dargebracht von Kollegen, Schülern und Freunden*, ed. D. F. W. Schmidt et al. (Berlin: Verlag Arthur Collignon, 1939) 379–93.

Preisker, Herbert
"Wundermächte und Wundermänner der helle-

nistisch-römischen Kultur und die Auferweckung des Lazarus in Joh 11." *Wissenschaftliche Zeitschrift der Martin-Luther-Universität Halle-Wittenberg* 6 (1952/ 1953) 519–23.

Preisker, Herbert
"Das Evangelium des Johannes als erster Teil eines apokalyptischen Doppelwerkes." *TBl* 15 (1936) 185–92.

Preiss, Théo
"Etude sur le chapitre 6 de l'Evangile de Jean." *ETR* 46 (1971) 143–67.

Preiss, Théo.
"Aramäisches in Joh 8, 30–36." *TZ* 3 (1947) 78–80.

Prete, Benedetto
"La concordanza del participio *erchomenon* in *Giov.* 1,9." *BeO* 17 (1975) 195–208.

Prete, Benedetto
"'I poveri' nel racconto giovanneo dell'unzione di Betania (Gv 12,1–8)." *Atti della settimana biblica* 24 (1978) 429–44.

Prete, Benedetto
"Beati coloro che non vedono e credono (Giov. 20,29)." *BeO* (1967) 97–114.

Prete, Benedetto
"La missione rivelatrice di Cristo secondo il quarto Evangelista." *Atti della settimana biblica* 20 (1970) 133–50.

Pribnow, H.
Die johanneische Anschauung vom "Leben." Eine biblisch-theologische Untersuchung in religionsgeschichtlicher Beleuchtung (Greifswald: Universitäts-verlag Ratsbuchhandlung L. Bamberg, 1934).

Price, J. L.
"The Search for the Theology of the Fourth Gospel." In *New Testament Issues*, ed. R. Batey. Harper Forum Books (New York: Harper & Row, 1970).

Price, J. L.
"Light from Qumran upon Some Aspects of Johannine Theology." In *John and Qumran*, ed. J. H. Charlesworth (London: Chapman, 1972) 30–35.

Pronobis, C.
"Bethesda zur Zeit Jesu." *TQ* 114 (1933) 181–207.

Proudman, C. L. J.
"The Eucharist in the Fourth Gospel." *CJT* 12 (1966) 212–16.

Proulx, P. and Alonso Schökel, L.
"Las Sandalias del Mesías Esposo." *Bib* 59 (1978) 1–37.

Prümm, K.
Der christliche Glaube und die altheidnische Welt. Vol. 1, *Der religionsgeschichtliche Hintergrund des johanneischen Logos* (Leipzig: J. Hegner, 1935).

Pujol, L.
"'In loco qui dicitur *Lithostrotos.*'" *VD* 15 (1935) 180–86, 204–7, 233–37.

Pulligny, J. de
"La première finale du quatrième évangile et l'épisode d'Emmaus dans Luc." *RHR* 95 (1927) 364–71.

Pulver, M.
"Die Lichterfahrung im Johannesevangelium, im Corpus Hermeticum, in der Gnosis und der Ostkirche." *ErJb* 10 (1943) 253–96.

Pulver, Max
"Die Lichterfahrung im Johannesevangelium, im Corpus Hermeticum, in der Gnosis und in der Ostkirche." *ErJb* 10 (1943) 253–96.

Purvis, James D.
"The Fourth Gospel and the Samaritans." *NovT* 17 (1975) 161–98.

Quasten, John
"The Parable of the Good Shepherd: Jn 10, 1–21." *CBQ* 10 (1948) 1–12, 151–69.

Quiévreux, François
"Le récit de la multiplication des pains dans le quatrième Evangile." *RSR* 41 (1967) 97–108.

Quiévreux, François
"La structure symbolique de l'évangile de saint Jean." *RHPR* 33 (1953) 123–65.

Quispel, Gilles
"Nathanael und der Menschensohn (Joh 1, 51)." *ZNW* 47 (1956) 281–83.

Radermakers, J.
"La prière de Jésus. Jn 17." *AsSeign* 29 (1973) 48–86.

Radermakers, Jean
"Je suis la vraie vigne Jn 15,1–8." *AsSeign* 26 (1973) 46–58.

Radermakers, Jean
"Mission et apostolat dans l'évangile johannique." *SE* 2 = TU 87 (Berlin: Akademie-Verlag, 1964) 100–121.

Rahner, Hugo
"Flumina de ventre Christi—Die patristische Auslegung von Joh 7, 37–38." *Bib* 22 (1941) 269–302, 367–403.

Ramos-Regidor, J.
"Signo y Poder—A proposito de la exegesis patristica de Jn 2,1–11." *Salesianum* 27 (1965) 499–562; 28 (1966) 3–64.

Randall, John F.
"The Theme of Unity in John 17:20–23." *ETL* 41 (1965) 373–94.

Raney, W. H.
The Relation of the Fourth Gospel to the Christian Cultus (Giessen: A. Töpelmann, 1933).

Raphael, Georg
Annotationes Philologicae in NT (Lüneburg: J. A. Langevak, 1747).

Rasco, Aemilius
"Christus granum frumenti (Jo 12,24)." *VD* 37 (1959) 12–25, 65–77.

Rau, Christoph
Struktur und Rhythmus im Johannes-Evangelium. Eine Untersuchung über die Komposition des vierten Evangeliums, Schriften zur Religionserkenntnis (Stuttgart: Urachhaus, 1972).

Redford, J.
"Preparing the Way: John the Baptist." *Clergy Review* 66 (1981) 193–200.

Redlich, E. Basil
"St John i–iii: A Study in Dislocations." *ExpTim* 55 (1943/1944) 89–92.

Reese, James M.
"Literary Structure of Jn 13:31–14:31; 16:5–6, 16–33." *CBQ* 34 (1972) 321–31.

Regul, J.
Die antimarcionitischen Evangelienprologe, Vetus Latina, Die Reste der altlateinischen Bibel, Aus der Geschichte der lateinischen Bibel 6 (Freiburg: Herder, 1969).

Reich, H.
"Der König mit der Dornenkrone." *Neue Jahrbücher für das klassische Altertum, Geschichte und deutsche Literatur* 13 (1904) 705–33.

Reim, Günter
"John iv, 44—Crux or Clue?" *NTS* 22 (1975/1976) 476–80.

Reim, Günter
"Joh 9—Tradition und zeitgenössische messianische Diskussion." *BZ* 22 (1978) 245–53.

Reim, Günter
Studien zum alttestamentlichen Hintergrund des Johannesevangeliums, SNTSMS 22 (New York: Cambridge University Press, 1974).

Reim, Günter
"Johannes 21—Ein Anhang?" In *Studies in New Testament Language and Text. Essays in Honour of George D. Kilpatrick on the Occasion of his sixty-fifth Birthday*, ed. J. K. Elliott. NovTSup 44 (Leiden: E. J. Brill, 1976) 330–37.

Reiser, William E.
"The Case of the Tidy Tomb: The Place of the Napkins of John 11:44 and 20:7." *HeyJ* 14 (1973) 47–57.

Rengstorf, Karl Heinrich
Johannes und sein Evangelium (Darmstadt: Wissenschaftliche Buchgesellschaft, 1973).

Rengstorf, Karl Heinrich
Die Anfänge der Auseinandersetzung zwischen Christusglaube und Asklepiosfrömmigkeit, Schriften der Gesellschaft zur Förderung der Westfälischen Landesuniversität zu Münster 30 (Münster: Aschendorff, 1953).

Rettig, Heinrich Christian Michael
De quatuor Evangeliorum canonicorum origine, 2 vols. (Giessen: Müller, 1824).

Reuss, Eduard
"Ideen zur Einleitung in das Evangelium Johannis." In *Denkschrift der Theologischen Gesellschaft zu Strassburg* 1 (Strasbourg, 1840) 7–60.

Reuss, Eduard
　　Die johanneische Theologie (Jena, 1847).
Reuss, Eduard
　　"Johannes der Apostel und Evangelist." In
　　*Allgemeine Encyklopädie der Wissenschaften und
　　Künste,* Zweite Sektion, Teil 22 (Leipzig: F. A.
　　Brockhaus, 1843) 1–94.
Reuter, Hans Richard
　　"Wider die Krankheit zum Tode." In *Schöpferische
　　Nachfolge,* ed. Ch. Frey and W. Huber (Heidelberg:
　　Forschungsstätte der Evangelischen Studien
　　gemeinschaft, 1978) 563ff.
Réville, Jean
　　Le quatrième évangile, son origine et sa valeur historique
　　(1901).
Réville, Jean
　　*La doctrine du logos dans le quatrième Evangile et dans
　　les oeuvres de Philon* (Paris: G. Fischbacher, 1881).
Reynolds, S. M.
　　"The Supreme Importance of the Doctrine of
　　Election and the Eternal Security of the Elect as
　　Taught in the Gospel of John." *WTJ* 28 (1965) 38–
　　41.
Rhodes, Erroll F.
　　"The Corrections of Papyrus Bodmer II." *NTS* 14
　　(1967/1968) 271–81.
Riaud, J.
　　"La gloire et la royauté de Jésus dans la Passion
　　selon saint Jean." *BVC* 56 (1964) 28–44.
Ricca, P.
　　Die Eschatologie des Vierten Evangeliums (Zurich and
　　Frankfurt: Gotthelf-Verlag, 1966).
Ricca, P.
　　"Note di ecclesiologia giovannica." *Protestantesimo*
　　22 (1967) 148–66.
Richmond, Wilfrid John
　　*The Gospel of the Rejection. A Study of the Relation of
　　the Fourth Gospel to the Three* (London: Murray,
　　1906).
Richter, Georg
　　"Zur sogenannten Semeia-Quelle des Johannes-
　　evangeliums." In his *Studien zum
　　Johannesevangelium,* 281–87.
Richter, Georg
　　"Die Fleischwerdung des Logos im Johannes-
　　evangelium." *NovT* 13 (1971) 81–126; 14 (1972)
　　257–76. In his *Studien zum Johannesevangelium,*
　　149–98.
Richter, Georg
　　"Ist *en* ein strukturbildendes Element im Logos-
　　hymnus?" *Bib* 51 (1970) 539–44. In his *Studien zum
　　Johannesevangelium,* 143–48.
Richter, Georg
　　"Bist du Elias? (Joh 1,21)." *BZ* 6 (1962) 79–92,
　　238–56; 7 (1963) 63–80. In his *Studien zum
　　Johannesevangelium,* 1–41.
Richter, Georg
　　"Zur Frage von Tradition und Redaktion in Joh
　　1,19–34." In his *Studien im Johannesevangelium,*

288–314.
Richter, Georg
　　"Zu den Tauferzählungen Mk 1,9–11 und Joh
　　1,32–34." *ZNW* 65 (1974) 43–56. In his *Studien
　　zum Johannesevangelium,* 315–26.
Richter, Georg
　　"Zum sogenannten Taufetext Joh 3,5." In his
　　Studien zum Johannesevangelium, 327–45.
Richter, Georg
　　"Zum gemeindebildenden Element in den johan-
　　neischen Schriften." In his *Studien zum Johannes-
　　evangelium,* 383ff.
Richter, Georg
　　"Präsentische und futurische Eschatologie im
　　vierten Evangelium." In *Jesus und der Menschensohn.
　　Für Anton Vögtle,* ed. R. Pesch and R. Schnacken-
　　burg (Freiburg: Herder, 1975) 117–52. In his
　　Studien zum Johannesevangelium, 346–82.
Richter, Georg
　　"Die Alttestamentlichen Zitate in der Rede vom
　　Himmelsbrot: Joh 6,26–51a." In his *Studien zum
　　Johannesevangelium,* 199–265.
Richter, Georg
　　"Zur Formgeschichte und literarischen Einheit von
　　Joh VI, 31–58." *ZNW* 60 (1969) 21–55. In his
　　Studien zum Johannesevangelium, 88–119.
Richter, Georg
　　"Die Fusswaschung: Joh 13,1–20." *MTZ* 16 (1965)
　　13–26. Now in his *Studien zum Johannesevangelium,*
　　42–57.
Richter, Georg
　　"Die Deutung des Kreuzestodes Jesu in der
　　Leidensgeschichte des Johannesevangeliums (Joh
　　13–19)." In his *Studien zum Johannesevangelium,*
　　58–73.
Richter, Georg
　　*Die Fusswaschung im Johannesevangelium. Geschichte
　　ihrer Deutung,* BU 1 (Regensburg: F. Pustet, 1967).
Richter, Georg
　　Studien zum Johannesevangelium, ed. J. Hainz. BU
　　13 (Regensburg: F. Pustet, 1977).
Richter, Georg
　　"Die Deutung des Kreuzestodes Jesu in der
　　Leidensgeschichte des Johannesevangeliums."
　　BibLeb 9 (1968) 21–36.
Richter, Georg
　　"Die Gefangennahme Jesu nach dem Johannes-
　　evangelium (18,1–12)." *BibLeb* 10 (1969) 26–39.
Richter, Georg
　　"Blut und Wasser aus der durchbohrten Seite
　　Jesu." In his *Studien zum Johannesevangelium,* 120–
　　42.
Richter, Georg
　　"Der Vater und Gott Jesu und seiner Brüder in Joh
　　20,17. Ein Beitrag zur Christologie des Johannes-
　　evangeliums." In his *Studien zum
　　Johannesevangelium,* 266–80.
Ridderbos, Hermann
　　"The Structure and Scope of the Prologue to the

Gospel of John." *NovT* 8 (1966) 180–201.

Ridderbos, Hermann
"On the Christology of the Fourth Gospel." In *Saved by Hope. Essays in Honor of Richard C. Oudersluys*, ed. J. I. Cook (Grand Rapids: Wm. B. Eerdmans, 1978) 15–26.

Riedl, Johannes
"Wenn ihr den Menschensohn erhöht habt, werdet ihr erkennen (Joh 8, 28)." In *Jesus und der Menschensohn. Für Anton Vögtle*, ed. R. Pesch and R. Schnackenburg (Freiburg: Herder, 1975) 355–70.

Riedl, Johannes
"Die Funktion der Kirche nach Johannes. 'Vater, wie du mich in die Welt gesandt hast, so habe ich auch sie in die Welt gesandt' (Joh 17,18)." *BK* 28 (1973) 12–14.

Riedl, Johannes
Das Heilswerk Jesu nach Johannes, Freiburger theologische Studien 93 (Freiburg: Herder, 1973).

Riehm, E.
Review of *Der johanneische Lehrbegriff*, by B. Weiss. *TSK* 37 (1864) 521–62.

Riesenfeld, Harald
"Die Perikope von der Ehebrecherin in der frühkirchlichen Tradition." *SEÅ* 17 (1952) 106–11.

Riesenfeld, Harald
"A Probable Background to the Johannine Paraclete." In *Ex Orbe Religionum. Studia Geo Widengren XXIV mense Apr. MCMLXXII quo die lustra tredecim feliciter explevit oblata ab collegis, discipulis, amicis, collegae magistro amico congratulantibus. Pars prior*, Studies in the History of Religion [Supplements to Numen] 21 (Leiden: E. J. Brill, 1972) 266–77.

Riesenfeld, Harald
"Zu den johanneischen ἵνα-Sätzen." *ST* 19 (1965) 213–20.

Riesenfeld, Harald
"Liknelserna i den synoptiska och i den johanneiska traditionen." *SEÅ* 25 (1960) 37–61. French: "Les paraboles dans la prédiction de Jésus selon les traditions synoptique et johannique." *Eglise et théologie* 22 (1959) 21–29.

Riga, P.
"Signs of Glory. The Use of 'Sēmeion' in St. John's Gospel." *Int* 17 (1963) 402–24.

Rigaux, Beda
"Die Jünger in Joh 17." *Tübinger theologische Quartalschrift* 150 (1970) 202–13.

Rigg, H.
"Was Lazarus 'the Beloved Disciple'?" *ExpTim* 33 (1921/1922) 232–34.

Rigg, W. H.
"The Purpose of the Fourth Gospel." *CQR* 61 (1935) 1–37.

Riggenbach, Christoph Johannes
"Johannes der Apostel und der Presbyter." *Jahrbücher für deutsche Theologie* 13 (1868) 319–34.

Riggenbach, Christoph Johannes
Die Zeugnisse für das Evangelium Johannis (Basel: Bahnmeier's Verlag, 1866).

Riggenbach, D.
"Neue Materialien zur Beleuchtung des Papiaszeugnisses über den Märtyrertod des Johannes." *NKZ* 32 (1921) 692–96.

Riggenbach, Eduard
"Die Quellen der Auferstehungsgeschichte, mit besonderer Berücksichtigung des Schauplatzes der Erscheinungen." In *Aus Schrift und Geschichte; Theologische Abhandlungen und Skizzen Herrn Prof. D. Conrad von Orelli zur Feier seiner 25-jährigen Lehrtätigkeit in Basel von Freunden und Schülern gewidmet* (Basel: R. Reich, 1898) 109–53.

Riggs, Don Richard
"John's Persecution Ethic: A Study in the Farewell Discourse." Dissertation, Vanderbilt University, 1969.

Riggs, James Stevenson
The Messages of Jesus According to the Gospel of John. The Discourses of Jesus in the Fourth Gospel (New York: Charles Scribner's Sons, 1907).

Ringgren, Helmer
Word and Wisdom. Studies in the hypostatization of divine qualities and functions in the ancient Near East (Lund: Olssons boktr, 1947).

Rissi, Mathias
"John 1,1–18." *Int* 31 (1977) 395–401.

Rissi, Mathias
"Die Logoslieder im Prolog des vierten Evangeliums." *TZ* 31 (1975) 321–36; 32 (1976) 1–13.

Rissi, Mathias
"Die Hochzeit in Kana Joh 2,1–11." In *Oikonomia. Heilsgeschichte als Thema der Theologie. Oscar Cullmann zum 65. Geburtstag gewidmet*, ed. F. Christ (Hamburg: Reich, 1967) 76–92.

Rissi, Mathias
"Voll grosser Fische, 153, Joh 21,1–14." *TZ* 35 (1979) 73–89.

Rist, John M.
"St. John and Amelius." *JTS*, n.s., 20 (1969) 230–31.

Ritschl, A.
"Zum Verständnis des Prologes des johanneischen Evangeliums." *TSK* 48 (1875) 576–82.

Ritt, Hubert
"'So sehr hat Gott die Welt geliebt . . .' (Joh 3,16)— Gotteserfahrung bei Johannes." In *"Ich will euer Gott werden . . . ." Beispiele biblischen Redens von Gott*, SBS 100 (Stuttgart: Katholisches Bibelwerk, 1981) 207–26.

Ritt, Hubert
Das Gebet zum Vater. Zur Interpretation von Joh 17, Forschung zur Bibel 36 (Würzburg: Echter Verlag, 1979).

Roberge, Michel
"Structures littéraires et christologie dans le quatrième évangile: Jean 1,29–34." In *Le Christ hier, aujourd'hui et demain. Colloque de christologie tenu à l'Université Laval*, ed. R. Laflamme and M.

Gervais (Québec: Les Presses de l'Université Laval, 1976) 467–78.

Roberge, Michel
"Jean VI, 22–24: Un problème de critique textuelle." *Laval Théologique et Philosophique* 34 (1978) 275–89.

Roberge, Michel
"Jean VI, 22–24: Un problème de critique littéraire." *Laval Théologique et Philosophique* 35 (1979) 139–51.

Roberge, Michel
"Le discours sur le pain de vie (Jean 6,22–59). Problèmes d'interprétation." *Laval Théologique et Philosophique* 38 (1982) 265–300.

Roberge, Michel
"Notices de conclusion et redaction du quatrième évangile." *Laval théologique et philosophique* 31 (1975) 49–53.

Roberts, C. H.
An Unpublished Fragment of the Fourth Gospel in the John Rylands Library (Manchester: Manchester University Press, 1935).

Roberts, J. H.
"The lamb of God." *Neot* 2 (1968) 41–56.

Roberts, R. L.
"The Rendering 'Only Begotton' in John 3:16." *Restoration Quarterly* 16 (1973) 2–22.

Robertson, Archibald Thomas
The Divinity of Christ in the Gospel of John (New York: Fleming H. Revell Co, 1916).

Robinson, D. W. B.
"Born of Water and Spirit: Does John 3:5 Refer to Baptism?" *Reformed Theological Review* 25 (1966) 15–23.

Robinson, J. A. T.
"The Relation of the Prologue to the Gospel of St. John." *NTS* 9 (1962/1963) 120–29.

Robinson, J. A. T.
"The 'Others' of John 4,38: A Test of Exegetical Method." *SE* 1 = TU 73 (Berlin: Akademie-Verlag, 1959) 510–15.

Robinson, J. A. T.
"The Destination and Purpose of St. John's Gospel." *NTS* 6 (1959/1960) 117–31.

Robinson, James M.
"Recent Research in the Fourth Gospel." *JBL* 78 (1959) 242–52.

Robinson, James M.
"The Johannine Trajectory." In J. M. Robinson and H. Koester, *Trajectories through Early Christianity* (Philadelphia: Fortress Press, 1971) 232–68.

Robinson, James M.
"Sethians and Johannine Thought: The *Trimorphic Protennoia* and the Prologue of the Gospel of John." In *The Rediscovery of Gnosticism*, 2 vols., ed. Bentley Layton. Studies in the History of Religions [Supplement to *Numen*] 41. Vol. 1, *The School of Valentinus;* Vol. 2, *Sethian Gnosticism.* (Leiden: E. J.

Brill, 1980–1981) 643–62.

Robinson, John Arthur Thomas
"The Parable of John 10, 1–5." *ZNW* 46 (1955) 233–40.

Robinson, John Arthur Thomas
"The Significance of the Foot-Washing." In *Neotestamentica et patristica. Eine Freundesgabe, Herrn Professor Dr. Oscar Cullmann zu seinem 60. Geburtstag überreicht,* NovTSup 6 (Leiden: E. J. Brill, 1962) 144–47.

Rogers, Donald G.
"Who Was the Beloved Disciple?" *ExpTim* 77 (1966) 214.

Röhricht, R.
"Zur johanneischen Logoslehre." *TSK* 41 (1868) 299–315; 44 (1871) 503–9.

Roloff, Jürgen
"Der johanneische 'Lieblingsjünger' und der Lehrer der Gerechtigkeit." *NTS* 15 (1968/1969) 129–51.

Romaniuk, Kazimierz
"'I am the Resurrection and the Life.'" *Concilium* 60 (1970) 68–77.

Romeo, Joseph A.
"Gematria and John 21:11—The Children of God." *JBL* 97 (1978) 263–64.

Ross, Alexander
"Displacements in the Fourth Gospel." *ExpTim* 58 (1946/1947) 250.

Rosscup, James E.
Abiding in Christ. Studies in John 15. (Grand Rapids: Zondervan, 1973).

Rossetto, G.
"La route vers le Père: Jn 14,1–12." *AsSeign* 26 (1973) 18–30.

Roth, C.
"The Cleansing of the Temple and Zechariah." *NovT* 4 (1960) 174–81.

Rottmanner, O.
"Joh 2,4: Eine mariologische Studie." *TQ* 74 (1892) 215–45.

Rousseau, François
"La femme adultère. Structure de Jn 7, 53–8,11." *Bib* 59 (1978) 463–80.

Roustang, F.
"L'entretien avec Nicodème [Jn 3:1–15]." *NRT* 78 (1956) 337–58.

Roustang, F.
"Les moments de l'Acte de Foi et ses conditions de possibilité." *RSR* 46 (1958) 344–78.

Ru, Gerrit de
"Einge notities bij de herinterpretaties van de voetwassing." *Kerk en theologie* 30 (1979) 89–104.

Ruager, Søren
"Johannes 6 og nadveren." *TTKi* 50 (1979) 81–92.

Rubio Morán, L.
"Revelación en enigmas y revelación en claridad. Análisis exegético de Jn 16,25." *Salmanticensis* 19 (1972) 107–44.

Ruckstuhl, Eugen

"Das Johannesevangelium und die Gnosis." In *Neues Testament und Geschichte. Historisches Geschehen und Deutung im Neuen Testament. Oscar Cullmann zum 70. Geburtstag*, ed. H. Baltensweiler and B. Reicke (Zurich: Theologischer Verlag; Tübingen: Mohr-Siebeck, 1972) 143–56.

Ruckstuhl, Eugen

"Abstieg und Erhöhung des johanneischen Menschensohnes." In *Jesus und der Menschensohn. Für Anton Vögtle*, ed. R. Pesch and R. Schnackenburg (Freiburg: Herder, 1975) 314–41.

Ruckstuhl, Eugen

"Die johanneische Menschensohnforschung." In *Theologische Berichte 1*, ed. J. Pfammatter and F. Fürger (Zurich and Cologne: Benziger, 1972) 171–284.

Ruckstuhl, Eugen

"Literarkritik am Johannesevangelium und eucharistische Rede (Jo 6, 51c–58)." *Divus Thomas* 23 (1945) 153–90, 301–33.

Ruckstuhl, Eugen

"Wesen und Kraft der Eucharistie in der Sicht des Johannesevangeliums." In *Das Opfer der Kirche. Exegetische, dogmatische und pastoraltheologische Studien zum Verständnis der Messe*, ed. R. Erni. Luzerner theologische Studien 1 (Lucerne: Rex-Verlag, 1954) 47–90.

Ruckstuhl, Eugen

"Johannine Language and Style. The Question of their Unity." In *L'Evangile de Jean. Sources, rédaction, théologie*, ed. M. de Jonge. BETL 44 (Gembloux: Duculot; Louvain: University Press, 1977) 125–47.

Ruckstuhl, Eugen

Die literarische Einheit des Johannesevangeliums; der gegenwärtige Stand der einschlägigen Forschungen (Fribourg: Paulusverlag, 1951).

Ruddick, C. T.

"Feeding and Sacrifice—The Old Testament Background of the Fourth Gospel." *ExpTim* 79 (1968) 340–41.

Rudel, W.

"Das Mißverständnis im Johannesevangelium." *NKZ* 32 (1921) 351–61.

Ruegg, U.

"Zur Freude befreit: Jesus auf der Hochzeit zu Kana." In *Die Wunder Jesu*, ed. Anton Steiner and Volker Weymann (Basel: F. Reinhardt Verlag; Zurich: Benziger, 1978) 147–66.

Rusch, Frederick A.

"The Signs and the Discourses: The Rich Theology of John 6." *CurTM* 5 (1978) 386–90.

Russell, Elbert

"Possible Influence of the Mysteries on the Form and Interrelation of the Johannine Writings." *JBL* 51 (1932) 336–51.

Russell, Ralph

"The Beloved Disciple and the Resurrection." *Scr* 8

(1956) 57–62.

Sabbe, M.

"Tempelreiniging en Tempellogion." *Collationes Brugenses et Gandavenses* 2 (1956) 289–99, 466–80.

Sabbe, M.

"The Arrest of Jesus in Jn 18,1–11 and its Relation to the Synoptic Gospels. A Critical Evaluation of A. Dauer's Hypothesis." In *L'Evangile de Jean. Sources, rédaction, théologie*, ed. M. de Jonge. BETL 44 (Gembloux: Duculot; Louvain: University Press, 1977) 203–34.

Sabourin, Leopold

"Resurrectio Lazari (Jo 11,1–44)." *VD* 46 (1968) 350–60.

Sabugal, S.

"El título Messías-Christos en el contexto del Relato sobre la Actividad de Jesús en Samaría: Jn 4,25.29." *Augustinianum* 12 (1972) 79–105.

Sabugal, S.

"Una contribución a la cristologia joannea." *Augustinianum* 12 (1972) 565–72.

Sabugal, S.

Christos: Investigación exegetica sobre la cristologia joannea (Barcelona: Herder, 1972).

Safrai, Shmuel

The Pilgrimage at the Time of the Second Temple (Tel Aviv: Am Hasserfer Publisher Ltd., 1965) [in Hebrew].

Sahlin, Harald

"Zwei Abschnitte aus Joh 1 rekonstruiert." *ZNW* 51 (1960) 64–69.

Sahlin, Harald

"Till förstaelsen av Joh 7,37–41." *SEÅ* 11 (1946) 77–90.

Sahlin, Harald

"Lasarus-gestalten (Die Gestalt des Lazarus)." *SEÅ* 37/38 (1972/1973) 167–74.

Sahlin, Harald

Zur Typologie des Johannesevangeliums (Uppsala: Lundequistska Bokhandeln, 1950).

Salmon, V.

Histoire de la tradition textuelle de l'original grec du quatrième évangile avec 64 illustrations (papyrus et manuscrits accompagnés d'une transcription complète) (Paris: Letouzey et Ané, 1969).

Salvoni, Fausto

"Textual Authority for Jn 7,53–8,11." *Restoration Quarterly* 4 (1960) 11–15.

Salvoni, Fausto

"The So-Called Jesus Resurrection Proof (John 20:7)." *Restoration Quarterly* 22 (1979) 72–76.

Sanday, W.

The Criticism of the Fourth Gospel (Oxford: Clarendon Press; New York: Charles Scribner's Sons, 1905).

Sanday, William M. A.

The Gospels in the Second Century. An Examination of the Critical Part of a Work Entitled "Supernatural Religion" (London: Macmillan, 1876).

Sanday, William M. A.
The Authorship and Historical Character of the Fourth Gospel Considered in Reference to the Contents of the Gospel Itself (London: Macmillan, 1872).

Sanders, Jack T.
The New Testament's Christological Hymns. Their Historical Religious Background, SNTSMS 15 (London: Cambridge University Press, 1971).

Sanders, Joseph N.
"Those Whom Jesus Loved: St. John 11,5." *NTS* 1 (1954/1955) 29–76.

Sanders, Joseph N.
The Fourth Gospel in the Early Church (Cambridge: Cambridge University Press, 1943).

Sanders, Joseph N.
"St. John on Patmos." *NTS* 9 (1962/1963) 75–85.

Sandvik, Björn
"Joh 15 als Abendmahlstext." *TZ* 23 (1967) 323–28.

Sass, Gerhard
Die Auferweckung des Lazarus. Eine Auslegung von Johannes 11, BibS(N) 51 (Neukirchen-Vluyn: Neukirchener Verlag, 1967).

Sasse, Hermann
"Κόσμος." *TDNT* 3: 891–92, 894–95.

Sauer, J.
"Die Exegese des Cyril von Alexandrien nach seinem Kommentar zum Johannesevangelium." Dissertation, Freiburg, 1965.

Sava, A. F.
"The Wound in the Side of Christ." *CBQ* 19 (1957) 343–46.

Schaeder, Hans Heinrich
"Der 'Mensch' im Prolog des IV. Evangeliums." In *Studien zum antiken Synkretismus aus Iran und Griechenland,* ed. H. H. Schaeder and R. Reitzenstein (Leipzig: B. G. Teubner, 1926; reprint Darmstadt: Wissenschaftliche Buchgesellschaft, 1965) 306–50.

Schaefer, O.
"Der Sinn der Rede Jesu von den vielen Wohnungen in seines Vaters Hause und von dem Weg zu ihm (Joh 14,1–7)." *ZNW* 32 (1933) 210–17.

Schäferdiek, K.
"Theodor von Mopsuestia als Exeget des vierten Evangeliums." *Studia patristica* 10,1 (Berlin: Akademie-Verlag, 1970) 242–46.

Schedl, Claus
"Zur Schreibung von Joh 1, 10A in Papyrus Bodmer XV." *NovT* 14 (1972) 238–40.

Scheffer, H.-L.
Examen critique et exégétique du XXI. Chap. de l'évangile selon S. Jean (Strassburg: F. G. Levrault, 1839).

Schein, Bruce E.
"Our Father Abraham." Dissertation, Yale University, 1972.

Schelkle, Karl Hermann
"Kirche im Johannesevangelium." *TQ* 156 (1976) 277–283.

Schelkle, Karl Hermann
"Die Leidensgeschichte Jesu nach Johannes. Motiv- und formgeschichtliche Betrachtung." In his *Wort und Schrift. Beiträge zur Auslegung und Auslegungsgeschichte des Neuen Testaments* (Düsseldorf: Patmos-Verlag, 1966) 76–80.

Schencke, Wilhelm
"Die 'Chokma' (Sophia) in der jüdischen Hypostasenspekulation: ein Beitrag zur Geschichte der religiösen Ideen im Zeitalter des Hellenismus." In *Videnskapsselskapets skrifter* 2: *Hist.-filos. Klasse,* 1912, no. 6 (Kristiania: Dybwad, 1913).

Schenke, Gesine
"'Die dreigestaltige Protennoia': Eine gnostische Offenbarungsrede in koptischer Sprache aus dem Fund von Nag Hammadi eingeleitet und übersetzt vom Berliner Arbeitskreis für koptisch-gnostische Schriften." *TLZ* 99 (1974) 731–46.

Schenke, Hans-Martin
"Jakobsbrunnen—Josephsgrab—Sychar. Topographische Untersuchungen und Erwägungen in der Perspektive von Joh 4,5.6." *ZDPV* 84 (1968) 159–84.

Schenke, Ludger
"Die formale und gedankliche Struktur von Joh 6,26–58." *BZ,* n.f., 24 (1980) 21–41.

Schenkel, Daniel
Das Christusbild der Apostel und der nachapostolischen Zeit aus den Quellen dargestellt (Leipzig: F. A. Brockhaus, 1879) 174–93, 203–13, 373–97.

Schepens, Prosper
"Pontifex anni illius (Ev. de saint Jean 11,49.51; 18,14)." *RSR* 11 (1921) 372–74.

Schille, Gottfried
"Prolegomena zur Jesusfrage." *TLZ* 93 (1968) 481–88.

Schille, Gottfried
"Das Leiden des Herrn. Die evanglische Passionstradition und ihr 'Sitz im Leben.'" *ZTK* 52 (1955) 161–205.

Schilling, F. A.
"The Story of Jesus and the Adulteress [Jn 8:1–11]." *ATR* 37 (1955) 91–106.

Schimanowski, G.
"Präexistenz und Christologie. Untersuchungen zur Präexistenz von Weisheit und Messias in der jüdischen Tradition." Dissertation, Tübingen, 1981.

Schirmer, Dietrich
Rechtsgeschichtliche Untersuchungen zum Johannes-Evangelium (Berlin: Erlangen, 1964).

Schlatter, Adolf
Der Evangelist Johannes (Stuttgart: Calwer Vereinsbuchhandlung, 1930) 1183–84 on John 3:1.

Schlatter, Adolf
"Der Bruch Jesu mit der Judenschaft." In *Aus Schrift und Geschichte. Theologische Abhandlungen und Skizzen Herrn Prof. D. Conrad von Orelli zur Feier*

seiner 25-jährigen Lehrtätigkeit in Basel von Freunden und Schülern gewidmet (Basel: B. Reich, 1898) 1–23.

Schlatter, Adolf
"Die Sprache und die Heimat des vierten Evangelisten." In *Johannes und sein Evangelium*, ed. K. H. Rengstorf. Wege der Forschung 82 (Darmstadt: Wissenschaftliche Buchgesellschaft, 1973) 28–201.

Schlatter, Adolf
Die Parallelen in den Worten Jesu bei Johannes und Matthäus (Gütersloh: C. Bertelsmann, 1898).

Schlatter, Frederic W.
"The Problem of Jn 1,3b–4a." *CBQ* 34 (1972) 54–58.

Schleiermacher, Friedrich
Homilien über das Evangelium des Johannes in den Jahren 1823–1826 gesprochen. Aus wortgetreuen Nachschriften, ed. Ad. Sydow. In his *Sämmtliche Werke*, Zweite Abtheilung, Predigten, vols. 8–9 (Berlin: G. Reimer, 1837 and 1847).

Schleiermacher, Friedrich
Über die Religion. Reden an die Gebildeten unter ihren Verächtern (Berlin: G. Reimer, ³1821).

Schleiermacher, Friedrich
The Life of Jesus, tr. S. MacLean Gilmour. Ed. with an introduction by Jack C. Verheyden. Lives of Jesus Series (Philadelphia: Fortress Press, 1975) = *Das Leben Jesu. Vorlesungen an der Universität zu Berlin in Jahr 1832 gehalten*, ed. K. A. Rütenick (Berlin: G. Reimer, 1864).

Schleiermacher, Friedrich
Einleitung ins Neue Testament. Aus Schleiermacher's handschriftlichem Nachlasse und nachgeschriebenen Vorlesungen, mit einer Vorrede von Dr. Friedrich Lücke, ed. G. Wolde (Berlin: G. Reimer, 1845).

Schlier, Heinrich
"Die Bruderliebe nach dem Evangelium und den Briefen des Johannes." In his *Ende der Zeit. Exegetische Aufsätze und Vorträge* 3 (Freiburg and Vienna: Herder, 1971) 124–35.

Schlier, Heinrich
"Glauben, Erkennen, Lieben nach dem Johannesevangelium." In his *Besinnung auf das Neue Testament. Exegetische Aufsätze und Vorträge* 2 (Freiburg and Vienna: Herder, 1964) 279–93.

Schlier, Heinrich
"Meditation über den johanneischen Begriff der Wahrheit." In his *Besinnung auf das Neue Testament. Exegetische Aufsätze und Vorträge* 2 (Freiburg and Vienna: Herder, 1964) 272–78.

Schlier, Heinrich
"'Im Anfang war das Wort' im Prolog des Johannesevangeliums." *Wort und Wahrheit* 9 (1954) 169–80.

Schlier, Heinrich
"Joh 6 und das johanneische Verständnis der Eucharisitie." In his *Das Ende der Zeit. Exegetische Aufsätze und Vorträge*, 2 (Freiburg and Vienna: Herder, 1971) 102–23.

Schlier, Heinrich
"Der Heilige Geist als Interpret nach dem Johannesevangelium." *Internationale Katholische Zeitschrift Communio* 2 (1973) 97–108.

Schlier, Heinrich
"Zum Begriff des Geistes nach dem Johannesevangelium." In *Neutestamentliche Aufsätze. Festschrift für Prof. Josef Schmid zum 70. Geburtstag*, ed. J. Blinzler et al. (Regensburg: F. Pustet, 1963) 233–39.

Schlier, Heinrich
"Jesus und Pilatus nach dem Johannesevangelium." In his *Die Zeit der Kirche. Exegetische Aufsätze und Vorträge* (Freiburg: Herder, 1956, ⁵1972) 56–74.

Schlier, Heinrich
"Zur Christologie des Johannesevangelium." In his *Das Ende der Zeit. Exegetische Aufsätze und Vorträge* 3 (Freiburg: Herder, 1971) 85–88.

Schmid, Josef
"Joh 1, 13." *BZ* 1 (1957) 118–25.

Schmid, L.
"Johannes und die Religionsgeschichte." Dissertation, Tübingen, 1933.

Schmid, Lothar
"Die Komposition der Samaria-Szene in Joh 4, 1–42." *ZNW* 28 (1929) 148–58.

Schmidt, Karl Ludwig
"Der johanneische Charakter der Erzählung vom Hochzeitswunder in Kana." In *Harnack-Ehrung. Beiträge zur Kirchengeschichte ihrem Lehrer Adolf von Harnack zu seinem 70. Geburtstag* (Leipzig: J. C. Hinrichs, 1921) 32–43.

Schmiedel, Paul W.
"Gospel." *Encyclopaedia Biblica*, ed. Thomas Kelly Cheyne and J. Sutherland Black (London: A. and C. Black; New York: Macmillan, 1901) 2: 1761–1898.

Schmiedel, Paul W.
"John, Son of Zebedee." *Encyclopaedia Biblica*, ed. Thomas Kelly Cheyne and J. Sutherland Black (London: A. and C. Black; New York: Macmillan, 1901) 2: 2503–62.

Schmiedel, Paul W.
The Johannine Writings, tr. Maurice A. Canney (London: A. & C. Black, 1908) = *Johannesschriften des Neuen Testaments*, (Tübingen: Mohr-Siebeck, 1906).

Schmithals, Walter
"Der Prolog des Johannesevangeliums." *ZNW* 70 (1979) 16–43.

Schmitt, J.
"Le groupe johannique et la chrétienté apostolique." In *Les groupes informels dans l'église*, ed. René Metz and Jean Schlick (Strasbourg: C. E. R. D. I. C., 1971) 169–79.

Schnackenburg, Rudolf
"Entwicklung und Stand der johanneischen Forschung seit 1955." In *L'Evangile de Jean. Sources, rédaction, théologie*, ed. M. de Jonge. BETL

44 (Gembloux: Duculot; Louvain: University Press, 1977) 19–44.

Schnackenburg, Rudolf
"Zur johanneischen Forschung." *BZ* 18 (1974) 273–87.

Schnackenburg, Rudolf
"Neue Arbeiten zu den johanneischen Schriften." *BZ* 11 (1967) 303–7; 12 (1968) 141–45.

Schnackenburg, Rudolf
"Das Johannesevangelium in der heutigen Forschung." Zentrale Forschung *Theologie der Gegenwart in Auswahl* (1976) 65–71.

Schnackenburg, Rudolf
"Neuere englische Literatur zum Johannes-evangelium." *BZ* 2 (1958) 144–54.

Schnackenburg, Rudolf
Christian Existence in the New Testament, vol. 1, tr. F. Wieck (Notre Dame, IN: University of Notre Dame Press, 1968).

Schnackenburg, Rudolf
"Der Glaube im vierten Evangelium." Dissertation, Breslau, 1937.

Schnackenburg, Rudolf
"Offenbarung und Glaube im Johannesevan-gelium." In his *Schriften zum Neuen Testament. Exegese in Fortschritt und Wandel* (Munich: Kösel, 1971) 78–96.

Schnackenburg, Rudolf
"Logos-Hymnus und johanneischer Prolog." *BZ* 1 (1957) 69–109.

Schnackenburg, Rudolf
"'Und das Wort ist Fleisch geworden.'" *Communio* 8 (1979) 1–9.

Schnackenburg, Rudolf
"Der Menschensohn im Johannesevangelium." *NTS* 11 (1964/1965) 123–37.

Schnackenburg, Rudolf
"Die Messiasfrage im Johannesevangelium." In *Neutestamentliche Aufsätze. Festschrift für Prof. Josef Schmid zum 70. Geburtstag*, ed. J. Blinzler, O. Kuss, F. Mussner (Regensburg: F. Pustet, 1963) 240–64.

Schnackenburg, Rudolf
Das erste Wunder Jesu (Johannes 2, 1–11) (Freiburg: Herder, 1951).

Schnackenburg, Rudolf
"Die Sakramente im Johannesevangelium." *Sacra Pagina. Miscellanea biblica congressus internationalis catholici de re biblica*, 2 vols., ed. J. Coppens, A. Descamps, and E. Massaux. BETL 12–13 (Paris: J. Gabalda; Gembloux: Duculot, 1959) 2: 235–54.

Schnackenburg, Rudolf
"Die 'situationsgelösten' Redestücke in Joh 3." *ZNW* 49 (1958) 88–99.

Schnackenburg, Rudolf
"Die 'Anbetung in Geist und Wahrheit' (Joh 4, 23) im Lichte von Qumrantexten." *BZ* 3 (1959) 88–94.

Schnackenburg, Rudolf
"Zur Traditionsgeschichte von Joh 4,46–54." *BZ* 8 (1964) 58–88.

Schnackenburg, Rudolf
"Zur Rede vom Brot aus dem Himmel: Eine Beobachtung zu Joh 6, 52." *BZ* 12 (1968) 248–52.

Schnackenburg, Rudolf
"Das Brot des Lebens." In *Tradition und Glaube. Das frühe Christentum in seiner Umwelt. Festgabe für Karl Georg Kuhn zum 65. Geburtstag*, ed. J. Jeremias, H.-W Kuhn, and H. Stegemann (Göttingen: Vandenhoeck & Ruprecht, 1971) 328–42.

Schnackenburg, Rudolf
"Der johanneische Bericht von der Salbung in Bethanien (Joh 12,1–8)." *MTZ* (1950) 48–52.

Schnackenburg, Rudolf
"Joh 12,39–41: Zur christologischen Schriftaus-legung des vierten Evangelisten." In *Neues Testament und Geschichte. Historisches Geschehen und Deutung im Neuen Testament. Oscar Cullman zum 70. Geburtstag*, ed. H. Baltensweiler and B. Reicke (Tübingen: Mohr-Siebeck; Zurich: Theologischer Verlag, 1972) 167–77.

Schnackenburg, Rudolf
"Johannes 14,7." In *Studies in New Testament Language and Text. Essays in Honour of George D. Kilpatrick on the Occasion of his sixty-fifth Birthday*, ed. J. K. Elliott. NovTSup 44 (Leiden: E. J. Brill, 1976) 345–56.

Schnackenburg, Rudolf
Die Kirche im Neuen Testament. Ihre Wirklichkeit und theologische Deutung, ihr Wesen und Geheimnis, Quaestiones Disputatae 14 (New York and Freiburg: Herder, 1961) 93–106.

Schnackenburg, Rudolf
"Die johanneischen Gemeinde und ihre Geister-fahrung." In *Die Kirche des Anfangs. Festschrift für Heinz Schürmann zum 65. Geburtstag*, ed. R. Schnackenburg, J. Ernst, and J. Wanke. Erfurter Theologische Studien 38 (Leipzig: St. Benno; Freiburg: Herder, 1977) 277–306.

Schnackenburg, Rudolf
"Strukturanalyse von Joh 17." *BZ* 17 (1973) 67–78, 196–202.

Schnackenburg, Rudolf
"Die Ecce-homo-Szene und der Menschensohn." In *Jesus und der Menschensohn. Für Anton Vögtle*, ed. R. Pesch and R. Schnackenburg (Freiburg: Herder, 1975) 371–86.

Schnackenburg, Rudolf
"Der Jünger, den Jesus liebte." In EKKNT Vorarbeiten 2 (Neukirchen-Vluyn: Neukirchener-Verlag; Cologne: Benziger, 1970) 97–117.

Schnackenburg, Rudolf
"Zur Herkunft des Johannesevangeliums." *BZ* 14 (1970) 1–23.

Schneider, H.
"'The Word Was Made Flesh.' An Analysis of the Theology of Revelation in the Fourth Gospel." *CBQ* 31 (1969) 344–56.

Schneider, Johannes
"Zur Frage der Komposition von Jo 6,27–58." In

In Memoriam Ernst Lohmeyer, ed. W. Schmauch (Stuttgart: Evangelische Verlagswerk, 1951) 132–42.

Schneider, Johannes
"Zur Komposition von Joh 7, I." *ZNW* 45 (1954) 108–19.

Schneider, Johannes
"Zur Komposition von Joh 10." *ConNT* 11 (1947) 220–25.

Schneider, Johannes
"Die Abschiedsreden Jesu. Ein Beitrag zur Frage der Komposition von Joh 13,31–17,26." In *Gott und die Götter.* [FS. E. Fascher] (Berlin: Evangelische Verlaganstalt, 1958) 103–12.

Schneider, Johannes
"Zur Komposition von Joh 18,12–27: Kaiphas und Hannas." *ZNW* 48 (1957) 111–19.

Schneider, Johannes
Die Christusschau des Johannesevangeliums (Berlin: Furche-Verlag, 1935).

Schneider, Karl Ferdinand Theodor
Die Echtheit des johanneischen Evangeliums nach den Quellen neu untersucht. Erster Beitrag: die äusseren Zeugnisse (Berlin: Wiegandt & Grieben, 1854–1855).

Schnider, Franz and Werner Stenger
Johannes und die Synoptiker. Vergleich ihrer Parallelen, Biblische Handbibliothek 9 (Munich: Kösel, 1971).

Schniewind, Julius Daniel
Die Parallelperikopen bei Lukas und Johannes (Hildesheim: G. Olms, ²1958).

Schnyder, C.
"Ankläger und Angeklagte (Joh 8, 1–11)." *Reformatio* 26 (1977) 641ff.

Scholten, Johannes Henricus
Die ältesten Zeugnisse betreffend die Schriften des Neuen Testaments, historisch untersucht (Bremen: H. Gesenius, 1867).

Scholten, Johannes Henricus
Der Apostel Johannes in Kleinasien; Historisch-kritische Untersuchung (Berlin: F. Henschel, 1872).

Schottroff, Luise
Der Glaubende und die feindliche Welt. Beobachtungen zum gnostichen Dualismus und seiner Bedeutung für Paulus und das Johannesevangelium, WMANT 37 (Neukirchen-Vluyn: Neukirchener Verlag, 1970).

Schottroff, Luise
"Heil als innerweltliche Entweltlichung. Der gnostische Hintergrund der johanneischen Vorstellung vom Zeitpunkt der Erlösung." *NovT* 11 (1969) 294-317.

Schottroff, Luise
"Johannes 4:5–15 und die Konsequenzen des johanneischen Dualismus." *ZNW* 60 (1969) 199–214.

Schram, Terry Leonard
"The Use of *Joudaioi* in the Fourth Gospel." Dissertation, Utrecht, 1974.

Schreiber, Johannes

"Das Schweigen Jesu." In *Theologie und Unterricht. Über die Repräsentanz des Christlichen in der Schule* [Festschrift H. Stock], ed. H. Wegenast (Gütersloh: Gerd Mohn, 1969) 79–87.

Schrenck, Erich von
Die johanneische Auffasung von "Leben" mit Berücksichtigung ihrer Vorgeschichte untersucht (Leipzig: A. Deichert, 1898).

Schulz, A.
"Das Wunder in Kana im Lichte des Alten Testaments." *BZ* 16 (1924) 93–96.

Schulz, Siegfried
"Die Komposition des Johannesprologs und die Zusammensetzung des vierten Evangeliums." *SE* 1 = TU 73 (Berlin: Akademie-Verlag, 1959) 351–62.

Schulz, Siegfried
Untersuchungen zur Menschensohn-Christologie im Johannesevangelium, zugleich ein Beitrag zur Methodengeschichte der Auslegung des 4. Evangeliums (Göttingen: Vandenhoeck & Ruprecht, 1957).

Schulz, Siegfried
Q—die Spruchquelle der Evangelisten (Zurich: Theologischer Verlag, 1972).

Schulz, Siegfried
"Die Komposition des Johannesprologs und die Zusammensetzung des vierten Evangeliums." *SE* 1 = TU 73 (Berlin: Akademie-Verlag, 1959) 351–62.

Schulz, Siegfried
Komposition und Herkunft der johanneischen Reden. BWANT 5 (Stuttgart: W. Kohlhammer, 1960).

Schulz, Siegfried
"Die Bedeutung neuer Gnosisfunde für die neutestamentliche Wissenschaft." *TRu* 26 (1960) 209–66, 301–34.

Schulze, Johann Daniel
Der schriftstellerische Charakter und Werth des Johannes zum Behuf der Specialhermeneutik seiner Schriften untersucht und bestimmt. Voran ein Nachtrag über die Quellen der Briefe von Petrus, Jakobus und Judas, und über das Verhältnis dieser Briefe zu andern neutestamentlichen Schriften (Weissenfels: In der Böseschen Buchhandlung, 1803).

Schulze, W. A.
"Das Johannesevangelium im deutschen Idealismus." *Zeitschrift für philosophische Forschung* 18 (1964) 85–118.

Schürer, E.
"Über den gegenwärtigen Stand der johanneischen Frage." In *Johannes und sein Evangelium,* ed. K. H. Rengstorf (Darmstadt: Wissenschaftliche Buchgesellschaft, 1973) 1–27. 1973:1–27.

Schürmann, Heinz
"Joh. 6, 51c—ein Schlüssel zur johanneischen Brotrede." *BZ* 2 (1958) 244–62.

Schürmann, Heinz
"Die Eucharistie als Repräsentation und Applikation des Heilsgeschehens nach Joh 6, 53-58." *TTZ*

68 (1959) 30–45, 108–18. In his *Ursprung und Gestalt. Erörterungen und Besinnungen zum Neuen Testament,* Kommentare und Beiträge zum Alten und Neuen Testament (Düsseldorf: Patmos Verlag, 1970) 167–84.

Schürmann, Heinz
"Jesu letzte Weisung: Joh 19,26–27a." In his *Ursprung und Gestalt. Erörterungen und Besinnungen zum Neuen Testament,* Kommentare und Beiträge zum Alten und Neuen Testament (Düsseldorf: Patmos-Verlag, 1970) 13–28.

Schütz, Roland
"Zum ersten Teil des Johannesevangeliums." *ZNW* 8 (1907) 243–55.

Schwank, Benedikt
"Das Wort vom Wort." *Erbe und Auftrag* 42 (1966) 183–87.

Schwank, Benedikt
"Efraim in Joh 11,54." *Erbe und Auftrag* 51 (1975) 346–51. Also in *L'Evangile de Jean. Sources, rédaction, théologie,* ed. M. de Jonge. BETL 44 (Gembloux: Duculot; Louvain: University Press, 1977) 377–83.

Schwank, Benedikt
"Was ist Wahrheit?" *Erbe und Auftrag* 47 (1971) 487–96.

Schwank, Benedikt
"Die Ostererscheinungen des Johannes-evangeliums und die Post-mortem-Erscheinungen der Parapsychologie." *Erbe und Auftrag* 44 (1968) 36–53.

Schwank, Benedikt
"Fortschritte in der Johannes-Exegese?" *Erbe und Auftrag* 43 (1967) 157–62.

Schwartz, Eduard
"Über den Tod der Söhne Zebedäi." In *Johannes und sein Evangelium,* ed. K. H. Rengstorf (Darmstadt: Wissenschaftliche Buchgesellschaft, 1973) 202–72.

Schwartz, Eduard
"Noch einmal der Tod der Söhne Zebedäi." *ZNW* 11 (1910) 89–104.

Schwartz, Eduard
"Johannes und Kerinthos." In his *Gesammelte Schriften,* 5 vols. (Berlin: Walter de Gruyter, 1938–1963), 5: 170–82.

Schwartz, Eduard
"Aporien im vierten Evangelium." NGG (1907) 1: 342–72; (1908) 2: 115–48, 3: 149–88, 4: 497–560.

Schwartz, Eduard
"Das philologische Problem des Johannesevangelium." In his *Gesammelte Schriften,* 5 vols. (Berlin: Walter de Gruyter, 1938–1963) 1: 131–36.

Schwegler, A.
"Die neueste Johanneische Litteratur." *Theologischer Jahrbücher* 1 (Tübingen, 1842) 140–70, 288–309.

Schwegler, Friedrich Carl Albert
Der Montanismus und die christliche Kirche des zweiten Jahrhunderts (Tübingen: L. F. Fues, 1841) 15–151.

Schwegler, Friedrich Carl Albert
Das nachapostolische Zeitalter in den Hauptmomenten seiner Entwicklung, 2 vols. (Tübingen: L. F. Fues, 1846) 338–74.

Schweizer, Alexander
Das Evangelium Johannes nach seinem innern Werthe und seiner Bedeutung für das Leben Jesu kritisch untersucht (Leipzig: Weidmann, 1841).

Schweizer, Eduard
Erniedrigung und Erhöhung bei Jesus und seinen Nachfolgern, ATANT 28 (Zurich: Zwingli Verlag, ²1962) 179f.

Schweizer, Eduard
"Zum religionsgeschichtlichen Hintergrund der Sendungsformel Gal 4,4; Röm 8,38; Jo 3,16f.; Jo 4,9." In his *Beiträge zur Theologie des Neuen Testaments. Neutestamentliche Aufsätze* (Zurich: Zwingli Verlag, 1970) 83–96.

Schweizer, Eduard
"Jesus der Zeuge Gottes." In *Studies in John Presented to Professor J. N. Sevenster on the Occasion of his Seventieth Birthday* (Leiden: E. J. Brill, 1970) 161–68.

Schweizer, Eduard
"Πνεῦμα." *TDNT* 6: 436–38.

Schweizer, Eduard
"Die Heilung der Königlichen: Joh 4, 46–54." *EvT* 11 (1951/1952) 64–71.

Schweizer, Eduard
"Das johanneische Zeugnis vom Herrenmahl." *EvT* 12 (1952/1953) 341–63.

Schweizer, Eduard
Neues Testament und heutige Verkündigung, BibS(N) 56 (Neukirchen: Neukirchener Verlag, 1969).

Schweizer, Eduard
"Der Kirchenbegriff im Evangelium und den Briefen des Johannes." *SE* 1 = TU 73 (Berlin: Akademie-Verlag, 1959) 363–81.

Schweizer, Eduard
Gemeinde und Gemeindeordnung im Neuen Testament, ATANT 35 (Zurich: Zwingli Verlag, 1959) 105–24.

Schweizer, Eduard
"Das johanneische Zeugnis vom Herrenmahl." *EvT* 12 (1952/53) 341–63.

Schweizer, Eduard
"Zu Apg 1,16–22." *TZ* 14 (1958) 46.

Schweizer, Eduard
Ego Eimi. Die religionsgeschichtliche Herkunft und theologische Bedeutung der johanneischen Bildreden, zugleich ein Beitrag zur Quellenfrage des vierten Evangeliums, FRLANT, n.s., 38 (Göttingen: Vandenhoeck & Ruprecht, ²1965).

Scognamiglio, A. R.
"La resurrezione di Lazzaro: un 'segno' tra passato

e presente." *Nicolaus* 5 (1977) 3–58.

Scognamiglio, R.
"Se uno non nasce da acqua e da spirito." *Nicolaus* 8 (1980) 301–10.

Scott, Ernest Findlay
The Fourth Gospel. Its Purpose and Theology (Edinburgh: T. & T. Clark, 1906, ²1923).

Scott, John A.
"The Words for 'Love' in John 21,25ff." *The Classical Weekly* 39 (1945/1946) 71–72; 40 (1946/1947) 60–61.

Seeberg, Reinhold
"Ὁ λόγος σὰρξ ἐγένετο." In *Festgabe von Fachgenossen und Freunde. A. von Harnack zum siebsigsten Geburtstag dargebracht* (Tübingen: Mohr-Siebeck, 1921) 263–81.

Segal, A. F.
"Two Powers in Heaven." Dissertation, Yale University, 1975.

Segalla, Giuseppe
"Preesistenza, incarnazione e divinità di Cristo in Giovanni (Vg e 1 Gv.)." *RivB* 22 (1974) 155–81.

Segalla, Giuseppe
"Tre personaggi in cerca di fede: un guideo, una samaritana, un pagano (Gv 3–4)." *Parole di Vita* 16 (1971) 29–49.

Segalla, Giuseppe
"La struttura circolare-chiasmatica di Gv 6,26–58 e il suo significato teologico." *BeO* 13 (1971) 191–98.

Segalla, Giuseppe
"Il libro dell'Addio di Gesú ai suoi." *Parole di Vita* 15 (1970) 356–76.

Segalla, Giuseppe
"La struttura chiastica di Giov 15,1–8." *BeO* 12 (1970) 129–131.

Segalla, Giuseppe
"L'esperienza cristiana in Giovanni." *Studia Patavina* 18 (1971) 299–342.

Segalla, Giuseppe
Volontà di Dio e dell'uomo in Giovanni (Brescia: Paideia, 1974).

Segalla, Giuseppe
"Rassengna di cristologia giovannea." *Studia Patavina* 18 (1972) 693–732.

Segovia, Fernando F.
"*Agape* and *agapan* in First John and the Johannine Tradition." Dissertation, Notre Dame University, 1978.

Sell, Jesse
"A Note on a striking Johannine Motif found at CG VI:6, 19." *NovT* 20 (1978) 232–40.

Selms, A. van
"The Best Man and the Bride—from Sumer to St. John with a new interpretation of Judges, Chapters 14 and 15." *JNES* 9 (1950) 65–75.

Selong, G.
The Cleansing of the Temple in Jn 2,13–22 with a Reconsideration of the Dependence of the Fourth Gospel Upon the Synoptics. Dissertation, Louvain, 1971.

Senft, Christophe
"L'évangile de Jean et la théologie de la croix." *Bulletin du Centre Protestant d'Etudes* 30 (1978) 31–37.

Serra, A.
Contributi dell'antica letteratura giudaica per l'esegesi di Giovanni 2, 1–12 e 19, 25–27, Scripta Pontificiae Facultatis Theologicae "Marianum" 31, n.s., 3 (Rome: Herder, 1977).

Seyffarth, Traugott August
Ein Beitrag zur Specialcharakteristik der johanneischen Schriften besonders des Johanneischen Evangeliums (Leipzig: C. H. Reclam, 1823).

Seynaeve, J.
"Le testament spirituel du Christ. Les discours de la denière Cène (Jn 13–17)." *Orientations Pastorales* 14 (1962) 66–75.

Seynaeve, Jaak
"Les citations scripturaires en Jn 19,36–37: Une preuve en faveur de la typologie de l'Agneau Pascal?" *Revue Africaine de Théologie* 1 (1977) 67–76.

Seynaeve, Jaak
"Les verbes ἀποστέλλω et πέμπω dans le vocabulaire théologique de Saint Jean." In *L'Evangile de Jean. Sources, rédaction, théologie*, ed. M. de Jonge. BETL 44 (Gembloux: Duculot; Louvain: University Press, 1977) 385–89.

Shaw, Alan
"The Breakfast by the Shore and the Mary Magdalene Encounter as Eucharistic Narratives." *JTS*, n.s., 25 (1974) 12–26.

Shaw, Alan
"Image and Symbol in John 21." *ExpTim* 86 (1975) 311.

Sheehan, John F. X.
"Feed my Lambs." *Scr* 16 (1964) 21–27.

Shepherd, Massey H., Jr.
"The Jews in the Gospel of John. Another Level of Meaning." ATR Supplement 3 (1974) 95–112.

Shorter, Mary
"The Position of Chapter VI in the Fourth Gospel." *ExpTim* 84 (1973) 181–83.

Sidebottom, E. M.
"The Son of Man as Man in the Fourth Gospel." *ExpTim* 68 (1956/1957) 213–35, 280–83.

Sidebottom, E. M.
"The Ascent and Descent of the Son of Man in the Gospel of St. John." *ATR* 39 (1957) 115–22.

Sidebottom, E. M.
The Christ of the Fourth Gospel in the Light of First-Century Thought (London: S. P. C. K., 1961).

Siegfried, Carl
Philo von Alexandrien (Jena: H. Dufft, 1875).

Siegman, Edward F.
"St. John's Use of the Synoptic Material." *CBQ* 30 (1968) 182–98.

Siegwalt, Gérard
"Introduction à une théologie chrétienne de la récapitulation." *RTP* 31 (1981) 259–78.

Sigge, Timotheus
Das Johannesevangelium und die Synoptiker; eine Untersuchung seiner Selbständigkeit und der gegenseitigen Beziehungen (Münster i.W: Aschendorff, 1935).

Sikes, Walter W.
"The Anti-Semitism of the Fourth Gospel." *JR* 21 (1941) 23–30.

Silva, Rafael
"Dos casos de exégesis evangélica de difícil solución (Mt 8,5–13; Lc 7,1–10; Jo 4,46–54)." *Compostellanum* 13 (1968) 89–107.

Simon, Marcel
"Retour du Christ et reconstruction du Temple dans la pensée chrétienne primitive." In *Aux sources de la tradition chrétienne. Mélanges offerts à M. Maurice Goguel à l'occasion do son soixante-dixième anniversaire* (Paris: Delachaux & Niestlé, 1950) 247–57.

Simonetti, Manlio
"Giovanni 14,28 nella controversia ariana." In *Kyriakon. Festschrift Johannes Quasten*, ed. P. Granfield and J. A. Jungmann. 2 vols. (Münster: Aschendorff, 1970) 151–61.

Simonis, A. J.
Die Hirtenrede im Johannes-Evangelium. Versuch einer Analyse von Johannes 10, 1–18 nach Entstehung, Hintergrund und Inhalt, AnBib 29 (Rome: Päpstliches Bibelinstitut, 1967).

Sjöberg, Erik
"Neuschöpfung in den Toten-Meer-Rollen." *ST* 9 (1959) 131–36.

Škrinjar, A.
"De terminologia sacrificiali in J 6,51–56." *Divus Thomas,* Piacenza (1971) 189–97.

Smalley, Stephen S.
"New Light on the Fourth Gospel." *TynB* 17 (1966) 35–62.

Smalley, Stephen S.
John: Evangelist and Interpreter (Exeter: Paternoster Press, 1978).

Smalley, Stephen S.
"Johannes 1,51 und die Einleitung zum vierten Evangelium." In *Jesus und der Menschensohn. Für Anton Vögtle,* ed. R. Pesch and R. Schnackenburg (Freiburg: Herder, 1975) 300–13.

Smalley, Stephen S.
"The Johannine Son of Man Sayings." *NTS* 15 (1968/1969) 278–301.

Smalley, Stephen S.
"Liturgy and Sacrament in the Fourth Gospel." *EvQ* 29 (1957) 159–70.

Smalley, Stephen S.
"The Sign in John xxi." *NTS* 20 (1973/1974) 275–88.

Smalley, Stephen S.

"Diversity and Development in John." *NTS* 17 (1970/1971) 276–92.

Smend, F.
"Die Behandlung alttestamentlicher Zitate als Ausgangspunkt der Quellenscheidungen im vierten Evangelium." *ZNW* 24 (1925) 147–50.

Smend, Rudolf
Wilhelm Martin Leberecht de Wettes Arbeit am Alten und am Neuen Testament (Basel: Helbing & Lichtenhahn, 1958).

Smith, C. Hughes
"Οὕτως ἐστιν πᾶς ὁ γεγεννημένος ἐκ τοῦ πνεύματος." *ExpTim* 81 (1969/1970) 181.

Smith, C. R.
"The Unfruitful Branches in John 15." *Grace Journal* 9 (1968) 3–22.

Smith, Charles W. F.
"Tabernacles in the Fourth Gospel and Mark." *NTS* 9 (1962/1963) 130–46.

Smith, D. Moody, Jr.
The Composition and Order of the Fourth Gospel: Bultmann's Literary Theory (New Haven and London: Yale University Press, 1965).

Smith, D. Moody, Jr.
"John 12:12ff. and the Question of John's Use of the Synoptics." *JBL* 82 (1963) 58–64.

Smith, D. Moody, Jr.
"The Milieu of the Johannine Miracle Source: a Proposal." In *Jews, Greeks and Christians. Religious Cultures in Late Antiquity. Essays in Honor of William David Davies,* ed. Robert Hamerton-Kelly and Robin Scroggs. SJLA 21 (Leiden: E. J. Brill, 1976) 164–80.

Smith, D. Moody, Jr.
"The Sources of the Gospel of John. An Assessment of the Present State of the Problem." *NTS* 10 (1963/1964) 336–51.

Smith, D. Moody, Jr.
"The Presentation of Jesus in the Fourth Gospel." *Int* 31 (1977) 367–78.

Smith, D. Moody, Jr.
"Johannine Christianity: Some Reflections on its Character and Delineation." *NTS* 21 (1974/1975) 222–48.

Smith, D. Moody, Jr.
"John 16,1–15." *Int* 33 (1979) 58–62.

Smith, D. Moody, Jr.
Review of *The Gospel of Signs,* by R. Fortna. *JBL* 89 (1970) 498–501.

Smith, Morton
"On the Wine-God in Palestine (Gen 18; Jn 2 and Achilles Tatius)." In *Salo Wittmayer Baron Jubilee Volume on the Occasion of his Eightieth Birthday,* ed. Saul Lieberman and A. Hyman (Jerusalem: American Academy for Jewish Research; New York: distributed by Columbia University Press, 1974) English section, 2: 815–29.

Smith, Morton
"Mark 6:32–15:47 and John 6:1–19:43." SBLASP

2 (Missoula: Scholars Press, 1978) 281–87.

Smith, Morton
"Collected Fragments: On the Priority of John 6 to Mark 6–8." SBLASP 1 (Missoula: Scholars Press, 1979) 105–8.

Smith, Taylor Clarence
"The Christology of the Fourth Gospel." *RevExp* 71 (1974) 19–30.

Smith, Taylor Clarence
Jesus in the Fourth Gospel (Nashville: Broadman Press, 1959).

Smitmans, Adolf
Das Weinwunder von Kana. Die Auslegung von Jo 2, 1–11 bei den Vätern und heute, BGBE 6 (Tübingen: Mohr-Siebeck, 1966).

Smothers, Edgar R.
"Two Readings in Papyrus Bodmer II." *HTR* 51 (1958) 109–22.

Smyth-Florentin, F.
"Jésus veut associer ses disciples à son amour: Jn 17,24–26." *AsSeign* 96 (1967) 40–48.

Snaith, Norman H.
"The Meaning of 'the Paraclete.'" *ExpTim* 57 (1945/1946) 47–50.

Snyder, Graydon F.
"John 13:16 and the Anti-Petrinism of the Johannine Tradition." *BR* 16 (1971) 5–15.

Soden, Hans von
"Was ist Wahrheit? Vom geschichtlichen Begriff der Wahrheit." In his *Gesammelte Aufsätze und Vorträge*, 2 vols., ed. Hans von Campenhausen. Vol. 1, *Grundsätzliches und Neutestamentliches* (Tübingen: Mohr-Siebeck, 1951) 1–24.

Solages, B. de
Jean et les Synoptiques (Leiden: E. J. Brill, 1979).

Solages, Bruno de
"Jean, fils de Zébédée et l'énigme du disciple que Jésus aimait." *BLE* 73 (1972) 41–50.

Solages, Bruno de and J. M. Vacherot
"Le Chapitre XXI de Jean est-il de la même plume que le reste de l'Evangile?" *BLE* 80 (1979) 96–101.

Soltau, Wilhelm
Das vierte Evangelium in seiner Entstehungsgeschichte dargelegt, SHAW.PH 7 (Heidelberg: Carl Winter, ⁶1916).

Soltau, Wilhelm
"Die Reden des vierten Evangeliums." *ZNW* 17 (1916) 49–60.

Soltau, Wilhelm
"Der eigenartige dogmatische Standpunkt der Johannesreden und seine Erklärung." *ZWT* 52 (1910) 341–58.

Soltau, Wilhelm
"Verwandtschaft zwischen Evangelium und dem 1. Johannesbrief." *TSK* 89 (1916) 228–33.

Soltau, Wilhelm
"Der eigenartige dogmatische Standpunkt der Johannesreden und seine Erklärung." *ZWT* 52 (1910) 341–58.

Soltau, Wilhelm
"Welche Bedeutung haben die synoptischen Berichte des 4. Evangeliums für die Feststellung seines Entstehens?" *ZWT* 52 (1910) 33–66.

Soltau, Wilhelm
Unsere Evangelien, ihre Quellen und ihr Quellenwert vom Standpunkt des Historikers aus betrachtet (Leipzig: H. Dieterich, 1901).

Soltau, Wilhelm
"Zum Johannesevangelium: Die Kritiker am Scheideweg." *Protestantische Monatshefte* 13 (1909) 436–47.

Soltau, Wilhelm
"Das Problem des Johannesevangeliums und der Weg zu seiner Lösung." *ZNW* 16 (1915) 24–53.

Soltau, Wilhelm
"Thesen über die Entwicklung einer johanneischen Literatur." *ZWT* 53 (1911) 167–70.

Soltau, Wilhelm
Das vierte Evangelium in seiner Entstehungsgeschichte dargelegt, SHAW.PH 7 (Heidelberg: C. Winter, ⁶1916).

Sortino, Placido M. Da
"La vocazione di Pietro secondo la tradizione sinottica e secondo San Giovanni." *San Pietro. Atti della XIX settimana Biblica, Associazione Biblica Italiana* (Brescia: Paideia, 1967) 27–57.

Sortino, Placido M. de
"La vocazione di Pietro secondo la tradizione sinottica e secondo S. Giovanni." *Atti della settimana biblica* 19 (1966) 27–57.

Soulier, Henry
La doctrine du Logos chez Philon d'Alexandrie (Turin: V. Bona, 1876).

Spaemann, Heinrich
"Stunde des Lammes. Meditationen über die ersten Jüngerberufungen (Joh. 1, 35–51)." *BibLeb* 7 (1966) 58–68.

Spaeth, H.
"Nathanael: Ein Beitrag zum Verständnis der Composition des Logos-Evangeliums." *ZWT* 11 (1868) 168–213, 309–43.

Sparks, H. F. D.
"St. John's Knowledge of Matthew. The Evidence of John 13,16 and 15,20." *JTS*, n.s., 3 (1952) 58–61.

Spengler, Oswald
The Decline of the West, 2 vols. Tr. Charles Francis Atkinson (New York: A. A. Knopf, 1926–1928).

Spicq, Ceslaus
Agape in the New Testament. Vol. 3, *Agape in the Gospel, Epistles and Apocalypse of St. John*, tr. M. A. McNamara and M. H. Richter (St. Louis and London: B. Herder Book Co., 1966).

Spicq, Ceslaus
"Le Siracide et la structure littéraire du Prologue de saint Jean." In *Memorial Lagrange. Cinquantenaire de l'école biblique et archéologique française de Jérusalem (15 novembre 1890–15 novembre 1940)*

(Paris: J. Gabalda, 1940) 183–95.

Spicq, Ceslaus
"Il primo miracolo di Gesú dovuto a sua Madre."
Sacra Doctrina 18 (1973) 125–44.

Spicq, Ceslaus
"Notes d'exégèse johannique: la charité est amour
manifeste." *RB* 65 (1958) 358–70.

Spitta, Friedrich
"Die Hirtengleichnisse des vierten Evangeliums."
ZNW 10 (1909) 59–80, 103–27.

Spitta, Friedrich
"Die neutestamentliche Grundlage der Ansicht
von E. Schwartz über den Tod der Söhne
Zebedäi." In *Johannes und sein Evangelium*, ed. K.
H. Rengstorf (Darmstadt: Wissenschaftliche
Buchgesellschaft, 1973) 291–313.

Spitta, Friedrich
"Julius Wellhausen in seiner Bedeutung für die
Evangelienkritik und Geschichte Jesu." In *Archiv
der Strassburger Pastoralkonferenz* (Strassburg, 1907)
293–317.

Spitta, Friedrich
"Unordnungen im Texte des vierten Evange-
liums." In his *Zur Geschichte und Literatur des
Urchristentums* (Göttingen: Vandenhoeck &
Ruprecht, 1893) 1: 155–204.

Spitta, Friedrich
"Das Verhältnis von Joh. 6 zum Passah." In his *Zur
Geschichte und Literatur des Urchristentums* (Göttingen: Vandenhoeck & Ruprecht, 1893) 1: 216–
21.

Spitta, Friedrich
"Johanneische Parallelen." In his *Zur Geschichte und
Literatur des Urchristentums* (Göttingen: Vanden-
hoeck & Ruprecht, 1907) 3, 2: 98–108.

Spitta, Friedrich
Streitfragen der Geschichte Jesu (Göttingen: Vandenhoeck & Ruprecht, 1907).

Spitta, Friedrich
Jesus und die Heidenmission (Giessen: A. Töpelmann, 1909) 87ff.

Spitta, Friedrich
*Das Johannes-Evangelium als Quelle der Geschichte
Jesu* (Göttingen: Vandenhoeck & Ruprecht, 1910).

Spriggs, G. D.
"Meaning of 'Water' in John 3:5." *ExpTim* 85
(1974) 149–50.

Springer, E.
"Die Einheit der Rede von Kaphernaum (Jo 6)."
BZ 15 (1918–1921) 319–34.

Stachel, Günter
"Die Einheit in Christus. Eine Katechese über Joh
17,20–23." *Katechetische Blätter* 90 (1965) 313–20.

Stachio, P.
"The Concept of Faith in the Johannine Writings."
Logos 22 (1971) 115–30.

Staerk, Willy
Der biblische Christus. Vol. 1 of *Soter, die biblische
Erlösererwartung als religionsgeschichtliches Problem;*

eine biblisch-theologische Untersuchung. BFCT, 2nd
series: Sammlung wissenschaftlicher Monographien 31 (Gütersloh: C. Bertelsmann, 1933).

Stagg, F.
"The Farewell Discourses—John 13–17." *RevExp*
62 (1965) 459–72.

Stählin, Gustav
"Ὀργή." *TDNT* 5: 430–34.

Stählin, Gustav
"Zum Problem der johanneischen Eschatologie."
ZNW 33 (1934) 225–59.

Stählin, Wilhelm
*Das johanneische Denken. Eine Einführung in die
Eigenart des vierten Evangleiums* (Witten-Ruhr:
Luther-Verlag, 1954).

Stamm, Raymond T.
"Luke-Acts and Three Cardinal Ideas of John." In
Biblical Studies in Memory of H. C. Alleman, eds. J. M.
Myers, O. Reimherr, H. N. Bream. Gettysburg
Theological Studies (Locust Valley, NY: J. J.
Augustin, 1960).

Stange, Carl
"Der Prolog des Johannes-Evangeliums." *ZST* 21
(1950/1952) 120–41.

Stange, Erich
*Die Eigenart der Johanneischen Produktion. Ein Beitrag
zur Kritik der neueren Quellenscheidungshypothesen
und zur Charakteristik der Johanneischen Psyche*
(Dresden: C. L. Ungelenk, 1915).

Stanks, T.
"The Servant of God in John I 29.36." Dissertation, Louvain, 1963.

Stanley, David Michael
"The Johannine Literature." *TS* 17 (1956) 516–
31.

Stanley, David Michael
"Israel's Wisdom Meets the Wisdom of God."
Worship 32 (1958) 280–87.

Stanley, David Michael
"The Bread of Life." *Worship* 32 (1957/1958)
477–88.

Stanley, David Michael
"Holy Scripture. The Feast of Tents: Jesus' Self-
Revelation." *Worship* 34 (1964) 20–27.

Stanley, David Michael
"The Passion according to St. John." *Worship* 33
(1959) 210–30.

Stanton, Vincent Henry
The Gospels As Historical Documents, 3 vols. Vol. 1,
The Early Use of the Gospels; Vol. 2, *The Synoptic
Gospels;* Vol. 3, *The Fourth Gospel* (Cambridge:
Cambridge University Press, 1903–1920).

Stanton, Vincent Henry
"Convince or convict (John 16,8)." *ExpTim* 33
(1921/1922) 278–79.

Stauffer, Ethelbert
"Die Hochzeit zu Kana." In *Neue Wege im kirchlichen
Unterricht*, ed. K. Frör. Hilfsbücher für den kirch-
lichen Unterricht 1 (Munich: Chr. Kaiser Verlag,

1949) 49–61.

Stauffer, Ethelbert
"Agnostos Christos. Joh 2,24 und die Eschatologie des vierten Evangeliums." In *The Background of the New Testament and its Eschatology* [in honor of Charles Harold Dodd], ed. W. D. Davies and D. Daube (Cambridge: Cambridge University Press, 1956) 281–99.

Steck, R.
"Die Perikope von der Ehebrecherin." In *Zur Feier des 50 jährigen Amtsjubiläums des Herrn Prof. Dr. A. Schweizer. Gratulationsschrift der ev. -theol. Fakultät an der Hochschule Bern zum 29.10.1884* (Bern, 1884).

Steiner, Rudolf
L'évangile de saint Jean dans ses rapports avec les trois autres Evangiles et notamment avec celui de saint Luc. Quatorze conférences faites à Cassel, du 24 juin au 8 Juillet 1909 (Paris: Association de la science spirituelle, 1934, 1945).

Steinmetz, Franz-Josef
"'. . . Und ich gehe nimmer, wann ich gehe—.' Zum Verständnis der johanneischen Abschiedsreden." *Geist und Leben* 51 (1978) 85–99.

Steinmeyer, Franz Karl Ludwig
Beiträge zum Verständnis des johanneischen Evangeliums. Vol. 4, *Das Nachtgespräch Jesu mit dem Nikodemus* (Berlin: Wiegandt & Grieben, 1889).

Steinmeyer, Franz Karl Ludwig
Beiträge zum Verständnis des johanneischen Evangeliums. Vol. 2, *Das Gespräch Jesu mit der Samariterin* (Berlin: Wiegandt & Grieben, 1887).

Steinmeyer, Franz Karl Ludwig
Die Rede Jesu in der Schule von Capernaum (Berlin: Wiegandt & Grieben, 1892).

Steinmeyer, Franz Karl Ludwig
Beiträge zum Verständnis des johanneischen Evangeliums. Vol. 6, *Die Aussagen Jesu im Zehnten Capitel des Johannes* (Berlin: Wiegandt und Grieben, 1891).

Steinmeyer, Franz Karl Ludwig
Beiträge zum Verständnis des johanneischen Evangeliums. Vol. 8, *Die Scheiderede Jesu an den Kreis der Seinen* (Berlin: Wiegandt & Grieben, 1893).

Steinmeyer, Franz Karl Ludwig
Das hohepriesterliche Gebet Jesu Christi (Berlin: Wiegandt, 1886).

Steitz, Georg Eduard
"Der classische und der johanneische Gebrauch von ἐκεῖνος," *TSK* 34 (1861) 267–310.

Steitz, Georg Eduard
"Über den Gebrauch des Pronomen ἐκεῖνος im vierten Evangelium." *TSK* 32 (1859) 497–506.

Stemberger, Günter
La symbolique du bien et du mal selon saint Jean, Parole de Dieu (Paris: Editions du Seuil, 1970).

Stemberger, Günter
"Les brebis du Bon Pasteur." *AsSeign* 25 (1969) 62–70.

Stemberger, Günter
"'Er kam in sein Eigentum.' Das Johannesevangelium im Dialog mit der Gnosis." *Wort und Wahrheit* 28 (1973) 435–52.

Stenger, Werner
"Die Auferweckung des Lazarus (Joh 11,1–45). Vorlage und johanneische Redaktion." *TTZ* 83 (1974) 17–37.

Stenger, Werner
"Δικαιοσύνη in Joh 16,8.10." *NovT* 21 (1979) 2–12.

Stier, Ewald Rudolf
The Words of the Lord Jesus, tr. Willam B. Pope, 8 vols. (Edinburgh: T. & T. Clark, 1888–1894) = *Die Reden des Herrn Jesu. Andeutungen für gläubiges Verständnis derselben* (Barmen: W. Langewiesche, ² 1851–53, ³1865–74).

Stiftinger, K.
"Exegesegeschichtliche Studie zu Joh. 7,37f." Dissertation, Graz, 1970/1971.

Stöger, Alois
"Das österliche Sakrament der Taufe. Meditation zu Joh 3,1–21." *BibLeb* 52 (1979) 121–24.

Stolz, Fritz
"Zeichen und Wunder. Die prophetische Legitimation und ihre Geschichte." *ZTK* 69 (1972) 125–44.

Storelli, F.
"Il prologo di Giovanni e il Logos origeniano." *Nicolaus* 5 (1977) 209–18.

Strachan, Robert Harvey
The Fourth Evangelist: Dramatist or Historian? (London: Hodder & Stoughton; New York: G. H. Doran, 1925).

Strachan, Robert Harvey
"The Development of Thought within the Fourth Gospel." *ExpTim* 34 (1922/1923) 228–32, 246–49.

Strathmann, H.
"Johannes." *Evangelisches Kirchenlexicon,* 4 vols. (Göttingen: Vandenhoeck & Ruprecht, 1955–1961) 2: 357–363.

Strauss, David Friedrich
The Life of Jesus Critically Examined, ed. with an introduction by Peter C. Hodgson; tr. George Eliot (Philadelphia: Fortress Press, 1972) = *Das Leben Jesu, kritisch bearbeitet* (Tübingen: C. F. Osiander, 1835 and 1836).

Suggit, J.
"The Eucharistic Significance of John 20.19–29." *Journal of Theology of South Africa* 16 (1976) 52–59.

Summers, Ray
"The Christ of John's Gospel." *Southwestern Journal of Theology* 8 (1965) 35–43.

Summers, Ray
"The Johannine View of the Future Life." *RevExp* 58 (1961) 331–47.

Sundberg, Albert C.
"*Isos tō Theō*: Christology in John 5.17–30." *BR* 15 (1970) 19–31

Sundberg, Albert C.
"Christology in the Fourth Gospel." *BR* 21 (1976) 29–37.

Suriano, T.
"Doubting Thomas: An Invitation to Belief." *Bible Today* 53 (1971) 309–15.

Süskind, F. G.
"Etwas ueber die neueren Ansichten der Stelle Joh 1,1–14." *Magazin für christliche Dogmatik und Moral* 10 (1803) 1–91.

Süß, W.
Review of *La questione Petroniana,* by E. von Mamorate. *Gnomon* 23 (1951) 312–17.

Swanson, D. C.
"Diminutives in the Greek New Testament." *JBL* 77 (1958) 134–51.

Sweeney, T. A.
"Jesus of the Fourth Gospel." Dissertation, Graduate Theological Union, 1974.

Swete, Henry Barclay
The Last Discourse and Prayer of Our Lord. A Study of St. John XIV–XVII (London: Macmillan, 1914).

Sybel, Ludwig von
"Die Salbungen." *ZNW* 23 (1924) 184–93.

Synge, F. C.
"The Holy Spirit in the Gospels and Acts." *CQR* (1935) 205–17.

Synge, F. C.
"Studies in Texts." *Theology* 50 (1947) 263–64.

Tabachovitz, David
"Ein paar Beobachtungen zum spätgriechischen Sprachgebrauch." *ErJb* 44 (1946) 296–305.

Talbert, Charles H.
"Artistry and Theology: An Analysis of the Architecture of Jn 1,19–5,47." *CBQ* 32 (1970) 341–66.

Talvero, S.
"Problemática de la unidad en Jn. 18–20." *Salmanticensis* 19 (1972) 513–75.

Tayler, John James
An Attempt to Ascertain the Character of the Fourth Gospel; Especially in its Relation to the Three First (London and Edinburgh: Williams & Norgate, 1867).

Taylor, E. K.
"The Lamb of God." *Clergy Review* 48 (1963) 285–92.

Taylor, Jefferson R.
"A Note on St. John i, 18." *ExpTim* 18 (1906/1907) 47.

Taylor, Vincent
"The Fourth Gospel and Some Recent Criticism." *HJ* 25 (1926/1927) 725–43.

Taylor, W. M.
Jesus at the Well: John IV, 1–42 (New York: A. D. F. Randolph & Co., 1884).

Teeple, Howard M.
"Methodology in Source Analysis of the Fourth Gospel." *JBL* 81 (1962) 279–86.

Teeple, Howard M.
The Literary Origin of the Gospel of John (Evanston, IL: Religion and Ethics Institute, 1974).

Temple, Patrick J.
"The Eucharist in St. John 6." *CBQ* 9 (1947) 442–52.

Temple, Sydney
"The Two Signs in the Fourth Gospel." *JBL* 81 (1962) 169–74.

Temple, Sydney
The Core of the Fourth Gospel (London and Oxford: A. R. Mowbray, 1975).

Temple, Sydney
"The Two Signs in the Fourth Gospel." *JBL* 81 (1962) 169–74.

Temple, Sydney
"A Key to the Composition of the Fourth Gospel." *JBL* 80 (1961) 220–32.

Tenney, Merrill C.
"Topics from the Gospel of John. Part II: The Meaning of the Signs." *BSac* 132 (1975) 145–60.

Tenney, Merrill C.
"Topics from the Gospel of John. Part IV: The Growth of Belief." *BSac* 132 (1975) 343–57.

Tenney, Merrill C.
"Topics from the Gospel of John. Part III: The Meaning of 'Witness' in John." *BSac* 132 (1975) 229–41.

Tenney, Merrill C.
"The Symphonic Structure of John." *BSac* 120 (1963) 117–25.

Theissen, Gerd
Urchristliche Wundergeschichten. Ein Beitrag zur formgeschichtlichen Erforschung der synoptischen Evangelien. SNT 8 (Gütersloh: Gerd Mohn, 1974).

Theobald, Michael
"Im Anfang war das Wort." Textlinguistische Studie zum Johannesprolog, SBS 106 (Stuttgart: Katholisches Bibelwerk, 1983).

Thils, G.
"De interpretatione Evangelii Sancti Johannis 13,31–14,31." *Collectanea Mechliniensia* 29 (1940) 33–36.

Thoma, Albrecht
"Das Alte Testament im Johannes-Evangelium." *ZWT* 22 (1879) 18–66, 171–223, 273–312.

Thoma, Albrecht
Die Genesis des Johannes-evangeliums. Ein Beitrag zu seiner Auslegung, Geschichte und Kritik (Berlin: G. Reimer, 1882).

Thoma, Albrecht
"Justins literarisches Verhältnis zu Paulus und zum Johannesevangelium." *ZWT* 18 (1875) 383–412, 490–566.

Thomas, J.
"Le discours dans la synagogue de Capharnaum. Note sur Jean 6,22–59." *Christus* 29 (1982) 218–22.

Thomas, J.
Le mouvement baptiste en Palestine et Syrie (150 av. J.-

C.–300 ap. J.-C.) (Gembloux: Duculot, 1935).

Thomas, J. D.
"A Translation Problem—John 3:8." *Restoration Quarterly* 24 (1981) 219–24.

Thomas, Richard W.
"The Meaning of the Terms 'Life' and 'Death' in the Fourth Gospel and in Paul." *SJT* 21 (1968) 199–212.

Thomas, W. H. Griffith
"The Plan of the Fourth Gospel." *BSac* 125 (1968) 313–23.

Thomas, W. H. Griffith
"The Purpose of the Fourth Gospel: John 21." *BSac* 125 (1968) 254–62.

Thompson, J. D.
"An Analysis of Present and Future in the Eschatology of the Fourth Gospel." Dissertation, Emory University, 1967.

Thompson, J. M.
"Accidental Disarrangement in the Fourth Gospel." *Expositor,* 8th ser., 17 (1919) 47–54.

Thompson, J. M.
"The Interpretation of the John VI." *Expositor,* 8th ser., 11 (1916) 337–48.

Thompson, J. M.
"Is John XXI an Appendix?" *Expositor,* 8th ser., 10 (1915) 139–47.

Thompson, J. M.
"Accidental Disarrangement in the Fourth Gospel." *Expositor,* 8th ser., 17 (1919) 47–54.

Thompson, J. M.
"The Structure of the Fourth Gospel." *Expositor,* 8th ser., 10 (1915) 512–26.

Thompson, L. M.
"The Multiple Uses of the Lazarus-Motif in Modern Literature." *Christian Scholar's Review* 7 (1978) 306–9.

Thurneysen, E.
"Der Prolog zum Johannesevangelium." *Zwischen den Zeiten* 3 (1925) 12–37.

Thüsing, Wilhelm
"Die johanneische Theologie als Verkündigung der Grösse Gottes." *TTZ* 74 (1965) 321–31.

Thüsing, Wilhelm
"'Wenn ich von der Erde erhöht bin . . .' (Joh 12,32). Die Erhöhung Jesu nach dem Johannesevangelium." *Bibel und Kirche* 20 (1965) 40–42.

Thüsing, Wilhelm
Herrlichkeit und Einheit. Eine Auslegung des Hohepriesterlichen Gebetes Jesu (Johannes 17), Die Welt der Bibel 14 (Düsseldorf: Patmos-Verlag, 1962).

Thüsing, Wilhelm
Die Erhöhung und Verherrlichung Jesu im Johannesevangelium. NTAbh 21, 1–2 (Münster: Aschendorff, 1960, ²1970).

Thyen, Hartwig
"Aus der Literatur zum Johannesevangelium." *TRu* 39 (1974) 1–69, 222–52, 289–330; 42 (1977) 211–70; 43 (1978) 328–59; 44 (1979) 97–134.

Thyen, Hartwig
"Auf neuen Wegen dem Rätsel des vierten Evangeliums auf der Spur? Überlegungen zu dem Buch von Birger Olsson." *SEÅ* 40 (1975) 136–43.

Thyen, Hartwig
"Das Heil kommt von den Juden." In *Kirche. Festschrift für Günther Bornkamm zum 75. Geburtstag* (Tübingen: Mohr-Siebeck, 1980) 163–84.

Thyen, Hartwig
"Johannes 13 und die 'kirchliche Redaktion' des vierten Evangeliums." In *Tradition und Glaube. Das frühe Christentum in seiner Umwelt. Festgabe für Karl Georg Kuhn zum 65. Geburtstag,* ed. G. Jeremias, H.-W. Kuhn, and H. Stegemann (Göttingen: Vandenhoeck & Ruprecht, 1971) 343–56.

Thyen, Hartwig
"'Niemand hat grössere Liebe als die, dass er sein Leben für seine Freunde hingibt' (Joh 15,13)." In *Theologia Crucis—Signum Crucis. Festschrift für Erich Dinkler zum 70. Geburtstag,* ed. C. Andersen and G. Klein (Tübingen: Mohr-Siebeck, 1979) 467–81.

Thyen, Hartwig
"Entwicklungen innerhalb der johanneischen Theologie und Kirche im Spiegel von Joh 21 und der Lieblingsjüngertexte des Evangeliums." In *L'Evangile de Jean. Sources, rédaction, théologie,* ed. M. de Jonge. BETL 44 (Gembloux: Duculot; Louvain: University Press, 1977) 259–99.

Thyen, Hartwig
Studien zur Sündenvergebung im Neuen Testament und seinen alttestamentlichen und jüdischen Voraussetzungen, FRLANT 96 (Göttingen: Vandenhoeck & Ruprecht, 1970).

Thyen, Hartwig
"Die Probleme der neueren Philo-Forschung." *TRu* 23 (1955/56) 230–46.

Tilborg, Sjef van
"'Neerdaling' en incarnatie: de christologie van Johannes. ['Katabasis' and Incarnation in the Gospel of John.]" *Tijdschrift voor Theologie* 13 (1973) 20–33.

Tittmann, Carl Christian
Tractatus de vestigiis gnosticorum in Novo Testamento frustra quaesitis (Leipzig: Breitkopf, 1773).

Titus, Eric L.
"The Identity of the Beloved Disciple." *JBL* 69 (1950) 323–28.

Tobler, Johannes Rudolf
Evangelium Johannis nach dem Grundtext getreu wiedergegeben (Schaffhausen: Brodtmann, 1867).

Tobler, Johannes T.
"Über den Ursprung des vierten Evangeliums." *ZWT* 3 (1860) 169–203.

Toit, A. B. du
"On Incarnate Word—A Study of John 1,14." *Neot* 2 (1968) 9–21.

Topel, L. John
"A Note on the Methodology of Structural Analysis in John 2:23–3:21." *CBQ* 33 (1971) 211–20.

Torrey, Charles C.
"When I am Lifted up from the Earth, John 12:32." *JBL* 51 (1932) 320–22.

Torrey, Charles Cutler
"The Aramaic Origin of the Gospel of John." *HTR* 16 (1923) 305–44.

Tosatto, G.
"La passione di Cristo in S. Giovanni." *Parole di Vita* 15 (1970) 377–88.

Toussaint, Stanley D.
"The Significance of the First Sign in John's Gospel." *BSac* 134 (1977) 45–51.

Traets, C.
Voir Jésus et le Père en lui selon l'Evangile de Saint Jean (Rome: Gregorian University, 1967).

Tragan, P. R., ed.
Segni e sacramenti nel Vangelo di Giovanni. Sacramentum 3, Studia Anselmiana 66 (Rome: Editrice Anselmiana, 1977).

Trémel, Y. B.
"Le Fils de l'homme selon saint Jean." *Lumière et vie* 12 (1962/1963) 65–92.

Trilling, W.
"Gegner Jesu—Widersachet der Gemeinde—Repräsentanten der Welt. Das Johannesevangelium und die Juden." In *Gottesverächter und Menschenfeinde? Juden zwischen Jesus und frühchristlicher Kirche,* ed. H. Goldstein (Düsseldorf: Patmos-Verlag, 1979) 190–210.

Trites, Allison A.
"The Woman Taken in Adultery." *BSac* 131 (1974) 137–46.

Troadec, Henry
"Le témoignage de la lumière. Jean 8, 12–59." *BVC* 49 (1963) 16–26.

Trocmé, Etienne
"Jean-Baptiste dans le quatrième évangile." *RHPR* 60 (1980) 129–51.

Trocmé, Etienne
"L'expulsion des marchands du Temple [Mt 21:12–17]." *NTS* 15 (1968/1969) 1–22.

Trudinger, Paul
"The Prologue of John's Gospel: Its Extent, Content and Intent." *Reformed Theological Review* 33 (1974) 11–17.

Trudinger, Paul
"The Seven Days of the New Creation in St. John's Gospel: Some Further Reflection." *EvQ* 44 (1972) 154–58.

Trudinger, Paul
"The Raising of Lazarus—A Brief Response." *Downside Review* 94 (1976) 287–90.

Trudinger, Paul
"A 'Lazarus Motif' in Primitive Christian Preaching." *ANQ* 7 (1966) 29–32.

Tsuchido, Kiyoshi
"The Composition of the Nicodemus-Episode, John 2,23–3,21." *Annual of the Japanese Biblical Institute* 1 (1975) 91–103.

Tuñí Vancells, J. O.
"La verdad os hará libres." Jn 8, 32. Liberación y libertad del creyente en el cuarto evangelio (Barcelona: Herder, 1973).

Turner, C. H.
"On the Punctation of John 7, 37–38." *JTS* 24 (1923) 66–70.

Turner, Nigel
Grammatical Insights into the New Testament (Edinburgh: T. & T. Clark, 1966) 135–54.

Turner, William
"Believing and Everlasting Life—A Johannine Inquiry." *ExpTim* 64 (1952/1953) 50–52.

Twomey, J. J.
"Barabbas was a Robber." *Scr* 8 (1956) 115–19.

Ullmann, C.
"Bemerkungen zu Joh IV 13,14 und VI,35." *TSK* 1 (1828) 791–94.

Unnik, Willem Cornelis van
"A Greek Characteristic of Prophecy in the Fourth Gospel." In *Text and Interpretation: Studies in the New Testament presented to Matthew Black,* ed. E. Best and R. McL. Wilson (London: Cambridge University Press, 1979) 211–30.

Unnik, Willem Cornelis van
"The purpose of St. John's Gospel." *SE* 1 = TU 73 (Berlin: Akademie-Verlag, 1959) 383–411.

Unnik, Willem Cornelis van
"The Gospel of Truth and the New Testament." In *The Jung Codex. A Newly Recovered Gnostic Papyrus,* ed. F. L. Cross (London: A. R. Mowbray, 1955) 79–129.

Unnik, Willem Cornelis van
"C. F. Burney's Hypothese aangaande de Aramaesche achtergrond van het Johannes-Evangelie." *Vox Theologica* 7 (1935) 123–31.

Unnik, Willem Cornelis van
"The Quotation from the Old Testament in Jn 12,34." *NovT* 3 (1959) 174–79.

Urbach, Efraim Elimelech
The Sages, their Concepts and Beliefs, tr. Israel Abrahams (Jerusalem: Magnes Press, Hebrew University, 1973).

Uricchio, N.
"La teoria delle trasposizioni nel Vangelo di S. Giovanni." *Bib* 31 (1950) 129–63; 32 (1951) 567f.

Usteri, Johann Martin
"Exegetische und historisch-kritische Bemerkungen zum Gespräch Jesu mit Nikodemus, Joh. 3, 1–21." *TSK* 63 (1890) 504–51.

Vaganay, Léon
"La finale du quatrième Evangile." *RB* 45 (1936) 512–28.

Valentin, Patrick
"Les comparutions de Jésus devant le Sanhédrin." *RSR* 59 (1971) 230–36.

Vanderlip, D. George
Christianity according to John (Philadelphia: Westminster Press, 1975).

Vanhoye, Albert
"Notre foi, oeuvre divine, d'après le quatrième évangile." *NRT* 86 (1964) 339–54.

Vanhoye, Albert
"Interrogation johannique et exégèse de Cana (Jn 2,4)." *Bib* 55 (1974) 157–67.

Vanhoye, Albert
"La composition de Jn 5,19–30." In *Mélanges bibliques en hommage au R. P. Béda Rigaux*, ed. A. Descamps and A. de Halleux (Gembloux: Duculot, 1970) 259–74.

Vanhoye, Albert
"Opera Jesu donum Patris [Jo 5,36; 17,4]." *VD* 36 (1958) 83–92.

Vanhoye, Albert
"L'oeuvre du Christ, don du Père (Jn v,36 et xvii,4)." *RSR* 48 (1960) 377–419.

Vanneste, A.
"Le pain de vie descendu du ciel (Jn 6,55–58)." *AsSeign* 54 (1966) 41–53.

Vardaman, E. J.
"The Pool of Bethesda." *BR* 14 (1963) 27–29.

Vawter, Bruce
"'What Came to be in Him was Life' (Jn 1,3b–4a)." *CBQ* 25 (1963) 401–6.

Vawter, Bruce
"The Johannine Sacramentary." *TS* 17 (1956) 151–66.

Vawter, Bruce
"Some Recent Developments in Johannine Theology." *BTB* 1 (1971) 30–58.

Velena, J. H.
"Adventsonthulling, Jo 1,26b." *Homiletica et biblica* 23 (1964) 266–69.

Vellanickal, Matthew
"Drink from the Source of the Living Water." *Biblebhashyam* 5 (1979) 309–18.

Vellanickal, Matthew
The Divine Sonship of Christians in the Johannine Writings, AnBib 72 (Rome: Pontifical Biblical Institute, 1977).

Vergote, A.
"L'exaltation du Christ en croix selon le quatrième évangile." *ETL* 28 (1952) 5–23.

Vermeil, Frank
Etude sur le 21. chapitre de l'évangile selon S. Jean (Strassbourg: Berger-Levrault, 1861).

Vielhauer, P.
Geschichte der urchristlichen Literatur. Einleitung in das Neue Testament, die Apokryphen und die Apostolischen Väter (Berlin and New York: Walter de Gruyter, 1975) 410–84.

Villain, Maurice
"Those Who Believe. A Meditation on John 17." *One in Christ* 6 (1970) 140–45, 547–53.

Villalón, J. R.
Sacrements dans l'Esprit. Existence humaine et théologie sacramentelle, Théologie historique 43 (Paris: Beauchesne, 1977) 277–82.

Villiers, J. L. de
"The Shepherd and the Flock." *Neot* 2 (1968) 89–103.

Vincent, L.-H.
"Le Lithostrotos évangélique." *RB* 59 (1952) 513–30.

Violet, Bruno
"Ein Versuch zu Joh 20,17." *ZNW* 24 (1925) 78–80.

Virgulin, Stephen
"Recent Discussion of the Title, Lamb of God." *Scr* 13 (1961) 74–80.

Vogel, Erhard Friedrich
Der Evangelist Johannes und seine Ausleger vor dem jüngsten Gericht (Hof: Grau, 1801).

Vogels, Heinrich Josef
"Die Tempelreinigung und Golgotha (Joh 2:19–22)." *BZ* 6 (1962) 102–7.

Voigt, Simão
"Topo-geografia et Teologia del Battista nel IV Vangelo." *SBFLA* 27 (1977) 69–101.

Völker, Walther
"Heracleons Stellung zu seiner Zeit im Lichte seiner Schriftauslegung." Dissertation, Halle, 1923.

Volkmar, G.
"Ein neu entdecktes Zeugnis für das Johannes-Evangelium." *Theologische Jahrbücher* 13 (Tübingen, 1854) 446–62.

Volkmar, G.
"Berichtigung zur äussern Bezeugung des Johannes-Evangeliums." *ZWT* 3 (1860) 293–300.

Vollmer, Hans
Jesus und das Sacaeenopfer. Religionsgeschichtliche Streiflichter (Giessen: A. Töpelmann, 1905).

Vollmer, Hans
"Nochmals: Jesus und das Sacaeenopfer." *ZNW* 8 (1907) 320–21.

Vorster, W. S.
"The Gospel of John as Language." *Neot* 6 (1972) 19–27.

Vouga, François
"'Aimez-vous les uns les autres.' Une étude sur l'église de Jean." *Bulletin de Centre Protestant d'Etudes* 26 (Geneva, 1974) 5–31.

Vouga, François
Le cadre historique et l'intention théologique de Jean (Paris: Beauchesne, 1977).

Vries, E. de
"Johannes 4:1–42 in geest en hoofdzaak." *Gereformeerd theologisch tijdschrift* 78 (1978) 93–114.

Wagenmann
"Zum johanneischen Prolog." *Jahrbücher für deutsche Theologie* 20 (1875) 441.

Wahlde, Urban C. von
"The Witnesses to Jesus in John 5:31–40 and Belief in the Fourth Gospel." *CBQ* 43 (1981) 385–404.

Wahlde, Urban C. von
"A Literary Analysis of the 'ochlos'-passages in the Fourth Gospel in their Relation to the Pharisees and Jews-material." Dissertation, Marquette University, 1975.

Wahlde, Urban C. von
"A Redactional Technique in the Fourth Gospel." *CBQ* 38 (1976) 520–33.

Wahlde, Urban C. von
"The Terms for Religious Authorities in the Fourth Gospel: A Key to Literary Strata?" *JBL* 98 (1979) 231–53.

Waitz, Eberhard
"Zur Erklärung von Joh 7, 22–24." *TSK* 54 (1881) 145–60.

Walker, Rolf
"Jüngerwort und Herrenwort. Zur Auslegung von Joh 4, 39–42." *ZNW* 57 (1966) 49–54.

Walter, Eugen
Die Mysterien des Wortes und der Liebe. Auslegung der Abschiedsreden des Herrn (Joh. 14–17) (Freiburg: Herder, 1964; Dusseldorf: Patmos Verlag, ²1967).

Walter, Nikolaus
"Die Auslegung überlieferter Wundererzählungen im Johannesevangelium." In *Theologische Versuche* 2, ed. J. Rogge et al. (Berlin-Ost: Evangelische Verlagsanstalt, 1970) 93–107.

Wanke, Joachim
"Die Zukunft des Glaubenden. Theologische Erwägungen zur johanneischen Eschatologie." *Theologie und Glauben* 71 (1981) 129–39.

Ward, A. Marcus
"The Fourth Gospel in the Recent Study." *ExpTim* 81 (1969/1970) 68–72.

Watkins, Henry William
Modern Criticism Considered in its Relation to the Fourth Gospel (London: J. Murray, 1890).

Watson, Wilfred G. E.
"Antecedents of a New Testament Proverb." *VT* 20 (1970) 368–70.

Watt, A. Crawford
"John's Difficulty in Knowing the Christ—'and I knew him not.'" *ExpTim* 19 (1907/1908) 93–94.

Watts, D. J.
"Eschatology in the Johannine Community. A Study of Diversity." Dissertation, Edinburgh, 1980.

Wead, David W.
"We have a Law." *NovT* 11 (1969) 185–89.

Wead, David W.
"The Johannine Double Meaning." *Restoration Quarterly* 13 (1970) 106–20.

Wead, David W.
"The Literary Devices in John's Gospel." Dissertation, Basel, 1970.

Weber, Michael
Authentia capitis ultimi evangelii Johannis hujusque evangelii totius et primae Joh. Epistolae, argumentorum internorum usu, vindicata, Miscellaneous dissertations 119 (Halle: Fr. Ruff, 1823).

Wedel, Alton F.
"John 4,5–26 (5–42)." *Int* 31 (1977) 406–12.

Wegscheider, Julius August Ludwig
Versuch einer vollstädigen Einleitung in das Evangelium des Johannes (Göttingen: J. F. Röwer, 1806).

Weifel, W.
"Bethabara jenseits des Jordan (Joh 1, 28)." *ZDPV* 83 (1967) 72–81.

Weigandt, Peter
"Zum Text von Joh 10, 7. Ein Beitrag zum Problem der koptischen Bibelübersetzung." *NovT* 9 (1967) 43–51.

Weise, Manfred
"Passionswoche und Epiphaniewoche im Johannesevangelium. Ihre Bedeutung für Komposition und Konzeption des vierten Evangeliums." *KD* 12 (1966) 48–62.

Weiser, Alfons
"Joh 13,12–20—Zufügung eines späteren Herausgebers?" *BZ* 12 (1968) 252–57.

Weiss, Bernhard
Der johanneische Lehrbegriff in seinen Grundzügen untersucht (Berlin: W. Hertz, 1862).

Weiss, Herold
"Foot Washing in the Johannine Community." *NovT* 21 (1979) 298–325.

Weiss, Johannes
"Zum Märtyrertod des Zebedäiden." *ZNW* 11 (1910) 167.

Weiss, Josef
Die Predigt Jesu vom Reiche Gottes, ed. F. Hahn (Göttingen: Vandenhoeck & Ruprecht, ³1964).

Weiss, K.
"Die 'Gnosis' im Hintergrund und im Spiegel der Johannesbriefe." In *Gnosis und Neues Testament. Studien aus Religionswissenschaft und Theologie,* ed. K.-W. Tröger (Gütersloh: Gerd Mohn, 1973) 341ff.

Weisse, Christian Hermann
Die evangelische Geschichte, kritisch und philosophisch bearbeitet, 2 vols. (Leipzig: Breitkopf & Härtel, 1838).

Weisse, Christian Hermann
Die Evangelienfrage in ihrem gegenwärtigen Stadium (Leipzig: Breitkopf & Härtel, 1856).

Weitzel, K. L.
"Das Selbstzeugnis des vierten Evangelisten über seine Person." *TSK* 22 (1849) 578–638.

Weizsäcker, Carl
"Die johanneische Logoslehre, mit besonderer Berücksichtigung der Schrift: Der johanneische Lehrbegriff, von Dr. B. Weiss." *Jahrbücher für deutsche Theologie* 7 (1862) 619–708.

Weizsäcker, Carl
"Beiträge zur Charakteristik des johanneischen Evangelium." *Jahrbücher für Deutsche Theologie* 4 (1859) 685–767.

Weizsäcker, Carl

"Das Selbstzeugnis des johanneischen Christus." *Jahrbücher für deutsche Theologie* 2 (1857) 154–208.

Weizsäcker, Karl Heinrich von
"Die Bezeugung des Evangeliums." In his *Untersuchungen über die evangelische Geschichte, ihre Quellen und den Gang ihrer Entwicklung* (Tübingen: Mohr-Siebeck, ²1901) 140–51.

Weizsäcker, Karl Heinrich von
Das apostolische Zeitalter der christlichen Kirche (Tübingen: Mohr-Siebeck, ³1902).

Weizsäcker, Karl Heinrich von
Untersuchungen über die evangelische Geschichte, ihre Quellen und den Gang ihrer Entwicklung (Tübingen: Mohr-Siebeck, ²1901) 172–84.

Welch, C. H.
Parable, Miracle and Sign of Matthew and John Considered Dispensationally (London: Berean Publ. Trust, ²1978).

Wellhausen, Julius
Erweiterungen und Änderungen im vierten Evangelium (Berlin: G. Reimer, 1907).

Wendland, Paul
"Σωτήρ." *ZNW* 5 (1904) 335–53.

Wendland, Paul
"Jesus als Saturnalienkönig." *Hermes* 33 (1898) 175–79.

Wendt, Hans Heinrich
Die Johannesbriefe und das johanneische Christentum (Halle: Buchhandlung des Waisenhauses, 1925).

Wendt, Hans Heinrich
Das Johannesevangelium. Eine Untersuchung seiner Entstehung und seines geschichtlichen Wertes (Göttingen: Vandenhoeck & Ruprecht, 1900).

Wendt, Hans Heinrich
Die Schichten im vierten Evangelium (Göttingen: Vandenhoeck & Ruprecht, 1911).

Wendt, Hans Heinrich
Die Lehre Jesu, 2 vols. Vol. 1, *Die evangelischen Quellenberichte über die Lehre Jesu;* Vol. 2, *Der Inhalt der Lehre Jesu* (Göttingen: Vandenhoeck & Ruprecht, 1886–1890).

Wengst, Klaus
Häresie und Orthodoxie im Spiegel des ersten Johannesbriefes (Gütersloh: Gerd Mohn, 1976).

Wengst, Klaus
Christologische Formeln und Lieder im Urchristentum, SNT 7 (Gütersloh: Gerd Mohn, 1972) 200–208.

Wennemer, Karl
"Theologie des 'Wortes' im Johannesevangelium. Das innere Verhältnis des verkündigten *logos theou* zum persönlichen *Logos*." *Scholastik* 38 (1963) 1–17.

Wensinck, A. J.
"John VIII, 6–8." In *Amicitiae Corolla. A Volume of Essays Presented to James Rendel Harris, D. Litt., on the Occasion of his Eightieth Birthday*, ed. H. G. Wood (London: University of London Press, 1933) 300–302.

Wenz, H.

"Sehen und Glauben bei Johannes." *TZ* 17 (1961) 17–25.

Wette, Wilhelm Martin Leberecht de
"Bemerkungen zu Stellen des Evangeliums Johannis." *TSK* 7 (1834) 924–44.

Wette, Wilhelm Martin Leberecht de
Biblische Dogmatik des Alten und Neuen Testamentes; oder, Kritische Darstellung der Religionslehre des Hebraismus, des Judenthums und Urchristenthums (Berlin: Realschulbuchhandlung, 1813).

Wette, Wilhelm Martin Leberecht de
Lehrbuch der historisch-kritischen Einleitung in die kanonischen Bücher des Neuen Testaments (Berlin: G. Reimer, ²1830).

Wetter, Gillis Petersson
"Die Verherrlichung im Johannesevangelium." *Beiträge zur Religionswissenschaft* 2 (1915) 32–113.

Wetter, Gillis Petersson
"Ich bin es." *TSK* 88 (1915) 224–38.

Wetter, Gillis Petersson
"Ich bin das Licht der Welt." *Beiträge zur Religionswissenschaft* 1,2 (1914).

Wetter, Gillis Petersson
"Eine gnostische Formel im vierten Evangelium." *ZNW* 18 (1917/1918) 49–63.

Wetter, Gillis Petersson
"*Phōs*. Eine Untersuchung über hellenistische Frömmigkeit, zugleich ein Beitrag zum Verständnis des Manichäismus." *Skrifter utgifna af (k.) Humanistiska Vetenskapssamfundet i Uppsala* 17:2 (Leipzig: Harrassowitz; Uppsala: A.-B. Akademiska Bokhandelung, 1917).

Wetter, Gillis Petersson
"Religionsgeschichtliche Studien zu dem vierten Evangelium mit Ausgangspunkt 'Verherrlichung.'" *Beiträge zur Religionswissenschaft* 2 (1918) 32–113.

Wetter, Gillis Petersson
"Der Sohn Gottes," eine Untersuchung über den Charakter und die Tendenz des Johannesevangeliums; zugleich ein Beitrag zur Kenntnis der Heilandsgestalten der Antike FRLANT, n.s., 9 (Göttingen: Vandenhoeck & Ruprecht, 1916).

Wetzel, G.
Die Echtheit und Glaubwürdigkeit des Evangeliums Johannes aufs neue untersucht und verteidigt (Leipzig: H. G. Wallmann, 1899).

White, H. J.
"On the Sayings Attributed to Our Lord in John II, 19." *Expositor*, 8th ser., 17 (1919) 415–23.

Whittacker, John
"A Hellenistic Context for Jo 10, 29." *VC* 24 (1970) 241–60.

Whittaker, M.
"'Signs and Wonders': The Pagan Background." *SE* 5 = TU 103 (Berlin: Akademie-Verlag, 1968) 155–58.

Widengren, Geo
"The Gathering of the Dispersed." *SEÅ* 41/42

(1976/1977) 224–34.

Widengren, Geo
"En la maison de mon Père sont demeures nombreuses." *SEÅ* 37/38 (1972/1973) 9–15.

Wieand, David J.
"John v. 2 and the Pool of Bethesda." *NTS* 12 (1965/1966) 392–404.

Wiefel, Wolfgang
"Die Scheidung von Gemeinde und Welt im Johannesevangelium auf dem Hintergrund der Trennung von Kirche und Synagoge." *TZ* 35 (1979) 213–27.

Wikgren, Allen Paul
"The Lectionary Text of the Pericope John 8:1–11." *JBL* 53 (1934) 188–98.

Wilckens, Ulrich
"Der eucharistische Abschnitt der johanneischen Rede vom Lebensbrot (Joh 6,51c–58)." In *Neues Testament und Kirche. Für Rudolf Schnackenburg*, ed. J. Gnilka (Freiburg and Vienna: Herder, 1974) 220–48.

Wilcox, Max
"The 'Prayer' of Jesus in John XI, 41b–42." *NTS* 24 (1977/1978) 128–32.

Wilcox, Max
"The Composition of Joh 13,21–30." In *Neotestamentica and Semitica. Studies in Honour of Matthew Black*, ed. E. E. Ellis and M. Wilcox (Edinburgh: T. & T. Clark, 1969) 143–56.

Wiles, Maurice Frank
The Spiritual Gospel. The Interpretation of the Fourth Gospel in the Early Church (Cambridge: Cambridge University Press, 1960).

Wilke, Christian Gottlieb
Der Urevangelist; oder, Exegetisch-kritische Untersuchung über das Verwandtschaftsverhältniss der drei ersten Evangelien (Dresden and Leipzig: G. Fleischer, 1838).

Wilken, Robert Louis
"Collegia, Philosophical Schools and Theology." In *The Catacombs and the Colosseum. The Roman Empire as the Setting of Primitive Christianity*, ed. S. Benko and J. J. O'Rourke (Valley Forge, PA: Judson, 1971) 268–91.

Wilkens, Wilhelm
"Evangelist und Tradition im Johannesevangelium." *TZ* 16 (1960) 81–90.

Wilkens, Wilhelm
"Das Abendmahlszeugnis im vierten Evangelium." *EvT* 18 (1958) 354–70.

Wilkens, Wilhelm
"Die Erweckung des Lazarus." *TZ* 15 (1959) 22–39.

Wilkens, Wilhelm
Die Entstehungsgeschichte des vierten Evangeliums (Zollikon: Evangelischer Verlag, 1958).

Wilkens, Wilhelm
"Evangelist und Tradition im Johannesevangelium." *TZ* 16 (1960) 81–90.

Wilkens, Wilhelm
Zeichen und Werke. Ein Beitrag zur Theologie des vierten Evangeliums in Erzählungs- und Redestoff, ATANT 55 (Zurich: Zwingli Verlag, 1969).

Wilkens, Wilhelm
Die Entstehungsgeschichte des vierten Evangeliums (Zollikon: Evangelischer Verlag, 1958).

Wilkinson, John
"The Incident of the 'Blood and Water' in John 19,34." *SJT* 28 (1975) 149–72.

Wilkinson, John
"A Study of Healing in the Gospel according to John." *SJT* 20 (1967) 442–61.

Willemese, J.
"Recente boeken over het vierde evangelie." *Tijdschrift voor Theologie* 6 (1966) 437–40.

Willemse, Johannes
"La patrie de Jésus selon Saint Jean iv. 44." *NTS* 11 (1964/1965) 349–64.

Willemse, Johannes
Het vierde evangelie, Een onderzoek naar zijn structuur (Hilversum: P. Brand, 1965).

Williams, Francis E.
"Fourth Gospel and Synoptic Tradition: Two Johannine Passages." *JBL* 86 (1967) 311–19.

Williams, J.
"Proposed Renderings for Some Johannine Passages." *BT* 25 (1974) 351–53.

Wilson, Jeffrey
"The Integrity of John 3:22–36." *JSNT* 10 (1871) 34–41.

Wilson, R. McL.
"Philo and the Fourth Gospel." *ExpTim* 65 (1953/1954) 47–49.

Wilson, W. G.
"The Original Text of the Fourth Gospel. Some Objective Evidence Against the Theory of Page Displacements." *JTS* 50 (1949) 59–60.

Wind, A.
"Destination and Purpose of the Gospel of John." *NovT* 14 (1972) 26–69.

Windisch, Hans
"Die Absolutheit des Johannesevangeliums." *ZST* 5 (1927/1928) 3–54.

Windisch, Hans
"Die Dauer der öffentlichen Wirksamkeit Jesu nach den vier Evangelisten." *ZNW* 12 (1911) 141–75.

Windisch, Hans
Die katholischen Briefe, HNT 15 (Tübingen: Mohr-Siebeck, 1930).

Windisch, Hans
"Angelophanien um den Menschensohn auf Erden. Zu Joh 1, 51." *ZNW* 30 (1931) 215–33.

Windisch, Hans
"Joh 1, 51 und die Auferstehung Jesu." *ZNW* 31 (1932) 199–204.

Windisch, Hans
"Die johanneische Weinregel." *ZNW* 14 (1913)

248–57.

Windisch, Hans
Johannes und die Synoptiker. Wollte der vierte Evangelist die älteren Evangelien ergänzen oder ersetzen?
UNT 12 (Leipzig: J. C. Hinrichs, 1926).

Windisch, Hans
"Das johanneische Christentum und sein Verhältnis zum Judentum und zu Paulus." *Christliche Welt* 47 (1933) 98–107, 147–54.

Windisch, Hans
"Die fünf johanneischen Parakletsprüche." In *Festgabe für Adolf Jülicher zum 70. Geburtstag 26. Januar 1927* (Tübingen: Mohr-Siebeck, 1927) 110–37.

Windisch, Hans
"Jesus und der Geist im Johannes-Evangelium." In *Amicitiae Corolla, A Volume of Essays presented to James Rendel Harris, D. Litt., on the Occasion of his Eightieth Birthday*, ed. H. G. Wood (London: University of London Press, 1933) 34–69.

Windisch, Hans
The Spirit-Paraclete in the Fourth Gospel, tr. J. W. Cox. Facet Books, Biblical Series 20 (Philadelphia: Fortress Press, 1968).

Windisch, Hans
"Der johanneische Erzählungsstil." In ΕΥΧΑΡΙΣ-ΤΗΡΙΟΝ; *Studien zur Religion und Literatur des Alten und Neuen Testaments Hermann Gunkel zum 60. Geburtstage, dem 23 Mai 1922, dargebracht von seinen Schülern und Freunden*, ed. Hans Schmidt. FRLANT, n.s., 19 (Göttingen: Vandenhoeck & Ruprecht, 1923) 174–213.

Windisch, Hans
Der Barnabasbrief, HNT, Ergänzungsband 3 (Tübingen: Mohr-Siebeck, 1920).

Wink, Walter
"John the Baptist in the Gospel Tradition." SNTSMS 7 (London: Cambridge University Press, 1968) 87–106.

Winter, Paul
"Zum Verständnis des Johannes-Evangelium." *Vox Theologica* 25 (1954) 149–59; *TLZ* 80 (1955) 141–50.

Winter, Paul
"Μονογενὴς παρὰ πατρός." *ZRGG* 5 (1953) 335–65.

Winter, Paul
On the Trial of Jesus, Studia Judaica, Forschungen zur Wissenschaft des Judentums 1 (Berlin: Walter de Gruyter, 1961).

Winter, Paul
"Marginal Notes on the Trial of Jesus, II." *ZNW* 50 (1959) 221–51.

Wittichen, C.
"Zur Markusfrage III: Die ursprüngliche Zugehörigkeit der Erzählung von der Ehebrecherin zum Markusevangelium." *Jahrbücher für protestantische Theologie* 5 (1879) 165–82; 7 (1881) 366–75.

Wolfson, Harry Austin
Philo. Foundations of Religious Philosophy in Judaism, Christianity, and Islam, 2 vols. (Cambridge: Harvard University Press, [2]1948).

Woodhouse, H.
"Hard Sayings—IX. John 7. 39." *Theology* 67 (1964) 310–12.

Woodhouse, H. F.
"The Paraclete as Interpreter." *Biblical Theology* 18 (1968) 51–53.

Wootton, R. W. F.
"The Implied Agent in Greek Passive Verbs in Mark, Luke, and John." *BT* 19 (1968) 159–64.

Worden, T.
"The Marriage Feast at Cana (John 3.1–11)." *Scr* 20 (1968) 97–106.

Worden, T.
"The Holy Eucharist in St. John—I." *Scr* 15 (1963) 97–103.

Worden, T.
"The Holy Eucharist in St. John—II." *Scr* 16 (1964) 5–16.

Worden, T.
"'Seigneur, à qui irions-nous?'" *Concilium* 50 (Paris, 1969) 105–81.

Worsley, Frederick William
The Fourth Gospel and the Synoptists. Being a Contribution to the Study of the Johannine Problem (Edinburgh: T. & T. Clark, 1909).

Wotherspoon, Arthur W.
"Concerning the Name 'Paraclete.'" *ExpTim* 34 (1922/1923) 43–44.

Wrede, William
Review of *Der Prolog des vierten Evangeliums*, by Wilhelm Baldensperger. *Göttingenische gelehrte Anzeigen* (1900) 1–26.

Wrede, William
Charakter und Tendenz des Johannesevangeliums (Tübingen: Mohr-Siebeck, 1903, [2]1933).

Wrege, Hans-Theo
"Jesusgeschichte und Jüngergeschichte nach Joh 12,20–38 und Hebr 5,7–10." In *Der Ruf Jesu und die Antwort der Gemeinde. Exegetische Untersuchungen Joachim Jeremias zum 70. Geburtstag gewidmet von seinen Schülern*, ed. E. Lohse et al. (Göttingen: Vandenhoeck & Ruprecht, 1970) 259–88.

Wulf, F.
"'Meister, wo wohnst du?' (Joh 1,38)." *Geist und Leben* 31 (1958) 241–44.

Wurm, Alois
Die Irrlehrer im ersten Johannesbrief, Biblische Studien 1,8 (Freiburg: Herder, 1903).

Würzburger, Karl
"Abrahams Kinder: Überlegungen zu Joh 8,30–39." *Kirchenblatt für die reformierte Schweiz* 124 (1968) 82–85.

Wurzinger, A.
"Glauben nach Johannes." *BLit* 39 (1966) 203–8.

Yamauchi, Edwin M.
"Jewish Gnosticism? The Prologue of John, Mandean Parallels and the Trimorphic Proten-

345

noia." In *Festschrift G. Quispel* (Leiden: E. J. Brill, 1981) 467–97.

Yamauchi, Edwin M.
"The Present Status of Mandaean Studies." *JNES* 25 (1966) 88–96.

York, Harry C.
"A Note on the Interpretation of the Fourth Gospel." *JBL* 37 (1918) 100–4.

Youtie, H. C.
"Σημεῖον in the Papyri and Its Significanc for Plato." *Zeitschrift für Papyrologie und Epigraphik* 6 (1970) 105–16.

Zahn, Theodor
"Das Evangelium des Johannes unter den Händen seiner neuesten Kritiker." *NKZ* 22 (1911) 28–58, 83–115.

Zahn, Theodor
"Zur Heimatkunde des Evangelisten Johannes." *NKZ* 18 (1907) 265–94, 593–608; 19 (1908) 31–39, 207–18.

Zarella, Pietro
"Gesú cammina sulle acque. Significato teologico di Giov 6,16–21." *Scuola Cattolica* 95 (1967) 146–60.

Zehrer, F.
"Das Gespräch Jesu mit seiner Mutter auf der Hochzeit zu Kana (Joh 2, 3f.) im Licht der traditions- und redaktionsgeschichtlichen Forschung." *BLit* 43 (1970) 14–27.

Zeitlin, Solomon
"The Date of the Crucifixion according to the Fourth Gospel." *JBL* 51 (1932) 263–71.

Zeller, Dieter
Die Passion nach Johannes. Sechs Wortgottesdienste für die Sonntage vor Ostern (Stuttgart: Katholisches Bibelwerk, 1969).

Zeller, Eduard
Review of *Der Lehrbegriff des Evangeliums und der Briefe Johannis*, by K. R. Köstlin. *Theologischer Jahrbücher* 4 (Tübingen, 1845) 75–100.

Zeller, Eduard
"Noch ein Wort über den Ausspruch Jesu bei Justin, Apol 1.61 über die Wiedergeburt." *Theologische Jahrbücher* 14 (Tübingen, 1855) 138–40.

Zeller, Eduard
"Die äusseren Zeugnisse über das Dasein und den Ursprung des vierten Evangeliums. Eine Prüfung der Kirchlichen Tradition bis auf Irenäus." *Theologische Jahrbücher* 4 (Tübingen, 1845) 579–656.

Zeller, Eduard
Die Philosophie der Griechen in ihrer geschichtlichen Entwicklung, 3 vols. (Leipzig: O. R. Reisland, 1903–1922).

Zerwick, Maximillian
"Vom Wirken des Heiligen Geistes in uns. Meditationsgedanken zu Jo 16,5–15." *Geist und Leben* 38 (1965) 224–30.

Ziegler, Carl Ludwig
"Erläuterung der schwierigen Stelle Joh 8, 12–59." *Magazin für Religionsphilosophie, Exegese und Kirchengeschichte* 5 (1796) 227–90.

Ziegler, Dr.
"Bemerkungen über das Evangelium des Johannes, und Erklärungen einzelner schwieriger Stellen desselben." *Neuestes theologisches Journal* 9, ed. J. P. Gabler (1802) 15–69.

Ziener, G.
"Weisheitsbuch und Johannesevangelium I." *Bib* 38 (1957) 396–418.

Ziener, G.
"Weisheitsbuch und Johannesevangelium II." *Bib* 39 (1958) 37–60.

Zimmermann, H.
"Das absolute *Ego Eimi* als die neutestamentliche Offenbarungsformel." *BZ* 4 (1960) 54–69, 266–76.

Zimmermann, H.
"Papyrus Bodmer II und seine Bedeutung für die Textgeschichte des Johannes-Evangeliums." *BZ* 2 (1958) 214–43.

Zimmermann, Heinrich
"Christushymnus und johanneischer Prolog." In *Neues Testament und Kirche. Für Rudolf Schnackenburg*, ed. J. Gnilka (Freiburg and Vienna: Herder, 1974) 220–48.

Zimmermann, Heinrich
"'Meister, wo wohnst Du?' (Joh 1,38)." *Lebendiges Zeugnis* (1962) 49–57.

Zimmermann, Heinrich
"Struktur und Aussageabsicht der johanneischen Abschiedsreden (Jo 13–17)." *BLit* 8 (1967) 279–90.

Zimmermann, Hellmuth
"Lukas und die johanneische Tradition." *TSK* 76 (1903) 586–605.

Zimmermann, J. O.
"Die johanneische aletheia." Dissertation, Fribourg, 1977/1978.

Zimolong, B.
"Die Nikodemus-Perikope nach dem syrosinaitischen Text." Dissertation, Breslau, 1919.

Zurhellen, Otto
"Die Heimat des vierten Evangeliums." In *Johannes und sein Evangelium*, ed. K. H. Rengstorf (Darmstadt: Wissenschaftliche Buchgesellschaft, 1973) 314–80.

Zwaan, J. de
"John Wrote in Aramaic." *JBL* 57 (1938) 155–71. 257–73.

Zweifel, Bertrand
"Jésus lave les pieds de ses disciples. Essai d'exégèse sur Jn 13,1–20." Dissertation, Lausanne, 1965.

1. Passages

a / New Testament

References to the Gospel of John indicate only those passages that are discussed out of order.

8:32	2:146	10:22–39	1:85	12:1	2:69, 93, 227
8:35	2:64	10:22	1:182, 243	12:2	2:69
8:36	2:146	10:24	1:144	12:3	2:70, 227
8:38	1:212, 260	10:25	1:212; 2:30	12:4	2:57
8:40	1:96, 212, 260	10:29	1:51	12:9	2:84
8:41ff.	1:49	10:30	1:51, 96, 254;	12:10	1:58, 301; 2:71
8:44	1:84		2:50	12:11	1:62; 2:20
8:46	2:143	10:31	2:30	12:12–19	1:85
8:47	1:96	10:32	1:62	12:12	2:84
8:50	1:212	10:34	1:256	12:17	2:90
8:52	1:252	10:36	2:154	12:18	1:89; 2:90
8:54	1:212	10:37	1:212; 2:30	12:19	1:218
8:57	1:15	10:39	2:30, 58	12:20ff.	2:238
8:59	1:96; 2:42, 58	10:40–42	1:37	12:20–36	1:85f.; 2:49
9	1:50, 76, 80, 84,	10:40	1:147; 2:58	12:22	1:271
	199, 247, 256;	10:41	1:83	12:25	2:32
	2:51, 66, 71, 146	11	1:37, 50, 76, 80,	12:27–28	2:157, 164
9:1	1:87, 245		84, 85, 87, 88,	12:27	2:150
9:2	1:77, 247		256, 302; 2:42,	12:31	2:30
9:3–7	1:87		84, 237	12:32–33	2:179
9:5	1:88, 95, 299;	11:2	1:218; 2:227	12:32	2:19
	2:46	11:3	2:237	12:33–36	1:49
9:6–7	1:87; 2:8	11:4	2:37	12:35	2:16
9:7	1:301	11:5	2:237	12:36	2:30
9:8–12	1:87	11:14	2:49	12:36b	2:51, 101
9:13–18a	1:87	11:15	1:62	12:37–42	2:186
9:13	1:218, 243	11:16	2:60, 76	12:37	1:192, 193, 234;
9:14	1:89	11:18–19	1:243		2:20
9:15	1:218	11:19	2:90	12:42	1:218; 2:18
9:16	1:87, 89	11:20–26	1:88	12:44–50	1:49, 51, 86; 2:51
9:17	1:144	11:23–27	2:78, 79	12:44	1:50; 2:16
9:18b–23	1:87	11:23–25	1:63	12:48	1:63; 2:238
9:22	1:202, 243; 2:8,	11:24	1:63, 88	12:49	2:125
	137	11:25–27	1:33, 95	13:1–3	1:57
9:24–34	1:87	11:25	1:63, 88, 235,	13:1	1:1, 173; 2:84
9:29	1:264		293, 299	13:2	2:57
9:31	1:200	11:31	2:90	13:3	2:150
9:32–33	1:200	11:33	1:56	13:5	1:58
9:34–35	1:277	11:41–44	2:78	13:16	2:137, 216
9:34	1:202, 243; 2:8,	11:42	2:156	13:18	1:298
	143	11:43–44	2:227	13:23ff.	2:227
9:35–38	1:87f.	11:45–53	1:85; 2:69	13:23–26	2:236
9:37	2:49	11:45	1:277; 2:20, 61,	13:23	2:57, 233
9:38	2:20		90	13:27	1:185
9:39	1:95	11:46–47	1:218	13:30	2:59, 164
9:40–41	2:51	11:46	2:90	13:31–17:26	1:86
9:41	1:50, 77; 2:26	11:47	1:89, 192	13:33	2:16
10	1:27, 49; 2:150	11:49–50	2:57, 167	13:36–38	2:172
10:1–21	1:84f.	11:50	2:169	13:36	2:143
10:1–18	1:51	11:52	1:275	13:37	2:232
10:4	1:58	11:54	2:84, 90	13:38	2:170
10:7	1:7	11:55	1:182, 218, 243	14–17	2:90
10:9	1:7	12	1:37; 2:90	14	2:164
10:16	2:238	12:1–11	1:85	14:5	2:60
10:18	1:185	12:1–8	1:75; 2:57, 69		

Reference	Page
20:30	1:89, 192, 193, 302; 2:230
21	1:41, 61, 76, 77, 88, 89, 116, 237, 280, 297; 2:215, 238
21:1	1:270
21:2	1:165, 172; 2:60
21:4	2:209
21:6	1:59
21:7	2:112, 237
21:12	1:58, 62
21:15–17	1:165
21:16	1:236
21:19	1:89
21:20	2:57, 112, 236
21:22–23	2:238
21:22	2:217
21:24	1:1; 2:201, 237, 239
21:25	1:77

Matthew

Reference	Page
2:11	1:166
2:22	1:270
2:23	1:166
3:1	1:149
3:5	1:158
3:7	1:148, 158
3:7b–10	1:148
3:7b	1:148
3:10	1:148
3:11	1:147, 148
3:12	1:148
3:14ff.	1:152
3:14–15	1:148, 152
3:16ff.	1:154
4:13	1:175
4:18	1:165
4:19	2:224
5:23–24	1:190
7:7	2:126
8:1–9a	1:274
8:5–13	1:78, 234, 236; 2:70
8:7ff.	1:235
8:8	1:66
8:28–34	1:86
9:4	1:271
10:2	1:165
10:3	2:60
10:4	2:80
10:5–6	1:225
10:16	2:155
10:25	1:66
10:34	1:189; 2:80

Reference	Page
10:40	2:110
11:11a	1:35
11:11b	1:35
11:19	1:126
11:21	2:71
11:22	1:249
11:23	1:165, 279, 296
12:28	2:38
12:40	1:185
13:28	1:59
14:13–21	1:273
14:21	1:273
14:22–33	1:237
14:22–27	1:281
14:30f.	1:280
15:21–28	1:176
15:26–27	1:60
15:29–30	1:271
15:29	1:270
15:32–39	1:273, 282
15:32–38	1:275
15:38	1:275
16:17–18	2:232, 234
16:17	1:164; 2:225
16:18	1:165
16:19	2:211
16:28	1:253
17:10–13	1:149
17:10	1:35
17:11	1:116
17:14–21	1:86
17:24–27	1:176, 190
18:6	1:192
18:18	1:76
18:19	2:211
20:20–23	1:10
20:22–23	2:238
21:1–11	2:93
21:12–13	1:186
21:23–27	1:186
21:23	1:184
23:24–26	1:126
23:37–38	1:190
23:37	1:62
24:1–3	1:190
24:2	2:80
24:15	1:190
24:26–27	1:253
24:26	2:16
24:30–31	1:253
24:34	1:253
26:6–13	2:83, 85
26:12	2:85
26:17–29	1:3
26:20–29	2:105

Reference	Page
26:21	2:110
26:25	2:110
26:26	1:294
26:28	1:294
26:30–35	2:171
26:33	2:225
26:46	2:164
26:48–49	2:165
26:51	2:80, 165
26:54	2.166
26:55	2.166
26:58	2:167, 171
26:60–61	1:184
26:61	1:190; 2:80
26:64	1:253
26:67–68	2:167, 181
26:69–75	2:171
27:11	2:79
27:19	2:184
27:27–31	2:180
27:29	2:181
27:33	2:192
27:34	2:198
27:37	2:192
27:40	1:184, 190
27:56	2:198
27:64	2:208
28:1	2:207
28:5	2:209
28:9	2:210
28:13–15	2:208
28:17	2:211, 215
28:18	1:253; 2:215
28:19ff.	1:249

Mark

Reference	Page
1:1–13	1:81
1:4	1:149
1:5	1:116
1:9–11	1:149
1:14–15	1:82
1:16–20	1:166, 167
1:16	2:224
1:29–31	1:247
1:29	1:76, 165
2:5	2:58
2:8	1:192, 271, 305
2:9	2:28
2:10	2:58
2:11	1:246, 257; 2:28
2:13–14	1:167
2:14	1:165
2:16b	2:28
2:18–22	1:146
2:19	1:149
2:20	2:6

352

Chrysostom
Hom.
43.1   1:280
53.1   2:28
82.1   2:154
In Joh.
11.1   1:266
Cicero
De off.
3.28.102   1:249
Nat. deor.
2.28.71   1:223
Clement of Alexandria
Strom.
4.41–42   2:16
Cyrillus of Jerusalem
Hom.
33.1133   1:244
Euripides
Bacchae
203   1:178
Ion
693   1:118
Eusebius
H.E.
1.13.4   2:60
3.23.1ff.   1:15
3.25.5–6   1:12
3.28.2   1:24
3.39.3   1:9, 13; 2:70
3.39.4   1:163
3.39.14   1:10
3.39.15–16   1:11
3.39.16   1:11
3.39.17   1:13
4.29.6   1:14
5.1.44   2:192
5.20.4ff.   1:15
6.14.7   1:23
Onomasticon
40.1   1:210
Hippolytus
Ref.
5.8.5   1:114
5.9.18,   1:221
5.26.25   2:105
5.26.29   2:48
7.20f.   2:105
27.2   1:220
Irenaeus
Adv. haer.
Preface 3   1:15
1.8.5   1:112
2.22.3   1:243
2.22.5   1:15, 184

2.22.6   1:15
3.3.3   1:16
3.3.4   1:16, 24
3.4   1:8
3.11.9   1:23
4.27ff.   1:16
4.27.1   1:16
4.27.2   1:16
4.28.1   1:16
4.30.1   1:16
4.30.4   1:16
4.31.1   1:16
4.33.3   1:16
5.33.3–4   1:10, 15
Isocrates
Paneg.
10.38   1:174
Jerome
Comm. in Mt.
9.9   1:190
Dialog. adv. Pelag.
3.2   1:12; 2:6
In Ezechielen
47.12   2:224
Vir. ill.
3   1:12
Josephus
Ant.
2.275f.   1:219
3.159ff.   2:197
3.224ff.   1:182
8.100   2:12
9.288   1:31
15.380   1:184
17.9.3   2:30
BJ
2.103–4   2:79
2.530   1:244
3.57   1:270
3.328   1:244
3.506   1:280
3.530   1:244
4.9.9   2:76
4.317   2:194
4.456   1:270
5.149–151   1:244
5.302   1:244
6.420   1:182
Dial.
8   2:16
27.5   2:15
Vita
269   1:218
420   1:24

Justin
First Apol.
1.35.6   2:187
61.4f.   1:13
66.1ff.   1:294
66.2   1:13
Dial.
8.3   1:153
81.4   1:13
108.2   2:208
Longus
Pastoralia
4.26.38   2:46
Maximus Tyre
Diss.
15.6.2   1:249
Origen
Comm. Joh.
2.2.13–15   1:109
2.14   1:112
61   1:244
C. Celsum
6.5   1:114
Philo
De cher.
87–90   1:248
90   1:249
De decal.
104   1:111
Det. Pot. Ins.
7.21   1:223
18   1:248
161   1:248
De ebr.
30   1:138
In. Flac.
6.36–39   2:180
De fuga
198   1:220
Leg. all.
1.3f.   1:248
2.49   1:138
3.82   1:178
De mut. nom.
154ff.   2:29
De post. Caini
145   1:120
De somn.
1.229f.   1:109
2.249   1:178
De spec. leg.
1.65   2:13
1.162f.   1:182
1.332   2:156
4.238   2:228

2. Foreign Words

a / Greek

ἀγαθά	1:88
ἀγαπάω	2:225, 237
ἁγιάζειν	2:155
ἅγιοι	2:154
ἀδελφοί	1:175; 2:229
ἀθρακία	2:224
αἷμα	1:118, 294, 295
αἴρειν	2:202
αἰτία	2:197
ἀκολουθέω	1:158; 2:233
ἀλάβαστρον	2:86
ἀλήθεια	1:223; 2:180
ἀληθινός	1:295; 2:131
ἁλιευτικά	2:224
ἀλλά	1:291
ἄλλος	1:59
ἀλλοχόθεν	2:46
ἀμὴν ἀμήν	1:64, 249, 252; 2:46, 232
ἀναβαίνω	1:182; 2:224, 231
ἀνάπαυσις	1:249; 2:131
ἀνθρακία	1:64; 2:232
ἄνθρωπος	1:210
ἄντλημα	1:226
ἀντί	1:120
ἀπό	2:229
ἀποδείκνυμι	1:199
ἀποκατάστασις πάντων	2:158
ἀποστέλλω	1:96
ἀρνία	2:225, 232
ἄρτος	1:291, 293
ἀρχή	1:113
ἀρχήν (τὴν)	2:28
ἀρχιτρίκλινος	1:173f.
ἄρχομαι	1:59, 279
ἄρχοντες	1:86, 1:199; 2:199
ἀρώματα	2:196
ἀφιέναι	1:58
βασιλεία τοῦ θεοῦ	1:200
βασιλεύς	1:273; 2:183
Βηθανία	1:146
βῆμα	2:187
βόσκω	2:225, 232
γάμος	1:172
γίνομαι	1:130
γινώσκω	1:218; 2:144
γράμματα	2:13
γραφή	1:185
γυμνός	2:223
γύναι	1:63f., 173, 222
διά	1:112, 296
διαζώννυμι	2:223
διακονέω	2:69
διάκονοι	1:176
διὰ τοῦτο	2:14f.
διδάσκαλε	1:168
διδάσκω	2:16
δίψα, δίψω	2:193, 198
δόξα	1:111, 119
δοξάζω	2:150
δοῦλοι	2:132
δυνάμεις	1:126
ἐὰν (μὴ) τις	1:64f.
ἐγγύς	1:64
ἐγείρω	1:185, 246, 249, 257, 258, 302
ἐγώ εἰμι	2:165
ἔθνος	2:75
εἰδώς	2:105, 106
εἰκών	1:95
εἶπον	2:50
εἰς	1:220
εἷς	1:59; 2:50
ἐκ	1:59, 62
ἐκβάλλω	1:58; 2:46f.
ἐκεῖνος	1:59, 61f.
ἐκλεκτός	1:154
Ἕλληνες	2:17
ἐμός	1:65
ἐν	1:59, 109
ἐνβριμάομαι	2:66
ἐν κόλπῳ	2:110
ἐνταφιασμός	2:89
ἐξετάζω	1:58, 89; 2:225, 229
ἐξουσία	2:182
ἐπαύριον	1:280
ἐπίγεια	1:202
ἐπιστρέφω	2:172
ἐπουράνια	1:202
ἐραυνάω	1:264
ἔργα	1:266
ἐργάζομαι	1:290
ἐρωτάω	1:58, 234; 2:145, 146, 225
ἐσθίω	1:295
ἔτι μικρόν	2:16
εὐαγγέλιον πνευματικόν	1:23
γραφή	1:185
Ζηλωτής, ὁ	2:80
ζῆν	1:235
ζωή	1:113, 114
ζώννυμι	2:223, 227
ἡμέρα	1:63
θεῖος	1:111
θεῖος ἀνήρ	1:32, 166, 192, 228, 231, 303; 2:67, 72, 74
θέλω	1:58; 2:157
θεός	1:109, 110f., 121, 126, 290
θεωρέω	1:270
θύρα	2:47, 48
θυρωρός	2:46, 47
Θωμᾶς	2:60
ἴδιος	1:59, 118, 164, 234; 2:46f.
ἱερόν	1:182
Ἱεροσόλυμα	1:62
Ἱερουσαλήμ	1:62
ἵνα	1:62, 65f., 225
ἰσχύω	1:89; 2:229
ἰχθύδιον	1:64
ἰχθύς	1:64
καθαρίσμα	1:210
καθίζω	2:187
καθώς	2:150
καί	1:143
καιρός	2:8
καίτοιγε	1:218
καίω	2:223f.
Καναναῖος, ὁ	2:80
καταλαμβάνω	1:114f.
κατηγορία	2:185
κεῖμαι	2:223f.
κένωσις	1:112
κεφαλή	2:88
Κηφᾶς	1:165
κλάσματα	1:272, 275
κοιλία	2:18
κόσμος	1:112, 113, 114, 118; 2:31, 153, 155
κρατέω	2:210
κρίσις	1:252; 2:27
κρυπτός	2:13
κύριος	1:218; 2:207f., 211
λαμβάνω	1:58, 118; 2:49

359

λαός	2:75	πηγή	1:229	φανερόω	1:64; 2:222, 225, 230
λέγειν	2:87	πιάζω	2:222		
λησταί	2:166, 197, 198	πιστεύω	1:174, 192	φαντασία	1:253
		πλευρὰν ἔνυξεν (τὴν)	2:195	φάντασμα	1:295
λιθόστρωτον	2:183	πλήρης	1:125	φάρμακον ἀθανασίας	1:294, 296
λόγος	1:109, 110, 111, 225, 263f., 300	πλήρωμα	1:125	φαῦλα	1:88f, 90
		πλοιάριον	1:280; 2:222	φιλέω	2:225, 237
		πλοῖον	2:222	φρέαρ	1:229, 230
ἄσαρκος	1:81	πνεῦμα	1:201, 203, 223; 2:31f.	φύσει σῳζόμενοι	1:203, 293, 308; 2:63
ἔνσαρκος	1:81				
		πνευματικὴ πέτρα	2:17	φῶς	1:117
μανθάνω	2:13	ποδονιπτήρ	2:107	φωτίζω	1:127
μαρτυρία	1:143	ποιμαίνω	2:46, 225, 232		
μένειν	1:159	πόλις	1:218; 2:69	χάρις	1:120, 125
μεταβαίνω	1:7; 2:6, 150, 158	πρόβατα	2:225, 232	χιτών	2:197
		προφήτης	1:146	χριστός	1:144, 164
μετὰ τοῦτο, ταῦτα	1:59, 175, 210, 243, 270; 2:58, 59, 221	προσκυνέω	2:215		
		προσφάγιον	2:223	ψωμίον	2:113
		πρῶτος	1:164		
μετρηταί	1:173			ὥρα	2:157
μονογενής	1:113, 120, 121	ῥαββί	1:58	ὡς (οὖν)	1:61, 159, 219; 2:61
		ῥαββουνί	2:209		
		ῥῆμα	1:212, 300; 2:158	ὥστε	1:225
Ναζωραῖος	2:197			ὠτάριον	1:60
ναός	1:182, 190				
νόμος	1:120	Σαμφουριν	2:76, 77		
Νικόδημος	1:199	σάρξ	1:118, 294, 295		
νύσσω	2:195, 201	σημεῖον	1:34, 39, 85, 89, 174, 192; 2:39, 71, 212, 289f., 300, 301, 302		
οἶδα	1:199, 223f., 262; 2:62, 213				
ὀστέα	1:295	σκηνόω	1:119		
ὅτι	1:58	σουδάριον	2:208		
οὐκ . . . οὐδείς	1:64	σοφία	1:126		
οὖν	1:61; 2:38, 77f., 208, 230	σπεῖρα	2:166		
		σῶμα	1:294, 295, 296; 2:88		
οὗτος	1:296				
ὀψάριον	1:64, 272; 2:223	σωματικά	1:23, 24		
		σωτήρ	1:226, 228		
ὄχλος	1:64; 2:90				
		τετέλεσται	2:125, 151, 158, 194		
παιδίον	1:235				
πάντα	1:112	τις	1:59		
παρά	1:109	τότε	1:59, 61		
παραδιδόναι	2:178, 179, 183	τρώγω	1:295		
παράκλητος	1:96	ὑδρία	1:226		
παριεπάτει	2:6	ὑπάγω	2:229		
παροιμία	2:47	ὑπέρ	1:59		
παρρησία	2:49, 60	ὑπό	1:58		
πάσης σαρκός	2:150	ὕσσωπος	2:194		
πατρίς	1:83, 234				
πέμπω	1:96, 154	φαίνω	1:114f., 117		
περί	1:58, 59				
πέτρα	1:165				

b / Hebrew and Aramaic

אוֹכֵל לַחְמִי	1:295
אות	1:95, 174
אני והוא	1:224
בית תפלה	1:186
ד	1:264
הג סוכות	2:12
היה	1:235
חד	1:59
טליא	1:152
יוחנן	1:164
כָּל בָּשָׂר	2:150
כפא	1:165
מימרא	1:136
משלח	1:96
נכבה	1:60
סכר	1:264
עבד	1:153
פת	2:113
קנא	2:80
רְבּוּנִי	2:209
תָּאוֹמָה	2:60

c / Latin

crurifragium	2:194
laesae majestatis	2:196
patibulum	2:192, 227

original language of
1:1, 55f., 75, 81, 110, 120,
124, 129, 153
and the Synoptics
1:1, 75f., 86f., 127, 153,
154, 160, 184, 186f., 210,
225, 234, 236, 238, 246,
247, 259, 274, 275f.,
281ff., 307; 2:20, 31, 42,
56, 66, 68, 69, 78, 79, 83f.,
85f., 86f., 90f., 93, 105,
107, 109f., 112f., 126,
128, 132, 139, 143, 155,
167, 168, 169, 170, 171–
174, 181, 184, 195, 196,
197f., 198, 200, 207, 208,
209, 211, 213, 216, 236,
237
style of
1:1, 57–59, 60–66, 86–90;
2:229f.
Gospel of Thomas
1:36; 2:63, 153

Heracleon
1:18f., 90, 112
Hermas, Shepherd of
1:9
Hippolytus
1:18
hour
1:178f., 253, 259f.; 2:6f.,
8, 96f., 105f., 150, 158,
165
hymns (in the NT)
1:112, 125, 130

icon, concept of
1:250
Ignatius
1:7f.
Irenaeus
1:12, 15f., 23, 37

James, son of Zebedee
1:158, 164; 2:6, 214, 229,
230
Jerome
1:12, 42f., 190
Jerusalem
2:6, 80f.
Jesus
as Christ
2:40, 49

death of
2:49, 75, 117, 125, 126f.,
143
earthly
1:94, 95, 96, 97, 148, 249,
251, 260; 2:20, 71, 114,
125f., 128, 139, 200
as God striding over the
earth
1:1, 94, 300, 301; 2:72,
132, 152, 156
historical (s. earthly)
message of
1:97, 250; 2:125, 144
as son
1:168
as son of man
1:110, 158, 253f., 267,
290; 2:40, 41
supernatural knowledge of
1:218, 221, 224, 227, 245,
271, 295; 2:37, 59, 66, 75,
172, 223
as teacher
2:152
as way to the Father
2:124f.
Jewish Christianity
1:123, 144, 272; 2:47, 49,
193, 238
"Jews," the
1:15, 26, 83, 84, 85, 96,
128, 143, 144, 148, 166,
184, 185, 186, 187, 202,
203, 207, 211, 212, 219f.,
222, 223, 230, 236, 243,
246, 247, 248, 249, 254,
255, 257, 258, 259, 262,
263, 264, 265, 266, 273,
277, 290, 292, 293, 294,
296, 310; 2:3, 7f., 14, 16,
19, 20, 29, 30, 39, 41, 50,
58, 61, 75, 80, 136f., 178,
181f., 183, 184, 185, 187,
188, 192, 201f., 210, 212
John the Baptist (and
movement)
1:35, 37, 65, 76, 77, 79,
80, 81ff., 90, 101, 110,
115, 116ff., 120, 122ff.,
127ff., 143–149, 152, 154,
156, 158, 160, 168, 209,
210, 211, 263, 266, 267,
274

John, the Presbyter
1:10
John, son of Zebedee
1:1, 6f., 9f., 11, 14, 18, 23,
46, 74, 135, 158, 164;
2:157, 229, 230
Jonah
1:164
Josephus
1:56f.
Judas
2:57
judgment
1:89, 205, 251f., 254, 259,
265, 267; 2:27, 238
Justin Martyr
1:13

language, Johannine (s.
Gospel of John)
life
2:32, 64, 79f., 131
light
1:126f., 205, 263; 2:26,
38, 101
logos
2:27
love
2:107, 109, 117f., 126,
127, 131, 132
Luke
1:94, 101, 124, 146;
2:69f., 74, 112, 166, 169,
184, 199f., 223
Luther, Martin
1:153, 292

Mandean(s)
1:34, 35, 36, 123ff., 192
Manichean(s)
1:34
Marcion
1:8, 12, 17, 18
Mark
1:124, 212; 2:71, 112,
164, 171, 184, 198f., 200
martyrdom
2:98
Matthew
1:94, 101, 124; 2:70, 113,
166, 184
original language of
1:12, 55f.

message of Jesus (s. Jesus)
messiah
1:110, 144, 164; 2:15f.,
18, 40, 49, 79, 98, 179
pseudo-
2:48
miracles
1:33, 78, 83, 86, 87, 90,
94f., 176, 192, 199f.,
205f., 234, 236, 237, 258,
266, 271, 290, 300, 301,
302; 2:6, 14, 20, 30f., 31,
38, 39, 40, 41, 42, 49, 56,
58, 60, 62, 66f., 68, 71,
74f., 78, 90, 212, 224
"miracles," gospel of (s. also
source, signs)
1:38f., 192, 237, 301;
2:71, 72, 78, 212
mission
1:160, 225, 226; 2:17, 137
misunderstanding
2:16, 17, 50, 59, 61, 72,
108
Montanus, Montanism
1:23
Muratori
1:14
mysticism, divine
2:127

Naassenes
1:114
Nathaniel
1:76, 158, 165, 166, 167,
172; 2:229, 230
Nazareth
1:166
Nicodemus
2:41f., 57

Ogdoad
1:112, 113
Origen
1:43, 90, 109, 114, 190,
244

Papias
1:9–13, 16, 18, 163f., 167;
2:85
paraclete (also s. spirit)
1:23, 96f.; 2:19f., 118,
126, 128, 138, 139

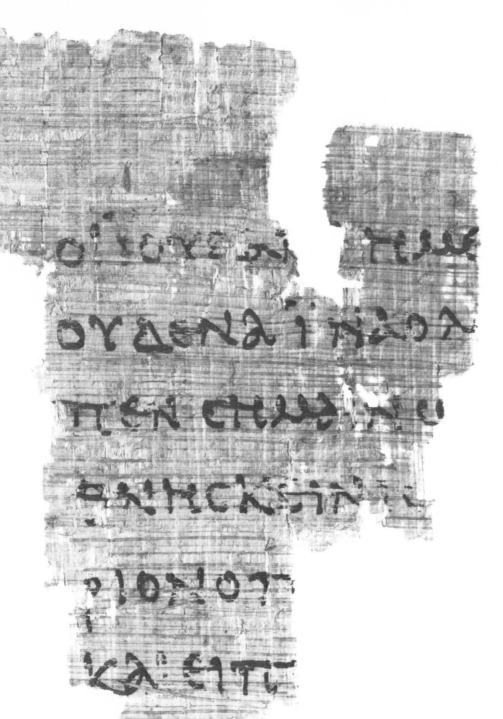

ΟΙ ΟΥ ΧΕ . . . ΠΕΜ
ΟΥΔΕΝΑΙ ΗΔΟΛ
ΠΕΝ ΕΙΝΑ . . .
ΘΝΗϹΚΕΙΝ . .
ΔΙΟΝΟΤ .
ΚΑ ΕΙΤ